The National Directory *of* Expert Witnesses

A Comprehensive National Guide to Experts, Consultants & Litigation Support Specialists

---

Engineers

Expert Witnesses

Scientific Advisors

Medical Specialists

Technical Consultants

2005

National Forensic Center
National Directory of Expert Witnesses
P.O. Box 270529 • San Diego, CA 92198-0529

Tel: (800) 735-6660
Fax: (858) 487-7747

Web Site: www.National-Experts.com
E-mail: info@National-Experts.com

Notice

The *National Directory of Expert Witnesses* is intended as a listing of individuals and organizations offering their services in specific areas of technical, scientific and medical expertise. The persons and firms listed in the directory complete a detailed questionnaire and pay a fee for their listings. National Forensic Center/Directory of Expert Witnesses has not investigated or evaluated the qualifications of any individual or organization listed in this directory. National Forensic Center/Directory of Expert Witnesses does not recommend or endorse the services of those listed, and no recommendation or endorsement is implied.

Great care has been taken in compiling the listings published in this directory. Despite these efforts, however, errors may occur. National Forensic Center/Directory of Expert Witnesses does not assume any liability and hereby disclaims any liability to any party for damage or loss because of errors or omissions in the *National Directory of Expert Witnesses* whether such errors are the result of negligence, accident or any other cause.

Published by

Claims Providers of America
National Forensic Center
P.O. Box 270529 • San Diego, CA 92198-0529
Tel: (800) 735-6660 • Tel: (800) 526-5177 • Fax: (858) 487-7747
E-mail: info@National-Experts.com • Web Site: www.National-Experts.com

ISBN 1-890714-09-7

Printed in the United States

To Order Additional Copies

Copies of *The National Directory of Expert Witnesses* or the *Forensic Services Directory* may be purchased directly from the National Forensic Center for $45 each (includes shipping and handling plus applicable sales taxes in California). To place an order or for additional information, contact:

National Directory of Expert Witnesses
(800) 735-6660

National Forensic Center
(800) 526-5177

Fax: (858) 487-7747
E-mail: info@National-Experts.com
Web Site: www.National-Experts.com

Copies of the directories also may be ordered online at National-Experts.com.

Internet Online Directory

A continuously updated online edition of the National Directory *of* Expert Witnesses/Forensic Services Directory is available on the Internet (see display ad on previous page). To access this free online database, visit our Web site at National-Experts.com and follow the links to the *Internet Online Directory*.

National-Experts.com

Experts and consultants are invited to register for the 2006 edition of the published directory and for listing in our Internet Online Directory

Contents

Introduction

The 2005 edition of the *National Directory of Expert Witnesses* includes over 1,500 expert and consultant listings from across the nation in more than 400 categories of technical, scientific and medical expertise. As an illustration of the breadth and depth of expertise available, the detailed subject index at the end of the directory includes over 6,000 separate entries, ranging from "Abdominal Surgery" to "Zoning."

The directory is designed primarily to be used by trial attorneys, paralegals, investigators, insurance claims adjusters and others as a resource for locating experts from many different fields to assist in the resolution of lawsuits and insurance claims. The individuals and organizations listed in the directory pay a fee for their listings and display ads. National Forensic Center/Directory of Expert Witnesses does not charge any additional fees or commissions for the services of experts contacted through the directory. We also have not investigated or evaluated the qualifications of any person or firm listed in the directory, and a listing does not imply certification or endorsement of the services of those listed.

Although we have taken great care in compiling the listings in this directory, some errors may occur. We request that errors or omissions be reported to us so that we can make the necessary corrections to our Internet online database and to future editions of the directory.

The following section explains how to use the Category Index and other indexes in the directory to locate an expert in a particular field or specialty.

How to Use the Directory

The *National Directory of Expert Witnesses* includes three separate indexes to help you locate an individual or organization in the directory:

The **Category Index** corresponds to the actual organization of expert listings in the directory. To locate the first page of the "forensic accountant" listings, for example, you would first look under the general heading of "ACCOUNTING," and then under the subheading of "Forensic Accounting."

The **Name/Organization Index**, which immediately follows the Category Index, provides an alphabetical listing of all individuals, firms and other organizations appearing in the directory. Use this index to locate a listing for a specific individual or organization.

The detailed **Subject Index**, located at the back of the directory, is useful for finding specialized areas of expertise not included in the Category Index. To find an expert with experience in "Hearing Loss," for example, you would locate this specialty in the Subject Index and then refer to the page number(s) shown for the listings in the directory that include this specialty.

Expert Referral Services

If you are unable to locate an expert in the directory, provide a brief description of your specific needs to National Forensic Center via fax, e-mail, or toll-free telephone call, and receive a direct referral from our current referrals database. A special online referral form is also available on our Internet web site. These referral services are provided at no charge to attorneys, claims adjusters and other authorized representatives of law firms and insurance companies.

Fax:	(858) 487-7747
E-mail:	info@national-experts.com
Web Site:	www.national-experts.com
Toll-free:	(800) 735-6660 or (800) 526-5177

Internet Online Directory

We also publish an Internet Online Directory, a continuously updated online edition of the *National Directory of Expert Witnesses/Forensic Services Directory*. The online directory can be accessed free of charge at National-Experts.com. *(See page iii for more information on the Internet Online Directory.)*

Category Index

ENGINEERING (cont.)

MEDICINE & HEALTH (cont.)

Name/Organization Index

A

B

C

D

E

NAME/ORGANIZATION INDEX

F

G

H

I

NAME/ORGANIZATION INDEX

J

K

L

NAME/ORGANIZATION INDEX

O

P

Q

R

S

NAME/ORGANIZATION INDEX

T

NAME/ORGANIZATION INDEX

NAME/ORGANIZATION INDEX

Expert Listings

ACCIDENT PREVENTION & SAFETY

General

Gary L. Buffington
President/CEO
American Safety Consulting, Inc.
P. O. Box 71017
Los Angeles, CA 90071
Tel: (661) 298-0006
(888) 828-1044
Fax: (661) 298-0311
E-mail: gbuff46@yahoo.com

Specialties: Safety Expert with 30+ years of consulting and expert witness experience in the following areas: Construction; Underground Construction; Tunneling, Mining & Mills; Risk Assessment; CAL/OSHA; IIPP, MSHA, NEC, NFPA, NRC Regs.; Safety Training. **Degrees/licenses:** MS; BS; CRSP; CSHM; CSP; WSO-CSE/CSM/CSS; Lic. PI; CIH; EMT.

Eric David
Liaicon
5280-128 Atherton St.
Long Beach, CA 90815-3957
Tel: (562) 597-1877
Fax: (562) 986-9548

Specialties: Electrical and General Contractor with 37+ years of trade. Consulting, and expert witness experience since 1980 in the following areas: Defect Construction; Customs & Practices; Injury/Fire Cause Investigation; Accident Reconstruction; Construction Claims; Electrical Trade; Accident Prevention/Safety. **Degrees/licenses:** BA; MA; Cert. Elec. Inspector ICC & IAEI #42820; Inactive Elec/Gen Contractor.

J. Nigel Ellis, PhD, CSP, PE, CPE
President
Dynamic Scientific Controls, Inc./
Ellis Litigation Support
306 Country Club Dr.
Wilmington, DE 19803
Tel: (302) 571-8470
Fax: (302) 571-0756
E-mail: Nigel@FallSafety.com
Web Site: www.FallSafety.com

Specialties: Consulting and forensic safety network specializing in fall hazards, fall protection and energy-related injuries and incidents; Safety engineering analysis and practical solutions based on 30+ years of training instruction including OSHA compliance courses, and industry and construction and commercial fall protection site assessment, engineering and site implementation; Legal consultation for over 18 years including courtroom experience; Author of the popular and authoritative text book "Introduction to Fall Protection 3rd. ed." published by American Society of Safety Engineers. **Degrees/licenses:** PhD, PE (Safety MA, CA), CSP, CPE.

ForensisGroup, Inc.
Mercy Steenwyk
3452 E. Foothill Blvd., Ste. 1160
Pasadena, CA 91107
Tel: (626) 795-5000
(800) 555-5422
Fax: (626) 795-1950
E-mail: experts@forensisgroup.com
Web Site: www.forensisgroup.com

Specialties: Thousands of our clients have gained the technical advantage and the edge in their cases from our multidisciplined group of experts in hundreds of disciplines. We have some of the best and the brightest at competitive rates backed by 14 years of excellent track record and the support of our trained staff. We assist you until you have the right expert. Some of our areas of exper

(Listing continued on next page)

General *(cont.)*

ForensisGroup, Inc. (cont.)

tise are: Construction, Safety, Engineering, Product Liability, Accident Reconstruction, Automotive, Environmental, Slip & Fall, Appraisal, Medical and other scientific disciplines. Unsurpassed standards. Clients actively evaluate our experts. **Degrees/licenses:** PE, GC, CSP, PhD, MD, GC, CIH, AIA.

Vincent A. Gallagher

Safety Expert
Safety Research, Inc.
739 White Horse Pike, Ste. 3
Audubon, NJ 08106
Tel: (856) 547-4884
Fax: (856) 547-5551
E-mail: safety@snip.net
Web Site: www.safetyresearchinc.com

Specialties: Former OSHA official. Served as safety expert for United Nations. Has consulted for major corporations and unions; Evaluated hazards related to hundreds of construction sites and manufacturing environments; Expert in construction safety management, fall hazard control, scaffolds, trench and excavations. Taught in ten colleges and universities; Received ten awards from OSHA and one from the United Nations. Certified hazard control manager and certified health and safety manager. **Degrees/licenses:** Masters Degree, Center for Safety, New York University.

See primary listing under CONSTRUCTION: Safety Engineering

J. Terrence Grisim, CSP, CDS, CPSM, ARM

President
Safety Management Consultants, Inc.
636 South Washington Street
Elmhurst, IL 60126-4347
Tel: (800) 726-1718
(630) 279-9499
Fax: (630) 279-9498
E-mail: jtgrisim@aol.com

Specialties: Premises Safety and Liability: retail store safety, retail display safety, slips/trips and falls, falling merchandise/top stock accidents, negligent maintenance, negligent method of operation; Transportation, Warehousing and Distribution: fleet safety, motor vehicle/fleet operations, forklifts, loading docks, warehouse safety, material handling DOT compliance, negligent entrustment/retention; Product Safety: product safety evaluation, product design review/hazard analysis, warning label development, product related literature and video, machine guarding; Automotive Service: automotive lifts, shop safety; Workplace Safety and Health: workplace accidents, OSHA compliance and citation issues. **Degrees/licenses:** BGS Aviation Engr. Technology, Psych & Sociology, Texas Field Safety Rep.

George S. Kennedy, CSP

Kennedy Safety Services, Inc.
137 Ruhle Road
Ballston Spa, NY 12020
Tel: (518) 885-2560
Fax: (518) 884-8756
E-mail: kssinc@aol.com

Specialties: Accident and safety specialist; Litigation consulting; Safety training and education issues; Safety management; Personal injury investigation; Accident investigation and reconstruction; OSHA compliance and regulations; Construction and industrial safety and health issues: e.g., trenching, excavation, confined space entry, stairways, scaffolds, ladders, slips, falls, fall protection, electrical hazards, materials handling, loading docks, forklifts, tools, equipment, machine guarding, lockout/tagout, personal protective equipment, hazard communication. Certified

Safety Professional, BS in Civil Engineering with 27 years safety and health experience. **Degrees/licenses:** CSP, CSHM, CHSP, BSCE, OSHA Instructor.

James M. Miller, PE, PhD

President
Miller Engineering Associates, Inc.
2392 Fuller Court
Ann Arbor, MI 48105
Tel: (734) 662-6822
Fax: (734) 747-9712
E-mail: jmiller@millerengineering.com
Web Site: www.millerengineering.com

Specialties: Mechanical Design Safety: Power Tools & Machine Guarding; OSHA/ANSI/ASTM Compliance; Warnings, Labels, Instructions & User Manuals: Health Hazard Warnings; Design of User Manuals & Warnings; Consumer Product Safety: Human Factors & Ergonomics, Slips, Falls-Premise, Vehicle, Ladder; Child, Home Appliances, Furniture; Vehicles: Auto, Truck, ATV, Boat, Jet Ski, Snowmobile; Seat Belts & Air Bags; Chemical, Fire, Environmental & Waste Disposal: Fires & Explosions-Vapors/Electrical/Chemical; Chemical Labeling Requirements; MSDS; Groundwater & Soil Contamination; Agricultural & Construction Safety: Tractor, Implement, Harvester & Grain Storage; Pesticides, Herbicides, Fungicides; Nursing Malpractice; Nursing Management. **Degrees/licenses:** James Miller, PE, PhD; Bradley Cook, PE; Rebecca Lehto, PhD, RN, OCN.

Jon J. Pina, MS, CSP

Safety, Health
& Environmental Professional
Evergreen Environmental Health
& Safety, Inc.
368 Rt. 110 Hwy.
Indiana, PA 15701
Tel: (724) 349-7029
Fax: (724) 349-3540
E-mail: jpina@adelphia.net

Specialties: Over 31 years experience; safety, industrial hygiene, environmental, PA state OSHA consultant, construction management, demolition, "hands-on" industrial and chemical plant operations; slip, trip, and falls; falls from elevations/trucks/mobile platforms; hot work/fires/explosions; machine-guarding; electrical hazards; Safety & Health Programs; asbestos identification/abatement; environmental surveys/assessments, hazardous waste site remediation; drilling, construction, excavation, utility location/isolation, tank cleaning, water treatment, boilers, confined space; off-road vehicles, defensive driving; emergency response/security/Local Emergency Planning Committee, LEPC member; safety professor; professionally published. **Degrees/licenses:** MS Safety Sci; MS Geol; BS Geosci Ed.; Cert Safety Prof; Cert Prof Instructor.

Safety Play, Inc.

Scott Burton
— Free Air Fare —
Main Office:
10460 Roosevelt Blvd., #295
St. Petersburg, FL 33716
Tel: (888) 878-0244 (Toll Free)
(727) 522-0061
Fax: (727) 522-0061
E-mail: safetyplay@mindspring.com
Web Site:
www.mindspring.com/~safetyplay

California Office:
7095 Hollywood Blvd., #1308
Los Angeles, CA 90028

Specialties: Free air fare (minor restrictions apply, one round trip). Instructor for safety courses. Expert in playground, sports, and recreation accidents including playgrounds, soccer, trampolines, water, baseball, football, softball, basketball, volleyball, fitness equipment, exercise trails, etc. Investigation of warnings, ADA compliance, supervision, hazards, layout, design, surfacing, and inspections for risk management, parks and recreation, schools, facilities, amusement parks, resorts, day care centers, hotels, restaurants, etc. Voting member on ASTM committees creating national standards and CPSC guidelines. Ex-manufacturer who is experienced in expert testimony, manufacturing, design, planning,

(Listing continued on next page)

General *(cont.)*

Safety Play, Inc. (cont.)

inspections, installations, recreational safety courses and manuals. Created Safety Signs and inspection tools. **Degrees/licenses:** Certified Playground Safety Inspector, Instructor, Bus. Deg.

See primary listing under RECREATION: General

Aquatics Safety & Water Rescue

Gerald M. Dworkin

Consultant, Aquatics Safety
& Water Rescue
Lifesaving Resources, Inc.
10 Main Street
P.O. Box 905
Harrisville, NH 03450
Tel: (603) 827-4139
Fax: (603) 827-4134
E-mail: admin@lifesaving.com
Web Site: www.lifesaving.com

Specialties: Drowning, Near Drowning, and Aquatic Injury Prevention and Emergency Management; Hazard and Risk Assessment, Victim and Incident Recognition, Emergency Protocols, and Aquatic Facility Operations; Lifeguard, Public Safety and Rescue Training and Supervision for Swimming Pools, Lakes, Oceans, Rivers and Waterparks, including specialties for Ice, Cold Water and Swiftwater Rescue. Authored numerous articles and several textbooks on Aquatics Safety, Water Rescue, and Pre-hospital Emergency Medical issues. Noted speaker and educator on Aquatics Safety and Water Rescue for Public Safety, Rescue and Aquatic Recreation organizations. Professional Firefighter, EMT, Lifeguard Instructor and Supervisor. **Degrees/licenses:** BS, EMT,NFPA FFIII, CPR/CPR Instruct, Lifeguard/Lifeguard Instruct, EMS Instruct.

See primary listing under RECREATION: Aquatics

Alan M. Steinman, MD, MPH

Rear Admiral (Ret.), USCG/USPHS
1135 Harrington Place
DuPont, WA 98327
Tel: (253) 229-4088
Fax: (253) 964-3549
E-mail: asteinman@aol.com

Specialties: Drowning, hypothermia, sea survival, maritime medicine, water survival, protective clothing, cold water immersion, water rescue, safety investigation, life jackets, life rafts; past Surgeon General of the U.S. Coast Guard; developed cold water survival time charts for USCG; widely published in areas of sea survival and hypothermia; chapter on immersion hypothermia in leading textbook of emergency medicine; lectures in drowning, hypothermia and sea survival; Board Certified in Occupational Medicine; MD from Stanford University; post-graduate training at Mayo Clinic and University of Washington; experience as expert witness in both state and federal courts. **Degrees/licenses:** MD, MPH, FACPM.

See primary listing under MEDICINE & HEALTH: Occup./Environ. Medicine

Kim W. Tyson

President
Tyson & Associates, Inc.
1102 Twin Creek Dr.
Pflugerville, TX 78660
Tel: (512) 990-9698
Fax: (512) 990-0865
E-mail: kimwtyson@aol.com

Specialties: Aquatic Safety; Accident Investigation - Aquatics; Drownings; Near-drownings; Spinal Cord Injury; Diving Accidents; Swimming Pool/Facility Operations; Aquatic Management; Lifeguard Training and Standard of Care for Swimming Pool, Open Water, and Surf. National Textbook Committee Member United States Lifesaving Association, American Red Cross, YMCA. National Standards Committees - State of Texas (ANSI/NSPI), World Waterpark Association. **Degrees/licenses:** BS, MS.

Children's Products

Paul Doppelt
Consultant
PD Consultant, Inc.
9330 Karlov
Skokie, IL 60076
Tel: (847) 674-6242
(847) 674-6236
Fax: (847) 674-6242
E-mail: pauldinc@aol.com

Specialties: Over 30 years experience evaluating children's products for safety and overall design integrity, including such product categories as toys, plush dolls, juvenile products, child car seats, tricycles, children's bicycles, wheeled riding vehicles, and indoor and outdoor playground equipment. Can also provide analysis of the product's user instructions, warnings, and age grading. Member of the ASTM committees on toy safety, juvenile products safety and playground equipment safety. Participant in the development of the CPSC's regulations on toy safety. Member of the Midwest Society of Professional Consultants. **Degrees/licenses:** BS Mech. Engr. (Design), IL Inst. of Tech.

Ergonomics

Alison Heller-Ono, MS, PT, CIE, CDA, CMC
President/CEO
Worksite International
887 Abrego Street
Monterey, CA 93940
Tel: (831) 648-8724
Fax: (831) 648-8330
E-mail: alisonh@worksiteinternational.com
Web Site: www.worksiteinternational.com

Specialties: Ergonomic Worksite Analysis: office, industrial and hospital; participatory ergonomics; consulting on work injury prevention and disability management; Workers' Compensation case management; work performance; facility design with ergonomics; musculoskeletal injury prevention; cumulative trauma disorders; repetitive motion injuries; back injury prevention, ergonomics education, ADA Title I disability issues, Reasonable Accommodation assessments, Workers' Compensation fraud. BS, MS, Licensed Physical Therapist, Certified Industrial Ergonomist, Ergonomics Education Program Specialist, Certified Disability Analyst, Certified Management Consultant. **Degrees/licenses:** BS, MS; See above for licenses & certifications.

Exercise Equipment

Frank J. Smith
Owner
Elite Fitness Consulting Services
1021 Highland Park
Fallbrook, CA 92028-5421
Tel: (760) 728-5212
Fax: (760) 728-5239
E-mail: fitwitness@aol.com
Web Site: www.fitwitness.com

Specialties: Twenty five years in Fitness Equipment design, use and operation; Fitness Center design; Certification of Instructors; Sauna Room design and operation; Steam Room design and operation; Flooring applications to fitness; designing Programs for Fitness Equipment Users; Lecturer on Fitness and Fitness Equipment use. Seven years as a consultant to the "President's Council on Physical Fitness and Sports." Published in the following areas: Fitness and Use of Equipment, Fitness Center design, Training Charts and Instruction Materials, Rehabilitation Programs, Instructional Videos. Designed Institutional and Retail Marketing Programs for Fitness Equipment. Fee: $150.00 per hr. **Degrees/licenses:** BA Education, Univ. of Washington; Provisional Teaching Cert., Education.

Fire Protection

Reed Fire Protection Engineering

Albert W. Reed, PE
President
4144 N. Central Expy., Ste. 510
Dallas, TX 75204-3140
Tel: (214) 638-7599
Fax: (214) 638-4710
E-mail: areed@reedfire.com
Web Site: www.reedfire.com

Specialties: Fire Alarm Systems, Automatic Sprinkler Systems, Building Code & Life Safety Consulting. Thirty years engineering experience, twenty three years as licensed engineer. All types of fire alarm and suppression systems knowledge. **Degrees/licenses:** Licensed in TX, FL, NV, AZ, NM, OK.

See primary listing under ENGINEERING: Fire Protection

Human Factors

Boster, Kobayashi & Associates

Michael Kreutzelman
Chief Operating Officer
59 Rickenbacker Circle
Livermore, CA 94550
Tel: (925) 447-6495
(925) 963-9653
Fax: (925) 447-6589
E-mail: michaelk@boster-kobayashi.com
Web Site: www.bosterkobayashi.com

Specialties: Accident reconstruction/automobiles, buses, trains, bicycles, motorcycles and tractor trailers. Highway design, biomedical analysis, machine guarding, product defects, seatbelts, airbags, elevator and escalators, tire failure, slip/trip and falls, lighting, nighttime photography, human factors, safety, construction safety, crashworthiness and recreational safety, amusement parks. Fifteen experts - firm has consulted on cases all over the United States. Senior experts have testified on average over 200 times. Fifty percent plaintiff and fifty percent defendant. Travel anywhere in the United States with 24-hour notice, if case warrants this emergency response. **Degrees/licenses:** PhD, PE, MS, ME, JD.

See primary listing under ACCIDENT RECONSTRUCTION: Automotive/Vehicular

Error Analysis, Inc.

Human Factors, Safety & Accident Reconstruction Consultants
Corporate Headquarters
5811 Amaya Drive, Ste. 205
La Mesa, CA 91942-4156
Tel: (619) 464-4427
Fax: (619) 464-4992
E-mail: info@erroranalysis.com
Web Site: www.erroranalysis.com

Specialties: Personal Injuries; Premises and Products Liability (all types); Warnings, Labels and Instructions; Slips, Trips and Falls; Commercial and Recreational Equipment; Motor Vehicle and Pedestrian Accidents; Visibility/Lighting; Perception - Reaction; Human Error; Reasonable Conduct; Safety Standards of Care, Codes and Standards; Negligent Supervision. **Degrees/licenses:** Experts available throughout the U.S. Resumes & fees available upon request.

Human Factors Consultants

Ralph N. Haber, Ph.D., Partner
Lyn Haber, Ph.D., Partner
313 Ridge View Drive
Swall Meadows, CA 93514
Tel: (760) 387-2458
Fax: (760) 387-2459
E-mail: Haberhfc@telis.org
Web Site:
www.humanfactorsconsultants.com

Specialties: Pretrial consultation and expert testimony on eyewitness perception and identification; fingerprint science; memory; language; and human factors of safety and accidents. (1) Eyewitness accuracy: effects of conditions of observation, intervening events, police procedures, lineup identifications, and earlier testimony. (2) Fingerprint science: accuracy of fingerprint comparisons; evaluation of comparison methods and laboratory procedures; underlying scientific assumptions and evidence; training and proficiency of examiners. (3) Memory: accuracy of recall by adults and by children, including recovery of memory. (4) Language: children and adults' comprehension; verbal and non-verbal harassment; factors of verbal interviewing that may alter memory; assessment of language disabilities. (5) Human factors: product safety; analyses of transportation, industrial and residential accidents in which equipment failure, human reaction/decision time, training adequacy, attention, error and warning signage may be implemented. Together, we have 45 years courtroom experience, 70 years research, 12 books, 250 published scientific articles. **Degrees/licenses:** PhD exptl psych; exptl linguistics; CCCSLP.

See primary listing under IDENTIFICATION: Eyewitness

Human Factors Engineering Services

Ezra S. Krendel
211 Cornell Avenue
Swarthmore, PA 19081-1933
Tel: (610) 543-9107
Fax: (610) 543-9107
E-mail: krendel@wharton.upenn.edu

Specialties: Construction and Industrial Equipment, Workplace, Recreation, and Highway Safety; Vehicular Control; Visual Search; Perception and Behavior; Product Liability; Warnings; Slip and Fall; Human Performance Reliability and Error. 30 years experience in litigation about 60/40 plaintiff/defendant. Professor Emeritus of Statistics and Operations Research, and of Systems Engineering; Human Factors Engineering and Ergonomics, University of Pennsylvania. Formerly Technical Director, Franklin Institute Research Laboratories, Philadelphia, PA. Consultant To U.S. Departments of Defense, Air Force, Army, Navy, Justice, Transportation, and to Industry. Labor Arbitrator, Federal Mediation and Conciliation Service. Fellow: IEEE, HFES, APA, APS, AAAS. **Degrees/licenses:** ScM.

Richard G. Pearson, PhD, F.Erg.S., CPE

Sage Forensics
5441 Blue Sage Drive
Raleigh, NC 27606
Tel: (919) 828-2443
Fax: (919) 836-8971
E-mail: rpearson@sageforensics.com
Web Site: www.sageforensics.com

Specialties: Forensic Consultant in Human Factors and Safety; Industrial and Consumer Products: design, safety, liability; Failure to Warn: signs, product labels, user manuals, instructions; Occupational Accidents: agriculture, construction, electrical; OSHA/Industry Standards; Machine Guarding; Highway Accidents: driver perception and reaction time; Human performance, attention, fatigue, human error. Professor Emeritus, Industrial Engineering, North Carolina State University; Consultant: National Institute of Occupational Safety and Health, Dupont, GE, Westinghouse; Fellow, four professional societies; Member ASTM, SAE, NSC. Over 60 publications. **Degrees/licenses:** MS, PhD, Cert. Prof. Ergonomist, F.Erg.S. (United Kingdom).

Safety Management Associates

Neil R. Temple, PE, CSP
Principal Consultant
11300 Lilting Lane
Fairfax Station, VA 22039-1718
Tel: (703) 978-3000
(703) 475-8590
Fax: (703) 978-3000 #51
E-mail: smasafety@compuserve.com
Web Site: www.sma-safety.com

Specialties: Accident causal determination, product design safety analysis, slip and fall dynamics, stair design and code compliance, walking surface characteristics and measurement, warning and instruction adequacy, electrical safety, machine guarding, building and safety code compliance. Scope of Services: Forensic safety analysis, accident investigation and reconstruction, product safety testing. Mr. Temple is a Registered Professional Engineer in Safety (PE) and a Board Certified Safety

(Listing continued on next page)

Human Factors *(cont.)*

Safety Management Associates (cont.)

Professional (CSP) in Comprehensive Practice. He has over 30 years of diverse safety engineering, human factors and environmental management experience and is certified by three additional competency boards. **Degrees/ licenses:** BS (VA Tech.), PE (Safety), CSP, CPSM, CHCM, CHSP.

See primary listing under ENGINEERING: Safety

Industrial Hygiene

Richard M. Lynch, PhD, CIH

President
Environmental Safety Management Corp.
21 E Scott Street
Riverside, NJ 08075
Tel: (856) 764-3557
Fax: (856) 764-3558
E-mail: rlynch@esmcorp.com
Web Site: www.esmcorp.com

Specialties: Indoor Air Quality, Mold, Ergonomics, Workers Compensation, Chemical Exposure Modeling, OSHA Compliance, Carpal Tunnel Syndrome, Back Injury, Industrial Hygiene, Safety. **Degrees/licenses:** PhD, MS, Certified Industrial Hygienist.

Rudy Von Burg, PhD

Principal
EnTox & Associates
230 Castro St.
Point Richmond, CA 94801
Tel: (510) 235-2969
(925) 288-2366
(415) 637-2402
Fax: (510) 235-2969
E-mail: rvonburg@entoxandassociates.com
Web Site: http://entoxandassociates.com

Specialties: Occupational & environmental toxicology Litigation Support and Expert Witness, petroleum products, pesticides, carbon monoxide, pharmaceutical agents, metals, asbestos, lead, indoor air, mold, household chemicals. OSHA training, plan preparation and compliance audits, worker protection, compensation claims. Board certified in Toxicology, Certified Industrial Hygiene, AHERA certified, Cal OSHA certified for asbestos, California certified for lead inspection and monitoring. **Degrees/licenses:** PhD, DABT, CIH, CEI, AHERA, CAC, CLI.

See primary listing under ENVIRONMENTAL: Toxicology

Toys & Juvenile Products

Reiner Associates, Inc.

Bert Reiner
President
10643 Angelo Tenero
Las Vegas, NV 89135
Tel: (702) 838-8997
(860) 716-4075 (Cell)
Fax: (702) 838-8669
E-mail: bert@reinerinc.com
Web Site: www.reinerinc.com/expert.html

Specialties: Playground equipment, infant/ juvenile furniture, sporting goods, swimming pools, bicycles, toys. Multifunctional engineering consulting firm providing in-depth expert testimony & research-development, engineering, model-making, quality assurance & manufacturing. 30+ years experience in design of toys, sporting goods, swimming pools, playground equipment & juvenile furniture. Standards: UL, CSA, ASTM, ANSI, CPSC. **Degrees/licenses:** BSME; Member: TIA, ASME, ACFE, IEEE, SPE.

See primary listing under RECREATION: General

Truck, Bus & Forklift Safety

V. Paul Herbert, CPSA

Director
Western Motor Carrier Safety Institute
954 Butterfly Valley Road
Quincy, CA 95971-9613
Tel: (530) 281-6565
(800) 875-7389
Fax: (530) 281-6566
E-mail: paulherbert@trucksafetyexpert.com
Web Site: http://www.trucksafetyexpert.com

Specialties: Truck and Bus Driver Selection, Training, Supervision and Qualification Standards; Commercial Vehicle Equipment, Inspection, Maintenance and Operation Standards; Commercial Vehicle Conspicuity/Visibility; Air Brake Systems, Coupling Devices - Fifth Wheels, Pintle Hooks, Steering Systems, Suspension Systems, Engines, Transmissions; Truck, Bus and Forklift Accident Analysis; Motor Carrier Safety Regulations; Loading/Load Securement Requirements; Hazardous Materials Transportation Regulations; Forklift, Loading Dock, Warehouse Operations. Certified Safety Coordinator, Certified Practicing Safety Administrator (CPSA), Certified Master Instructor (Commercial Drivers License), Certified National Safety Council DDC-8 Instructor, Certified Forklift Instructor, Former Truck Driver, Former State Trooper, Former Trucking Company Safety & Personnel Director. **Degrees/licenses:** See above for Qualifications & Certifications.

See primary listing under TRANSPORTATION: Truck, Bus & Forklift Safety

National Transportation Consultants, Inc.

Joseph Y. Morrison
President
1109 South 10th Street
Noblesville, IN 46060
Tel: (317) 770-0953
Fax: (317) 770-0954
E-mail: jmorrison@ntconsult.com
Web Site: http://www.ntconsult.com

Specialties: Over 150 years of transportation safety experience. Motor Carrier Safety Regulations; Safety Program Development; DOT Audits; Hazardous Materials Training; Accident Investigation and Reconstruction. Member of Commercial Vehicle Safety Alliance; Indiana Motor Truck Association; American Society of Safety Engineers; IACAI; IATAI, ACTAR.

See primary listing under TRANSPORTATION: Trucking

Merlyn Robert "Bob" Wilson

Transportation Safety, Inc.
Sacramento Office
2377 Gold Meadow Way, Suite 100
Gold River, CA 95670
Tel: (916) 526-2845
Fax: (916) 631-1515
E-mail: Bob-Wilson@msn.com
Web Site: http://www.transafetyinc.com

Los Angeles Office
13104 Philadelphia St., Suite 218
Whittier, CA 90601
Tel: (562) 698-0040
Fax: (562) 698-0139

Specialties: Diesel Engine Electronic Control Modules; Black Box Downloads; Tachograph Analysis; Hydraulic & Air Brakes Systems; Driver's Hours of Service and Log Books; Commercial Driver Qualification; Preventative Maintenance Inspections; Driver Pre-trip Inspections; Loading, Unloading and Cargo Securement; Hazardous Materials; Off-Tracking or Trailer Cheat; Out of Service Criteria; Permit Loads; Transport of Intermodal Freight Containers. Mr. Wilson is certified through

(Listing continued on next page)

Truck, Bus & Forklift Safety
(cont.)

Merlyn Robert "Bob" Wilson (cont.)

"ASE" as a truck technician specializing in hydraulic and air brake equipped trucks and buses. Past instructor for the Federal Transit Administration, University of California at Riverside, and the Northern California Public Safety Training & Education Center through Sacramento City College. Licensed forklift driver. **Degrees/licenses:** BS; AA (Admin. of Justice); Licensed private investigator, CA 13828.

ACCIDENT RECONSTRUCTION

General

Accident and Injury Analytica

Kenneth W. Luther, DC, QME
649 W. Maple Ave.
El Segundo, CA 90245
Tel: (310) 322-2233
Fax: (310) 322-6955
E-mail: k.luther@reconanalysis.com
Web Site: www.reconanalysis.com

Specialties: Chiropractor with 25 years of extensive consulting and expert witness experience in the following areas: Physical Medicine; Chiropractic Medicine; Accident Reconstruction; Injury Reconstruction; Qualified Medical Evaluation; Forensic Analysis. **Degrees/licenses:** BS; DC; QME.

A. William Breyer III, CHCM

Principal Consultant
Safety Consulting Services
178 Martesia Way
Indian Harbour Beach, FL 32937-3573
Tel: (321) 777-8599
E-mail: wbreyer@cfl.rr.com

Specialties: Occupational/Industrial Safety; Accident Investigations; OSHA Standards; Slips, Falls & Trips; Building Design Safety; Machine Guarding; National Fire Codes; National Electrical Code (NEC); NFPA Life Safety Code/NFPA #101; Plaintiff & Defense Strategies; Job Hazard Analyses; "In-the-Home" Accidents; Construction Safety; Safety Inspections/Techniques; Accident Prevention; Walking/Working Surfaces; Litigation Consulting; Personal Injury Investigations & Reconstruction; Fall Protection; Personal Protective Equipment; Safety Program Evaluation; Risk Assessment of Processes, Plants & Facilities; Material Handling Safety; Workplace safety; Electrical/Mechanical Design Safety. DEGREES/LICENSES: BA; CHCM-#143-Master Level; NFPA Mem.: Arch., Engrs. & Bldg. Officials Section. **Degrees/licenses:** See above. Cirriculum Vitae/Consulting Resume Provided Upon Request.

Carr & Associates Engineers, Inc.

Ben F. Carr, Jr., PE, RLS (President)
Bart Carr, RLS (Vice President)
2052 Oak Mountain Drive
Pelham, AL 35124
Tel: (205) 664-8498
Fax: (205) 664-9685
E-mail:
CarrAsso@aol.com or caebfcj@aol.com

Specialties: Carr & Associates, a thirty person civil/structural and surveying firm, established 1974, with civil, structural, environmental, and mechanical engineers, and surveyors. Approximately eighty percent of our work load is design, so that our forensic engineering is "real world" and not theory. Ben Carr has investigated over 300 vehicle and industrial accidents, and testified in depositions and court numerous times for defense and plaintiffs. He has developed computer programs for accident reconstruction, complimenting use of authoritative procedures and programs. Our surveying capabilities assure accurate, useful accident maps, where appropriate. **Degrees/licenses:** BCE, MS, PE (AL, MS, TN, SC, GA, FL), RLS (AL, FL, MS, TN, SC).

C. Michael Dickinson

President, Principal Engineer
Dickinson & Associates, Inc.
608-G Matthews-Mint Hill Rd. (28105)
P.O. Box 3093
Matthews, NC 28106-3093
Tel: (704) 847-4040
Fax: (704) 847-0788
E-mail:
mdickinson@dickinson-associates.com
Web Site: www.dickinson-associates.com

Specialties: Reconstruction and analysis of on- and off-road accidents involving automobiles, light trucks, SUV's, Tractor-trailers, heavy trucks and buses, motorcycles, bicycles, go-karts, pedestrians, and forklifts; High and low speed (soft tissue) accidents; Computer-assisted vehicle dynamics and collision analysis; 2D and 3D modeling and animation using EDVAP, HVE-2D, PC-CRASH, and 3D-Studio; Vision and visibility analysis; Vehicle system design and failure analysis including brakes, steering, suspension, and drive system components; Machinery and equipment accident reconstruction and failure analysis; machine design; fatigue and fracture mechanics analysis; FEA (ANSYS and ALGOR); reliability and risk analysis. **Degrees/licenses:** MSME, PE.

Error Analysis, Inc.

Human Factors, Safety & Accident
Reconstruction Consultants
Corporate Headquarters
5811 Amaya Drive, Ste. 205
La Mesa, CA 91942-4156
Tel: (619) 464-4427
Fax: (619) 464-4992
E-mail: info@erroranalysis.com
Web Site: www.erroranalysis.com

Specialties: Personal Injuries; Premises and Products Liability (all types); Warnings, Labels and Instructions; Slips, Trips and Falls; Commercial and Recreational Equipment; Motor Vehicle and Pedestrian Accidents; Visibility/Lighting; Perception - Reaction; Human Error; Reasonable Conduct; Safety Standards of Care, Codes and Standards; Negligent Supervision. **Degrees/licenses:** Experts available throughout the U.S. Resumes & fees available upon request.

See primary listing under ACCIDENT PREVENTION & SAFETY: Human Factors

ForensisGroup, Inc.

Mercy Steenwyk
3452 E. Foothill Blvd., Ste. 1160
Pasadena, CA 91107
Tel: (626) 795-5000
(800) 555-5422
Fax: (626) 795-1950
E-mail: experts@forensisgroup.com
Web Site: http://forensisgroup.com

Specialties: Thousands of our clients have gained the technical advantage and the edge in their cases from our multidisciplined group of experts in hundreds of disciplines. We have some of the best and the brightest at competitive rates backed by 14 years of excellent track record and the support of our trained staff. We assist you until you have the right expert. Some of our areas of expertise are: Construction, Safety, Engineering, Product Liability, Accident Reconstruction, Automotive, Environmental, Slip & Fall, Appraisal, Medical and other scientific disciplines. Unsurpassed standards. Clients actively evaluate our experts. **Degrees/licenses:** PE, GC, CSP, PhD, MD, GC, CIH, AIA.

See primary listing under ACCIDENT PREVENTION & SAFETY: General

John C. Glennon, Chartered

6917 W. 76th Street
Overland Park, KS 66204
Tel: (913) 383-3856
Fax: (913) 383-2277
E-mail: experts@johncglennon.com
Web Site: www.johncglennon.com

Specialties: Motor Vehicle Accident Investigation; Accident Reconstruction; Vehicle Crush Analysis; Vehicular Mechanical and

(Listing continued on next page)

General *(cont.)*

John C. Glennon, Chartered (cont.)
Structural Failure Analysis for Automobiles, Trucks, and Motorcycles; Testing Capabilities for Air Brakes, Hydraulic Brakes, Suspension Systems, Steering Systems, Tires, and Wheels; Determination if Proper Maintenance and Repair Procedures were Followed; Identification of Previous Body Structural Damage; Motor Carrier Safety and Compliance; Commercial Driver Responsibilities and Qualifications; Commercial Driver Hours of Service and Daily Logs; Proper Load Securement Procedures; Fleet Maintenance Requirements; Computer Animation; Forensic Mapping; Photo Modeling; Downloading of Crash Data Retrieval Systems (Automobile "BLACK BOX"). **Degrees/licenses:** D. Engr., PE, BS Automotive Technology, ASE Cert., CDL.

Thomas Gunzler, PE

Principal Consultant
Gunzler & Associates
P.O. Box 5848
Santa Monica, CA 90409
Tel: (310) 454-9614
(866) 326-7170

Specialties: Forensic engineering consultants, since 1973, with competence over a wide range of engineering expertise. Our consultants average thirty years in their respective specialties, have post-graduate diplomas and professional engineering registrations, where appropriate. Specialties include: safety engineering, product defect analysis, mechanical design, industrial and construction accidents, pedestrian safety, traffic accident reconstruction, fire cause analysis and chemical hazards. We are ready to discuss, in strict confidence, any matters which may lie in our areas of competence and will furnish resumes of our associates, terms of employment and fees on request.

InterCity Testing & Consulting

167 Willis Avenue
Mineola, NY 11501
Tel: (516) 747-8400 (NY)
(800) 822-1515 (Outside NYS)
Fax: (516) 746-0121/0111 (NY)
Tel: (561) 745-7940 (FL)
Fax: (561) 745-7939 (FL)
E-mail: exptl@aol.com
Web Site: http://www.InterCityTesting.com

3550 Watt Ave., Ste. 5
Sacramento, CA 95821
Tel: (916) 481-3093
(800) 500-5561 (Toll Free)
Fax: (916) 481-3095

Specialties: Visit our web site for condensed expert CV's in: Amusement Parks & Rides; Automotive Safety & Accident Reconstruction; Biomedical/Biomechanical Injury Analysis; Biomechanics; Boating & Marine Safety; Chemicals & Chemical Engineering; Civil Engineering/Structural Failures; Construction Accidents; Electrical & Mechanical Engineering; Firearms & Explosives; Fire Investigations; Flammable Fabrics; Helmets/ Motorcycle, Bicycle, Sports & Industrial; Machine Guarding; Medical Devices; Medical Emergency/EMT; Metallurgy & Material Sciences; Parks & Playgrounds; Slips, Trips & Falls; Sports/Recreation/Aquatics; Toxicology; Transportation & Highway Safety; Warnings & Instructions. INTERCITY IS NOT AN EXPERT REFERRAL SERVICE. **Degrees/licenses:** PE's / degrees thru PhD's in above specialties.

IPEC

Institute for Products,
Engineering & Construction
A Consortium of Engineers,
Construction & Safety Professionals
34522 N. Scottsdale Rd., Ste. D-8 #160
Scottsdale, AZ 85262
Tel: (888) 212-1155
Fax: (888) 414-1155
E-mail: ipec@forensicengineers.com
Web Site:
http://www.forensicengineers.com

666 Fifth Ave., #122
New York, NY 10103
Tel: (212) 315-9523

1429 G St. NW, #415
Washington, DC 20005
Tel: (202) 822-9660

231 North Ave. West, #134
Westfield, NJ 07090
Tel: (908) 233-2973

1920 Abrams Pkwy., #95
Dallas, TX 75214
Tel: (214) 827-9892

Specialties: Airbags; Seatbelts; Tires; Automobiles; Trucks; Trailers; Amusement Rides; Carnival Rides; Product Defects; Electrocution; Shock; Burns; Fires; Slips; Falls; Elevators; Ladders; Scaffolds; Cranes; Loading Docks; Safety Engineering; Human Factors; Repair Shop Practices; Construction Site Accidents; OSHA; Chemical Corrosion; Packaging; Oil Spills; Construction Equipment; Steel Mills; Industrial Machines; Hydraulic Lifts; Automatic Doors; Tractors; Forklifts; Recreational Vehicles; Golf Carts; ATVs; Motorcycles; Snow Plows; Off-road Vehicles; Bicycles; Lawnmowers; Saws; Grinders; Power Tools; Meat Slicers; Overhead Electric Lines; Manholes; Utility Poles; Carbon Monoxide; Red Tags; Aboriculture; Trees; Retail Stores; Furnaces; Flues; Appliances. Contact: Ned Howell. **Degrees/licenses:** Engineers: Auto, Constr, Mech, Elec, Struct, Civil, Chem, Safety, Arch, Aero.

See primary listing under CONSTRUCTION: General

R. Craig Jerner, PhD, PE

President
J.E.I. Metallurgical, Inc.
7703 Queens Ferry Lane
Dallas, TX 75248
Tel: (972) 934-0493
Fax: (972) 233-5909
E-mail: r.c.jerner@metallurgist.com
Web Site: http://www.metallurgist.com

Specialties: 35+ years experience conducting failure analysis, accident investigations, and metallurgical engineering. Expert testimony and litigation support in 65+ trials, 225 depositions, and 1,000+ failure investigations. EXPERTISE: Accident investigation & reconstruction; failure analysis; consumer & industrial products; vehicular & heavy equipment; gas, oil & tubular products; corrosion; welding design; testing and evaluation; micro/macro photography. HONORS: "Who's Who in Science & Engineering," "Who's Who in Executives & Professionals," The Sigma Xi Society. Professor (Tenured) University of Oklahoma 1965-78. Registered consultant OSHA, U. S. Dept. of Defense, U. S. Coast Guard, and NTSB. Registered Professional Engineer in Texas and Oklahoma. **Degrees/licenses:** PhD, Metallurgy; MS & BS, Metallurgical Engineering.

Wilbur R. Meredith, III

Owner
Meredith Enterprises
16040 Wake Robin Drive
Newbury, OH 44065-9160
Tel: (440) 564-7173
(440) 564-7174
(440) 567-1330 (Cellular)
Fax: (440) 564-7175
E-mail: v7cat@aol.com
Web Site: http://meredithenterprises.com

Specialties: Specializing in Automotive, Heavy Trucks, School Buses, Commercial

(Listing continued on next page)

General *(cont.)*

Wilbur R. Meredith, III (cont.)

Buses, Trailers, and Marine (Small Boats under 100-feet). Mechanical Engineer, National Association of Professional Accident Reconstruction Specialist (1992). Society of Automotive Engineers, American Institute of Industrial Engineers, Society of Manufacturing Engineers, Society of Naval Architects and Marine Engineers, American Boat and Yacht Council, Powerboat Manufacturer-U.S.C.G. certified, U.S. Patents on boat hull design, Industrial Machinery and Shop Equipment secondary specialty. In business since 1987. Utilize computer simulations for dynamics of automotive accidents. Free case review. Retainage or hourly billing available. **Degrees/licenses:** BSME (1959), Case Institute of Technology.

James M. Miller, PE, PhD

President
Miller Engineering Associates, Inc.
2392 Fuller Court
Ann Arbor, MI 48105
Tel: (734) 662-6822
Fax: (734) 747-9712
E-mail: jmiller@millerengineering.com
Web Site:
http://www.millerengineering.com

Specialties: Mechanical Design Safety: Power Tools & Machine Guarding; OSHA/ANSI/ASTM Compliance; Warnings, Labels, Instructions & User Manuals: Health Hazard Warnings; Design of User Manuals & Warnings; Consumer Product Safety: Human Factors & Ergonomics, Slips, Falls-Premise, Vehicle, Ladder; Child, Home Appliances, Furniture; Vehicles: Auto, Truck, ATV, Boat, Jet Ski, Snowmobile; Seat Belts & Air Bags; Chemical, Fire, Environmental & Waste Disposal: Fires & Explosions-Vapors/Electrical/Chemical; Chemical Labeling Requirements; MSDS; Groundwater & Soil Contamination; Agricultural & Construction Safety: Tractor, Implement, Harvester & Grain Storage; Pesticides, Herbicides, Fungicides; Nursing Malpractice; Nursing Management. **Degrees/licenses:** James Miller, PE, PhD; Bradley Cook, PE; Rebecca Lehto, PhD, RN, OCN.

See primary listing under ACCIDENT PREVENTION & SAFETY: General

Packer Engineering

Penny Rusch
Director of Business Development
1950 N. Washington St.
Naperville, IL 60563
Tel: (800) 323-0114
Fax: (630) 505-1986
E-mail: peinfo@packereng.com
Web Site: http://www.packereng.com

Specialties: Packer Engineering, a multidisciplinary engineering consulting company, provides expertise in the areas of failure analysis, accident investigation & reconstruction, cause & origin investigations, research & development, risk mitigation, and custom & routine testing. Packer offers a wide range of services in the following areas: Aviation, Biomechanical/Biomedical, Construction Technology, Chemical, Fire & Explosions, Electrical, Human Factors, Ergonomics, Machinery & Equipment, Materials, Occupational Safety, Product & Process Safety, System Failure Analysis & Recovery, Technology Assessment & Intellectual Property, and Transportation Systems. Our emergency response team is available 24 hours, 7 days a week.

See primary listing under ENGINEERING: Consulting

Pro/Consul Technical and Medical Experts

1945 Palo Verde Ave., Suite 200
Long Beach, CA 90815-3443
Tel: (800) 392-1119
(562) 799-0116
Fax: (562) 799-8821
E-mail: eexperts@msn.com
Web Site: http://www.expertinfo.com

Specialties: RIGHT EXPERT RIGHT AWAY!® 15,000 experts in 7,000 fields. Listed and recommended by the A. M. Best Company. Full-time research staff. We welcome your RUSH cases! TECHNICAL:

Fast inspections. Categories from Accident Reconstruction to Zoology, also including appraisal, economics, employment, human factors, insurance, premises liability, security, and many more. MEDICAL: IME's. Inexpensive insurance medical records reviews by MDs. Categories from Addiction Medicine to Zooplasty, including board certified physicians in all fields, dentistry, geriatrics, neuropsychology, neurosurgery, nursing, orthopedics, psychiatry and many more. Reasonable fees. Free initial consultation. Free resume binder. Free CLE classes. **Degrees/licenses:** MD, PhD, DDS, DVM, DO, DPM, PE, CPA, ME, CE, CRC, MAI, et al.

Safety Engineering Associates, Inc.

2798 S. Fish Hatchery Road
Madison, WI 53711-5398
Tel: (608) 271-7884
(888) 723-3834
Fax: (608) 271-3720
E-mail: office@safetyengineering.com
Web Site:
http://www.safetyengineering.com

Specialties: Accident reconstruction, analysis, laboratory testing, video animation and expert witness services regarding: Automobiles; Trucks; Motorcycles; Farm machinery; Industrial machinery; Consumer products; Highway and rail crossing design; Motor vehicle fire cause and origin analysis. Over 20,000 accidents analyzed since 1947. Eight licensed professional engineers. **Degrees/licenses:** PhD, MS, ME, CE, PE.

Seasoned Engineering Consultants, Inc.

C. Michael Neal, PE
President
500 N. Shoreline Blvd., Ste. 709 (78471)
P.O. Box 4276
Corpus Christi, TX 78469-4276
Tel: (361) 887-9388
Fax: (361) 881-9899
E-mail: sec_inc@msn.com

Specialties: Experienced professional engineers and architects, qualified technicians and dedicated staff performing forensic investigations for the legal, insurance, real estate, industry and private businesses in the areas of: industrial and commercial accidents; vehicle accidents; product and equipment failure analysis (vehicle, appliances, tools, machinery, equipment, firearms, industrial, commercial, oil field, marine, residential); piping/piping components/pressure vessel design/failure analysis; fire cause and origin; foundation distress; slip, trip & fall/building code compliance/ADA compliance/premises liability; catastrophe and storm damage evaluations; demonstrative exhibits; expert witness report/testimony; litigation support. **Degrees/licenses:** BSME, MSME, BSEE, BSA, MSA / PADI, PE & RA in Texas.

Technology Associates

Dr. I.U. Ojalvo
President
137 E. 36th St., Ste. 7K
New York, NY 10016
Tel: (800) 358-9909
Fax: (888) 358-9901
E-mail: iuo@Technology-Assoc.com
Web Site:
http://www.Technology-Assoc.com

1011 High Ridge Rd., 2nd Floor
Stamford, CT 06905
Tel: (203) 329-9909

5030 Champion Blvd., PMB 315
Boca Raton, FL 33496
Tel: (800) 358-9909

Specialties: Vehicles; Roadways; Pedestrians; Machinery; Fall downs; Structures; Construction; Ladders; Shopping Carts; Warnings; Human factors; Biomechanics; Sports & Playgrounds; Swimming pools; Codes & standards; Computer animation; Electric shock; etc. (over 1,400 cases); Testing; Consulting and testimony for defendants & plaintiffs in metropolitan NY area, New England, Florida & surrounding areas; Professors and licensed Professionals in Mechanical, Biomechanical and Electrical Engineering with many publications; Additional specialties in fires, floods, whiplash and other forms of soft tissue and skeletal injuries; Clients include most

(Listing continued on next page)

General *(cont.)*

Technology Associates (cont.)

major insurance companies, municipalities and numerous private law firms (See listings under Engineering & Product Liability). **Degrees/licenses:** BS, MS, PhD, Lic. PE, Fellow ASME, US Fulbright.

See display advertisement on page 18

James O. Yule, BSME, PE

Co-owner
Yule Engineering, Translating,
& Interpreting
6600 NW Sweetbriar Ln.
Kansas City, MO 64151-2354
Tel: (816) 741-9441
Fax: (816) 741-9482
E-mail: Only for certain clients

Specialties: TYPICAL VEHICULAR CASES: Semi/pickup/pole; Truck/Reliant rear; Diesel air filter; Car/pedestrian, stoplight & street lighting; Pickup lapbelt head-on; Cub Cadet mower fire; Ram/ditch airbag; Chrysler/pedestrian, street lighting; Corsica/ pedestrian, intersection; Sundance/Lumina T-bone; Motorcycle/car T-bone; Racecar trailer fire; John Deere cottonpicker fire; Mustang rear/light pole; Car door roller/finger; Parking-lot T-bone; Tag axle & logs rollover; Tool under driver seat; Curve, T-Bird/pole; Belt fail, rear-ending; Mine water-tanker rollover; Forklift driver pinned; Motorcyclist's neck/guy wire; Brake-disc failure, rollover; Forklift/pedestrian; Bronco rollover; Airbag non-deployment; Car/bridge pillar; Car/signpost; Steering bolt dropped out; Accelerator stuck. DEGREES/LICENSES: BSME; Post-graduate work equivalent to a second degree; PE registration by examination in Mechanical and Civil Engineering. Also see "Engineering, General". **Degrees/licenses:** See above.

Accident Photo Analysis & Mapping

Ebert & Associates, Inc.

Dr. James I. Ebert
Chief Scientist
3700 Rio Grande Blvd. NW, Ste. 3
Albuquerque, NM 87107
Tel: (505) 344-2345
(866) 503-9776 Toll Free
Fax: (505) 344-2444
E-mail: jebert@ebert.com
Web Site: http://www.ebert.com

Specialties: We specialize in developing and supporting legal arguments based on spatial and other data derived from photographs and maps through scientific analyses and expert witness testimony. Historic aerial photointerpretation, photo analysis, digital mapping, geographic information systems - GIS - database compilation and analysis, and subsurface contaminant modeling at Superfund, waste disposal, and other sites involved in environmental, land rights, and water rights litigation. Photo interpretation, photogrammetry, and 3-dimensional measurement and mapping from scene and evidence photographs and video for reconstruction of accident, fire, explosion, crime and other scenes in forensic cases. **Degrees/licenses:** BA, MA, PhD, Certified Photogrammetrist (ASPRS).

See primary listing under ENVIRONMENTAL: Aerial Photo Analysis & Mapping

Analysis

Ira S. Kuperstein

219 Penn Avenue
Dover, NJ 07801
Tel: (973) 283-2420
(800) 526-5177, Ext. 102
Fax: (973) 366-2104

Specialties: Traffic accident analysis; Accident reconstruction & analysis; Collision dynamics; Highway design & engineering; Traffic control devices & engineering.

Affiliation: Independent Consultant. **Degrees/licenses:** PhD; PE.

See primary listing under ACCIDENT RECONSTRUCTION: Automotive/Vehicular

Safety Consulting Engineers, Inc.

C. James Dahn
Registered Professional Engineer
2131 Hammond Drive
Schaumburg, IL 60173
Tel: (847) 925-8100
Fax: (847) 925-8120
E-mail: sceinc@sceinc.com
Web Site: http://www.sceinc.com

Specialties: Consulting, research & testing for fire and explosion hazards involving chemical, propellant, pyrotechnic and explosives manufacturing. Testing includes dust explosibility, electrostatics, thermal stability and mechanical sensitivity. Outdoor test site available for large-scale processing and testing. **Degrees/licenses:** BS Aeronautical Engineering.

Automotive/Vehicular

Aronberg & Associates Consulting Engineers, Inc.

Ralph Aronberg, PE
1304 SW 160th Ave., #220
Fort Lauderdale, FL 33326-1902
Tel: (954) 236-6605
E-mail: aronconeng@prodigy.net
Web Site:
http://pages.prodigy.net/aronconeng

Specialties: Traffic accident reconstruction (cars, trucks, motorcycles and pedestrians); Vehicle occupant kinematics (seatbelts); Biomechanics; Traffic engineering design (geometrics, signing, markings, signals and lighting); Sight distance analysis; Hazardous roadway conditions; Work zone traffic control evaluation; Evaluation of roadway curvature; Pedestrian safety; Computerized accident reconstruction and simulation; vehicle "black box" analysis; Fraud evaluation; 3D computer animations. Mr. Aronberg is a Professional Engineer with 25 years of government and private consulting experience. He has reconstructed over 1000 traffic accidents and testified in over 100 trials; Published through the Society of Automotive Engineers. **Degrees/licenses:** BSCE, MS, PE.

Automotive Engineering Consultants, Inc.

Donald B.H. Jeffers, PE
Principal Consultant
P.O. Box 7391
Ann Arbor, MI 48107-7391
Tel: (734) 994-0494
(800) 924-0494
Fax: (734) 994-0494
E-mail:
donjeffers@automotive-engineers.com
Web Site:
http://www.automotive-engineers.com

Specialties: ACCIDENT INVESTIGATION & RECONSTRUCTION: Trucks from Small Pickups to Multiple Unit Tractor-Trailers; Automobiles; Sport Utility Vehicles; Buses; Motor Homes; Vans; Pedestrians; Bicycles; Motorcycles; All Terrain Vehicles; Farm Machinery; Skidders; Self-Propelled Cranes; Trains; Boats; Light Aircraft; Pre- and Post-Accident Fire; Industrial Machinery. Computerized Vehicle Accident Analysis, Video Animation. PRODUCT LIABILITY: Component Failure Analysis; Brakes; Wheels; Tires; Steering; Engines; Transmissions; Drive Trains; Crashworthiness; Air Bags; Seat Belts; Fuel Tank and Fuel System Fires; Electrical Fires; Unexplained Acceleration; Cruise Controls; Computer controls; Vehicle and Component Structural Failure. SERVICES: Engineering Consultation, Litigation Assistance, Expert Witness. **Degrees/licenses:** University of Michigan BSE(ME), MSE(ME), PE.

See primary listing under ENGINEERING: Automotive

Automotive/Vehicular *(cont.)*

Boster, Kobayashi & Associates
Michael Kreutzelman
Chief Operating Officer
59 Rickenbacker Circle
Livermore, CA 94550
Tel: (925) 447-6495
(925) 963-9653
Fax: (925) 447-6589
E-mail: michaelk@boster-kobayashi.com
Web Site: http://www.bosterkobayashi.com

Specialties: Accident reconstruction/automobiles, buses, trains, bicycles, motorcycles and tractor trailers. Highway design, biomedical analysis, machine guarding, product defects, seatbelts, airbags, elevator and escalators, tire failure, slip/trip and falls, lighting, nighttime photography, human factors, safety, construction safety, crashworthiness and recreational safety, amusement parks. Fifteen experts - firm has consulted on cases all over the United States. Senior experts have testified on average over 200 times. Fifty percent plaintiff and fifty percent defendant. Travel anywhere in the United States with 24-hour notice, if case warrants this emergency response. **Degrees/licenses:** PhD, PE, MS, ME, JD.

John Forester
7585 Church St.
Lemon Grove, CA 91945-2306
Tel: (619) 644-5481
E-mail: forester@johnforester.com
Web Site: http://www.johnforester.com

Specialties: Bicycles; Bicycle traffic engineering; Bikeways; Bike paths; Bicyclist performance. Affiliation: Independent Consultant. **Degrees/licenses:** MS; PE.

See primary listing under ENGINEERING: Civil

John C. Glennon, Chartered
6917 W. 76th Street
Overland Park, KS 66204
Tel: (913) 383-3856
Fax: (913) 383-2277
E-mail: experts@johncglennon.com
Web Site: http://www.johncglennon.com

Specialties: Motor Vehicle Accident Investigation; Accident Reconstruction; Vehicle Crush Analysis; Vehicular Mechanical and Structural Failure Analysis for Automobiles, Trucks, and Motorcycles; Testing Capabilities for Air Brakes, Hydraulic Brakes, Suspension Systems, Steering Systems, Tires, and Wheels; Determination if Proper Maintenance and Repair Procedures were Followed; Identification of Previous Body Structural Damage; Motor Carrier Safety and Compliance; Commercial Driver Responsibilities and Qualifications; Commercial Driver Hours of Service and Daily Logs; Proper Load Securement Procedures; Fleet Maintenance Requirements; Computer Animation; Forensic Mapping; Photo Modeling; Downloading of Crash Data

Retrieval Systems (Automobile "BLACK BOX"). **Degrees/licenses:** D. Engr., PE, BS Automotive Technology, ASE Cert., CDL.

See primary listing under ACCIDENT RECONSTRUCTION: General

InterCity Testing & Consulting

167 Willis Avenue
Mineola, NY 11501
Tel: (516) 747-8400 (NY)
(800) 822-1515 (Outside NYS)
Fax: (516) 746-0121/0111 (NY)
Tel: (561) 745-7940 (FL)
Fax: (561) 745-7939 (FL)
E-mail: expt1@aol.com
Web Site: http://www.InterCityTesting.com

3550 Watt Ave., Ste. 5
Sacramento, CA 95821
Tel: (916) 481-3093
(800) 500-5561 (Toll Free)
Fax: (916) 481-3095

Specialties: Visit our web site for condensed expert CV's in: Amusement Parks & Rides; Automotive Safety & Accident Reconstruction; Biomedical/Biomechanical Injury Analysis; Biomechanics; Boating & Marine Safety; Chemicals & Chemical Engineering; Civil Engineering/Structural Failures; Construction Accidents; Electrical & Mechanical Engineering; Firearms & Explosives; Fire Investigations; Flammable Fabrics; Helmets/Motorcycle, Bicycle, Sports & Industrial; Machine Guarding; Medical Devices; Medical Emergency/EMT; Metallurgy & Material Sciences; Parks & Playgrounds; Slips, Trips & Falls; Sports/Recreation/Aquatics; Toxicology; Transportation & Highway Safety; Warnings & Instructions. INTERCITY IS NOT AN EXPERT REFERRAL SERVICE. **Degrees/licenses:** PE's / degrees thru PhD's in above specialties.

See primary listing under ACCIDENT RECONSTRUCTION: General

Ira S. Kuperstein

219 Penn Avenue
Dover, NJ 07801
Tel: (973) 283-2420
(800) 526-5177, Ext. 102
Fax: (973) 366-2104

Specialties: Collision dynamics; Computer simulation; Accident reconstruction & analysis; Traffic accident analysis; Highway design & engineering; Traffic control devices & engineering. Affiliation: Independent Consultant. **Degrees/licenses:** PhD; PE.

Zachary Parker

President
Parker Enterprises
310 Boundary Place
Roswell, GA 30075-6876
Tel: (805) 236-4532
Fax: (256) 500-9604
E-mail: zach.parker@ngc.com

Specialties: Human factors; Forensic perception/response; biodynamics. **Degrees/licenses:** Licensed Reliability Engineer.

See primary listing under ACCIDENT RECONSTRUCTION: Slip & Fall

TASA

(Technical Advisory Service for Attorneys)
1166 DeKalb Pike
Blue Bell, PA 19422-1853
Tel: (800) 523-2319
Fax: (800) 329-8272
E-mail: experts@tasanet.com
Web Site: http://www.tasanet.com

Specialties: Save search time! Contact TASA first. Benefit from 44 years of referral expertise. We assess your individual needs and refer experienced Local, Regional, or National professionals for Consulting, Testifying, and ADR in areas including Air Bags; Auto Crashworthiness, Impact, Lighting, and Restraints; Automotive Engineering; Aviation; Bicycles; Boat Accidents, Buses; Construction; Farm Equipment; Guardrails; Highway Design & Construction; Industrial Accidents; Meteorology; Motorcycles; Railroads; Rec-

(Listing continued on next page)

Automotive/Vehicular *(cont.)*

TASA (cont.)

reational Vehicles; Roll-Overs; Tires; Traffic; Trucks; Visual Perception; Hundreds More. SERVICES INCLUDE prompt customized searches, referrals, resumes, and your initial interview calls with experts. Exceptional personal service. **Degrees/licenses:** All prof. degrees, licenses, certifications represented.

See primary listing under EXPERT WITNESS REFERRALS: General

Antonio Villalobos, PhD, PE

Forensic Engineering, Accident Reconstruction & Biomechanics
410 Castle Place
Beverly Hills, CA 90210
Tel: (310) 550-7746
Fax: (310) 550-6824
E-mail: villalob@ucla.edu
Web Site: http://www.theaccidentexpert.net

Specialties: Traffic/vehicular accident reconstruction: auto, truck, pedestrian, occupant kinematics, low speed impacts; Biomechanics: bone & soft tissue injury, back & neck injuries, extremities, industrial, construction & recreational accidents, personal altercations; Slip & Fall Analysis (friction testing); Failure of mechanical equipment, machine components, rotating machinery, power presses, machine guards, forklifts; Heat Transfer analysis. Listed in Who's Who in Engineering. **Degrees/licenses:** PhD Engineering, MS & BA Physics, PE Mechanical.

Automotive/Vehicular, Defects

Safety Engineering Associates, Inc.

2798 S. Fish Hatchery Road
Madison, WI 53711-5398
Tel: (608) 271-7884
(888) 723-3834
Fax: (608) 271-3720
E-mail: office@safetyengineering.com
Web Site:
http://www.safetyengineering.com

Specialties: Accident reconstruction, analysis, laboratory testing, video animation and expert witness services regarding: Automobiles; Trucks; Motorcycles; Farm machinery; Industrial machinery; Consumer products; Highway and rail crossing design; Motor vehicle fire cause and origin analysis. Over 20,000 accidents analyzed since 1947. Eight licensed professional engineers. **Degrees/ licenses:** PhD, MS, ME, CE, PE.

See primary listing under ACCIDENT RECONSTRUCTION: General

Automotive/Vehicular, Lighting

Walter J. Kosmatka

390 Sandhurst Drive
Highland Heights, OH 44143
Tel: (440) 461-7862
Fax: (440) 461-0311

Specialties: (1) Discernibility - nighttime detection of roadway obstacles by drivers; Roadway terrain, inclement weather, site lighting and obstacle coloration are taken into account; Common "obstacles" are pedestrians, animals, stopped vehicles, trailers, debris, construction barricades; (2) Automotive lamp failure analysis for the purpose of determining the illuminated state of the light devices, or direction of impact; (3) Light output measurements of automotive lamps; (4) Site/area lighting measurements and specification for same. Holds 17 U.S. and foreign patents; Chair SAE Road Illumination

Devices (RID) Sub Committee; Consultant NHTSA/U. of Mich. Transportation Research Inst. **Degrees/licenses:** B. Chem. Eng.; BBA; Prov Member AAFS.

See primary listing under ACCIDENT RECONSTRUCTION: Visibility

Biodynamics of Injury

Zachary Parker

President
Parker Enterprises
310 Boundary Place
Roswell, GA 30075-6876
Tel: (805) 236-4532
Fax: (256) 500-9604
E-mail: zach.parker@ngc.com

Specialties: Human factors; Reliability engineering; Personal injury; Product liability. **Degrees/licenses:** Licensed Reliability Engineer.

See primary listing under ACCIDENT RECONSTRUCTION: Slip & Fall

Transamerican Consultant Engineers, Inc.

Roderick Stroud, PhD
President
P.O. Box 3033
Thousand Oaks, CA 91359
Tel: (818) 889-9986
Fax: (818) 889-9505
E-mail: tce@transameng.com
Web Site: http://www.transameng.com

Specialties: TCE provides an analytical engineering service for the insurance industry and legal profession, with expert witness testimony when required. All of our engineers have university degrees in engineering, industrial backgrounds and extensive forensic engineering experience. All have appeared many times as engineering experts in arbitration and in court. All qualify repeatedly as accident reconstruction/biomechanical engineers. Areas of expertise include: injury causation - failure analysis, motor vehicle accident, pedestrian accident, automotive, biomechanics, medical devices, orthopedic instrumentation, construction, machines, hardware, toys, marine, plumbing, fires, tools, slip/trip and fall. **Degrees/licenses:** AB, BSME, MSME, BSAE, MSAE, MS (Mtls. Sci.), PhD (BME), PE.

Biomechanics

Wilson C. "Toby" Hayes, PhD

President
Hayes + Associates, Inc.
301 SW 4th St., Suite 160
Corvallis, OR 97333
Tel: (541) 754-9645
(541) 912-7222
Fax: (541) 754-9949
E-mail: wch@hayesassoc.com
Web Site: http://www.hayesassoc.com

Specialties: Expertise: injury biomechanics, accident reconstruction and failure analysis; personal injury, products liability, wrongful death, premises liability, medical malpractice; motor vehicle accidents; slips, trips, falls; sports injuries, recreation and safety equipment, industrial injuries, ergonomics and repetitive stress syndromes. Background: (1979-98) Director, Orthopedic Biomechanics Laboratory, Mueller Professor Biomechanics, Harvard Medical School/MIT; (1998-present) Professor Exercise and Sports Science/Mechanical Engineering, Oregon State University; Orthopedics & Rehabilitation, Oregon Health Sciences University. Awards: (1995) American Society Biomechanics Borelli; (1996) Bristol-Myers Squibb/Zimmer Research. Excellence Orthopedic Treatment. **Degrees/licenses:** BS, MS (Stanford '64, '66); PhD (Northwestern '70).

Biomechanics *(cont.)*

InterCity Testing & Consulting

167 Willis Avenue
Mineola, NY 11501
Tel: (516) 747-8400 (NY)
(800) 822-1515 (Outside NYS)
Fax: (516) 746-0121/0111 (NY)
Tel: (561) 745-7940 (FL)
Fax: (561) 745-7939 (FL)
E-mail: expt1@aol.com
Web Site: http://www.InterCityTesting.com

3550 Watt Ave., Ste. 5
Sacramento, CA 95821
Tel: (916) 481-3093
(800) 500-5561 (Toll Free)
Fax: (916) 481-3095

Specialties: Visit our web site for condensed expert CV's in: Amusement Parks & Rides; Automotive Safety & Accident Reconstruction; Biomedical/Biomechanical Injury Analysis; Biomechanics; Boating & Marine Safety; Chemicals & Chemical Engineering; Civil Engineering/Structural Failures; Construction Accidents; Electrical & Mechanical Engineering; Firearms & Explosives; Fire Investigations; Flammable Fabrics; Helmets/ Motorcycle, Bicycle, Sports & Industrial; Machine Guarding; Medical Devices; Medical Emergency/EMT; Metallurgy & Material Sciences; Parks & Playgrounds; Slips, Trips & Falls; Sports/Recreation/Aquatics; Toxicology; Transportation & Highway Safety; Warnings & Instructions. INTERCITY IS NOT AN EXPERT REFERRAL SERVICE. **Degrees/licenses:** PE's / degrees thru PhD's in above specialties.

See primary listing under ACCIDENT RECONSTRUCTION: General

Chandler A. Phillips

Phillips & Phillips Associates
7200 Peters Road
Tipp City, OH 45371
Tel: (937) 667-6047
Fax: (937) 667-7717
E-mail: chandler.phillips@wright.edu

Specialties: Medical device injury analysis; Consumer product safety & hazard analysis; Injury biomechanics & injury causation; Forensic biomedical engineering; ergonomics & workplace safety; Human factors engineering. **Degrees/licenses:** MD; PE.

Pro/Consul Technical and Medical Experts

1945 Palo Verde Ave., Suite 200
Long Beach, CA 90815-3443
Tel: (800) 392-1119
(562) 799-0116
Fax: (562) 799-8821
E-mail: eexperts@msn.com
Web Site: http://www.expertinfo.com

Specialties: RIGHT EXPERT RIGHT AWAY!® 15,000 experts in 7,000 fields. Listed and recommended by the A. M. Best Company. Full-time research staff. We welcome your RUSH cases! TECHNICAL: Fast inspections. Categories from Accident Reconstruction to Zoology, also including appraisal, economics, employment, human factors, insurance, premises liability, security, and many more. MEDICAL: IME's. Inexpensive insurance medical records reviews by MDs. Categories from Addiction Medicine to Zooplasty, including board certified physicians in all fields, dentistry, geriatrics, neuropsychology, neurosurgery, nursing, orthopedics, psychiatry and many more. Reasonable fees. Free initial consultation. Free resume binder. Free CLE classes. **Degrees/licenses:** MD, PhD, DDS, DVM, DO, DPM, PE, CPA, ME, CE, CRC, MAI, et al.

See primary listing under ACCIDENT RECONSTRUCTION: General

Antonio Villalobos, PhD, PE

Forensic Engineering, Accident
Reconstruction & Biomechanics
410 Castle Place
Beverly Hills, CA 90210
Tel: (310) 550-7746
Fax: (310) 550-6824
E-mail: villalob@ucla.edu
Web Site: http://www.theaccidentexpert.net

Specialties: Traffic/vehicular accident reconstruction: auto, truck, pedestrian, occupant kinematics, low speed impacts; Biomechanics: bone & soft tissue injury, back & neck injuries, extremities, industrial, construction & recreational accidents, personal altercations; Slip & Fall Analysis (friction testing); Failure of mechanical equipment, machine components, rotating machinery, power presses, machine guards, forklifts; Heat Transfer analysis. Listed in Who's Who in Engineering. **Degrees/licenses:** PhD Engineering, MS & BA Physics, PE Mechanical.

See primary listing under ACCIDENT RECONSTRUCTION: Automotive/Vehicular

Chemical

Chemical Accident Reconstruction Services, Inc.

Michael Fox, PhD
Founder
9121 E. Tanque Verde Rd., #105
Tucson, AZ 85749-8391
Tel: (800) 645-3369
Fax: (520) 749-0861
E-mail: services@chemaxx.com
Web Site: http://www.chemaxx.com

Specialties: Complex industrial chemical accidents, fires and explosions as well as chemical-related consumer product injuries. The founder of the company has his PhD in Physical Chemistry, is a Certified Fire & Explosion Investigator and Certified or Accredited in Hazardous Chemicals, OSHA Process Hazard Analysis Team Leader, DOT Hazardous Materials, Corrosion, Metallurgy, Failure Analysis and Aerosols. Other specialties include: Propane, plastics, water chemistry, skin burns, acids, alkalis, carbon monoxide, flammable liquids, gasoline, scanning microscopy, MSDSs, natural gas, solvents, warning labels, PEX, welding, construction, chemical packaging & transport. For more specialties see web site. **Degrees/licenses:** PhD, Physical Chemistry; See certifications above.

See primary listing under CHEMISTRY/ CHEMICALS: General

Compressed Gases & Equipment

Gas Technology Consultants, Inc.

Joe Golemi
President
PO Box 6317
Metairie, LA 70009-6317
Tel: (504) 885-9600
(800) 721-4240
Fax: (504) 466-7922 or (866) GTC-CRYO
E-mail: joecryogtc@aol.com
Web Site:
http://www.gastechnologyconsultants.com

Specialties: Explosion/Accident Reconstruction involving oxygen, Acetylene, Propylene, Propane, Argon, Nitrogen, Hydrogen, Helium & C02, Compressed gas cylinders, Torches, Regulators & related equipment, Cryogenic Cylinders & vessels, bulk & high & low Pressure Gas Distribution Piping Systems, Oxygen cleaning services, Welding Engineering, AWS & ASTM registered, Insurance/Litigation Support, Board Certified Forensic Examination, Technical Reports/Testing, Reprographics, Trial preparation & Expert Witnesses. Continental United States.

Construction

Wexco International Corporation

Dr. Stephen C. Wexler, PE
3226 Thatcher Avenue
Marina del Rey, CA 90292
Tel: (800) 559-3877
(310) 306-3877
(415) 281-3877
Fax: (310) 306-7480
E-mail: wexco@wexco.net
Web Site: http://www.wexco.net

Specialties: Construction consulting, engineering, safety and management; Construction defects and damages, costs to repair, policy coverage; Construction claims, delay impact analysis, CPM scheduling, contract disputes, damage calcs; Earthquake damage analysis and appraisal; Fire and flood damage apprais-

(Listing continued on next page)

Construction *(cont.)*

Wexco International Corporation (cont.)

als; Safety Engineering, building codes and safety regulation compliance; Construction accidents (falls from height, scaffolds, ladders, use of tools and equipment); Slips, Trips and Falls (stairs, ramps, walkways). All California and other states. In business since 1969. Calif . Contractor's License B-1. Licensed Safety & Civil Engineers. Have testified in over 150 trials. **Degrees/licenses:** PE, CPE, CCE, CCS, CPMP, CVS, CMC, CBO, CSP.

See primary listing under CONSTRUCTION: Safety Engineering

Construction Equipment

Ronald L. Spear

President
R.L. Spear & Associates, Inc.
5249 Killdeer Place
Rockford, IL 61114-7083
Tel: (815) 282-9239
(815) 282-9238
Fax: (815) 282-9248
E-mail: SpearAssociates@aol.com

Specialties: Engineering advisor providing expert consultation and litigation support on agricultural tractors, asphalt paving equipment, forklift trucks, and other material handling and heavy construction equipment. Services provided include review of—vehicle design for standard and code compliance (ANSI, ASME, OSHA, SAE, ASAE), operator training, safe use and application, accident investigation, product liability, manufacturing and/or quality control deficiencies, and dealer or distributor performance in sales and service. Thirty-two years management experience within various engineering development and product support departments of a major manufacturer. **Degrees/licenses:** BSME.

See primary listing under ENGINEERING: Product Liability

Cutting Torches & Regulators

Gas Technology Consultants, Inc.

Joe Golemi
President
PO Box 6317
Metairie, LA 70009-6317
Tel: (504) 885-9600
(800) 721-4240
Fax: (504) 466-7922 or (866) GTC-CRYO
E-mail: joecryogtc@aol.com
Web Site:
http://www.gastechnologyconsultants.com

Specialties: Explosion/Accident Reconstruction involving oxygen, Acetylene, Propylene, Propane, Argon, Nitrogen, Hydrogen, Helium & C02, Compressed gas cylinders, Torches, Regulators & related equipment, Cryogenic Cylinders & vessels, bulk & high & low Pressure Gas Distribution Piping Systems, Oxygen cleaning services, Welding Engineering, AWS & ASTM registered, Insurance/Litigation Support, Board Certified Forensic Examination, Technical Reports/Testing, Reprographics, Trial preparation & Expert Witnesses. Continental United States.

See primary listing under ACCIDENT RECONSTRUCTION: Compressed Gases & Equipment

Electrical Incidents

Dr. Eugene W. Bartel

President
Bartel, Rudolf & Associates
5578 Aiken Road
McKees Rocks, PA 15136
Tel: (412) 787-8166
Fax: (412) 787-5506
E-mail: eugenebartel@aol.com

Specialties: Professional Accidental Fire Origin and Cause Investigation; Forensic Engineering Evaluation of Fire Evidence; Electrical Accident Investigation; Engineering Evaluation of Products Relative to Defects as related to Liability Analysis; Laboratory Testing & X-Ray Analysis; Subrogation Specialists; Trial

Exhibit Preparation Services. Over 30 years of experience in Fire and Accident Investigation and Trial Testimony. **Degrees/licenses:** BSEE, MSEE, PhDEE, PE, CFI.

See primary listing under ENGINEERING: Electrical

Robert C. Ender, PE

30 Fairfield Drive
Kennebunk, ME 04043
Tel: (207) 967-0728
Fax: (207) 967-0728
E-mail: rcender@ieee.org

Specialties: Consulting engineer with over 40 years experience specializing in: Electric power (utility, industrial, commercial & residential electric systems); Electrical accident & equipment failure analyses; Safety codes - NEC, NESC, OSHA; Electric system design, costs & operating performance; Electric power regulatory issues; Evaluations of service interruptions & voltage quality; Testimony in both Federal and state jurisdictions; Alternative dispute resolution. **Degrees/licenses:** BSEE, MS, PE.

See primary listing under ENGINEERING: Electrical

A.D. Patton, PhD, PE

President
Associated Power Analysts, Inc.
303 Anderson Street
College Station, TX 77840
Tel: (979) 696-0010
Fax: (979) 696-7071
E-mail: adpatton@tca.net
Web Site: http://member.expertpages.com/assocpwranalysts

Specialties: Electric Power System Analysis; Power System Reliability and Failure Analysis; High- and Low-Voltage Equipment Failure Analysis; Electrical Accident and Failure Reconstruction; Electrical Standards and Operating Practices; Electric Utility Deregulation; Personal Injury and Property Loss Investigations; Engineering Reports and Expert Witness Testimony. Extensive Expert Witness Experience: State and Federal Courts and Regulatory Bodies. Author of more than 100 Papers and Reports on Electric Power Systems. Professor of Electrical Engineering at Texas A&M University - 31 years; Engineer, Westinghouse Electric Corp. - 8 years; Consulting Practice - 31 years. Life Fellow of IEEE. **Degrees/licenses:** PhD, PE.

See primary listing under ENGINEERING: Electrical

John C. Pfeiffer

President
Pfeiffer Engineering Co.
2701 Lindsay Ave.
Louisville, KY 40206-2222
Tel: (502) 897-1630
Fax: (502) 895-3894
E-mail: jcp@pfeiffereng.com
Web Site: http://www.pfeiffereng.com

Specialties: Electrical incidents; injuries, electrocution, shock, arc flash hazards, fires, power surges, lightning damage, static electricity & explosions. Failures due to computer software problems. Electrical Engineer with over 35 years experience, over 140 accidents investigated, specializing in grounding, lightning protection, electrical surge protection, power systems, industrial control systems, instrumentation, and computer based systems. Primary experience in heavy industry-chemical & manufacturing. **Degrees/licenses:** BSEE; PE.

See primary listing under ENGINEERING: Electrical

Thomas P. Shefchick

President
Shefchick Associates
PO Box 62284
Sunnyvale, CA 94088-2284
Tel: (800) 321-4TOM
Fax: (408) 615-8300
E-mail: shefchick@comcast.net
Web Site: http://www.shefchick.com

Specialties: Electrical engineering investigation & analysis; Damage to electrical equipment; Electrical injury; Court qualified.

(Listing continued on next page)

Electrical Incidents *(cont.)*

Thomas P. Shefchick (cont.)

Degrees/licenses: BSEE; PE (CA, DE, HI, NJ, NY, PA).

See primary listing under ACCIDENT RECONSTRUCTION: Electrocutions & Shocks

Electrocutions & Shocks

Thomas P. Shefchick
President
Shefchick Associates
PO Box 62284
Sunnyvale, CA 94088-2284
Tel: (800) 321-4TOM
Fax: (408) 615-8300
E-mail: shefchick@comcast.net
Web Site: http://www.shefchick.com

Specialties: Electrical engineering; Wiring; Circuit breakers; Power distribution; Controls; Appliances; Air conditioning; Heating; Court qualified. **Degrees/licenses:** BSEE; PE (CA, DE, HI, NJ, NY, PA).

Elevators/Escalators

John L. Donnelly
President
Donnelly & Associates, Inc.
1807 Glenview Rd., Suite 207
Glenview, IL 60025-2944
Tel: (847) 729-7911
Fax: (847) 729-7919
E-mail: john.l.donnelly@att.net

Specialties: Elevators; Escalators; Personnel hoists; Safety code for elevators & escalators. **Degrees/licenses:** BSEE.

Farm Machinery

Dale M. Gumz
Owner
Inductive Engineering
10805 230th St.
Cadott, WI 54727
Tel: (715) 289-4721
Fax: (715) 289-4722

Specialties: Engineering Consultant for: Agriculture, Construction, Consumer Products, Specialty Machines. Forensic & Safety Services: Safety Responsibilities, Accident Reconstruction, Design Analysis, Expert Witness, Human Factors, Manufacturing Processes, Mechanical & Electrical, Occupational Safety, Product Liability, Product & Machine Design. In business since 1970. **Degrees/ licenses:** BSME, PE, CSP.

Ronald L. Spear
President
R.L. Spear & Associates, Inc.
5249 Killdeer Place
Rockford, IL 61114-7083
Tel: (815) 282-9239
(815) 282-9238
Fax: (815) 282-9248
E-mail: SpearAssociates@aol.com

Specialties: Engineering advisor providing expert consultation and litigation support on agricultural tractors, asphalt paving equipment, forklift trucks, and other material handling and heavy construction equipment. Services provided include review of—vehicle design for standard and code compliance (ANSI, ASME, OSHA, SAE, ASAE), operator training, safe use and application, accident investigation, product liability, manufacturing and/or quality control deficiencies, and dealer or distributor performance in sales and service. Thirty-two years management experience within various engineering development and product support departments of a major manufacturer. **Degrees/licenses:** BSME.

See primary listing under ENGINEERING: Product Liability

Firearms

Richard N. Ernest

Forensic Consultant
7413 Arcadia Trail
Fort Worth, TX 76137
Tel: (817) 228-6526
Fax: (817) 498-6375
E-mail: rernest@e-gunlab.com
Web Site: http://www.e-gunlab.com

Specialties: Ballistics; Shooting Scene Reconstructions; Accidental Shootings; Firearms Examination; Microscopic Examination of Bullets, Cartridge Cases & Shotshells; Toolmark Examination; Trigger Pull Analysis; Ejection Pattern Testing; Gunshot Residues Consulting & Distance Determinations; Crime Scene Reconstructions; General Criminalistics Examinations including hair, fibers, tire tracks, shoe prints, lamp filament examinations; Forensic Casework Review. Extensive courtroom testimony experience. Testified over 1,000 times in several states & in Federal courts. Distinguished Member of Association of Firearms & Toolmarks Examiners, American Academy of Forensic Sciences, Charter Member of Association for Crime Scene Reconstruction, International Wound Ballistics Association. **Degrees/licenses:** BS- Univ. of GA, AFTE, AAFS, SAFS, SWAFS, ACSR & IWBA.

See primary listing under FIREARMS & BALLISTICS: General

Fires & Explosions

John Michael Agosti & Associates, Inc.

John Michael Agosti
Fire Analyst & Consultant
23808 N. Overhill
Lake Zurich, IL 60047
Tel: (847) 682-6793
Fax: (847) 540-6297
E-mail: johnagosti@earthlink.net
Web Site: http://www.arsonexpert.com

Specialties: Fire Cause & Origin; Arson Defense; Fire Related Injury/Death Cases; Vehicle Fires; Explosion & Gas Fires; Building & Fire Code Research; Fire Department Operations; Fire Department Management/Labor Consulting. Over 28 years of fire dept. experience blended with 10 years of private investigations for insurance companies, attorneys and as an expert witness. Over 1,400 fires investigated. Experienced in plaintiff/defense/criminal/civil cases. Qualified in state and federal courts. Free initial phone consultation. **Degrees/licenses:** Fire Science Degree, State Certified Fire Investigator.

Dr. Eugene W. Bartel

President
Bartel, Rudolf & Associates
5578 Aiken Road
McKees Rocks, PA 15136
Tel: (412) 787-8166
Fax: (412) 787-5506
E-mail: eugenebartel@aol.com

Specialties: Professional Accidental Fire Origin and Cause Investigation; Forensic Engineering Evaluation of Fire Evidence; Electrical Accident Investigation; Engineering Evaluation of Products Relative to Defects as related to Liability Analysis; Laboratory Testing & X-Ray Analysis; Subrogation Specialists; Trial Exhibit Preparation Services. Over 30 years of experience in Fire and Accident Investigation and Trial Testimony. **Degrees/licenses:** BSEE, MSEE, PhDEE, PE, CFI.

See primary listing under ENGINEERING: Electrical

Chemical Accident Reconstruction Services, Inc.

Michael Fox, PhD
Founder
9121 E. Tanque Verde Rd., #105
Tucson, AZ 85749-8391
Tel: (800) 645-3369
Fax: (520) 749-0861
E-mail: services@chemaxx.com
Web Site: http://www.chemaxx.com

Specialties: Complex industrial chemical accidents, fires and explosions as well as chemical-related consumer product injuries.

(Listing continued on next page)

Fires & Explosions *(cont.)*

Chemical Accident Reconstruction Services, Inc. (cont.)

The founder of the company has his PhD in Physical Chemistry, is a Certified Fire & Explosion Investigator and Certified or Accredited in Hazardous Chemicals, OSHA Process Hazard Analysis Team Leader, DOT Hazardous Materials, Corrosion, Metallurgy, Failure Analysis and Aerosols. Other specialties include: Propane, plastics, water chemistry, skin burns, acids, alkalis, carbon monoxide, flammable liquids, gasoline, scanning microscopy, MSDSs, natural gas, solvents, warning labels, PEX, welding, construction, chemical packaging & transport. For more specialties see web site. **Degrees/licenses:** PhD, Physical Chemistry; See certifications above.

See primary listing under CHEMISTRY/ CHEMICALS: General

Robert E. Engberg, PE

President
Gas Dynamics Corporation
810 No. Lilac Dr., Ste. 205
Golden Valley, MN 55422-4672
Tel: (763) 521-8306
Fax: (763) 521-8306
E-mail: rengberg@aol.com
Web Site:
http://www.gasdynamicscorp.com

Specialties: Fire and Explosion Investigations; Propane, Butane, Natural Gas & Ammonia System Analysis & Design; Burner, Boiler & Dryer Systems; HVAC & Stress Analysis; Machine Design & Crane Component Stress Analysis; Fire Sprinkler & Monitoring Systems; Cathodic Protection Analysis; LP-Gas Standby & Storage Plants; Ammonia Storage & Petrochemical Plants; Lab Facilities for Pressure & Flow Analysis. **Degrees/licenses:** BS Math & Mech. Engr.; PE (MN & WI).

Fire & Risk Engineering

Robert Malanga, PE
President
9 Flintlock Drive, Ste. 100
Long Valley, NJ 07853
Tel: (908) 876-3255
Fax: (908) 876-4299
E-mail: email@fire-risk.com
Web Site: http://www.fire-risk.com

Specialties: Fire protection engineering - Investigation, forensic reconstruction of major fires/explosions; Evaluation of fire protection systems; Fire defense analysis; Application and interpretation of fire and building codes; Fire hazard analysis and risk assessment consulting. Experienced in wide range of industrial, commercial and chemical exposures; Corporate risk management and municipal fire service experience; Master planning and emergency response planning. **Degrees/licenses:** BS-Fire Protection Engr.; MS-Tech. Mgt.; AAS Elec. Engr.

See primary listing under ENGINEERING: Fire Protection

Russell R. Fote

Principal
Russell Fote & Associates, Inc.
3635 Stonebrook Court
Brookfield, WI 53005
Tel: (262) 781-4496
Fax: (262) 783-4312
E-mail: rfote@execpc.com
Web Site: http://www.fote-engineering.com

Specialties: Scalds; Fires; Explosions; Carbon monoxide; Flammable fabrics, liquids & gases; Water heaters, appliances & furnaces; Mechanical failures; Government regulations; Industry standards. Certified Fire & Explosion Investigator (CFEI). **Degrees/licenses:** MSEM; BSME; PE; CSP.

Interactive Consulting, Inc.

Meyer R. Rosen
President
P.O. Box 66
East Norwich, NY 11732
Tel: (516) 922-2167
Fax: (516) 922-3830
E-mail: meyer.rosen@chemicalconsult.com
Web Site: http://www.chemicalconsult.com

Specialties: With over thirty-five years industrial experience in chemistry and chemical engineering and fifteen years as Adjunct Professor of Fire Chemistry (Westchester Community College), Mr. Rosen has consulted for hundreds of domestic and international corporations in the development, optimization, safety, technical marketing and quality control of new and existing consumer and industrial products. He specializes in technical product liability related to personal injuries resulting from fires and explosions, chemical burns, toxic exposures, and hazardous chemicals in household and industrial products. He performs strategic pre-trial planning, deposition support and accident reconstruction. Mr. Rosen is experienced in design safety, formulation, packaging, product handling, codes & standards, intellectual property management, patent analysis/infringement litigation issues, safer alternatives, warnings, instructions and labeling. **Certifications include:** Fellow, American College of Forensic Examiners; Fellow, Royal Society of Chemistry (London); Diplomate, American Board of Forensic Engineering and Technology; Certified Professional Chemist and Chemical Engineer; Fellow, American Institute of Chemists; Technical Journalist for major chemical trade publications. Editor, "Handbook of Delivery Systems" and co-author of "Rheology Modifier Handbook". **Degrees/licenses:** BS, MS.

See primary listing under CHEMISTRY/ CHEMICALS: General

InterCity Testing & Consulting

167 Willis Avenue
Mineola, NY 11501
Tel: (516) 747-8400 (NY)
(800) 822-1515 (Outside NYS)
Fax: (516) 746-0121/0111 (NY)
Tel: (561) 745-7940 (FL)
Fax: (561) 745-7939 (FL)
E-mail: expt1@aol.com
Web Site: http://www.InterCityTesting.com

3550 Watt Ave., Ste. 5
Sacramento, CA 95821
Tel: (916) 481-3093
(800) 500-5561 (Toll Free)
Fax: (916) 481-3095

Specialties: Visit our web site for condensed expert CV's in: Amusement Parks & Rides; Automotive Safety & Accident Reconstruction; Biomedical/Biomechanical Injury Analysis; Biomechanics; Boating & Marine Safety; Chemicals & Chemical Engineering; Civil Engineering/Structural Failures; Construction Accidents; Electrical & Mechanical Engineering; Firearms & Explosives; Fire Investigations; Flammable Fabrics; Helmets/ Motorcycle, Bicycle, Sports & Industrial; Machine Guarding; Medical Devices; Medical Emergency/EMT; Metallurgy & Material Sciences; Parks & Playgrounds; Slips, Trips & Falls; Sports/Recreation/Aquatics; Toxicology; Transportation & Highway Safety; Warnings & Instructions. INTERCITY IS NOT AN EXPERT REFERRAL SERVICE. **Degrees/licenses:** PE's / degrees thru PhD's in above specialties.

See primary listing under ACCIDENT RECONSTRUCTION: General

Gregory K. Marsh

Gregory K. Marsh & Assoc., LLC
7700 West 61st Ave., Suite #12
Arvada, CO 80004-5635
Tel: (303) 421-3383
Fax: (303) 421-3383 (Call first)
E-mail: greg_marsh@ekit.com
Web Site: http://www.forensic-pro.com

Specialties: Arson investigation & oversight; Fire investigation evaluation & oversight;

(Listing continued on next page)

Fires & Explosions *(cont.)*

Gregory K. Marsh, (cont.)
Root cause analysis; Water damage; Indoor air quality (IAQ), including microbes; Sick Building Syndrome (SBS) analysis; Odors & tobacco smoke; Regulatory compliance; Environmental chemistry; Industrial hygiene; Power plants; Poisonings (chemical & pesticide); Water & general contamination evaluation; Product liability; Fraud; Personal injury; Workman's Compensation; Spoilage during sea transit. Affiliation: Gregory K. Marsh & Associates (President). Degrees and Licenses: Graduate level courses in Civil Engineering, Environmental Engineering & Chemistry. **Degrees/licenses:** BS (Chemistry).

Glenn D. Peterson, PE

2651 Carisbrook Drive
Oakland, CA 94611
Tel: (510) 482-2704
Fax: (510) 482-2704
E-mail: GlennPeterson@msn.com

Specialties: Investigation of fire protection systems design (sprinklers, standpipes, pumps, fire alarms, foam, halon, dry chemical & others); Fire protection equipment failures; Fires-cause and spread; Propane & natural gas fires & explosions; Furnace and water heater fires; Construction defects; Expert testimony; Computer simulations of fire spread; Analysis of fire hazards and burning characteristics of various materials; Building and fire code analysis; Fire Protection and Mechanical Engineer licenses; Over 30 years experience. **Degrees/licenses:** BS, FPE, ME.

See primary listing under ENGINEERING: Fire Protection

John W. Poole, III, PE

Principal
Poole Consulting Services, Inc.
1317 S. Fountain Drive
Olathe, KS 66061
Tel: (913) 829-8650
Fax: (913) 829-8690
E-mail: jack@pcsinkc.com
Web Site: http://www.pcsinkc.com

Specialties: Building and Fire Code Analyses and Consulting; Fire Suppression Design and Evaluation; Fire Alarm and Detection System Design and Evaluation; Fire or Explosion Cause and Origin Evaluation; Fire Protection/ Safety/Health Program Design and Evaluation; Fire Hazard Mitigation; Life Safety Code Analysis; Fire Incident Investigations; Flammable and/or Explosive Atmosphere Evaluations; Computer Fire and Egress Modeling; Fire Hazard Evaluations; Hydraulic Analysis; Forensic Fire Safety Analysis; Facility Safety and Fire Protection Audits; Wrongful Death Matters; Fire Reconstruction and Evaluation; Product and Equipment Liability Matters. **Degrees/licenses:** BS Fire Protection Engr., Lic. Prof. Engr. (PE).

See primary listing under ENGINEERING: Fire Protection

Thomas P. Shefchick

President
Shefchick Associates
PO Box 62284
Sunnyvale, CA 94088-2284
Tel: (800) 321-4TOM
Fax: (408) 615-8300
E-mail: shefchick@comcast.net
Web Site: http://www.shefchick.com

Specialties: Electrical fires: residential, commercial, industrial; Wiring; Circuit breakers; Power distribution; Controls; Appliances; Air conditioning; Heating; Court qualified. **Degrees/licenses:** BSEE; PE (CA, DE, HI, NJ, NY, PA).

See primary listing under ACCIDENT RECONSTRUCTION: Electrocutions & Shocks

L. Douglas Smoot

Senior Consultant
Combustion Resources, LLC
1453 West 820 North
Provo, UT 84601
Tel: (801) 422-8930 or 374-5474
Fax: (801) 422-0152 or 343-0687
E-mail: LDS@byu.edu or
dsmoot@combustionresources.com
Web Site:
http://www.combustionresources.com

Specialties: Fires; Gas, dust, vapor explosions, combustion, fossil fuels; Cause, origin, incident reconstruction, computer modeling; Pollutant formation. Professor emeritus - Chem. Eng., Dean Emeritus, Founding Director - Advanced Combustion Engineering Research Center, BYU; Consultant, 65 organizations; Extensive expert witness experience in fires/explosions: buildings, fireplaces, vehicles, coal mines, firearms; Member AIChE, ASME, NFPA, Combustion Institute: Author, 4 books, 220 papers; Distinguished Faculty Award, 1985; Governor's Medal, 1987; 2002 Homer H. Lowry Gold Medal, Dept. of Energy; 2002 Percy Nicholls Award, ASME; Colleagues: Dr. Scott Hill, Modeling, Dr. Craig Eatough, testing. **Degrees/licenses:** BS, Chemistry; BES, MS,PhD Chem Eng., PE.

Thielsch Engineering, Inc.

Ara Nalbandian, PE, Vice President
Bob Basile, PE
Florence Cone
195 Frances Avenue
Cranston, RI 02910
Tel: (401) 467-6454
Fax: (401) 467-2398
E-mail: nalbandiana@thielsch.com
Web Site: http://www.thielsch.com

Specialties: Failure analyses and forensic investigations of equipment and products in many different industries including power generation, pulp and paper, petroleum and chemical, process industries, mining, manufacturing, transportation, electronics, medical devices, failures or condition assessments of vessel, piping, bridges, building structures, electrical components/systems, pumps, water transmission, fire protection piping, compressors and other rotating equipment. Extensive laboratory testing facilities include full spectrum analyses, metallurgical, mechanical, chemical , analytical, bacteriological, environmental, structural and corrosion testing services. Registered Professional Engineers in Rhode Island, Massachusetts, Maine, New Jersey, Georgia, Florida, Indiana and California. **Degrees/licenses:** BS, PE, BS Mech. Engr. MS (RI, MA, ME, NJ, GA, FL, IN & CA).

See primary listing under ENGINEERING: Consulting

Fitness Equipment/Products

Frank J. Smith

Owner
Elite Fitness Consulting Services
1021 Highland Park
Fallbrook, CA 92028-5421
Tel: (760) 728-5212
Fax: (760) 728-5239
E-mail: fitwitness@aol.com
Web Site: http://www.fitwitness.com

Specialties: Twenty five years in Fitness Equipment design, use and operation; Fitness Center design; Certification of Instructors; Sauna Room design and operation; Steam Room design and operation; Flooring applications to fitness; designing Programs for Fitness Equipment Users; Lecturer on Fitness and Fitness Equipment use. Seven years as a consultant to the "President's Council on Physical Fitness and Sports." Published in the following areas: Fitness and Use of Equipment, Fitness Center design, Training Charts and Instruction Materials, Rehabilitation Programs, Instructional Videos. Designed Institutional and Retail Marketing Programs for Fitness Equipment. Fee: $150.00 per hr. **Degrees/licenses:** BA Education, Univ. of Washington; Provisional Teaching Cert., Education.

See primary listing under ACCIDENT PREVENTION & SAFETY: Exercise Equipment

Industrial

Joseph R. Driear, PE

612 Alta Loma Drive
Thiensville, WI 53092
Tel: (262) 242-2078
Fax: (262) 242-3736
E-mail: drieng@execpc.com

Specialties: Consulting engineering: Mechanical, metallurgical, structural, hydraulic & pneumatic. Expert witness, plaintiff or defense. Experienced in Industrial Accident Reconstruction; Causation; Product & Machine Design; Failure Analysis. Experienced with aerial work platforms; air compressors; docklevelers and truck loading dock equipment; conveyors; fires in vehicles, machines & buildings; hydraulic construction machines; machine electrical control; auto & truck engine, gear and part failures; household appliances; orthopedic devices. Experienced in deposition and trial. Engineering experience is in industry — 20 years in materials and processes engineering plus 20 years in machine/ product design and development engineering. 7 patents. **Degrees/licenses:** MetEng., MS; Licensed PE (WI, PA & IL).

Industrial Forklift Trucks

Ronald L. Spear

President
R.L. Spear & Associates, Inc.
5249 Killdeer Place
Rockford, IL 61114-7083
Tel: (815) 282-9239
(815) 282-9238
Fax: (815) 282-9248
E-mail: SpearAssociates@aol.com

Specialties: Engineering advisor providing expert consultation and litigation support on agricultural tractors, asphalt paving equipment, forklift trucks, and other material handling and heavy construction equipment. Services provided include review of—vehicle design for standard and code compliance (ANSI, ASME, OSHA, SAE, ASAE), operator training, safe use and application, accident investigation, product liability, manufacturing and/or quality control deficiencies, and dealer or distributor performance in sales and service. Thirty-two years management experience within various engineering development and product support departments of a major manufacturer. **Degrees/licenses:** BSME.

See primary listing under ENGINEERING: Product Liability

Lifting Equipment

CRAFT Forensic Services

Bradley D. Closson
180 Otay Lakes Road, Suite 109
Bonita, CA 91902
Tel: (619) 737-9563
Fax: (619) 737-9564
E-mail: bclosson@craftforensic.com
Web Site: http://www.craftforensic.com

Specialties: Crane, rigging, aerial devices, forklift accident investigation and reconstruction. All environments and jurisdictions. Extensive practical operation experience. Member ASME B30, SAE, ASCE, ASSE, ASNE, SAME, ACRP and CCAA. Previously accepted as expert in federal and numerous state jurisdictions. Active on state and federal advisory boards relevant to material handling safety, have trained equipment operators and riggers in all aspects of equipment and environmental safety, have trained equipment managers in operation safety. Speak at industry meetings on related safety issues. Perform material handling safety calculations and analysis as well as equipment condition inspections. **Degrees/licenses:** BS; California Crane, Nevada Crane, Maritime Crane Inspector.

Frederick G. Heath

Principal
Heath and Associates
3316 Springcrest Drive
Louisville, KY 40241
Tel: (502) 425-2385
Fax: (502) 339-0729
E-mail: fgheath@bellsouth.net
Web Site:
http://www.heathandassociates.com

Specialties: Expert services covering industrial machines, lifts, hoists, jacks, cranes and material handling equipment. Heath and Associates draws on 40 years of engineering, manufacturing and management experience to provide services relating to product safety analysis and planning, accident investigation and reconstruction, product design, documentation and cost reduction and quality assurance and manufacturing. Heath and Associates can assist in product evaluations, testing, compliance with applicable standards, compliance with applicable regulations (OSHA, EPA & DOT), adequacy of instructional materials and labeling, development of explanatory exhibits and preparation of evidence for trial. **Degrees/licenses:** BSME, CHMM, CSS.

Marine

Hector V. Pazos, PE

Ocean-Oil Expert Witness, Inc.
& Yachts Unlimited, Inc.
P.O. Box 47188
St. Petersburg, FL 33743-7188
Tel: (727) 347-2556
(504) 367-4072
Fax: (727) 343-9717 or (504) 367-3790
E-mail: Oceanoilpazos@cs.com or
Hectorpazos75597@aol.com
Web Site: http://www.siterrific.com/pazos

Specialties: Expert Witness; Maritime accident reconstruction; Personal injury; Slip and fall; Inclined and vertical ladders; Safety; Product liability; Design and latent defects; Structural and equipment failure; Fires and explosions; Power and sail pleasure boats; Passenger and cargo vessels; Offshore platforms; Drilling rigs; Pipelines; Barges and tugboats; Floating cranes; Container ships; Dredges; Fishing vessels; Noise and vibrations; Diving accidents; Human errors regarding vessel design, construction and operations; Marine surveying; Expert reports. Expert witness testimony provided in over 400 cases and analysis and/or investigation participation in over 1,200 cases. Boat owner and operator. **Degrees/licenses:** MS Naval Architect, Marine & Mechanical Engineer, PE.

See primary listing under MARITIME & ADMIRALTY: General

Capt. Mitchell S. Stoller

President
MAREX
30021 Tomas St., Ste. 300
Rancho Santa Margarita, CA 92688
Tel: (949) 858-5475
Fax: (949) 858-5477
E-mail: marexco@aol.com

Specialties: Expert Witness to the marine industry. Experience in Federal and State court, judicial arbitration, mediation services, and represents both plaintiff and defense. Consultant to the United States Coast Guard. Captain Stoller is the President and founder of Marex, a marine consulting company designed to market the safety expertise that enabled him to become the youngest captain of Exxon Shipping Company, U.S.A. He also holds an outstanding tanker safety operational record both at the Company and as a Los Angeles Harbor Pilot. Capt. Stoller has written and/or consulted on Safety and procedural manuals for numerous shipping companies and has been retained in over 800 blue/brown water cases across the nation from jet skis to pleasure crafts to super tankers. **Degrees/licenses:** Unlimited Master Mariner's Lic., Extensive Pilotage Lic., BS Nautical Sci.

See primary listing under MARITIME & ADMIRALTY: General

Marine *(cont.)*

Trident Marine Safety Associates

Henry S. Woods III
16850 Saturn Lane, #100
Houston, TX 77058
Tel: (281) 486-4552
Fax: (281) 486-9295
E-mail: hsw123@earthlink.net
Web Site:
http://www.tridentmarinesafety.com

P.O. Box 435
East Boothbay, ME 04544
Tel: (800) 580-BUOY

Specialties: Litigation support services for plaintiff and defense counsel and insurers in the following areas: Accident causation; Boating safety; Marine safety; Marine standards/codes/regulations; Rules of the Road ("right-of-way" issues); Collisions; Groundings; Hazards to navigation; Cargo loss/damage; Coast Guard regulations; Carbon monoxide poisoning; Jetski accidents; Water skiing accidents. **Degrees/licenses:** BS, MS.

Microwave Heating

R.F. Schiffmann Associates, Inc.

Robert F. Schiffmann
President
149 West 88 Street
New York, NY 10024-2401
Tel: (212) 362-7021
Fax: (212) 769-4630
E-mail: microwaves@juno.com
Web Site:
http://www.microwaveinnovations.com

Specialties: Microwave Heating; Microwave Ovens; Microwave Foods; Microwave Packaging; Microwave Cookware; Microwave oven accidents and injuries; Microwave fires; Microwave patents and infringement; Industrial Microwave Processing Systems. Independent consultant since 1971; Contract R&D Laboratory; Teach two international courses on Microwave Technology annually; Lecture worldwide on Microwave Technology; Fellow of the International Microwave Power Institute (IMPI); Past Chairman, President & Board member of IMPI for 18 years; Over 30 U.S. patents; Scientific Lecturer on Microwave Technology for Institute of Food Technologists; Extensive Expert Witness Testimony. **Degrees/licenses:** BS, MS, FIMPI.

Pedestrian

Aronberg & Associates Consulting Engineers, Inc.

Ralph Aronberg, PE
1304 SW 160th Ave., #220
Fort Lauderdale, FL 33326-1902
Tel: (954) 236-6605
E-mail: aronconeng@prodigy.net
Web Site:
http://pages.prodigy.net/aronconeng

Specialties: Traffic accident reconstruction (cars, trucks, motorcycles and pedestrians); Vehicle occupant kinematics (seatbelts); Biomechanics; Traffic engineering design (geometrics, signing, markings, signals and lighting); Sight distance analysis; Hazardous roadway conditions; Work zone traffic control evaluation; Evaluation of roadway curvature; Pedestrian safety; Computerized accident reconstruction and simulation; vehicle "black box" analysis; Fraud evaluation; 3D computer animations. Mr. Aronberg is a Professional Engineer with 25 years of government and private consulting experience. He has reconstructed over 1000 traffic accidents and testified in over 100 trials; Published through the Society of Automotive Engineers. **Degrees/licenses:** BSCE, MS, PE.

See primary listing under ACCIDENT RECONSTRUCTION: Automotive/Vehicular

Personal Injury

A. C. T. International

Bernd S. Givon, PE & Associates
8306 Wilshire Blvd., #88
Beverly Hills, CA 90211
Tel: (310) 652-3221
Fax: (310) 652-3291
E-mail: actintl@netscape.com

Specialties: Forty-five years experience in consumer products evaluation, testing, failure analysis, industrial, commercial & domestic accident reconstruction; Investigate misuse, abuse, hazards & safety; Slip, trip & fall; Chairs, appliances, office & juvenile furniture; Playground and exercise equipment injuries; Bicycles and wheelchairs; Toys; Conveyors, power tools & ladders; Glass breakage; Textiles and fabric flammability, burn & scalding mishaps; Building materials; Gates, doors, windows & hardware; Damage assessment; Automotive accessories defects; Critique instructions & warnings; Detailed CV & fee schedule available upon request. **Degrees/licenses:** PhD, MS Mech Eng., PE (CA & NJ).

See primary listing under ENGINEERING: Forensic

Capt. Mitchell S. Stoller

President
MAREX
30021 Tomas St., Ste. 300
Rancho Santa Margarita, CA 92688
Tel: (949) 858-5475
Fax: (949) 858-5477
E-mail: marexco@aol.com

Specialties: Expert Witness to the marine industry. Experience in Federal and State court, judicial arbitration, mediation services, and represents both plaintiff and defense. Consultant to the United States Coast Guard. Captain Stoller is the President and founder of Marex, a marine consulting company designed to market the safety expertise that enabled him to become the youngest captain of Exxon Shipping Company, U.S.A. He also holds an outstanding tanker safety operational record both at the Company and as a Los Angeles Harbor Pilot. Capt. Stoller has written and/or consulted on Safety and procedural manuals for numerous shipping companies and has been retained in over 800 blue/brown water cases across the nation from jet skis to pleasure crafts to super tankers. **Degrees/licenses:** Unlimited Master Mariner's Lic., Extensive Pilotage Lic., BS Nautical Sci.

See primary listing under MARITIME & ADMIRALTY: General

Playgrounds

Safety Play, Inc.

Scott Burton
— Free Air Fare —
Main Office:
10460 Roosevelt Blvd., #295
St. Petersburg, FL 33716
Tel: (888) 878-0244 (Toll Free)
(727) 522-0061
Fax: (727) 522-0061
E-mail: safetyplay@mindspring.com
Web Site:
http://www.mindspring.com/~safetyplay

California Office:
7095 Hollywood Blvd., #1308
Los Angeles, CA 90028

Specialties: Free air fare (minor restrictions apply, one round trip). Instructor for safety courses. Expert in playground, sports, and recreation accidents including playgrounds, soccer, trampolines, water, baseball, football, softball, basketball, volleyball, fitness equipment, exercise trails, etc. Investigation of warnings, ADA compliance, supervision, hazards, layout, design, surfacing, and inspections for risk management, parks and recreation, schools, facilities, amusement parks, resorts, day care centers, hotels, restaurants, etc. Voting member on ASTM committees creating national standards and CPSC guidelines. Ex-manufacturer who is experienced in expert testimony, manufacturing, design, planning, inspections, installations, recreational safety courses and manuals. Created Safety Signs

(Listing continued on next page)

Playgrounds *(cont.)*

Safety Play, Inc. (cont.)
and inspection tools. **Degrees/licenses:** Certified Playground Safety Inspector, Instructor, Bus. Deg.

See primary listing under RECREATION: General

Pressure Regulators

Robert W. Lindner, PE

President
Lindner Consulting Services, Inc.
7 Westmount Drive
Livingston, NJ 07039-4212
Tel: (973) 740-1319
Fax: (973) 740-1319
E-mail: boblindner@aol.com

Specialties: Natural Gas Industry: Transmission, Distribution and Operations; Pressure Regulators: Appliance, House Service, Commercial/Industrial, Distribution, M&R Station, High Pressure, Low Pressure, Installation & Design/Maintenance; Safety Relief Valves; Accident/Failure Analysis, Expert Witness Report/Testimony. Over 44 years engineering expertise in the application, operation, maintenance and design of all types of pressure regulator installations. Over 34 years engineering experience in process control and control valves. Lectured on pressure regulators at numerous seminars and gas utility training sessions. Career includes management & engineering experience plus leadership positions in national professional organizations. **Degrees/licenses:** BS, MS, PE.

Railroads

Ronald H. Dunn, PE, FASCE

President
R.H. Dunn & Associates, Inc.
112 Lely
Williamsburg, VA 23188
Tel: (757) 253-1453
Fax: (757) 253-1162
E-mail: rhdunninc@tni.net

Specialties: Professional Engineer with 40 years experience in design, construction, maintenance and operation of railroads/rail transit systems; personally involved in major projects of 18 railroads/17 rail transit properties in 45+ states, DC and 6 provinces. Railway consulting/forensic engineering services include investigations of track failures, derailments, crossing accidents, construction claims, track construction/maintenance problems, and technical input/expert witness testimony for plaintiffs or defendants, in wrongful death, personal injury and FELA claims. COURT EXPERIENCE: Federal, State, ICC, Surface Transportation Board, Army Corps of Engineers - BCA, AAA, and Queen's Bench, Canada. **Degrees/licenses:** BS Engr., Johns Hopkins Univ.; PE; Fellow ASCE, NAFE, ITE, AREMA.

Allan M. Zarembski, PhD, PE

President
ZETA-TECH Associates, Inc.
900 Kings Hwy. N., Ste. 208
Cherry Hill, NJ 08034
Tel: (856) 779-7795
Fax: (856) 779-7436
E-mail: zarembski@zetatech.com
Web Site: http://www.zetatech.com

Specialties: Railroad Engineering, vehicle/track dynamics, derailment analysis, failure analysis, track and track systems, track/train interaction, railroad operations analysis, costing, economics of railroad operations, maintenance, failure, railroad safety, risk analysis and risk management. Testifying before Federal and Local court, ICC. PhD Civil Engineering, Princeton University; MS, Princeton; MS,

BS, New York University; Registered Prof. Engineer, 5 States. 120+ technical papers, 2 books, AMSE Rail Transportation Award 1992. **Degrees/licenses:** PhD, PE.

Shooting Reconstruction

John H. Dillon, Jr.

Forensic Consultant
7007 Trails End Road
Manassas, VA 20112-3602
Tel: (703) 791-5559
Fax: (703) 791-6712
E-mail: jhdillonjr@aol.com

Specialties: Ballistics; Microscopic Examinations of Bullets, Cartridge Cases, Shotshells; Firearms Operability, Accidental Discharges, Trigger Pull Analyses; Shooting Reconstruction; Gunshot Residues; Muzzle-to-Victim Distance Determinations; Shotgun Shooting Distance Determinations; Ejection Pattern Testing; Crime Scene Documentation and Laboratory Procedures Review. Court Qualified, 24 States, 12 Federal Courts. U.S. Naval Academy, BS; University of Virginia, MEd; Numerous articles in forensic journals. Retired FBI Agent, former Chief FBI Ballistics Unit. Member, American Academy of Forensic Sciences, Association for Crime Scene Reconstruction and Mid-Atlantic Association of Forensic Scientists. Distinguished/Life Member and Past President, Association of Firearm and Toolmark Examiners. Consultant, Forensic Technology, Inc. Consultant, The Academy Group. **Degrees/licenses:** BS, MEd, D-ABFE, FBI Lab Certified Ballistics & Toolmarks.

See primary listing under FIREARMS & BALLISTICS: General

Slip & Fall

Randall Atlas, PhD, AIA, CPP

Atlas Safety & Security Design, Inc.
770 Palm Bay Lane, Ste. 4-I
Miami, FL 33138
Tel: (305) 756-5027
(800) 749-6029
Fax: (305) 754-1658
E-mail: ratlas@ix.netcom.com
Web Site: http://www.cpted-security.com

Specialties: Providing expert services in Architecture, Security Systems Design, Criminal Justice Facility Design & Accessibility, and Premises Liability involving Hotels, Office Buildings, Parking Lots/Garages, Shopping Centers, Gas Stations, Apartment Buildings, and University/School Campuses; Slip and Fall Forensic Analysis; Inmate Suicide Negligence; Building Code Review; Stair, Step and Ramp Design; Prison Violence and Jail Conditions; Americans with Disabilities (ADA) Compliance for Accessibility; Registered Architect (FL); Certified Protection Professional (CPP); Adjunct Professor in Architecture & Criminal Justice at Florida Atlantic University & Florida International University; Author of over 50 articles and books on bldg. security/safety and suicide prevention, Amer. with Disabilities Act. **Degrees/licenses:** PhD Crim.; Masters, Architecture; AIA, CPP; Lic. Architect (FL), NCARB Regis.

See primary listing under SECURITY: Premises Liability

Milton Bailey

18 Bayfield Rd.
Wayland, MA 01778
Tel: (508) 653-9489
Fax: (508) 653-9489
E-mail: milbbbb@hotmail.com
Web Site: http://www.baileystc.com

Specialties: Slip, trip & fall; Walkways; Ramps; Shoes; Safety shoes; Sports; Recreation; Dance floors; Mats & carpets; Handicapped; Stairs; Escalators; Playing surfaces; Accident reconstruction; Accident analysis;

(Listing continued on next page)

Slip & Fall *(cont.)*

Milton Bailey (cont.)

Material evaluation; Foot protection; Roller skating rinks; Human factors; Ergonomics; Bathtubs; Showers; Grates; Ladders; Scaffolds; Review experts' work (Daubert, Kumho, Lanigan). Affiliation: Independent Consultant; AAA Arbitrator. **Degrees/licenses:** MS.

J. Nigel Ellis, PhD, CSP, PE, CPE

President
Dynamic Scientific Controls, Inc./Ellis Litigation Support
306 Country Club Dr.
Wilmington, DE 19803
Tel: (302) 571-8470
Fax: (302) 571-0756
E-mail: Nigel@FallSafety.com
Web Site: http://www.FallSafety.com

Specialties: Consulting and forensic safety network specializing in fall hazards, fall protection and energy-related injuries and incidents; Safety engineering analysis and practical solutions based on 30+ years of training instruction including OSHA compliance courses, and industry and construction and commercial fall protection site assessment, engineering and site implementation; Legal consultation for over 18 years including courtroom experience; Author of the popular and authoritative text book "Introduction to Fall Protection 3rd. ed." published by American Society of Safety Engineers. **Degrees/licenses:** PhD, PE (Safety MA, CA), CSP, CPE.

See primary listing under ACCIDENT PREVENTION & SAFETY: General

Russell R. Fote

Principal
Russell Fote & Associates, Inc.
3635 Stonebrook Court
Brookfield, WI 53005
Tel: (262) 781-4496
Fax: (262) 783-4312
E-mail: rfote@execpc.com
Web Site: http://www.fote-engineering.com

Specialties: Walks, ramps, steps, illumination, walk surface friction testing, automatic doors, ladders, building codes, consensus standards, ADA regulations. **Degrees/licenses:** MSEM; BSME; PE; CSP.

See primary listing under ACCIDENT RECONSTRUCTION: Fires & Explosions

Thomas Gunzler, PE

Principal Consultant
Gunzler & Associates
P.O. Box 5848
Santa Monica, CA 90409
Tel: (310) 454-9614
(866) 326-7170

Specialties: Forensic engineering consultants, since 1973, with competence over a wide range of engineering expertise. Our consultants average thirty years in their respective specialties, have post-graduate diplomas and professional engineering registrations, where appropriate. Specialties include: safety engineering, product defect analysis, mechanical design, industrial and construction accidents, pedestrian safety, traffic accident reconstruction, fire cause analysis and chemical hazards. We are ready to discuss, in strict confidence, any matters which may lie in our areas of competence and will furnish resumes of our associates, terms of employment and fees on request.

See primary listing under ACCIDENT RECONSTRUCTION: General

Zachary Parker

President
Parker Enterprises
310 Boundary Place
Roswell, GA 30075-6876
Tel: (805) 236-4532
Fax: (256) 500-9604
E-mail: zach.parker@ngc.com

Specialties: All aspects. **Degrees/licenses:** Licensed Reliability Engineer.

Jon J. Pina, MS, CSP
Safety, Health
& Environmental Professional
Evergreen Environmental Health
& Safety, Inc.
368 Rt. 110 Hwy.
Indiana, PA 15701
Tel: (724) 349-7029
Fax: (724) 349-3540
E-mail: jpina@adelphia.net

Specialties: Over 31 years experience; safety, industrial hygiene, environmental, PA state OSHA consultant, construction management, "hands-on" industrial and chemical operations; slip, trip, and falls; falls from elevations; falls from trucks, mobile platforms; fall prevention/protection, nursing home falls/strains, hunting tree stand falls; demolition; material handling; asbestos abatement; environmental surveys/assessments, hazardous waste site remediation; drilling, construction, excavation, utility location/isolation, tank cleaning, water treatment, boilers, confined space, electrical hazards; off-road vehicles, defensive driving; emergency response/security, LEPC member; safety professor; professionally published. **Degrees/licenses:** MS Safety Sci; MS Geol; BS Geosci Ed.; Cert Safety Prof; Cert Prof Instructor.

See primary listing under ACCIDENT PREVENTION & SAFETY: General

Mark S. Sanders, PhD, CHFP
Professor Emeritus, CSU Northridge
17060 Rancho Street
Encino, CA 91316
Tel: (818) 784-7041
Fax: (818) 784-4453

Specialties: Human Factors specialist with extensive consulting and expert witness experience in the following: Human Factors; Perception; Information Processing; Reaction Time; Risk Perception; Decision Making; Behavioral Expectations; Slips/Trips/Falls; Warning Effectiveness; Driver Performance; Product Safety. 1000+ cases and 150+ court appearances. 90+ Human Factors textbooks. Professor Emeritus, CSU Northridge; Senior Staff Scientist, Essex Corporation. Fellow and Past President, Human Factors & Ergonomics Society; Member, Society of Automotive Engineers; Ergonomics Society; Illuminating Engineer Society; National Safety Council. **Degrees/licenses:** PhD & MS Human Factors, Purdue University; Certified Human Factors Professional.

Antonio Villalobos, PhD, PE
Forensic Engineering, Accident
Reconstruction & Biomechanics
410 Castle Place
Beverly Hills, CA 90210
Tel: (310) 550-7746
Fax: (310) 550-6824
E-mail: villalob@ucla.edu
Web Site: http://www.theaccidentexpert.net

Specialties: Traffic/vehicular accident reconstruction: auto, truck, pedestrian, occupant kinematics, low speed impacts; Biomechanics: bone & soft tissue injury, back & neck injuries, extremities, industrial, construction & recreational accidents, personal altercations; Slip & Fall Analysis (friction testing); Failure of mechanical equipment, machine components, rotating machinery, power presses, machine guards, forklifts; Heat Transfer analysis. Listed in Who's Who in Engineering. **Degrees/licenses:** PhD Engineering, MS & BA Physics, PE Mechanical.

See primary listing under ACCIDENT RECONSTRUCTION: Automotive/Vehicular

Trucks, Buses & Forklifts

CRAFT Forensic Services
Bradley D. Closson
180 Otay Lakes Road, Suite 109
Bonita, CA 91902
Tel: (619) 737-9563
Fax: (619) 737-9564
E-mail: bclosson@craftforensic.com
Web Site: http://www.craftforensic.com

Specialties: Crane, rigging, aerial devices, forklift accident investigation and reconstruction. All environments and jurisdictions. Extensive practical operation experience. Member ASME B30, SAE, ASCE, ASSE, ASNE, SAME, ACRP and CCAA. Previously

(Listing continued on next page)

Trucks, Buses & Forklifts
(cont.)

CRAFT Forensic Services (cont.)
accepted as expert in federal and numerous state jurisdictions. Active on state and federal advisory boards relevant to material handling safety, have trained equipment operators and riggers in all aspects of equipment and environmental safety, have trained equipment managers in operation safety. Speak at industry meetings on related safety issues. Perform material handling safety calculations and analysis as well as equipment condition inspections. **Degrees/licenses:** BS; California Crane, Nevada Crane, Maritime Crane Inspector.

See primary listing under ACCIDENT RECONSTRUCTION: Lifting Equipment

John C. Glennon, Chartered
6917 W. 76th Street
Overland Park, KS 66204
Tel: (913) 383-3856
Fax: (913) 383-2277
E-mail: experts@johncglennon.com
Web Site: http://www.johncglennon.com

Specialties: Motor Vehicle Accident Investigation; Accident Reconstruction; Vehicle Crush Analysis; Vehicular Mechanical and Structural Failure Analysis for Automobiles, Trucks, and Motorcycles; Testing Capabilities for Air Brakes, Hydraulic Brakes, Suspension Systems, Steering Systems, Tires, and Wheels; Determination if Proper Maintenance and Repair Procedures were Followed; Identification of Previous Body Structural Damage; Motor Carrier Safety and Compliance; Commercial Driver Responsibilities and Qualifications; Commercial Driver Hours of Service and Daily Logs; Proper Load Securement Procedures; Fleet Maintenance Requirements; Computer Animation; Forensic Mapping; Photo Modeling; Downloading of Crash Data Retrieval Systems (Automobile "BLACK BOX"). **Degrees/licenses:** D. Engr., PE, BS Automotive Technology, ASE Cert., CDL.

See primary listing under ACCIDENT RECONSTRUCTION: General

National Transportation Consultants, Inc.
Joseph Y. Morrison
President
1109 South 10th Street
Noblesville, IN 46060
Tel: (317) 770-0953
Fax: (317) 770-0954
E-mail: jmorrison@ntconsult.com
Web Site: http://www.ntconsult.com

Specialties: Over 150 years of transportation safety experience. Motor Carrier Safety Regulations; Safety Program Development; DOT Audits; Hazardous Materials Training; Accident Investigation and Reconstruction. Member of Commercial Vehicle Safety Alliance; Indiana Motor Truck Association; American Society of Safety Engineers; IACAI; IATAI, ACTAR.

See primary listing under TRANSPORTATION: Trucking

Merlyn Robert "Bob" Wilson
Transportation Safety, Inc.
Sacramento Office
2377 Gold Meadow Way, Suite 100
Gold River, CA 95670
Tel: (916) 526-2845
Fax: (916) 631-1515
E-mail: Bob-Wilson@msn.com
Web Site: http://www.transafetyinc.com

Los Angeles Office
13104 Philadelphia St., Suite 218
Whittier, CA 90601
Tel: (562) 698-0040
Fax: (562) 698-0139

Specialties: Diesel Engine Electronic Control Modules; Black Box Downloads; Tachograph Analysis; Hydraulic & Air Brakes Systems; Driver's Hours of Service and Log Books; Commercial Driver Qualification; Preventative Maintenance Inspections; Driver Pre-trip Inspections; Loading, Unloading and Cargo Securement; Hazardous Materials; Off-Tracking or Trailer Cheat; Out of Service Criteria; Permit Loads; Transport of Intermodal Freight Containers. Mr. Wilson is certified through "ASE" as a truck technician specializing in hydraulic and air brake equipped trucks and buses. Past instructor for the Federal Transit Administration, University of California at Riverside, and the Northern California Public Safety Training & Education Center through Sacramento City College. Licensed forklift driver. **Degrees/licenses:** BS; AA (Admin. of Justice); Licensed private investigator, CA 13828.

See primary listing under ACCIDENT PREVENTION & SAFETY: Trucks, Buses & Forklifts

Visibility

Darrell Carter

Clinical Professor, Emeritus
University of California - Berkeley
P.O. Box 1025
Glen Ellen, CA 95442
Tel: (707) 935-8908
Fax: (707) 938-9372
E-mail: dbcarter@uclink.berkeley.edu

Specialties: Optometry; Optometric standard of care; Examination and prescription procedures - tonometry, ophthalmoscopy, visual fields, etc.; Detection and management of ocular diseases; Contact lens procedures; Ocular pharmacology; Vision loss and economic effects; Visibility in auto and other accidents. **Degrees/licenses:** AB-UCLA, OD-SCCO, MS & PhD - UC; Optometry Licenses CA & NV.

See primary listing under MEDICINE & HEALTH: Optometry

Harris Visibility Studies, Inc.

James L. Harris, Sr.
2699 Camino Artemisa
Alpine, CA 91901
Tel: (619) 659-3827
Fax: (619) 659-3824
E-mail: JSr@hvsi.com

Specialties: Visibility issues in aviation (midairs & wirestrikes), automobile, motorcycle, pedestrian, and railroad crossing accidents; Sun/moon calculations, measurements of natural and artificial lighting including street lights and headlights; Characteristics of the human visual system such as foveal and peripheral contrast detection thresholds, fixations and visual search, the role of expectancy and its impact on perception-reaction; Nighttime photography using technique published in the Journal of Forensic Sciences; Quality computer animations and static simulations designed to accurately illustrate visibility issues; Defense against inaccurate computer animations. **Degrees/licenses:** BSEE.

Walter J. Kosmatka

390 Sandhurst Drive
Highland Heights, OH 44143
Tel: (440) 461-7862
Fax: (440) 461-0311

Specialties: (1) Discernibility - nighttime detection of roadway obstacles by drivers; Roadway terrain, inclement weather, site lighting and obstacle coloration are taken into account; Common "obstacles" are pedestrians, animals, stopped vehicles, trailers, debris, construction barricades; (2) Automotive lamp failure analysis for the purpose of determining the illuminated state of the light devices, or direction of impact; (3) Light output measurements of automotive lamps; (4) Site/area lighting measurements and specification for same. Holds 17 U.S. and foreign patents; Chair SAE Road Illumination Devices (RID) Sub Committee; Consultant NHTSA/U. of Mich. Transportation Research Inst. **Degrees/licenses:** B. Chem. Eng.; BBA; Prov Member AAFS.

ACCOUNTING

General

Advisors/Experts @ MCS Associates

Norman Katz
Managing Partner
18881 Von Karman Ave., Ste. 1175
Irvine, CA 92612-1569
Tel: (949) 263-8700
Fax: (949) 263-0770
E-mail: info@mcsassociates.com
Web Site: http://www.mcsassociates.com

Specialties: Nationally recognized banking, financial services, real estate consulting group; Experienced expert witnesses and consultants include bankers, lenders, insurance managers, brokers, agents, economists, securities brokers, trust fiduciaries, appraisers, accountants. Expertise: Bank operations, check fraud; Lending policies, procedures; Loan administration, foreclosures, bankruptcy; Lender liability; D&O Liability; Insurance (Life, Disability, Property & Casualty, Reinsurance, Surplus) underwriting, claims handling, bad faith; Broker duties, agency management; Title insurance & escrow; R/E brokerage, leasing, property management, appraisal, development, construction defects; Business valuation, lost profits, damages assessment; Forensic accounting; Securities brokerage, trading, investment suitability; Economic & statistical analysis. **Degrees/licenses:** MBA, PhD, CPA, CLU, CPCU, CFP, CFA, CREA, MAI, ASA.

See primary listing under FINANCE: Commercial Banking

Bay Sherman Craig & Goldstein, LLP

Peter M. Craig
Hal Jaffe
11845 W. Olympic Blvd. #845
Los Angeles, CA 90064
Tel: (310) 477-1400
Fax: (310) 479-0720
E-mail: craigp@bscgllp.com
Web Site: http://magazineconsulting.com or http://baysherman.com

Specialties: All aspects of publishing litigation support and expert witness services including valuations, forensic accounting and financial analysis, damages, mergers and acquisitions; Experienced in testimony; Over 50 years combined experience; Published book on magazine finance, accounting and valuation; Over 150 seminars on various publishing financial topics. **Degrees/licenses:** BS, CPA.

See primary listing under PUBLISHING: General

Campos & Stratis, P.A.

Chris Campos, CPA
Certified Public Accountants
310 Cedar Lane
Teaneck, NJ 07666
Tel: (201) 692-0300
Fax: (201) 692-0722
E-mail: CCampos@campos-stratis.com or info@campos-stratis.com
Web Site: http://www.campos-stratis.com

Specialties: Chris Campos, CPA: Forensic accounting, investigative accounting, damages and lost profits calculations, business interruption arising from fires, hurricanes, etc., general accounting, accounting malpractice, anti-trust, patents, construction, breach of contract, business losses; Rutgers University, BS Bus. Admin.; American Institute of Certified Public Accountants, New York; New Jersey and Pennsylvania Societies of Certified Public Accountants; Testified in Federal and State courts, deposed hundreds of times. **Degrees/licenses:** BS, CPA.

Jonathan E. Cohen

Jonathan E. Cohen,
an Accountancy Corporation
5850 Canoga Ave. Ste 200
Woodland Hills, CA 91367
Tel: (818) 340-9272
Fax: (818) 883-8126
E-mail: jeccpa@pacbell.net

Specialties: CPA with more than 24 years experience in the following areas: Litigation Support and Forensic Accounting Services in Connection with Personal Injury, Business Interruption, Disability, Wrongful Death and Termination Incidents and Income Tax Consequences of Securities Transactions. Expert Witness Testimony/Reports; Pre-trial Preparation; Assistance in Development of Case Strategy; Damage and Lost Profits Calculation; Loss of Earnings Analysis; Discovery and Deposition Assistance; Investigative Accounting; Accounting and Financial Statement Analysis. **Degrees/licenses:** BS Accounting; MBA Corporate Finance; CPA.

See primary listing under ECONOMICS: Economic Losses/Damages

Cohen, Miskei & Mowrey, LLP

Scott Mowrey
15303 Ventura Blvd., Suite 1150
Sherman Oaks, CA 91505
Tel: (818) 986-5070
Fax: (818) 986-5034
E-mail: cmm@cmmpas.com

Specialties: Forensic Accountants and Finance Experts with extensive experience in the following areas: Forensic Accounting, Fraud Investigation, Economic Damages, Business Valuation, Family Law, Bankruptcy, Reorganization, Lost Earnings/Profits Analysis. **Degrees/licenses:** CPAs; CFEs; MBAs.

Fulcrum Financial Inquiry

David Nolte
Principal
1000 Wilshire Blvd., Ste. 1650
Los Angeles, CA 90017
Tel: (213) 787-4111
(213) 787-4100
Fax: (213) 787-4141
E-mail: dnolte@fulcruminquiry.com
Web Site: http://www.fulcruminquiry.com

Specialties: Our analysis and research combined with unique presentation techniques have resulted in an unequaled track record in successful court cases and client recoveries. Our personnel are full time and fully focused on the services we provide. We thoughtfully incorporate technology into our work to provide great results at a more reasonable cost. Our expertise encompasses damages analysis, lost profit studies, business & intangible asset valuations, fraud investigations, statistics, forensic economic analysis, royalty audits, strategic & market assessments, competitive surveys, analysis of computerized data including computer forensics, and a wide range of other financial advisory services. **Degrees/ licenses:** CPA, ASA, CMA, MBA, CFA.

Glenn M. Gelman & Associates

Glenn M. Gelman, CPA, MS Tax
Managing Director
1940 East 17th St.
Santa Ana, CA 92705-8606
Tel: (714) 667-2600
Fax: (714) 667-2636
E-mail: ggel@gmgcpa.com
Web Site: http://www.gmgcpa.com

Specialties: Expert Testimony, Forensic Accounting, Litigation Consulting, Deposition Strategy, Arbitrations, Business Interruption, Lost Profits, Business Valuations, Marital Dissolution, Construction Claims, Fraud, Alter Ego, Financial Analysis, Financial Modeling, Consumer Lending. Nationally recognized expertise in Construction Accounting. Memberships: American Institute of Certified Public Accountants, California Society of CPAs, National Litigation Support Services Association, Forensic Expert Witness As-

(Listing continued on next page)

General *(cont.)*

Glenn M. Gelman & Associates (cont.)
sociation, Engineering Contractors Association, American Subcontractors Association, Southern California Contractors Association. Awards: Digest 50 award as one of the top fifty medium sized CPA firms, named Best Accounting Firm for the Construction Industry by Construction Link. **Degrees/licenses:** CPA, Masters Degree in Taxation, others.

Gumbiner, Savett, Finkel, Fingleson & Rose, Inc.

Ronald S. Greene, CPA
Executive Vice President
1723 Cloverfield Blvd.
Santa Monica, CA 90404
Tel: (310) 828-9798
Fax: (310) 829-7853

Specialties: Business, legal, and accounting specialist with extensive consulting and expert witness experience in the following areas: Lost Profit, Damages and Calculations; Fraud Analyses & Audits; Assets & Income Tracing; Litigation Strategy Consulting; Tax Support; Family Law Accounting; Business Valuations; Royalty & Contract Audits; Standard of Care Analyses. **Degrees/licenses:** CPA, MBA, CVA, MBT, JD.

Legier & Materne, apac

Consultants and CPAs
William R. Legier, CPA, CFE
Managing Director
Energy Centre
1100 Poydras St., 34th Floor
New Orleans, LA 70163
Tel: (504) 561-0020
Fax: (504) 561-0023
E-mail: legier@lmcpa.com
Web Site: http://www.lmcpa.com

Specialties: Certified Public Accountant; Certified Fraud Examiner; Extensive Testifying in Federal and State Courts for leading national law firms and Fortune 500 companies in areas including accounting, calculating and refuting financial damages including lost profits, fraud detection and recovery, mismanagement, appointment of receiver, business valuations, shareholder disputes, evidence of ownership, identification of hidden assets, corporate veil piercing, analysis and explanation of complex financial transactions, bankruptcies, forensic accounting, accounting malpractice, marital dissolutions, document control, advanced automated graphic design and display techniques. **Degrees/licenses:** CPA, CFE.

Mayer Hoffman McCann PC

Steve Franklin
Jeff Freeman
11601 Wilshire Blvd, Ste. 2300
Los Angeles, CA 90025
Tel: (310) 268-2000
Fax: (310) 268-2001
E-mail: sfranklin@cbiz.com or jfreeman@cbiz.com
Web Site: http://www.cbiz.com or http://www.mhm-pc.com

Specialties: Business and Accounting firm with extensive consulting and expert witness experience in the following areas: Business Litigation; Business Valuation & Appraisal; Financial Reconstruction; Family Limited Partnerships; Marital Dissolutions; Transactional Due Diligence; Business Interruption; Commercial Damage & Lost Profits; Fraud Investigations; Tax Controversies. **Degrees/licenses:** CPA; CFE; ABV.

David Ostrove, Attorney-CPA

5757 Wilshire Blvd., Ste. 535
Los Angeles, CA 90036-3600
Tel: (323) 939-3400
Fax: (323) 939-3500
E-mail: dostrove@comcast.net
Web Site: http://www.lawyers.com/ok&olaw

Specialties: Special master, arbitrator, mediator, law school professor, author, lecturer; Forensic accounting; Experienced witness 40+ years; Accounting malpractice; Lawyer malpractice; Litigation support; Books, records & accounting issues; Consulting & evaluation; Damages assessment and computations; Tax issues; Breach of fiduciary duties; Real estate transactions; Malpractice arising out of probate, wills, trusts; Leveraged buyouts; Exchanges of properties; Corporate transactions;

Reasonable value of services; Business valuation; Financial statement analysis; Wrongful discharge; Tax preparer negligence; Case review, analysis and consulting; 50 years combined history in the professions of accounting and law. **Degrees/licenses:** JD, CPA.

UHY Mann Frankfort Stein & Lipp Advisors

Saul Solomon
Dir. of Forensic, Litigation & Business Valuation Services
12 Greenway Plaza, 8th Floor
Houston, TX 77046-1291
Tel: (713) 960-1706
Fax: (713) 968-7140
E-mail: ssolomon@uhy-us.com
Web Site: http://www.uhy-us.com

Specialties: Loss/Damage Determination: Antitrust and Class Action Analysis, Bankruptcy Matters, Breach of Contract, Business Interruption, Fraud and Forensic Accounting, Lender Liability, Intellectual Property, Professional Malpractice, Securities Fraud, Shareholder Disputes; Lost Earnings, Profits, Value; Personal Injury; Family Law: Asset Tracing, Characterization; Business Valuations For Public And Private Entities, Mergers & Acquisitions Due Diligence, Financial and Economic Analysis; Trial Services in State and Federal Courts: Evidence Evaluation, Expert Witnesses, Planning And Strategy During Trial. Consulted with all Major Industries: Construction, Consumer Products, Government, Health Care, Oil and Gas, Technology, Manufacturing, etc. **Degrees/licenses:** BBA, CPA, CFE, CVA.

Business Interruption/ Lost Profits

Robert W. Berliner, CPA, CFE

Director of Litigation Services
Marks Paneth & Shron LLP
622 Third Avenue
New York, NY 10017
Tel: (212) 503-8853
Fax: (212) 503-8852
E-mail: rberliner@markspaneth.com
Web Site: http://www.markspaneth.com

Specialties: Securities Fraud; Accounting Malpractice; Post Acquisition Disputes; Forensic Accounting; Fraud Investigation; Contract Disputes; Damages and Lost Profit Calculations. Former National Office Accounting and Auditing Partner at a "Big 8" CPA firm; has served as a member of the Auditing Standards Board and the FASB Emerging Issues Task Force; was the Chairman of the Professional Ethics Committee of the New York State Society of CPAs; was an adjunct professor of accounting at NYU's Stern School of Business; and has testified in a variety of cases in Federal and State Courts throughout the country. **Degrees/licenses:** BS, MBA, CPA, CFE.

See primary listing under ACCOUNTING: Malpractice

Campos & Stratis, P.A.

Chris Campos, CPA
Certified Public Accountants
310 Cedar Lane
Teaneck, NJ 07666
Tel: (201) 692-0300
Fax: (201) 692-0722
E-mail: CCampos@campos-stratis.com or info@campos-stratis.com
Web Site: http://www.campos-stratis.com

Specialties: Chris Campos, CPA: Forensic accounting, investigative accounting, damages and lost profits calculations, business interruption arising from fires, hurricanes, etc., general accounting, accounting malpractice, anti-trust, patents, construction, breach of

(Listing continued on next page)

Business Interruption/ Lost Profits *(cont.)*

Campos & Stratis, P. A. (cont.)
contract, business losses; Rutgers University, BS Bus. Admin.; American Institute of Certified Public Accountants, New York; New Jersey and Pennsylvania Societies of Certified Public Accountants; Testified in Federal and State courts, deposed hundreds of times. **Degrees/licenses:** BS, CPA.

See primary listing under ACCOUNTING: General

DiGabriele, McNulty & Co. LLC

James A. DiGabriele, CPA, CFE, DABFA, MSM, MST, Cr. FA, CVA
Managing Partner
414 Eagle Rock Ave., Ste. 305
West Orange, NJ 07052
Tel: (973) 243-2600
Fax: (973) 243-2646
E-mail: jim@dmcpa.com
Web Site: http://www.dmcpa.com

Specialties: Forensic Accounting, Investigative Accounting, Business Interruption, Financial Analysis, Damages and Lost Profits Calculations, Structured Settlements, Inventory Observations, Property Losses, Subrogation, Fraud Detection, Wage Losses, Fidelity/Surety Claims, Expert Testimony. Diplomates, American Board of Forensic Accounting; Member, Association of Certified Fraud Examiners; Former Federal Treasury Agents; Former State Auditor. **Degrees/ licenses:** BS, CFE, CPA, DABFA, CFSA, MSM, MST, Cr. FA, CVA.

See primary listing under ACCOUNTING: Forensic Accounting

Litigation Economics, LLC

Stanley P. Stephenson, PhD
One Embarcadero Center, Suite 500
San Francisco, CA 94111
Tel: (415) 835-1212
Fax: (415) 835-1213
E-mail: stan@litigationeconomics.com
Web Site: http://litigationeconomics.com

Specialties: Since 1985, experts at Litigation Economics, LLC have provided economic, accounting, and financial consulting in complex litigation. Credibility before judges, jurors, mediators, and arbitrators is the most essential factor a Litigation Economics expert provides. We develop damage reports for plaintiffs or critique such reports for defense counsel. Specializations include: breach of contract, business interruption, construction, franchise, intellectual property, products liability, and lost earnings capacity. We have provided assistance in more than 150 cases and testified in 25 cases in various legal hearings. Member: National Association of Certified Valuation Analysts; Financial Management Association. **Degrees/licenses:** PhD, MS (Indiana University), BA (Ball State University).

See primary listing under ECONOMICS: Economic Losses/Damages

Matson, Driscoll & Damico

John A. Damico, PC, CPA
Managing Partner
750 Hammond Dr. NE, Bldg. 14
Atlanta, GA 30328
Tel: (404) 252-0085
Fax: (404) 255-0673
E-mail: jdamico@mdd.net
Web Site: http://www.mdd.net

Specialties: Matson, Driscoll, and Damico is an international forensic accounting and consulting firm with a specialty in business interruption/lost profits, insurance loss accounting and litigation services. There are currently 28 MD&D offices across the world. MD&D's analysis and verification of the facts and reporting pave the way for prompt and equitable resolutions of each case. Skill, proven expertise and total dedication to this special area of accounting are the characteristics that separate MD&D professionals from other accountants. Professional excellence in forensic insurance claims accounting and litigation services is the distinguishing hallmark of the firm. For more information, visit www.mdd.net. **Degrees/licenses:** The firm: BA, MBA, CFE, CPA, CMA, CVA, MCP.

Thomas M. Neches

Managing Partner
Thomas Neches & Company LLP
Biltmore Court, Ste. 350
520 South Grand Ave.
Los Angeles, CA 90071-2662
Tel: (213) 624-8150
Fax: (213) 624-8152
E-mail: tmn@thomasneches.com
Web Site: http://www.thomasneches.com

Specialties: Expert testimony regarding: accounting, financial, business valuation, statistical, computer database issues. Certified Public Accountant, accredited in business valuation, Certified Valuation Analyst, Certified Fraud Examiner. Provided trial testimony on behalf of plaintiffs and defendants regarding: lost profits, fraud, breach of contract, lost business value, intellectual property, antitrust, personal injury. Representative industries include: manufacturing, entertainment, banking, insurance, wholesale, retail, securities, construction, professional services. BA, Mathematics, University of California San Diego; MS, Operations Research, University of California Los Angeles. Prior Big "5" accounting firm partner specializing in litigation services. **Degrees/licenses:** MS, CPA/ABV, CVA, CFE.

Michael David Pakter, CPA, CFE, CIRA, CA

Managing Member
G & P Financial Litigation Advisors, LLC
205 West Wacker Drive, Suite 918
Chicago, IL 60606
Tel: (312) 229-1720
Fax: (312) 229-1725
E-mail: mpakter@litcpa.com
Web Site: http://www.litcpa.com

Specialties: Michael Pakter is a Certified Public Accountant, Certified Fraud Examiner, Certified Insolvency and Restructuring Advisor and Chartered Accountant. He has over 25 years experience providing financial analysis, accounting, auditing and investigative services. Michael performs financial analysis and forensic accounting for distressed and reorganizing companies, especially those with incomplete or falsified records. He provides bankruptcy and reorganization services to debtors and creditors, focusing on fraudulent conveyances and litigation during bankruptcy proceedings. Michael has provided consulting services and expert testimony to trial lawyers to assist with accountants' malpractice, damages determination, discovery, forensic accounting, lost profits and commercial litigation. **Degrees/licenses:** CPA, CFE, CIRA, CA.

See primary listing under ACCOUNTING: Forensic Accounting

Business Valuation

Matson, Driscoll & Damico

John A. Damico, PC, CPA
Managing Partner
750 Hammond Dr. NE, Bldg. 14
Atlanta, GA 30328
Tel: (404) 252-0085
Fax: (404) 255-0673
E-mail: jdamico@mdd.net
Web Site: http://www.mdd.net

Specialties: Matson, Driscoll, and Damico is an international forensic accounting and consulting firm with a specialty in business valuation through its Certified Valuation Analyst professionals. There are currently 28 MD&D offices across the world. MD&D's analysis and verification of the facts and reporting pave the way for prompt and equitable resolutions of each case. Skill, proven expertise and total dedication to this special area of accounting are the characteristics that separate MD&D professionals from other accountants. Professional excellence in forensic accounting and business valuations is the distinguishing hallmark of the firm. For more information, visit www.mdd.net. **Degrees/licenses:** The firm: BA, MBA, CFE, CPA, CMA, CVA, MCP.

See primary listing under ACCOUNTING: Business Interruption/Lost Profits

Business Valuation *(cont.)*

Thomas M. Neches
Managing Partner
Thomas Neches & Company LLP
Biltmore Court, Ste. 350
520 South Grand Ave.
Los Angeles, CA 90071-2662
Tel: (213) 624-8150
Fax: (213) 624-8152
E-mail: tmn@thomasneches.com
Web Site: http://www.thomasneches.com

Specialties: Expert testimony regarding: accounting, financial, business valuation, statistical, computer database issues. Certified Public Accountant, accredited in business valuation, Certified Valuation Analyst, Certified Fraud Examiner. Provided trial testimony on behalf of plaintiffs and defendants regarding: lost profits, fraud, breach of contract, lost business value, intellectual property, antitrust, personal injury. Representative industries include: manufacturing, entertainment, banking, insurance, wholesale, retail, securities, construction, professional services. BA, Mathematics, University of California San Diego; MS, Operations Research, University of California Los Angeles. Prior Big "5" accounting firm partner specializing in litigation services. **Degrees/licenses:** MS, CPA/ABV, CVA, CFE.

See primary listing under ACCOUNTING: Business Interruption/Lost Profits

Financial Statements, GAAP/GAAS & SEC

Donald L. Brenner
President/Founder
The Brenner Group
345 North Canal St., #802
Chicago, IL 60606
Tel: (312) 382-8918
(312) 671-6010
Fax: (312) 382-8959
E-mail: brennergrp@cs.com or
dlpb@msn.com
Web Site: http://www.thebrennergroup.org

Specialties: Over 35 years of consulting and management experience, with specialized expertise in litigation support, economic damages, forensic accounting, auditing, fraud investigations, business valuations, crisis management, business consulting and expert witness testimony. Acted as expert witness and provided other litigation support services for a variety of legal proceedings including breach of contract and other business damage claims, wrongful death, commercial matters, construction issues, professional malpractice, fraud, matrimonial, economic damages, and personal injury. **Degrees/licenses:** BS, MBA, CPA, CVA, CFE, CMC.

See primary listing under ECONOMICS: Economic Losses/Damages

Forensic Accounting

Robert W. Berliner, CPA, CFE
Director of Litigation Services
Marks Paneth & Shron LLP
622 Third Avenue
New York, NY 10017
Tel: (212) 503-8853
Fax: (212) 503-8852
E-mail: rberliner@markspaneth.com
Web Site: http://www.markspaneth.com

Specialties: Securities Fraud; Accounting Malpractice; Post Acquisition Disputes; Forensic Accounting; Fraud Investigation; Contract Disputes; Damages and Lost Profit Calculations. Former National Office Accounting and Auditing Partner at a "Big 8" CPA firm; has served as a member of the Auditing Standards Board and the FASB Emerging Issues Task Force; was the Chairman of the Professional Ethics Committee of the New York State Society of CPAs; was an adjunct professor of accounting at NYU's Stern School of Business; and has testified in a variety of cases in Federal and State Courts throughout the country. **Degrees/licenses:** BS, MBA, CPA, CFE.

See primary listing under ACCOUNTING: Malpractice

Peter H. Burgher

2 Brambleberry Dr.
Howell, MI 48843-8738
Tel: (517) 546-6330
Fax: (517) 546-9565
E-mail: pete@marelco.com
Web Site: http://www.expertpages.com/cv/burgher.htm

Specialties: Accounting; Auditing; Securities Fraud; Lost Profits; Damage Claims; Finance Evaluations of Businesses especially Professional Firms, Lawyers Divorce and Law Firm Divisions. Experienced in Insurance, Manufacturing, Aviation, Aircraft Mfr. and Airlines, Fast Foods, Securities Law 10 (b) 5, Malpractice Defense and Prosecution. **Degrees/licenses:** AB, MBA, CPA, A&P, DAR.

Campos & Stratis, P.A.

Chris Campos, CPA
Certified Public Accountants
310 Cedar Lane
Teaneck, NJ 07666
Tel: (201) 692-0300
Fax: (201) 692-0722
E-mail: CCampos@campos-stratis.com or info@campos-stratis.com
Web Site: http://www.campos-stratis.com

Specialties: Chris Campos, CPA: Forensic accounting, investigative accounting, damages and lost profits calculations, business interruption arising from fires, hurricanes, etc., general accounting, accounting malpractice, anti-trust, patents, construction, breach of contract, business losses; Rutgers University, BS Bus. Admin.; American Institute of Certified Public Accountants, New York; New Jersey and Pennsylvania Societies of Certified Public Accountants; Testified in Federal and State courts, deposed hundreds of times. **Degrees/licenses:** BS, CPA.

See primary listing under ACCOUNTING: General

Cohen, Miskei & Mowrey, LLP

Scott Mowrey
15303 Ventura Blvd., Suite 1150
Sherman Oaks, CA 91505
Tel: (818) 986-5070
Fax: (818) 986-5034
E-mail: cmm@cmmpas.com

Specialties: Forensic Accountants and Finance Experts with extensive experience in the following areas: Forensic Accounting, Fraud Investigation, Economic Damages, Business Valuation, Family Law, Bankruptcy, Reorganization, Lost Earnings/Profits Analysis. **Degrees/licenses:** CPAs; CFEs; MBAs.

See primary listing under ACCOUNTING: General

DiGabriele, McNulty & Co. LLC

James A. DiGabriele, CPA, CFE, DABFA, MSM, MST, Cr. FA, CVA
Managing Partner
414 Eagle Rock Ave., Ste. 305
West Orange, NJ 07052
Tel: (973) 243-2600
Fax: (973) 243-2646
E-mail: jim@dmcpa.com
Web Site: http://www.dmcpa.com

Specialties: Forensic Accounting, Investigative Accounting, Business Interruption, Financial Analysis, Damages and Lost Profits Calculations, Structured Settlements, Inventory Observations, Property Losses, Subrogation, Fraud Detection, Wage Losses, Fidelity/Surety Claims, Expert Testimony. Diplomates, American Board of Forensic Accounting; Member, Association of Certified Fraud Examiners; Former Federal Treasury Agents; Former State Auditor. **Degrees/licenses:** BS, CFE, CPA, DABFA, CFSA, MSM, MST, Cr. FA, CVA.

Forensic Accounting *(cont.)*

Forensic Accounting Consultants, PC

Victor C. Moore, CPA
President
2904 White Oak Drive
Houston, TX 77007
Tel: (713) 426-3444
Fax: (713) 426-3031
E-mail: vmoore@facpc.com
Web Site: http://www.facpc.com

Specialties: Litigation consulting, forensic accounting, expert witness testimony, class-action securities fraud, derivative actions, damages calculations, business valuation. Extensive experience: SEC reporting, banking, trusts, mortgage companies, real estate, sub-prime lending, oil & gas, fiduciary conduct, pension plans, regulatory & statutory accounting, auditing & accounting malpractice, high-tech manufacturing, utilities, state & municipal governments, lost profits claims. **Degrees/licenses:** Firm Members Hold CPA, MSA, MA Licenses/Degrees.

Stephen R. Gross, CPA, CFE, CVA

Forensic Specialist
HLB Gross Collins, PC
2625 Cumberland Pkwy., Ste. 400
Atlanta, GA 30339
Tel: (770) 433-1711
Fax: (770) 432-3473
E-mail: sgross@grosscollins.com
Web Site: http://www.grosscollins.com

Specialties: Duke University - undergraduate degree, Management Sciences; Georgia State University, graduate studies in Accounting. Speaker, trainer and National Partner in Charge of Business Consulting for international accounting firm. Experienced in litigation support cases spanning 30 years. Cases have included valuations of domestic assets in divorce cases of wealthy litigants, valuation and location of hidden assets, business and contract disputes, damages calculations, future earnings, etc. **Degrees/licenses:** CPA, CFE, CVA.

Gumbiner, Savett, Finkel, Fingleson & Rose, Inc.

Ronald S. Greene, CPA
Executive Vice President
1723 Cloverfield Blvd.
Santa Monica, CA 90404
Tel: (310) 828-9798
Fax: (310) 829-7853

Specialties: Business, legal, and accounting specialist with extensive consulting and expert witness experience in the following areas: Lost Profit, Damages and Calculations; Fraud Analyses & Audits; Assets & Income Tracing; Litigation Strategy Consulting; Tax Support; Family Law Accounting; Business Valuations; Royalty & Contract Audits; Standard of Care Analyses. **Degrees/licenses:** CPA, MBA, CVA, MBT, JD.

See primary listing under ACCOUNTING: General

Matson, Driscoll & Damico

John A. Damico, PC, CPA
Managing Partner
750 Hammond Dr. NE, Bldg. 14
Atlanta, GA 30328
Tel: (404) 252-0085
Fax: (404) 255-0673
E-mail: jdamico@mdd.net
Web Site: http://www.mdd.net

Specialties: Matson, Driscoll, and Damico is an international forensic accounting and consulting firm with a specialty in insurance claims accounting, litigation services, damage calculations and fraud examinations. There are currently 28 MD&D offices across the world. MD&D's analysis and verification of the facts and reporting pave the way for prompt and equitable resolutions of each case. Skill, proven expertise and total dedication to this special area of accounting are the characteristics that separate MD&D professionals from other accountants. Professional excellence in forensic accounting is the distinguishing hallmark of the firm. For more information, visit www.mdd.net. **Degrees/licenses:** The firm: BA, MBA, CFE, CPA, CMA, CVA, MCP.

See primary listing under ACCOUNTING: Business Interruption/Lost Profits

Mayer Hoffman McCann PC

Steve Franklin
Jeff Freeman
11601 Wilshire Blvd, Ste. 2300
Los Angeles, CA 90025
Tel: (310) 268-2000
Fax: (310) 268-2001
E-mail: sfranklin@cbiz.com or jfreeman@cbiz.com
Web Site: http://www.cbiz.com or http://www.mhm-pc.com

Specialties: Business and Accounting firm with extensive consulting and expert witness experience in the following areas: Business Litigation; Business Valuation & Appraisal; Financial Reconstruction; Family Limited Partnerships; Marital Dissolutions; Transactional Due Diligence; Business Interruption; Commercial Damage & Lost Profits; Fraud Investigations; Tax Controversies. **Degrees/ licenses:** CPA; CFE; ABV.

See primary listing under ACCOUNTING: General

Donald John Miod, CPA, ABV, CVA, CBA

Partner
Miod & Company, LLP
Certified Public Accountants
11600 Indian Hills Rd., #300
Mission Hills, CA 91345-1225
Tel: (818) 905-5822
Fax: (818) 905-5867
E-mail: dmiod@miod-cpa.com
Web Site: http://www.miod-cpa.com

Specialties: Forensic Accounting and Financial Analysis; Business Valuations; Estate Valuations; Market Analysis; Litigation Support; Damage and Lost Profits Calculations; Investigative Accounting; Employee Dishonesty; Embezzlement; Fraud Investigations; Comprehensive Evaluation of Internal Controls; Identification of Unreported or Diverted Income; Loss of Earnings Calculations; Cash Flow Analysis; Spousal Support Determinations; Lifestyle Analysis; Hidden Asset Tracing ; Settlement Assessments; Reimbursement Claims and Analysis; Tax Consultation; Business Management; Business Planning; Claims Accounting; Inventory Losses; Reconstruction of Accounting Records; Tax and Estate Planning; Breach of Contract; Insurance Defense; Construction Defects; Bankruptcy. Over 29 years experience. **Degrees/licenses:** BS, CPA, ABV, CVA, CBA, CFS, DABFA.

Thomas M. Neches

Managing Partner
Thomas Neches & Company LLP
Biltmore Court, Ste. 350
520 South Grand Ave.
Los Angeles, CA 90071-2662
Tel: (213) 624-8150
Fax: (213) 624-8152
E-mail: tmn@thomasneches.com
Web Site: http://www.thomasneches.com

Specialties: Expert testimony regarding: accounting, financial, business valuation, statistical, computer database issues. Certified Public Accountant, accredited in business valuation, Certified Valuation Analyst, Certified Fraud Examiner. Provided trial testimony on behalf of plaintiffs and defendants regarding: lost profits, fraud, breach of contract, lost business value, intellectual property, antitrust, personal injury. Representative industries include: manufacturing, entertainment, banking, insurance, wholesale, retail, securities, construction, professional services. BA, Mathematics, University of California San Diego; MS, Operations Research, University of California Los Angeles. Prior Big "5" accounting firm partner specializing in litigation services. **Degrees/licenses:** MS, CPA/ABV, CVA, CFE.

See primary listing under ACCOUNTING: Business Interruption/Lost Profits

Forensic Accounting *(cont.)*

Michael David Pakter, CPA, CFE, CIRA, CA

Managing Member
G & P Financial Litigation Advisors, LLC
205 West Wacker Drive, Suite 918
Chicago, IL 60606
Tel: (312) 229-1720
Fax: (312) 229-1725
E-mail: mpakter@litcpa.com
Web Site: http://www.litcpa.com

Specialties: Michael Pakter is a Certified Public Accountant, Certified Fraud Examiner, Certified Insolvency and Restructuring Advisor and Chartered Accountant. He has over 25 years experience providing financial analysis, accounting, auditing and investigative services. Michael performs financial analysis and forensic accounting for distressed and reorganizing companies, especially those with incomplete or falsified records. He provides bankruptcy and reorganization services to debtors and creditors, focusing on fraudulent conveyances and litigation during bankruptcy proceedings. Michael has provided consulting services and expert testimony to trial lawyers to assist with accountants' malpractice, damages determination, discovery, forensic accounting, lost profits and commercial litigation. **Degrees/ licenses:** CPA, CFE, CIRA, CA.

Rimkus Consulting Group, Inc.

Curtis R. Brown
Senior Vice President
8 Greenway Plaza, Ste. 500
Houston, TX 77046
Tel: (713) 621-3550
(800) 580-3228
Fax: (713) 623-4357
E-mail: expert@rimkus.com
Web Site: http://www.rimkus.com

Specialties: Rimkus Consulting Group, Inc., established in 1983, is a worldwide provider of independent, professional consulting services to insurance companies, law firms, corporations and government agencies. Rimkus assists clients in the responsive and timely resolution of claims and disputes. Our team of educated and experienced engineers, scientists, accountants, and technical specialists, is recognized for excellence in service by local, national, and international business communities. Primary areas of expertise include industrial, vehicular and worker accident investigation and reconstruction; failure analysis; product liability; industrial, commercial and residential environmental analysis; and forensic accounting.

See primary listing under ENGINEERING: General

TASA

(Technical Advisory Service for Attorneys)
1166 DeKalb Pike
Blue Bell, PA 19422-1853
Tel: (800) 523-2319
Fax: (800) 329-8272
E-mail: experts@tasanet.com
Web Site: http://www.tasanet.com

Specialties: Save search time! Contact TASA first. Benefit from 44 years of referral expertise. We assess your individual needs and refer experienced Local, Regional, or National professionals for Consulting, Testifying, and ADR in Forensic Accounting areas including Antitrust; Auditing; Bankruptcy; Business Dissolution; Business Valuations; Damages; Estates; Insurance; Inventory Fraud; Limited Partnerships; Mergers-Acquisitions; Mortgage-Bank Lending; Patents; Pension Funds; Property and Wage Losses; Real Estate; Royalties; Sales; Securities; Small Business; Taxes; Trademarks; Wages-Hours; Hundreds More. SERVICES INCLUDE prompt customized searches, referrals, resumes, and your initial interview calls with experts. Exceptional personal service. **Degrees/licenses:** All prof. degrees, licenses, certifications represented.

See primary listing under EXPERT WITNESS REFERRALS: General

Malpractice

Robert W. Berliner, CPA, CFE
Director of Litigation Services
Marks Paneth & Shron LLP
622 Third Avenue
New York, NY 10017
Tel: (212) 503-8853
Fax: (212) 503-8852
E-mail: rberliner@markspaneth.com
Web Site: http://www.markspaneth.com

Specialties: Securities Fraud; Accounting Malpractice; Post Acquisition Disputes; Forensic Accounting; Fraud Investigation; Contract Disputes; Damages and Lost Profit Calculations. Former National Office Accounting and Auditing Partner at a "Big 8" CPA firm; has served as a member of the Auditing Standards Board and the FASB Emerging Issues Task Force; was the Chairman of the Professional Ethics Committee of the New York State Society of CPAs; was an adjunct professor of accounting at NYU's Stern School of Business; and has testified in a variety of cases in Federal and State Courts throughout the country. **Degrees/licenses:** BS, MBA, CPA, CFE.

Peter H. Burgher
2 Brambleberry Dr.
Howell, MI 48843-8738
Tel: (517) 546-6330
Fax: (517) 546-9565
E-mail: pete@marelco.com
Web Site: http://www.expertpages.com/cv/burgher.htm

Specialties: Accounting; Auditing; Securities Fraud; Lost Profits; Damage Claims; Finance Evaluations of Businesses especially Professional Firms, Lawyers Divorce and Law Firm Divisions. Experienced in Insurance, Manufacturing, Aviation, Aircraft Mfr. and Airlines, Fast Foods, Securities Law 10 (b) 5, Malpractice Defense and Prosecution. **Degrees/licenses:** AB, MBA, CPA, A&P, DAR.

See primary listing under ACCOUNTING: Forensic Accounting

ACOUSTICS

General

Jack E. Randorff, PhD, PE, FASA
Principal-in-Charge
Randorff and Associates, Inc.
11 West Canyon View Drive
Ransom Canyon, TX 79366
Tel: (806) 829-2521
Fax: (806) 829-2527

Specialties: Environmental noise assessments; sound level survey; train horn loudness assessments; employee hearing damage-risk assessments; vibration assessments; highway noise assessment; aircraft/airport noise assessment; architectural sound isolation assessments; industrial noise assessments; testimony - plaintiffs & defendants; clients - major companies, federal agencies, state agencies, local municipalities, private industry, schools, universities, national architectural/engineering firms; National Council of Acoustical Consultants, President (1992-1994), Vice President - membership (1998-2002), Vice President - finance (2002-2004); Fellow - Acoustical Society of America, American Institute of Physics; President - Engineers Council of Houston (1985-1986), Science Engineering Fair of Houston (1986-1988). **Degrees/licenses:** BS, MS, PhD, PE (Texas).

ADVERTISING

General

Robert A. Grayson, PhD
President
Grayson Associates
30728 Paseo Elegancia
San Juan Capistrano, CA 92675-5426
Tel: (949) 487-9970
Fax: (949) 487-9975
E-mail: bob@graysonassociates.com
Web Site:
http://www.marketingexpertwitness.com

136 East 56th Street
New York, NY 10022
Tel: (212) 688-6175

Specialties: Internationally known marketing consultant: 35 years experience, big and little companies, Fortune 500, advertising agency/ marketing company experience, prof. Graduate School, author, publisher, lecturer. Specialty: consumer products, services. Expert testimony: advertising, promotion, trademark, packaging, acquisitions, all marketing mix. **Degrees/licenses:** MBA, PhD.

See primary listing under MARKETING: General

Performance Analysis Group, Inc.
Richard Shain, President
Pamela Shain, Managing Director
100 Wells Ave., Ste 202
Newton, MA 02459-3210
Tel: (617) 244-5700
Fax: (617) 527-2422
E-mail: richard@pag-adsave.com
Web Site: http://www.pag-adsave.com

Specialties: Determination of advertising and marketing effectiveness. Advertising/Media Auditing. Specializing in Spot TV, Network Television, Cable, Radio, Magazines, Newspapers; Evaluation of budgets and plans; Billing reconciliations, audience delivery evaluations; Customized analysis. A nationally recognized firm with a broad range of industry experience auditing many market leaders. Experience in many industries including pharmaceuticals, entertainment, automotive, financial, and fast foods. Legal references available. Principals are former senior level advertising and media executives at top advertising agencies and multi-national corporations with extensive industry knowledge. **Degrees/licenses:** BA - Math, BS - Economics, MBA - Marketing Program.

AGRICULTURE

General

House Agricultural Consultants
Gregory A. House
Agricultural Consultant
1105 Kennedy Place, Ste. 1
P.O. Box 1615
Davis, CA 95617
Tel: (530) 753-3361
Fax: (530) 753-0464
E-mail: gahouse@houseag.com
Web Site: http://www.houseag.com

Specialties: Twenty-five years experience in agricultural consulting; Accredited farm manager; Accredited rural appraiser; Certified professional agronomist. Specialties: Crop production, Farm business management, Fruit and nut crops, Vegetable crops, Field crops, Crop valuation and loss, Rangeland and pasture management, Soil management and conservation, Irrigation practices, Crop marketing, Agricultural economics. **Degrees/licenses:** BS, Crop Ecology; AFM, ARA, CPAg.

James M. Miller, PE, PhD
President
Miller Engineering Associates, Inc.
2392 Fuller Court
Ann Arbor, MI 48105
Tel: (734) 662-6822
Fax: (734) 747-9712
E-mail: jmiller@millerengineering.com
Web Site:
http://www.millerengineering.com

Specialties: Agricultural & Construction Safety: Tractor, Implement, Harvester & Grain Storage; Pesticides, Herbicides, Fungicides; Mechanical Design Safety: Power Tools & Machine Guarding; OSHA/ANSI/ASTM Compliance; Warnings, Labels, Instructions & User Manuals: Health Hazard Warnings; Design of User Manuals & Warnings; Consumer Product Safety: Human Factors & Ergonomics, Slips, Falls-Premise, Vehicle, Ladder; Child, Home Appliances, Furniture; Vehicles: Auto, Truck, ATV, Boat, Jet Ski, Snowmobile; Seat Belts & Air Bags; Chemical, Fire, Environmental & Waste Disposal: Fires & Explosions-Vapors/Electrical/Chemical; Chemical Labeling Requirements; MSDS; Groundwater & Soil Contamination; Nursing Malpractice; Nursing Management. **Degrees/licenses:** James Miller, PE, PhD; Bradley Cook, PE; Rebecca Lehto, PhD, RN, OCN.

See primary listing under ACCIDENT PREVENTION & SAFETY: General

Forestry

Thomas A. Sturza, Safety Engineer
Joseph A. Sturza, Logging Engineer
Sturza Safety, Inc.
376 Avery Road West
Winlock, WA 98596
Tel: (360) 262-3202
Fax: (360) 740-0387
E-mail: sturza@localaccess.com

Specialties: Expert Witness; Product Liability, Compliance Inspections; Safety Code Development; Accident Investigation; Forest Road Design & Inspection; Logging System Analyses; Timber Felling Practices; OSHA Code Interpretation; Forest Products; Logging & Sawmills. **Degrees/licenses:** BS - Logging Engineering.

Horses

CeCe Younger
Equine Litigation Consultant & Appraiser
CeCe Younger Bloodstock
3906 Mont Blanc Ter.
Bakersfield, CA 93306-7566
Tel: (661) 873-0224
(661) 747-4394 (Cellular)
Fax: (661) 873-0944
E-mail: clyhorse@aol.com
Web Site: http://www.bannerfarms.com or
http://www.CeCeYounger.com

Specialties: 35 years experience: Horse Behavior; Farm Operations; Stable Management; Safety, Standard of Care; Accident Reconstruction; Litigation Support; Insurance Claims; Certified Horse Appraisals; Estate and Donations; Show Horses, Race Horses, Rental Horses; Breeding Quarter Horses, Warmbloods, Miniature Horses, Ponies and Thoroughbreds. Professional Trainer of Horses & Riders; Senior Life Member Amer. Society of Equine Appraisers; Youngest woman admitted to and life member of the U.S. Equestrian Team; Member of Pacific Coast Horse Show Assn., USA Equestrian Assn., Amer. Quarter Horse Assn., Amer. Society of Appraisers, Calif. Thoroughbred Breeders Assn., Amer. Assn. for Horsemanship Safety. **Degrees/licenses:** BA, Drew University; Licensed USA Equestrian Judge. See above.

See primary listing under ANIMALS: Horses

ALCOHOL/DRUGS

General

Esam Z. Dajani, PhD, FACG

President
IDDC Corporation
1549 RFD
Long Grove, IL 60047-9532
Tel: (847) 634-9586
E-mail: EsamD@aol.com
Web Site: http://www.edajani.com

Specialties: Clinical pharmacology, toxicology, drug development, regulatory affairs, pharmaceutical R & D and contract research organizations (CROs). Dr. Dajani has expertise in alcohol, drugs (prescription & OTC), driving under the influence, industrial chemicals, health & beauty products, product liability, labeling and medical malpractice. He provides research, analysis, merit statement, and testimony for plaintiff and defense. Dr. Dajani directed clinical research at major pharmaceutical companies and held academic appointments. He is currently serving as the president of a CRO group and Adjunct Professor of Medicine at Loyola University. He has 260 publications, presentations and patents. **Degrees/licenses:** BS, MS & PhD (Pharmacol. & Toxicol.). Licensed Pharmacist.

H.H. Miller Consulting

Harold H. Miller
2816 Ironwood Drive
Grand Prairie, TX 75052
Tel: (972) 660-1614
E-mail: hhpm@sbcglobal.net

Specialties: Consulting services, Toxicology, Pharmacology, Expert Testimony, Quality Assurance, Quality Control, Hazardous Materials, Facility Inspections and Regulatory Affairs. Dr. Miller has academic training in chemistry, medical technology and pharmacology. Assistant Professor in college of pharmacy, Toxicologist with major petrochemical company and Director of Toxicology with national reference laboratory. Experienced in assessment of effects of prescribed medications, drugs of abuse and alcohol, in relation to alleged malpractice, accidents and investigations. Numerous inspections of facilities for regulatory compliance. Experienced as expert witness in administrative hearings, depositions and courtroom testimony. **Degrees/licenses:** BA Chemistry; MT (ASCP) Medical Technology; PhD Pharmacology.

See primary listing under MEDICINE & HEALTH: Toxicology

Douglas Severance, MD

5601 Norris Canyon Rd., Ste. 330
San Ramon, CA 94583
Tel: (925) 275-0400
Fax: (925) 327-7155
E-mail: poprocks120@earthlink.net

Specialties: Certified by the American Society of Addictive Medicine. Twenty years of work in chemical dependency. Medical director of several detox/rehabilitation programs. Contracted as a chemical dependency expert in multiple cases. **Degrees/licenses:** BS, MD, ABFP, ASAM.

S. Franklin Sher, MD

Toxicology & Family Physician & Surgeon
1150 Civic Drive
Walnut Creek, CA 94596
Tel: (925) 935-3113
Fax: (925) 935-4482
E-mail: franklinsher@yahoo.com

Specialties: Impaired performance from alcohol or drugs; pedestrian, bicyclist or operator of any motorized transport for commercial/personal use. Forty five years experience. Over 2000 court trials (including federal and state) as qualified expert in 31 California counties; Review police, coroner, accident, reconstruction reports; depositions, interviews, transcripts; hospital and physician's records. Literature search; analysis and evaluation of evidence; retrograde extrapolations, dose/drink calculations; changes in human factors from alcohol/drug impairment; influence of body trauma/blood losses on alcohol/drugs levels. Clients include Caltrans, Attorney General, many major Law Firms; Defense 85%, Plaintiff 15%. **Degrees/licenses:** BS, MD, FAAFP.

Chemical Dependence

Douglas Severance, MD
5601 Norris Canyon Rd., Ste. 330
San Ramon, CA 94583
Tel: (925) 275-0400
Fax: (925) 327-7155
E-mail: poprocks120@earthlink.net

Specialties: Certified by the American Society of Addictive Medicine. Twenty years of work in chemical dependency. Medical director of several detox/rehabilitation programs. Contracted as a chemical dependency expert in multiple cases. **Degrees/licenses:** BS, MD, ABFP, ASAM.

See primary listing under ALCOHOL/DRUGS: General

Driving Under the Influence

Ali Z. Hameli, MD
Consultant, Forensic Pathology
3005 Silverside Road
Wilmington, DE 19810
Tel: (302) 478-3341
Fax: (302) 478-3341

Specialties: Forensic Pathology, Forensic Medicine, Forensic Toxicology; Professional Consultation/Case Management in Forensic Medicine/Pathology/Toxicology; Case review, verbal/written reports, deposition/trial testimony. Chief Medical Examiner 1964-1997; Director, Forensic Sciences Laboratory 1970-1997, State of Delaware; Clinical Associate Professor, Forensic Pathology, Jefferson Medical College; President, National Association of Medical Examiners 1973-1975; Vice President, American Academy of Forensic Sciences, 1992-1993; President Medical Society of Delaware, 1990-1991; Consultant, U.S. Justice Department, identification of Josef Mengele, 1985; Consultant, Mayoral Commission, MOVE Bombing, Philadelphia, 1985. Recipient of many prestigious awards. **Degrees/licenses:** MD, Board Certified, Anatomic & Forensic Pathology.

See primary listing under MEDICINE & HEALTH: Forensic Pathology

Karl Verebey, PhD, DABFT
President & Director
Forensic Toxicology Associates
638 Debchar Court
River Vale, NJ 07675
Tel: (908) 862-4404
(201) 391-0015
Fax: (908) 862-4405
E-mail: k.verebey@att.net
Web Site: http://home.att.net/~k.verebey

Specialties: Alcohol & Drugs of Abuse Testing: Disputes of laboratory results; Interpretation of laboratory and behavioral data; Psychopharmacology & Clinical Pharmacology: Interpretation of drugs and/or alcohol toxicity based on concentration and time/action parameters; Toxicology of alcohol, drugs and metals. Cornell University Medical College, PhD, Pharmacology, Biochemistry; Board Certified in Forensic Toxicology & Clinical Laboratory Sciences; High Complexity Laboratory Director, ABB. Over 30 years experience drug abuse pharmacology, alcohol & psychopharmacology. Former Chief Toxicologist, City of New York. Over 100 publications. Over 300 cases since 1981; in court testimony accepted in 7 states as an expert. **Degrees/licenses:** PhD; DABFT (Amer. Bd. of Forensic Tox.); HCLD (ABB); Clin. Lab Direc. NY, NJ, PA.

ANIMALS

General

Richard H. Polsky, PhD, CAAB
President
Animal Behavior Counseling Services, Inc.
2288 Manning Avenue
Los Angeles, CA 90064
Tel: (310) 474-3776
Fax: (310) 475-9659
E-mail: dr.polsky@verizon.net
Web Site: http://www.dogexpert.com

Specialties: Expert on dog behavior and cat behavior with reference to dog bites and cat bites and personal injury due to the behavior

(Listing continued on next page)

General *(cont.)*

Richard H. Polsky (cont.)
of a dog or cat. Assessment and reconstruction of pet-related injuries/dog bites or dog attacks. Dr. Polsky is available to render expert opinion about dogs and cats with reference to their dangerous or aggressive propensities. Third party/landlord cases. Experienced in both civil and criminal litigation in animal behavior as it applies to dogs and cats. Plaintiff and defense. **Degrees/licenses:** PhD Animal Behavior, Certified Applied Animal Behaviorist (CAAB).

See primary listing under ANIMALS: Dogs & Cats

Dogs & Cats

Richard H. Polsky, PhD, CAAB

President
Animal Behavior Counseling Services, Inc.
2288 Manning Avenue
Los Angeles, CA 90064
Tel: (310) 474-3776
Fax: (310) 475-9659
E-mail: dr.polsky@verizon.net
Web Site: http://www.dogexpert.com

Specialties: Expert on dog behavior and cat behavior with reference to dog bites and cat bites and personal injury due to the behavior of a dog or cat. Assessment and reconstruction of pet-related injuries/dog bites or dog attacks. Dr. Polsky is available to render expert opinion about dogs and cats with reference to their dangerous or aggressive propensities. Third party/landlord cases. Experienced in both civil and criminal litigation in animal behavior as it applies to dogs and cats. Plaintiff and defense. **Degrees/licenses:** PhD Animal Behavior, Certified Applied Animal Behaviorist (CAAB).

Horses

Kathy Kusner

1049 N. Stanley Ave., #6
West Hollywood, CA 90046
Tel: (323) 654-7266
Web Site: http://kathykusner.com

Specialties: Horses: Show Horses (Hunters and Jumpers); Racing; Rental Horses and Pleasure Horses; Cross Country Riding; All levels of Riding, Training and Instruction; Stable Management; Horse and Equipment Appraisal; Horse Behavior; Safety Procedures; Industry Standards; Accident Prevention and Reconstruction. Rider in three Olympic Games - Tokyo, Mexico City, and Munich (silver medal), and two Pan American Games - Sao Paulo (gold medal) and Winnipeg (silver medal). First licensed female jockey. Gives clinics nationally and internationally on training, riding, and showing. Named Horsewoman of the Year; inducted into the Show Jumping Hall of Fame and was chosen as one of the 50 most influential horsemen of the 20th Century. Horse Expert Witness since 1983.

CeCe Younger

Equine Litigation Consultant & Appraiser
CeCe Younger Bloodstock
3906 Mont Blanc Ter.
Bakersfield, CA 93306-7566
Tel: (661) 873-0224
(661) 747-4394 (Cellular)
Fax: (661) 873-0944
E-mail: clyhorse@aol.com
Web Site: http://www.bannerfarms.com or http://www.CeCeYounger.com

Specialties: 35 years experience: Horse Behavior; Farm Operations; Stable Management; Safety, Standard of Care; Accident Reconstruction; Litigation Support; Insurance Claims; Certified Horse Appraisals; Estate and Donations; Show Horses, Race Horses, Rental Horses; Breeding Quarter Horses, Warmbloods, Miniature Horses, Ponies and Thoroughbreds. Professional Trainer of Horses & Riders; Senior Life Member Amer. Society of Equine Appraisers; Youngest woman admitted to and life member of the U.S. Equestrian Team; Member of Pacific Coast Horse Show

Assn., USA Equestrian Assn., Amer. Quarter Horse Assn., Amer. Society of Appraisers, Calif. Thoroughbred Breeders Assn., Amer. Assn. for Horsemanship Safety. **Degrees/ licenses:** BA, Drew University; Licensed USA Equestrian Judge. See above.

Veterinary Medicine

Bruce S. Putchat, VMD

Pleasant Valley Animal Hospital
Lucky Chance Pet Resort & Spa
AnWell Veterinary Rehab
& Conditioning Center
1945 State Road
Quakertown, PA 18951
Tel: (610) 346-7854
Fax: (610) 346-8752
E-mail: drbru@epix.net
Web Site: http://www.pvah.com or
http://www.anwellveterinaryrehab.com

Specialties: Facility design; Veterinary practice; Animal health, care & welfare; Marketing consultant to the pet industry; Animal legislation & regulation. Affiliation: Nathan Putchat Associates (Director, Life Sciences Division).
Biographical Information: Bruce S. Putchat was born 1942, Trenton, NJ; BS (Zoology & Entomology) 1964, PA State University. Graduate studies in Cytogenetics 1964, PA State University. Veterinariae Medicinae Doctoris (1968), University of Pennsylvania. Owner, Administrative Head & Chief of Medicine & Surgery, Pleasant Valley Animal Hospital. Principal, Nathan Putchat Associates, P.A. Licenses: Veterinary Medicine & Surgery (FL, NY, PA). Accredited by National Board of Veterinary Examiners. Member: American Animal Hospital Association; American Veterinary Medical Association; American Association of Equine Practitioners; American Association of Sheep & Goat Practitioners. Founding member: American Association of Avian Practitioners; Veterinary Cancer Society. Member: PA State Veterinary Association; FL Veterinary Association; Lehigh Valley Veterinary Medical Association; Lehigh Valley Humane Society. Specialties: Medical Management & Administration of Animal Health & Welfare Problems; Veterinary Facility Design & Practice; Marketing Problems in the Pet Industry; Genetics; Orthopedics & Cardiovascular Disease; Exotic Animal Health & Management; Medical & Legal Ramifications of Animal Welfare Legislation; Forensic & Legal support for the Veterinary Profession. President, Lehigh Valley Veterinary Medical Association. Trustee, PA Veterinary Medical Association, Consultant & Liaison Agent between the PA Veterinary Medical Association & the University of PA School of Veterinary Medicine; Consultant to the PA Association of Animal Health Technicians; Consultant to the Pet Industry Joint Advisory Council. Lecturer. Publications incl: The General Veterinary Hospital Concept (1981). Investigations & Research, Reports, Consultation, Arbitration, Expert Testimony, Seminars.
Degrees/licenses: BS; VMD.

Veterinary Physical Rehab/ Conditioning

Bruce S. Putchat, VMD

Pleasant Valley Animal Hospital
Lucky Chance Pet Resort & Spa
AnWell Veterinary Rehab
& Conditioning Center
1945 State Road
Quakertown, PA 18951
Tel: (610) 346-7854
Fax: (610) 346-8752
E-mail: drbru@epix.net
Web Site: http://www.pvah.com or
http://www.anwellveterinaryrehab.com

Specialties: Facility design; Veterinary practice; Animal health, care & welfare; Marketing consultant to the pet industry; Animal legislation & regulation. Affiliation: Nathan Putchat Associates (Director, Life Sciences Division). See Dr. Putchat's biographical information under his primary listing of ANIMALS-Veterinary Medicine on this page.
Degrees/licenses: BS; VMD.

See primary listing under ANIMALS: Veterinary Medicine

APPRAISAL & VALUATION

General

BTI Appraisal

Ben F. Tunnell III
Chairman
605 West Olympic Blvd., Ste. 820
Los Angeles, CA 90015
Tel: (213) 532-3800
Fax: (213) 532-3807
E-mail: ben@btiappraisal.com
Web Site: http://www.btiappraisal.com

Specialties: BTI Appraisal offers litigation and appraisal experience, nationally and internationally, since 1974 in the areas of: Real Estate, Machinery & Equipment, and Business Valuation. We represent attorneys, insurance companies, governments, financial institutions and corporations for insurance claims, condemnations, and IRS and SEC issues. Well-written and documented reports reduce litigation costs and speed dispute resolution. Our work has passed the most rigorous scrutiny of the IRS, the SEC, government condemning agencies and state and federal courts. The collective experience of our nationally regarded professionals can address projects of all sizes and locations.

Business Matters in the Visual Arts

Jeremy Stone
Accredited Member,
American Society of Appraisers
4034 20th Street, 2nd Floor
San Francisco, CA 94114
Tel: (415) 252-1010
Fax: (415) 436-9241
E-mail: jstone@jeremystone.biz
Web Site: http://www.jeremystone.biz

Specialties: Extensive expertise in the following areas: 20th Century American art & artists; Exhibition, contract & sales records; plaintiff & defense work involving artists, galleries, collectors/clients & landlord/tenant studio issues; Professional practices of the Art world; Appraisal reports (tax, insurance & litigation); Deposition questions. Former Positions: Director, Jeremy Stone Gallery, San Francisco, CA; Executive Director, LEAP (Learning Through Education in the Arts Projects) San Francisco, CA; Consultant, The Jewish Museum, San Francisco, CA; Curator, Nestle Beverage Company, San Francisco, CA; Career Resources Program Director, San Francisco Art Institute; Visiting Faculty, San Francisco Art Institute. Published 15 articles, 3 catalogs, and 2 books. Accredited member, American Society of Appraisers. **Degrees/licenses:** Exec. Cert., Nonprofit Mgmt, Univ. San Francisco; BS, Org. Behavior, USF, USPAP.

ForensisGroup, Inc.

Mercy Steenwyk
3452 E. Foothill Blvd., Ste. 1160
Pasadena, CA 91107
Tel: (626) 795-5000
(800) 555-5422
Fax: (626) 795-1950
E-mail: experts@forensisgroup.com
Web Site: http://forensisgroup.com

Specialties: Thousands of our clients have gained the technical advantage and the edge in their cases from our multidisciplined group of experts in hundreds of disciplines. We have some of the best and the brightest at competitive rates backed by 14 years of excellent track record and the support of our trained staff. We assist you until you have the right expert. Some of our areas of expertise are: Construction, Safety, Engineering, Product Liability, Accident Reconstruction, Automotive, Environmental, Slip & Fall, Appraisal, Medical and other scientific disciplines. Unsurpassed standards. Clients actively evaluate our experts. **Degrees/licenses:** PE, GC, CSP, PhD, MD, GC, CIH, AIA.

See primary listing under ACCIDENT PREVENTION & SAFETY: General

Fulcrum Financial Inquiry

David Nolte
Principal
1000 Wilshire Blvd., Ste. 1650
Los Angeles, CA 90017
Tel: (213) 787-4111
(213) 787-4100
Fax: (213) 787-4141
E-mail: dnolte@fulcruminquiry.com
Web Site: http://www.fulcruminquiry.com

Specialties: Our analysis and research combined with unique presentation techniques have resulted in an unequaled track record in successful court cases and client recoveries. Our personnel are full time and fully focused on the services we provide. We thoughtfully incorporate technology into our work to provide great results at a more reasonable cost. Our expertise encompasses damages analysis, lost profit studies, business & intangible asset valuations, fraud investigations, statistics, forensic economic analysis, royalty audits, strategic & market assessments, competitive surveys, analysis of computerized data including computer forensics, and a wide range of other financial advisory services. **Degrees/licenses:** CPA, ASA, CMA, MBA, CFA.

See primary listing under ACCOUNTING: General

UHY Mann Frankfort Stein & Lipp Advisors

Saul Solomon
Dir. of Forensic, Litigation
& Business Valuation Services
12 Greenway Plaza, 8th Floor
Houston, TX 77046-1291
Tel: (713) 960-1706
Fax: (713) 968-7140
E-mail: ssolomon@uhy-us.com
Web Site: http://www.uhy-us.com

Specialties: Loss/Damage Determination: Antitrust and Class Action Analysis, Bankruptcy Matters, Breach of Contract, Business Interruption, Fraud and Forensic Accounting, Lender Liability, Intellectual Property, Professional Malpractice, Securities Fraud, Shareholder Disputes; Lost Earnings, Profits, Value; Personal Injury; Family Law: Asset Tracing, Characterization; Business Valuations For Public And Private Entities, Mergers & Acquisitions Due Diligence, Financial and Economic Analysis; Trial Services in State and Federal Courts: Evidence Evaluation, Expert Witnesses, Planning And Strategy During Trial. Consulted with all Major Industries: Construction, Consumer Products, Government, Health Care, Oil and Gas, Technology, Manufacturing, etc. **Degrees/licenses:** BBA, CPA, CFE, CVA.

See primary listing under ACCOUNTING: General

Antiques

O'Toole-Ewald Art Associates, Inc.

Elin Lake Ewald, PhD, ASA
1133 Broadway, Suite 1107
New York, NY 10010
Tel: (212) 989-5151
Fax: (212) 242-1629
E-mail: ele@otoole-ewald.com
Web Site: http://www.otoole-ewald.com

Specialties: Appraisals for damage/loss, equitable distributions, estates, insurance, and fraud cases relating to fine and/or decorative arts. O'Toole-Ewald has an in-house staff with expertise in painting, sculpture, antiques, Asian art, works on paper, photography, furniture, ceramics, glassware, rugs, textiles, silver, et al. We provide excellent analytical reports including fully documented forensic appraisals. All of our reports adhere to U.S.P.A.P. standards and include photography. Expert witness testimony and consultation available. Established in 1932.

See primary listing under APPRAISAL & VALUATION: Fine/Decorative Art

Business & Corporate

Arnold D. Brown

Principal
Brown CPA Group, Ltd.
Northbrook Office Court
666 Dundee Rd., Suite 1603
Northbrook, IL 60062-2737
Tel: (847) 509-4100
Fax: (847) 509-1040
E-mail: arnieb@browncpagroup.com
Web Site: http://www.browncpagroup.com

Specialties: Forensic accounting; Business valuations; Estate & gift tax valuations; Malpractice claims; Damage claims; Shareholder disputes; Stock options; Analysis of documents & structuring of divorce settlements; Trial strategy; Expert testimony; Deposition & cross examination assistance to counsel. **Degrees/licenses:** BBA; CPA; CVA.

See primary listing under LITIGATION SUPPORT: General

BTI Appraisal

Ben F. Tunnell III
Chairman
605 West Olympic Blvd., Ste. 820
Los Angeles, CA 90015
Tel: (213) 532-3800
Fax: (213) 532-3807
E-mail: ben@btiappraisal.com
Web Site: http://www.btiappraisal.com

Specialties: BTI Appraisal offers litigation and appraisal experience, nationally and internationally, since 1974 in the areas of: Real Estate, Machinery & Equipment, and Business Valuation. We represent attorneys, insurance companies, governments, financial institutions and corporations for insurance claims, condemnations, and IRS and SEC issues. Well-written and documented reports reduce litigation costs and speed dispute resolution. Our work has passed the most rigorous scrutiny of the IRS, the SEC, government condemning agencies and state and federal courts. The collective experience of our nationally regarded professionals can address projects of all sizes and locations.

See primary listing under APPRAISAL & VALUATION: General

The Center for Forensic Economic Studies

Jerome M. Staller, PhD, President
Brian P. Sullivan, PhD, VP
Pia Di Girolamo, PhD, Sr. Economist
Lawrence M. Santucci, MA, Sr. Economist
Donald F. Gurian, CPA,
Sr. Business Consultant
1608 Walnut Street, Ste. 801
Philadelphia, PA 19103
Tel: (215) 546-5600
Fax: (215) 732-8158
E-mail: cfes@cfes.com
Web Site: http://www.cfes.com

Specialties: Economic & Statistical Analysis in Personal Injury, Commercial, Employment and Civil Rights matters; Business Valuations. PhD-level economists & full-time support staff. **Degrees/licenses:** Staff members hold PhDs.

See primary listing under ECONOMICS: General

Cohen, Miskei & Mowrey, LLP

Scott Mowrey
15303 Ventura Blvd., Suite 1150
Sherman Oaks, CA 91505
Tel: (818) 986-5070
Fax: (818) 986-5034
E-mail: cmm@cmmpas.com

Specialties: Forensic Accountants and Finance Experts with extensive experience in the following areas: Forensic Accounting, Fraud Investigation, Economic Damages, Business Valuation, Family Law, Bankruptcy, Reorganization, Lost Earnings/Profits Analysis. **Degrees/licenses:** CPAs; CFEs; MBAs.

See primary listing under ACCOUNTING: General

Higgins, Marcus & Lovett, Inc.

Mark C. Higgins, ASA
President
800 S. Figueroa St., Ste. 710
Los Angeles, CA 90017
Tel: (213) 617-7775
Fax: (213) 617-8372
E-mail: mhiggins@hmlinc.com
Web Site: http://www.hmlinc.com

Specialties: The firm has over 20 years of litigation support and expert testimony experience in matters involving business valuation, economic damages, intellectual property, loss of business goodwill and lost profits. Areas of practice include business disputes, eminent domain, bankruptcy, tax disputes, and corporate and marital dissolution. **Degrees/licenses:** MBAs, ASAs, CFAs.

Holt Media Group

Arthur H. Holt, President, CEO
Christine Borger, EVP
2178 Industrial Drive, Suite 914
Bethlehem, PA 18017
Tel: (610) 814-2821
Fax: (610) 814-2826
E-mail: artholt@holtmedia.com <u>or</u>
ceborger@holtmedia.com
Web Site: http://www.holtmedia.com

Specialties: Communications: radio & television; Cable, Internet, television & related fields; Media analysis & research; Appraisals. **Degrees/licenses:** BFA; FCC 1st Class Engineer - Arthur; MBA - Christine.

See primary listing under COMMUNICATIONS/TELECOMMUNICATIONS: General

Michael G. Kaplan, CPA, CVA, CFFA

Kaplan Abraham Burkert & Company
5950 Canoga Ave., Ste 200
Woodland Hills, CA 91367
Tel: (818) 888-0066
Fax: (818) 888-8860
E-mail: michael@forensicvalue.com
Web Site: http://www.kab-bv.com

Specialties: Accountant with extensive consulting and expert witness experience in the following areas: Business Disputes; Economic Damages; Goodwill; Fraud & Embezzlement; Loss of Earnings & Profits; Business Valuation; Forensic Accounting; Wrongful Termination; Infringement; Legal & Accountants' Malpractice. **Degrees/licenses:** MBA; CPA.

Litigation Economics, LLC

Stanley P. Stephenson, PhD
One Embarcadero Center, Suite 500
San Francisco, CA 94111
Tel: (415) 835-1212
Fax: (415) 835-1213
E-mail: stan@litigationeconomics.com
Web Site: http://litigationeconomics.com

Specialties: Since 1985, experts at Litigation Economics, LLC have provided economic, accounting, and financial consulting in complex litigation. Credibility before judges, jurors, mediators, and arbitrators is the most essential factor a Litigation Economics expert provides. We develop damage reports for plaintiffs or critique such reports for defense counsel. Specializations include: breach of contract, business interruption, construction, franchise, intellectual property, products liability, and lost earnings capacity. We have provided assistance in more than 150 cases and testified in 25 cases in various legal hearings. Member: National Association of Certified Valuation Analysts; Financial Management Association. **Degrees/licenses:** PhD, MS (Indiana University), BA (Ball State University).

See primary listing under ECONOMICS: Economic Losses/Damages

Business & Corporate *(cont.)*

Mayer Hoffman McCann PC

Steve Franklin
Jeff Freeman
11601 Wilshire Blvd, Ste. 2300
Los Angeles, CA 90025
Tel: (310) 268-2000
Fax: (310) 268-2001
E-mail: sfranklin@cbiz.com or jfreeman@cbiz.com
Web Site: http://www.cbiz.com or http://www.mhm-pc.com

Specialties: Business and Accounting firm with extensive consulting and expert witness experience in the following areas: Business Litigation; Business Valuation & Appraisal; Financial Reconstruction; Family Limited Partnerships; Marital Dissolutions; Transactional Due Diligence; Business Interruption; Commercial Damage & Lost Profits; Fraud Investigations; Tax Controversies. **Degrees/licenses:** CPA; CFE; ABV.

See primary listing under ACCOUNTING: General

Donald John Miod, CPA, ABV, CVA, CBA

Partner
Miod & Company, LLP
Certified Public Accountants
11600 Indian Hills Rd., #300
Mission Hills, CA 91345-1225
Tel: (818) 905-5822
Fax: (818) 905-5867
E-mail: dmiod@miod-cpa.com
Web Site: http://www.miod-cpa.com

Specialties: Forensic Accounting and Financial Analysis; Business Valuations; Estate Valuations; Market Analysis; Litigation Support; Damage and Lost Profits Calculations; Investigative Accounting; Employee Dishonesty; Embezzlement; Fraud Investigations; Comprehensive Evaluation of Internal Controls; Identification of Unreported or Diverted Income; Loss of Earnings Calculations; Cash Flow Analysis; Spousal Support Determinations; Lifestyle Analysis; Hidden Asset Tracing ; Settlement Assessments; Reimbursement Claims and Analysis; Tax Consultation; Business Management; Business Planning; Claims Accounting; Inventory Losses; Reconstruction of Accounting Records; Tax and Estate Planning; Breach of Contract; Insurance Defense; Construction Defects; Bankruptcy. Over 29 years experience. **Degrees/licenses:** BS, CPA, ABV, CVA, CBA, CFS, DABFA.

See primary listing under ACCOUNTING: Forensic Accounting

Laura Jane Tindall, CPA

President
Laura J. Tindall & Company PA
3780 A Road
Loxahatchee, FL 33470
Tel: (561) 795-1965
Fax: (561) 793-3131
E-mail: ljt@ljtindall.com
Web Site: http://www.businessdamagevalue.com

Specialties: Breach of contract, Lost Profits, Business Valuation, Lost Wages, Eminent Domain Business Damages. **Degrees/licenses:** Doctorate in Business Admin, CPA/ABV, BVAL, CVA, MCBA.

Computers

NACOMEX USA, Inc.

Robert J. Zises, ASA
President
230 Park Avenue, 10th Floor
New York, NY 10169
Tel: (800) 622-6639
Fax: (212) 681-9211
E-mail: zises@nacomex.com
Web Site: http://www.nacomex.com

Specialties: Computer hardware appraisal & valuation for corporate & governmental clients since 1987. Experienced in present-day, historical retrospective, mass appraisals, residual value forecasts, & depreciation schedules for: municipalities, corporate ad valorem appeals, property taxes, lease termination & buy-out issues, contract evaluation, purchase money allocation, bankruptcy, loss replacement. Litigation & expert witness testimony references available. Critique & analysis of opposing experts' reports. All our reports are USPAP-compliant. **Degrees/licenses:** ASA, IAAO, IPT, AIA, National Forensic Centre.

Fine/Decorative Art

Business Matters in the Visual Arts

Jeremy Stone
Accredited Member,
American Society of Appraisers
4034 20th Street, 2nd Floor
San Francisco, CA 94114
Tel: (415) 252-1010
Fax: (415) 436-9241
E-mail: jstone@jeremystone.biz
Web Site: http://www.jeremystone.biz

Specialties: Extensive expertise in the following areas: 20th Century American art & artists; Exhibition, contract & sales records; plaintiff & defense work involving artists, galleries, collectors/clients & landlord/tenant studio issues; Professional practices of the Art world; Appraisal reports (tax, insurance & litigation); Deposition questions. Former Positions: Director, Jeremy Stone Gallery, San Francisco, CA; Executive Director, LEAP (Learning Through Education in the Arts Projects) San Francisco, CA; Consultant, The Jewish Museum, San Francisco, CA; Curator, Nestle Beverage Company, San Francisco, CA; Career Resources Program Director, San Francisco Art Institute; Visiting Faculty, San Francisco Art Institute. Published 15 articles, 3 catalogs, and 2 books. Accredited member, American Society of Appraisers. **Degrees/ licenses:** Exec. Cert., Nonprofit Mgmt, Univ. San Francisco; BS, Org. Behavior, USF, USPAP.

See primary listing under APPRAISAL & VALUATION: General

O'Toole-Ewald Art Associates, Inc.

Elin Lake Ewald, PhD, ASA
1133 Broadway, Suite 1107
New York, NY 10010
Tel: (212) 989-5151
Fax: (212) 242-1629
E-mail: ele@otoole-ewald.com
Web Site: http://www.otoole-ewald.com

Specialties: Appraisals for damage/loss, equitable distributions, estates, insurance, and fraud cases relating to fine and/or decorative arts. O'Toole-Ewald has an in-house staff with expertise in painting, sculpture, antiques, Asian art, works on paper, photography, furniture, ceramics, glassware, rugs, textiles, silver, et al. We provide excellent analytical reports including fully documented forensic appraisals. All of our reports adhere to U.S.P.A.P. standards and include photography. Expert witness testimony and consultation available. Established in 1932.

Horses

CeCe Younger

Equine Litigation Consultant & Appraiser
CeCe Younger Bloodstock
3906 Mont Blanc Ter.
Bakersfield, CA 93306-7566
Tel: (661) 873-0224
(661) 747-4394 (Cellular)
Fax: (661) 873-0944
E-mail: clyhorse@aol.com
Web Site: http://www.bannerfarms.com or http://www.CeCeYounger.com

Specialties: 35 years experience: Horse Behavior; Farm Operations; Stable Management; Safety, Standard of Care; Accident Reconstruction; Litigation Support; Insurance Claims; Certified Horse Appraisals; Estate and Donations; Show Horses, Race Horses, Rental Horses; Breeding Quarter Horses, Warmbloods, Miniature Horses, Ponies and Thoroughbreds. Professional Trainer of Horses & Riders; Senior Life Member Amer. Society of Equine Appraisers; Youngest woman admitted to and life member of the U.S. Equestrian

(Listing continued on next page)

Horses *(cont.)*

CeCe Younger (cont.)
Team; Member of Pacific Coast Horse Show Assn., USA Equestrian Assn., Amer. Quarter Horse Assn., Amer. Society of Appraisers, Calif. Thoroughbred Breeders Assn., Amer. Assn. for Horsemanship Safety. **Degrees/licenses:** BA, Drew University; Licensed USA Equestrian Judge. See above.

See primary listing under ANIMALS: Horses

Machinery & Equipment

BTI Appraisal

Ben F. Tunnell III
Chairman
605 West Olympic Blvd., Ste. 820
Los Angeles, CA 90015
Tel: (213) 532-3800
Fax: (213) 532-3807
E-mail: ben@btiappraisal.com
Web Site: http://www.btiappraisal.com

Specialties: BTI Appraisal offers litigation and appraisal experience, nationally and internationally, since 1974 in the areas of: Real Estate, Machinery & Equipment, and Business Valuation. We represent attorneys, insurance companies, governments, financial institutions and corporations for insurance claims, condemnations, and IRS and SEC issues. Well-written and documented reports reduce litigation costs and speed dispute resolution. Our work has passed the most rigorous scrutiny of the IRS, the SEC, government condemning agencies and state and federal courts. The collective experience of our nationally regarded professionals can address projects of all sizes and locations.

See primary listing under APPRAISAL & VALUATION: General

Personal Property

R. Maurice Robinson, ISHC, CRE, ASA

President
Maurice Robinson & Associates, LLC
880 Apollo St. #125
El Segundo, CA 90245
Tel: (310) 640-9656
Fax: (310) 640-9276
E-mail: Maurice@MauriceRobinson.com
Web Site: http://www.mauricerobinson.com

Specialties: CRE, ASA, ISHC, trained arbitrator & mediator, certified appraiser. Recipient of top award for real estate consultants and appraisers for valuing the Grand Canyon National Park in 2000. Hotel and real estate industry business issues expert with 25 years consulting experience resolving disputes between owner-operator, borrower-lender and franchisee-franchisor. Fluent in ground & building leases; management contracts; franchise agreements; partnership & JV agreements; concession contracts; development agreements and loan docs. Expert witness testimony; damage calculations; lost profits analysis; deal structuring; workouts; bankruptcy; new development planning; market demand assessment; acquisition due diligence; and economic, market, financial & investment analysis. **Degrees/licenses:** MPA; BA Economics; State Certified General Real Estate Appraiser.

Real Estate

BTI Appraisal

Ben F. Tunnell III
Chairman
605 West Olympic Blvd., Ste. 820
Los Angeles, CA 90015
Tel: (213) 532-3800
Fax: (213) 532-3807
E-mail: ben@btiappraisal.com
Web Site: http://www.btiappraisal.com

Specialties: BTI Appraisal offers litigation and appraisal experience, nationally and internationally, since 1974 in the areas of: Real Estate, Machinery & Equipment, and

Business Valuation. We represent attorneys, insurance companies, governments, financial institutions and corporations for insurance claims, condemnations, and IRS and SEC issues. Well-written and documented reports reduce litigation costs and speed dispute resolution. Our work has passed the most rigorous scrutiny of the IRS, the SEC, government condemning agencies and state and federal courts. The collective experience of our nationally regarded professionals can address projects of all sizes and locations.

See primary listing under APPRAISAL & VALUATION: General

Robert W. Thorpe, AICP

President
R.W. Thorpe & Associates, Inc.
(Seattle/Anchorage/Denver/Winthrop)
705 2nd Ave., Ste. 710, Hoge Bldg.
Seattle, WA 98104
Tel: (206) 624-6239
Fax: (206) 625-0930
E-mail: rwta@rwta.com
Web Site: http://www.rwta.com

Specialties: Expert Witness, Courts, Quasi-judicial; Highest & Best Use, Land Use, Zoning; Development Permits; Instructor at Universities, Community Colleges & NAHB: Land Economics/Planning; Masters degrees in Urban Planning & Urban Development. **Degrees/licenses:** AICP, BS Business & Economics, M-Urb.Dev/Urb. Plng, NAHB, College & Univ. Inst.

Charles B. Warren, ASA

Principal
Warren & Warren
2033 Powell Street
San Francisco, CA 94133
Tel: (415) 433-0959
Fax: (415) 982-1441
E-mail: cbw@apo.com
Web Site: http://www.slip.net/~cjwarren

Specialties: Appraisal Standards; Assessment Appeals; Forensic Appraisal of unusual properties. Senior member American Society of Appraisers in urban real property. California State Licensed. Qualified expert in Federal District Court, Superior Court, Bankruptcy Court, and before assessments appeals boards. **Degrees/licenses:** BA, Univ. of Calif.-Berkeley; Post Grad. Studies; Cert. General Appraisal Lic.

Vehicles

J.A. "Doc" Watson

P.O. Box 758
Humble, TX 77347
Tel: (281) 540-8257
Fax: (281) 446-5212
E-mail: theautoexpert@aol.com
Web Site: http://www.theautoexpert.com

Specialties: Automotive consumer fraud, deceptive trade practices. Opinions, depositions and testimony which have led to successful solutions in mediation, arbitration, pre-trial settlements and trials. Ten+ years' experience expert witness plaintiff and defense. Expertise - sales and finance tactics, leasing, diminished value, rebates, curbstoning, odometers, repossession, salvage, credit procedures, vehicle appraisals, mechanical and body repair fraud, previous damage, trucks, lemon law, title kiting, program cars, bad credit, service contracts, life and accident & health policies, auto auctions, wholesaling, manufacturers' warranties, lender fraud, flood damage, class action, personal injury. 40+ years automotive employment history.

ARBITRATION/ MEDIATION

General

Molly M. Murphy

Trial Consultant - Mediator
1541 Ocean Ave., 2nd Floor
Santa Monica, CA 90401
Tel: (310) 458-7720
Fax: (310) 458-7298
E-mail: mickeyslaw@yahoo.com
Web Site:
http://www.jury-trialconsultant.com

Specialties: Trial Consultant and Mediator with extensive consulting and expert witness experience in the following areas: Theme Development, Trial/Evidence Strategy; Preparation of Expert/Lay Witnesses; Mock Trials; Voir Dire Strategy; Jury Questions and Questionnaires; Jury Selection; Jury Monitoring and Post-Trial Interviews; Elmo System for Trial Presentation.. **Degrees/licenses:** Dispute Resolution Masters Program; Pepperdine U. Law School Mediation Training.

ARCHITECTURE

General

ForensisGroup, Inc.

Mercy Steenwyk
3452 E. Foothill Blvd., Ste. 1160
Pasadena, CA 91107
Tel: (626) 795-5000
(800) 555-5422
Fax: (626) 795-1950
E-mail: experts@forensisgroup.com
Web Site: http://forensisgroup.com

Specialties: Thousands of our clients have gained the technical advantage and the edge in their cases from our multidisciplined group of experts in hundreds of disciplines. We have some of the best and the brightest at competitive rates backed by 14 years of excellent track record and the support of our trained staff. We assist you until you have the right expert. Some of our areas of expertise are: Construction, Safety, Engineering, Product Liability, Accident Reconstruction, Automotive, Environmental, Slip & Fall, Appraisal, Medical and other scientific disciplines. Unsurpassed standards. Clients actively evaluate our experts. **Degrees/licenses:** PE, GC, CSP, PhD, MD, GC, CIH, AIA.

See primary listing under ACCIDENT PREVENTION & SAFETY: General

Philip Kroeze, AIA

Principal
Consulting Architectural Services
19 Summerside
Coto de Caza, CA 92679
Tel: (949) 589-0554
Fax: (949) 589-4351
E-mail: kroeze@cox.net
Web Site: http://www.jurispro.com/mem/kroeze

Specialties: Licensed Architect (CA); Member: American Institute of Architects (AIA), Construction Specifications Institute (CSI), International Congress of Building Officials (ICBO), National Council of Architectural Registration Boards (NCARB). Architectural/Engineering standard of care; moisture intrusion; construction documents. 35+ years experience in design, working drawings, specifications, construction; litigation support; single & multi-family residential, commercial, offices; personal injury; ADA compliance; UBC types I-V; wood, steel & concrete structures; models, charts, renderings, & other exhibits; photographs. **Degrees/licenses:** Licensed Architect (CA); Bachelor of Architecture; US Army Corps of Engineers.

KULWIEC GROUP/ ARCHITECTS

W. John Kulwiec,
AIA, CSI, NCARB, ICC, AAMA
532 Glade Drive
Santa Paula, CA 93060-1617
Tel: (877) 774-6500 ext. 109
Fax: (805) 525-5105
E-mail: John@KulwiecGroup.com
Web Site: http://www.KulwiecGroup.com

Specialties: 35+YEARS of PROFESSIONAL EXPERIENCE and current practice utilized to effectively provide Forensic and Expert Witness expertise in: Standard of Care, Post Construction Building Autopsy, Destructive Testing, Scope of Work Definition, Scheduling Analysis of Contractor & Architect, Change Order Disputes, Drawings and Documents Analysis, Communication Analysis between Client, Architect & Contractor, Waterproofing Issues, Mold Issues, Roofing Issues, Code Compliance: ADA, Title 24, ICC, Local, OSHPD, Construction Defects & Negligence. LITIGATION EXPERIENCE: Mediation, Arbitration, Superior and Federal Court, Plaintiff and Defense for Architects, Owners and Contractors. For complete CV visit www.KulwiecGroup.com. **Degrees/licenses:** BArch, Illinois Inst Tech; Arch Lic: CA #C-3978, AZ, CO, NV, WA, MI.

Ian Mackinlay Architecture, Inc.

Ian Mackinlay, FAIA
President
26 O'Farrell St., Ste. 200
San Francisco, CA 94108
Tel: (415) 243-4191
Fax: (415) 243-9769
E-mail: ian@ima-arch.com
Web Site: http://www.ima-arch.com

Specialties: Architecture; Expert analysis and testimony regarding architectural design and construction defects; Building code compliance; Roofing and waterproofing systems; Problems related to building in the snow and cold; Litigation strategy and organization; Product research and documentation; Alternative dispute resolution; Remedial design and reconstruction; Design review/quality assurance; Design related accident; Trial graphics. 450+ cases since 1979. Licensed in 17 states as listed below plus MT, NY, OH, NM. **Degrees/licenses:** Arch. Lic.: CA, WA, NV, UT, WY, AK, CO, GU, HI, ID, IL, MD, MN, NCARB #5408.

Glenn A. Marin

Vice President
IXP Corp.
8256 Enramada Ave.
Whittier, CA 90605
Tel: (562) 696-1286
Fax: (562) 693-5002
E-mail: glennm8256@aol.com

Specialties: Public Safety Systems (EMS, fire, police): Computer Aided Dispatch, Records Management, Mobile Data Terminal Systems; Two-way mobile radio: design and operational use parameters; Emergency Dispatching: practices and operations; Staffing, working environment, facility requirements; Jail Systems: computer support requirements, inmate housing analysis; Court Master for Jail overcrowding; Computer simulation analysis of radio systems channel loading, fire move-up analysis, dispatch staffing requirements. Retired Police Lieutenant. 22 years serving hundreds of public safety clients from small to very large. International experience. Extensive expert witness cases in Federal and State Courts. **Degrees/licenses:** BS, CSU - LA (1966); MPA, USC (1972); Grad. work, Comp. Sci., UC - Fullerton.

See primary listing under LAW ENFORCEMENT: General

Ron Travers, AIA

La Jolla Pacific, Ltd.
460 Goddard
Irvine, CA 92618-4610
Tel: (949) 645-8900
Fax: (949) 645-8813
E-mail: rtravers@ljpltd.com
Web Site: http://www.ljpltd.com

Specialties: Extensive experience in Planning, Zoning, Design and Construction Administration of wood frame, suburban, density, residential, and high rise towers of concrete pre-stressed, post-tension, steel construction,

(Listing continued on next page)

General *(cont.)*

Ron Travers (cont.)
and related defects pertaining to the above. Knowledge of major weatherproofing designs and concepts. Mold expert in construction related matters, requiring assessment of cause, condition, extent of mold, and recommendation of restoration methods, and repair processes. If hygienic and laboratory analysis is deemed necessary, refer to other known professionals. Success in managing investigations of various structural defect situations. Considerable in-court expert witness experience. **Degrees/licenses:** AIA, Lic. in WA, OR, CA, AZ, NV, CO, HI; NCARB Certified.

WWCOT

Dean Vlahos, AIA, NCARB, CCCA
David Sakaguchi, AIA
3130 Wilshire Blvd., 6th Floor
Santa Monica, CA 90403
Tel: (310) 828-0040
Fax: (310) 453-9432
Web Site: http://www.wwcot.com

Specialties: On site observations; destructive investigations; analysis; research; expert testimony on design, building codes, general construction defects and repair methods. **Degrees/licenses:** AIA, NCARB, CCCA, LEEO.

ATTORNEY

Legal Malpractice

Phillip Feldman

Law Offices of Phillip Feldman
15250 Ventura Blvd. Ste. 610
Sherman Oaks, CA 91403
Tel: (310) LEG-MALP (534-6257)
Fax: (818) 986-1757
E-mail: LegMalpExpert@aol.com
Web Site:
http://www.LegalMalpracticeExperts.com

Specialties: Thirty-seven years Legal Malpractice, professional liability, ethics & professional responsibility; fee disputes; with experience on both sides of the bar. Hands-on experience in almost all transactional & trial lawyering underlying matters ("case within a case," causation issues) including over 25 years as a Judge Pro Temp & Attorney/Client Fee Dispute Arbitrator (accounting degree). Former State Bar Prosecutor, present Attorney Discipline & Ethics Defense counsel. Prolific national author & lecturer. Never disqualified or failed to qualify in any jurisdiction. Testimony, reports & consults have been used in almost all jurisdictions (state & federal) for twenty-three years. **Degrees/licenses:** BS, MBA, JD, Bd. Cert. Legal & Med. Malpractice, ABA, ABPLA, CA.

See primary listing under MEDICAL-LEGAL: Legal Malpractice

Samuel K. Freshman, BA, JD

President
Standard Management Company
6151 W. Century Blvd., Suite 300
Los Angeles, CA 90045
Tel: (310) 410-2300
Fax: (310) 410-2919
E-mail:
sfreshman@standardmanagement.com

Specialties: Attorney, Real Estate Broker, Banker, Professor, Legal Malpractice, Arbitration, Brokerage, Malpractice, Leases, Syndication, Construction, Property Management, Finance, Due Diligence, Conflict of Interest, Title Insurance, Banking, Escrow. 32 years State & Federal Courts. 29 articles. Mediator, Fiduciary Duties, Lease Inerpretation, Banking Title Company President. **Degrees/licenses:** BA, JD, California Bar, U. S. Supreme Court & District Court, U. S. Tax Court.

See primary listing under REAL ESTATE: General

Malpractice/Liability/ Litigation

Lewis Laska

Attorney
901 Church Street
Nashville, TN 37203
Tel: (800) 298-6288
Fax: (615) 255-6289
E-mail: mail@verdictslaska.com
Web Site: http://www.verdictslaska.com

Specialties: Medical Malpractice, Products Liability and Railroad litigation. Publisher of "Medical Malpractice Verdicts, Settlements and Experts," "National Products Liability Database Report," and "FELA Reporter and Railroad Liability Monitor." All are monthly publications reporting verdicts and settlements on a national basis. In-house databases can be searched for identification of experts used in cases reported in the newsletters. Identify experts for your cases, or retrieve case reports identifying a specific expert expected to be used in your case. Help evaluate the value of your case by finding similar cases that have been tried. The national database of verdicts and settlements contains over 25,000 cases. Call for a quote on the cost of searching the database.
See display advertisement above

AUDIO/VIDEO EVIDENCE

General

Audio Forensic Center

Durand R. Begault, PhD
130 Sutter Street, Ste. 500
San Francisco, CA 94104
Tel: (800) 257-7706 (Ext. 261)
Fax: (415) 397-0454
E-mail: dbegault@cmsalter.com
Web Site: http://www.audioforensics.com

Specialties: Acoustics; audibility; audio demonstrations; audio and video tape enhancement; voice identification and elimination; audio tape authentication; intellectual property and patent claims; acoustical compliance; acoustical gunshot analysis; transcripts from noisy tapes. **Degrees/licenses:** BA UC - Santa Cruz; MFA Mills College, Oakland, CA; PhD UC - San Diego.

General *(cont.)*

Bill Krone

Legal Video Expert
Deja View Video
417 S. El Dorado St.
San Mateo, CA 94402
Tel: (800) 416-5608
(650) 343-8899
E-mail: bill@dejaview.com
Web Site: http://www.dejaview.com

Specialties: Analysis of video recordings as to authenticity, consistency, veracity, and identification. Video measurement for character identification. Edits, erasures, alterations or anomalies or recordings addressed and resolved. Evaluation of video recordings and cameras. Special emphasis on field recording procedures and specifications of camera and recording media in order to provide an opinion as to reasonable depiction of what could have been seen by the participants. Trial Testimony and Consultation in State and Federal Courts. Extensive trial list and references upon request. Synchronized transcript and video to CD-ROM and DVD. Prints and image enhancements from video. Visual site surveys, reconstructions, visibility studies, field production, opposition expert services available. **Degrees/licenses:** BA, SMPTE, NABET, Notary Public (CA).

AUTOMOTIVE

General

Al Axelrod

President
Al Axelrod, Inc.
22661 Crespi St.
Woodland Hills, CA 91364-1310
Tel: (818) 224-2116
Fax: (818) 224-2116
E-mail: axelsmart@aol.com

Specialties: Inspections, service/repair issues, shop practice, standards, product liability, root cause defect analysis, safety systems including brakes, steering, airbags, seat belts, ABS, speed control; lemon law/fraudulent claims, tire defects and wheel defects - fire cause and origin; fleet maintenance and management, alternative dispute resolution. Over 20,000 road test for defects; 40 years automotive industry experience. Initial case conference, no charge. **Degrees/licenses:** ASE Certified Master Tech (CMAT)(L1-Adv.); BS; Qualified Expert, SAE/BAR.

Michael D. Haslam

AFS Risk Management Services
3540 Simsbury Court
Carlsbad, CA 92008
Tel: (760) 729-8457
Fax: (760) 729-8581
E-mail: BLCexpert@aol.com

Specialties: Auto Industry expert with 40+ years of consulting and expert witness experience in the following areas: Auto Financing/ Leasing; Regulation Z & M; FCRA; ECOA; FDCPA; UCC; Portfolio Management; Lender Due Diligence; Repossessions/Asset Disposal; Consumer/Commercial Transactions.

Lewis R. Linet Jr., PhD

President
American Auto Seminars
c/o American Auto Seminars
19355 Sherman Way #22
Reseda, CA 91335
Tel: (818) 772-6464
Fax: (818) 772-6464
E-mail:
Lew@AmericanAutoSeminars.com or
http://www.AmericanAutoSeminars.com

Specialties: Expert witness and case preparation services provided to attorneys in the field of "Automobile Dealership Standards & Practices" - New and used cars, sales, leasing, finance, service, parts. Sales and management training. Twenty-six years experience. CV and references available upon request. Visit www.AmericanAutoSeminars.com. **Degrees/licenses:** BA in Economics; PhD in Business-Marketing; Los Angeles Business & Retail lic.

Pro/Consul Technical and Medical Experts

1945 Palo Verde Ave., Suite 200
Long Beach, CA 90815-3443
Tel: (800) 392-1119
(562) 799-0116
Fax: (562) 799-8821
E-mail: eexperts@msn.com
Web Site: http://www.expertinfo.com

Specialties: RIGHT EXPERT RIGHT AWAY!® 15,000 experts in 7,000 fields. Listed and recommended by the A. M. Best Company. Full-time research staff. We welcome your RUSH cases! TECHNICAL: Fast inspections. Categories from Accident Reconstruction to Zoology, also including appraisal, economics, employment, human factors, insurance, premises liability, security, and many more. MEDICAL: IME's. Inexpensive insurance medical records reviews by MDs. Categories from Addiction Medicine to Zooplasty, including board certified physicians in all fields, dentistry, geriatrics, neuropsychology, neurosurgery, nursing, orthopedics, psychiatry and many more. Reasonable fees. Free initial consultation. Free resume binder. Free CLE classes. **Degrees/licenses:** MD, PhD, DDS, DVM, DO, DPM, PE, CPA, ME, CE, CRC, MAI, et al.

See primary listing under ACCIDENT RECONSTRUCTION: General

Robert J. Waters

Consultant
Waters Consulting
2188 Monterey Drive
Fairfield, CA 94534-1723
Tel: (707) 421-2278
(707) 479-3574
Fax: (707) 421-2278
E-mail: info@autolitigationsupport.com
Web Site:
http://www.autolitigationsupport.com

Specialties: Since 1992 providing thorough technical assistance in all areas of automotive engineering and technologies. My experience includes cases related to small claims, Lemon Law, personal injury, unsafe vehicle sales, dealership and repair shop practices, product liability, failure analysis, flat rate and standards of care. Clients include law enforcement agencies, insurance carriers, law firms, manufacturers and individuals. Certified Master Automobile Technician since 1982. Member Society of Automotive Engineers. Ford Motor Company Master technician. Plaintiff and Defense. **Degrees/licenses:** ASE A1, A2, A3, A4, A5, A6, A7, A8, L1, SAE.

AVIATION

General

Dellem Associates, Inc.

Larry S. Weaver
President
14023 No. Dale Mabry Hwy
Tampa, FL 33618-2401
Tel: (813) 963-5353
Fax: (813) 962-3164
E-mail: lweaver@dellem.com
Web Site: http://www.dellem.com

Specialties: Fuel storage facilities (specializing in Aviation Fuel facilities both on and off airports), including the construction, maintenance and operation of various types of petroleum facilities and the training and testing of personnel in handling petroleum products. Specifically for Aviation Fuel, we provide verification of specifications; determination of composition and potential sources of contamination; aircraft fueling procedures; operational safety and training of personnel. Member, ASTM Tech J - Development of aviation fuel specifications. **Degrees/licenses:** United States Naval Academy, BS; New York University, MBA.

See primary listing under PRODUCT LIABILITY: Petroleum Products

General *(cont.)*

Robert "Bob" Norris, Captain
Aviation Consulting Services
P.O. Box 1522
San Carlos, CA 94070
Tel: (650) 508-1079
Fax: (650) 508-9005
E-mail: avconsult@aol.com
Web Site: http://www.avconsult.com

Specialties: Expert Witness for Plaintiff or Defendant; General Aviation Flight and Ground Training Schools; Air Carrier Training Programs for Pilots, Flight Engineers, Aircraft Dispatchers, Flight Attendants, Check Airman and Flight Instructors; Career Advancement Counseling; Captain Interview Board; Crew Resource Management (CRM) Programs; Wrongful Termination; Discrimination. Engineering Psychologist, Hughes Aircraft Company: Space Systems, Flight Simulation, Weapons Development; United Airlines: Flight Manager, Flight & Simulator Instructor, FAA Check Airman; Captain Qualified: DC-8, DC-10, B-737, B-757, B-767; Flight Dispatcher, Owner FAA-141 Flight School and FAA Maintenance Repair Station. Author. **Degrees/licenses:** BS, ATP, FE, CFI, CFII, MEI.

Wrongful Termination

Don A. Brigham
President
Aviation Forensics, LLC
3423 Seabreeze Lane
Corona Del Mar, CA 92625
Tel: (949) 720-8126
Fax: (786) 549-0751
E-mail: opg333@cox.net

Specialties: Forensic evaluation and expert testimony relating to commercial flight crew training, aviation ground school and line operation of commercial aircraft; flight simulator training; accident and incident evaluation all relating to wrongful termination of professional aviator. Former U.S. Marine Naval Aviator; Captain and FAA proficiency check pilot designee for both Western Airlines and Delta Air Lines; facilitator for Delta Air Lines Cockpit Resource Management (CRM) to over 10,000 pilots. Expert in assembling, certifying, testifying to training, commercial flight record performance before formal and informal judicial boards of inquiry and review. **Degrees/licenses:** Airline Transport Pilot; Multi-Single Engine Land; Flight Engr.,Turbojet.

BIOLOGICAL SCIENCES

Serology

Brian Wraxall
Chief Forensic Serologist
Serological Research Institute
3053 Research Dr.
Richmond, CA 94806
Tel: (510) 223-7374
Fax: (510) 222-8887
E-mail: bwraxall@serological.com
Web Site: http://www.serological.com

Specialties: Forensic serology; Forensic serology analysis; Proficiency Provider; DNA testing; Paternity testing; Bodily fluids: saliva, semen, blood; Technical support & training; Forensic serology research & development; Laboratory analysis, ASCLD/LAB® Accredited. **Degrees/licenses:** Fellow, American Board of Criminalistics; HNC (Applied Biology); DABFE.

BUSINESS

General

Mayer Hoffman McCann PC

Steve Franklin
Jeff Freeman
11601 Wilshire Blvd, Ste. 2300
Los Angeles, CA 90025
Tel: (310) 268-2000
Fax: (310) 268-2001
E-mail: sfranklin@cbiz.com or jfreeman@cbiz.com
Web Site: http://www.cbiz.com or http://www.mhm-pc.com

Specialties: Business and Accounting firm with extensive consulting and expert witness experience in the following areas: Business Litigation; Business Valuation & Appraisal; Financial Reconstruction; Family Limited Partnerships; Marital Dissolutions; Transactional Due Diligence; Business Interruption; Commercial Damage & Lost Profits; Fraud Investigations; Tax Controversies. **Degrees/licenses:** CPA; CFE; ABV.

See primary listing under ACCOUNTING: General

Rochelle B. Spandorf, Esq.

Sonnenschein, Nath & Rosenthal
601 South Figueroa Street
Los Angeles, CA 90017-5704
Tel: (213) 892-5036
Fax: (213) 623-9924
E-mail: rspandorf@sonnenschein.com
Web Site: http://www.sonnenschein.com

Specialties: Franchising specialist with extensive consulting and expert witness experience in the following areas: Business Franchising; Dealer & Distribution Law; Registration & Disclosure; Earnings Claims; Contract Disputes; Supplier Limitations; Performance Disputes; Encroachment; Non-compete Agreements; Alternative Distribution; Termination, Non-Renewal & Transfer; Franchisee Association Rights. **Degrees/licenses:** BS, Cornell University; JD, Washington University.

Franchises

Rochelle B. Spandorf, Esq.

Sonnenschein, Nath & Rosenthal
601 South Figueroa Street
Los Angeles, CA 90017-5704
Tel: (213) 892-5036
Fax: (213) 623-9924
E-mail: rspandorf@sonnenschein.com
Web Site: http://www.sonnenschein.com

Specialties: Franchising specialist with extensive consulting and expert witness experience in the following areas: Business Franchising; Dealer & Distribution Law; Registration & Disclosure; Earnings Claims; Contract Disputes; Supplier Limitations; Performance Disputes; Encroachment; Non-compete Agreements; Alternative Distribution; Termination, Non-Renewal & Transfer; Franchisee Association Rights. **Degrees/licenses:** BS, Cornell University; JD, Washington University.
See primary listing under BUSINESS: General

BUSINESS VALUATION

General

Gumbiner, Savett, Finkel, Fingleson & Rose, Inc.

Ronald S. Greene, CPA
Executive Vice President
1723 Cloverfield Blvd.
Santa Monica, CA 90404
Tel: (310) 828-9798
Fax: (310) 829-7853

Specialties: Business, legal, and accounting specialist with extensive consulting and expert witness experience in the following areas: Lost Profit, Damages and Calculations; Fraud Analyses & Audits; Assets & Income Tracing; Litigation Strategy Consulting; Tax Support; Family Law Accounting; Business Valuations; Royalty & Contract Audits; Standard of Care Analyses. **Degrees/licenses:** CPA, MBA, CVA, MBT, JD.
See primary listing under ACCOUNTING: General

CHEMICAL PLANT & SAFETY MANAGEMENT

General

Expert Witness Chemical Plant & Safety Management

James J. "Jim" Gadwood
Expert Witness - Consultant
590 Pheasant Ridge Drive
Lake Zurich, IL 60047
Tel: (847) 438-0528
E-mail: jimgadwood@aol.com
Web Site: http://hometown.aol.com/jimgadwood/myhomepage/resume.html

Specialties: Business Experience: Jim Gadwood has successfully completed 38 years of experience within the Chemical Process Industry. An experienced Plant Manager with an extensive background in Chemical Plant and Safety Management. Expert Witness Experience: Industrial-Contractor Accidents plus EPA & OSHA requirements. Define Industry Standards & GMP-Good Manufacturing Practices. Accident Causation and Safety & Accident Research. Determine Responsibilities within an Accident. Deposition and Trial Experience. References, Business Resume, Case History: available upon request. **Degrees/licenses:** BS Chemistry & MBA Courses; ACS, AICHE, ASTM.

See primary listing under CHEMISTRY/ CHEMICALS: General

CHEMISTRY

Industrial Chemistry

Arthur S. Diamond

President
Diamond Research Corp.
530 West Ojai Avenue, Suite 108
Ojai, CA 93023-2471
Tel: (805) 640-7177
Fax: (805) 640-7178
E-mail: drc@west.net
Web Site: http://www.imagingnews.com

Specialties: Chemical research for graphic communication: Paper chemistry; Paper & film coatings; Imaging materials; Toners; Inkjet inks. **Degrees/licenses:** BS; MS; PE

CHEMISTRY/ CHEMICALS

General

Chemical Accident Reconstruction Services, Inc.

Michael Fox, PhD
Founder
9121 E. Tanque Verde Rd., #105
Tucson, AZ 85749-8391
Tel: (800) 645-3369
Fax: (520) 749-0861
E-mail: services@chemaxx.com
Web Site: http://www.chemaxx.com

Specialties: Complex industrial chemical accidents, fires and explosions as well as chemical-related consumer product injuries. The founder of the company has his PhD in Physical Chemistry, is a Certified Fire & Explosion Investigator and Certified or Accredited in Hazardous Chemicals, OSHA Process Hazard Analysis Team Leader, DOT Hazardous Materials, Corrosion, Metallurgy, Failure Analysis and Aerosols. Other specialties include: Propane, plastics, water chemistry, skin burns, acids, alkalis, carbon monoxide, flammable liquids, gasoline, scanning microscopy, MSDSs, natural gas, solvents, warning labels, PEX, welding, construction, chemical packaging & transport. For more specialties see web site. **Degrees/licenses:** PhD, Physical Chemistry; See certifications above.

Chemir Analytical Services

Shri Thanedar, PhD
CEO
2672 Metro Blvd.
Maryland Heights, MO 63043
Tel: (800) 659-7659
Fax: (314) 291-6630
E-mail: info@chemir.com
Web Site: http://www.chemir.com

Specialties: Materials Identification - identify and quantify components in an unknown sample; Deformulation - reverse engineering of a product; Failure Analysis - material and product failures; Comparative Analysis - product contamination and "good vs. bad" product comparison. Experienced in the chemical analysis of polymers, plastics, paints, coatings, drugs, adhesives and rubbers. Recent cases include patent infringement; product liability and failure; arson investigation; insurance claim validation. Experienced PhD chemists available for consultation including expert witness and testimony to back up laboratory data. In business since 1959.

Expert Witness Chemical Plant & Safety Management

James J. "Jim" Gadwood
Expert Witness - Consultant
590 Pheasant Ridge Drive
Lake Zurich, IL 60047
Tel: (847) 438-0528
E-mail: jimgadwood@aol.com
Web Site: http://hometown.aol.com/jimgadwood/myhomepage/resume.html

Specialties: Business Experience: Jim Gadwood has successfully completed 38 years of experience within the Chemical Process Industry. An experienced Plant Manager with an extensive background in Chemical Plant and Safety Management. Expert Witness Experience: Industrial-Contractor Accidents plus EPA & OSHA requirements. Define Industry Standards & GMP-Good Manufacturing Practices. Accident Causation and Safety & Accident Research. Determine Responsibilities within an Accident. Deposition and Trial Experience. References, Business Resume, Case History: available upon request. **Degrees/licenses:** BS Chemistry & MBA Courses; ACS, AICHE, ASTM.

Interactive Consulting, Inc.

Meyer R. Rosen
President
P.O. Box 66
East Norwich, NY 11732
Tel: (516) 922-2167
Fax: (516) 922-3830
E-mail: meyer.rosen@chemicalconsult.com
Web Site: http://www.chemicalconsult.com

Specialties: With over thirty-five years industrial experience in chemistry and chemical engineering and fifteen years as Adjunct Professor of Fire Chemistry (Westchester Community College), Mr. Rosen has consulted for hundreds of domestic and international corporations in the development, optimization, safety, technical marketing and quality control of new and existing consumer and industrial products. He specializes in technical product liability related to personal injuries resulting from fires and explosions, chemical burns, toxic exposures, and hazardous chemicals in household and industrial products. He performs strategic pre-trial planning, deposition support and accident reconstruction. Mr. Rosen is experienced in design safety, formulation, packaging, product handling, codes & standards, intellectual property management, patent analysis/infringement litigation issues, safer alternatives, warnings, instructions and labeling. **Certifications include:** Fellow, American College of Forensic Examiners; Fellow, Royal Society of Chemistry (London); Diplomate, American Board of Forensic Engineering and Technology; Certified Professional Chemist and Chemical Engineer; Fellow, American Institute of Chemists; Technical Journalist for major chemical trade publications. Editor, "Handbook of Delivery Systems" and co-author of "Rheology Modifier Handbook." **Degrees/licenses:** BS, MS.

General *(cont.)*

InterCity Testing & Consulting

167 Willis Avenue
Mineola, NY 11501
Tel: (516) 747-8400 (NY)
(800) 822-1515 (Outside NYS)
Fax: (516) 746-0121/0111 (NY)
Tel: (561) 745-7940 (FL)
Fax: (561) 745-7939 (FL)
E-mail: exptl@aol.com
Web Site: http://www.InterCityTesting.com

3550 Watt Ave., Ste. 5
Sacramento, CA 95821
Tel: (916) 481-3093
(800) 500-5561 (Toll Free)
Fax: (916) 481-3095

Specialties: Visit our web site for condensed expert CV's in: Amusement Parks & Rides; Automotive Safety & Accident Reconstruction; Biomedical/Biomechanical Injury Analysis; Biomechanics; Boating & Marine Safety; Chemicals & Chemical Engineering; Civil Engineering/Structural Failures; Construction Accidents; Electrical & Mechanical Engineering; Firearms & Explosives; Fire Investigations; Flammable Fabrics; Helmets/ Motorcycle, Bicycle, Sports & Industrial; Machine Guarding; Medical Devices; Medical Emergency/EMT; Metallurgy & Material Sciences; Parks & Playgrounds; Slips, Trips & Falls; Sports/Recreation/Aquatics; Toxicology; Transportation & Highway Safety; Warnings & Instructions. INTERCITY IS NOT AN EXPERT REFERRAL SERVICE. **Degrees/licenses:** PE's / degrees thru PhD's in above specialties.

See primary listing under ACCIDENT RECONSTRUCTION: General

RJ Lee Group, Inc.

5 Nationwide locations:
CA, NY, PA, VA, WA
Keith Rickabaugh
Director of Sales and Marketing
350 Hochberg Road
Monroeville, PA 15146
Tel: (800) 860-1775
(724) 325-1776
Fax: (724) 733-1799
E-mail: krickabaugh@rjlg.com
Web Site: http://www.rjlg.com

Specialties: COMPANY INFORMATION: Independent laboratory and consulting group specializing in application of instrumental techniques to solve problems. Over 250 employees and 20 years litigation support experience. FAILURE ANALYSIS: materials, metals, polymers, and ceramics. CONSTRUCTION MATERIALS/DEFECT IDENTIFICATION: concrete and cement, aggregates, and fill materials. FORENSICS: gun shot residue, hair, fiber, and other trace evidence. ENVIRONMENTAL: disaster/ impact assessment and remediation, receptor modeling, particulate characterization, air and dust analysis, and diesel particulate characterization. EXPANDED SERVICES: auger spectroscopy (AES), optical and electron microscopy (SEM & TEM), inorganic chemistry (AA/ICP & X-ray diffraction), organic chemistry (GC-ECD, GC-FID, GC/MS, FTIR & HPLC), thermal analysis (TGA, DSC, DTA), industrial hygiene, asbestos, silica, method development, product testing, software development, x-ray photoelectron spectroscopy, x-ray diffraction, and x-ray fluorescence (XPS, XRD, XRF). **Degrees/licenses:** BS, CIH, CSP, MA, MBA, MS, MSFS, PE, PhD; AIHA & NVLAP + Other Accred.

See primary listing under FAILURE ANALYSIS: General

A. Andrew Shores, PhD

212 Carroll Canal
Venice, CA 90291
Tel: (310) 578-5783
Fax: (310) 306-3789
E-mail: aShores@mediaone.net
Web Site:
http://people.we.mediaone.net/aShores

Specialties: Credible and persuasive witness testimonies on Chemicals, Hazardous Materials, Coatings/Paints, Adhesives, Plastics, Rubbers, Inks; Corrosion, Testing & Analysis, Weathering & Degradation, Slipperiness, Product Liability and Failure, Patent Infringements. Former Senior Scientist and Research Director at major corporations. **Degrees/ licenses:** PhD Chemistry.

See primary listing under CHEMISTRY/ CHEMICALS: Paints & Coatings

John E. Spessard, PhD, PE, CSP

P.O. Box 835901
Richardson, TX 75083-5901
Tel: (972) 867-8989
Fax: (972) 599-1338
E-mail: johnspessard@yahoo.com

Specialties: Expert Witness; Technical/ Economic Evaluations of Proposed Claim Resolutions; Environmental Claims; OSHA Compliance and Employee Safety; Chemical Exposures to Public and Employees; Hazardous Wastes Treatment and Disposal; Applicable Federal, State and Local Regulations; Accident Investigations: Hazardous Material Generation and Releases, Workplace Injuries, Safety Practices and Programs, Evaluation of Opposing Expert's Reports. **Degrees/licenses:** PhD, MBA, PE, CSP.

See primary listing under ENGINEERING: Chemical, Safety

Adhesives

Richard P. Muny

President
Chemsultants International, Inc.
9349 Hamilton Drive
Mentor, OH 44060
Tel: (440) 352-0218
Fax: (440) 352-8572
E-mail: rmuny@chemsultants.com
Web Site: http://www.chemsultants.com

Specialties: Adhesives, sealants and coatings of all types: Epoxies, Acrylics, Urethanes, Natural Rubber, Styrene Butadiene, Polyvinyl Acetates & others; Pressure Sensitive, Heat seal and Contact Adhesives: Water-based, Hotmelt, 100% solids and solvent adhesives; Thermal and UV drying and curing; Extensive laboratory and coating facility: activities include benchmarking, quality evaluation, physical and analytical testing; product formulation, development, litigation support and expert witness. Markets include PSA tapes and labels, graphic arts, medical, electronics, consumer products, automotive and industrial coatings. **Degrees/licenses:** Ten degreed chemists and engineers; A2LA laboratory accreditation.

Environmental Chemistry

A. Dallas Wait

Principal/Environmental Chemist
Gradient Corporation
20 University Rd.
Cambridge, MA 02138-5756
Tel: (617) 395-5000
Fax: (617) 395-5001
E-mail: dwait@gradientcorp.com
Web Site: http//www.gradientcorp.com

Specialties: Environmental chemistry; Petroleum & PCB chemistry; Analytical chemistry; Forensic chemistry; Chemical fingerprinting; Product characterization; Quality assurance; Data usability & integrity; Method design & evaluation; Lab fraud investigations; Historical analytical chemistry practices; Regulatory comment; Agency negotiations; Sampling techniques; Laboratory auditing & management. **Degrees/licenses:** PhD (Organic Chemistry); BS (Chemistry).

Fire Investigation

Chemical Accident Reconstruction Services, Inc.

Michael Fox, PhD
Founder
9121 E. Tanque Verde Rd., #105
Tucson, AZ 85749-8391
Tel: (800) 645-3369
Fax: (520) 749-0861
E-mail: services@chemaxx.com
Web Site: http://www.chemaxx.com

Specialties: Complex industrial chemical accidents, fires and explosions as well as chemical-related consumer product injuries. The founder of the company has his PhD in Physical Chemistry, is a Certified Fire & Explosion Investigator and Certified or Accredited in Hazardous Chemicals, OSHA Process Hazard Analysis Team Leader, DOT Hazardous Materials, Corrosion, Metallurgy, Failure Analysis and Aerosols. Other specialties include: Propane, plastics, water chemistry, skin burns, acids, alkalis, carbon monoxide, flammable liquids, gasoline, scanning microscopy, MSDSs, natural gas, solvents, warning labels, PEX, welding, construction, chemical packaging & transport. For more specialties see web site. **Degrees/licenses:** PhD, Physical Chemistry; See certifications above.

See primary listing under CHEMISTRY/CHEMICALS: General

Paints & Coatings

Edward D. Cohen, PhD

President
Edward D. Cohen Consulting Services, Inc.
15638 E. Cerro Alto Drive
Fountain Hills, AZ 85268-1720
Tel: (480) 836-9452
Fax: (480) 836-9453
E-mail: cohened146@aol.com
Web Site:
http://www.edcohenconsulting.com

Specialties: Specializes in all aspects of the web coating process; coating and drying of thin films, process development and scale-up; polyester base development; film defect mechanisms; coating analytical characterization techniques; process analysis; coating line design, coating formulation development. Many publications and lecturers. Co-editor and co-author of two books on coating technology. Founding President of the International Society of Coating Science and Technology. Received the John A. Tallmadge Award for Contribution to Coating Technology Sponsored by the American Institute of Chemical Engineers and the President's Award from AIMCAL. Contributing author to several trade journals. **Degrees/licenses:** BSChE, PhD.

Consolidated Research, Inc.

Darlene R. Brezinski, PhD
President
P.O. Box 2190
Kingsford, MI 49802
Tel: (906) 779-9498
Fax: (906) 779-9787
E-mail: darpaint@aol.com

Specialties: Consolidated Research is a technical consulting firm for the paint and coatings industry. Staff have career backgrounds with firms within the industry. These include raw materials suppliers, coatings manufacturers and end-use applicators. We offer expertise in paint, polymers, pigments, additives, failure analysis, liability, toxic issues, patent infringement, analysis and identification of paint, and expert witness services. **Degrees/licenses:** PhD, DABFE, FACFE.

A. Andrew Shores, PhD

212 Carroll Canal
Venice, CA 90291
Tel: (310) 578-5783
Fax: (310) 306-3789
E-mail: aShores@mediaone.net
Web Site:
http://people.we.mediaone.net/aShores

Specialties: Credible and persuasive witness testimonies on Coatings/Paints, Adhesives, Sealants, Chemicals, Plastics, Rubbers, Inks, Hazardous Materials, Corrosion, Testing & Analysis, Weathering & Degradation, Slipperiness, Product Liability and Failure, Patent Infringements. Former Senior Scientist and Research Director at major corporations. **Degrees/licenses:** PhD Chemistry.

Petroleum

Ely and Associates, Inc.

John W. Ely
President
14343-G Torrey Chase Blvd.
Houston, TX 77014-1630
Tel: (281) 580-4646
Fax: (281) 580-3999
E-mail: elyfracs@sbcglobal.net
Web Site: http://www.elyfrac.com

Specialties: All aspects of petroleum engineering with specialties in stimulation, design and implementation. Over 60 publications to books including "Engineer's Guide to Stimulation." Member of Society of Petroleum Engineers, American Chemical Society, Fellow of American Institute of Chemists. Our company includes personnel with a multitude of training and experience including PhD in chemistry, reservoir engineering and a particularly deep understanding of the chemistry of stimulation fluids and their effect on formations, and stimulation techniques and processes. Testimony in more than 25 cases involving service company pumping operations and reservoir damage.

See primary listing under ENGINEERING: Petroleum

Maurice E. Le Pera

President
Le Pera and Associates
1050 Kiln Drive
Harrisonburg, VA 22801-8577
Tel: (540) 432-0991
Fax: (540) 432-0989
E-mail: melepera@aol.com
Web Site: http://www.melepera.com

Specialties: Petroleum product applications; gasoline; diesel fuels; turbine fuels; alternate fuels; engine and gear oils; hydraulic and brake fluids; greases; lubricants; preservatives; antifreeze and coolants; automotive applications; specification development; utilization criteria; quality assurance and testing; engineering evaluations; field problem solving; product substitutions; compatibility assessments; engine performance testing; validation of product claims; energy conservation and pollution prevention; recycling and reclamation; storage procedures. University of Delaware, BS chemistry; University of Delaware Graduate School, MS course work completed; Recipient of DOD Defense Standardization and Meritorious Civilian Service Awards; Numerous publications; member of professional societies. **Degrees/licenses:** BS.

See primary listing under PRODUCT LIABILITY: Petroleum Products

James G. Speight, PhD, DSc

Consultant
2476 Overland Road
Laramie, WY 82070-4808
Tel: (307) 745-6069
Fax: (307) 721-3128
E-mail: jamessp8@aol.com
Web Site:
http://www.drjamesspeight.qpg.com

Specialties: More than 35 years experience with fossil fuels, especially petroleum technology, coal, and natural gas. See web page for more details. **Degrees/licenses:** PhD, DSc.

See primary listing under ENGINEERING: Petroleum

Polymers

Edward W. Funk, PhD

EWF Consulting
676 DeTamble Ave.
Highland Park, IL 60035
Tel: (847) 433-5659
Fax: (847) 433-2837
E-mail: ewf@ewfconsulting.net
Web Site: http://www.ewfconsulting.net

Specialties: Chemical processes and products, polymers, resins, membranes, films, composites, coatings, plastic products, industrial chemicals, consumer chemicals, solvents, vapor and water emissions. Experience in cases involving patent infringement, chemical accidents, product liability, and environmental issues. Dr. Funk has 20 years industrial experi-

(Listing continued on next page)

Polymers *(cont.)*

Edward W. Funk (cont.)
ence with Exxon and Honeywell and is also a Professor of Chemical Engineering at University of Illinois. He is the author of 6 U.S. patents and 70 technical publications. He has been a consultant to numerous chemical companies, law firms, and national laboratories. **Degrees/licenses:** BS, Yale; PhD, University of California, Berkeley.

COMMUNICATIONS/ TELECOMMUNICATIONS

General

The Chatham Group

Jerry A. Klein
President
101 First Street, Ste. 477
Los Altos, CA 94022
Tel: (650) 948-1243
Fax: (650) 949-0534
E-mail: jaklein@chathamlaw.com
Web Site: http://www.chathamlaw.com

Specialties: Silicon Valley based consulting organization specializing in litigation support services for intellectual property litigation matters in state, federal and international proceedings. Our group consists of senior scientists, engineers, managers and experts in the fields of: Electronics, Semiconductors, Computer Hardware and Software, Telecommunications, Office Automation, Communications, Medical Electronics, Biotechnology, Materials, Manufacturing Processes, Industry Custom and Practice, Marketing. Expert witnesses, technical consulting, tutorials, discovery assistance, trial aids, market studies, patent portfolio strategy, damage determinations, investment banking and venture capital due diligence, witness location, prior art search and evaluation for domestic and international matters. **Degrees/licenses:** BSME, Patent Agent, PhDs in Computer Science, etc.

See primary listing under INTELLECTUAL PROPERTY: Patent Infringement

Arthur S. Diamond

President
Diamond Research Corp.
530 West Ojai Avenue, Suite 108
Ojai, CA 93023-2471
Tel: (805) 640-7177
Fax: (805) 640-7178
E-mail: drc@west.net
Web Site: http://www.imagingnews.com

Specialties: Toner chemistry & manufacturing technology; Photographic & electrostatic imaging technology; Reprographic copying & duplicating; Fine particle technology; Ink jet ink technology. **Degrees/licenses:** BS; MS; PE.

See primary listing under CHEMISTRY: Industrial Chemistry

John C. Donovan

President
Telecom Visions, Inc.
11 Osborne Rd.
Garden City, NY 11530
Tel: (516) 739-3565
Fax: (516) 739-0181
E-mail: donovan@speakeasy.org
Web Site: http://telecomexpertwitness.com

Specialties: Nationally recognized telecommunications expert witness before FCC and 44 jurisdictions throughout USA. 40 personal appearances; 60 affidavits, expert reports, and prefiled testimony. Dozens of lawyers as references. See website for 14-page CV. Expert in telephone industry planning, engineering, construction, customer service, operating support systems, field operations, and many other skill-sets as indicated at www.telecomexpertwitness.com. Experienced with pricing and estimating telecommunications construction, cable damage assessment and litigation, class action lawsuits against major regional telephone companies, investment due diligence investigations, patent infringement lawsuits, and other telecommunications projects. **Degrees/licenses:** BSEE - West Point, MBA - Purdue, Mgt. Dev.- Penn State.

Forensic Analyst

Roger L. Boyell
416 Parry Drive
Moorestown, NJ 08057-2877
Tel: (856) 234-5800
Fax: (856) 234-9539
E-mail: boyell@ieee.org
Web Site: http://www.boyell.com

Specialties: Expertise in electronic control and communication systems, 30 years experience in industry. Cases deal with machinery electronic controls, audio-video systems, tape recording, traffic radar and lidar, cellular phones, electric shock, radio interference, electrical malfunctions, wireless communications, automobile electronics, surveillance systems, electronic circuits, paging systems, sound systems, telephone communication, security and alarm systems, remote controls. Services include site inspection, field measurement, lab analysis, test reports, technical findings, consultation, and expert testimony for civil, criminal, insurance, and patent cases. **Degrees/licenses:** BEE, MS, MBA, SMIEEE, FACFE, DABFET, PE.

See primary listing under ENGINEERING: Electronic

Holt Media Group

Arthur H. Holt, President, CEO
Christine Borger, EVP
2178 Industrial Drive, Suite 914
Bethlehem, PA 18017
Tel: (610) 814-2821
Fax: (610) 814-2826
E-mail: artholt@holtmedia.com or ceborger@holtmedia.com
Web Site: http://www.holtmedia.com

Specialties: Communications: radio & television; Cable, Internet, television & related fields; Media analysis & research; Appraisals. **Degrees/licenses:** BFA; FCC 1st Class Engineer - Arthur; MBA - Christine.

COMPUTERS/ SOFTWARE

General

Berg Software Design

Brian A. Berg
President
14500 Big Basin Way, Ste. F
Saratoga, CA 95070
Tel: (408) 741-5010
Fax: (408) 741-5234
E-mail: bberg@bswd.com
Web Site: http://www.bswd.com

Specialties: Computer software and firmware; Device drivers; Real-time software; SCSI; ATAPI/IDE; Fibre Channel; Storage devices: optical storage (WORM, rewritable, M-O, CD-ROM, jukeboxes); Windows, UNIX, Silicon Graphics (SGI) IRIX, embedded operating systems; Software comparison; Patent infringement investigation. Books: "Software for Optical Storage," "Rewritable Optical Storage Technology." Articles: "SCSI: An Integrator's Resource Guide," and eight others. Professional Affiliations: IEEE, ACM, CPSR, IDEMA, PATCA. Conference chair, speaker and session chair: Asilomar Microcomputer Workshop; Conference speaker, session chair, and conference advisory board member: Storage Area Networks (SAN) Conference and Server Blade Summit. **Degrees/licenses:** BS Mathematics.

The Chatham Group

Jerry A. Klein
President
101 First Street, Ste. 477
Los Altos, CA 94022
Tel: (650) 948-1243
Fax: (650) 949-0534
E-mail: jaklein@chathamlaw.com
Web Site: http://www.chathamlaw.com

Specialties: Silicon Valley based consulting organization specializing in litigation support services for intellectual property litigation

(Listing continued on next page)

General *(cont.)*

The Chatham Group (cont.)

matters in state, federal and international proceedings. Our group consists of senior scientists, engineers, managers and experts in the fields of: Electronics, Semiconductors, Computer Hardware and Software, Telecommunications, Office Automation, Communications, Medical Electronics, Biotechnology, Materials, Manufacturing Processes, Industry Custom and Practice, Marketing. Expert witnesses, technical consulting, tutorials, discovery assistance, trial aids, market studies, patent portfolio strategy, damage determinations, investment banking and venture capital due diligence, witness location, prior art search and evaluation for domestic and international matters. **Degrees/licenses:** BSME, Patent Agent, PhDs in Computer Science, etc.

See primary listing under INTELLECTUAL PROPERTY: Patent Infringement

Delos Research Group

W.M. vanCleemput, PhD
President
333 Maude Avenue
Sunnyvale, CA 94085
Tel: (408) 733-8000
Fax: (408) 733-8008
E-mail: wmvc@acm.org
Web Site: http://www.delosresearch.com

Specialties: Technical Expertise: Computer engineering, emphasis on software, computer architecture, computer-aided design, hardware testing, software development methodology, management of large software development projects; Ex Stanford University faculty; Founder of several software companies. Functional Expertise: Prior art searches, patent validity searches, database searches, patent claim analysis, copyright and trade secret issues, expert witness testimonial, discovery phase investigations, deposition assistance, patent portfolio evaluation, contract disputes, intellectual property protection: audits, creation of policies and procedures. Special Areas: European prior art searches; Extensive collection of software prior art. **Degrees/licenses:** PhD.

John T. Dorsey

Principal
Dorsey-Pages LLC
P.O. Box 760397
Lathrup Village, MI 48076
Tel: (248) 642-2420
Fax: (248) 642-7475
E-mail: jtdorsey@dorsey-pages.com
Web Site: http://Dorsey-Pages.com

Specialties: Governmental Systems Expert. Served as Expert Witness and developed Expert Reports and Rebuttal in Federal and State cases involving Public Safety Computer Aided Dispatch and Records Management Systems. General expertise in: Systems Development, EDP/MIS Systems, Data Networking, EDP/MIS Audit, Equipment Evaluation and Selection, Financial Information and Reporting, Information Technology Strategic Planning, Records Management, Computer Contracts, Courts and Criminal Justice System. Thirty years of computer industry and consulting experience; awarded ICCP's CDP (Certificate in Data Processing), 1978. Twenty five years of management consulting experience; awarded IMC's CMC (Certified Management Consultant), 1986. **Degrees/licenses:** BS, Math - UD (1968); MBA Wash. U (1973); CMC; CDP.

Robert Gezelter, CDP

Principal
Robert Gezelter Software Consultant
35-20 167th Street, Ste. 215
Flushing, NY 11358-1731
Tel: (718) 463-1079
Fax: On Request
E-mail: gezelter@rlgsc.com
Web Site: http://www.rlgsc.com

Specialties: Mr. Gezelter has been in practice for over 25 years. His practice ranges from mainframes to embedded microprocessors including all aspects of hardware and software. He has worked extensively in architectures, operating system internals, security, performance, and networks. He has worked in environments from real-time process control to time-sharing. He has published several book chapters and many articles on technical topics. He has spoken locally, nationally, and internationally for IEEE, DECUS, ISSA, and

ISACA. His litigation related practice includes all stages, from pre-filing to appellate level, including reports and testimony. **Degrees/licenses:** BA (CS)/MS CS (NYU/Courant Institute); CDP (ICCP).

Great Scott Enterprises, Inc.

Scott Greene
Senior Computer Forensics Examiner
P.O. Box 42047
Tucson, AZ 85733-2047
Tel: (866) 795-7166
Fax: (520) 722-6796
E-mail: scott@Great-Scott.com
Web Site: http://www.Great-Scott.com/indexndew.html

Specialties: 20+ Years Experience. Computer Forensics consulting specializing in Recovery, Acquisition, Preservation and Analysis of data as evidence, including data purposefully destroyed. Proper handling techniques can save data from websites, computer files, fax machines and emails. Expert witness testimony for both plaintiffs and defendants in court and arbitration cases. We are highly skilled at Databases, applications, documents, e-mails, images, accounting systems, hacking events, intrusions, Custom Software Design and Development, password cracking, Source code analysis and more. Experienced in Insurance, Civil, Corporate and Criminal cases. Management of large projects with multiple disciplines. **Degrees/licenses:** Studied Systems Eng. @ U of AZ, ISSP, Novell, AccPac.

Glenn A. Marin

Vice President
IXP Corp.
8256 Enramada Ave.
Whittier, CA 90605
Tel: (562) 696-1286
Fax: (562) 693-5002
E-mail: glennm8256@aol.com

Specialties: Public Safety Systems (EMS, fire, police): Computer Aided Dispatch, Records Management, Mobile Data Terminal Systems; Two-way mobile radio: design and operational use parameters; Emergency Dispatching: practices and operations; Staffing, working environment, facility requirements; Jail Systems: computer support requirements, inmate housing analysis; Court Master for Jail overcrowding; Computer simulation analysis of radio systems channel loading, fire move-up analysis, dispatch staffing requirements. Retired Police Lieutenant. 22 years serving hundreds of public safety clients from small to very large. International experience. Extensive expert witness cases in Federal and State Courts. **Degrees/licenses:** BS, CSU - LA (1966); MPA, USC (1972); Grad. work, Comp. Sci., UC - Fullerton.

See primary listing under LAW ENFORCEMENT: General

Ron Russ, CDP

CEO
RLRA, Inc.
3813 Easy Street
Alvarado, TX 76009
Tel: (817) 790-6556
Fax: (817) 783-2268
E-mail: ron@rlruss.com
Web Site: http://www.rlruss.com

Specialties: Expert Witness: Computer Litigation, 70+ cases (civil and criminal). Breach of Contract (hardware/software), Data Recovery and Analysis, Equipment Appraisal and Valuation, Internet, Insurance Misrepresentation, Project Analysis and Evaluation, Forms Alteration, Internet Pornography, and Class Action related to Telecom matters. Preparation of extensive reports to support Deposition and Trial testimony. Experienced in Federal and District Courts and Arbitration. 40+ years computer industry experience. Degree and Certified. Chairman and CEO of multiple computer firms serving clients in 25+ states and 7 countries. No geographic limitations. Reasonable rates. Case history available. **Degrees/licenses:** BS Math-Computer Science, Cert. in Data Processing.

General *(cont.)*

Samuel J. Simms, Jr.
President/COO
Simms Inc dba Simms Financials
2030 Butternut Drive
Huntingdon Valley, PA 19006-1733
Tel: (215) 674-0731
Fax: (425) 645-2534
E-mail: ssimms1949@yahoo.com

Specialties: Over thirty years experience designing, coding, test and implementing a wide variety of commercial business applications in progressively responsible positions. Proficient in COBOL, CICS, CB2/SQL, and DATACOM/DB, IMS, EASYTRIEVE PLUS, VSAM, TSO, SMS Macro Assembler, MVS & DOS JCL. As an IT professional in a variety of business environments such as life, health & casualty insurance, the Federal Reserve Banking System, manufacturing, commercial banking, pharmaceuticals, transportation, and State Government and data processing settings, e.g., development, design and analysis, conversions, maintenance and performed various other data processing activities. These included writing and debugging programs in both the batch and online environments, testing JCL procedures, writing specifications, test plans, documentation and performing tasks related to analysis. **Degrees/licenses:** BA, PA State University (PA); MS in Computer Science, Villanova University (PA).

Barry Strock
President
Barry Strock Consulting Associates, Inc.
464 Pond Hill Rd.
Rensselaerville, NY 12147
Tel: (518) 797-3954
Fax: (518) 797-5282
E-mail: barry@strock.com
Web Site: http://www.strock.com

Specialties: Government Technology Procurement and Implementation Experts. Co-author "THE MUNICIPAL COMPUTER SYSTEMS HANDBOOK." 30 years government systems experience. 300 needs assessments, system procurements, implementations. Best practices for municipal systems; Financials, HRIS, CIS, CRM, Electric/Water Utilities, Police/Fire/EMS CAD/RMS, Courts, Housing Authorities, School Districts, Colleges, Health Care. Expert witness services, mediation, dispute resolution, legal oversight for over 100 clients. County, State, Federal court actions. College, attorney and hands-on educated and trained in contract law, public law, depositions, expert testimony. Specialize in City, County, Town, Village, Borough, State systems. Software, hardware, networks, telecom specialists. **Degrees/licenses:** BS, Finance/Economics; MPA/MURP; PhD, (abd) Health.

Appraisal & Valuation

NACOMEX USA, Inc.
Robert J. Zises, ASA
President
230 Park Avenue, 10th Floor
New York, NY 10169
Tel: (800) 622-6639
Fax: (212) 681-9211
E-mail: zises@nacomex.com
Web Site: http://www.nacomex.com

Specialties: Computer hardware appraisal & valuation for corporate & governmental clients since 1987. Experienced in present-day, historical retrospective, mass appraisals, residual value forecasts, & depreciation schedules for: municipalities, corporate ad valorem appeals, property taxes, lease termination & buy-out issues, contract evaluation, purchase money allocation, bankruptcy, loss replacement. Litigation & expert witness testimony references available. Critique & analysis of opposing experts' reports. All our reports are USPAP-compliant. **Degrees/licenses:** ASA, IAAO, IPT, AIA, National Forensic Centre.

See primary listing under APPRAISAL & VALUATION: Computers

Ron Russ, CDP
CEO
RLRA, Inc.
3813 Easy Street
Alvarado, TX 76009
Tel: (817) 790-6556
Fax: (817) 783-2268
E-mail: ron@rlruss.com
Web Site: http://www.rlruss.com

Specialties: Expert Witness: Computer Litigation, 70+ cases (civil and criminal). Breach of Contract (hardware/software), Data Recovery and Analysis, Equipment Appraisal and Valuation, Internet, Insurance Misrepresentation, Project Analysis and Evaluation, Forms Alteration, Internet Pornography, and Class Action related to Telecom matters. Preparation of extensive reports to support Deposition and Trial testimony. Experienced in Federal and District Courts and Arbitration. 40+ years computer industry experience. Degree and Certified. Chairman and CEO of multiple computer firms serving clients in 25+ states and 7 countries. No geographic limitations. Reasonable rates. Case history available. **Degrees/licenses:** BS Math-Computer Science, Cert. in Data Processing.
See primary listing under COMPUTERS/SOFTWARE: General

Computer Forensics

Forensic Recovery, LLC
Robert F. DeYoung, PhD
President and Founder
15010 Durham Lane
Davie, FL 33331-2964
Tel: (954) 610-4136
Fax: (954) 252-5027
E-mail: rdeyoung@forensicrecovery.com
Web Site: http://www.forensicrecovery.com

Specialties: FORENSIC RECOVERY provides the legal and corporate communities the finest in computer forensic examination processes of computer systems and related media for criminal, civil or administrative investigations. FORENSIC RECOVERY is recognized by the Federal Courts as an expert in the field of computer forensic procedures and electronic data recovery. Backed by fifteen years of investigative experience, nine years dedicated specifically to the computer forensic processes, FORENSIC RECOVERY offers assistance with all aspects of investigative and computer forensic needs. Specializing in professional computer forensic capabilities, case review and analysis, expert testimony. **Degrees/licenses:** PhD, MS, BA, HTCN-Advanced Computer Forensic Tech.

Johnette Hassell, PhD
President
Electronic Evidence Retrieval, LLC
141 Robert E. Lee Blvd., Ste. 108
New Orleans, LA 70124-2534
Tel: (504) 483-0201
(970) 923-1561 (Rocky Mtn. Office)
Fax: (281) 966-1854
E-mail:
JHassell@ElectronicEvidenceRetrieval.com
Web Site:
http://ElectronicEvidenceRetrieval.com

Specialties: Computer science, computer software; forensic investigation of computer media; deleted file recovery; "undeleting" computer files; imaging computer media; software copyright infringement; theft of intellectual property. More than twenty years experience in serving as expert in computer-related cases; accepted as expert in Louisiana, Texas, and New York. Deposition and testimony experience. Case-related industries include oil field tools, medical record keeping, telecommunication, oil platform engineering, non-profit. College professor, textbook author, consultant to private industry on software engineering and software testing, administrative and managerial experience, software design and development. **Degrees/licenses:** PhD, MA, BS Mathematics.

Zvi Herschman, MD
346 Wilson Street
West Hempstead, NY 11552
Tel: (516) 486-7384
Fax: (516) 486-2743
E-mail: hesh346@juno.com

Specialties: Computer Forensics such as data retrieval for case preparation, support for Forensic Accounting, Medical Malprac-
(Listing continued on next page)

Computer Forensics *(Cont.)*

Zvi Herschman (cont.)
tice, Device Failure, Fraud cases, Corporate Espionage, Inappropriate Internet Access and General Data/Media searches. **Degrees/ licenses:** MD, DABA.

See primary listing under MEDICINE & HEALTH: Pain Management

TASA

(Technical Advisory Service for Attorneys)
1166 DeKalb Pike
Blue Bell, PA 19422-1853
Tel: (800) 523-2319
Fax: (800) 329-8272
E-mail: experts@tasanet.com
Web Site: http://www.tasanet.com

Specialties: Save search time! Contact TASA first. Benefit from 44 years of referral expertise. We assess your needs and refer experienced Local, Regional, or National professionals in every Computer expertise area you require for Consulting and Litigation, including Data Recovery; Embedded Systems; Firewalls; Fraud; Graphics; Hacking; Hard-Drive Recovery; Illustration; Internet Commerce, Law, Marketing, Music, News, Relationships, Security; On-line Services; Security; Simulations; Software Copyright Infringement; Tape Restoration; Viruses; Workplace Internet and E-mail Policies; Hundreds More. SERVICES INCLUDE prompt customized searches, referrals, resumes, and your initial interview calls with experts. Exceptional personal service. **Degrees/licenses:** All prof. degrees, licenses, certifications represented.

See primary listing under EXPERT WITNESS REFERRALS: General

Richard Van Leer, PhD

President/Master Data Analyst
ENTERPRIT.COM CORP
15841 Pines Blvd., #400
Pembroke Pines, FL 33027
Tel: (954) 450-0745
Fax: (954) 450-3065
E-mail: rvl@enterprit.com
Web Site: http://www.enterprit.com

Specialties: Dr. Van Leer has been providing technical expertise to industry leaders, fortune 500 companies, manufacturers world-wide and the legal profession on most areas of Information Technology for 38 years. Currently he is prominently situated in the nation's highest-profile Email and SPAM litigations. His company, Enterprit.com Corporation provides the extensive data analysis that makes the difference in winning the case, and defending/prosecuting it. Dr. Van Leer consults routinely on the Internet and intranets to corporate executives and attorneys between speaking engagements around the country. **Degrees/licenses:** Msc, PhD Information Technology.

See primary listing under INTERNET: Email/ SPAM

Information Systems

Barry Strock

President
Barry Strock Consulting Associates, Inc.
464 Pond Hill Rd.
Rensselaerville, NY 12147
Tel: (518) 797-3954
Fax: (518) 797-5282
E-mail: barry@strock.com
Web Site: http://www.strock.com

Specialties: Government Technology Procurement and Implementation Experts. Co-author "THE MUNICIPAL COMPUTER SYSTEMS HANDBOOK." 30 years government systems experience. 300 needs assessments, system procurements, implementations. Best practices for municipal systems; Financials, HRIS, CIS, CRM, Electric/Water Utilities, Police/Fire/EMS CAD/RMS, Courts, Housing Authorities, School Districts, Colleges, Health Care. Expert witness services, mediation, dispute resolution, legal oversight for over 100 clients. County, State, Federal court actions. College, attorney and hands-on educated and trained in contract law, public law, depositions, expert testimony. Specialize in City, County, Town, Village, Borough, State systems. Software, hardware, networks, telecom specialists. **Degrees/licenses:** BS, Finance/Economics; MPA/MURP; PhD, (abd) Health.

See primary listing under COMPUTERS/ SOFTWARE: General

Internet Technology

Robert Gezelter, CDP

Principal
Robert Gezelter Software Consultant
35-20 167th Street, Ste. 215
Flushing, NY 11358-1731
Tel: (718) 463-1079
Fax: On Request
E-mail: gezelter@rlgsc.com
Web Site: http://www.rlgsc.com

Specialties: Mr. Gezelter has been in practice for over 25 years. His practice ranges from mainframes to embedded microprocessors including all aspects of hardware and software. He has worked extensively in architectures, operating system internals, security, performance, and networks. He has worked in environments from real-time process control to time-sharing. He has published several book chapters and many articles on technical topics. He has spoken locally, nationally, and internationally for IEEE, DECUS, ISSA, and ISACA. His litigation related practice includes all stages, from pre-filing to appellate level, including reports and testimony. **Degrees/ licenses:** BA (CS)/MS CS (NYU/Courant Institute); CDP (ICCP).

See primary listing under COMPUTERS/ SOFTWARE: General

Investigation

Forensic Recovery, LLC

Robert F. DeYoung, PhD
President and Founder
15010 Durham Lane
Davie, FL 33331-2964
Tel: (954) 610-4136
Fax: (954) 252-5027
E-mail: rdeyoung@forensicrecovery.com
Web Site: http://www.forensicrecovery.com

Specialties: FORENSIC RECOVERY provides the legal and corporate communities the finest in computer forensic examination processes of computer systems and related media for criminal, civil or administrative investigations. FORENSIC RECOVERY is recognized by the Federal Courts as an expert in the field of computer forensic procedures and electronic data recovery. Backed by fifteen years of investigative experience, nine years dedicated specifically to the computer forensic processes, FORENSIC RECOVERY offers assistance with all aspects of investigative and computer forensic needs. Specializing in professional computer forensic capabilities, case review and analysis, expert testimony. **Degrees/licenses:** PhD, MS, BA, HTCN-Advanced Computer Forensic Tech.

See primary listing under COMPUTERS/ SOFTWARE: Computer Forensics

Johnette Hassell, PhD

President
Electronic Evidence Retrieval, LLC
141 Robert E. Lee Blvd., Ste. 108
New Orleans, LA 70124-2534
Tel: (504) 483-0201
(970) 923-1561 (Rocky Mtn. Office)
Fax: (281) 966-1854
E-mail:
JHassell@ElectronicEvidenceRetrieval.com
Web Site:
http://ElectronicEvidenceRetrieval.com

Specialties: Computer science, computer software; forensic investigation of computer media; deleted file recovery; "undeleting" computer files; imaging computer media;

(Listing continued on next page)

Investigation *(cont.)*

Johnette Hassell (cont.)
software copyright infringement; theft of intellectual property. More than twenty years experience in serving as expert in computer-related cases; accepted as expert in Louisiana, Texas, and New York. Deposition and testimony experience. Case-related industries include oil field tools, medical record keeping, telecommunication, oil platform engineering, non-profit. College professor, textbook author, consultant to private industry on software engineering and software testing, administrative and managerial experience, software design and development. **Degrees/licenses:** PhD, MA, BS Mathematics.

See primary listing under COMPUTERS/SOFTWARE: Computer Forensics

Software

Samuel J. Simms, Jr.
President/COO
Simms Inc dba Simms Financials
2030 Butternut Drive
Huntingdon Valley, PA 19006-1733
Tel: (215) 674-0731
Fax: (425) 645-2534
E-mail: ssimms1949@yahoo.com

Specialties: Over thirty years experience designing, coding, test and implementing a wide variety of commercial business applications in progressively responsible positions. Proficient in COBOL, CICS, CB2/SQL, and DATACOM/DB, IMS, EASYTRIEVE PLUS, VSAM, TSO, SMS Macro Assembler, MVS & DOS JCL. As an IT professional in a variety of business environments such as life, health & casualty insurance, the Federal Reserve Banking System, manufacturing, commercial banking, pharmaceuticals, transportation, and State Government and data processing settings, e.g., development, design and analysis, conversions, maintenance and performed various other data processing activities. These included writing and debugging programs in both the batch and online environments, testing JCL procedures, writing specifications, test plans, documentation and performing tasks related to analysis. **Degrees/licenses:** BA, PA State University (PA); MS in Computer Science, Villanova University (PA).

See primary listing under COMPUTERS/SOFTWARE: General

CONSTRUCTION

General

Ralph A. Adams, PE
President
Prestige Construction Services
1414 Castlerock Road
Houston, TX 77090
Tel: (281) 444-8404
Fax: (281) 444-1630
E-mail:
RADAMS53@HOUSTON.RR.COM

Specialties: PROJECT AND CONSTRUCTION MANAGEMENT: project planning and schedule, CPM scheduling, pre-construction services, management and staffing for heavy/highway construction, industrial and petrochemical plant construction, commercial and residential construction. CONSTRUCTION REPORTS: construction quality studies and reports, construction specification compliance reports, condition of sales inspection and reports for commercial and residential properties, construction accident and slip/fall studies. FORENSIC ENGINEERING: investigations, reports and testimony for plaintiff/defendant, construction planning and scheduling, construction changes, termination, delays and suspension, differing site conditions, breach of contract, construction accidents and slip/falls. CONSTRUCTION ENGINEERING: construction plant layout and planning, detail design of construction plant facilities. **Degrees/licenses:** AB, MSCE, Board Certified Diplomat in Forensic Engineering.

Steven Cohen, Esq.

President
Cohen & Associates, Inc.
2530 Wilshire Blvd, 3rd Floor
Santa Monica, CA 90403
Tel: (310) 315-5404
Fax: (310) 315-5408
E-mail: scohen@litigationbusters.com
Web Site: http://www.litigationbusters.com

Specialties: Real Estate/Construction Specialist and Attorney with extensive experience in the following areas: Construction Defects; Construction Contract Disputes; Mold Inspection/Remediation; Risk Analysis; Mechanical Defects; Electrical Defects; Structural Defects; Real Estate; HOA, DRE, CSLB Rules & UBC Compliance. General/Electrical Contractor; Graduate level certified in Dispute Resolution. **Degrees/licenses:** Atty; JD-MBA; RE Broker; Gen/Electric Contractor.

DPM National Consulting

Buildings, Bridges, Elevators, Roofing
Daniel Koffler, PE
234 Philadelphia Pike
Wilmington, DE 19809
Tel: (302) 762-3352
Fax: (302) 762-3353
E-mail: koda@iopener.net

Specialties: Elevators and Escalators, Roofing, Structural, Masonry, Formwork & Shoring, Building Defects, Building Code Violations, Building Failures, Construction Accidents, Personal Injury, Fire Damage Survey & Reconstruction. Forensic Engineering, Arbitration and Expert Witness. Extensive court experience. Nationwide service. **Degrees/licenses:** BCE, PE - 35 Years Experience.

ForensisGroup, Inc.

Mercy Steenwyk
3452 E. Foothill Blvd., Ste. 1160
Pasadena, CA 91107
Tel: (626) 795-5000
(800) 555-5422
Fax: (626) 795-1950
E-mail: experts@forensisgroup.com
Web Site: http://forensisgroup.com

Specialties: Thousands of our clients have gained the technical advantage and the edge in their cases from our multidisciplined group of experts in hundreds of disciplines. We have some of the best and the brightest at competitive rates backed by 14 years of excellent track record and the support of our trained staff. We assist you until you have the right expert. Some of our areas of expertise are: Construction, Safety, Engineering, Product Liability, Accident Reconstruction, Automotive, Environmental, Slip & Fall, Appraisal, Medical and other scientific disciplines. Unsurpassed standards. Clients actively evaluate our experts. **Degrees/licenses:** PE, GC, CSP, PhD, MD, GC, CIH, AIA.

See primary listing under ACCIDENT PREVENTION & SAFETY: General

General *(cont.)*

IPEC

Institute for Products, Engineering & Construction
A Consortium of Engineers, Construction & Safety Professionals
34522 N. Scottsdale Rd., Ste. D-8 #160
Scottsdale, AZ 85262
Tel: (888) 212-1155
Fax: (888) 414-1155
E-mail: ipec@forensicengineers.com
Web Site: http://www.forensicengineers.com

666 Fifth Ave., #122
New York, NY 10103
Tel: (212) 315-9523

1429 G St. NW, #415
Washington, DC 20005
Tel: (202) 822-9660

231 North Ave. West, #134
Westfield, NJ 07090
Tel: (908) 233-2973

1920 Abrams Pkwy., #95
Dallas, TX 75214
Tel: (214) 827-9892

Specialties: Construction; Contractual Relationships; Construction Defects; Construction Delays, Claims; Codes; Construction Site Safety; Engineering, Architecture; Fire Alarm & Sprinkler Systems; Electrical; HVAC; Air Conditioning; Heating; Bridges; Tunnels; Parking Garages; Cranes; Scaffolds; Standard of Care; Boilers, Architecture, Project Management; Facilities Management; Maintenance; Water Damage, Pipe Failure; Condominium & Home Owner Associations; Residential Development, Lease Closeout; Chemical, Commercial & Industrial Facilities; Roof Collapse; Concrete, Steel, Wood; Playgrounds; Docks; Foundations; Pilings; Trusses; Landscape Architecture; Trenching; Excavation; Underground Utilities; Underground Tanks; Overhead Electric Lines; Storm Water; Soils; Sitework; Roads; Sidewalks; Paving; Doors; Windows; Stairs; Floors; Steam Systems; Plumbing; Cooling Towers; Chillers; Flues; Furnaces; Natural Gas & Electric Utility Company Standard Practice; OSHA. Contact: Ned Howell. **Degrees/ licenses:** Engineers: Auto, Constr, Mech, Elec, Struct, Civil, Chem, Safety, Arch, Aero.

KULWIEC GROUP/ ARCHITECTS

W. John Kulwiec, AIA, CSI, NCARB, ICC, AAMA
532 Glade Drive
Santa Paula, CA 93060-1617
Tel: (877) 774-6500 ext. 109
Fax: (805) 525-5105
E-mail: John@KulwiecGroup.com
Web Site: http://www.KulwiecGroup.com

Specialties: 35+YEARS of PROFESSIONAL EXPERIENCE and current practice utilized to effectively provide Forensic and Expert Witness expertise in: Standard of Care, Post Construction Building Autopsy, Destructive Testing, Scope of Work Definition, Scheduling Analysis of Contractor & Architect, Change Order Disputes, Drawings and Documents Analysis, Communication Analysis between Client, Architect & Contractor, Waterproofing Issues, Mold Issues, Roofing Issues, Code Compliance: ADA, Title 24, ICC, Local, OSHPD, Construction Defects & Negligence. LITIGATION EXPERIENCE: Mediation, Arbitration, Superior and Federal Court, Plaintiff and Defense for Architects, Owners and Contractors. For complete CV visit www.KulwiecGroup.com. **Degrees/licenses:** BArch, Illinois Inst Tech; Arch Lic: CA #C-3978, AZ, CO, NV, WA, MI.

See primary listing under ARCHITECTURE: General

Julius J. Kummerman, FACFE, DABFE

President
California Construction Forensics, Inc.
16633 Gilmore St.
Van Nuys, CA 91406
Tel: (818) 908-9966
E-mail: jkummerman@juno.com
Web Site: http://www.jkummerman.com

Specialties: Property damage causation, defect, negligence, subrogation & liability evaluation; Construction contracts; Code requirements; Industry standards & practices. Affiliation: State Panel of Consumer Arbitrators; Fellow, American College of Forensic Examiners; National Forensic Center. **Degrees/licenses:** General Contractor (Licensed CA), B379076; Asbestos Certified.

Ian Mackinlay Architecture, Inc.

Ian Mackinlay, FAIA
President
26 O'Farrell St., Ste. 200
San Francisco, CA 94108
Tel: (415) 243-4191
Fax: (415) 243-9769
E-mail: ian@ima-arch.com
Web Site: http://www.ima-arch.com

Specialties: Architecture; Expert analysis and testimony regarding architectural design and construction defects; Building code compliance; Roofing and waterproofing systems; Problems related to building in the snow and cold; Litigation strategy and organization; Product research and documentation; Alternative dispute resolution; Remedial design and reconstruction; Design review/quality assurance; Design related accident; Trial graphics. 450+ cases since 1979. Licensed in 17 states as listed below plus MT, NY, OH, NM. **Degrees/licenses:** Arch. Lic.: CA, WA, NV, UT, WY, AK, CO, GU, HI, ID, IL, MD, MN, NCARB #5408.

See primary listing under ARCHITECTURE: General

Frank McDonough

Chairman of the Board
McDonough Bolyard Peck, Inc.
8315 Lee Highway
Suite 400
Fairfax, VA 22031-4513
Tel: (703) 641-9088
Fax: (703) 641-8965
E-mail: fmcdonough@mbpce.com
Web Site: http://www.mbpce.com

Specialties: Construction delay analysis; Construction impact analysis; construction claims analysis; Dispute resolution; Engineering expert testimony; Litigation support. Affiliation: Construction Expert Witness, Third Party Neutral: DRB, Arbitrator/Mediator. **Degrees/licenses:** BE; PE (AL, DE, DC, GA, MD, MA, PA, VA, UK).

See primary listing under CONSTRUCTION: Consulting

Ted S. Merrill

General Contractor and Consultant
Ted S. Merrill & Sons, Inc.
Building Surgeons (Lic. #345079)
7907 North Ave.
Lemon Grove, CA 91945-1827
Tel: (619) 464-3997
Fax: (619) 464-8581
E-mail: ted@tsm-sons.com

Specialties: 50 years Construction experience in positions ranging from laborer, apprentice carpenter, carpenter, superintendent, estimator to general contractor. Including all phases of construction contracting, but specializing in damage repair work, including experience in estimating and reconstruction of building damaged by fire, wind, motor vehicles, earth movement and construction defects. This type of work is estimated and contracted by Ted S. Merrill & Sons, Inc., with Federal and State governments local cities, school districts, insurance companies and individual owners of residential, commercial and industrial buildings. 32 years experience in cost estimating structures with construction defect problems. Giving testimony at settlement conferences and depositions. Qualified and testified as an

(Listing continued on next page)

General *(cont.)*

Ted S. Merrill (cont.)
expert in Municipal, Superior and Federal Courts.. **Degrees/licenses:** State of California Contractor, B-1 Licenses #275171 & 345079.

Frederick A. Porcello, PE, PP

President
Porcello Engineering, Inc.
PO Box 728
Pine Brook, NJ 07058
Tel: (973) 882-8377
Fax: (973) 882-8478
E-mail: fporcellopei@verizon.net

Specialties: Claims and Delay Analysis, Failure Analysis, Curtain Walls, Windows, Roofs, Masonry, Demolition, Soil, Deep and Shallow Foundations, Structural Steel, Asbestos, Lead Paint, Groundwater, Licensed NJ UST Consultant, Licensed NYC and NJ Testing Laboratory, Fireproofing, Asphalt, Indoor Air Quality, Non-Destructive Weld Testing. **Degrees/licenses:** BS CE, PE in NJ, NY, CT, MA, VT, FL.

Pro/Consul Technical and Medical Experts

1945 Palo Verde Ave., Suite 200
Long Beach, CA 90815-3443
Tel: (800) 392-1119
(562) 799-0116
Fax: (562) 799-8821
E-mail: eexperts@msn.com
Web Site: http://www.expertinfo.com

Specialties: RIGHT EXPERT RIGHT AWAY!® 15,000 experts in 7,000 fields. Listed and recommended by the A. M. Best Company. Full-time research staff. We welcome your RUSH cases! TECHNICAL: Fast inspections. Categories from Accident Reconstruction to Zoology, also including appraisal, economics, employment, human factors, insurance, premises liability, security, and many more. MEDICAL: IME's. Inexpensive insurance medical records reviews by MDs. Categories from Addiction Medicine to Zooplasty, including board certified physicians in all fields, dentistry, geriatrics, neuropsychology, neurosurgery, nursing, orthopedics, psychiatry and many more. Reasonable fees. Free initial consultation. Free resume binder. Free CLE classes. **Degrees/licenses:** MD, PhD, DDS, DVM, DO, DPM, PE, CPA, ME, CE, CRC, MAI, et al.

See primary listing under ACCIDENT RECONSTRUCTION: General

Zallen Engineering

Rubin M. Zallen
Principal
1101 Worcester Road
Framingham, MA 01701
Tel: (508) 875-1360
Fax: (508) 875-1369
E-mail: rmzallen@zallenengineering.com
Web Site:
http://www.zallenengineering.com

Specialties: STRUCTURAL FAILURES, PROBLEM STRUCTURES and CONSTRUCTION: Structural engineering, forensic engineering, earthquake engineering, and construction engineering for buildings, bridges, and special structures. Investigation of structural failures and problem structures; recommendations and design for reconstruction and repair; investigation and consulting on construction problems, claims, and procedures; consulting on earthquake analysis and design; structural design review; consulting in structural engineering; technical assistance to attorneys; expert testimony. Keywords: seismic; wind; civil; analysis; test; failure; foundation; settlement; pile; caisson; underpinning; shoring; steel; metal; welding; concrete; prestressing; post-tensioning; masonry; wood; timber; plastic; code; inspection; defects; dynamic. **Degrees/licenses:** PE, SE, MS, B of CE.

See primary listing under ENGINEERING: Structural

Accounting

Glenn M. Gelman & Associates

Glenn M. Gelman, CPA, MS Tax
Managing Director
1940 East 17th St.
Santa Ana, CA 92705-8606
Tel: (714) 667-2600
Fax: (714) 667-2636
E-mail: ggel@gmgcpa.com
Web Site: http://www.gmgcpa.com

Specialties: Expert Testimony, Forensic Accounting, Litigation Consulting, Deposition Strategy, Arbitrations, Business Interruption, Lost Profits, Business Valuations, Marital Dissolution, Construction Claims, Fraud, Alter Ego, Financial Analysis, Financial Modeling, Consumer Lending. Nationally recognized expertise in Construction Accounting. Memberships: American Institute of Certified Public Accountants, California Society of CPAs, National Litigation Support Services Association, Forensic Expert Witness Association, Engineering Contractors Association, American Subcontractors Association, Southern California Contractors Association. Awards: Digest 50 award as one of the top fifty medium sized CPA firms, named Best Accounting Firm for the Construction Industry by Construction Link. **Degrees/licenses:** CPA, Masters Degree in Taxation, others.

See primary listing under ACCOUNTING: General

Arbitration

Boyken International, Inc.

Donald R. Boyken, FCCC
Chairman & CEO
400 Northridge Rd., Ste. 1200
Atlanta, GA 30350-3356
Tel: (770) 992-3210
Fax: (770) 992-1489
E-mail: dboyken@boyken.com
Web Site: http://www.boyken.com

Specialties: Manage the development and construction of large commercial projects including airports, hotels & resorts, universities, theme parks and medical facilities. Expertise includes cost and schedule management, contract requirements, design management, construction management, and hurricane damage assessments. Projects include: The Four Seasons Resort, Nevis, West Indies; Atlantis Resort - Phase II & III, Bahamas; The Venetian Resort & Casino, Las Vegas, Nevada; Disney Hotels and Theme Parks; Hartsfield Jackson Atlanta International Airport; London Heathrow Airport - Terminal 5; Bay Hotel & Resort - Turks & Caicos Islands; Duke University Medical Center; Georgia Board of Regents Development Program. **Degrees/licenses:** BS, MBA, Certified Cost Consultant; Certified Arbitrator for AAA.

See primary listing under CONSTRUCTION: Claims

Cousino Consulting & Professional Services

Michael T. Cousino
President, Certified Restorer
26901 Eckel Rd.
Perrysburg, OH 43551
Tel: (800) 874-2122
Fax: (419) 874-0601
E-mail:
mcousino@cousinoconstruction.com
Web Site:
http://www.cousinoconstruction.com

Specialties: All types of disaster property restoration, evaluation, analysis and cost valuations; analysis and control of odors, mold and mildew testing and remediation; feasibility and analysis of loss repairs; construction claims analysis; traveling consulting services; complete disaster planning and control services; contingency planning; appraisals, umpiring, dispute resolution and arbitration. Expert witness and testimony reporting. Member: ASCR (Associated Specialties of Cleaning and Restoration); DKI (Disaster Kleenup International); NIDR (National Institute of Disaster Restoration, Certified Restorer); WLI (Water Loss Institute); NFPA (National Fire Protection Association); Certified Technology Restorer (CTR). **Degrees/licenses:** CR, OH License 70-74210, MI License 2102-130597, CTR.

See primary listing under CONSTRUCTION: Disaster Reconstruction

Arbitration *(cont.)*

Julius J. Kummerman, FACFE, DABFE

President
California Construction Forensics, Inc.
16633 Gilmore St.
Van Nuys, CA 91406
Tel: (818) 908-9966
E-mail: jkummerman@juno.com
Web Site: http://www.jkummerman.com

Specialties: Property damage causation, defect, negligence, subrogation & liability evaluation; Construction contracts; Code requirements; Industry standards & practices. Affiliation: State Panel of Consumer Arbitrators; Fellow, American College of Forensic Examiners; National Forensic Center. **Degrees/licenses:** General Contractor (Licensed CA), B379076; Asbestos Certified.

See primary listing under CONSTRUCTION: General

Building Codes

Ralph A. Adams, PE

President
Prestige Construction Services
1414 Castlerock Road
Houston, TX 77090
Tel: (281) 444-8404
Fax: (281) 444-1630
E-mail:
RADAMS53@HOUSTON.RR.COM

Specialties: PROJECT AND CONSTRUCTION MANAGEMENT: project planning and schedule, CPM scheduling, pre-construction services, management and staffing for heavy/highway construction, industrial and petrochemical plant construction, commercial and residential construction. CONSTRUCTION REPORTS: construction quality studies and reports, construction specification compliance reports, condition of sales inspection and reports for commercial and residential properties, construction accident and slip/fall studies. FORENSIC ENGINEERING: investigations, reports and testimony for plaintiff/defendant, construction planning and scheduling, construction changes, termination, delays and suspension, differing site conditions, breach of contract, construction accidents and slip/falls. CONSTRUCTION ENGINEERING: construction plant layout and planning, detail design of construction plant facilities. **Degrees/licenses:** AB, MSCE, Board Certified Diplomat in Forensic Engineering.

See primary listing under CONSTRUCTION: General

J. Robert Nelson, PE

Senior Vice President
PFS Corporation
3637 Motor Ave., Ste. 380
Los Angeles, CA 90034
Tel: (310) 559-7287
Fax: (310) 559-1368
E-mail: rnelson@pfscorporation.com
Web Site: http://www.pfscorporation.com

Specialties: Building and Fire Code expert; 35 years experience in code enforcement and construction (ten years with ICBO/Uniform Building Code and Uniform Fire Code; five years with LA County Building Dept.) Technical Investigations and Test Laboratory available; Civil, Structural and Fire Protection Engineering. Construction defects/forensics; gypsum wallboard, drywall, plaster, stucco, shear walls, seismic/earthquake, sheet metal flashing, decking, roofing, wood framing & siding. Slip & fall, fire investigation & testing lab. **Degrees/licenses:** Registered Civil & Fire Protection Engineer.

PFS Corporation

Michael J. Slifka, PE
2402 Daniels Street
Madison, WI 53718
Tel: (608) 224-5512
Fax: (608) 223-5560
E-mail: mslifka@pfscorporation.com
Web Site: http://www.pfscorporation.com

Specialties: Fire protection engineering; Forensic investigations of fire growth, development and spread; Fire origin; Building design; Building codes; Life safety codes and standards; BS in Fire Protection and Safety Engineering. **Degrees/licenses:** BS, PE

See primary listing under ENGINEERING: Fire Protection

John D. Shepherd, RRC, RRO

President
Shepherd Consulting Services
P. O. Box 10010
Torrance, CA 90505
Tel: (310) 378-0791
Fax: (310) 378-0794
E-mail: jds@shepherdconsulting.com
Web Site:
http://www.shepherdconsulting.com

Specialties: SCS specializes in the investigation and analysis of water intrusion, construction failure, standard of care and building code issues related to roofing, sheet metal, waterproofing, and the building envelope for construction defect litigation, property damage claims and personal injury claims. Support services include visual inspections, intrusive testing, leak investigations, water testing, report development, documentation, document review, research, mediation, expert witness testimony and cost estimating. **Degrees/licenses:** RCI Reg. Roof consultant #212/Observer #19. CA Roofing Contr. Lic.# 557494.

Building Failures

Heino Ainso, PE, PhD

Chief Engineer
Ainso & Associates, Inc.
61 Highbrook Ave.
Pelham, NY 10803
Tel: (914) 738-6323
Fax: (914) 738-6323
E-mail: heinoainso@aol.com

Specialties: Forensic investigations, failure analysis, damages quantification, building code compliance verification, preparation and analysis of construction claims, documentation, expert testimony. Member: Am Soc. of Civil Engineers, Am Conc. Institute; Published papers on shell theory and structural analysis. **Degrees/licenses:** BME, MME, PhD in Applied Mechanics; PE in NY and NJ.

Robert G. Cox

Owner
Cox & Associates
11321 Trade Center Dr., Ste. 215
Rancho Cordova, CA 95742
Tel: (916) 638-4771
Fax: (916) 638-5058
E-mail: cox-rg@att.net

Specialties: Forensic inspection and reporting; construction document review; specification preparation; inspection - hospitals, schools, high rises; roofing, waterproofing; concrete; building system failures; construction claims, expert witness superior court; property inspection, California licensed inspector. Member ICBO; member Earthquake Response Team, CSI, AIA Associate. **Degrees/licenses:** Contractor A B C-8; Inspector Hospitals, Schools; Solar Engineer.

See primary listing under CONSTRUCTION: Consulting

Harlan W. Fair

President
H. Fair Associates, Inc.
3 Browns Lane
Hawthorne, NY 10532-1520
Tel: (914) 592-1999
Fax: (914) 592-3247

Specialties: Construction claims; Delay claim analysis; Building & construction inspection; Construction management; Construction accident investigation; Expert testimony; Schedule/CPM analyses; Material failures; Structural & foundation investigation & analyses; Roof & drainage problems; Cash flow analysis (construction); Claims preparation; Exhibits & models. **Degrees/licenses:** MS; PE.

Claims

Ralph A. Adams, PE

President
Prestige Construction Services
1414 Castlerock Road
Houston, TX 77090
Tel: (281) 444-8404
Fax: (281) 444-1630
E-mail:
RADAMS53@HOUSTON.RR.COM

Specialties: PROJECT AND CONSTRUCTION MANAGEMENT: project planning and schedule, CPM scheduling, pre-construction services, management and staffing for heavy/highway construction, industrial and petrochemical plant construction, commercial and residential construction. CONSTRUCTION REPORTS: construction quality studies and reports, construction specification compliance reports, condition of sales inspection and reports for commercial and residential properties, construction accident and slip/fall studies. FORENSIC ENGINEERING: investigations, reports and testimony for plaintiff/defendant, construction planning and scheduling, construction changes, termination, delays and suspension, differing site conditions, breach of contract, construction accidents and slip/falls. CONSTRUCTION ENGINEERING: construction plant layout and planning, detail design of construction plant facilities. **Degrees/licenses:** AB, MSCE, Board Certified Diplomat in Forensic Engineering.

See primary listing under CONSTRUCTION: General

Boyken International, Inc.

Donald R. Boyken, FCCC
Chairman & CEO
400 Northridge Rd., Ste. 1200
Atlanta, GA 30350-3356
Tel: (770) 992-3210
Fax: (770) 992-1489
E-mail: dboyken@boyken.com
Web Site: http://www.boyken.com

Specialties: Manage the development and construction of large commercial projects including airports, hotels & resorts, universities, theme parks and medical facilities. Expertise includes cost and schedule management, contract requirements, design management, construction management, and hurricane damage assessments. Projects include: The Four Seasons Resort, Nevis, West Indies; Atlantis Resort - Phase II & III, Bahamas; The Venetian Resort & Casino, Las Vegas, Nevada; Disney Hotels and Theme Parks; Hartsfield Jackson Atlanta International Airport; London Heathrow Airport - Terminal 5; Bay Hotel & Resort - Turks & Caicos Islands; Duke University Medical Center; Georgia Board of Regents Development Program. **Degrees/licenses:** BS, MBA, Certified Cost Consultant; Certified Arbitrator for AAA.

Construction Control Dynamics, Inc.

Ronald S. Majors, PE
President
260 Peachtree St., #1401
Atlanta, GA 30303-1237
Tel: (404) 688-8409
Fax: (404) 524-5427
E-mail: info@concondyn.com
Web Site: http://www.concondyn.com

Specialties: Delay, Disruption, Acceleration Claim Analyses; Productivity Loss; CPM Scheduling; Damage Calculations; E&O Defense; Out-of-Sequence Work; Pre-Claim Consultation; Project Monitoring. Testimony before State and Federal Courts, Arbitration Panels. Mediation presentation. Extensive service as Arbitrator and Mediator. Member: American Arbitration Association, American Association of Cost Engineers, American Society of Civil Engineers, National Society of Professional Engineers, Associated Builders & Contractors, Project Management Institute, Dispute Avoidance and Resolution Task Force, National Academy of Forensic Engineers. **Degrees/licenses:** BSCE, BA, MEA, PE, PMP.

See primary listing under CONSTRUCTION: Consulting

Harlan W. Fair

President
H. Fair Associates, Inc.
3 Browns Lane
Hawthorne, NY 10532-1520
Tel: (914) 592-1999
Fax: (914) 592-3247

Specialties: Building & construction inspection; Construction claims; Delay claim analysis; Construction management; Construction accident investigation; Crane over-turn analysis; Scaffold & ladder accident investigations; Expert testimony; Schedule/CPM analyses; Material failures; Structural & foundation investigation & analyses; Roof & drainage problems; Cash flow analysis (construction); Claims preparation; Exhibits & models. **Degrees/licenses:** MS; PE.

See primary listing under CONSTRUCTION: Building Failures

Ted S. Merrill

General Contractor and Consultant
Ted S. Merrill & Sons, Inc.
Building Surgeons (Lic. #345079)
7907 North Ave.
Lemon Grove, CA 91945-1827
Tel: (619) 464-3997
Fax: (619) 464-8581
E-mail: ted@tsm-sons.com

Specialties: 50 years Construction experience in positions ranging from laborer, apprentice carpenter, carpenter, superintendent, estimator to general contractor. Including all phases of construction contracting, but specializing in damage repair work, including experience in estimating and reconstruction of building damaged by fire, wind, motor vehicles, earth movement and construction defects. This type of work is estimated and contracted by Ted S. Merrill & Sons, Inc., with Federal and State governments local cities, school districts, insurance companies and individual owners of residential, commercial and industrial buildings. 32 years experience in cost estimating structures with construction defect problems. Giving testimony at settlement conferences and depositions. Qualified and testified as an expert in Municipal, Superior and Federal Courts.. **Degrees/licenses:** State of California Contractor, B-1 Licenses #275171 & 345079.

See primary listing under CONSTRUCTION: General

The Nielsen-Wurster Group, Inc.

Patricia Galloway, CEO
Kris R. Nielsen, Chairman
Reza Nikain, President
Jack L. Dignum, Senior VP
345 Wall Street
Princeton, NJ 08540
Tel: (609) 497-7300
Fax: (609) 497-3412
E-mail: njnwg@aol.com
Web Site: http://www.nielsen-wurster.com

Specialties: Dispute resolution; Litigation support; Schedule delay analyses; Geotechnical evaluations; Forensic investigations; Damage Quantification; Arbitration, mediation and dispute review boards; Management consulting; Audits; Risk Evaluations; Training seminars; Risk management; Project planning; Project execution; Risk assessments; Trend evaluations; Risk reduction strategies; Systems implementation; Services worldwide; Licensed professional engineers in all states; CPAs, Project management professionals; Extensive experience in project management and project controls. Authored numerous professional papers on Project Management, Risk Management and Analysis of Project Delay. Serving private and public companies throughout the power, building, transportation, infrastructure, telecommunications and process industries. **Degrees/licenses:** MSCE, BSCE, MBA, PE, PMP, P.Eng., CCE, PSP, C.Eng., JD, CPA, F.ICE.

See primary listing under CONSTRUCTION: Consulting

Claims *(cont.)*

PCCI (Pacific Construction Consultants, Inc.)

Marketing Director
3083 Gold Canal Drive, Suite 100
Rancho Cordova, CA 95670-6129
Tel: (916) 638-4848
(800) 655-PCCI (7224)
Fax: (916) 638-5124
E-mail: pcci@pcci.biz
Web Site: http://www.pcci.biz

Specialties: Construction contract disputes, claims defense and preparation, CPM scheduling, delay analyses, productivity analyses, scope disputes, standard of care, expert witness and litigation support. Engineers and other construction professionals. Extensive negotiation, mediation, arbitration and litigation experience. In-house graphics department. Seminars. Training. **Degrees/licenses:** Eng., Contracting.

See primary listing under CONSTRUCTION: Consulting

PMA Consultants LLC

Dr. Gui Ponce de Leon, PE
Managing Principal
One Woodward Ave., Suite 1400
Detroit, MI 48226
Tel: (313) 963-8863
Fax: (313) 963-8918
E-mail: info@pmaconsultants.com
Web Site: http://www.pmaconsultants.com

Specialties: PMA is a national project management consulting firm founded in 1971. The latest survey by Engineering News Record ranks PMA 29th largest CM for-fee firm in the U.S. We have provided consulting and expert services on architectural, infrastructure, transportation, water/wastewater, power, and corporate projects exceeding $80 billion. PMA's services include: Project Management, Claims Avoidance & Management, Change Order Analysis, Contract Review & Administration, Schedule & Cost Management, VE & IT Services, Expert Witness. PMA has 13 offices nationwide. Visit www.PMAConsultants.com. **Degrees/licenses:** PhD, PE, JD, MBA, RA, CPA, CVS, CCC, CCE, EIT, PMI, PMP.

Raths, Raths & Johnson, Inc.

Otto C. "Chuck" Guedelhoefer
Senior Principal
835 Midway Drive
Willowbrook, IL 60527
Tel: (630) 325-6160
Fax: (630) 325-2866
E-mail: ocguedelhoefer@rrj.com
Web Site: http://www.rrj.com

Specialties: Forensic Engineering; Failure Analysis; Structural Problem Analysis; Construction Problem Resolution; Extensive Expert Witness Testimony: State and Federal Courts; Performance Evaluation; Structural Repair Design; Material Evaluation & Testing; Full Scale Testing; Mock-up Testing; Models for Courtroom Exhibits; Presentation Graphics; Condition Assessment and Repair of Distressed or Aged Structures. Managed investigations of disputes involving a variety of complaints and assisted a diverse set of clients. Licensed Structural Engineer in Illinois; Professional Engineer in 17 states. Contributed articles to many technical and industry publications and lectured on various facets of engineering practice. **Degrees/licenses:** BSCE, MSCE Structures, PE, SE.

See primary listing under ENGINEERING: Structural

William A. Rutherford, PE

10 Peach Drive
Lititz, PA 17543
Tel: (717) 627-3368
E-mail: stmusic@worldnet.att.net

Specialties: Qualified Expert Witness; Civil; Structural; Cooling Towers; Design; Estimating; Forensic; Construction Practices; Construction Management; Project Management; Project Planning & Controls; Schedule Analysis; System Turn-Over; Structural Welding; Claims; Concrete; Steel; Timber; Defects; Municipal; Disputes; Infrastructure; Personal Injury; Quality Control; Roads; Heavy Construction; Scaffold Safety; Site Work; Grading;

Bridge Inspection; Storm Water; Earthwork; Utilities; Nuclear Plants; Operations; Maintenance; Rigging; Cranes; Accidents; Structural Failures; Plant Engineering; Equipment Accidents; Contracts; Material Storage; Site Inspection; Trench Collapse; Falls; Electrocutions; Schools; Commercial; Residential; Plaintiff and Defendant experience. Case Reconstruction experience. Worcester Polytechnic Institute (73). **Degrees/licenses:** BSCE, PE; Civil/Structural (PA, MA).

Trauner Consulting Services, Inc.

Theodore J. Trauner Jr., PE, PP
CEO
One Penn Center
1617 JFK Blvd., Ste. 600
Philadelphia, PA 19103
Tel: (215) 814-6400
Fax: (215) 814-6440
E-mail: ted.trauner@traunerconsulting.com
Web Site:
http://www.traunerconsulting.com

Specialties: Construction claims prevention/resolution; forensic engineering; dispute resolution; multimedia/graphics/models; mediation; litigation support; computerized document retrieval; construction management/owners representation; surety completion/claims; construction scheduling/control; partnering/facilitation; design/constructability review; construction/cost audits; estimating; project monitoring; project status reports; procedure/procurement manuals; seminars/in-house training; expert testimony before various tribunals; 5 published construction texts; membership in CMAA, ACFE, ASCE, SAME, PMI, CSI, NSPE, AAA, American Board of Forensic Examiners, The Beavers, Inc., Dispute Review Foundation, Inc. **Degrees/licenses:** BS, Masters of Eng. in Struc. Eng. & Struc. Mech., MBA, PE, PP.

Concrete/Foundations

Kirby T. Meyer

President
MLAW Consulting Engineers
2804 Longhorn Blvd.
Austin, TX 78758
Tel: (512) 835-7000
Fax: (512) 651-0098
E-mail: ktmeyer@mlaw-eng.com
Web Site: http://www.mlaw-eng.com

Specialties: Soil mechanics & foundations; Foundation engineering; Structural failure; Blasting & construction damage; Foundation movement; Materials testing. **Degrees/licenses:** MS; PE.

See primary listing under ENGINEERING: Civil

Consulting

Boyken International, Inc.

Donald R. Boyken, FCCC
Chairman & CEO
400 Northridge Rd., Ste. 1200
Atlanta, GA 30350-3356
Tel: (770) 992-3210
Fax: (770) 992-1489
E-mail: dboyken@boyken.com
Web Site: http://www.boyken.com

Specialties: Manage the development and construction of large commercial projects including airports, hotels & resorts, universities, theme parks and medical facilities. Expertise includes cost and schedule management, contract requirements, design management, construction management, and hurricane damage assessments. Projects include: The Four Seasons Resort, Nevis, West Indies; Atlantis Resort - Phase II & III, Bahamas; The Venetian Resort & Casino, Las Vegas, Nevada; Disney Hotels and Theme Parks; Hartsfield Jackson Atlanta International Airport; London Heathrow Airport - Terminal 5; Bay Hotel & Resort - Turks & Caicos Islands; Duke University Medical Center; Georgia Board of Regents Development Program. **Degrees/licenses:** BS, MBA, Certified Cost Consultant; Certified Arbitrator for AAA.

See primary listing under CONSTRUCTION: Claims

Consulting *(cont.)*

Bynum & Associates Corporation

James L. Bynum, President
H. Fred Uttke II, Vice President
16182 Construction Circle W., Ste. A
Irvine, CA 92606
Tel: (949) 653-8300
(949) 439-1988
Fax: (949) 653-8383
E-mail: jim@b-a-c.com
Web Site: http://www.b-a-c.com

Specialties: General Contracting, Construction Management, Construction Consulting and Foundation Specialties; Forensic investigation and analysis; Design, Code and Industry Standard Compliance; Cost Estimating, Property Loss Analysis; New, Repair and Replacement; Certified Mold Inspection and Remediation; Value Engineering means and methods. Construction Experience exceeds thirty years, Forensic Investigation and Analysis experience exceeds eleven years. Services available throughout the Western United States. Licenses include; B-1 General Building, C-8 Concrete and C-12 Grading State of California, B-2 General Building State of Nevada and General Building State of North Carolina. **Degrees/licenses:** B-1, C-8 and C-12 State of California.

See primary listing under CONSTRUCTION: Defects

Construction Control Dynamics, Inc.

Ronald S. Majors, PE
President
260 Peachtree St., #1401
Atlanta, GA 30303-1237
Tel: (404) 688-8409
Fax: (404) 524-5427
E-mail: info@concondyn.com
Web Site: http://www.concondyn.com

Specialties: Delay, Disruption, Acceleration Claim Analyses; Productivity Loss; CPM Scheduling; Damage Calculations; E&O Defense; Out-of-Sequence Work; Pre-Claim Consultation; Project Monitoring. Testimony before State and Federal Courts, Arbitration Panels. Mediation presentation. Extensive service as Arbitrator and Mediator. Member: American Arbitration Association, American Association of Cost Engineers, American Society of Civil Engineers, National Society of Professional Engineers, Associated Builders & Contractors, Project Management Institute, Dispute Avoidance and Resolution Task Force, National Academy of Forensic Engineers. **Degrees/licenses:** BSCE, BA, MEA, PE, PMP.

Robert G. Cox

Owner
Cox & Associates
11321 Trade Center Dr., Ste. 215
Rancho Cordova, CA 95742
Tel: (916) 638-4771
Fax: (916) 638-5058
E-mail: cox-rg@att.net

Specialties: Forensic inspection and reporting; construction document review; specification preparation; inspection - hospitals, schools, high rises; roofing, waterproofing; concrete; building system failures; mold-mildew construction claims, expert witness superior court; property inspection, California licensed inspector. Member ICBO; member Earthquake Response Team, CSI, AIA Associate. **Degrees/licenses:** Contractor A B C-8; Inspector Hospitals, Schools; Solar Engineer.

Harlan W. Fair

President
H. Fair Associates, Inc.
3 Browns Lane
Hawthorne, NY 10532-1520
Tel: (914) 592-1999
Fax: (914) 592-3247

Specialties: Building & construction inspection; Construction claims; Delay claim analysis; Construction management; Construction accident investigation; Expert testimony; Schedule/CPM analyses; Material failures; Structural & foundation investigation & analyses; Roof & drainage problems; Cash flow analysis (construction); Claims preparation; Exhibits & models. **Degrees/licenses:** MS; PE.

See primary listing under CONSTRUCTION: Building Failures

Frank McDonough

Chairman of the Board
McDonough Bolyard Peck, Inc.
8315 Lee Highway
Suite 400
Fairfax, VA 22031-4513
Tel: (703) 641-9088
Fax: (703) 641-8965
E-mail: fmcdonough@mbpce.com
Web Site: http://www.mbpce.com

Specialties: Construction delay analysis; Construction impact analysis; construction claims analysis; Dispute resolution; Engineering expert testimony; Litigation support. Affiliation: Construction Expert Witness, Third Party Neutral: DRB, Arbitrator/Mediator. **Degrees/licenses:** BE; PE (AL, DE, DC, GA, MD, MA, PA, VA, UK).

The Nielsen-Wurster Group, Inc.

Patricia Galloway, CEO
Kris R. Nielsen, Chairman
Reza Nikain, President
Jack L. Dignum, Senior VP
345 Wall Street
Princeton, NJ 08540
Tel: (609) 497-7300
Fax: (609) 497-3412
E-mail: njnwg@aol.com
Web Site: http://www.nielsen-wurster.com

Specialties: Dispute resolution; Litigation support; Schedule delay analyses; Geotechnical evaluations; Forensic investigations; Damage Quantification; Arbitration, mediation and dispute review boards; Management consulting; Audits; Risk Evaluations; Training seminars; Risk management; Project planning; Project execution; Risk assessments; Trend evaluations; Risk reduction strategies; Systems implementation; Services worldwide; Licensed professional engineers in all states; CPAs, Project management professionals; Extensive experience in project management and project controls. Authored numerous professional papers on Project Management, Risk Management and Analysis of Project Delay. Serving private and public companies throughout the power, building, transportation, infrastructure, telecommunications and process industries. **Degrees/licenses:** MSCE, BSCE, MBA, PE, PMP, P.Eng., CCE, PSP, C.Eng., JD, CPA, F.ICE.

PCCI (Pacific Construction Consultants, Inc.)

Marketing Director
3083 Gold Canal Drive, Suite 100
Rancho Cordova, CA 95670-6129
Tel: (916) 638-4848
(800) 655-PCCI (7224)
Fax: (916) 638-5124
E-mail: pcci@pcci.biz
Web Site: http://www.pcci.biz

Specialties: Construction contract disputes, claims defense and preparation, CPM scheduling, delay analyses, productivity analyses, scope disputes, standard of care, expert witness and litigation support. Engineers and other construction professionals. Extensive negotiation, mediation, arbitration and litigation experience. In-house graphics department. Seminars. Training. **Degrees/licenses:** Eng., Contracting.

CPM Scheduling

Trauner Consulting Services, Inc.

Theodore J. Trauner Jr., PE, PP
CEO
One Penn Center
1617 JFK Blvd., Ste. 600
Philadelphia, PA 19103
Tel: (215) 814-6400
Fax: (215) 814-6440
E-mail: ted.trauner@traunerconsulting.com
Web Site:
http://www.traunerconsulting.com

Specialties: Construction claims prevention/resolution; forensic engineering; dispute resolution; multimedia/graphics/models; mediation; litigation support; computerized document retrieval; construction manage-

(Listing continued on next page)

CPM Scheduling *(cont.)*

Trauner Consulting Services, Inc. (cont.)
ment/owners representation; surety completion/claims; construction scheduling/control; partnering/facilitation; design/constructability review; construction/cost audits; estimating; project monitoring; project status reports; procedure/procurement manuals; seminars/in-house training; expert testimony before various tribunals; 5 published construction texts; membership in CMAA, ACFE, ASCE, SAME, PMI, CSI, NSPE, AAA, American Board of Forensic Examiners, The Beavers, Inc., Dispute Review Foundation, Inc. **Degrees/licenses:** BS, Masters of Eng. in Struc. Eng. & Struc. Mech., MBA, PE, PP.

See primary listing under CONSTRUCTION: Claims

Wexco International Corporation

Dr. Stephen C. Wexler, PE
3226 Thatcher Avenue
Marina del Rey, CA 90292
Tel: (800) 559-3877
(310) 306-3877
(415) 281-3877
Fax: (310) 306-7480
E-mail: wexco@wexco.net
Web Site: http://www.wexco.net

Specialties: Construction consulting, engineering, safety and management; Construction defects and damages, costs to repair, policy coverage; Construction claims, delay impact analysis, CPM scheduling, contract disputes, damage calcs; Earthquake damage analysis and appraisal; Fire and flood damage appraisals; Safety Engineering, building codes and safety regulation compliance; Construction accidents (falls from height, scaffolds, ladders, use of tools and equipment); Slips, Trips and Falls (stairs, ramps, walkways). All California and other states. In business since 1969. Calif. Contractor's License B-1. Licensed Safety & Civil Engineers. Have testified in over 150 trials. **Degrees/licenses:** PE, CPE, CCE, CCS, CPMP, CVS, CMC, CBO, CSP.

See primary listing under CONSTRUCTION: Safety Engineering

Defects

Bynum & Associates Corporation

James L. Bynum, President
H. Fred Uttke II, Vice President
16182 Construction Circle W., Ste. A
Irvine, CA 92606
Tel: (949) 653-8300
(949) 439-1988
Fax: (949) 653-8383
E-mail: jim@b-a-c.com
Web Site: http://www.b-a-c.com

Specialties: General Contracting, Construction Management, Construction Consulting and Foundation Specialties; Forensic investigation and analysis; Design, Code and Industry Standard Compliance; Cost Estimating, Property Loss Analysis; New, Repair and Replacement; Certified Mold Inspection and Remediation; Value Engineering means and methods. Construction Experience exceeds thirty years, Forensic Investigation and Analysis experience exceeds eleven years. Services available throughout the Western United States. Licenses include; B-1 General Building, C-8 Concrete and C-12 Grading State of California, B-2 General Building State of Nevada and General Building State of North Carolina. **Degrees/licenses:** B-1, C-8 and C-12 State of California.

Calcoast Labs / DL Labs, Inc.

D. Patrick Fairley, Pres. - Lab Director
Antoine Chamsi, VP Materials Chemistry
Thomas Sliva, VP - Tech. Direc. (DL Labs)
4072 Watts Street
Emeryville, CA 94608
Tel: (510) 652-2979
Fax: (510) 652-3085
E-mail: ccoastlabs@aol.com or
dllabs@aol.com
Web Site: http://www.calcoastlabs.com or
http://www.dllabs.com

DL Labs, Inc.
74 Kent Street
Brooklyn, NY 11222
Tel: (718) 383-5080
Fax: (718) 383-7445

Specialties: Calcoast Labs, Inc. of Emeryville, California, has acquired DL Labs of New York City, formerly David Litter Laboratories. The acquisition makes Calcoast/DL Labs one of the largest independent paint, coatings, sealant & materials testing laboratories in North America. The California/New York locations also provide for universal coverage of our domestic and foreign client base. We provide analytical & expert services to the legal community. DL Labs is accredited by NVLAP (Code 100252-0), CGSB, ISO/IEC25. Calcoast Labs is accredited by DEA & Los Angeles Department of Building & Safety. **Degrees/licenses:** BS, MS, PhD.

See primary listing under FAILURE ANALYSIS: Materials

Steven Cohen, Esq.

President
Cohen & Associates, Inc.
2530 Wilshire Blvd, 3rd Floor
Santa Monica, CA 90403
Tel: (310) 315-5404
Fax: (310) 315-5408
E-mail: scohen@litigationbusters.com
Web Site: http://www.litigationbusters.com

Specialties: Real Estate/Construction Specialist and Attorney with extensive experience in the following areas: Construction Defects; Construction Contract Disputes; Mold Inspection/Remediation; Risk Analysis; Mechanical Defects; Electrical Defects; Structural Defects; Real Estate; HOA, DRE, CSLB Rules & UBC Compliance. General/Electrical Contractor; Graduate level certified in Dispute Resolution. **Degrees/licenses:** Atty; JD-MBA; RE Broker; Gen/Electric Contractor.

See primary listing under CONSTRUCTION: General

Ivey Engineering, Inc.

HVAC, Plumbing, Piping
& Fire Sprinkler Experts
6390 Greenwich Drive, Ste. 240
San Diego, CA 92122
Tel: (858) 587-2874
Fax: (858) 587-6749
E-mail: info@iveyengineering.com
Web Site: http://www.iveyengineering.com

Specialties: Ivey Engineering is a forensic engineering, failure analysis and construction claims consulting firm specializing in HVAC, plumbing, fire sprinkler and process piping systems. The staff is comprised of professional engineers, former construction executives and service and repair professionals. Clients include contractors, architectural and engineering firms, facility owners, law firms and insurance companies. The experts have managed over 1,000 construction projects, designed over 1,000 projects, estimated and bid over 3,000 projects, prepared and negotiated over 10,000 change orders and prepared or defended over 50 construction claims. For more information go to www.iveyengineering.com. **Degrees/licenses:** PEs in 10 States, ICBO Cert. Inspectors, BSMEs; Contractors two states.

See primary listing under CONSTRUCTION: Mechanical/Plumbing

Defects *(cont.)*

Josephson-Werdowatz & Associates, Inc.

Carl H. Josephson, SE
Principal Structural Engineer
6370 Lusk Blvd., Ste. F200
San Diego, CA 92121-2753
Tel: (858) 558-2181
Fax: (858) 558-2188
E-mail: cjosephson@jwa-se.com
Web Site: http://www.jwa-se.com

6900 E. Camelback Rd., Ste. 522
Scottsdale, AZ 85251-2442
Tel: (480) 945-5337
Fax: (480) 945-5499

2110 East Flamingo Rd., Ste. 203
Las Vegas, NV 89119-5192
Tel: (702) 733-6500
Fax: (702) 733-6555

Specialties: Construction defect investigations/evaluations; Structural design & analysis; Wood frame, steel, masonry & concrete structures; Building code review & analysis; Computer presentations & animations; Alternative dispute resolution. Carl Josephson and Dan Werdowatz of Josephson-Werdowatz & Associates (JW&A) have been retained on over 500 cases as expert witnesses for construction litigation. JW&A works as both plaintiff and defense experts for a wide range of clients, and has been jointly retained on a number of cases by both plaintiff and defendant. JW&A strives for a reasoned, accurate and practical solution to construction litigation problems. DEGREES/LICENSES: Mr. Josephson: BSCE (Structures), PE/SE (CA, AZ, ID, NV & WA); PE (UT, CO, FL, & NM). Mr. Werdowatz: BSCE, MS (Structures), PE/SE (CA, WA, AZ, OR, NV & HI); PE (CO & TX). **Degrees/licenses:** BSCE, MS, PE, SE (See above).

See primary listing under ENGINEERING: Structural

Philip Kroeze, AIA

Principal
Consulting Architectural Services
19 Summerside
Coto de Caza, CA 92679
Tel: (949) 589-0554
Fax: (949) 589-4351
E-mail: kroeze@cox.net
Web Site:
http://www.jurispro.com/mem/kroeze

Specialties: Licensed Architect (CA); Member: American Institute of Architects (AIA), Construction Specifications Institute (CSI), International Congress of Building Officials (ICBO), National Council of Architectural Registration Boards (NCARB). Architectural/Engineering standard of care; moisture intrusion; construction documents. 35+ years experience in design, working drawings, specifications, construction; litigation support; single & multi-family residential, commercial, offices; personal injury; ADA compliance; UBC types I-V; wood, steel & concrete structures; models, charts, renderings, & other exhibits; photographs. **Degrees/licenses:** Licensed Architect (CA); Bachelor of Architecture; US Army Corps of Engineers.

See primary listing under ARCHITECTURE: General

Ted S. Merrill

General Contractor and Consultant
Ted S. Merrill & Sons, Inc.
Building Surgeons (Lic. #345079)
7907 North Ave.
Lemon Grove, CA 91945-1827
Tel: (619) 464-3997
Fax: (619) 464-8581
E-mail: ted@tsm-sons.com

Specialties: 50 years Construction experience in positions ranging from laborer, apprentice carpenter, carpenter, superintendent, estimator to general contractor. Including all phases of construction contracting, but specializing in damage repair work, including experience in estimating and reconstruction of building damaged by fire, wind, motor vehicles, earth movement and construction defects. This type of work is estimated and contracted by Ted S.

Merrill & Sons, Inc., with Federal and State governments local cities, school districts, insurance companies and individual owners of residential, commercial and industrial buildings. 32 years experience in cost estimating structures with construction defect problems. Giving testimony at settlement conferences and depositions. Qualified and testified as an expert in Municipal, Superior and Federal Courts.. **Degrees/licenses:** State of California Contractor, B-1 Licenses #275171 & 345079.

See primary listing under CONSTRUCTION: General

J. Robert Nelson, PE

Senior Vice President
PFS Corporation
3637 Motor Ave., Ste. 380
Los Angeles, CA 90034
Tel: (310) 559-7287
Fax: (310) 559-1368
E-mail: rnelson@pfscorporation.com
Web Site: http://www.pfscorporation.com

Specialties: Building and Fire Code expert; 35 years experience in code enforcement and construction (ten years with ICBO/Uniform Building Code and Uniform Fire Code; five years with LA County Building Dept.) Technical Investigations and Test Laboratory available; Civil, Structural and Fire Protection Engineering. Construction defects/forensics; gypsum wallboard, drywall, plaster, stucco, shear walls, seismic/earthquake, sheet metal flashing, decking, roofing, wood framing & siding. Slip & fall, fire investigation & testing lab. **Degrees/licenses:** Registered Civil & Fire Protection Engineer.

See primary listing under CONSTRUCTION: Building Codes

Richard E. Norris, PE, RRC

Principal
Norris Consulting Services
43255 Mission Boulevard, Ste. 203
Fremont, CA 94539-5826
Tel: (510) 440-0141
Fax: (510) 440-0142
E-mail: norris@members.asce.org
Web Site: http://www.renorris.com

Specialties: Expert consultant providing full litigation support with extensive expertise in cases involving: Bituminous materials; Construction project management; Decay; Forensic investigation of construction defects; Mold; Roofing; Waterproofing. **Degrees/licenses:** D. Eng. MS, BS, PE, RRC.

RJ Lee Group, Inc.

5 Nationwide locations:
CA, NY, PA, VA, WA
Keith Rickabaugh
Director of Sales and Marketing
350 Hochberg Road
Monroeville, PA 15146
Tel: (800) 860-1775
(724) 325-1776
Fax: (724) 733-1799
E-mail: krickabaugh@rjlg.com
Web Site: http://www.rjlg.com

Specialties: COMPANY INFORMATION: Independent laboratory and consulting group specializing in application of instrumental techniques to solve problems. Over 250 employees and 20 years litigation support experience. FAILURE ANALYSIS: materials, metals, polymers, and ceramics. CONSTRUCTION MATERIALS/DEFECT IDENTIFICATION: concrete and cement, aggregates, and fill materials. FORENSICS: gun shot residue, hair, fiber, and other trace evidence. ENVIRONMENTAL: disaster/impact assessment and remediation, receptor modeling, particulate characterization, air and dust analysis, and diesel particulate characterization. EXPANDED SERVICES: auger spectroscopy (AES), optical and electron microscopy (SEM & TEM), inorganic chemistry (AA/ICP & X-ray diffraction), organic chemistry (GC-ECD, GC-FID, GC/MS,

(Listing continued on next page)

Defects *(cont.)*

RJ Lee Group, Inc. (cont.)
FTIR & HPLC), thermal analysis (TGA, DSC, DTA), industrial hygiene, asbestos, silica, method development, product testing, software development, x-ray photoelectron spectroscopy, x-ray diffraction, and x-ray fluorescence (XPS, XRD, XRF). **Degrees/licenses:** BS, CIH, CSP, MA, MBA, MS, MSFS, PE, PhD; AIHA & NVLAP + Other Accred.

See primary listing under FAILURE ANALYSIS: General

Ron Travers, AIA

La Jolla Pacific, Ltd.
460 Goddard
Irvine, CA 92618-4610
Tel: (949) 645-8900
Fax: (949) 645-8813
E-mail: rtravers@ljpltd.com
Web Site: http://www.ljpltd.com

Specialties: Extensive experience in Planning, Zoning, Design and Construction Administration of wood frame, suburban, density, residential, and high rise towers of concrete pre-stressed, post-tension, steel construction, and related defects pertaining to the above. Knowledge of major weatherproofing designs and concepts. Mold expert in construction related matters, requiring assessment of cause, condition, extent of mold, and recommendation of restoration methods, and repair processes. If hygienic and laboratory analysis is deemed necessary, refer to other known professionals. Success in managing investigations of various structural defect situations. Considerable in-court expert witness experience. **Degrees/licenses:** AIA, Lic. in WA, OR, CA, AZ, NV, CO, HI; NCARB Certified.

See primary listing under ARCHITECTURE: General

Demolition

Jon J. Pina, MS, CSP

Safety, Health
& Environmental Professional
Evergreen Environmental Health
& Safety, Inc.
368 Rt. 110 Hwy.
Indiana, PA 15701
Tel: (724) 349-7029
Fax: (724) 349-3540
E-mail: jpina@adelphia.net

Specialties: Over 31 years experience; safety, industrial hygiene, environmental, PA state OSHA consultant, construction management, "hands-on" industrial/chemical operations; slip, trip, and falls; falls from elevation/ trucks/moble platforms; hot work/fires/explosives; asbestos identification, abatement, disposal, final clearance; asbestos awareness training; environmental surveys/Phase I & II environmental assessments; hazardous waste site remediation; RCRA, CERCLA; mixed wastes, PCBs, USTs, , heavy metals, unexploded ordnances, etc.; drum, soil, water, and air sampling; construction, excavation, utility location/isolation, tank cleaning, confined space, electrical hazards; emergency response, LEPC member; safety professor; professionally published. Demolished many steel, coke, and chemical facilities. **Degrees/licenses:** MS Safety Sci; MS Geol; BS Geosci Ed.; Cert Safety Prof; Cert Prof Instructor.

See primary listing under ACCIDENT PREVENTION & SAFETY: General

Disaster Reconstruction

Bynum & Associates Corporation

James L. Bynum, President
H. Fred Uttke II, Vice President
16182 Construction Circle W., Ste. A
Irvine, CA 92606
Tel: (949) 653-8300
(949) 439-1988
Fax: (949) 653-8383
E-mail: jim@b-a-c.com
Web Site: http://www.b-a-c.com

Specialties: General Contracting, Construction Management, Construction Consulting and Foundation Specialties; Forensic investigation and analysis; Design, Code and Industry Standard Compliance; Cost Estimating, Property Loss Analysis; New, Repair and Replacement; Certified Mold Inspection and Remediation; Value Engineering means and methods. Construction Experience exceeds thirty years, Forensic Investigation and Analysis experience exceeds eleven years. Services available throughout the Western United States. Licenses include; B-1 General Building, C-8 Concrete and C-12 Grading State of California, B-2 General Building State of Nevada and General Building State of North Carolina. **Degrees/licenses:** B-1, C-8 and C-12 State of California.

See primary listing under CONSTRUCTION: Defects

Cousino Consulting & Professional Services

Michael T. Cousino
President, Certified Restorer
26901 Eckel Rd.
Perrysburg, OH 43551
Tel: (800) 874-2122
Fax: (419) 874-0601
E-mail:
mcousino@cousinoconstruction.com
Web Site:
http://www.cousinoconstruction.com

Specialties: All types of disaster property restoration, evaluation, analysis and cost valuations; analysis and control of odors, mold and mildew testing and remediation; feasibility and analysis of loss repairs; construction claims analysis; traveling consulting services; complete disaster planning and control services; contingency planning; appraisals, umpiring, dispute resolution and arbitration. Expert witness and testimony reporting. Member: ASCR (Associated Specialties of Cleaning and Restoration); DKI (Disaster Kleenup International); NIDR (National Institute of Disaster Restoration, Certified Restorer); WLI (Water Loss Institute); NFPA (National Fire Protection Association); Certified Technology Restorer (CTR). **Degrees/licenses:** CR, OH License 70-74210, MI License 2102-130597, CTR.

Disputes

Geno Maniago

Construction Consultation & Scaffold Safety
1130 Links Way
Gibsonia, PA 15044
Tel: (724) 265-9967
Fax: (724) 265-9967
E-mail: geno@genomaniago.com
Web Site: http://genomaniago.com

244 St. Augustine Ave., 801 W.
Venice, FL 34285-1844
Tel: (941) 488-1805
Fax: (941) 488-1805

Specialties: Fifty years experience in all phases of construction; Journeyman Bricklayer; General Superintendent large construction company; Divisional Vice President Waco Scaffold & Equipment Company; Twenty five years experience designing, erecting, and supervising scaffold erection crews; Experienced in standard, Morgan, suspended, tube and clamp, and system scaffold; Represented the American Subcontractors Association on Disputes Review Boards; Conducted scaffold safety seminars for apprentices and journeymen tradesmen; Member Akron Builders Exchange; Life member American Subcontractors Association; Arbitration and Mediation classes - Kent State University and American Arbitration Society; Scaffold safety

(Listing continued on next page)

Disputes *(cont.)*

Geno Maniago (cont.)
and engineering courses by Waco Engineering Department.

See primary listing under CONSTRUCTION: Scaffold Safety

The Nielsen-Wurster Group, Inc.

Patricia Galloway, CEO
Kris R. Nielsen, Chairman
Reza Nikain, President
Jack L. Dignum, Senior VP
345 Wall Street
Princeton, NJ 08540
Tel: (609) 497-7300
Fax: (609) 497-3412
E-mail: njnwg@aol.com
Web Site: http://www.nielsen-wurster.com

Specialties: Dispute resolution; Litigation support; Schedule delay analyses; Geotechnical evaluations; Forensic investigations; Damage Quantification; Arbitration, mediation and dispute review boards; Management consulting; Audits; Risk Evaluations; Training seminars; Risk management; Project planning; Project execution; Risk assessments; Trend evaluations; Risk reduction strategies; Systems implementation; Services worldwide; Licensed professional engineers in all states; CPAs, Project management professionals; Extensive experience in project management and project controls. Authored numerous professional papers on Project Management, Risk Management and Analysis of Project Delay. Serving private and public companies throughout the power, building, transportation, infrastructure, telecommunications and process industries. **Degrees/licenses:** MSCE, BSCE, MBA, PE, PMP, P.Eng., CCE, PSP, C.Eng., JD, CPA, F.ICE.

See primary listing under CONSTRUCTION: Consulting

Electrical

Eric David

Liaicon
5280-128 Atherton St.
Long Beach, CA 90815-3957
Tel: (562) 597-1877
Fax: (562) 986-9548

Specialties: Electrical and General Contractor with 37+ years of trade. Consulting, and expert witness experience since 1980 in the following areas: Defect Construction; Customs & Practices; Injury/Fire Cause Investigation; Accident Reconstruction; Construction Claims; Electrical Trade; Accident Prevention/Safety. **Degrees/licenses:** BA; MA; Cert. Elec. Inspector ICC & IAEI #42820; Inactive Elec/Gen Contractor.

See primary listing under ACCIDENT PREVENTION & SAFETY: General

Failure Analysis

Dr. Fari Barzegar, PE

Principal
Habitat Engineering & Forensics
446 17th Street, Suite 300
Oakland, CA 94612
Tel: (510) 891-0300
(510) 717-3600 (mobile)
Fax: (510) 891-0333
E-mail: Fari@HabitatEngineering.com
Web Site:
http://www.HabitatEngineering.com

Specialties: Building Design & Construction (Residential, Commercial, Industrial and Institutional); Seismic Resistant Design; Code Compliance; Construction Defects and Accidents; Repair & Retrofit Cost Estimates; Performance Evaluation of Bridges, Water Treatment and Sanitary Structures, Pavements, Retaining Walls, Underground Conduits and Pipelines; Diagnostic & Failure Investigations; Concrete and Repair Materials; Analysis of Damage due to Vibration, Blast, Impact, Wind and Earthquake; Finite Element Analysis of Structural/Mechanical Components; 21 years of experience in Consulting, Research and

Teaching; 43 publications; Reviewer of Technical Articles for Prestigious Journals; Member: ASCE, SEAONC, ACI, EERI, AISC, ICC, FEWA. **Degrees/licenses:** BS, MS, PhD, Reg. Prof. Engr. & Bldg. Contractor (CA).

See primary listing under ENGINEERING: Structural

Inspection

John D. Shepherd, RRC, RRO

President
Shepherd Consulting Services
P. O. Box 10010
Torrance, CA 90505
Tel: (310) 378-0791
Fax: (310) 378-0794
E-mail: jds@shepherdconsulting.com
Web Site:
http://www.shepherdconsulting.com

Specialties: SCS specializes in the investigation and analysis of water intrusion, construction failure, standard of care and building code issues related to roofing, sheet metal, waterproofing, and the building envelope for construction defect litigation, property damage claims and personal injury claims. Support services include visual inspections, intrusive testing, leak investigations, water testing, report development, documentation, document review, research, mediation, expert witness testimony and cost estimating. **Degrees/licenses:** RCI Reg. Roof consultant #212/Observer #19. CA Roofing Contr. Lic.# 557494.

See primary listing under CONSTRUCTION: Building Codes

Management

Al Alesi

President
Roofing Solutions, Inc.
7045 Corporate Way, Suite 2
Dayton, OH 45459
Tel: (937) 433-1880
Fax: (937) 433-9441

Specialties: Engineering & management of roofing & waterproofing systems; condition surveys, failure analysis & moisture surveys; Design of new or retrofit roof systems; Value engineering, roof installation inspections, insurance claim analysis, expert testimony for arbitration or litigation. **Degrees/licenses:** BS; CPRC; CCI; CSI.

See primary listing under CONSTRUCTION: Roofing/Waterproofing

Bruce Baron

President/Owner
Baron Consulting
1315 Hobart Street
Menlo Park, CA 94025
Tel: (650) 280-2863
Fax: (650) 326-8933 (call first)
E-mail: bbaron@juno.com

Specialties: Over 35 years experience in the structural steel industry, first working in a fabrication plant. In 1972 Mr. Baron found his own company, primarily working on structural steel projects for buildings, large custom homes, bridges, and marine applications. Specialized in large and small turnkey projects including project design conception, sharp drawings for design team review, fabrication and field installation; fabrication of other specialized ferrous metals, including stainless steel; worked with non ferrous metals, including aluminum and bronze. The company was involved in the forming, bending, rolling, shearing, punching, drilling, welding, and bolting of a variety of shapes, hollow sections and plate. Has worked on projects from design development phase through project management coordination, to final completion. Projects include wind tunnel, hotels, college buildings, hospitals, Stanford linear accelerator, bridges, water treatment plants and reservoirs. **Degrees/licenses:** California Contractors Lic. C-51, Structural Steel, C60.

Mechanical/Plumbing

William J. Goode
President
W.J. Goode Corporation
1600 Providence Highway
Walpole, MA 02081
Tel: (508) 668-9995
Fax: (508) 668-9996
E-mail: wjgoode@wjgoodecorp.com
Web Site: http://www.wjgoodecorp.com

Specialties: Provide post fire analysis, expert witness, discovery, deposition and trial services for plaintiffs and defendants involved in claims regarding Heating, Ventilation and Air Conditioning (HVAC) systems in buildings and thermal distribution systems. Mr. Goode's expert experience includes college campuses, office buildings, hotels, housing, retail, physical fitness facilities, research buildings, performing arts centers, heating and cooling plants, hospitals, medical support buildings, industrial and manufacturing facilities. He is a member of the American Society of Heating Refrigeration and Air Conditioning Engineers, the Association for Facilities Engineering and the National Academy of Forensic Engineers. **Degrees/licenses:** BSME, MSEM, Reg. Prof. Engineer, Lic. Master Pipe Ftr.

See primary listing under ENGINEERING: HVAC

Ivey Engineering, Inc.
HVAC, Plumbing, Piping
& Fire Sprinkler Experts
6390 Greenwich Drive, Ste. 240
San Diego, CA 92122
Tel: (858) 587-2874
Fax: (858) 587-6749
E-mail: info@iveyengineering.com
Web Site: http://www.iveyengineering.com

Specialties: Ivey Engineering is a forensic engineering, failure analysis and construction claims consulting firm specializing in HVAC, plumbing, fire sprinkler and process piping systems. The staff is comprised of professional engineers, former construction executives and service and repair professionals. Clients include contractors, architectural and engineering firms, facility owners, law firms and insurance companies. The experts have managed over 1,000 construction projects, designed over 1,000 projects, estimated and bid over 3,000 projects, prepared and negotiated over 10,000 change orders and prepared or defended over 50 construction claims. For more information go to www.iveyengineering.com. **Degrees/licenses:** PEs in 10 States, ICBO Cert. Inspectors, BSMEs; Contractors two states.

Metals/Metallurgy

Bruce Baron
President/Owner
Baron Consulting
1315 Hobart Street
Menlo Park, CA 94025
Tel: (650) 280-2863
Fax: (650) 326-8933 (call first)
E-mail: bbaron@juno.com

Specialties: Over 35 years experience in the structural steel industry, first working in a fabrication plant. In 1972 Mr. Baron found his own company, primarily working on structural steel projects for buildings, large custom homes, bridges, and marine applications. Specialized in large and small turnkey projects including project design conception, sharp drawings for design team review, fabrication and field installation; fabrication of other specialized ferrous metals, including stainless steel; worked with non ferrous metals, including aluminum and bronze. The company was involved in the forming, bending, rolling, shearing, punching, drilling, welding, and bolting of a variety of shapes, hollow sections and plate. Has worked on projects from design development phase through project management coordination, to final completion. Projects include wind tunnel, hotels, college buildings, hospitals, Stanford linear accelerator, bridges, water treatment plants and reservoirs. **Degrees/licenses:** California Contractors Lic. C-51, Structural Steel, C60.

See primary listing under CONSTRUCTION: Management

Mobile Homes/ Manufactured Housing

Dan M. Pate
President
Dan Pate Enterprises, Inc.
P.O. Box 691991
Tulsa, OK 74169-1991
Tel: (918) 234-2556
Fax: (918) 234-2556
E-mail: DanPateInc@aol.com

Specialties: Litigation, Arbitration, Mediation as Expert Witness in Manufactured Home (mobilehome) cases; Technical assistance for depositions; Inspections of factory-built homes; Investigation of transportation, foundation and installation issues; Inspections of delivery sites; Assessment of warranty repairs by industry standards; Certified manufactured housing appraisals. Thirty-year veteran of manufactured housing (mobilehome) industry as retailer, transporter, installer, inspector and consultant. Experienced in recovery and refurbishing of repossessed manufactured homes. State Licensed Mechanical Contractor, Certified Home Installation Technician, Specialized Training in installation per ANSI 225.1 code, Certified by National Society of Appraiser Specialists.

See primary listing under MANUFACTURED HOUSING INDUSTRY: General

Personal Injury

Darrell L. Henderson, MD
Plastic Surgeon
Plastic Surgery Associates
1101 South College Rd., Ste. 400
Lafayette, LA 70503
Tel: (337) 233-5025
Fax: (337) 233-5054
E-mail: plasticsx@aol.com
Web Site: http://www.psassoc.com

Specialties: Hand/wrist surgeon, general plastic surgeon; Six-year residency at Mayo Clinic; General Surgery, Plastic Surgery. Fellowship in surgery of the hand and wrist with Dr. Frackelton, Milwaukee, WS. Vast experience in forensic evaluations of injuries and the impact disability has on the ability to work and problems, future medical, surgeries and expenses caused by the injury. Qualified as defense and plaintiff expert in many federal and state courts in the U.S. and Australia. American Society of Plastic Surgeons, American Board of Plastic surgeons, American Board of Forensic Examiners. **Degrees/licenses:** MD.

See primary listing under MEDICINE & HEALTH: Plastic & Reconstructive Surgery

William A. Rutherford, PE
10 Peach Drive
Lititz, PA 17543
Tel: (717) 627-3368
E-mail: stmusic@worldnet.att.net

Specialties: Qualified Expert Witness; Civil; Structural; Cooling Towers; Design; Estimating; Forensic; Construction Practices; Construction Management; Project Management; Project Planning & Controls; Schedule Analysis; System Turn-Over; Structural Welding; Claims; Concrete; Steel; Timber; Defects; Municipal; Disputes; Infrastructure; Personal Injury; Quality Control; Roads; Heavy Construction; Scaffold Safety; Site Work; Grading; Bridge Inspection; Storm Water; Earthwork; Utilities; Nuclear Plants; Operations; Maintenance; Rigging; Cranes; Accidents; Structural Failures; Plant Engineering; Equipment Accidents; Contracts; Material Storage; Site Inspection; Trench Collapse; Falls; Electrocutions; Schools; Commercial; Residential; Plaintiff and Defendant experience. Case Reconstruction experience. Worcester Polytechnic Institute (73). **Degrees/licenses:** BSCE, PE; Civil/Structural (PA, MA).

See primary listing under CONSTRUCTION: Claims

Roads/Heavy Construction

John F. Robertson, PE

President
JFRA
16219 Taylorsville Rd.
Fisherville, KY 40023
Tel: (502) 267-9230
Fax: (502) 267-4966
E-mail: johnexpert@aol.com

Specialties: Expert witness in Heavy/Highway Construction; Roads; Earthworks; Siteworks; Underground Utilities; Watermains; Storm; Sanitary; Curbs & Gutter; Concrete & Asphalt Paving; Grading; Foundations; Delay Claims; Changed Conditions; Traffic Controls; Estimating, Management; Project Planning & Control; Safety; Scheduling. **Degrees/licenses:** BS Civil Engr.; M. Engr. Mgt.; PE (KY); ASCE, AACE.

Roofing/Waterproofing

Al Alesi

President
Roofing Solutions, Inc.
7045 Corporate Way, Suite 2
Dayton, OH 45459
Tel: (937) 433-1880
Fax: (937) 433-9441

Specialties: Engineering & management of roofing & waterproofing systems; condition surveys, failure analysis & moisture surveys; Design of new or retrofit roof systems; Value engineering, roof installation inspections, insurance claim analysis, expert testimony for arbitration or litigation. **Degrees/licenses:** BS; CPRC; CCI; CSI.

Joseph C. Chew

President
J.C. Chew Consulting, Inc.
8691 Westfield Rd.
P.O. Box 215
Westfield Center, OH 44251
Tel: (330) 887-1400
Fax: (330) 887-5120
E-mail: jcchewjr@hotmail.com
Web Site:
http://www.firms.findlaw.com/jcchew

Specialties: Industrial/commercial roofing; Expertise includes: single-ply roofing, modified bitumen, BUR, metal building roof coatings, sprayed-in-place foam, exterior masonry sidewall coatings. Litigation assistance to attorneys, insurance companies, & industry in roofing litigation; including project file review, specification review, roof inspection & recommendations. Expert witness testimony for deposition, mediation, arbitration & trial. **Degrees/licenses:** Resume & CV available upon request; Over 20 yrs. indust. exp.

Dedicated Roof and Hydro-Solutions

David R. Hawn, RRC, CEM
President
6500 Harvest Mill Ct.
Centreville, VA 20121-4819
Tel: (703) 266-6638
Fax: (703) 266-1660
E-mail: drhawn@worldnet.att.net
Web Site: http://www.drhroofsolutions.com

Specialties: Roof and waterproofing forensic investigations and failure analysis; warranty issues; insurance issues; construction issues; wind; hail; and water entry damage. All roof and waterproofing types: low slope, steep slope, plaza decks, and sub-grade systems. All building types: commercial, industrial, institutional, and multi-residential. Experienced on a nationwide and international basis. Roof and waterproofing consultation services provided since 1982. Expert testimony provided over the last 16 years on numerous occasions. Serves on the Ethics and "Interface" peer review committees of the Roof Consultants Institute (RCI). **Degrees/licenses:** BSConE, Iowa State Univ.; Reg. Roof Consultant (RRC), Cert. Energy Mgr. (CEM).

DPM National Consulting

Buildings, Bridges, Elevators, Roofing
Daniel Koffler, PE
234 Philadelphia Pike
Wilmington, DE 19809
Tel: (302) 762-3352
Fax: (302) 762-3353
E-mail: koda@iopener.net

Specialties: Elevators and Escalators, Roofing, Structural, Masonry, Formwork & Shoring, Building Defects, Building Code Violations, Building Failures, Construction Accidents, Personal Injury, Fire Damage Survey & Reconstruction. Forensic Engineering, Arbitration and Expert Witness. Extensive court experience. Nationwide service. **Degrees/licenses:** BCE, PE - 35 Years Experience.

See primary listing under CONSTRUCTION: General

Ian Mackinlay Architecture, Inc.

Ian Mackinlay, FAIA
President
26 O'Farrell St., Ste. 200
San Francisco, CA 94108
Tel: (415) 243-4191
Fax: (415) 243-9769
E-mail: ian@ima-arch.com
Web Site: http://www.ima-arch.com

Specialties: Architecture; Expert analysis and testimony regarding architectural design and construction defects; Building code compliance; Roofing and waterproofing systems; Problems related to building in the snow and cold; Litigation strategy and organization; Product research and documentation; Alternative dispute resolution; Remedial design and reconstruction; Design review/quality assurance; Design related accident; Trial graphics. 450+ cases since 1979. Licensed in 17 states as listed below plus MT, NY, OH, NM. **Degrees/licenses:** Arch. Lic.: CA, WA, NV, UT, WY, AK, CO, GU, HI, ID, IL, MD, MN, NCARB #5408.

See primary listing under ARCHITECTURE: General

Richard E. Norris, PE, RRC

Principal
Norris Consulting Services
43255 Mission Boulevard, Ste. 203
Fremont, CA 94539-5826
Tel: (510) 440-0141
Fax: (510) 440-0142
E-mail: norris@members.asce.org
Web Site: http://www.renorris.com

Specialties: Expert consultant providing full litigation support with extensive expertise in cases involving: Bituminous materials; Construction project management; Decay; Forensic investigation of construction defects; Mold; Roofing; Waterproofing. **Degrees/licenses:** D. Eng. MS, BS, PE, RRC.

See primary listing under CONSTRUCTION: Defects

John D. Shepherd, RRC, RRO

President
Shepherd Consulting Services
P. O. Box 10010
Torrance, CA 90505
Tel: (310) 378-0791
Fax: (310) 378-0794
E-mail: jds@shepherdconsulting.com
Web Site:
http://www.shepherdconsulting.com

Specialties: SCS specializes in the investigation and analysis of water intrusion, construction failure, standard of care and building code issues related to roofing, sheet metal, waterproofing, and the building envelope for construction defect litigation, property damage claims and personal injury claims. Support services include visual inspections, intrusive testing, leak investigations, water testing, report development, documentation, document review, research, mediation, expert witness testimony and cost estimating. **Degrees/licenses:** RCI Reg. Roof consultant #212/Observer #19. CA Roofing Contr. Lic.# 557494.

See primary listing under CONSTRUCTION: Building Codes

Safety Engineering

Gary L. Buffington

President/CEO
American Safety Consulting, Inc.
P. O. Box 71017
Los Angeles, CA 90071
Tel: (661) 298-0006
(888) 828-1044
Fax: (661) 298-0311
E-mail: gbuff46@yahoo.com

Specialties: Safety Expert with 30+ years of consulting and expert witness experience in the following areas: Construction; Underground Construction; Tunneling, Mining & Mills; Risk Assessment; CAL/OSHA; IIPP, MSHA, NEC, NFPA, NRC Regs.; Safety Training. **Degrees/licenses:** MS; BS; CRSP; CSHM; CSP; WSO-CSE/CSM/CSS; Lic. PI; CIH; EMT.

See primary listing under ACCIDENT PREVENTION & SAFETY: General

John P. Coniglio, PhD, CSP, CHMM

Exec. VP - OPS
Occupational Safety
& Environmental Assoc., Inc.
3748 So. Park Ave.
Blasdell, NY 14219-1802
Tel: (716) 821-0091
Fax: (716) 821-0232
E-mail: johnconiglio@osea.com or
experts@osea.com
Web Site: http://johnconiglio.com

Specialties: Occupational safety & health specialist with 30 years experience working in heavy industry, process chemical, & construction. Testified in Federal, state and various regulatory courts and venues. Frequently called upon for NYS Labor Law and Federal OSHA matters. Areas of expertise include: Accident Investigation and Reconstruction, Indoor Air/Industrial Hygiene, Toxic Substances Control, Process Chemical, Construction, Demolition, Heavy Equipment, Machine Guarding, Excavation, Flammable/Combustible Materials, Fumes & Dusts, Confined Spaces, Fall Protection, Noise, Lockout/Tagout, Slip & Falls, Scaffold, Ladder Stairs, Competent Person, Overhead Cranes, Man Lifts, Industrial Practices, Process Safety. **Degrees/licenses:** AAS(2), BS, MS, PhD, CSP, CHMM, RPIH, CHCM, COHC.

See primary listing under ENGINEERING: Safety

Vincent A. Gallagher

Safety Expert
Safety Research, Inc.
739 White Horse Pike, Ste. 3
Audubon, NJ 08106
Tel: (856) 547-4884
Fax: (856) 547-5551
E-mail: safety@snip.net
Web Site: http://www.safetyresearchinc.com

Specialties: Former OSHA official. Served as safety expert for United Nations. Has consulted for major corporations and unions; Evaluated hazards related to hundreds of construction sites and manufacturing environments; Expert in construction safety management, fall hazard control, scaffolds, trench and excavations. Taught in ten colleges and universities; Received ten awards from OSHA and one from the United Nations. Certified hazard control manager and certified health and safety manager. **Degrees/licenses:** Masters Degree, Center for Safety, New York University.

George S. Kennedy, CSP

Kennedy Safety Services, Inc.
137 Ruhle Road
Ballston Spa, NY 12020
Tel: (518) 885-2560
Fax: (518) 884-8756
E-mail: kssinc@aol.com

Specialties: Accident and safety specialist; Litigation consulting; Safety training and education issues; Safety management; Personal injury investigation; Accident investigation and reconstruction; OSHA compliance and regulations; Construction and industrial safety and health issues: e.g., trenching, excavation, confined space entry, stairways, scaffolds, ladders, slips, falls, fall protection, electrical hazards, materials handling, loading docks, forklifts, tools, equipment, machine guarding, lockout/tagout, personal protective equipment, hazard communication. Certified Safety Professional, BS in Civil Engineering with 27 years safety and health experience. **Degrees/licenses:** CSP, CSHM, CHSP, BSCE, OSHA Instructor.

See primary listing under ACCIDENT PREVENTION & SAFETY: General

Twomey Safety Engineering

Richard E. Twomey, CSP
147 Grassy Hill Road
East Lyme, CT 06333
Tel: (860) 442-8340
(860) 867-7511
Fax: (860) 444-1602
E-mail: rettse@snet.net
Web Site: http://www.twomeysafety.com

Specialties: OSHA compliance, general and products liability, slips and falls, accident reconstruction, safety audits. Ergonomics: risk assessments, work-site analysis, accident investigations, ergonomic program development and equipment. Industrial Hygiene: OSHA compliance - indoor air quality, industrial air contaminants, noise and personal protective equipment. Safety Engineering: OSHA compliance - chemical process safety management, control of hazardous energy (lockout-tagout), electrical, fire protection and life safety, machine guarding, walking/working surfaces, vehicles and construction safety standards. Products Liability: Safety standards - boiler and pressure vessel, chemical containers and labeling, elevators, equipment and machine tools, and vehicles. DEGREES/LICENSES: BS, Marine Engineer; BS, Mechanical Engineer; MS, Occupational Safety & Health; Certified Safety Professional. **Degrees/licenses:** See above.

See primary listing under ENGINEERING: Safety

Wexco International Corporation

Dr. Stephen C. Wexler, PE
3226 Thatcher Avenue
Marina del Rey, CA 90292
Tel: (800) 559-3877
(310) 306-3877
(415) 281-3877
Fax: (310) 306-7480
E-mail: wexco@wexco.net
Web Site: http://www.wexco.net

Specialties: Construction consulting, engineering, safety and management; Construction defects and damages, costs to repair, policy coverage; Construction claims, delay impact analysis, CPM scheduling, contract disputes, damage calcs; Earthquake damage analysis and appraisal; Fire and flood damage appraisals; Safety Engineering, building codes and safety regulation compliance; Construction accidents (falls from height, scaffolds, ladders, use of tools and equipment); Slips, Trips and Falls (stairs, ramps, walkways). All California and other states. In business since 1969. Calif. Contractor's License B-1. Licensed Safety & Civil Engineers. Have testified in over 150 trials. **Degrees/licenses:** PE, CPE, CCE, CCS, CPMP, CVS, CMC, CBO, CSP.

Scaffold Safety

Geno Maniago

Construction Consultation & Scaffold Safety
1130 Links Way
Gibsonia, PA 15044
Tel: (724) 265-9967
Fax: (724) 265-9967
E-mail: geno@genomaniago.com
Web Site: http://genomaniago.com

244 St. Augustine Ave., 801 W.
Venice, FL 34285-1844
Tel: (941) 488-1805
Fax: (941) 488-1805

Specialties: Fifty years experience in all phases of construction; Journeyman Bricklayer; General Superintendent large construction company; Divisional Vice President Waco Scaffold & Equipment Company; Twenty five

(Listing continued on next page)

Scaffold Safety *(cont.)*

Geno Maniago (cont.)

years experience designing, erecting, and supervising scaffold erection crews; Experienced in standard, Morgan, suspended, tube and clamp, and system scaffold; Represented the American Subcontractors Association on Disputes Review Boards; Conducted scaffold safety seminars for apprentices and journeymen tradesmen; Member Akron Builders Exchange; Life member American Subcontractors Association; Arbitration and Mediation classes - Kent State University and American Arbitration Society; Scaffold safety and engineering courses by Waco Engineering Department.

Sitework/Grading

William B. Wigginton, RG, CEG, CHG
Geolex, Inc.
P.O. Box 374
Aptos, CA 95001
Tel: (831) 662-0609
Fax: (831) 662-0609
E-mail: wwigginton@aol.com

Specialties: Landslide identification and repair; Foundation failure; Construction failure analysis; Groundwater resources and studies; Soil testing; Roadway construction and failure investigations; Insurance causation studies. **Degrees/licenses:** MS Geology, RG (CA), CEG (CA), Cert. Hydrogeologist (CA).

See primary listing under GEOLOGY/HYDROLOGY: General

CRIMINALISTICS/ CRIMINOLOGY

General

Technical Associates, Inc.
Marc Scott Taylor
4125 Market Street, Ste. 3
Ventura, CA 93003
Tel: (805) 677-2155
Fax: (805) 676-1638
E-mail: info@tai-labs.com
Web Site: http://www.tai-labs.com

Specialties: Criminalistics firm with extensive experience in the following areas: Criminalistics & DNA Analysis; PCR & RFLP Consultation and Testing; Crime Scene Reconstruction; Gunshot Residue; Toolmarks; Shoeprints; Tiretracks; Firearms; Blood Splatter. Extremely sensitive testing of all types of forensic samples. **Degrees/licenses:** BS Zoology; MS.

DNA - Forensics

Dean A. Wideman
Consulting Forensic Scientist
and Criminal Profiler
NucleoGenix LLC
12000 Network Blvd., Suite B-200
San Antonio, TX 78249
Tel: (210) 336-7285
Fax: (210) 877-0200
E-mail: dwideman@forensic-profiler.com
Web Site: http://www.forensic-profiler.com
or http://www.nucleo-genix.com

Specialties: forensic DNA analysis, DNA mixtures, DNA statistics, physical evidence examination, bloodstain pattern analysis, crime scene investigation, expert witness testimony, trial preparation, criminal profiling, crime analysis and reconstruction, evidence collection procedures, forensic laboratory operations, second opinion, crime mapping, violent and sexual crime investigation, population genetics, forensic serology, review of laboratory data and protocols, case review and evaluation, investigative strategies and support. **Degrees/licenses:** Master of Science (MSc) - Forensic Science; Master of Business Admin. (MBA).

Brian Wraxall

Chief Forensic Serologist
Serological Research Institute
3053 Research Dr.
Richmond, CA 94806
Tel: (510) 223-7374
Fax: (510) 222-8887
E-mail: bwraxall@serological.com
Web Site: http://www.serological.com

Specialties: Forensic serology; Forensic serology analysis; Proficiency Provider; DNA testing; Paternity testing; Bodily fluids: saliva, semen, blood; Technical support & training; Forensic serology research & development; Laboratory analysis, ASCLD/LAB®Accredited. **Degrees/licenses:** Fellow, American Board of Criminalistics; HNC (Applied Biology); DABFE.

See primary listing under BIOLOGICAL SCIENCES: Serology

CRIMINOLOGY

Gangs

Dr. Lewis Yablonsky, PhD

Emeritus Professor of Criminology
California State University - Northridge
2311 4th St., Ste. 312
Santa Monica, CA 90405
Tel: (310) 450-3697
Fax: (310) 450-3697
E-mail: expertwitness@lewyablonsky.com
Web Site: http://www.lewyablonsky.com

Specialties: Former Director, Crime Prevention program for Security in NYC sponsored by Columbia Univ. and others. Author of 17 books including the textbooks: "Criminology" (Harper Collins, 1990), "Gangsters" (NYU Press, 1997), and "Gangs In Court" (Lawyers & Judges Publishers, 2005). Expert witness in over 150 cases involving gang behavior, substance abuse, violence, family violence, company security/liability and related criminal subjects. Expert witness for corporations on legal/financial responsibility when crimes occurred on their property. Participated as an E-W in courts: LA, NY, AZ, Fla., San Jose, San Diego, San Francisco, Orange, Riverside, Sacramento, U.S. Federal. For complete resume, contact Dr. Lewis Yablonsky or check website (see above). **Degrees/licenses:** PhD, NYU; Calif. Licensed Therapist (#21997).

CRISIS/EMERGENCY MANAGEMENT

Search & Rescue

Robert J. Koester

President
dbS Productions
University Station
P.O. Box 1894
Charlottesville, VA 22903
Tel: (434) 293-5502
(434) 989-5502
Fax: (800) 745-1581
E-mail: Robert@dbs-sar.com
Web Site: http://www.dbs-sar.com

Specialties: Nursing home wandering cases, Search and Rescue management evaluation, Alzheimer's disease and related dementia wandering cases, Search and Rescue research, behavioral profiles of lost people, dementia profile, psychotic profile, despondent profile, mental retardation profile. Initial law enforcement first response to missing person incidents, search and rescue training. President, dbS Production 89; Lead instructor course developer, Virginia Department of Emergency Management; Editor-in-chief, SARNEWS. Numerous papers and publications. **Degrees/licenses:** MS, EMT-C, Incident Commander Type I.

DEMONSTRATIVE EVIDENCE

Audio/Video Evidence

Brunette & Associates

Leo L. Brunette
Certified voice stress Analyst
P O Box 590
La Center, WA 98629-0590
Tel: (360) 263-2209
(360) 910-4770
E-mail: diogeneswest@tds.net
Web Site: http://www.truthsearch.net

Specialties: Mr. Brunette has 44 years law enforcement experience in both public and private sectors as well as 27 in voice stress analysis where he has worked with all voice stress systems. He is both a Polygrapher and voice stress analyst certified by the ISSA College of Analysts and qualified instructor in voice stress analysis. Currently the Vice President of Training for the Diogenes Company, he designed the latest high speed computerized systems on the market today, currently used by many Government agencies in the USA and the free world. **Degrees/licenses:** ISSA, CFE, KofC, Nebraska VSA, Lic. #24 since 1984.

See primary listing under LITIGATION SUPPORT: Polygraph/Lie Detection

Bill Krone

Legal Video Expert
Deja View Video
417 S. El Dorado St.
San Mateo, CA 94402
Tel: (800) 416-5608
(650) 343-8899
E-mail: bill@dejaview.com
Web Site: http://www.dejaview.com

Specialties: Analysis of video recordings as to authenticity, consistency, veracity, and identification. Video measurement for character identification. Edits, erasures, alterations or anomalies or recordings addressed and resolved. Evaluation of video recordings and cameras. Special emphasis on field recording procedures and specifications of camera and recording media in order to provide an opinion as to reasonable depiction of what could have been seen by the participants. Trial Testimony and Consultation in State and Federal Courts. Extensive trial list and references upon request. Synchronized transcript and video to CD-ROM and DVD. Prints and image enhancements from video. Visual site surveys, reconstructions, visibility studies, field production, opposition expert services available. **Degrees/licenses:** BA, SMPTE, NABET, Notary Public (CA).

See primary listing under AUDIO/VIDEO EVIDENCE: General

Graphics/Exhibits

LegalVision

Jonathan Carey
Creative Director
Twelve Geary Street, 3rd Floor
San Francisco, CA 94108-5710
Tel: (415) 834-0123
Fax: (415) 834-1869
E-mail: jcarey@legalvisionsf.com

Specialties: We have provided demonstrative exhibit experience in over 1000 business, personal injury and criminal trials. We create: Case-specific charts, Scale maps, Magnetic presentation boards, 3-D models, Illustrations, Photographs, Video documentaries, Animated simulations. Our clear, compelling presentation materials make it easy for you and your experts to explain complex information to a jury in a way they understand and remember. No matter your case, type or budget, our experienced designers work closely with you to develop persuasive exhibits for settlement discussions and trial. **Degrees/licenses:** JD, BSME, MBA, MS Medical & Biological Illustration.

Photography

LegalVision
Jonathan Carey
Creative Director
Twelve Geary Street, 3rd Floor
San Francisco, CA 94108-5710
Tel: (415) 834-0123
Fax: (415) 834-1869
E-mail: jcarey@legalvisionsf.com

Specialties: We have provided demonstrative exhibit experience in over 1000 business, personal injury and criminal trials. We create: Case-specific charts, Scale maps, Magnetic presentation boards, 3-D models, Illustrations, Photographs, Video documentaries, Animated simulations. Our clear, compelling presentation materials make it easy for you and your experts to explain complex information to a jury in a way they understand and remember. No matter your case, type or budget, our experienced designers work closely with you to develop persuasive exhibits for settlement discussions and trial. **Degrees/licenses:** JD, BSME, MBA, MS Medical & Biological Illustration.

See primary listing under DEMONSTRATIVE EVIDENCE: Graphics/Exhibits

DENTISTRY

General

Harry I. Aronowitz
Orthodontics Exclusively
465 N. Roxbury Drive, Ste. 1011
Beverly Hills, CA 90210
Tel: (310) 246-0100
Fax: (310) 246-0106
E-mail: aronowitz@usc.edu

Specialties: Extensive consulting and expert experience in the field of Orthodontics. USC Professor and Chairman, Orthodontic Peer Review Committee. Board certified in both Orthodontics & Pain. **Degrees/licenses:** DMD, QME, ABO, OKU; Board Certified Orthodontist.

Parviz Azar-Mehr, DMD
Prosthodontist,
Prof. of Clinical Dentistry, USC
10921 Wilshire Blvd., Ste. 501
Los Angeles, CA 90024
Tel: (310) 443-3030
Fax: (310) 443-5660
Web Site: http://www.azarmehr.com

Specialties: More than 25 years of consulting and expert witness experience in Clinical Dentistry. Court appearances in over 100 criminal cases including Dental Malpractice and TMJ Disorders. Member of the American College of Prosthodontics. **Degrees/licenses:** Advanced Prosthodontics, USC; DMD, NYU & University of Michigan.

Damian L. Newhart, DDS
Scott G. Newhart, DMD (DDS)
Beverly Hills/Santa Monica/Los Angeles
Inglewood/Westchester
Tel: (310) 550-1533
Fax: (310) 274-9756

Specialties: Doctors of Dental Surgery with extensive consulting and expert witness experience in the following areas: Dental Trauma, TMJ Injuries, Evaluation/Treatment. Cert. Spec. Orthodontics; Diplomate, American Academy of Pain Management; Qualified Medical Examiner (QME); Independent Medical Evaluator (IME); Agreed Medical Evaluator (AME); American Academy Head, Neck & Facial & TMJ Orthopedics. **Degrees/licenses:** DMD.

Ronald O. Segall, DMD, MS
Endodontist
196 Thomas Johnson Dr., Ste. 235
Frederick, MD 21702
Tel: (301) 663-5133
Fax: (301) 663-6943
E-mail: sr1234@erols.com

Specialties: Endodontics; Board Certified Endodontist (root canal specialist). Clinical rotating Internship prior to residency. Published author of scientific articles in "Journal of Endodontics" and "Oral Surgery, Oral Medicine, and Oral Pathology." Nine years

(Listing continued on next page)

General *(cont.)*

Ronald O. Segall (cont.)
military service, twenty-six years and currently in private practice. Past president of Maryland Endodontic Association and Edward C. Penick Endodontic study Club. Available for diagnosis and treatment evaluation for root canal therapy, consultation, malpractice case review, expert testimony. Previous legal experience. Knowledgeable about computers, digital radiography, and surgical microscopes. **Degrees/licenses:** DMD; MS; Licensed in MD, DC, PA.

See primary listing under DENTISTRY: Endodontics

Endodontics

Ronald O. Segall, DMD, MS

Endodontist
196 Thomas Johnson Dr., Ste. 235
Frederick, MD 21702
Tel: (301) 663-5133
Fax: (301) 663-6943
E-mail: sr1234@erols.com

Specialties: Endodontics; Board Certified Endodontist (root canal specialist). Clinical rotating Internship prior to residency. Published author of scientific articles in "Journal of Endodontics" and "Oral Surgery, Oral Medicine, and Oral Pathology." Nine years military service, twenty-six years and currently in private practice. Past president of Maryland Endodontic Association and Edward C. Penick Endodontic study Club. Available for diagnosis and treatment evaluation for root canal therapy, consultation, malpractice case review, expert testimony. Previous legal experience. Knowledgeable about computers, digital radiography, and surgical microscopes. **Degrees/licenses:** DMD; MS; Licensed in MD, DC, PA.

Oral Surgery

Robert J. Fish

Professional Centre at Woodmont
7737 North University Drive, Suite 100
Fort Lauderdale, FL 33321-2968
Tel: (954) 720-7700
Fax: (954) 724-4448
E-mail: DrSmile604@aol.com

Specialties: TMJ; Oral surgery; Oral rehabilitation & reconstruction; General dentistry; Cosmetic dentistry; Restorative dentistry; Personal injury; Dental malpractice; Dental negligence. Affiliation: Academy of General Dentistry; Private Practice (General, Cosmetic & Restorative Dentistry). Degrees and Licenses: Diplomate, Board Certified in Forensic Dentistry, American Board of Forensic Dentistry; Diplomate, Board Certified in Forensic Medicine, American Board of Forensic Medicine; Diplomate, Board Certified Forensic Examiner, American Board of Forensic Examiners; Fellow, The Royal Society of Medicine, Odontology Section; Fellow, Academy of General Dentistry; Fellow, American College of Forensic Examiners. **Degrees/licenses:** DDS (Licensed in DC, FL, MA, MI, NY, OH, PA); JD.

Oral/Maxillofacial Surgery

Charles S. Syers, DDS - San Francisco, CA

Oral & Maxillofacial Surgeon
P. O. Box 1879
San Mateo, CA 94401-0946
Tel: (650) 347-2614
Fax: (650) 347-2680
E-mail: legaldent@aol.com

Specialties: Extensive experience in the following areas: Anesthesia; Dental implants; Dental infection; Dental injury; Dental pain; Dento-facial nerve injury; Dento-facial trauma; Orthognathic surgery; Pain management; Temporomandibular Joint Injury (TMJ). Professional Experience: Chief, Oral-Maxillofacial Surgery, French Medical Dental Center; Visiting Lecturer, University of Pacific Dental School; Lecturer with MediLegal Institute; Associate Clinical Professor, University of CA, Dental School; Associate Clinical Professor, University of Pacific School of Dentistry. Assoc. Editor of The American Journal of Pain Management. Professional Societies: American Board of Oral and Maxillofacial Surgeons; American Dental Society of Anesthesiology; The American Fellowship of Oral-Maxillofacial Surgeons; International Congress of Oral Implantologists; American Academy of Pain Management; American Trauma society; American Forensic Examiners. **Degrees/licenses:** MA, DDS; DDS (CA, MI, IL).

Orthodontics

Harry I. Aronowitz

Orthodontics Exclusively
465 N. Roxbury Drive, Ste. 1011
Beverly Hills, CA 90210
Tel: (310) 246-0100
Fax: (310) 246-0106
E-mail: aronowitz@usc.edu

Specialties: Extensive consulting and expert experience in the field of Orthodontics. USC Professor and Chairman, Orthodontic Peer Review Committee. Board certified in both Orthodontics & Pain. **Degrees/licenses:** DMD, QME, ABO, OKU; Board Certified Orthodontist.

See primary listing under DENTISTRY: General

TMJ

Parviz Azar-Mehr, DMD

Prosthodontist,
Prof. of Clinical Dentistry, USC
10921 Wilshire Blvd., Ste. 501
Los Angeles, CA 90024
Tel: (310) 443-3030
Fax: (310) 443-5660
Web Site: http://www.azarmehr.com

Specialties: More than 25 years of consulting and expert witness experience in Clinical Dentistry. Court appearances in over 100 criminal cases including Dental Malpractice and TMJ Disorders. Member of the American College of Prosthodontics. **Degrees/licenses:** Advanced Prosthodontics, USC; DMD, NYU & University of Michigan.

See primary listing under DENTISTRY: General

Damian L. Newhart, DDS

Scott G. Newhart, DMD (DDS)
Beverly Hills/Santa Monica/Los Angeles
Inglewood/Westchester
Tel: (310) 550-1533
Fax: (310) 274-9756

Specialties: Doctors of Dental Surgery with extensive consulting and expert witness experience in the following areas: Dental Trauma, TMJ Injuries, Evaluation/Treatment. Cert. Spec. Orthodontics; Diplomate, American Academy of Pain Management; Qualified Medical Examiner (QME); Independent Medical Evaluator (IME); Agreed Medical Evaluator (AME); American Academy Head, Neck & Facial & TMJ Orthopedics. **Degrees/licenses:** DMD.

See primary listing under DENTISTRY: General

Charles S. Syers, DDS - San Francisco, CA

Oral & Maxillofacial Surgeon
P. O. Box 1879
San Mateo, CA 94401-0946
Tel: (650) 347-2614
Fax: (650) 347-2680
E-mail: legaldent@aol.com

Specialties: Extensive experience in the following areas: Anesthesia; Dental implants; Dental infection; Dental injury; Dental pain; Dento-facial nerve injury; Dento-facial trauma; Orthognathic surgery; Pain management; Temporomandibular Joint Injury (TMJ). Professional Experience: Chief, Oral-Maxillofacial Surgery, French Medical Dental Center; Visiting Lecturer, University of Pacific Dental School; Lecturer with MediLegal Institute; Associate Clinical Professor, University of CA, Dental School; Associate Clinical Professor, University of Pacific School of Dentistry. Assoc. Editor of The American Journal of Pain Management. Professional Societies: American Board of Oral and Maxillofacial Surgeons;

(Listing continued on next page)

TMJ *(cont.)*

Charles S. Syers (cont.)
American Dental Society of Anesthesiology; The American Fellowship of Oral-Maxillofacial Surgeons; International Congress of Oral Implantologists; American Academy of Pain Management; American Trauma society; American Forensic Examiners. **Degrees/licenses:** MA, DDS; DDS (CA, MI, IL).

See primary listing under DENTISTRY: Oral/Maxillofacial Surgery

DISTRIBUTION OPERATIONS

General

Distribution Assistance

Arthur T. Silk
President
P O Box 1418
East Dennis, MA 02641-1418
Tel: (508) 385-9802
Fax: (508) 385-9802
E-mail: atsilk@gis.net
Web Site:
http://www.distributionassistance.com

Specialties: Established in 1985, we are a management consulting logistics/expert witness firm devoted to helping clients create and improve cost effective/service enhancing solutions to issues in the areas of contract logistics, contract carrier transportation, customer service, distribution operations, import/export, incentive programs, inventory management, logistics audits and benchmarks, material handling, on time delivery, operating services, plant facilities, productivity improvements, safety, supply chain, third party logistics, traffic/transportation and warehousing. Industries serviced include active wear, athletic shoes/sneakers, automotive parts, beer/wine/ liquor, beverage, books, building products, clothing, consumer products, contract warehousing, distributors, drug stores, electronic parts, footwear, food, hardware, import/export, insurance, leather, non-profit, optical, paper, packaging, refrigerated/frozen retail, software, supermarket, suppliers, third party and wholesalers. **Degrees/licenses:** AB Honors-Boston College; MBA-Harvard Graduate School of Business Admin.

See primary listing under WAREHOUSING: General

DOCUMENT EXAMINATION

General

Gary Herbertson

Forensic Document Examiner
2203 McKinley Avenue
Berkeley, CA 94703
Tel: (510) 845-4482
Fax: (510) 845-4673
E-mail: herbertson4n6@earthlink.net

Specialties: Broad range of document examinations including: Identification of writers, typewriters, copy machine, rubber stamps. Determination of forgery, alterations, obliterations. Comparison of paper, ink, cut marks, stains. Fully equipped laboratory. Affiliation: Retired Unit Chief of FBI Laboratory, Fellow of American Academy of Forensic Sciences. **Degrees/licenses:** BA, MS, Forensic Science. Certified by FBI Laboratory.

Moore Document Laboratory

David S. Moore, BS, MEd
9010 Barrhill Way
Fair Oaks, CA 95628
Tel: (800) 989-3205
Fax: (916) 989-9674
E-mail: dmoore@mooredocs.com
Web Site: http://www.mooredocs.com

Specialties: All aspects of Forensic Questioned Documents, including: Identification of Signatures, Handwriting & Handprinting; Typewriter & Business Machine identification; Ink & Paper examinations; Examinations for

Alterations, Indentations and Obliterations; Photography for Court Demonstration; Fully Equipped Document Laboratory & Reference Materials; Expert Testimony in excess of 575 times in more than 20 states in Civil & Criminal Trials, Administrative Hearings, Arbitrations and Depositions; CV & fee schedule upon request; 25+ years experience; Full-time private practice; Formerly employed in Questioned Document labs of U.S. Army, U.S. Postal Inspection Service and California Department of Justice. **Degrees/licenses:** Certified by ABFDE since 1978.

See primary listing under LITIGATION SUPPORT: Questioned Documents

Farrell C. Shiver

Shiver & Nelson Document
Investigation Laboratory, Inc.
1903 Lilac Ridge Drive
Woodstock, GA 30189
Tel: (770) 517-6008
Fax: (678) 494-9283
E-mail: shiver@documentlab.com
Web Site: http://www.documentlab.com

Specialties: Former Chief Document Examiner, U.S. Army Crime Lab, Certified by the American Board of Forensic Document Examiners, Treasurer of the American Society of Questioned Document Examiners, member of the Questioned Document Section of the American Academy of Forensic Sciences. Handwriting comparison and forgery detection; Detection and decipherment of alterations; Decipherment of faint, faded, altered or obliterated entries; Identification of typewriters, photocopiers and other office machines; Nondestructive ink examination; Detection and decipherment of indented writing impressions; Typical cases - medical malpractice (alteration of medical record), signatures on documents, anonymous letters. **Degrees/licenses:** BS, MS, Diplomate - ABFDE.

Richard Van Leer, PhD

President/Master Data Analyst
ENTERPRIT.COM CORP
15841 Pines Blvd., #400
Pembroke Pines, FL 33027
Tel: (954) 450-0745
Fax: (954) 450-3065
E-mail: rvl@enterprit.com
Web Site: http://www.enterprit.com

Specialties: Dr. Van Leer has been providing technical expertise to industry leaders, fortune 500 companies, manufacturers world-wide and the legal profession on most areas of Information Technology for 38 years. Currently he is prominently situated in the nation's highest-profile Email and SPAM litigations. His company, Enterprit.com Corporation provides the extensive data analysis that makes the difference in winning the case, and defending/prosecuting it. Dr. Van Leer consults routinely on the Internet and intranets to corporate executives and attorneys between speaking engagements around the country. **Degrees/licenses:** Msc, PhD Information Technology.

See primary listing under INTERNET: Email/SPAM

Handwriting/Typewriting

Gary Herbertson

Forensic Document Examiner
2203 McKinley Avenue
Berkeley, CA 94703
Tel: (510) 845-4482
Fax: (510) 845-4673
E-mail: herbertson4n6@earthlink.net

Specialties: Broad range of document examinations including: Identification of writers, typewriters, copy machine, rubber stamps. Determination of forgery, alterations, obliterations. Comparison of paper, ink, cut marks, stains. Fully equipped laboratory. Affiliation: Retired Unit Chief of FBI Laboratory, Fellow of American Academy of Forensic Sciences. **Degrees/licenses:** BA, MS, Forensic Science. Certified by FBI Laboratory.

See primary listing under DOCUMENT EXAMINATION: General

ECONOMICS

General

Anderson Economic Group, LLC

Patrick L. Anderson
Principal
260 East Saginaw Street
East Lansing, MI 48823
Tel: (517) 333-6984
Fax: (517) 333-7058
E-mail: webmaster@AndersonEconomicGroup.com
Web Site: http://www.AndersonEconomicGroup.com

Specialties: Since 1996, Anderson Economic Group has provided economic, finance, market and policy analyses for businesses, state governments, municipalities, and trade associations throughout the U.S. We also provide expert testimony in matters of business valuation, lost profit calculations, economic and fiscal impacts, market area identification, antitrust analysis, and "good cause" grounds in business decisions. Our Economists and CPAs specialize in communicating complex issues. We have extensive knowledge of retail, real estate, franchised distribution (automobile, alcoholic beverage, rental car, and hospitality), telecommunications, and manufacturing industries; and of tax and regulatory policy. **Degrees/licenses:** CVs & publication list available upon request.

The Center for Forensic Economic Studies

Jerome M. Staller, PhD, President
Brian P. Sullivan, PhD, VP
Pia Di Girolamo, PhD, Sr. Economist
Lawrence M. Santucci, MA, Sr. Economist
Donald F. Gurian, CPA, Sr. Business Consultant
1608 Walnut Street, Ste. 801
Philadelphia, PA 19103
Tel: (215) 546-5600
Fax: (215) 732-8158
E-mail: cfes@cfes.com
Web Site: http://www.cfes.com

Specialties: Economic & Statistical Analysis in Personal Injury, Commercial, Employment and Civil Rights matters; Business Valuations. PhD-level economists & full-time support staff. **Degrees/licenses:** Staff members hold PhDs.

Fulcrum Financial Inquiry

David Nolte
Principal
1000 Wilshire Blvd., Ste. 1650
Los Angeles, CA 90017
Tel: (213) 787-4111
(213) 787-4100
Fax: (213) 787-4141
E-mail: dnolte@fulcruminquiry.com
Web Site: http://www.fulcruminquiry.com

Specialties: Our analysis and research combined with unique presentation techniques have resulted in an unequaled track record in successful court cases and client recoveries. Our personnel are full time and fully focused on the services we provide. We thoughtfully incorporate technology into our work to provide great results at a more reasonable cost. Our expertise encompasses damages analysis, lost profit studies, business & intangible asset valuations, fraud investigations, statistics, forensic economic analysis, royalty audits, strategic & market assessments, competitive surveys, analysis of computerized data including computer forensics, and a wide range of other financial advisory services. **Degrees/licenses:** CPA, ASA, CMA, MBA, CFA.

See primary listing under ACCOUNTING: General

Robert A. Sherwin

Managing Principal
Analysis Group, Inc.
601 South Figueroa Street, Suite 1300
Los Angeles, CA 90017
Tel: (213) 896-4500
Fax: (213) 623-4112
E-mail: rsherwin@analysisgroup.com
Web Site: http://www.analysisgroup.com

Specialties: Mr. Sherwin specializes in applied microeconomics and finance. He has performed research and given testimony in antitrust, tax, regulatory, intellectual property infringement, capital adequacy and commercial damage matters. Mr. Sherwin's antitrust experience includes analysis of price fixing, price discrimination, market definition, market power, monopolization and damages. He has written on the subject of market definition and has conducted numerous cost-based predatory pricing studies. **Degrees/licenses:** JD, University of Chicago Law School; AB, Wabash College; CPA.

David Singh, PhD

Economics Expert/Professor
1945 Palo Verde Ave., Ste. 200
Long Beach, CA 90815-3443
Tel: (800) 392-1119
Fax: (562) 799-8821
E-mail: eexperts@msn.com
Web Site: http://www.expertinfo.com

Specialties: Dr. Singh has been retained as an expert witness in over 300 cases. He is also a Professor of Economics at California State University, Long Beach. Dr. Singh's areas of specialty include (but are not limited to): Economic Damages, Loss of Earnings, Lost Profits, Business Interruption, Business Valuation, Wrongful Termination, Personal Injury, Wrongful Death. Excellent references are available upon request. Dr. Singh is a MCLE provider. He is also the author of a number of professional publications, some of which have appeared in nationally renowned journals. **Degrees/licenses:** MA Economics, PhD Economics.

Daryl Winn

Associate Professor
University of Colorado
1475 Moss Rock Place
Boulder, CO 80304
Tel: (303) 449-7276
Fax: (303) 449-1584
E-mail: winn@colorado.edu

Specialties: Economic analysis; Cost analysis. **Degrees/licenses:** PhD.

Agricultural Economics

House Agricultural Consultants

Gregory A. House
Agricultural Consultant
1105 Kennedy Place, Ste. 1
P.O. Box 1615
Davis, CA 95617
Tel: (530) 753-3361
Fax: (530) 753-0464
E-mail: gahouse@houseag.com
Web Site: http://www.houseag.com

Specialties: Twenty-five years experience in agricultural consulting; Accredited farm manager; Accredited rural appraiser; Certified professional agronomist. Specialties: Crop production, Farm business management, Fruit and nut crops, Vegetable crops, Field crops, Crop valuation and loss, Rangeland and pasture management, Soil management and conservation, Irrigation practices, Crop marketing, Agricultural economics. **Degrees/licenses:** BS, Crop Ecology; AFM, ARA, CPAg.

See primary listing under AGRICULTURE: General

Business Interruption/ Lost Profits

Technical Associates, Inc.

Michael J. Ileo, PhD
President/Chief Economist
James Center III, Ste. 601
1051 East Cary St.
Richmond, VA 23219
Tel: (804) 644-4000
(888) 923-3423
Fax: (804) 644-2977
E-mail: Mike.Ileo@tai-econ.com
Web Site: http://www.tai-econ.com

Specialties: Business Interruption/Lost Profits, Economic Losses/Damages, Business Valuation, Bankruptcy, Mergers & Acquisitions, Due Diligence, Antitrust, Insurance Rate Filings, Utility Regulation, Statistics, Telecommunications. Accepted as an expert on these and related matters during a 35-year professional career by state and federal courts, regulatory bodies, and administrative agencies throughout the U.S. and Canada regarding numerous products and services at the manufacturing, wholesale, distribution, and retail trade levels, including motor vehicles, natural resources, utilities, banking, finance, petrochemicals, insurance, transportation, and housing. Taught economics at several colleges and universities in MO, RI and VA. **Degrees/licenses:** BS, MS, PhD.
See primary listing under ECONOMICS: Economic Losses/Damages

Business Valuation

David N. Fuller

Founding Principal
Value Incorporated
5221 N. O'Connor Blvd., Ste. 830
Irving, TX 75039
Tel: (972) 831-7907
Fax: (972) 831-7901
E-mail: dfuller@valueinc.com
Web Site: http://www.valueinc.com

Specialties: Specializing in valuation of businesses, assets and securities, as well as determination of economic loss/damages. Experience includes a broad spectrum of industries and ranges from small companies to Fortune 100. Qualified as an expert in numerous state and courts throughout the country. Earned BA Economics from Austin College and MBA Finance from SMU. Consult in M&A, financial reporting and tax reporting areas in addition to the litigation arena. **Degrees/licenses:** MBA, CFA, ASA.

Lee A. Gould, CPA, CFE, JD

Managing Member
G & P Financial Litigation Advisors, LLC
205 West Wacker Drive, Suite 918
Chicago, IL 60606
Tel: (312) 229-1770
Fax: (312) 229-1725
E-mail: lgould@litcpa.com
Web Site: http://www.litcpa.com

Specialties: Mr. Gould provides business valuation and forensic accounting services to trial lawyers and their clients. He performs business valuations for estate and gift tax, matrimonial dissolution and shareholder dissent and oppression purposes. He performs forensic accounting to assist in locating hidden assets, investigate claims of asset misappropriation or determine the source of funds used to acquire assets. Mr. Gould provides consulting and expert witness testimony to assist trial lawyers with damages measurement and financial analysis. He specializes in lost profit calculations and breach of contract damages. **Degrees/licenses:** CPA, CFE, JD.

Higgins, Marcus & Lovett, Inc.

Mark C. Higgins, ASA
President
800 S. Figueroa St., Ste. 710
Los Angeles, CA 90017
Tel: (213) 617-7775
Fax: (213) 617-8372
E-mail: mhiggins@hmlinc.com
Web Site: http://www.hmlinc.com

Specialties: The firm has over 20 years of litigation support and expert testimony experience in matters involving business valuation, economic damages, intellectual property, loss of business goodwill and lost profits. Areas of practice include business disputes, eminent domain, bankruptcy, tax disputes, and corporate and marital dissolution. **Degrees/licenses:** MBAs, ASAs, CFAs.

See primary listing under APPRAISAL & VALUATION: Business & Corporate

Mayer Hoffman McCann PC

Steve Franklin
Jeff Freeman
11601 Wilshire Blvd, Ste. 2300
Los Angeles, CA 90025
Tel: (310) 268-2000
Fax: (310) 268-2001
E-mail: sfranklin@cbiz.com or
jfreeman@cbiz.com
Web Site: http://www.cbiz.com or
http://www.mhm-pc.com

Specialties: Business and Accounting firm with extensive consulting and expert witness experience in the following areas: Business Litigation; Business Valuation & Appraisal; Financial Reconstruction; Family Limited Partnerships; Marital Dissolutions; Transactional Due Diligence; Business Interruption; Commercial Damage & Lost Profits; Fraud Investigations; Tax Controversies. **Degrees/licenses:** CPA; CFE; ABV.

See primary listing under ACCOUNTING: General

Joseph R. Mulhern, EDD, CRC

Vocational/Economic Expert
MCS Rehabilitation
6130 Elton Ave. #110
Las Vegas, NV 89107
Tel: (702) 216-0330
Fax: (702) 216-0331

Specialties: Loss of capacity to work and earn money. **Degrees/licenses:** EDD, CRC.

See primary listing under VOCATIONAL REHABILITATION: General

Compensation

James F. Carey, CMC

30 Mosswood Road
Burlingame, CA 94010
Tel: (650) 347-3633
Fax: (650) 347-2442
E-mail: jfcarey@aol.com

Specialties: Executive compensation; sales pay; reasonable compensation, lost earnings. Certified Management Consultant. Experienced in Federal and state courts. Author of books and articles on compensation. **Degrees/licenses:** MA, CMC.

Economic Losses/Damages

Advisors/Experts @ MCS Associates

Norman Katz
Managing Partner
18881 Von Karman Ave., Ste. 1175
Irvine, CA 92612-1569
Tel: (949) 263-8700
Fax: (949) 263-0770
E-mail: info@mcsassociates.com
Web Site: http://www.mcsassociates.com

Specialties: Nationally recognized banking, financial services, real estate consulting group; Experienced expert witnesses and consultants include bankers, lenders, insurance managers, brokers, agents, economists, securities brokers, trust fiduciaries, appraisers, accountants. Expertise: Bank operations, check fraud; Lending policies, procedures; Loan administration, foreclosures, bankruptcy; Lender liability; D&O Liability; Insurance (Life, Disability, Property & Casualty, Reinsurance, Surplus) underwriting, claims handling, bad faith; Broker duties, agency management; Title insurance & escrow; R/E brokerage, leasing, property management, appraisal, development, construction defects; Business valuation, lost profits, damages assessment; Forensic accounting; Securities brokerage, trading, investment suitability; Economic & statistical analysis. **Degrees/licenses:** MBA,

(Listing continued on next page)

Economic Losses/Damages
(cont.)

Advisors/Experts @ MCS Associates (cont.) PhD, CPA, CLU, CPCU, CFP, CFA, CREA, MAI, ASA.

See primary listing under FINANCE: Commercial Banking

Anderson Economic Group, LLC

Patrick L. Anderson
Principal
260 East Saginaw Street
East Lansing, MI 48823
Tel: (517) 333-6984
Fax: (517) 333-7058
E-mail: webmaster@AndersonEconomicGroup.com
Web Site: http://www.AndersonEconomicGroup.com

Specialties: Our Economists and CPAs provide expert testimony regarding lost earnings, reductions in business value, and other economic losses that occur from business interruptions, loss of franchises, lost lines of business, breach of contract, statutory impediments, work stoppages, and policy changes. We use state-of-the-art analytical techniques, including geographic analysis of trade areas, proper apportionment of costs and revenue, modeling of alternative cash flow scenarios, and acute industry analyses. Principal Patrick Anderson is the award-winning author of over 90 published articles and the book "Business Economics and Finance". **Degrees/licenses:** CVs & publication list available upon request.

See primary listing under ECONOMICS: General

Donald L. Brenner

President/Founder
The Brenner Group
345 North Canal St., #802
Chicago, IL 60606
Tel: (312) 382-8918
(312) 671-6010
Fax: (312) 382-8959
E-mail: brennergrp@cs.com or dlpb@msn.com
Web Site: http://www.thebrennergroup.org

Specialties: Over 35 years of consulting and management experience, with specialized expertise in litigation support, economic damages, forensic accounting, auditing, fraud investigations, business valuations, crisis management, business consulting and expert witness testimony. Acted as expert witness and provided other litigation support services for a variety of legal proceedings including breach of contract and other business damage claims, wrongful death, commercial matters, construction issues, professional malpractice, fraud, matrimonial, economic damages, and personal injury. **Degrees/licenses:** BS, MBA, CPA, CVA, CFE, CMC.

James F. Carey, CMC

30 Mosswood Road
Burlingame, CA 94010
Tel: (650) 347-3633
Fax: (650) 347-2442
E-mail: jfcarey@aol.com

Specialties: Executive compensation; sales pay; reasonable compensation, lost earnings. Certified Management Consultant. Experienced in Federal and state courts. Author of books and articles on compensation. **Degrees/licenses:** MA, CMC.

See primary listing under ECONOMICS: Compensation

Jonathan E. Cohen

Jonathan E. Cohen,
an Accountancy Corporation
5850 Canoga Ave. Ste 200
Woodland Hills, CA 91367
Tel: (818) 340-9272
Fax: (818) 883-8126
E-mail: jeccpa@pacbell.net

Specialties: CPA with more than 24 years experience in the following areas: Litigation Support and Forensic Accounting Services in Connection with Personal Injury, Business Interruption, Disability, Wrongful Death and Termination Incidents and Income Tax Consequences of Securities Transactions. Expert Witness Testimony/Reports; Pre-trial Preparation; Assistance in Development of Case Strategy; Damage and Lost Profits Calculation; Loss of Earnings Analysis; Discovery and Deposition Assistance; Investigative Accounting; Accounting and Financial Statement Analysis. **Degrees/licenses:** BS Accounting; MBA Corporate Finance; CPA.

Cohen, Miskei & Mowrey, LLP

Scott Mowrey
15303 Ventura Blvd., Suite 1150
Sherman Oaks, CA 91505
Tel: (818) 986-5070
Fax: (818) 986-5034
E-mail: cmm@cmmpas.com

Specialties: Forensic Accountants and Finance Experts with extensive experience in the following areas: Forensic Accounting, Fraud Investigation, Economic Damages, Business Valuation, Family Law, Bankruptcy, Reorganization, Lost Earnings/Profits Analysis. **Degrees/licenses:** CPAs; CFEs; MBAs.

See primary listing under ACCOUNTING: General

The Fontana Group, Inc.

Ernest H. Manuel, Jr., PhD, President
Joseph F. Roesner, Vice President
3509 N. Campbell Ave.
Tucson, AZ 85719
Tel: (520) 325-9800
Fax: (520) 325-9847
E-mail: tfgi@fontanagroup.com
Web Site: http://www.fontanagroup.com

Specialties: Marketing and economic impact studies in automotive retailing; Largest specialist with state and federal litigation experience (since 1973) in terminations, relocations, new dealerships, allocation systems, business valuations and economic damages; All linemakes; US and Canada. Outstanding references. **Degrees/licenses:** PhD, DBA, MBA, CMA.

David N. Fuller

Founding Principal
Value Incorporated
5221 N. O'Connor Blvd., Ste. 830
Irving, TX 75039
Tel: (972) 831-7907
Fax: (972) 831-7901
E-mail: dfuller@valueinc.com
Web Site: http://www.valueinc.com

Specialties: Specializing in valuation of businesses, assets and securities, as well as determination of economic loss/damages. Experience includes a broad spectrum of industries and ranges from small companies to Fortune 100. Qualified as an expert in numerous state and courts throughout the country. Earned BA Economics from Austin College and MBA Finance from SMU. Consult in M&A, financial reporting and tax reporting areas in addition to the litigation arena. **Degrees/licenses:** MBA, CFA, ASA.

See primary listing under ECONOMICS: Business Valuation

Economic Losses/Damages
(cont.)

Lee A. Gould, CPA, CFE, JD

Managing Member
G & P Financial Litigation Advisors, LLC
205 West Wacker Drive, Suite 918
Chicago, IL 60606
Tel: (312) 229-1770
Fax: (312) 229-1725
E-mail: lgould@litcpa.com
Web Site: http://www.litcpa.com

Specialties: Mr. Gould provides business valuation and forensic accounting services to trial lawyers and their clients. He performs business valuations for estate and gift tax, matrimonial dissolution and shareholder dissent and oppression purposes. He performs forensic accounting to assist in locating hidden assets, investigate claims of asset misappropriation or determine the source of funds used to acquire assets. Mr. Gould provides consulting and expert witness testimony to assist trial lawyers with damages measurement and financial analysis. He specializes in lost profit calculations and breach of contract damages. **Degrees/licenses:** CPA, CFE, JD.

See primary listing under ECONOMICS: Business Valuation

Gumbiner, Savett, Finkel, Fingleson & Rose, Inc.

Ronald S. Greene, CPA
Executive Vice President
1723 Cloverfield Blvd.
Santa Monica, CA 90404
Tel: (310) 828-9798
Fax: (310) 829-7853

Specialties: Business, legal, and accounting specialist with extensive consulting and expert witness experience in the following areas: Lost Profit, Damages and Calculations; Fraud Analyses & Audits; Assets & Income Tracing; Litigation Strategy Consulting; Tax Support; Family Law Accounting; Business Valuations; Royalty & Contract Audits; Standard of Care Analyses. **Degrees/licenses:** CPA, MBA, CVA, MBT, JD.

See primary listing under ACCOUNTING: General

Michael G. Kaplan, CPA, CVA, CFFA

Kaplan Abraham Burkert & Company
5950 Canoga Ave., Ste 200
Woodland Hills, CA 91367
Tel: (818) 888-0066
Fax: (818) 888-8860
E-mail: michael@forensicvalue.com
Web Site: http://www.kab-bv.com

Specialties: Accountant with extensive consulting and expert witness experience in the following areas: Business Disputes; Economic Damages; Goodwill; Fraud & Embezzlement; Loss of Earnings & Profits; Business Valuation; Forensic Accounting; Wrongful Termination; Infringement; Legal & Accountants' Malpractice. **Degrees/licenses:** MBA; CPA.

See primary listing under APPRAISAL & VALUATION: Business & Corporate

Litigation Economics, LLC

Stanley P. Stephenson, PhD
One Embarcadero Center, Suite 500
San Francisco, CA 94111
Tel: (415) 835-1212
Fax: (415) 835-1213
E-mail: stan@litigationeconomics.com
Web Site: http://litigationeconomics.com

Specialties: Since 1985, experts at Litigation Economics, LLC have provided economic, accounting, and financial consulting in complex litigation. Credibility before judges, jurors, mediators, and arbitrators is the most essential factor a Litigation Economics expert provides. We develop damage reports for plaintiffs or critique such reports for defense counsel. Specializations include: breach of contract, business interruption, construction, franchise, intellectual property, products liability, and lost earnings capacity. We have provided assistance in more than 150 cases and testified in 25 cases in various legal hearings. Member: National Association of Certified Valuation Analysts; Financial Management Association. **Degrees/licenses:** PhD, MS (Indiana University), BA (Ball State University).

Mayer Hoffman McCann PC

Steve Franklin
Jeff Freeman
11601 Wilshire Blvd, Ste. 2300
Los Angeles, CA 90025
Tel: (310) 268-2000
Fax: (310) 268-2001
E-mail: sfranklin@cbiz.com or
jfreeman@cbiz.com
Web Site: http://www.cbiz.com or
http://www.mhm-pc.com

Specialties: Business and Accounting firm with extensive consulting and expert witness experience in the following areas: Business Litigation; Business Valuation & Appraisal; Financial Reconstruction; Family Limited Partnerships; Marital Dissolutions; Transactional Due Diligence; Business Interruption; Commercial Damage & Lost Profits; Fraud Investigations; Tax Controversies. **Degrees/licenses:** CPA; CFE; ABV.

See primary listing under ACCOUNTING: General

David Singh, PhD

Economics Expert/Professor
1945 Palo Verde Ave., Ste. 200
Long Beach, CA 90815-3443
Tel: (800) 392-1119
Fax: (562) 799-8821
E-mail: eexperts@msn.com
Web Site: http://www.expertinfo.com

Specialties: Dr. Singh has been retained as an expert witness in over 300 cases. He is also a Professor of Economics at California State University, Long Beach. Dr. Singh's areas of specialty include (but are not limited to): Economic Damages, Loss of Earnings, Lost Profits, Business Interruption, Business Valuation, Wrongful Termination, Personal Injury, Wrongful Death. Excellent references are available upon request. Dr. Singh is a MCLE provider. He is also the author of a number of professional publications, some of which have appeared in nationally renowned journals. **Degrees/licenses:** MA Economics, PhD Economics.

See primary listing under ECONOMICS: General

Technical Associates, Inc.

Michael J. Ileo, PhD
President/Chief Economist
James Center III, Ste. 601
1051 East Cary St.
Richmond, VA 23219
Tel: (804) 644-4000
(888) 923-3423
Fax: (804) 644-2977
E-mail: Mike.Ileo@tai-econ.com
Web Site: http://www.tai-econ.com

Specialties: Business Interruption/Lost Profits, Economic Losses/Damages, Business Valuation, Bankruptcy, Mergers & Acquisitions, Due Diligence, Antitrust, Insurance Rate Filings, Utility Regulation, Statistics, Telecommunications. Accepted as an expert on these and related matters during a 35-year professional career by state and federal courts, regulatory bodies, and administrative agencies throughout the U.S. and Canada regarding numerous products and services at the manufacturing, wholesale, distribution, and retail trade levels, including motor vehicles, natural resources, utilities, banking, finance, petrochemicals, insurance, transportation, and housing. Taught economics at several colleges and universities in MO, RI and VA. **Degrees/licenses:** BS, MS, PhD.

Laura Jane Tindall, CPA

President
Laura J. Tindall & Company PA
3780 A Road
Loxahatchee, FL 33470
Tel: (561) 795-1965
Fax: (561) 793-3131
E-mail: ljt@ljtindall.com
Web Site:
http://www.businessdamagevalue.com

Specialties: Breach of contract, Lost Profits, Business Valuation, Lost Wages, Eminent Domain Business Damages. **Degrees/licenses:** Doctorate in Business Admin, CPA/ABV, BVAL, CVA, MCBA.

See primary listing under APPRAISAL & VALUATION: Business & Corporate

EDUCATION/SCHOOLS

General

Education Management Consulting, LLC

Edward F. Dragan, EdD
Owner/Principal Consultant
Diamond Silver Office Complex
24 Arnett Ave., Ste. 102
Lambertville, NJ 08530
Tel: (609) 397-8989
Fax: (609) 397-1999
E-mail: edragan@edmgt.com
Web Site: http://www.edmgt.com

Specialties: Consultation and expert services to lawyers on cases involving schools and education nationally. Standard of care, child custody, special education, security, hiring, etc. Court qualified liability, education, education administration and supervision, special education and special education administration and supervision expert. Certified School Administrator; Certified Management Consultant. 30+ years experience as public, private and state education administrator and adjunct professor. Doctor of Education, Education Administration and Supervision, Rutgers University; Master of Arts, Special Education, The College of New Jersey; Master of Education Law, Franklin Pierce Law Center. **Degrees/licenses:** BA, MA, MEL, EdD, CMC, CPM, ACD.

See primary listing under EDUCATION/SCHOOLS: Standard of Care

Child Custody School Evaluation

William L. Bainbridge, PhD, FACFE

President, CEO
and Distinguished Research Professor
SchoolMatch Institute -
University of Dayton
Blendonview Office Park
5027 Pine Creek Dr.
Westerville, OH 43081-4849
Tel: (614) 890-1573
Fax: (614) 890-3294
E-mail: bainbridge@schoolmatch.com
Web Site: http://www.childcustody.com
or http://www.educationexpert.com

Specialties: Child custody: schools issues, educational quality issues, school comparisons issues, relocation issues, school data issues, adolescent adjustment; Child custody in divorce; relocating children because of divorce. School based accidents. Affiliation: University of Dayton (Distinguished Research Professor). **Degrees/licenses:** PhD; FACFE.

Consulting

Academic Guidance Services (since 1960)

6399 Wilshire Blvd., Suite 515
Los Angeles, CA 90048
Tel: (310) 435-1129
(949) 833-9444
Fax: (213) 483- 4839
E-mail: davidhung8@cs.com
Web Site: http://childtreatment.com
or http://specialedu.net

Specialties: Educational evaluation, IEP analysis, appropriateness of school and home; Family dispute re: school and home placement, family counseling, child rearing practices, behavior management, diagnoses; Treatment of learning disabilities, attention deficit and hyperactivity disorders (ADHD), dyslexia; School selection, intensive tutoring of academic skills, individual school for credits. **Degrees/licenses:** PhD (Psychology); MA (Psychology); BSc.

Safety Consulting

Marc A. Rabinoff

President
Rabinoff Consulting Services, Inc.
7600 W. Coal Mine Ave., Unit "A"
Littleton, CO 80123
Tel: (303) 972-3428
Fax: (303) 972-3428
E-mail: marc62aus@aol.com

Specialties: Personal injuries: gymnastics & trampolines, aquatics, health clubs, playgrounds, weight rooms, athletics, physical education and educational administration; Sports facilities (injuries & risk management); Product liability (sports injuries). Affiliation: Metropolitan State College of Denver (Professor and Chair, Department of Human Performance, Sport & Leisure Studies). **Degrees/licenses:** EdD.

See primary listing under RECREATION: General

Standard of Care

William L. Bainbridge, PhD, FACFE

President, CEO
and Distinguished Research Professor
SchoolMatch Institute -
University of Dayton
Blendonview Office Park
5027 Pine Creek Dr.
Westerville, OH 43081-4849
Tel: (614) 890-1573
Fax: (614) 890-3294
E-mail: bainbridge@schoolmatch.com
Web Site: http://www.childcustody.com or
http://www.educationexpert.com

Specialties: Accidents in schools or on school activities; Child custody in divorce; Relocating children because of divorce; Child custody: schools issues, educational quality issues, school comparisons issues, relocation issues, school data issues, adolescent adjustment. Affiliation: University of Dayton (Distinguished Research Professor). **Degrees/licenses:** PhD; FACFE.

See primary listing under EDUCATION/SCHOOLS: Child Custody School Evaluation

Education Management Consulting, LLC

Edward F. Dragan, EdD
Owner/Principal Consultant
Diamond Silver Office Complex
24 Arnett Ave., Ste. 102
Lambertville, NJ 08530
Tel: (609) 397-8989
Fax: (609) 397-1999
E-mail: edragan@edmgt.com
Web Site: http://www.edmgt.com

Specialties: Consultation and expert services to lawyers on cases involving schools and education nationally. Standard of care, child custody, special education, security, hiring, etc. Court qualified liability, education, education administration and supervision, special education and special education administration and supervision expert. Certified School Administrator; Certified Management Consultant. 30+ years experience as public, private and state education administrator and adjunct professor. Doctor of Education, Education Administration and Supervision, Rutgers University; Master of Arts, Special Education, The College of New Jersey; Master of Education Law, Franklin Pierce Law Center. **Degrees/licenses:** BA, MA, MEL, EdD, CMC, CPM, ACD.

EMPLOYMENT

General

William P. Anthony, PhD, SPHR

Professor of Management
The Carl De Santis Professor
of Business Administration
Florida State University
College of Business
Tallahassee, FL 32306-1110
Tel: (850) 644-7844
Fax: (850) 644-0588
E-mail: banthon@cob.fsu.edu
Web Site:
http://garnet.acns.fsu.edu/~banthon/

Specialties: Consulting, advice and testimony in numerous areas of employment: Discrimination; Wrongful discharge; Sexual harassment; FMLA; ADA; Negligent hire; Negligent retention; Human resource policy, and organization design and strategy. Have published extensively and am involved on the side of both plaintiff and defendants on various cases. Major strength is employment policy development and implementation. **Degrees/licenses:** PhD, MBA, SPHR.

Richard B. Danehy, JD, SPHR

Vice President
Fraser Richards, LLC
7922 Winchester Circle
Goleta, CA 93117-1067
Tel: (805) 968-9606
Fax: (805) 968-9807
E-mail: HRexperts@aol.com

Specialties: Standard of care in Human Resource policies, practices, procedures, ethics, forms, sexual harassment, sex, race, national origin, age, religious, disability discrimination; At Will; Retaliation. Adequacy of Investigations. Fact finding & Discipline. Wrongful Termination. FMLA. Negligent hiring, training, supervision & retention; Ratification. Wage-Hour. 150+ cases - both plaintiff and defense. **Degrees/licenses:** BBA, JD Licensed to practice law in NJ.

ForensisGroup, Inc.

Mercy Steenwyk
3452 E. Foothill Blvd., Ste. 1160
Pasadena, CA 91107
Tel: (626) 795-5000
(800) 555-5422
Fax: (626) 795-1950
E-mail: experts@forensisgroup.com
Web Site: http://forensisgroup.com

Specialties: Thousands of our clients have gained the technical advantage and the edge in their cases from our multidisciplined group of experts in hundreds of disciplines. We have some of the best and the brightest at competitive rates backed by 14 years of excellent track record and the support of our trained staff. We assist you until you have the right expert. Some of our areas of expertise are: Construction, Safety, Engineering, Product Liability, Accident Reconstruction, Automotive, Environmental, Slip & Fall, Appraisal, Medical and other scientific disciplines. Unsurpassed standards. Clients actively evaluate our experts. **Degrees/licenses:** PE, GC, CSP, PhD, MD, GC, CIH, AIA.

See primary listing under ACCIDENT PREVENTION & SAFETY: General

Brian H. Kleiner, PhD, MBA

Professor of Human Resource Management
California State University
800 N. State College Blvd.
Fullerton, CA 92834
Tel: (714) 879-9705
(714) 879-6050
Fax: (714) 879-5600
E-mail: BrianHKleiner@aol.com

Specialties: Sexual harassment, workplace investigations, progressive discipline, wrongful termination, discrimination, ADA, recruiting, improper employment screening, compensation, wages & hours, benefits & retirement plans, ERISA, workers' compensation, workplace violence, labor/management relations, FMLA/CFRA, OSHA, negligent supervision, performance appraisals, promotion selections, training, workplace reductions, and statistical analysis of employment data. Former human resource manager at Ford Motor Company. 100+ business and governmental consulting clients. Trained thousands of managers. Substantial experience giving testimony and preparing deposition questions for defendants and plaintiffs throughout the U.S. 500+ publications. Many honors. Taught first publicly televised graduate "Managing Human Resources" course. **Degrees/licenses:** PhD in Management (UCLA); MBA (UCLA).

Robert "Bob" Norris, Captain

Aviation Consulting Services
P.O. Box 1522
San Carlos, CA 94070
Tel: (650) 508-1079
Fax: (650) 508-9005
E-mail: avconsult@aol.com
Web Site: http://www.avconsult.com

Specialties: Expert Witness for Plaintiff or Defendant; General Aviation Flight and Ground Training Schools; Air Carrier Training Programs for Pilots, Flight Engineers, Aircraft Dispatchers, Flight Attendants, Check Airman and Flight Instructors; Career Advancement Counseling; Captain Interview Board; Crew Resource Management (CRM) Programs; Wrongful Termination; Discrimination. Engineering Psychologist, Hughes Aircraft Company: Space Systems, Flight Simulation, Weapons Development; United Airlines: Flight Manager, Flight & Simulator Instructor, FAA Check Airman; Captain Qualified: DC-8, DC-10, B-737, B-757, B-767; Flight Dispatcher, Owner FAA-141 Flight School and FAA Maintenance Repair Station. Author. **Degrees/licenses:** BS, ATP, FE, CFI, CFII, MEI.

See primary listing under AVIATION: General

ADA

Biddle Consulting Group, Inc.

Daniel Biddle, PhD
President
2868 Prospect Park Dr., Ste. 110
Rancho Cordova, CA 95670
Tel: (916) 266-6722
Fax: (916) 266-4170
E-mail: staff@biddle.com
Web Site: http://www.biddle.com

Specialties: The Biddle Consulting Group, Inc. specializes in disparate impact cases for hiring, layoffs, transfers, or promotions. Other specialties include job relatedness studies (content, criterion, construct validation); Affirmative Action and Equal Employment Opportunity compliance; selection plan development and validation. **Degrees/licenses:** PhD, 30 staff with various degrees.

See primary listing under EMPLOYMENT: Discrimination

Mary Ciddio, MA, CRC, CDMS, ABVE

Vocational Rehabilitation Consultant
Ciddio-Morris Associates, Inc.
1611 Telegraph Ave., #808
Oakland, CA 94612
Tel: (510) 208-7100 Ext. 101
Fax: (510) 208-7107
E-mail: mciddio@ciddiomorris.com
Web Site: http://www.ciddiomorris.com

Specialties: Vocational Expert Witness: Determination of residual/potential earning capacity, testing, evaluation, plan development and job placement. Experienced in testimony on ADA, FEHA, Wrongful Termination, Marriage Dissolution, Personal Injury and Third Party cases. Over 25 years experience as a Vocational Rehabilitation Counselor. Founder and President of Ciddio-Morris Associates. Over 10 years experience in courtroom and deposition testimony. Educator and presenter for professional groups including San Francisco Bar Association, Insurance Education Association and Industrial Claims Association. Experienced with a wide range of disabilities

(Listing continued on next page)

ADA *(cont.)*

Mary Ciddio (cont.)

including brain injury and psychiatric issues. **Degrees/licenses:** MA Vocational Rehab. Counseling, CRC, CDMS, ABVE, MA Sociology.

Alison Heller-Ono, MS, PT, CIE, CDA, CMC

President/CEO
Worksite International
887 Abrego Street
Monterey, CA 93940
Tel: (831) 648-8724
Fax: (831) 648-8330
E-mail: alisonh@worksiteinternational.com
Web Site:
http://www.worksiteinternational.com

Specialties: Ergonomic Worksite Analysis: office, industrial and hospital; participatory ergonomics; consulting on work injury prevention and disability management; Workers' Compensation case management; work performance; facility design with ergonomics; musculoskeletal injury prevention; cumulative trauma disorders; repetitive motion injuries; back injury prevention, ergonomics education, ADA Title I disability issues, Reasonable Accommodation assessments, Workers' Compensation fraud. BS, MS, Licensed Physical Therapist, Certified Industrial Ergonomist, Ergonomics Education Program Specialist, Certified Disability Analyst, Certified Management Consultant. **Degrees/licenses:** BS, MS; See above for licenses & certifications.

See primary listing under ACCIDENT PREVENTION & SAFETY: Ergonomics

Brian H. Kleiner, PhD, MBA

Professor of Human Resource Management
California State University
800 N. State College Blvd.
Fullerton, CA 92834
Tel: (714) 879-9705
(714) 879-6050
Fax: (714) 879-5600
E-mail: BrianHKleiner@aol.com

Specialties: ADA; FEHA; reasonable accommodation; EEOC guidelines; determination of essential and marginal job functions; interactive process; undue hardship, policy development and implementation; FMLA; CFRA. Former human resource manager at Ford Motor Company. Over 100 business and governmental consulting clients. Trained thousands of managers. Substantial experience giving testimony and preparing deposition questions for defendants and plaintiffs throughout the U.S. 500+ publications. Many honors. Taught first publicly televised graduate "Managing Human Resources" course. **Degrees/licenses:** PhD in Management (UCLA); MBA (UCLA).

See primary listing under EMPLOYMENT: General

Benefits & Retirement Plans

Brian H. Kleiner, PhD, MBA

Professor of Human Resource Management
California State University
800 N. State College Blvd.
Fullerton, CA 92834
Tel: (714) 879-9705
(714) 879-6050
Fax: (714) 879-5600
E-mail: BrianHKleiner@aol.com

Specialties: ERISA; operation and termination of pension plans; operation of employee benefit plans; administration and enforcement; fiduciary duties; prohibited transactions; prohibited transactions exemptions; funding benefits through a Voluntary Employee Benefits Association; costing benefits; flexible compensation/benefits plans (cafeteria plans). Former human resource manager at Ford Motor Company. Over 100 business and governmental consulting clients. Trained thousands of managers. Substantial experience giving testimony and preparing deposition questions for defendants and plaintiffs throughout the U.S. 500+ publications. Many honors. Taught first publicly televised graduate "Managing Human Resources" course. **Degrees/licenses:** PhD in Management (UCLA); MBA (UCLA).

See primary listing under EMPLOYMENT: General

Compensation

James F. Carey, CMC

30 Mosswood Road
Burlingame, CA 94010
Tel: (650) 347-3633
Fax: (650) 347-2442
E-mail: jfcarey@aol.com

Specialties: Executive compensation; sales pay; reasonable compensation, lost earnings. Certified Management Consultant. Experienced in Federal and state courts. Author of books and articles on compensation. **Degrees/licenses:** MA, CMC.

See primary listing under ECONOMICS: Compensation

Brian H. Kleiner, PhD, MBA

Professor of Human Resource Management
California State University
800 N. State College Blvd.
Fullerton, CA 92834
Tel: (714) 879-9705
(714) 879-6050
Fax: (714) 879-5600
E-mail: BrianHKleiner@aol.com

Specialties: Jobs and pay in the United States; executive compensation; job analysis, defining job content, job evaluation systems for measuring job differences; the Hay System; surveying market pay and compensation practices; designing a base pay structure; merit pay and performance appraisal; incentives. Former human resource manager at Ford Motor Company. Over 100 business and governmental consulting clients. Trained thousands of managers. Substantial experience giving testimony and preparing deposition questions for defendants and plaintiffs throughout the U.S. 500+ publications. Many honors. Taught first publicly televised graduate "Managing Human Resources" course. **Degrees/licenses:** PhD in Management (UCLA); MBA (UCLA).

See primary listing under EMPLOYMENT: General

Disability Evaluation

Leonard Kalfuss, MD

Bone & Joint Medical Clinic
225 S. Civic Dr., Ste. 1
Palm Springs, CA 92262
Tel: (760) 327-8595
Fax: (760) 327-8597
E-mail: DrLKalfuss@dc.rr.com

Specialties: Forensic Orthopedics - 35 years. AME, IME, QME. Testimony experience: trial, deposition, complex cases for plaintiff/ defense, P.I.-medical record review malpractice. Available throughout California. Prompt response and reports. **Degrees/licenses:** BSc, MD, FICS; Board Certified Orthopedic Surgery, Forensic Medicine.

See primary listing under MEDICINE & HEALTH: Orthopedic Surgery

Stephen Morewitz, PhD & Associates

Tel: (312) 263-9160
(415) 252-0569
(818) 594-1587
E-mail: morewitz@earthlink.net
Web Site:
http://home.earthlink.net/~morewitz

Specialties: Assesses disability, quality of life losses, rehabilitation, sexual harassment policies and procedures, sexual harassment/ assault impact, and profiles of sexual harassment/assault offenders and victims. Also provides medical record and employment record reviews, technical research, and experts in other fields. Over 18 years experience. Professor, former Dean, author of 5 books, including "Chronic Disease and Health Care" (forthcoming, 2005), "Sexual Harassment & Social Change" (1996), and more than 70 other publications. Secured major federal research and training grants. Presented research papers at national and international conferences and reviewer of conference research papers. Management consultant. 2 Outstanding Scholar Book Awards, 2003 and 2004, American Public Health Association, Top Ten Injury Research Poster, "Who's Who in Medicine &

(Listing continued on next page)

Disability Evaluation *(cont.)*

Stephen Morewitz (cont.)
Healthcare," and other honors. Offices in Buffalo Grove, IL, San Francisco & Tarzana, CA. **Degrees/licenses:** PhD, Certified Behavioral Scientist (CPSP).

See primary listing under EMPLOYMENT: Sexual Harassment

Robert J. Shorr, MD

RJS Medical
18455 Burbank Blvd. #105
Tarzana, CA 91356
Tel: (818) 776-9555
Fax: (818) 776-8883
E-mail: Robert.Shorr@att.com

Specialties: Certified (Neurology), American Board of Psychiatry and Neurology: highly experienced in electrodiagnostic testing. Workers Compensation and Personal Injury specialist; California State Qualified Medical Examiner; more than twenty years experience as an Independent Medical Examiner, Defense Medical Evaluator; Court Expert Witness testimony; Plaintiff and Defense, BA, University of California, Berkeley, M.D., University of California, Academy of Neurology, Association of California Neurologist, American Medical Association, California Medical Association, Los Angeles County Medical Association, California Society of Industrial Medicine and Surgery. Locations: Tarzana (San Fernando Valley) and Lancaster (Antelope Valley), California. Several other locations available in Ventura and Santa Barbara counties. **Degrees/licenses:** MD; QME; IME; AME; DME.

See primary listing under MEDICINE & HEALTH: Neurology

Vocational Consulting Group

Charles A. Kincaid,
PhD, CRC, ATP, CVE, CLCP
Vocational Rehabilitation Counselor
11 Dundar Rd., Ste. 101
Springfield, NJ 07081
Tel: (973) 564-9538
Fax: (973) 564-8182
E-mail: vocg@aol.com
Web Site: http://www.vocationalcg.com

Specialties: Determining Worker Employability & Earning Capacity - Vocational Testing, Earning Capacity Studies, Vocational Rehabilitation, Assistive Technology Evaluations, Job Analysis, Workplace Accommodation Services, Expert Witness Testimony in divorce, personal injury, discrimination, wrongful termination, Workers' Compensation including repetitive stress (ergonomic injuries), medical/hospital malpractice cases. Earning Capacity Studies include Transferable Skills Analysis, Labor Market Surveys, Pre-injury Earning Assessments, and Life Care Planning. Extensive experience in vocational rehabilitation - public, non-profit and private sectors. Unique expertise in recommending workplace accommodations and Assistive Technology to aid in returning to work. Certified Life Care Planner. **Degrees/licenses:** PhD Rehab. Counseling; Cert. Rehab. Cnslr; ATP; Cert. Voc. Expert.

See primary listing under EMPLOYMENT: Employability/Earning Capacity

Discrimination

Biddle Consulting Group, Inc.

Daniel Biddle, PhD
President
2868 Prospect Park Dr., Ste. 110
Rancho Cordova, CA 95670
Tel: (916) 266-6722
Fax: (916) 266-4170
E-mail: staff@biddle.com
Web Site: http://www.biddle.com

Specialties: The Biddle Consulting Group, Inc. specializes in disparate impact cases for hiring, layoffs, transfers, or promotions. Other specialties include job relatedness studies (content, criterion, construct validation);

Affirmative Action and Equal Employment Opportunity compliance; selection plan development and validation. **Degrees/licenses:** PhD, 30 staff with various degrees.

JorgensenHR

Karen Jorgensen, MBA
28494 Westinghouse Place, #212
Valencia, CA 91355
Tel: (661) 600-2070
Fax: (661) 600-2040

Specialties: Employment Specialist with extensive consulting and expert witness experience in the following areas: Human Resources; Policies & Procedures; Harassment; Employee Handbooks; Terminations; Training; Equal Employment; Compensation; Investigations. **Degrees/licenses:** MBA, Anderson Graduate School UCLA; PIHRA; SHRM; ACA.

Brian H. Kleiner, PhD, MBA

Professor of Human Resource Management
California State University
800 N. State College Blvd.
Fullerton, CA 92834
Tel: (714) 879-9705
(714) 879-6050
Fax: (714) 879-5600
E-mail: BrianHKleiner@aol.com

Specialties: Discrimination based on age, race, national origin, religion, sexual orientation, disability and sex, including pregnancy and equal pay. Steps to prevent discrimination including policy formulation, training, complaint investigation, and appropriate corrective action. Statistical analysis of employment data for assessing disparate impact. Former human resource manager at Ford Motor Company. Over 100 business and governmental consulting clients. Trained thousands of managers. Substantial experience giving testimony and preparing deposition questions for defendants and plaintiffs throughout the U.S. 500+ publications. Many honors. Taught first publicly televised graduate "Managing Human Resources" course. **Degrees/licenses:** PhD in Management (UCLA); MBA (UCLA).

See primary listing under EMPLOYMENT: General

Amy Oppenheimer, JD

878 Spruce St.
Berkeley, CA 94707
Tel: (510) 393-4212
E-mail: amy@amyopp.com
Web Site: http://www.amyopp.com

Specialties: Expert witness on employment policies and procedures, investigation, corrective action; Neutral investigations and fact finding; Mediation & internal dispute resolution; Case evaluation; Training on preventing workplace harassment & discrimination, investigations and employment discrimination. Testified as expert on sexual harassment policies and procedures in federal & state cases for both plaintiff and defense. Administrative Law Judge, California Unemployment Insurance Appeals Board, 1992-present; Arbitrator and Mediator, American Arbitration Association, 1989-present; Partner, Levy & Oppenheimer, 1984-1992. Co-author of "Investigating Workplace Harassment: How to be Fair, Thorough and Legal" (Shrm, 2002). **Degrees/licenses:** BA, UC Berkeley (1975); JD, UC Davis (1980); State Bar of Calif.

See primary listing under EMPLOYMENT: Sexual Harassment

Employability/ Earning Capacity

Leona H. Liberty, Ed.D., CRC, NCC, CLCP

Director
Capabilities Evaluation Center, Inc.
120 DeFreest Drive
Rensselaer Technology Park
Troy, NY 12180-7608
Tel: (518) 283-7148
Fax: (518) 283-7168
E-mail: T20@msn.com

Specialties: Address the employability and vocational potential, earnings capacity and other needs or losses of individuals who suffered personal injury through work, motor vehicle accidents, developmental or progressive diseases, or other conditions; the result of

(Listing continued on next page)

Employability/ Earning Capacity *(cont.)*

Leona H. Liberty (cont.)
divorce, employment discrimination, or other separation from the workplace. The method to do the aforementioned includes face-to-face or hypothetical Vocational Evaluations, with testing, if permitted, to assess strengths and limitations for gainful or other employment; Labor Market Surveys to assess and determine pre-post employability opportunities and earnings capacity. Life Care Plans are developed that identify projected needs and costs for individuals who suffer catastrophic injuries. **Degrees/licenses:** Doctor of Education, Ed.D., CRC, NCC, CLCP.

Eugene E. Van de Bittner, PhD, CRC

President/Rehabilitation Consultant
Mirfak Associates, Inc.
577 Ygnacio Valley Road
Walnut Creek, CA 94596
Tel: (925) 296-0300
Fax: (925) 296-0301
E-mail: drgene@mirfak.com
Web Site: http://www.mirfak.com

Specialties: Rehabilitation consulting and expert witness services regarding employability, earning capacity, and life care needs and costs. Vocational rehabilitation evaluations, plan development, and monitoring. Return to work services to arrange modified or alternate employment through an interactive process. Evaluating the adequacy of job search efforts. Labor market research and job placement services. Life care planning and management. **Degrees/licenses:** Ph.D., Rehabilitation; M.Ed., Vocational Rehabilitation; CRC, CLCP, ABVE.

Vocational Consulting Group

Charles A. Kincaid,
PhD, CRC, ATP, CVE, CLCP
Vocational Rehabilitation Counselor
11 Dundar Rd., Ste. 101
Springfield, NJ 07081
Tel: (973) 564-9538
Fax: (973) 564-8182
E-mail: vocg@aol.com
Web Site: http://www.vocationalcg.com

Specialties: Determining Worker Employability & Earning Capacity - Vocational Testing, Earning Capacity Studies, Vocational Rehabilitation, Assistive Technology Evaluations, Job Analysis, Workplace Accommodation Services, Expert Witness Testimony in divorce, personal injury, discrimination, wrongful termination, Workers' Compensation including repetitive stress (ergonomic injuries), medical/hospital malpractice cases. Earning Capacity Studies include Transferable Skills Analysis, Labor Market Surveys, Pre-injury Earning Assessments, and Life Care Planning. Extensive experience in vocational rehabilitation - public, non-profit and private sectors. Unique expertise in recommending workplace accommodations and Assistive Technology to aid in returning to work. Certified Life Care Planner. **Degrees/licenses:** PhD Rehab. Counseling; Cert. Rehab. Cnslr; ATP; Cert. Voc. Expert.

Sexual Harassment

Richard B. Danehy, JD, SPHR

Vice President
Fraser Richards, LLC
7922 Winchester Circle
Goleta, CA 93117-1067
Tel: (805) 968-9606
Fax: (805) 968-9807
E-mail: HRexperts@aol.com

Specialties: Standard of care in Human Resource policies, practices, procedures, ethics, forms, sexual harassment, sex, race, national origin, age, religious, disability discrimination; At Will; Retaliation. Adequacy of Investigations. Fact finding & Discipline. Wrongful Termination. FMLA. Negligent hiring, training, supervision & retention; Ratification.

Wage-Hour. 150+ cases - both plaintiff and defense. **Degrees/licenses:** BBA, JD Licensed to practice law in NJ.

See primary listing under EMPLOYMENT: General

Brian H. Kleiner, PhD, MBA

Professor of Human Resource Management
California State University
800 N. State College Blvd.
Fullerton, CA 92834
Tel: (714) 879-9705
(714) 879-6050
Fax: (714) 879-5600
E-mail: BrianHKleiner@aol.com

Specialties: Steps to prevent sexual harassment from occurring in the workplace, including policy formulation, training, and monitoring; how to conduct a sexual harassment investigation and take appropriate corrective action; EEOC guidelines; reasons why victims are reluctant to make complaints. Former human resource manager at Ford Motor Company. Over 100 business and governmental consulting clients. Trained thousands of managers. Substantial experience giving testimony and preparing deposition questions for defendants and plaintiffs throughout the U.S. 500+ publications. Many honors. Taught first publicly televised graduate "Managing Human Resources" course. **Degrees/licenses:** PhD in Management (UCLA); MBA (UCLA).

See primary listing under EMPLOYMENT: General

Stephen Morewitz, PhD & Associates

Tel: (312) 263-9160
(415) 252-0569
(818) 594-1587
E-mail: morewitz@earthlink.net
Web Site:
http://home.earthlink.net/~morewitz

Specialties: Assesses sexual harassment policies and procedures, sexual harassment/assault impact, profiles of sexual harassment/assault offenders and victims, disability, quality of life losses, and rehabilitation. Also provides employment record and medical record reviews, technical research, and experts in other fields. Over 18 years experience. Professor, former Dean, author of 5 books, including "Sexual Harassment & Social Change" (1996), and more than 70 other publications. Secured major federal research and training grants. Presented research papers at national and international conferences and reviewer of conference research papers. Management consultant. 2 Outstanding Scholar Book Awards, 2003 and 2004, American Public Health Association, Top Ten Injury Research Poster, "Who's Who in Medicine & Healthcare," and other honors. Offices in Buffalo Grove, IL, San Francisco & Tarzana, CA. **Degrees/licenses:** PhD, Certified Behavioral Scientist (CPSP).

Amy Oppenheimer, JD

878 Spruce St.
Berkeley, CA 94707
Tel: (510) 393-4212
E-mail: amy@amyopp.com
Web Site: http://www.amyopp.com

Specialties: Expert witness on employment policies and procedures, investigation, corrective action; Neutral investigations and fact finding; Mediation & internal dispute resolution; Case evaluation; Training on preventing workplace harassment & discrimination, investigations and employment discrimination. Testified as expert on sexual harassment policies and procedures in federal & state cases for both plaintiff and defense. Administrative Law Judge, California Unemployment Insurance Appeals Board, 1992-present; Arbitrator and Mediator, American Arbitration Association, 1989-present; Partner, Levy & Oppenheimer, 1984-1992. Co-author of "Investigating Workplace Harassment: How to be Fair, Thorough and Legal" (Shrm, 2002). **Degrees/licenses:** BA, UC Berkeley (1975); JD, UC Davis (1980); State Bar of Calif.

Sexual Harassment *(cont.)*

Martin H. Williams, PhD

Clinical & Forensic Psychologist
P.O. Box 62439
Sunnyvale, CA 94088
Tel: (888) 225-9957
Fax: (888) 225-9957
E-mail: mw@drmwilliams.com
Web Site: http://drmwilliams.com

Specialties: Dr. Williams is a psychologist and psychotherapist who testifies on malpractice and emotional damages. He is an expert on sexual harassment, boundary violations, therapist patient sex, malingering, post traumatic stress disorder and borderline personality disorder. He has published in refereed journals on harmfulness of therapist-patient sexual involvement, ethics, risk management and malpractice. He is in full-time clinical practice, is licensed in California and testifies nationally. Offices in Los Angeles, San Jose, Orange County and San Diego. **Degrees/ licenses:** PhD in Psychology (1975); Calif. Licensed Psychologist (1976).

See primary listing under MEDICINE & HEALTH: Psychology

Vocational Rehabilitation

Mary Ciddio, MA, CRC, CDMS, ABVE

Vocational Rehabilitation Consultant
Ciddio-Morris Associates, Inc.
1611 Telegraph Ave., #808
Oakland, CA 94612
Tel: (510) 208-7100 Ext. 101
Fax: (510) 208-7107
E-mail: mciddio@ciddiomorris.com
Web Site: http://www.ciddiomorris.com

Specialties: Vocational Expert Witness: Determination of residual/potential earning capacity, testing, evaluation, plan development and job placement. Experienced in testimony on ADA, FEHA, Wrongful Termination, Marriage Dissolution, Personal Injury and Third Party cases. Over 25 years experience as a Vocational Rehabilitation Counselor. Founder and President of Ciddio-Morris Associates. Over 10 years experience in courtroom and deposition testimony. Educator and presenter for professional groups including San Francisco Bar Association, Insurance Education Association and Industrial Claims Association. Experienced with a wide range of disabilities including brain injury and psychiatric issues. **Degrees/licenses:** MA Vocational Rehab. Counseling, CRC, CDMS, ABVE, MA Sociology.

See primary listing under EMPLOYMENT: ADA

Howard Goldfarb, MA, CRC

Vocational Rehabilitation Consultant
Goldfarb and Associates
1101 Fremont Avenue, Suite 103
South Pasadena, CA 91030
Tel: (626) 441-9687
Fax: (626) 799-8736
E-mail: goldfarbassociates@yahoo.com

Specialties: Twenty years of experience providing expert witness testimony as a vocational rehabilitation and employability consultant. Involved with personal injury, third party litigation and marriage dissolution matters. Evaluate long-term disability and ERISA cases. Testify as a Vocational Expert for the Social Security Administration. Certified to provide counseling services to injured workers through the U. S. Department of Labor, Office of Workers Compensation programs. Independent Vocational Evaluator. Instructor at the California State University, Los Angeles. Administer and interpret vocational testing. **Degrees/licenses:** MA, New York University; Certified Rehabilitation Counselor.

Richard K. Smith, PhD
Clinical Director
Back in the Saddle
Long-term Residential Services
for Head Injured Adults
9775 Mockingbird Ave.
Apple Valley, CA 92308
Tel: (760) 240-3217 & (909) 980-3567
Fax: (760) 240-3274 & (909) 989-3932
E-mail: staff@thesaddle.com
Web Site: http://www.thesaddle.com

Specialties: Head injury, CVA, spinal and other catastrophic pictures. Vocational and transitional design for adult head injured at Rancho Los Amigos Med. Center. Co-director, Back in the Saddle, long-term community residential setting for brain damaged adults. Private practice: domestic violence, vocational rehabilitation and community re-entry. PhD (USIU, 1991); MS Rehabilitation Counseling, Calif. State Univ., Los Angeles (1974). Formerly: So. Calif. Head Injury Foundation Board of Directors; San Bernardino County Dept. of Mental Health Commission. Currently, member San Bernardino County Domestic Violence Consortium; National Brain Injury Foundation; American and Calif. Psychological Assoc. **Degrees/licenses:** PhD, Licensed Clinical Psych., Certified Rehab. Counselor (CRC).

Wages & Hours

Brian H. Kleiner, PhD, MBA
Professor of Human Resource Management
California State University
800 N. State College Blvd.
Fullerton, CA 92834
Tel: (714) 879-9705
(714) 879-6050
Fax: (714) 879-5600
E-mail: BrianHKleiner@aol.com

Specialties: Coverage; employment relationship; maximum hours; employment of minors; minimum wages; hours worked; overtime compensation; flexible scheduling arrangements; exemptions; state and local government employers; payment of wages; records and posting requirements; enforcement. Former human resource manager at Ford Motor Company. Over 100 business and governmental consulting clients. Trained thousands of managers. Substantial experience giving testimony and preparing deposition questions for defendants and plaintiffs throughout the U.S. 500+ publications. Many honors. Taught first publicly televised graduate "Managing Human Resources" course. **Degrees/licenses:** PhD in Management (UCLA); MBA (UCLA).

See primary listing under EMPLOYMENT: General

Workers' Compensation

Peter N. Rogers, JD
Senior Partner
Rogers, Booker & Trevino, PC
901 Waterfall Way, #105
Richardson, TX 75080
Tel: (972) 644-1111
Fax: (972) 644-7600
E-mail: Peter@workerscomppubs.com
Web Site:
http://www.workerscomppubs.com

Specialties: Workers' compensation in Texas. Mr. Rogers is a retired Air Force Colonel who served 23 years as a judge advocate. After retiring from the Air Force in 1991, Mr. Rogers became an Administrative Law Judge in workers' compensation courts in Dallas, Texas. After entering private practice in 1995, Mr. Rogers built a successful workers' compensation law firm. He is a published author of workers' compensation handbooks, has developed and lectured in over 50 continuing legal education courses on workers' compensation topics, and has provided expert opinions and/or deposition testimony in over 30 cases involving workers' compensation in Texas. **Degrees/licenses:** BA, JD, Board Certified - Workers' Compensation - TBLS.

Workplace Violence

Brian H. Kleiner, PhD, MBA
Professor of Human Resource Management
California State University
800 N. State College Blvd.
Fullerton, CA 92834
Tel: (714) 879-9705
(714) 879-6050
Fax: (714) 879-5600
E-mail: BrianHKleiner@aol.com

Specialties: Recognizing signs of imminent violence; employer responsibilities and liability for acts of employees; OSHA guidelines; violence prevention policies and programs versus employee privacy rights; implementing preventive procedures and strategies; special issues for healthcare workers; statutory prohibition against hate; restraining orders and injunctive relief. Former human resource manager at Ford Motor Company. Over 100 business and governmental consulting clients. Trained thousands of managers. Substantial experience giving testimony and preparing deposition questions for defendants and plaintiffs throughout the U.S. 500+ publications. Many honors. Taught first publicly televised graduate "Managing Human Resources" course. **Degrees/licenses:** PhD in Management (UCLA); MBA (UCLA).

See primary listing under EMPLOYMENT: General

Wrongful Termination

Martin Blinder, MD
Assistant Clinical Professor, Psychiatry
50 Idalia Road
San Anselmo, CA 94960
Tel: (415) 453-8920

Specialties: Extensive experience with nationwide court appearances in the following areas: Criminal responsibility; Eye witness identification; Head injuries; Malingering; Psychiatric malpractice; Sexual harassment/molestation; Testamentary capacity and undue influence; Wrongful termination. Professional Experience: (Adjunct) Assistant Professor of Law, Hastings; Supervising Psychiatist, Inpatient Psychiatric Service, UC Hospital; Psychiatric Consultant; FAA, U. S. Department of Justice, USPHS, U. S. Postal Service, Government of New Zealand; Qualified Medical Examiner, CA Department of Industrial Relations. Fellow, APA. Professional Societies: AMA, CMA, NCPS. More than 100 publications, including 6 books. **Degrees/licenses:** BA, Cornell University; MD, Chicago Medical School; Lic. (CA, GA, HI, KY).

See primary listing under IDENTIFICATION: Eyewitness

Don A. Brigham
President
Aviation Forensics, LLC
3423 Seabreeze Lane
Corona Del Mar, CA 92625
Tel: (949) 720-8126
Fax: (786) 549-0751
E-mail: opg333@cox.net

Specialties: Forensic evaluation and expert testimony relating to commercial flight crew training, aviation ground school and line operation of commercial aircraft; flight simulator training; accident and incident evaluation all relating to wrongful termination of professional aviator. Former U.S. Marine Naval Aviator; Captain and FAA proficiency check pilot designee for both Western Airlines and Delta Air Lines; facilitator for Delta Air Lines Cockpit Resource Management (CRM) to over 10,000 pilots. Expert in assembling, certifying, testifying to training, commercial flight record performance before formal and informal judicial boards of inquiry and review. **Degrees/licenses:** Airline Transport Pilot; Multi-Single Engine Land; Flight Engr.,Turbojet.

See primary listing under AVIATION: Wrongful Termination

Richard B. Danehy, JD, SPHR

Vice President
Fraser Richards, LLC
7922 Winchester Circle
Goleta, CA 93117-1067
Tel: (805) 968-9606
Fax: (805) 968-9807
E-mail: HRexperts@aol.com

Specialties: Standard of care in Human Resource policies, practices, procedures, ethics, forms, sexual harassment, sex, race, national origin, age, religious, disability discrimination; At Will; Retaliation. Adequacy of Investigations. Fact finding & Discipline. Wrongful Termination. FMLA. Negligent hiring, training, supervision & retention; Ratification. Wage-Hour. 150+ cases - both plaintiff and defense. **Degrees/licenses:** BBA, JD Licensed to practice law in NJ.

See primary listing under EMPLOYMENT: General

JorgensenHR

Karen Jorgensen, MBA
28494 Westinghouse Place, #212
Valencia, CA 91355
Tel: (661) 600-2070
Fax: (661) 600-2040

Specialties: Employment Specialist with extensive consulting and expert witness experience in the following areas: Human Resources; Policies & Procedures; Harassment; Employee Handbooks; Terminations; Training; Equal Employment; compensation; Investigations. **Degrees/licenses:** MBA, Anderson Graduate School UCLA; PIHRA; SHRM; ACA.

See primary listing under EMPLOYMENT: Discrimination

Brian H. Kleiner, PhD, MBA

Professor of Human Resource Management
California State University
800 N. State College Blvd.
Fullerton, CA 92834
Tel: (714) 879-9705
(714) 879-6050
Fax: (714) 879-5600
E-mail: BrianHKleiner@aol.com

Specialties: Employment-at-will; evaluating and administering disciplinary action; progressive discipline; practical guidelines for avoiding unfair dismissed claims; post termination actions and procedures; performance evaluation and appraisal systems; layoffs and staff reductions. Former human resource manager at Ford Motor Company. Over 100 business and governmental consulting clients. Trained thousands of managers. Substantial experience giving testimony and preparing deposition questions for defendants and plaintiffs throughout the U.S. 500+ publications. Many honors. Taught first publicly televised graduate "Managing Human Resources" course. **Degrees/licenses:** PhD in Management (UCLA); MBA (UCLA).

See primary listing under EMPLOYMENT: General

ENGINEERING

General

The Chatham Group

Jerry A. Klein
President
101 First Street, Ste. 477
Los Altos, CA 94022
Tel: (650) 948-1243
Fax: (650) 949-0534
E-mail: jaklein@chathamlaw.com
Web Site: http://www.chathamlaw.com

Specialties: Silicon Valley based consulting organization specializing in litigation support services for intellectual property litigation matters in state, federal and international proceedings. Our group consists of senior

(Listing continued on next page)

General *(cont.)*

The Chatham Group (cont.)
scientists, engineers, managers and experts in the fields of: Electronics, Semiconductors, Computer Hardware and Software, Telecommunications, Office Automation, Communications, Medical Electronics, Biotechnology, Materials, Manufacturing Processes, Industry Custom and Practice, Marketing. Expert witnesses, technical consulting, tutorials, discovery assistance, trial aids, market studies, patent portfolio strategy, damage determinations, investment banking and venture capital due diligence, witness location, prior art search and evaluation for domestic and international matters. **Degrees/licenses:** BSME, Patent Agent, PhDs in Computer Science, etc.

See primary listing under INTELLECTUAL PROPERTY: Patent Infringement

Chemical Accident Reconstruction Services, Inc.

Michael Fox, PhD
Founder
9121 E. Tanque Verde Rd., #105
Tucson, AZ 85749-8391
Tel: (800) 645-3369
Fax: (520) 749-0861
E-mail: services@chemaxx.com
Web Site: http://www.chemaxx.com

Specialties: Complex industrial chemical accidents, fires and explosions as well as chemical-related consumer product injuries. The founder of the company has his PhD in Physical Chemistry, is a Certified Fire & Explosion Investigator and Certified or Accredited in Hazardous Chemicals, OSHA Process Hazard Analysis Team Leader, DOT Hazardous Materials, Corrosion, Metallurgy, Failure Analysis and Aerosols. Other specialties include: Propane, plastics, water chemistry, skin burns, acids, alkalis, carbon monoxide, flammable liquids, gasoline, scanning microscopy, MSDSs, natural gas, solvents, warning labels, PEX, welding, construction, chemical packaging & transport. For more specialties see web site. **Degrees/licenses:** PhD, Physical Chemistry; See certifications above.

See primary listing under CHEMISTRY/ CHEMICALS: General

ForensisGroup, Inc.

Mercy Steenwyk
3452 E. Foothill Blvd., Ste. 1160
Pasadena, CA 91107
Tel: (626) 795-5000
(800) 555-5422
Fax: (626) 795-1950
E-mail: experts@forensisgroup.com
Web Site: http://forensisgroup.com

Specialties: Thousands of our clients have gained the technical advantage and the edge in their cases from our multidisciplined group of experts in hundreds of disciplines. We have some of the best and the brightest at competitive rates backed by 14 years of excellent track record and the support of our trained staff. We assist you until you have the right expert. Some of our areas of expertise are: Construction, Safety, Engineering, Product Liability, Accident Reconstruction, Automotive, Environmental, Slip & Fall, Appraisal, Medical and other scientific disciplines. Unsurpassed standards. Clients actively evaluate our experts. **Degrees/licenses:** PE, GC, CSP, PhD, MD, GC, CIH, AIA.
See primary listing under ACCIDENT PREVENTION & SAFETY: General

Edward L. Guess, PE

Principal
Alpha Design & Engineering
2707 N. Xenophon Ave.
Tulsa, OK 74127
Tel: (918) 695-0618
Fax: (918) 582-9553
E-mail: eguess@galstar.com
Web Site:
http://www.guessengineering.com

Specialties: Heating, Ventilation, Air Conditioning (HVAC), Failure analysis, Pressure vessels, pumps and pumping systems, construction, lighting/Illumination, pipelines, petroleum, noise, vibration, boat and system design, valves, fire protection, electrical systems-worked in the Power, Oil and Architectural/Engineering Industries. Services to Legal Profession include information for legal briefs investigations, research, depositions, court appearances, arbitration. **Degrees/licenses:** BSME, MSME, PE.

InterCity Testing & Consulting

167 Willis Avenue
Mineola, NY 11501
Tel: (516) 747-8400 (NY)
(800) 822-1515 (Outside NYS)
Fax: (516) 746-0121/0111 (NY)
Tel: (561) 745-7940 (FL)
Fax: (561) 745-7939 (FL)
E-mail: expt1@aol.com
Web Site: http://www.InterCityTesting.com

3550 Watt Ave., Ste. 5
Sacramento, CA 95821
Tel: (916) 481-3093
(800) 500-5561 (Toll Free)
Fax: (916) 481-3095

Specialties: Visit our web site for condensed expert CV's in: Amusement Parks & Rides; Automotive Safety & Accident Reconstruction; Biomedical/Biomechanical Injury Analysis; Biomechanics; Boating & Marine Safety; Chemicals & Chemical Engineering; Civil Engineering/Structural Failures; Construction Accidents; Electrical & Mechanical Engineering; Firearms & Explosives; Fire Investigations; Flammable Fabrics; Helmets/ Motorcycle, Bicycle, Sports & Industrial; Machine Guarding; Medical Devices; Medical Emergency/EMT; Metallurgy & Material Sciences; Parks & Playgrounds; Slips, Trips & Falls; Sports/Recreation/Aquatics; Toxicology; Transportation & Highway Safety; Warnings & Instructions. INTERCITY IS NOT AN EXPERT REFERRAL SERVICE. **Degrees/licenses:** PE's / degrees thru PhD's in above specialties.

See primary listing under ACCIDENT RECONSTRUCTION: General

IPEC

Institute for Products, Engineering & Construction
A Consortium of Engineers, Construction & Safety Professionals
34522 N. Scottsdale Rd., Ste. D-8 #160
Scottsdale, AZ 85262
Tel: (888) 212-1155
Fax: (888) 414-1155
E-mail: ipec@forensicengineers.com
Web Site: http://www.forensicengineers.com

666 Fifth Ave., #122
New York, NY 10103
Tel: (212) 315-9523

1429 G St. NW, #415
Washington, DC 20005
Tel: (202) 822-9660

231 North Ave. West, #134
Westfield, NJ 07090
Tel: (908) 233-2973

1920 Abrams Pkwy., #95
Dallas, TX 75214
Tel: (214) 827-9892

Specialties: Product Liability; Product Defect; Machine Design; Warnings & Labels; Guarding; Safety; Saws; Ladders; Natural Gas; HVAC; Lighting; Heavy Equipment; Construction Equipment; Welding; Utility Company Practices; Pipe Failure; Plumbing; Plastics; Underground Tanks; Water Treatment; Sewage Systems; Electrical Overhead Lines & Electric Power Distribution; Telephone Poles; Electrocution; Shock; Transformers; Power Tools; Industrial Machines; Conveyors; Telecommunications; Portable Heaters; Pumps; Boilers; Aeronautical; Helicoptors; Shipbuilding; Metal Fatigue; Corrosion; Valves; Engineering-Mechanical, Electrical, Civil, Structural, Chemical, Architectural, Environmental, Construction, Automotive, Safety, Geotechnical, Industrial, Metallurgical; OSHA; Codes & Standards; Fire Protection Systems. Contact: Ned Howell. **Degrees/licenses:** Engineers: Auto, Constr, Mech, Elec, Struct, Civil, Chem, Safety, Arch, Aero.
See primary listing under CONSTRUCTION: General

General *(cont.)*

Wilbur R. Meredith, III

Owner
Meredith Enterprises
16040 Wake Robin Drive
Newbury, OH 44065-9160
Tel: (440) 564-7173
(440) 564-7174
(440) 567-1330 (Cellular)
Fax: (440) 564-7175
E-mail: v7cat@aol.com
Web Site: http://meredithenterprises.com

Specialties: Specializing in Automotive, Heavy Trucks, School Buses, Commercial Buses, Trailers, and Marine (Small Boats under 100-feet). Mechanical Engineer, National Association of Professional Accident Reconstruction Specialist (1992). Society of Automotive Engineers, American Institute of Industrial Engineers, Society of Manufacturing Engineers, Society of Naval Architects and Marine Engineers, American Boat and Yacht Council, Powerboat Manufacturer-U.S.C.G. certified, U.S. Patents on boat hull design, Industrial Machinery and Shop Equipment secondary specialty. In business since 1987. Utilize computer simulations for dynamics of automotive accidents. Free case review. Retainage or hourly billing available. **Degrees/licenses:** BSME (1959), Case Institute of Technology.

See primary listing under ACCIDENT RECONSTRUCTION: General

John J. Oransky, PE, CIH, CSP, DEE, DABFET

Founder
Oransky Engineering & Consulting
374 West Ridge Street
Lansford, PA 18232
Tel: (570) 645-3582
Fax: (570) 645-4533

Specialties: Significant experience in hazardous and solid waste management, hazardous materials control, engineering studies and evaluations, industrial ventilation, safety and environmental audits, storage tank inspection, evaluation and certification, process development, design and optimization, air pollution system evaluation and design, wastewater system characterization and design, permit application assistance, technical training, environmental and safety program development and upgrade, waste minimization engineering, process modification assistance, industrial hygiene, material reuse and chemical substitution studies. Member of the American College of Forensic Examiners. **Degrees/licenses:** BSCHE, MSCHE, PE, CIH, CSP, DEE, DABFET.

See primary listing under ENVIRONMENTAL: General

Pro/Consul Technical and Medical Experts

1945 Palo Verde Ave., Suite 200
Long Beach, CA 90815-3443
Tel: (800) 392-1119
(562) 799-0116
Fax: (562) 799-8821
E-mail: eexperts@msn.com
Web Site: http://www.expertinfo.com

Specialties: RIGHT EXPERT RIGHT AWAY!® 15,000 experts in 7,000 fields. Listed and recommended by the A. M. Best Company. Full-time research staff. We welcome your RUSH cases! TECHNICAL: Fast inspections. Categories from Accident Reconstruction to Zoology, also including appraisal, economics, employment, human factors, insurance, premises liability, security, and many more. MEDICAL: IME's. Inexpensive insurance medical records reviews by MDs. Categories from Addiction Medicine to Zooplasty, including board certified physicians in all fields, dentistry, geriatrics, neuropsychology, neurosurgery, nursing, orthopedics, psychiatry and many more. Reasonable fees. Free initial consultation. Free resume binder. Free CLE classes. **Degrees/licenses:** MD, PhD, DDS, DVM, DO, DPM, PE, CPA, ME, CE, CRC, MAI, et al.

See primary listing under ACCIDENT RECONSTRUCTION: General

Rimkus Consulting Group, Inc.

Curtis R. Brown
Senior Vice President
8 Greenway Plaza, Ste. 500
Houston, TX 77046
Tel: (713) 621-3550
(800) 580-3228
Fax: (713) 623-4357
E-mail: expert@rimkus.com
Web Site: http://www.rimkus.com

Specialties: Rimkus Consulting Group, Inc., established in 1983, is a worldwide provider of independent, professional consulting services to insurance companies, law firms, corporations and government agencies. Rimkus assists clients in the responsive and timely resolution of claims and disputes. Our team of educated and experienced engineers, scientists, accountants, and technical specialists, is recognized for excellence in service by local, national, and international business communities. Primary areas of expertise include industrial, vehicular and worker accident investigation and reconstruction; failure analysis; product liability; industrial, commercial and residential environmental analysis; and forensic accounting.

Schutz Engineering Corp.

Peter K. Schutz, PE
President
45 River Road
Summit, NJ 07901
Tel: (908) 638-3300
Fax: (908) 277-6256
E-mail: SchutzE@compuserve.com

Specialties: Mechanical engineering design, analysis, testing; new product development; electro-mechanical equipment; special machinery; medical, office, and laboratory equipment, instrumentation, and devices; electronics; electronics packaging and enclosure design; electro-magnetics; fluid systems (incl. gas and air) and components; analysis and modeling of dynamic systems, computer modeling of fluid flows (CFD) and temperature distributions; heat transfer analysis; mechanical systems and components, plastic and metal parts; testing, measurements, drawings. Member of ASME, IEEE; Former Adjunct Instructor: CCM and Stevens Inst. of Technology; 2 patents; Expert Witness: patent infringement, copied products, machinery, product safety analysis. **Degrees/licenses:** BSME, MSME, PE, Grad. Dale Carnegie Course (Pub. Speaking & Human Relations).

See primary listing under ENGINEERING: Design

Technology Associates

Dr. I.U. Ojalvo
President
137 E. 36th St., Ste. 7K
New York, NY 10016
Tel: (800) 358-9909
Fax: (888) 358-9901
E-mail: iuo@Technology-Assoc.com
Web Site:
http://www.Technology-Assoc.com

1011 High Ridge Rd., 2nd Floor
Stamford, CT 06905
Tel: (203) 329-9909

5030 Champion Blvd., PMB 315
Boca Raton, FL 33496
Tel: (800) 358-9909

Specialties: Vehicles; Roadways; Pedestrians; Machinery; Fall downs; Structures; Construction; Ladders; Shopping Carts; Warnings; Human factors; Biomechanics; Sports & Playgrounds; Swimming pools; Codes & standards; Computer animation; Electric shock; etc. (over 1,400 cases); Testing; Consulting and testimony for defendants & plaintiffs in metropolitan NY area, New England, Florida & surrounding areas; Professors and licensed Professionals in Mechanical, Biomechanical and Electrical Engineering with many publications; Additional specialties in fires, floods, whiplash and other forms of soft tissue and skeletal injuries; Clients include most major insurance companies, municipalities and numerous private law firms (See listings under Accident Reconstruction & Product Liability). **Degrees/licenses:** BS, MS, PhD, Lic. PE, Fellow ASME, US Fulbright.

See primary listing under ACCIDENT RECONSTRUCTION: General
See display advertisement on page 18

General *(cont.)*

James O. Yule, BSME, PE

Co-owner
Yule Engineering, Translating, & Interpreting
6600 NW Sweetbriar Ln.
Kansas City, MO 64151-2354
Tel: (816) 741-9441
Fax: (816) 741-9482
E-mail: Only for certain clients

Specialties: TYPICAL COMMERCIAL/ INDUSTRIAL/FARM CASES: Sidewalk tripping, street lighting; Concrete fell on man; Car fell on man; Gas explosion; Conveyor fault; House fire; Confined space; Car lift; Car ramp; Stepladder twist; Deflesher caught arm; Farm combine ladder; Defective curb; Defective steps; Ammonia/eyes; Bakery auger/arm; Freight-elevator doors/hand; Rotating shaft/arm; Boat-mast electrocution; Ammonia/ face; Extension ladder slip; Blowmolder/hand; Tile stair slip; Folding-ladder collapse; Cooling-tower ladder; Crane-cable electrocution; Sidewalk lighting; Wheelchair ramp; Jack failure; Center-pivot irrigator; Garage-door crush; Wet floor; Farm auger shock; Substation shock; Skyhook fall; Curb trip; Mower threw missile; Dumpster lid/child neck; Motel stair; RR pit steps. DEGREES/LICENSES: BSME; Post-graduate work equivalent to a second degree; PE registration by examination in Mechanical and Civil Engineering. **Degrees/licenses:** See above.

See primary listing under ACCIDENT RECONSTRUCTION: General

Acoustical

Jack E. Randorff, PhD, PE, FASA

Principal-in-Charge
Randorff and Associates, Inc.
11 West Canyon View Drive
Ransom Canyon, TX 79366
Tel: (806) 829-2521
Fax: (806) 829-2527

Specialties: Environmental noise assessments; sound level survey; train horn loudness assessments; employee hearing damage-risk assessments; vibration assessments; highway noise assessment; aircraft/airport noise assessment; architectural sound isolation assessments; industrial noise assessments; testimony - plaintiffs & defendants; clients - major companies, federal agencies, state agencies, local municipalities, private industry, schools, universities, national architectural/engineering firms; National Council of Acoustical Consultants, President (1992-1994), Vice President - membership (1998-2002), Vice President - finance (2002-2004); Fellow - Acoustical Society of America, American Institute of Physics; President - Engineers Council of Houston (1985-1986), Science Engineering Fair of Houston (1986-1988). **Degrees/ licenses:** BS, MS, PhD, PE (Texas).

See primary listing under ACOUSTICS: General

Airports

Helmer Engineering, Inc.

Ray G. Helmer, PE
9314 Bankside
Houston, TX 77031
Tel: (713) 777-7611
Fax: (713) 774-6881
E-mail: HelmerEng@Houston.RR.com
Web Site:
http://www.helmer-engineering.com

Specialties: Civil engineering; FAA standards; Airport pavement, lighting, signing; Highway geometry, intersections, street engineering, grading, earthwork; Sight distance; Transportation/traffic engineering; Traffic accidents; Traffic signals, signs; Pavement marking, highway lighting; Train, automobile, bicycle, pedestrian accidents; Traffic accident expert testimony involving city, county, state DOTs; Construction accidents; Hydraulics, hydrology; Drainage, flooding, stormwater management; Sanitary engineering; Sewer lines, pump stations, wastewater treatment plants; Sewer overflows; Water lines, pump stations, water treatment plants, Water Disinfection Byproducts (DBPs); plumbing; Firewater pressure, volume, adequacy; Tornado, hurricane, earthquake damage; Structures; Foundation failure, structural damage, water intrusion; Engineered product liability/defects; Soil expansion, contraction, settlement. **Degrees/licenses:** BS (Civil Engineering); Registered Professional Engineer.

See primary listing under ENGINEERING: Water Resources

Architectural

Thornton-Tomasetti Group, Inc.

LZA Technology Division
Emmanuel E. Velivasakis, PE
President
641 Avenue of the Americas
New York, NY 10011-2014
Tel: (917) 661-7800
Fax: (917) 661-7801
E-mail: Expert@LZATechnology.com
Web Site: http://www.TheTTGroup.com

Specialties: LZA Technology Division of Thornton-Tomasetti Group, has extensive experience in assisting attorneys and insurance companies in the evaluation of claims, and providing expert witness reports and testimony based on our analyses and forensic investigations. Our expertise includes IAQ and mold; structural failures, including safety and damage assessment surveys; dynamic testing and analysis; reliability; failure and risk analysis; fire materials testing; and evaluation of damage caused by both man-made and natural causes. Offices in NY, NJ, CT, MA, PA, DC, FL, IL, TX, MO, and CA. **Degrees/licenses:** PE, RA, CIH, PhD, RS.

Automotive

Automotive Engineering Consultants, Inc.

Donald B.H. Jeffers, PE
Principal Consultant
P.O. Box 7391
Ann Arbor, MI 48107-7391
Tel: (734) 994-0494
(800) 924-0494
Fax: (734) 994-0494
E-mail:
donjeffers@automotive-engineers.com
Web Site:
http://www.automotive-engineers.com

Specialties: A small group of highly competent engineers and technicians, we conduct forensic engineering studies of automobiles and trucks. Services include: Vehicle Accident Investigation and Reconstruction; Computerized Accident Analysis; Expert Witness Services; Vehicle Systems Failure Analysis: Brakes, Wheels, Tires, Steering, Engines, Transmissions, Electrical, Fuel, Crashworthiness. Our Ann Arbor, Michigan, location puts us in the center of some of the foremost automotive test facilities and research libraries in the world. Our automotive engineering basis is in prototype research, design and construction. Founded 1975. See our listings under Accident Reconstruction and Failure Analysis. **Degrees/licenses:** University of Michigan BSE(ME), MSE(ME), PE.

John C. Glennon, Chartered

6917 W. 76th Street
Overland Park, KS 66204
Tel: (913) 383-3856
Fax: (913) 383-2277
E-mail: experts@johncglennon.com
Web Site: http://www.johncglennon.com

Specialties: Motor Vehicle Accident Investigation; Accident Reconstruction; Vehicle Crush Analysis; Vehicular Mechanical and Structural Failure Analysis for Automobiles, Trucks, and Motorcycles; Testing Capabilities for Air Brakes, Hydraulic Brakes, Suspension Systems, Steering Systems, Tires, and Wheels;

(Listing continued on next page)

Automotive *(cont.)*

John C. Glennon, Chartered (cont.)
Determination if Proper Maintenance and Repair Procedures were Followed; Identification of Previous Body Structural Damage; Motor Carrier Safety and Compliance; Commercial Driver Responsibilities and Qualifications; Commercial Driver Hours of Service and Daily Logs; Proper Load Securement Procedures; Fleet Maintenance Requirements; Computer Animation; Forensic Mapping; Photo Modeling; Downloading of Crash Data Retrieval Systems (Automobile "BLACK BOX"). **Degrees/licenses:** D. Engr., PE, BS Automotive Technology, ASE Cert., CDL.

See primary listing under ACCIDENT RECONSTRUCTION: General

William D. Guentzler

President
Forensics International
10298 Hawley Road
El Cajon, CA 92021
Tel: (619) 390-9081
Fax: (619) 390-9086
E-mail: forensicsintl@msn.com

Specialties: Thirty six years as university professor, twenty five years as forensic examiner. Failure analysis of automotive, truck, ATV/ ATC, motorcycle, golf cart and recreational vehicles; Specialist in braking systems, cooling systems, steering, suspension, fuel systems including gas, diesel, propane, CNG, LNG, and electric; Vehicle fire cause and origin and tires. **Degrees/licenses:** BS, MA, PhD.

See primary listing under FAILURE ANALYSIS: Automotive/Vehicular

Bioengineering

Wilson C. "Toby" Hayes, PhD

President
Hayes + Associates, Inc.
301 SW 4th St., Suite 160
Corvallis, OR 97333
Tel: (541) 754-9645
(541) 912-7222
Fax: (541) 754-9949
E-mail: wch@hayesassoc.com
Web Site: http://www.hayesassoc.com

Specialties: Expertise: injury biomechanics, accident reconstruction and failure analysis; personal injury, products liability, wrongful death, premises liability, medical malpractice; motor vehicle accidents; slips, trips, falls; sports injuries, recreation and safety equipment, industrial injuries, ergonomics and repetitive stress syndromes. Background: (1979-98) Director, Orthopedic Biomechanics Laboratory, Mueller Professor Biomechanics, Harvard Medical School/MIT; (1998-present) Professor Exercise and Sports Science/Mechanical Engineering, Oregon State University; Orthopedics & Rehabilitation, Oregon Health Sciences University. Awards: (1995) American Society Biomechanics Borelli; (1996) Bristol-Myers Squibb/Zimmer Research. Excellence Orthopedic Treatment. **Degrees/licenses:** BS, MS (Stanford '64, '66); PhD (Northwestern '70).

See primary listing under ACCIDENT RECONSTRUCTION: Biomechanics

Dr. Raphael Katzen

Consulting Engineer
Raphael Katzen, PE
9220 Bonita Beach Rd., Ste. 200
Bonita Springs, FL 34135
Tel: (239) 498-2552
Fax: (239) 498-2551
E-mail: RKatzenpe@aol.com

Specialties: Chemical and Biochemical Process Technology; Organism Propagation; Fermentation; Environmental Aspects; Reaction Technology; Separations Technology; Plant Design; Extensive experience in chemical and biochemical plant process design, construction, operation world-wide; Member National Academy of Engineering, American Institute of Chemical Engineers, American Chemical Society, American Institute of Chemists, TAPPI, CPPA; Expert Witness in Federal Court cases concerning Patents, Contracts, Performance, formerly National Panel AAA (Chief Arbitrator); Author of more than 50 articles; Inventor on more than 30 patents. **Degrees/licenses:** BChE, MChE, DChE Polytechnic Univ.; PE License 16 States.

See primary listing under ENGINEERING: Chemical

Biomechanics

Transamerican Consultant Engineers, Inc.

Roderick Stroud, PhD
President
P.O. Box 3033
Thousand Oaks, CA 91359
Tel: (818) 889-9986
Fax: (818) 889-9505
E-mail: tce@transameng.com
Web Site: http://www.transameng.com

Specialties: TCE provides an analytical engineering service for the insurance industry and legal profession, with expert witness testimony when required. All of our engineers have university degrees in engineering, industrial backgrounds and extensive forensic engineering experience. All have appeared many times as engineering experts in arbitration and in court. All qualify repeatedly as accident reconstruction/biomechanical engineers. Areas of expertise include: injury causation - failure analysis, motor vehicle accident, pedestrian accident, automotive, biomechanics, medical devices, orthopedic instrumentation, construction, machines, hardware, toys, marine, plumbing, fires, tools, slip/trip and fall. **Degrees/licenses:** AB, BSME, MSME, BSAE, MSAE, MS (Mtls. Sci.), PhD (BME), PE.

See primary listing under ACCIDENT RECONSTRUCTION: Biodynamics of Injury

Biomedical

Boster, Kobayashi & Associates

Michael Kreutzelman
Chief Operating Officer
59 Rickenbacker Circle
Livermore, CA 94550
Tel: (925) 447-6495
(925) 963-9653
Fax: (925) 447-6589
E-mail: michaelk@boster-kobayashi.com
Web Site: http://www.bosterkobayashi.com

Specialties: Accident reconstruction/automobiles, buses, trains, bicycles, motorcycles and tractor trailers. Highway design, biomedical analysis, machine guarding, product defects, seatbelts, airbags, elevator and escalators, tire failure, slip/trip and falls, lighting, nighttime photography, human factors, safety, construction safety, crashworthiness and recreational safety, amusement parks. Fifteen experts - firm has consulted on cases all over the United States. Senior experts have testified on average over 200 times. Fifty percent plaintiff and fifty percent defendant. Travel anywhere in the United States with 24-hour notice, if case warrants this emergency response. **Degrees/licenses:** PhD, PE, MS, ME, JD.

See primary listing under ACCIDENT RECONSTRUCTION: Automotive/Vehicular

Joseph F. Dyro, PhD, CCE

21 Bob's Lane
Setauket, NY 11733
Tel: (631) 751-7244
Fax: (631) 751-7802
E-mail: dyro@alum.mit.edu
Web Site: http://www.dyro.org/brg.htm

Specialties: Medical Devices Product Liability, Patent Infringement; Forensic Clinical Engineering; Biomedical Instrumentation; Biomechanics; Electrocution and Shock Accident Reconstruction; Human Factors; Hospital Accident Analysis. Editor-in-Chief of The Clinical Engineering Handbook. Wrote FDA Infant Incubator Standard. MIT SB Electrical Engineering; University of Pennsylvania

(Listing continued on next page)

Biomedical *(cont.)*

Joseph F. Dyro (cont.)
MS, PhD, Biomedical Engineering. Editor, "Journal of Clinical Engineering." American College of Clinical Engineering, President, 1992-94. Director Biomedical Engineering and Associate Research Professor of Anesthesiology, SUNY, Stony Brook University Hospital, 1980-94; Fellow, American Institute for Medical and Biological Engineering. Over 25 years litigation experience. Certified Clinical Engineer. **Degrees/licenses:** SBEE, MS, PhD, CCE.

Alexander G. Sensenbrenner, CBET

The Sensenbrenner Corporation
P. O. Box 5098
Crestline, CA 92325-5098
Tel: (909) 338-0858
Fax: (909) 338-9079
E-mail: wysiwyg51@earthlink.net

Specialties: Medical Devices and Systems to include anesthesia equipment; ventilators; respiratory therapy equipment; electrosurgical units; cautery; pulse oximetry; patient monitoring; telemetry; radiological/x-ray imaging; hyperbaric chambers; ultrasound imaging; medical gases; hospital beds; laboratory equipment; end tidal CO2 monitoring; surgical instrumentation; lasers; insufflators; endoscopic instrumentation; endoscopes; hysteroscopes; laparoscopes; cystoscopes; sterilization/decontamination equipment; infusion pumps; syringe pumps; infusion controllers; patient-controlled anesthesia pumps; perfusion pumps; clinical engineering practices; Joint Commission for the Accreditation of Healthcare Organizations standards compliance. **Degrees/licenses:** Certified Biomedical Equipment Technician.

See primary listing under MEDICINE & HEALTH: Medical Devices, Equip.

David Yadin

President
Biomedical Engineering Consultants
1111 Hermann Dr., Ste. 12B
Houston, TX 77004
Tel: (713) 522-6666
Fax: (713) 522-6686
E-mail:
ybdavid@texaschildrenshospital.org
Web Site: http://www.biomedeng.com

Specialties: Testing, evaluating, servicing, & repairs of Medical Devices & accessories. Over 25 years of expertise practicing at the world's largest medical center. Failure analysis & electromagnetic (EMI) compatibility investigation & assessment of infusion pumps, anesthesia machines, lasers & telemedicine. Directing comprehensive biomedical engineering program within hospital & home-care environments. Member of regulatory agency (FDA) panel & standards developing association (NFPA). Past president & founder of American College of Clinical Engineering (ACCE). President, Center for Telemedicine Law (CTL). Registered professional engineer (PE), certified clinical engineer (CCE), certified healthcare safety executive (HSPC), Fellow American Institute of Medical & Biological Engineering (AIMBE). **Degrees/ licenses:** BSc, MSc, EdD, PE, CCE, HSPC, FAIMBE, FACCE. See above.

See primary listing under MEDICINE & HEALTH: Medical Devices, Equip.

Boilers & Power Plants

L. Douglas Smoot

Senior Consultant
Combustion Resources, LLC
1453 West 820 North
Provo, UT 84601
Tel: (801) 422-8930 or 374-5474
Fax: (801) 422-0152 or 343-0687
E-mail: LDS@byu.edu
or dsmoot@combustionresources.com
Web Site:
http://www.combustionresources.com

Specialties: Fires; Gas, dust, vapor explosions, combustion, fossil fuels; Cause, origin, incident reconstruction, computer modeling;

Pollutant formation. Professor emeritus - Chem. Eng., Dean Emeritus, Founding Director - Advanced Combustion Engineering Research Center, BYU; Consultant, 65 organizations; Extensive expert witness experience in fires/explosions: buildings, fireplaces, vehicles, coal mines, firearms; Member AIChE, ASME, NFPA, Combustion Institute: Author, 4 books, 220 papers; Distinguished Faculty Award, 1985; Governor's Medal, 1987; 2002 Homer H. Lowry Gold Medal, Dept. of Energy; 2002 Percy Nicholls Award, ASME; Colleagues: Dr. Scott Hill, Modeling, Dr. Craig Eatough, testing. **Degrees/licenses:** BS, Chemistry; BES, MS,PhD Chem Eng., PE.

See primary listing under ACCIDENT RECONSTRUCTION: Fires & Explosions

A. Henry Studebaker, PE

Boiler Expert & Consultant
2946 Windsor Drive
Saint Joseph, MI 49085-9484
Tel: (269) 428-1709
Fax: (269) 429-8409
E-mail: Henrynavy@aol.com

Specialties: Litigation Support; Expert Witness Testimony; Casualty and Failure Analysis; Design, Code and Construction Review; Construction Dispute; Claim Evaluation. Principal has spent the major portion of lifetime career in matters dealing with boilers and pressure vessels. Boilers include residential, commercial, industrial and utility service of firetube and watertube types utilizing all types of fuels. Also, low, medium and high temperature water generators and cogeneration plants. **Degrees/licenses:** BSME, Purdue University; MBA, The University of Chicago.

Chemical

Edward D. Cohen, PhD

President
Edward D. Cohen Consulting Services, Inc.
15638 E. Cerro Alto Drive
Fountain Hills, AZ 85268-1720
Tel: (480) 836-9452
Fax: (480) 836-9453
E-mail: cohened146@aol.com
Web Site:
http://www.edcohenconsulting.com

Specialties: Specializes in all aspects of the web coating process; coating and drying of thin films, process development and scale-up; polyester base development; film defect mechanisms; coating analytical characterization techniques; process analysis; coating line design, coating formulation development. Many publications and lecturers. Co-editor and co-author of two books on coating technology. Founding President of the International Society of Coating Science and Technology. Received the John A. Tallmadge Award for Contribution to Coating Technology Sponsored by the American Institute of Chemical Engineers and the President's Award from AIMCAL. Contributing author to several trade journals. **Degrees/licenses:** BSChE, PhD.

See primary listing under CHEMISTRY/ CHEMICALS: Paints & Coatings

Dr. Raphael Katzen

Consulting Engineer
Raphael Katzen, PE
9220 Bonita Beach Rd., Ste. 200
Bonita Springs, FL 34135
Tel: (239) 498-2552
Fax: (239) 498-2551
E-mail: RKatzenpe@aol.com

Specialties: Chemical Process Technology; Design; Corrosion; Safety; Environmental Aspects; Reaction Technology; Separations Technology; Plant Design; Extensive experience in chemical plant process design, construction, operation world-wide; Member National Academy of Engineering, American

(Listing continued on next page)

Chemical *(cont.)*

Dr. Raphael Katzen (cont.)
Institute of Chemical Engineers, American Chemical Society, American Institute of Chemists, TAPPI, CPPA; Expert Witness in Federal Court cases concerning Patents, Contracts, Performance, formerly National Panel AAA (Chief Arbitrator); Author of more than 50 articles; Inventor on more than 30 patents. **Degrees/licenses:** BChE, MChE, DChE Polytechnic Univ.; PE License 16 States.

Michael G. Kesler

President
Kesler Engineering, Inc.
133 South Main St., Ste 2
Milltown, NJ 08850-1856
Tel: (732) 296-9910
Fax: (732) 296-9920
E-mail: mike@keslerengineering.com
Web Site:
http://www.keslerengineering.com

Specialties: Process analysis/computer modeling of petroleum/petrochemical plants; Engineering design & product quality liability; Process-patent infringement. Twenty five years tech/executive experience with MW Kellogg, Exxon, Mobil. Founder & president for 20 years of engineering consulting firm. **Degrees/licenses:** PhD, PE.

Ronald D. Ostermiller, PE

President
Quad Consulting, Inc.
1500 S. Dairy Ashford, Ste. 125
Houston, TX 77077
Tel: (281) 679-1406
Fax: (281) 679-1409
E-mail: oquad@ev1.net

Specialties: Professional Chemical Engineers competent and experienced in the refining, petrochemical, chemical, polymer/plastics, and oil/gas industries. Expert witness experienced in the fields of accident/incident investigation/litigation as well as a broad range of technical/commercial issues. Expert in strategic planning, project development, financial analysis, and risk assessment. Extensive experience in the areas of conceptual planning, project direction/management, process design, construction and construction management, plant start-up and plant operations/maintenance. We serve the process industries, the legal profession, the insurance industry, and the financial community. **Degrees/licenses:** BSChE Univ. of Colorado 1961; PE (TX, ID, LA, AL).

Chemical, Safety

John E. Spessard, PhD, PE, CSP

P.O. Box 835901
Richardson, TX 75083-5901
Tel: (972) 867-8989
Fax: (972) 599-1338
E-mail: johnspessard@yahoo.com

Specialties: Expert Witness; Technical/Economic Evaluations of Proposed Claim Resolutions; Environmental Claims; OSHA Compliance and Employee Safety; Chemical Exposures to Public and Employees; Hazardous Wastes Treatment and Disposal; Applicable Federal, State and Local Regulations; Accident Investigations: Hazardous Material Generation and Releases, Workplace Injuries, Safety Practices and Programs, Evaluation of Opposing Expert's Reports. **Degrees/licenses:** PhD, MBA, PE, CSP.

Civil

Cotton, Shires & Associates, Inc.

Patrick O. Shires
330 Village Lane
Los Gatos, CA 95030-7218
Tel: (408) 354-5542
Fax: (408) 354-1852
E-mail: pshires@cottonshires.com
Web Site: http://www.cottonshires.com

Specialties: Full service Geotechnical Engineering Consulting Firm specializing in Investigation, Design, Arbitration and Expert Witness Testimony with offices in Los Gatos and San Andreas, California. Earth Movement (settlement, soil creep, landslides, tunneling and expansive soil); Foundation Distress (movement and cracking of structures); Drainage and Grading (seeping slabs and ponding water in crawlspace); Pavement and Slabs (cracking and separating); Retaining Walls (movement, cracking and failures); Pipelines; Flooding and Hydrology; Design and Construction Deficiencies; Expert Testimony at over 70 trials (Municipal, Superior and Federal); 100+ depositions; 200+ settlement conferences in northern and southern California and Hawaii. **Degrees/licenses:** BS, MS/RCE, GE, GP.

See primary listing under ENGINEERING: Geotechnical

Vincent A. Ettari, PE

CEO: NY City Expeditor
Vincent A. Ettari, PE, PC
1065 Spillway Road
Shrub Oak, NY 10588
Tel: (914) 245-6320
Fax: (914) 245-6335
E-mail: ettari@ettari.com
Web Site: http://www.ettari.com

Specialties: Sanitary Waste Systems; Septic Systems; Water Supply Systems; Storm Drainage Systems; Flood Plain Analysis; Site Planning; Land Development; Subdivisions; Sitework; Parking Lots; Rock Cuts and Blasting; Soils and Slope Analyses; Geotechnical Engineering; Retaining Walls; Wetlands Issues; Groundwater Issues; Marine and Marinas; Dredging; Design of Small Dams, Retaining Walls, and Underground Chambers; Structural Design of Houses and Commercial Buildings; Building Codes Issues; Building Failures; Failure Analysis; Concrete, Steel, and Wood Design (member: ACI, AISC, AWC); Fire Protection (member NFPA); Supervision of Construction Sites; Slip, Trip and Fall; Personal Injury Investigations; House Inspections. **Degrees/licenses:** West. Co. Mun. Plan. Fed. Fallout Shelter Tech. (FEMA); Water Sys. Op. (NYSDOH).

John Forester

7585 Church St.
Lemon Grove, CA 91945-2306
Tel: (619) 644-5481
E-mail: forester@johnforester.com
Web Site: http://www.johnforester.com

Specialties: Bicycle traffic engineering; Bicycles; Bikeways; Bike paths; Bicyclist performance. Affiliation: Independent Consultant. **Degrees/licenses:** MS; PE.

Helmer Engineering, Inc.

Ray G. Helmer, PE
9314 Bankside
Houston, TX 77031
Tel: (713) 777-7611
Fax: (713) 774-6881
E-mail: HelmerEng@Houston.RR.com
Web Site:
http://www.helmer-engineering.com

Specialties: Civil engineering; FAA standards; Airport pavement, lighting, signing; Highway geometry, intersections, street engineering, grading, earthwork; Sight distance; Transportation/traffic engineering; Traffic accidents; Traffic signals, signs; Pavement marking, highway lighting; Train, automobile, bicycle, pedestrian accidents; Traffic accident expert testimony involving city, county, state DOTs; Construction accidents; Hydraulics, hydrology; Drainage, flooding, stormwater management; Sanitary engineering; Sewer lines, pump stations, wastewater treatment plants; Sewer overflows; Water lines, pump stations, water treatment plants, Water Disinfection Byproducts (DBPs); plumbing; Firewater pressure, volume, adequacy; Tornado, hurricane, earthquake damage; Structures; Foundation failure, structural damage, water intrusion; Engineered product liability/defects; Soil expansion, contraction, settlement. **Degrees/licenses:** BS (Civil Engineering); Registered Professional Engineer.

See primary listing under ENGINEERING: Water Resources

Civil *(cont.)*

Scott A. Johnson, PE, RLS

President
Rick Engineering Company
6150 N. 16th Street
Phoenix, AZ 85016-1705
Tel: (602) 957-3350
Fax: (602) 285-2396
E-mail: sjohnson@rickengineering.com
Web Site: http://www.rickengineering.com

Specialties: Land Development Civil Engineering and Land Surveying, Storm Drainage and Storm Water Management, Street and Highway Design, Sanitary Sewer and Water System Design, Topographic, ALTA, and Boundary Surveys, Grading and Earthwork. BSCE - San Diego State University, 1982; PE - California, Arizona, Nevada, New Mexico; RLS - California. **Degrees/licenses:** BSCE, PE, RLS.

Kirby T. Meyer

President
MLAW Consulting Engineers
2804 Longhorn Blvd.
Austin, TX 78758
Tel: (512) 835-7000
Fax: (512) 651-0098
E-mail: ktmeyer@mlaw-eng.com
Web Site: http://www.mlaw-eng.com

Specialties: Civil engineering; Structural failures; Structures; Geotechnical; Blasting & construction damage; Foundation movement; Materials testing; Water Intrusion; pavements. **Degrees/licenses:** MS; PE.

John F. Robertson, PE

President
JFRA
16219 Taylorsville Rd.
Fisherville, KY 40023
Tel: (502) 267-9230
Fax: (502) 267-4966
E-mail: johnexpert@aol.com

Specialties: Expert witness in Heavy/Highway Construction; Roads; Earthworks; Siteworks; Underground Utilities; Watermains; Storm; Sanitary; Curbs & Gutter; Concrete & Asphalt Paving; Grading; Foundations; Delay Claims; Changed Conditions; Estimates; Scheduling; Project Management; Traffic Controls. **Degrees/licenses:** BS Civil Engr.; M. Engr. Mgt.; PE (KY); ASCE, AACE.

See primary listing under CONSTRUCTION: Roads/Heavy Construction

Civil, Structural, Consulting

James J. Mallett, PE, PA

Civil/Structural Consulting Engineer
416 N. Baylen St.
Pensacola, FL 32501
Tel: (850) 438-7794
Fax: (850) 438-7839
E-mail: malletteng@mallett-eng.com

Specialties: Civil/Structural Construction Documents, Reports, Investigations, Limited Litigation. Professional Organizations: FES, NSPE, AWS, PCI, ACI, ASCE, CRSI, AISC, SBCCI, and AIA. **Degrees/licenses:** BCE, MSCE, MBA - Registered AL, FL, GA, KY, LA, MS, SC, TN.

Construction

Carr & Associates Engineers, Inc.

Ben F. Carr, Jr., PE, RLS (President)
Bart Carr, RLS (Vice President)
2052 Oak Mountain Drive
Pelham, AL 35124
Tel: (205) 664-8498
Fax: (205) 664-9685
E-mail: CarrAsso@aol.com
or caebfcj@aol.com

Specialties: Carr & Associates, a thirty person civil/structural and surveying firm, established 1974, with civil, structural, environmental, and mechanical engineers, and surveyors. Approximately eighty percent of our work load is design, so that our forensic engineering is "real world" and not theory. The firm's engineers have managed over 900 construction projects and testified in depositions and court numerous times for defense and plaintiffs. The firm has civil, topographic, and surveying computer software in house. Our surveying capabilities assure accurate, useful site and construction maps, where appropriate. **Degrees/licenses:** BCE, MS, PE (AL, MS, TN, SC, GA, FL), RLS (AL, FL, MS, TN, SC).

See primary listing under ACCIDENT RECONSTRUCTION: General

PMA Consultants LLC

Dr. Gui Ponce de Leon, PE
Managing Principal
One Woodward Ave., Suite 1400
Detroit, MI 48226
Tel: (313) 963-8863
Fax: (313) 963-8918
E-mail: info@pmaconsultants.com
Web Site: http://www.pmaconsultants.com

Specialties: PMA is a national project management consulting firm founded in 1971. The latest survey by Engineering News Record ranks PMA 29th largest CM for-fee firm in the U.S. We have provided consulting and expert services on architectural, infrastructure, transportation, water/wastewater, power, and corporate projects exceeding $80 billion. PMA's services include: Project Management, Claims Avoidance & Management, Change Order Analysis, Contract Review & Administration, Schedule & Cost Management, VE & IT Services, Expert Witness. PMA has 13 offices nationwide. Visit www.PMAConsultants.com. **Degrees/licenses:** PhD, PE, JD, MBA, RA, CPA, CVS, CCC, CCE, EIT, PMI, PMP.

See primary listing under CONSTRUCTION: Claims

Wexco International Corporation

Dr. Stephen C. Wexler, PE
3226 Thatcher Avenue
Marina del Rey, CA 90292
Tel: (800) 559-3877
(310) 306-3877
(415) 281-3877
Fax: (310) 306-7480
E-mail: wexco@wexco.net
Web Site: http://www.wexco.net

Specialties: Construction consulting, engineering, safety and management; Construction defects and damages, costs to repair, policy coverage; Construction claims, delay impact analysis, CPM scheduling, contract disputes, damage calcs; Earthquake damage analysis and appraisal; Fire and flood damage appraisals; Safety Engineering, building codes and safety regulation compliance; Construction accidents (falls from height, scaffolds, ladders, use of tools and equipment); Slips, Trips and Falls (stairs, ramps, walkways). All California and other states. In business since 1969. Calif . Contractor's License B-1. Licensed Safety & Civil Engineers. Have testified in over 150 trials. **Degrees/licenses:** PE, CPE, CCE, CCS, CPMP, CVS, CMC, CBO, CSP.

See primary listing under CONSTRUCTION: Safety Engineering

Zallen Engineering

Rubin M. Zallen
Principal
1101 Worcester Road
Framingham, MA 01701
Tel: (508) 875-1360
Fax: (508) 875-1369
E-mail: rmzallen@zallenengineering.com
Web Site:
http://www.zallenengineering.com

Specialties: STRUCTURAL FAILURES, PROBLEM STRUCTURES and CONSTRUCTION: Structural engineering, forensic engineering, earthquake engineering, and construction engineering for buildings, bridges, and special structures. Investigation of structural failures and problem structures; recommendations and design for reconstruction and repair; investigation and consulting on construction problems, claims, and procedures; consulting on earthquake analysis and design; structural design review; consulting in structural engineering; technical assistance to attorneys; expert testimony. Keywords: seismic; wind; civil; analysis; test; failure; foundation; settlement; pile; caisson; underpinning; shoring; steel; metal; welding; concrete; prestressing; post-tensioning; masonry; wood; timber; plastic; code; inspection; defects; dynamic. **Degrees/licenses:** PE, SE, MS, B of CE.

See primary listing under ENGINEERING: Structural

Consulting

AINSLIE

Alan Broadwin
Principal
27 Pine Ridge Road
Larchmont, NY 10538-2616
Tel: (914) 833-2649
Fax: (914) 833-5037
E-mail: broadwin@ainslie.com
Web Site:
http://www.lawinfo.com/biz/ainslie

Specialties: Design and litigation consultant; Patent and Technology evaluation; Regulatory Compliance Assessment of ISO and GMP Quality Systems; Evaluation of adequacy of medical devices and disposables; Assistance in discovery and depositions as fact or expert witness; Engineering and due diligence investigations; Surgeon/hospital interface; Review of clinical/technical reports. **Degrees/licenses:** BA, BSME Columbia; MSIE Stevens; ASQ CQA; RAB cert. auditor; RAC.

See primary listing under MEDICINE & HEALTH: Medical Devices, Equip.

GTS Global Turbine Specialists

Arthur Eckstat, BSME, MBA, DBA
President
P.O. Box 130
Chandler, AZ 85244-0130
Tel: (602) 670-9651
Fax: (480) 380-2551
E-mail: GTSeckstat@qwest.net
Web Site: http://www.JurisPro.com/mem/ArthurEckstat

Specialties: Dr. Eckstat has over 30 years experience in all facets of gas turbine engine design, manufacture, use and support. He was honored as a Contributor to Aviation History at the Smithsonian National Air & Space Museum in Washington, DC. He is the world's expert on the Garrett/AlliedSignal/Honeywell 85-series Auxiliary Power Units (APU) used in commercial and military aircraft and ground power. Dr. Eckstat is an experienced Forensic Investigator and Expert Witness for a variety of industrial and consumer products ranging from appliances to watercraft, including firearms. **Degrees/licenses:** BSME, MBA, DBA.

See primary listing under PRODUCT LIABILITY: General

Packer Engineering

Penny Rusch
Director of Business Development
1950 N. Washington St.
Naperville, IL 60563
Tel: (800) 323-0114
Fax: (630) 505-1986
E-mail: peinfo@packereng.com
Web Site: http://www.packereng.com

Specialties: Packer Engineering, a multidisciplinary engineering consulting company, provides expertise in the areas of failure analysis, accident investigation & reconstruction, cause & origin investigations, research & development, risk mitigation, and custom & routine testing. Packer offers a wide range of services in the following areas: Aviation, Biomechanical/Biomedical, Construction Technology, Chemical, Fire & Explosions, Electrical, Human Factors, Ergonomics, Machinery & Equipment, Materials, Occupational Safety, Product & Process Safety, System Failure Analysis & Recovery, Technology Assessment & Intellectual Property, and Transportation Systems. Our emergency response team is available 24 hours, 7 days a week.

Thielsch Engineering, Inc.

Ara Nalbandian, PE, Vice President
Bob Basile, PE
Florence Cone
195 Frances Avenue
Cranston, RI 02910
Tel: (401) 467-6454
Fax: (401) 467-2398
E-mail: nalbandiana@thielsch.com
Web Site: http://www.thielsch.com

Specialties: Failure analyses and forensic investigations of equipment and products in many different industries including power generation, pulp and paper, petroleum and chemical, process industries, mining, manufacturing, transportation, electronics, medical devices, failures or condition assessments of vessel, piping, bridges, building structures, electrical components/systems, pumps, water transmission, fire protection piping, compressors and other rotating equipment. Extensive laboratory testing facilities include full spectrum analyses, metallurgical, mechanical, chemical , analytical, bacteriological, environmental, structural and corrosion testing services. Registered Professional Engineers in Rhode Island, Massachusetts, Maine, New Jersey, Georgia, Florida, Indiana and California. **Degrees/licenses:** BS, PE, BS Mech. Engr. MS (RI, MA, ME, NJ, GA, FL, IN & CA).

David Yadin

President
Biomedical Engineering Consultants
1111 Hermann Dr., Ste. 12B
Houston, TX 77004
Tel: (713) 522-6666
Fax: (713) 522-6686
E-mail:
ybdavid@texaschildrenshospital.org
Web Site: http://www.biomedeng.com

Specialties: Testing, evaluating, servicing, & repairs of Medical Devices & accessories. Over 25 years of expertise practicing at the world's largest medical center. Failure analysis & electromagnetic (EMI) compatibility investigation & assessment of infusion pumps, anesthesia machines, lasers & telemedicine. Directing comprehensive biomedical engineering program within hospital & home-care environments. Member of regulatory agency (FDA) panel & standards developing association (NFPA). Past president & founder of American College of Clinical Engineering (ACCE). President, Center for Telemedicine Law (CTL). Registered professional engineer (PE), certified clinical engineer (CCE), certified healthcare safety executive (HSPC), Fellow American Institute of Medical & Biological Engineering (AIMBE). **Degrees/ licenses:** BSc, MSc, EdD, PE, CCE, HSPC, FAIMBE, FACCE. See above.

See primary listing under MEDICINE & HEALTH: Medical Devices, Equip.

Corrosion

Chemical Accident Reconstruction Services, Inc.

Michael Fox, PhD
Founder
9121 E. Tanque Verde Rd., #105
Tucson, AZ 85749-8391
Tel: (800) 645-3369
Fax: (520) 749-0861
E-mail: services@chemaxx.com
Web Site: http://www.chemaxx.com

Specialties: Complex industrial chemical accidents, fires and explosions as well as chemical-related consumer product injuries. The founder of the company has his PhD in Physical Chemistry, is a Certified Fire & Explosion Investigator and Certified or Accredited in Hazardous Chemicals, OSHA Process Hazard Analysis Team Leader, DOT Hazardous Materials, Corrosion, Metallurgy, Failure Analysis and Aerosols. Other specialties include: Propane, plastics, water chemistry, skin burns, acids, alkalis, carbon monoxide, flammable liquids, gasoline, scanning microscopy, MSDSs, natural gas, solvents, warning labels, PEX, welding, construction, chemical packaging & transport. For more specialties see web site. **Degrees/licenses:** PhD, Physical Chemistry; See certifications above.

See primary listing under CHEMISTRY/ CHEMICALS: General

Richard F. Lynch, PhD

Lynch & Associates, Inc.
377 Sicomac Avenue
Wyckoff, NJ 07481-2128
Tel: (201) 891-8399
Fax: (201) 891-8398
E-mail: richardflynch@aol.com
Web Site: http://www.JurisPro.com/mem/
RichardFLynch

Specialties: Expert witness in nonferrous and steel metallurgy including failure analysis. Metallurgical failure investigation/test interpretation for legal profession. Effective court testimony. Specialties in fracture and corrosion failure of nonferrous metal and steel, structural

(Listing continued on next page)

Corrosion *(cont.)*

Richard F. Lynch (cont.)
materials and fabricated products. Zinc, aluminum, brass/bronze and galvanized steel expert. Extensive background in nonferrous castings/wrought products including manufacture and performance. Expert in surface preparation, metal pretreatments and painting of galvanized steel including white rust formation and paint failure. Experienced in writing and interpreting standards and specifications for bare, painted and galvanized steel, and nonferrous products. ASTM Fellow. **Degrees/licenses:** PhD, MS & BS in Metallurgy & Materials Science, Lehigh University.

See primary listing under ENGINEERING: Metallurgical

Design

Robert D. Hookway

President/Sr. Consultant
Hookway Engineering PC
115 Kristin Drive
Chelmsford, MA 01824
Tel: (978) 256-4852
Fax: (978) 244-0392
E-mail: hookwayeng@comcast.net

Specialties: EXPERT CATEGORY: ENGINEERING CONSULTING. Design, analysis and evaluation of piping systems, pressure vessels and structures considering temperature (1400 F to -320F), pressure, earthquake etc, loadings. Condition assessment - piping installation and equipment in consideration of fatigue, corrosion, load capacity and demand. Failure analysis. Litigation support. Registered professional engineer. Service to the power generation, petroleum and process industries. Member of ASME B31.3 Process Piping Main Committee and past member of ASME Section III (ASME Boiler and Pressure Vessel Code) Working Group on Piping and Special Working Group on Seismic Design Rules. **Degrees/licenses:** BS, MS Mech. Eng.; P.E. MA, VA.

Schutz Engineering Corp.

Peter K. Schutz, PE
President
45 River Road
Summit, NJ 07901
Tel: (908) 638-3300
Fax: (908) 277-6256
E-mail: SchutzE@compuserve.com

Specialties: Mechanical engineering design, analysis, testing; new product development; electro-mechanical equipment; special machinery; medical, office, and laboratory equipment, instrumentation, and devices; electronics; electronics packaging and enclosure design; electro-magnetics; fluid systems (incl. gas and air) and components; analysis and modeling of dynamic systems, computer modeling of fluid flows (CFD) and temperature distributions; heat transfer analysis; mechanical systems and components, plastic and metal parts; testing, measurements, drawings. Member of ASME, IEEE; Former Adjunct Instructor: CCM and Stevens Inst. of Technology; 2 patents; Expert Witness: patent infringement, copied products, machinery, product safety analysis. **Degrees/licenses:** BSME, MSME, PE, Grad. Dale Carnegie Course (Pub. Speaking & Human Relations).

Electrical

David Alley

President
ANNA Inc.
626 Admiral Drive
Suite C-537
Annapolis, MD 21401
Tel: (410) 268-6321
Fax: (410) 268-3505
E-mail: info@annainc.com
Web Site: http://www.annainc.com

Specialties: Root Cause Investigation; Analysis of Power Plant Failures; Expert Opinions and Testimony on Electrical and Mechanical Failures. **Degrees/licenses:** PE, MBA, BSEE.

Dr. Eugene W. Bartel

President
Bartel, Rudolf & Associates
5578 Aiken Road
McKees Rocks, PA 15136
Tel: (412) 787-8166
Fax: (412) 787-5506
E-mail: eugenebartel@aol.com

Specialties: Professional Accidental Fire Origin and Cause Investigation; Forensic Engineering Evaluation of Fire Evidence; Electrical Accident Investigation; Engineering Evaluation of Products Relative to Defects as related to Liability Analysis; Laboratory Testing & X-Ray Analysis; Subrogation Specialists; Trial Exhibit Preparation Services. Over 30 years of experience in Fire and Accident Investigation and Trial Testimony. **Degrees/licenses:** BSEE, MSEE, PhDEE, PE, CFI.

Robert C. Ender, PE

30 Fairfield Drive
Kennebunk, ME 04043
Tel: (207) 967-0728
Fax: (207) 967-0728
E-mail: rcender@ieee.org

Specialties: Consulting engineer with over 40 years experience specializing in: Electric power (utility, industrial, commercial & residential electric systems); Electrical accident & equipment failure analyses; Safety codes - NEC, NESC, OSHA; Electric system design, costs & operating performance; Electric power regulatory issues; Evaluations of service interruptions & voltage quality; Testimony in both Federal and state jurisdictions; Alternative dispute resolution. **Degrees/licenses:** BSEE, MS, PE.

Forensic Analyst

Roger L. Boyell
416 Parry Drive
Moorestown, NJ 08057-2877
Tel: (856) 234-5800
Fax: (856) 234-9539
E-mail: boyell@ieee.org
Web Site: http://www.boyell.com

Specialties: Expertise in electronic control and communication systems, 30 years experience in industry. Cases deal with machinery electronic controls, audio-video systems, tape recording, traffic radar and lidar, cellular phones, electric shock, radio interference, electrical malfunctions, wireless communications, automobile electronics, surveillance systems, electronic circuits, paging systems, sound systems, telephone communication, security and alarm systems, remote controls. Services include site inspection, field measurement, lab analysis, test reports, technical findings, consultation, and expert testimony for civil, criminal, insurance, and patent cases. **Degrees/licenses:** BEE, MS, MBA, SMIEEE, FACFE, DABFET, PE.

See primary listing under ENGINEERING: Electronic

Gene Haynes

President
Matrix Engineering
97 Lang Road
Suite 2A
Ft. Walton Beach, FL 32547
Tel: (850) 864-1699
(256) 642-9090
Fax: (850) 864-3699
E-mail: gene@rapidexperts.com
Web Site: http://www.rapidexperts.com

Specialties: Complete engineering services and analysis involving Automotive Electrical Components and Systems, Industrial, Commercial, and Residential Circuit Breakers, Switchgear and Ground Fault Protectors, AC and DC Motors, Batteries, Battery Chargers, Starters and Alternators, Hand tools and Appliances, Fluorescent Lighting Ballasts, Switches/Relays, Sensors and Electromechanical Products. Director of Engineering

(Listing continued on next page)

Electrical *(cont.)*

Gene Haynes (cont.)
and Product Development, Prestolite Electric, 1994-1998; Director of Engineering, ABB, 1992-1994; Division Engineering and Quality Manager, Siemens Energy and Automation, 1989-1992. Published: "Have We Sparked Our Last Home Fire?" and "Magnetic Speed Sensor Design and Applications." **Degrees/licenses:** BSEE.

A.D. Patton, PhD, PE

President
Associated Power Analysts, Inc.
303 Anderson Street
College Station, TX 77840
Tel: (979) 696-0010
Fax: (979) 696-7071
E-mail: adpatton@tca.net
Web Site: http://member.expertpages.com/assocpwranalysts

Specialties: Electric Power System Analysis; Power System Reliability and Failure Analysis; High- and Low-Voltage Equipment Failure Analysis; Electrical Accident and Failure Reconstruction; Electrical Standards and Operating Practices; Electric Utility Deregulation; Personal Injury and Property Loss Investigations; Engineering Reports and Expert Witness Testimony. Extensive Expert Witness Experience: State and Federal Courts and Regulatory Bodies. Author of more than 100 Papers and Reports on Electric Power Systems. Professor of Electrical Engineering at Texas A&M University - 31 years; Engineer, Westinghouse Electric Corp. - 8 years; Consulting Practice - 31 years. Life Fellow of IEEE. **Degrees/licenses:** PhD, PE.

John C. Pfeiffer

President
Pfeiffer Engineering Co.
2701 Lindsay Ave.
Louisville, KY 40206-2222
Tel: (502) 897-1630
Fax: (502) 895-3894
E-mail: jcp@pfeiffereng.com
Web Site: http://www.pfeiffereng.com

Specialties: Electrical incidents; injuries, electrocution, shock, arc flash hazards, fires, power surges, lightning damage, static electricity & explosions. Failures due to computer software problems. Electrical Engineer with over 35 years experience, over 140 accidents investigated, specializing in grounding, lightning protection, electrical surge protection, power systems, industrial control systems, instrumentation, and computer based systems. Primary experience in heavy industry-chemical & manufacturing. **Degrees/licenses:** BSEE; PE.

Tasco Engineering, Inc.

Gary D. Tassainer
President
3375 Mayflower Way, #A
Lehi, UT 84043-2900
Tel: (801) 766-9500
Fax: (801) 766-9100
E-mail: mail@tascoengineering.com
Web Site: www.tascoengineering.com

Specialties: Electrical Generation, Distribution, Transmission, and SCADA Control System Analysis; Code Violations; Power System Integration with Distributed Generation or Cogeneration Facilities; Wind Power System Integration. **Degrees/licenses:** BS, EE, PE (Most States).

Electrical Utility

Robert C. Peters

Owner
RCP Engineering
11 Kenny Drive
Mohnton, PA 19540
Tel: (610) 775-2003
Fax: (610) 775-7044
E-mail: rcpengineering@verizon.net

Specialties: Member National Electrical Safety Code Subcommittee 5. Wood pole expert, overhead power lines, transmission line routing, overhead line failures, high voltage, steel towers and steel poles. Senior member IEEE, Life member ASCE. ANSI 05 wood standards, power line electric magnetic fields (EMF), clearances and safety of overhead electric power lines. Chairman IEEE Overhead Line Structural Material and Hardware Working Group. **Degrees/licenses:** BSCE, MSCE, Professional Engineer in 16 states.

Tasco Engineering, Inc.

Gary D. Tassainer
President
3375 Mayflower Way, #A
Lehi, UT 84043-2900
Tel: (801) 766-9500
Fax: (801) 766-9100
E-mail: mail@tascoengineering.com
Web Site: www.tascoengineering.com

Specialties: Electrical Generation, Distribution, Transmission, and SCADA Control System Analysis; Code Violations; Power System Integration with Distributed Generation or Cogeneration Facilities; Wind Power System Integration. **Degrees/licenses:** BS, EE, PE (Most States).

See primary listing under ENGINEERING: Electrical

Electromechanical

Schutz Engineering Corp.

Peter K. Schutz, PE
President
45 River Road
Summit, NJ 07901
Tel: (908) 638-3300
Fax: (908) 277-6256
E-mail: SchutzE@compuserve.com

Specialties: Mechanical engineering design, analysis, testing; new product development; electro-mechanical equipment; special machinery; medical, office, and laboratory equipment, instrumentation, and devices; electronics; electronics packaging and enclosure design; electro-magnetics; fluid systems (incl. gas and air) and components; analysis and modeling of dynamic systems, computer modeling of fluid flows (CFD) and temperature distributions; heat transfer analysis; mechanical systems and components, plastic and metal parts; testing, measurements, drawings. Member of ASME, IEEE; Former Adjunct Instructor: CCM and Stevens Inst. of Technology; 2 patents; Expert Witness: patent infringement, copied products, machinery, product safety analysis. **Degrees/licenses:** BSME, MSME, PE, Grad. Dale Carnegie Course (Pub. Speaking & Human Relations).

See primary listing under ENGINEERING: Design

Electronic

Forensic Analyst

Roger L. Boyell
416 Parry Drive
Moorestown, NJ 08057-2877
Tel: (856) 234-5800
Fax: (856) 234-9539
E-mail: boyell@ieee.org
Web Site: http://www.boyell.com

Specialties: Expertise in electronic control and communication systems, 30 years experience in industry. Cases deal with machinery electronic controls, audio-video systems,

(Listing continued on next page)

Electronic *(cont.)*

Forensic Analyst (cont.)
tape recording, traffic radar and lidar, cellular phones, electric shock, radio interference, electrical malfunctions, wireless communications, automobile electronics, surveillance systems, electronic circuits, paging systems, sound systems, telephone communication, security and alarm systems, remote controls. Services include site inspection, field measurement, lab analysis, test reports, technical findings, consultation, and expert testimony for civil, criminal, insurance, and patent cases. **Degrees/licenses:** BEE, MS, MBA, SMIEEE, FACFE, DABFET, PE.

Jack Goldberg
President
Metrionix, Inc.
9340 Carmel Mountain Rd., Ste. E
San Diego, CA 92129-2161
Tel: (858) 780-9311
Fax: (858) 780-9312
E-mail: info@metrionix.com
Web Site: http://www.metrionix.com

Specialties: Metrionix, Inc. provides expert witness, consulting and design services with expertise in medical and scientific instruments, audio and acoustics. Mr. Goldberg has 30 years of engineering experience and has served as an expert in patent litigation, trade secrets, criminal earwitness, failure analysis, and product liability, many cases involving medical instruments. Detailed knowledge includes circuit and system design, measurement and control, embedded software, signal processing, vital signs, infusion pumps and hearing. Trial experience includes testimony for plaintiff in medical instrument patent case which successfully led to award exceeding $100M. **Degrees/licenses:** MIT: MS and BS Elec Eng & Comp Sci; Sr. member IEEE.

See primary listing under MEDICINE & HEALTH: Medical Devices, Equip.

Innovation
An Engineering Firm
Ron Tolmei
Principal Investigator
1399 Ygnacio Valley Rd., Ste. 32
Walnut Creek, CA 94598
Tel: (925) 943-1604
Fax: (925) 943-1008
E-mail: rtolmei@earthlink.net

Specialties: Electrical/Electronic equipment design, medical electronics, computers, failure analysis, mass transit systems, patent infringement, auditing of engineering fees and charges; Modeling, simulations & technical exhibits. Negligence and liability assessments of design and manufacturing defects. Underwriters laboratories certification. Extensive experience with European product development for use in U.S.A. Expert analysis and testimony by former research, analysis and development director with 25 years professional experience at Johns Hopkins Applied Physics laboratory, Rockwell International (Rocketdyne), Bay Area Rapid Transit District (BART), Teknekron & Innovation. Authored patents, technical papers, articles and reports for publication in the United States and Europe. **Degrees/licenses:** BSEE, MSEE & PhD in Electronic Engineering.

Environmental

Alberto A. Gutierrez, RG
President
GEOLEX, Inc.
500 Marquette Ave. NW, Ste. 1350
Albuquerque, NM 87102
Tel: (505) 842-8000
Fax: (505) 842-7380
E-mail: aag@geolex.com
Web Site: http://www.geolex.com

Specialties: Environmental litigation support; Hydrogeology; Contaminant fate and transport modeling; Hazardous waste management; Site investigation and remediation; RCRA and Superfund cost allocation/analysis; Forensic geochemistry and source identification of soil and groundwater contamination; Aerial photography interpretation/waste management practice documentation; Environmental liability assessment and forensic accounting; Asset evaluation for corporate mergers and acquisitions. Registered professional geologist with AIPG and in 18 states. Extensive expert witness experience in state and federal court and hearings before regulatory bodies. Former chairman of New Mexico Environmental Improvement Board. Former Commissioner, NM Water Quality Control Commission. Extensively published. **Degrees/licenses:** BS Geomorphology (magna cum laude); MS (cum laude); RG, CPG, REA.

See primary listing under ENVIRONMENTAL: General

Jon Guerry Taylor, PE

Vice President
Zande-Jon Guerry Taylor, PE, Inc.
P.O. Box 1082
Mt. Pleasant, SC 29465
Tel: (843) 884-6415
Fax: (843) 856-1043
E-mail: guerryt@jgtinc.com
Web Site: http://www.jgtinc.com

Specialties: Marina planning and design - floating docks, piers, gangways, bulkheads, dredging, hurricane and storm structural damage and failure issues, environmental permitting issues, contracts, insurance claims; Environmental - wetlands, water resources, drainage, erosion, flooding, permitting. Over 30 years experience as a design professional. 15 years as owner. Expert testimony/depositions in federal and state court. Lectured in US, England, France, Australia, Mexico and New Zealand. Authored technical papers on marinas, hurricane damage and design, timber pier, dock and bulkhead design. **Degrees/licenses:** Professional Engineer - FL, GA, SC, NC, OH, VA & MI.

See primary listing under ENGINEERING: Marine

Thornton-Tomasetti Group, Inc.

LZA Technology Division
Emmanuel E. Velivasakis, PE
President
641 Avenue of the Americas
New York, NY 10011-2014
Tel: (917) 661-7800
Fax: (917) 661-7801
E-mail: Expert@LZATechnology.com
Web Site: http://www.TheTTGroup.com

Specialties: LZA Technology Division of Thornton-Tomasetti Group, has extensive experience in assisting attorneys and insurance companies in the evaluation of claims, and providing expert witness reports and testimony based on our analyses and forensic investigations. Our expertise includes IAQ and mold; structural failures, including safety and damage assessment surveys; dynamic testing and analysis; reliability; failure and risk analysis; fire materials testing; and evaluation of damage caused by both man-made and natural causes. Offices in NY, NJ, CT, MA, PA, DC, FL, IL, TX, MO, and CA. **Degrees/licenses:** PE, RA, CIH, PhD, RS.

See primary listing under ENGINEERING: Architectural

Failure Analysis

Anamet, Inc.

Kenneth R. Pytlewski
Director of Engineering and Laboratories
26102 Eden Landing Rd., Ste. 3
Hayward, CA 94545
Tel: (800) 377-7768
Fax: (510) 887-8427
E-mail: info@anametinc.com
Web Site: http://www.anametinc.com

Specialties: Engineers in most major disciplines. Professional engineers with extensive experience as experts for litigation support. On-site laboratory capabilities include, but not limited to, inorganic chemical analysis, mechanical testing and metallurgical evaluation including mechanical and materials failure analysis. **Degrees/licenses:** BS, MS, PE.

Failure Analysis *(cont.)*

IMR Test Labs, Inc.

Ronald J. Parrington, PE
President
131 Woodsedge Drive
Lansing Business & Tech. Park
Lansing, NY 14882
Tel: (607) 533-7000
Fax: (607) 533-9210
E-mail: ron.parrington@imrtest.com
Web Site: http://www.imrtest.com

Specialties: Received BS and MS degrees in Materials Engineering from Rensselaer Polytechnic Institute. Worked for General Electric and Dresser-Rand before joining IMR Test Labs in 1998. IMR Test Labs is a fully equipped materials testing laboratory specializing in failure analysis of metallic and nonmetallic materials. Has twenty years experience in materials failure analysis and testing. Is former chairman of the ASM International Failure Analysis Committee and an editor of "ASM Handbook," Volume 11 ("Failure Analysis and Prevention"). Has published several papers and teaches materials failure analysis and testing. **Degrees/licenses:** PE, MS, BS.

Innovation

An Engineering Firm
Ron Tolmei
Principal Investigator
1399 Ygnacio Valley Rd., Ste. 32
Walnut Creek, CA 94598
Tel: (925) 943-1604
Fax: (925) 943-1008
E-mail: rtolmei@earthlink.net

Specialties: Electrical/Electronic equipment design, medical electronics, computers, failure analysis, mass transit systems, patent infringement, auditing of engineering fees and charges; Modeling, simulations & technical exhibits. Negligence and liability assessments of design and manufacturing defects. Underwriters laboratories certification. Extensive experience with European product development for use in U.S.A. Expert analysis and testimony by former research, analysis and development director with 25 years professional experience at Johns Hopkins Applied Physics laboratory, Rockwell International (Rocketdyne), Bay Area Rapid Transit District (BART), Teknekron & Innovation. Authored patents, technical papers, articles and reports for publication in the United States and Europe. **Degrees/licenses:** BSEE, MSEE & PhD in Electronic Engineering.

See primary listing under ENGINEERING: Electronic

The Nielsen-Wurster Group, Inc.

Patricia Galloway, CEO
Kris R. Nielsen, Chairman
Reza Nikain, President
Jack L. Dignum, Senior VP
345 Wall Street
Princeton, NJ 08540
Tel: (609) 497-7300
Fax: (609) 497-3412
E-mail: njnwg@aol.com
Web Site: http://www.nielsen-wurster.com

Specialties: Dispute resolution; Litigation support; Schedule delay analyses; Geotechnical evaluations; Forensic investigations; Damage Quantification; Arbitration, mediation and dispute review boards; Management consulting; Audits; Risk Evaluations; Training seminars; Risk management; Project planning; Project execution; Risk assessments; Trend evaluations; Risk reduction strategies; Systems implementation; Services worldwide; Licensed professional engineers in all states; CPAs, Project management professionals; Extensive experience in project management and project controls. Authored numerous professional papers on Project Management, Risk Management and Analysis of Project Delay. Serving private and public companies throughout the power, building, transportation, infrastructure, telecommunications and process industries. **Degrees/licenses:** MSCE, BSCE, MBA, PE, PMP, P.Eng., CCE, PSP, C.Eng., JD, CPA, F.ICE.

See primary listing under CONSTRUCTION: Consulting

Fire Protection

Fire & Risk Engineering

Robert Malanga, PE
President
9 Flintlock Drive, Ste. 100
Long Valley, NJ 07853
Tel: (908) 876-3255
Fax: (908) 876-4299
E-mail: email@fire-risk.com
Web Site: http://www.fire-risk.com

Specialties: Fire protection engineering - Investigation, forensic reconstruction of major fires/explosions; Evaluation of fire protection systems; Fire defense analysis; Application and interpretation of fire and building codes; Fire hazard analysis and risk assessment consulting. Experienced in wide range of industrial, commercial and chemical exposures; Corporate risk management and municipal fire service experience; Master planning and emergency response planning. **Degrees/licenses:** BS-Fire Protection Engr.; MS-Tech. Mgt.; AAS Elec. Engr.

J. Robert Nelson, PE

Senior Vice President
PFS Corporation
3637 Motor Ave., Ste. 380
Los Angeles, CA 90034
Tel: (310) 559-7287
Fax: (310) 559-1368
E-mail: rnelson@pfscorporation.com
Web Site: http://www.pfscorporation.com

Specialties: Building and Fire Code expert; 35 years experience in code enforcement and construction (ten years with ICBO/Uniform Building Code and Uniform Fire Code; five years with LA County Building Dept.) Technical Investigations and Test Laboratory available; Civil, Structural and Fire Protection Engineering. Construction defects/forensics; gypsum wallboard, drywall, plaster, stucco, shear walls, seismic/earthquake, sheet metal flashing, decking, roofing, wood framing & siding. Slip & fall, fire investigation & testing lab. **Degrees/licenses:** Registered Civil & Fire Protection Engineer.

See primary listing under CONSTRUCTION: Building Codes

NRG Consultants Incorporated

Richard J. Hallowell Jr.
Registered Professional Engineer
110 Trenton Road
Fairless Hills, PA 19030
Tel: (215) 946-6741
Fax: (215) 946-6182
E-mail: nrgrjh@aol.com

Specialties: Property loss or damage related to failure of fire protection systems; Personal injury caused by fire protection equipment; Design analysis of fire protection systems; Product analysis of fire protection equipment; Code and standards compliance for fire protection systems and components; Testing of fire protection equipment and components; Construction contracts and bid documents. Richard J. Hallowell Jr. has over 45 years of experience in the building industry. He is qualified as an expert in his field and is experienced in investigative work involving report writing, depositions and expert witness testimony. **Degrees/licenses:** BSME; Reg. Prof. Engineer (PE).

See primary listing under ENGINEERING: HVAC

Glenn D. Peterson, PE

2651 Carisbrook Drive
Oakland, CA 94611
Tel: (510) 482-2704
Fax: (510) 482-2704
E-mail: GlennPeterson@msn.com

Specialties: Investigation of fire protection systems design (sprinklers, standpipes, pumps, fire alarms, foam, halon, dry chemical & others); Fire protection equipment failures; Fires-cause and spread; Propane & natural gas fires & explosions; Furnace and water heater fires; Construction defects; Expert testimony; Computer simulations of fire spread; Analysis of fire hazards and burning characteristics

(Listing continued on next page)

Fire Protection *(cont.)*

Glenn D. Peterson (cont.)
of various materials; Building and fire code analysis; Fire Protection and Mechanical Engineer licenses; Over 30 years experience. **Degrees/licenses:** BS, FPE, ME.

PFS Corporation

Michael J. Slifka, PE
2402 Daniels Street
Madison, WI 53718
Tel: (608) 224-5512
Fax: (608) 223-5560
E-mail: mslifka@pfscorporation.com
Web Site: http://www.pfscorporation.com

Specialties: Fire protection engineering; Forensic investigations of fire growth, development and spread; Fire origin; Building design; Building codes; Life safety codes and standards; BS in Fire Protection and Safety Engineering. **Degrees/licenses:** BS, PE

John W. Poole, III, PE

Principal
Poole Consulting Services, Inc.
1317 S. Fountain Drive
Olathe, KS 66061
Tel: (913) 829-8650
Fax: (913) 829-8690
E-mail: jack@pcsinkc.com
Web Site: http://www.pcsinkc.com

Specialties: Building and Fire Code Analyses and Consulting; Fire Suppression Design and Evaluation; Fire Alarm and Detection System Design and Evaluation; Fire or Explosion Cause and Origin Evaluation; Fire Protection/Safety/Health Program Design and Evaluation; Fire Hazard Mitigation; Life Safety Code Analysis; Fire Incident Investigations; Flammable and/or Explosive Atmosphere Evaluations; Computer Fire and Egress Modeling; Fire Hazard Evaluations; Hydraulic Analysis; Forensic Fire Safety Analysis; Facility Safety and Fire Protection Audits; Wrongful Death Matters; Fire Reconstruction and Evaluation; Product and Equipment Liability Matters. **Degrees/licenses:** BS Fire Protection Engr., Lic. Prof. Engr. (PE).

Reed Fire Protection Engineering

Albert W. Reed, PE
President
4144 N. Central Expy., Ste. 510
Dallas, TX 75204-3140
Tel: (214) 638-7599
Fax: (214) 638-4710
E-mail: areed@reedfire.com
Web Site: http://www.reedfire.com

Specialties: Fire Alarm Systems, Automatic Sprinkler Systems, Building Code & Life Safety Consulting. Thirty years engineering experience, twenty three years as licensed engineer. All types of fire alarm and suppression systems knowledge. **Degrees/licenses:** Licensed in TX, FL, NV, AZ, NM, OK.

Flood/Hydraulic

Anthony O. Righellis, PE

Principal
Righellis PC
2328 Timberline Way
Las Vegas, NV 89117-5808
Tel: (702) 240-0443
Fax: (702) 240-0443
E-mail: righellis@cox.net
Web Site: http://www.righellis.com

Specialties: Flood Damage; Drainage Deficiencies; Flood Plain Analysis; Site Civil Design; Roadway Design. Provided expert witness services since 1983. Provides services regionally throughout the western states. Registered professional engineer in California, Nevada, Oregon, and Washington. **Degrees/licenses:** PE, MSCE, BSCE.

Water Resources Consulting Services

Rick Van Bruggen, MS, PE
President
P.O. Box 19
Guerneville, CA 95446
Tel: (800) 776-3070 (Toll Free)
(707) 604-0050 (Office)
Fax: (707) 604-0051
E-mail: rvb@waterengr.com
Web Site: http://www.hydrologyexpert.com

Specialties: Mr. Van Bruggen has twenty-four years of engineering experience specializing in the use of systems engineering and modeling techniques to define and evaluate surface water resource systems, forensic hydrology and hydraulics, and alternative flood control measures. He has performed numerous studies of watershed hydrology, floodplain and storm drain system hydraulics, reservoir and flood control operations, and the hydraulics behind drownings. He is a founding Board Member and the San Francisco Chapter President of the Forensic Expert Witness Association, reflecting his considerable experience testifying as an expert in Water Resources Engineering. **Degrees/licenses:** BSCE, MSCE, PE (CA, AZ, NV).

WEST Consultants, Inc.

Jeffrey B. Bradley, PhD, PE
President
2601 25th Street SE, #450
Salem, OR 97302
Tel: (425) 646-8806
(858) 487-9378
(480) 345-2155
Fax: (503) 485-5491
Web Site: http://www.westconsultants.com

Specialties: Registered Professional Engineer five states. Nationally recognized expert with 29 years experience hydraulics, hydrology and sedimentation. Lectured in many short courses, including Bridge Scour and HEC-RAS for ASCE. Written over 100 professional papers and reports. Editor of the books, "The Physics of Sediment Transport by Wind and Water: A Collection of Hallmark Papers" by R. A. Bagnold and "Gravel Bed Rivers and the Environment." Past chair ASCE Water Resources Engineering Division, and Sedimentation Committee. Past President of the ASCE Environmental and Water Resources Institute. President of ASCE's American Academy of Water Resources Engineers. **Degrees/licenses:** BSCE, MSCE, PhD Hydraulics.

Forensic

A. C. T. International

Bernd S. Givon, PE & Associates
8306 Wilshire Blvd., #88
Beverly Hills, CA 90211
Tel: (310) 652-3221
Fax: (310) 652-3291
E-mail: actintl@netscape.com

Specialties: Forty-five years experience in consumer products evaluation, testing, failure analysis, industrial, commercial & domestic accident reconstruction; Investigate misuse, abuse, hazards & safety; Slip, trip & fall; Chairs, appliances, office & juvenile furniture; Playground and exercise equipment injuries; Bicycles and wheelchairs; Toys; Conveyors, power tools & ladders; Glass breakage; Textiles and fabric flammability, burn & scalding mishaps; Building materials; Gates, doors, windows & hardware; Damage assessment; Automotive accessories defects; Critique instructions & warnings; Detailed CV & fee schedule available upon request. **Degrees/licenses:** PhD, MS Mech Eng., PE (CA & NJ).

Audio Forensic Center

Durand R. Begault, PhD
130 Sutter Street, Ste. 500
San Francisco, CA 94104
Tel: (800) 257-7706 Ext. 261
Fax: (415) 397-0454
E-mail: dbegault@cmsalter.com
Web Site: http://www.audioforensics.com

Specialties: Acoustics; audibility; audio demonstrations; audio and video tape enhancement; voice identification and elimination; audio tape authentication; intellectual property and patent claims; acoustical compliance; acoustical gunshot analysis; transcripts from

(Listing continued on next page)

Forensic *(cont.)*

Audio Forensic Center (cont.)
noisy tapes. **Degrees/licenses:** BA UC - Santa Cruz; MFA Mills College, Oakland, CA; PhD UC - San Diego.

See primary listing under AUDIO/VIDEO EVIDENCE: General

J. Dennis Bruner, PhD, PE

J. Dennis Bruner, PhD, PE, PC
6054 S. Krameria St.
Englewood, CO 80111-4274
Tel: (303) 771-0047
(303) 771-9306
Fax: (303) 771-0047 *51
E-mail: dennisbruner@att.net

Specialties: Quality/Regulatory Compliance: FDA Medical Device Regulatory Compliance and Quality System Consulting. Expert Witness: Medical devices used in Cardiovascular Surgery, Hemodialysis, Surgical Blood Salvage, Physiologic Pressure Monitoring and Pulmonary Disease. Experience: 30+ years of medical device manufacturing (Quality, Regulatory Compliance, ISO 9001, CE Marking, Top Management) experience. Products Liability defense experience in over 20 medical device law suits. Memberships: NAFE (Sr. Member), NSPE, ASME, ASQ, RAPS. Board Certified Diplomate in Forensic Engineering by NAFE, a CASB Member Board. Post Doctoral Research: Harvard Medical School. **Degrees/licenses:** BS, MS, PhD, Mechanical/Biomed Engr., Reg. Prof. Engr.

Dr. W. Gene Corley

Senior Vice President
CTL Group
5400 Old Orchard Road
Skokie, IL 60077-1030
Tel: (847) 965-7500
Fax: (847) 965-6541
E-mail: gcorley@ctlgroup.com
Web Site: http://www.ctlgroup.com

Specialties: Expert witness testimony/litigation support in construction matters, structural/architectural engineering, and materials technology; Analysis of structural failures, collapse, buckling, cracking, vibrations, wind load, deformations, earthquakes, fire damage, and construction irregularities; Design methodology and code review; Forensic materials investigations; Structural documents, evaluation; In-house laboratory analysis; Report preparation; Color graphics, animated presentations; Post-tensioned concrete slabs; Reinforced concrete deflections/failures; Masonry; Explosion. Memberships include ASCE, ACI, NSPE, PCI, National Academy of Engineering. Numerous court appearances. Over 160 technical papers published. **Degrees/licenses:** BS, MS, PhD - Civil/Struct. Engr. PE in 22 States.

Joseph R. Driear, PE

612 Alta Loma Drive
Thiensville, WI 53092
Tel: (262) 242-2078
Fax: (262) 242-3736
E-mail: drieng@execpc.com

Specialties: Consulting engineering: Mechanical, metallurgical, structural, hydraulic & pneumatic. Expert witness, plaintiff or defense. Experienced in Industrial Accident Reconstruction; Causation; Product & Machine Design; Failure Analysis. Experienced with aerial work platforms; air compressors; docklevelers and truck loading dock equipment; conveyors; fires in vehicles, machines & buildings; hydraulic construction machines; machine electrical control; auto & truck engine, gear and part failures; household appliances; orthopedic devices. Experienced in deposition and trial. Engineering experience is in industry — 20 years in materials and processes engineering plus 20 years in machine/product design and development engineering. 7 patents. **Degrees/licenses:** MetEng., MS; Licensed PE (WI, PA & IL).

See primary listing under ACCIDENT RECONSTRUCTION: Industrial

Robert E. Engberg, PE

President
Gas Dynamics Corporation
810 No. Lilac Dr., Ste. 205
Golden Valley, MN 55422-4672
Tel: (763) 521-8306
Fax: (763) 521-8306
E-mail: rengberg@aol.com
Web Site:
http://www.gasdynamicscorp.com

Specialties: Fire and Explosion Investigations; Propane, Butane, Natural Gas & Ammonia System Analysis & Design; Burner, Boiler & Dryer Systems; HVAC & Stress Analysis; Machine Design & Crane Component Stress Analysis; Fire Sprinkler & Monitoring Systems; Cathodic Protection Analysis; LP-Gas Standby & Storage Plants; Ammonia Storage & Petrochemical Plants; Lab Facilities for Pressure & Flow Analysis. **Degrees/licenses:** BS Math & Mech. Engr.; PE (MN & WI).

See primary listing under ACCIDENT RECONSTRUCTION: Fires & Explosions

Geology

Cotton, Shires & Associates, Inc.

William R. Cotton
330 Village Lane
Los Gatos, CA 95030-7218
Tel: (408) 354-5542
Fax: (408) 354-1852
E-mail: bcotton@cottonshires.com
Web Site: http://www.cottonshires.com

Specialties: Full service Engineering Geologic and Geotechnical Engineering Consulting Firm specializing in Investigation, Design, Arbitration and Expert Witness Testimony with offices in Los Gatos and San Andreas, California. Earth Movement (settlement, soil creep, landslides, tunneling and expansive soil); Foundation Distress (movement and cracking of structures); Drainage and Grading (seeping slabs and ponding water in crawlspace); Pavement and Slabs (cracking and separating); Retaining Walls (movement, cracking and failures); Pipelines; Flooding and Hydrology; Design and Construction Deficiencies; Expert Deposition, Settlement Conference and Trial Testimony. **Degrees/ licenses:** MS, BA/RG, CEG, CPG.

Geotechnical

Cotton, Shires & Associates, Inc.

William R. Cotton
330 Village Lane
Los Gatos, CA 95030-7218
Tel: (408) 354-5542
Fax: (408) 354-1852
E-mail: bcotton@cottonshires.com
Web Site: http://www.cottonshires.com

Specialties: Full service Engineering Geologic and Geotechnical Engineering Consulting Firm specializing in Investigation, Design, Arbitration and Expert Witness Testimony with offices in Los Gatos and San Andreas, California. Earth Movement (settlement, soil creep, landslides, tunneling and expansive soil); Foundation Distress (movement and cracking of structures); Drainage and Grading (seeping slabs and ponding water in crawlspace); Pavement and Slabs (cracking and separating); Retaining Walls (movement, cracking and failures); Pipelines; Flooding and Hydrology; Design and Construction Deficiencies; Expert Deposition, Settlement Conference and Trial Testimony. **Degrees/ licenses:** MS, BA/RG, CEG, CPG.

See primary listing under ENGINEERING: Geology

Cotton, Shires & Associates, Inc.

Patrick O. Shires
330 Village Lane
Los Gatos, CA 95030-7218
Tel: (408) 354-5542
Fax: (408) 354-1852
E-mail: pshires@cottonshires.com
Web Site: http://www.cottonshires.com

Specialties: Full service Geotechnical Engineering Consulting Firm specializing in Investigation, Design, Arbitration and Expert Witness Testimony with offices in Los Gatos and San Andreas, California. Earth Movement (settlement, soil creep, landslides, tunneling and expansive soil); Foundation Distress

(Listing continued on next page)

Geotechnical *(cont.)*

Cotton, Shires & Associates (cont.)
(movement and cracking of structures); Drainage and Grading (seeping slabs and ponding water in crawlspace); Pavement and Slabs (cracking and separating); Retaining Walls (movement, cracking and failures); Pipelines; Flooding and Hydrology; Design and Construction Deficiencies; Expert Testimony at over 70 trials (Municipal, Superior and Federal); 100+ depositions; 200+ settlement conferences in northern and southern California and Hawaii. **Degrees/licenses:** BS, MS/RCE, GE, GP.

Environmental Geology Services

Marc Seeley, CEG, REA-II
1695 Willowside Road
Santa Rosa, CA 95401
Tel: (707) 528-0810
Fax: (707) 528-1956
E-mail: egs@ap.net

Specialties: 25+ years experience; Engineering geology, hazardous materials, environmental assessments; Causation and failure analysis, peer review, expert consulting; Civil Trial Science Panelist, 30+ depositions, contract management; Fault studies, earth movement and landslide investigations, air photo interpretation, underground storage tank investigations, ground water investigations and remediation; Land development/planning studies. Registered Geologist (CA, OR, ID), Certified Engineering Geologist (OR), Certified Environmental Manager (NV), Registered Environmental Assessor II (CA). **Degrees/licenses:** BA, MS Geology. See above for certifications.

Groundwater Remediation

Nicholas Albergo

Chairman & CEO
HSA Environmental
4019 East Fowler Avenue
Tampa, FL 33617
Tel: (813) 971-3882
Fax: (813) 971-1862
E-mail: nalbergo@hsa-env.com
Web Site: http://www.hsa-env.com

Specialties: Groundwater remediation, soil and water quality evaluations, contamination assessment, degradation and migration analysis, contaminant modeling, industrial wastewater treatment design, hazardous waste management, disposal and remedial strategy. Prior testimony includes cases involving difficult or unusual hazardous wastes, advanced hydrogeology, landfill gas and leachate assessment, geochemistry, water quality impact analysis, water resource management, and sensitive regulatory compliance issues. Has chaired several major scientific conferences, and has over 150 technical publications. Internationally recognized in the area of contamination assessment and remedial strategies associated with chlorinated solvents and other dense nonaqueous-phase liquids. **Degrees/licenses:** BSES, MSCE, PhDc, DEE, PE, REP.

David R. Hargis, PhD, RG

Principal Hydrogeologist
Hargis + Associates, Inc.
2365 Northside Dr., #C100
San Diego, CA 92108-2709
Tel: (619) 521-0165
Fax: (619) 521-8580
E-mail: drhargis@hargis.com
Web Site: http://www.hargis.com

Specialties: Hydrology/Hydrogeology; Contaminant Fate and Transport; Source Evaluation and Timing; Groundwater Modeling; Contaminant Transport Modeling; Groundwater and Soil Remediation; Litigation Support; Expert Witness Testimony; Cost Allocation Analysis; Water Resources Exploration, Design and Development. Provides expert witness testimony, technical counsel, litigation support concerning hydrological conditions and assessment of soil/groundwater contamination at complex industrial, commercial, or Superfund sites. Also provides technical support for PRP identification, cost allocation, negotiations with USEPA and state agencies involving site cleanup levels and approval of RI/FS/RD/RA documents, cost recovery issues, and toxic tort litigation. **Degrees/licenses:** PhD, MS, BS, Registered Geologist (CA, AZ, VA & TX).

See primary listing under GEOLOGY/ HYDROLOGY: Groundwater & Hydrogeology

Highway/Traffic

Boster, Kobayashi & Associates

Michael Kreutzelman
Chief Operating Officer
59 Rickenbacker Circle
Livermore, CA 94550
Tel: (925) 447-6495
(925) 963-9653
Fax: (925) 447-6589
E-mail: michaelk@boster-kobayashi.com
Web Site: http://www.bosterkobayashi.com

Specialties: Accident reconstruction/automobiles, buses, trains, bicycles, motorcycles and tractor trailers. Highway design, biomedical analysis, machine guarding, product defects, seatbelts, airbags, elevator and escalators, tire failure, slip/trip and falls, lighting, nighttime photography, human factors, safety, construction safety, crashworthiness and recreational safety, amusement parks. Fifteen experts - firm has consulted on cases all over the United States. Senior experts have testified on average over 200 times. Fifty percent plaintiff and fifty percent defendant. Travel anywhere in the United States with 24-hour notice, if case warrants this emergency response. **Degrees/ licenses:** PhD, PE, MS, ME, JD.

See primary listing under ACCIDENT RECONSTRUCTION: Automotive/Vehicular

James C. Jeffery III, PE

Traffic & Civil Engineering
Consulting Services
P. O. Box 961
Los Gatos, CA 95031
Tel: (408) 377-6222
Fax: (by request)

Specialties: Roadway design defect review to determine possible dangerous condition and liability. Adequacy of design, construction and maintenance of traffic control devices and systems, including compliance with standards of practice to meet existing conditions. Analysis of need for roadway accident mitigation measures related to highway design and construction, access, parking, and all land use types. Public and private experience with pedestrian, bicycle, motorbike, auto, bus and trucks. Consulting City Traffic Engineer. Plaintiff and defense consulting and expert witness (Municipal, Superior & Magistrate courts). Case evaluation can be rendered at a minimal fee. CV, case roster, and fee schedule available upon request. Fellow, Institute of Transportation Engineers. California Board of Registration Technical Expert. California Commercial, Vehicle, and Motorcycle licenses. **Degrees/licenses:** BS, Engineering; Environmental Studies; CA Reg. Traffic Engineer & Civil Eng..

HVAC

William J. Goode

President
W.J. Goode Corporation
1600 Providence Highway
Walpole, MA 02081
Tel: (508) 668-9995
Fax: (508) 668-9996
E-mail: wjgoode@wjgoodecorp.com
Web Site: http://www.wjgoodecorp.com

Specialties: Provide post fire analysis, expert witness, discovery, deposition and trial services for plaintiffs and defendants involved in claims regarding Heating, Ventilation and Air Conditioning (HVAC) systems in buildings and thermal distribution systems. Mr. Goode's expert experience includes college cam-

(Listing continued on next page)

HVAC *(cont.)*

William J. Goode (cont.)
puses, office buildings, hotels, housing, retail, physical fitness facilities, research buildings, performing arts centers, heating and cooling plants, hospitals, medical support buildings, industrial and manufacturing facilities. He is a member of the American Society of Heating Refrigeration and Air Conditioning Engineers, the Association for Facilities Engineering and the National Academy of Forensic Engineers. **Degrees/licenses:** BSME, MSEM, Reg. Prof. Engineer, Lic. Master Pipe Ftr.

Ivey Engineering, Inc.

HVAC, Plumbing, Piping
& Fire Sprinkler Experts
6390 Greenwich Drive, Ste. 240
San Diego, CA 92122
Tel: (858) 587-2874
Fax: (858) 587-6749
E-mail: info@iveyengineering.com
Web Site: http://www.iveyengineering.com

Specialties: Ivey Engineering is a forensic engineering, failure analysis and construction claims consulting firm specializing in HVAC, plumbing, fire sprinkler and process piping systems. The staff is comprised of professional engineers, former construction executives and service and repair professionals. Clients include contractors, architectural and engineering firms, facility owners, law firms and insurance companies. The experts have managed over 1,000 construction projects, designed over 1,000 projects, estimated and bid over 3,000 projects, prepared and negotiated over 10,000 change orders and prepared or defended over 50 construction claims. For more information go to www.iveyengineering.com. **Degrees/licenses:** PEs in 10 States, ICBO Cert. Inspectors, BSMEs; Contractors two states.

See primary listing under CONSTRUCTION: Mechanical/Plumbing

NRG Consultants Incorporated

Richard J. Hallowell Jr.
Registered Professional Engineer
110 Trenton Road
Fairless Hills, PA 19030
Tel: (215) 946-6741
Fax: (215) 946-6182
E-mail: nrgrjh@aol.com

Specialties: Property loss or damage related to failure of mechanical systems; Personal injury caused by mechanical equipment; Design analysis of mechanical systems; Product analysis of mechanical equipment; Code and standards compliance for mechanical systems and components; Testing of mechanical equipment and components; Indoor air quality testing and analysis; Construction contracts and bid documents. Richard J. Hallowell Jr. has over 45 years of experience in the building industry. He is qualified as an expert in his field and is experienced in investigative work involving report writing, depositions and expert witness testimony. **Degrees/licenses:** BSME; Reg. Prof. Engineer (PE).

Edward Saltzberg

President
Edward Saltzberg & Associates
14733 Oxnard Street
Van Nuys, CA 91411
Tel: (818) 994-2613
(323) 873-4752
Fax: (818) 782-7792
E-mail: ed@esaltzberg.com
Web Site: http://esaltzberg.com

Specialties: Nationally recognized mechanical engineer with over 50 years experience with plumbing, piping, HVAC, and fire protection for all types of projects. Registered mechanical engineer in approximately 16 states, as well as licensed plumber. Active in numerous technical societies, involved with code writing authority, has taught plumbing and mechanical engineering, and has designed and specified all types of plumbing and mechanical systems. Worked with plaintiffs or defendants on over 300 cases. Excellent credentials, CV, and references. In-house capability for preparing court presentation exhibits and meeting all your Expert Witness needs. **Degrees/licenses:** BSME, PE, FP, CIPE, CEM & PIPE.

See primary listing under ENGINEERING: Plumbing

Samuel T. Wineman, PE

Principal
Wineman Engineering
P.O. Box 251928
West Bloomfield, MI 48325-1928
Tel: (248) 926-0896
E-mail: stwineman@cs.com
Web Site: www.winemanengineering.com

14545 "J" Military Trail #134
Delray Beach, FL 33484
Tel: (561) 638-6634

Specialties: Expert Witness for Trial, Mediation & Arbitration. Forensic for Engineering Design and Construction of Mechanical systems including HVAC, boilers, pumps, Carbon Monoxide causes, ASHRAE standards, plumbing, gas piping, steam piping, and fire protection systems. Experience in industrial, utility, hospitals, institutional, schools, colleges, residential, and power plants. Building code review. Michigan Tech University 1956. Consultant in private practice 45 years. ASME, ASHRAE, NSPE, MSPE, ASPE & ACFE. **Degrees/licenses:** BSME, PE (MI, OH, WI, MO, KY, NY, KS, DC).

See primary listing under ENGINEERING: Mechanical

Indoor Air Quality

The Whitman Companies, Inc.

Barry Skoultchi, PE
116 Tices Lane, Unit B-1
East Brunswick, NJ 08816-2014
Tel: (732) 390-5858
Fax: (732) 390-9496
E-mail: bskoultchi@whitmanco.com
Web Site: http://www.whitmanco.com

Specialties: Asbestos, Mold Assessments, Lead Assessments, Environmental Health & Safety, Environmental Compliance; Ground Water; Wetland and Ecological Assessments; Urban Industrial Brownfields Restoration; Insurance and Predecessor Liability; USTs; Site Assessments; Indoor Air Quality. Expert Reports and Testimony. **Degrees/licenses:** PhD, PE, CIH, AST.

See primary listing under ENVIRONMENTAL: Engineering

Industrial

Conrad R. Hilpert, PhD, PE

President/Principal
CRH Engineers
1300 West Aluminum St.
Butte, MT 59701-2104
Tel: (406) 782-0328
Fax: (406) 782-3303
E-mail: crhconeng@in-tch.com

Specialties: Design, analysis, improvement, modification, of large, heavy dynamic machinery for basic industry, railroad, construction, mining, petroleum, logging, marine, heavy manufacturing, large diesel engines, transmissions, torque converters, hydrostatic drives, hydraulic power systems, retarders, brakes. Resume: First Lt. United States Army Corps of Engineers WWII, ETO. Engineer US Army Research & Development Laboratories Ft. Belvoir VA, Chief Engineer Hodgkins Proving Grounds the International Harvester Company, Chief Engineer Research and Development Twin Disc Incorporated, 30 company sponsored profitable patents (no ego trips), full professor Montana College of Mineral Science and Industry. **Degrees/licenses:** BS, MS, ME, PhD Engr., PE in 5 States.

See primary listing under ENGINEERING: Mechanical

Instrumentation

Billy I. Bonds, PE
Instrumentation Consultant
BJB Enterprises, LLC
6329 Double Tree Dr.
Baton Rouge, LA 70817
Tel: (225) 752-1326
Fax: (225) 752-1326
E-mail: bbonds@eatel.net

Specialties: Measuring; sensing; detecting, pneumatic devices; analytical; flow; level; pressure; temperature; thermowells; orifice plates; switches; ultrasonic; radar; thermocouples; RTDs; gas detection, toxic and combustible. Over 40 years experience; Completed four year apprenticeship as instrument repairman sanctioned by U.S. Department of Labor before attending college; Passed the CSE examination in 2002; Member of Louisiana Engineering Society; Member of National Society of Professional Engineers; Served two year term as Executive Board Member of ISA (The Instrumentation, Systems, and Automation Society); Life member of ISA. **Degrees/licenses:** BSEE; PE (CSE), State of Louisiana #30456.

Lighting/Illumination

Walter J. Kosmatka
390 Sandhurst Drive
Highland Heights, OH 44143
Tel: (440) 461-7862
Fax: (440) 461-0311

Specialties: (1) Discernibility - nighttime detection of roadway obstacles by drivers; Roadway terrain, inclement weather, site lighting and obstacle coloration are taken into account; Common "obstacles" are pedestrians, animals, stopped vehicles, trailers, debris, construction barricades; (2) Automotive lamp failure analysis for the purpose of determining the illuminated state of the light devices, or direction of impact; (3) Light output measurements of automotive lamps; (4) Site/area lighting measurements and specification for same. Holds 17 U.S. and foreign patents; Chair SAE Road Illumination Devices (RID) Sub Committee; Consultant NHTSA/U. of Mich. Transportation Research Inst. **Degrees/licenses:** B. Chem. Eng.; BBA; Prov Member AAFS.

See primary listing under ACCIDENT RECONSTRUCTION: Visibility

Manufacturing

Chandler & Associates
Richard Chandler
P. O. Box 6088
Huntington Beach, CA 92615-6088
Tel: (714) 963-8088
Fax: (714) 963-6499
E-mail: rchandler@justice.com

Specialties: Machinery Related Accidents; Mechanical Design; Power Tools; Product Liability; Custom testing and test apparatus; Working Models for courtroom demonstrations. 30 years experience as a mechanical engineer in the manufacturing sector including 15+ years 'hands on' experience in the design, manufacture and operation of a large variety of machinery and equipment: Power press, sheet metal, metalworking, woodworking, packaging, conveyors, hydraulic and plastics machinery, power tools, concrete machinery, machine guarding, material handling, printing presses, industrial equipment. **Degrees/licenses:** BS, Mechanical Engineering.

Frederick C. Kucklick
President
IMT Consulting, Inc.
21274 Sail Bay Drive
Cassopolis, MI 49031
Tel: (269) 445-8826
E-mail: kucklick@imtcusa.com
Web Site: http://www.imtcusa.com

Specialties: Engineering, Management and Litigation Support - Industrial Machinery and Complex Manufacturing Issues. My expertise is based on a mechanical engineering degree and over 25 years' ownership, top management, international sales, field startup, troubleshooting & installation, design engineering and project management positions with automotive component and heavy industrial machinery manufacturing companies in US and Europe. Cases handled include breaches of contracts (manufacturing production equipment and lines, vehicle components, failed joint venture), products liabilities (machine tools), trade secrets (machine designs, machine parts), bankruptcy administrative and transportation damage claims involving machine tools. **Degrees/licenses:** BSME.

See primary listing under MACHINERY: Industrial Manufacturing

Francis H. Raven

52740 Brandel Ave.
South Bend, IN 46635
Tel: (574) 272-7865
Fax: (574) 631-8341
E-mail: fraven@nd.edu

Specialties: Mechanical engineering; Mechanical design; Machines; Robots; Robotic systems; Hydraulic & pneumatic systems; Controls; Control systems; Mechanisms; Instrumentation. Affiliation: University of Notre Dame (Professor Emeritus, Aerospace & Mechanical Engineering). Listed in Marquis Who's Who in America and Who's Who in Science and Engineering. **Degrees/licenses:** PhD.

See primary listing under ENGINEERING: Mechanical

Marine

Jon Guerry Taylor, PE

Vice President
Zande-Jon Guerry Taylor, PE, Inc.
P.O. Box 1082
Mt. Pleasant, SC 29465
Tel: (843) 884-6415
Fax: (843) 856-1043
E-mail: guerryt@jgtinc.com
Web Site: http://www.jgtinc.com

Specialties: Marina planning and design - floating docks, piers, gangways, bulkheads, dredging, hurricane and storm structural damage and failure issues, environmental permitting issues, contracts, insurance claims; Environmental - wetlands, water resources, drainage, erosion, flooding, permitting. Over 30 years experience as a design professional. 15 years as owner. Expert testimony/depositions in federal and state court. Lectured in US, England, France, Australia, Mexico and New Zealand. Authored technical papers on marinas, hurricane damage and design, timber pier, dock and bulkhead design. **Degrees/licenses:** Professional Engineer - FL, GA, SC, NC, OH, VA & MI.

Materials Handling

CRAFT Forensic Services

Bradley D. Closson
180 Otay Lakes Road, Suite 109
Bonita, CA 91902
Tel: (619) 737-9563
Fax: (619) 737-9564
E-mail: bclosson@craftforensic.com
Web Site: http://www.craftforensic.com

Specialties: Crane, rigging, aerial devices, forklift accident investigation and reconstruction. All environments and jurisdictions. Extensive practical operation experience. Member ASME B30, SAE, ASCE, ASSE, ASNE, SAME, ACRP and CCAA. Previously accepted as expert in federal and numerous state jurisdictions. Active on state and federal advisory boards relevant to material handling safety, have trained equipment operators and riggers in all aspects of equipment and environmental safety, have trained equipment managers in operation safety. Speak at industry meetings on related safety issues. Perform material handling safety calculations and analysis as well as equipment condition inspections. **Degrees/licenses:** BS; California Crane, Nevada Crane, Maritime Crane Inspector.

See primary listing under ACCIDENT RECONSTRUCTION: Lifting Equipment

Mechanical

Chandler & Associates

Richard Chandler
P. O. Box 6088
Huntington Beach, CA 92615-6088
Tel: (714) 963-8088
Fax: (714) 963-6499
E-mail: rchandler@justice.com

Specialties: Machinery Related Accidents; Mechanical Design; Power Tools; Product Liability; Custom testing and test apparatus; Working Models for courtroom demonstrations. 30 years experience as a mechanical engineer in the manufacturing sector including 15+ years 'hands on' experience in the design, manufacture and operation of a large variety of machinery and equipment: Power press, sheet metal, metalworking, woodworking, packaging, conveyors, hydraulic and plastics machinery, power tools, concrete machinery, machine guarding, material handling, printing presses, industrial equipment. **Degrees/licenses:** BS, Mechanical Engineering.

See primary listing under ENGINEERING: Manufacturing

C. Michael Dickinson

President, Principal Engineer
Dickinson & Associates, Inc.
608-G Matthews-Mint Hill Rd. (28105)
P.O. Box 3093
Matthews, NC 28106-3093
Tel: (704) 847-4040
Fax: (704) 847-0788
E-mail:
mdickinson@dickinson-associates.com
Web Site:
http://www.dickinson-associates.com

Specialties: Mechanical system and component design and failure analysis; machinery and equipment accident reconstruction and failure analysis; industrial accident reconstruction; facility and equipment safety and code/standard compliance evaluations; machine design; fatigue and fracture mechanics analysis; experimental and analytical stress analysis including FEA; fracture surface analysis including SEM; reliability and risk analysis. Specialties include: machine guarding and safety; textile-processing equipment; mechanical drive components including gears, bearings, and shafts; manlifts; material handling equipment including conveyors, AGV's, forklifts, and boom trucks; consumer products; vehicle systems including brakes, suspension, steering, and drive system components. **Degrees/licenses:** MSME, PE.

See primary listing under ACCIDENT RECONSTRUCTION: General

Engineering Associate Services

Michael B. Plunkett, PE
President
P.O. Box 5420
Wakefield, RI 02880-5420
Tel: (401) 783-1591
(401) 935-6557 (Cell)
Fax: (801) 729-0611
E-mail: eas302@aol.com
Web Site: http://www.engineeringassociateservices.com

Specialties: Engineering Associate Services has been in the Engineering Consultant business for over 25 years and its key consultants have over 30 years of experience in failure analysis, product liability, pressure vessel & boiler analysis and evaluation of mechanical and structural components. Specializing in: seismic, pipelines, construction claims, product failure, product related injuries, design & construction, industrial accidents, mechanical/structural evaluation, patent infringement, failure analysis, power plants - piping - valves - tanks. **Degrees/licenses:** BSME, MSME, PE in numerous States.

Dale M. Gumz

Owner
Inductive Engineering
10805 230th St.
Cadott, WI 54727
Tel: (715) 289-4721
Fax: (715) 289-4722

Specialties: Engineering Consultant for: Agriculture, Construction, Consumer Products, Specialty Machines. Forensic & Safety Services: Accident Reconstruction, Design

Analysis, Expert Witness, Human Factors, Manufacturing Processes, Mechanical & Electrical, Occupational Safety, Product Liability, Safety Responsibilities, Product & Machine Design. In business since 1970. **Degrees/ licenses:** BSME, PE, CSP.

See primary listing under ACCIDENT RECONSTRUCTION: Farm Machinery

Conrad R. Hilpert, PhD, PE

President/Principal
CRH Engineers
1300 West Aluminum St.
Butte, MT 59701-2104
Tel: (406) 782-0328
Fax: (406) 782-3303
E-mail: crhconeng@in-tch.com

Specialties: Design, analysis, improvement, modification, of large, heavy dynamic machinery for basic industry, railroad, construction, mining, petroleum, logging, marine, heavy manufacturing, large diesel engines, transmissions, torque converters, hydrostatic drives, hydraulic power systems, retarders, brakes. Resume: First Lt. United States Army Corps of Engineers WWII, ETO. Engineer US Army Research & Development Laboratories Ft. Belvoir VA, Chief Engineer Hodgkins Proving Grounds the International Harvester Company, Chief Engineer Research and Development Twin Disc Incorporated, 30 company sponsored profitable patents (no ego trips), full professor Montana College of Mineral Science and Industry. **Degrees/licenses:** BS, MS, ME, PhD Engr., PE in 5 States.

Frederick C. Kucklick

President
IMT Consulting, Inc.
21274 Sail Bay Drive
Cassopolis, MI 49031
Tel: (269) 445-8826
E-mail: kucklick@imtcusa.com
Web Site: http://www.imtcusa.com

Specialties: Engineering, Management and Litigation Support - Industrial Machinery and Complex Manufacturing Issues. My expertise is based on a mechanical engineering degree and over 25 years' ownership, top management, international sales, field startup, troubleshooting & installation, design engineering and project management positions with automotive component and heavy industrial machinery manufacturing companies in US and Europe. Cases handled include breaches of contracts (manufacturing production equipment and lines, vehicle components, failed joint venture), products liabilities (machine tools), trade secrets (machine designs, machine parts), bankruptcy administrative and transportation damage claims involving machine tools. **Degrees/licenses:** BSME.

See primary listing under MACHINERY: Industrial Manufacturing

Steven B. Kushnick, PE, Inc.

Steven B. Kushnick, PE
Principal Engineer
P.O. Box 670084
Marietta, GA 30066-0119
Tel: (770) 591-1720
Fax: (770) 591-7996
E-mail: sbk@sbkushnick.com
Web Site: http://www.sbkushnick.com

Specialties: Failure analysis, durability assessment, mechanical design, and performance analysis and optimization of turbines, turbine engines, turbocompressors, reciprocating compressors, expanders, and ancillary equipment including diesel engines; Analyze equipment failures to determine cause and recommend preventive action; Reverse-engineer hardware for users and manufacturers; Assess hardware durability; Develop component inspections and repairs; Analyze stress, creep, fatigue, vibration, heat transfer, temperature, pressure, and flow. Experienced expert witness, expert consultant, and third-party engineering consultant. Access to metallurgical laboratory. Two patents in the field of turbine engines. **Degrees/licenses:** BSME, PE.

Mechanical *(cont.)*

Francis H. Raven
52740 Brandel Ave.
South Bend, IN 46635
Tel: (574) 272-7865
Fax: (574) 631-8341
E-mail: fraven@nd.edu

Specialties: Mechanical engineering; Mechanical design; Machines; Robots; Robotic systems; Hydraulic & pneumatic systems; Controls; Control systems; Mechanisms; Instrumentation. Affiliation: University of Notre Dame (Professor Emeritus, Aerospace & Mechanical Engineering). Listed in Marquis Who's Who in America and Who's Who in Science and Engineering. **Degrees/licenses:** PhD.

John R. Toth
John Toth Engineering, Inc.
11651 Osprey Pointe Blvd.
Clermont, FL 34711
Tel: (352) 536-9757
Fax: (352) 536-9349
E-mail: JohnToth@TothEngineering.com
Web Site: http://www.TothEngineering.com

Specialties: Mechanical and marine engineering-underwater equipment and materials, fiber optics, high-tension cables, machine design, tool & die, theme park equipment and amusement rides, elastomers, and fracture mechanics in concrete and rock. Senior consulting engineer with 20 years professional, industrial and marine based custom product engineering experience in mechanical, electromechanical, and optical engineering fields. Experience includes product design, research & development, technical program management, engineering management, and business management. Failure analysis and expert evaluation of mechanical systems, high tolerance machinery electromechanical devices, and underwater equipment for commercial, military and legal clients. **Degrees/licenses:** BS, MS, PE.

Samuel T. Wineman, PE
Principal
Wineman Engineering
P.O. Box 251928
West Bloomfield, MI 48325-1928
Tel: (248) 926-0896
E-mail: stwineman@cs.com
Web Site: www.winemanengineering.com

14545 "J" Military Trail #134
Delray Beach, FL 33484
Tel: (561) 638-6634

Specialties: Expert Witness for Trial, Mediation & Arbitration. Forensic for Engineering Design and Construction of Mechanical systems including HVAC, boilers, pumps, Carbon Monoxide causes, ASHRAE standards, plumbing, gas piping, steam piping, and fire protection systems. Experience in industrial, utility, hospitals, institutional, schools, colleges, residential, and power plants. Building code review. Michigan Tech University 1956. Consultant in private practice 45 years. ASME, ASHRAE, NSPE, MSPE, ASPE & ACFE. **Degrees/licenses:** BSME, PE (MI, OH, WI, MO, KY, NY, KS, DC).

Metallurgical

Anamet, Inc.
Kenneth R. Pytlewski
Director of Engineering and Laboratories
26102 Eden Landing Rd., Ste. 3
Hayward, CA 94545
Tel: (800) 377-7768
Fax: (510) 887-8427
E-mail: info@anametinc.com
Web Site: http://www.anametinc.com

Specialties: Engineers in most major disciplines. Professional engineers with extensive experience as experts for litigation support. On-site laboratory capabilities include, but not limited to, inorganic chemical analysis, mechanical testing and metallurgical evaluation including mechanical and materials failure analysis. **Degrees/licenses:** BS, MS, PE.

See primary listing under ENGINEERING: Failure Analysis

Engel Metallurgical Ltd.

Lester B. Engel,
PE, CEO/Metallurgical Engineer
James A. Brusso,
PhD, PE, Metallurgical Engineer
P.O. Box 6100
St. Cloud, MN 56302
Tel: (320) 253-7968
(800) 258-7968
Fax: (320) 253-7917
E-mail: info@engelmet.com
Web Site: http://www.engelmet.com

Specialties: Failure Analysis; Product Liability; Materials Evaluation; Trial Experience; Corrosion Testing; Product Development; Mechanical and Chemical Testing; Product Failure Simulations; Fracture Evaluations; Microstructural Studies; Scanning Electron Microscopy; Photographic Documentation; Product Design Evaluation; Specifications. Over 40 years experience as metallurgical engineers. Twenty years as a consulting and testing firm to a broad range of manufacturing, insurance and legal clientele. Extensive gas turbine, bearing, and steel products experience. ISO 17025 accredited. **Degrees/licenses:** MS, PhD, Metallurgical Engineering, Professional Engineer (PE).

IMR Test Labs, Inc.

Ronald J. Parrington, PE
President
131 Woodsedge Drive
Lansing Business & Tech. Park
Lansing, NY 14882
Tel: (607) 533-7000
Fax: (607) 533-9210
E-mail: ron.parrington@imrtest.com
Web Site: http://www.imrtest.com

Specialties: Received BS and MS degrees in Materials Engineering from Rensselaer Polytechnic Institute. Worked for General Electric and Dresser-Rand before joining IMR Test Labs in 1998. IMR Test Labs is a fully equipped materials testing laboratory specializing in failure analysis of metallic and nonmetallic materials. Has twenty years experience in materials failure analysis and testing. Is former chairman of the ASM International Failure Analysis Committee and an editor of "ASM Handbook," Volume 11 ("Failure Analysis and Prevention"). Has published several papers and teaches materials failure analysis and testing. **Degrees/licenses:** PE, MS, BS.

See primary listing under ENGINEERING: Failure Analysis

R. Craig Jerner, PhD, PE

President
J.E.I. Metallurgical, Inc.
7703 Queens Ferry Lane
Dallas, TX 75248
Tel: (972) 934-0493
Fax: (972) 233-5909
E-mail: r.c.jerner@metallurgist.com
Web Site: http://www.metallurgist.com

Specialties: 35+ years experience conducting failure analysis, accident investigations, and metallurgical engineering. Expert testimony and litigation support in 65+ trials, 225 depositions, and 1,000+ failure investigations. EXPERTISE: Accident investigation & reconstruction; failure analysis; consumer & industrial products; vehicular & heavy equipment; gas, oil & tubular products; corrosion; welding design; testing and evaluation; micro/macro photography. HONORS: "Who's Who in Science & Engineering," "Who's Who in Executives & Professionals," The Sigma Xi Society. Professor (Tenured) University of Oklahoma 1965-78. Registered consultant OSHA, U. S. Dept. of Defense, U. S. Coast Guard, and NTSB. Registered Professional Engineer in Texas and Oklahoma. **Degrees/licenses:** PhD, Metallurgy; MS & BS, Metallurgical Engineering.

See primary listing under ACCIDENT RECONSTRUCTION: General

Metallurgical *(cont.)*

Richard F. Lynch, PhD

Lynch & Associates, Inc.
377 Sicomac Avenue
Wyckoff, NJ 07481-2128
Tel: (201) 891-8399
Fax: (201) 891-8398
E-mail: richardflynch@aol.com
Web Site: http://www.JurisPro.com/mem/RichardFLynch

Specialties: Expert witness in nonferrous and steel metallurgy including failure analysis. Metallurgical failure investigation/test interpretation for legal profession. Effective court testimony. Specialties in fracture and corrosion failure of nonferrous metal and steel, structural materials and fabricated products. Zinc, aluminum, brass/bronze and galvanized steel expert. Extensive background in nonferrous castings/wrought products including manufacture and performance. Expert in surface preparation, metal pretreatments and painting of galvanized steel including white rust formation and paint failure. Experienced in writing and interpreting standards and specifications for bare, painted and galvanized steel, and nonferrous products. ASTM Fellow. **Degrees/licenses:** PhD, MS & BS in Metallurgy & Materials Science, Lehigh University.

Materials Evaluation and Engineering, Inc.

Larry D. Hanke, PE
Principal Engineer
13805 1st Ave. N., Ste. 400
Plymouth, MN 55441-5447
Tel: (763) 449-8870
(888) 349-8870
Fax: (763) 449-8699
E-mail: hanke@mee-inc.com
Web Site: http://www.mee-inc.com

Specialties: Failure analysis of metal, plastic, paints, coatings including: medical devices, consumer products, vehicles, industrial machines, industrial systems, tanks, pipelines. Expert in materials behavior; fracture; corrosion; wear; environmental degradation. Comprehensive laboratory: light and scanning electron microscopy; mechanical tests; chemical analysis; surface analysis. Experienced with insurance cases and testimony for deposition and trial. Excellent communications, written and verbal, to clearly explain complex technical issues in layman terms. Twenty years experience as a failure analyst and expert witness. **Degrees/licenses:** BS Met. E, PE.

See primary listing under FAILURE ANALYSIS: General

Marc H. Richman

One Richmond Square
Providence, RI 02906
Tel: (401) 751-9656
Fax: (401) 751-9210
E-mail: MHRichman@aol.com
Web Site: http://www.marchrichmanengineering.com

Specialties: Failure of metal parts: gas explosions, bridge & structural failures; Failures due to overloading; Failure of medical devices, orthopedic prostheses. Affiliation: Brown University (Professor Emeritus, Engineering); Marc H. Richman, Inc. (President). **Degrees/licenses:** ScD; PE.

SEAL Laboratories

Arun Kumar, PhD
250 North Nash Street
El Segundo, CA 90245
Tel: (310) 322-2011
Fax: (310) 322-2243
E-mail: akumar@seallabs.com
Web Site: http://www.seallabs.com

Specialties: Fully equipped failure analysis laboratory with qualified PhD Metallurgists and Chemists, available to perform failure analysis and to determine cause of failures of aircraft and automobile components, machineries, tools, medical devices, implants, etc.; Experienced staff for product liability and patent infringement litigation support, to act as expert witness and for trial testimony; 1 mile from Los Angeles International Airport. **Degrees/licenses:** PhD.

See primary listing under FAILURE ANALYSIS: General

Alan D. Zunkel, D.Sc., PE
President
A.D. Zunkel Consultants Inc.
8020 NE 71st Loop
Vancouver, WA 98662
Tel: (360) 896-5301
Fax: (360) 896-2180
E-mail: DZunkel@aol.com

Specialties: Historical and modern minerals processing and extraction metallurgy of primary and secondary zinc, lead, copper, precious metals, cadmium, arsenic and by products. Extensive investigation, research, deposition and expert witness testimony in state and federal environmental cases. BS, Missouri School of Mines; MS and D.Sc., Colorado School of Mines. Past president, TMS of AIME; Fellow, IMM; Member: CIM, SME of AIME, AISE, MMSA. Over 30 publications in extraction metallurgy. **Degrees/licenses:** BS, MS, D.Sc., PE, Chartered Engineer (UK).

Mining

Gary L. Buffington
President/CEO
American Safety Consulting, Inc.
P. O. Box 71017
Los Angeles, CA 90071
Tel: (661) 298-0006
(888) 828-1044
Fax: (661) 298-0311
E-mail: gbuff46@yahoo.com

Specialties: Safety Expert with 30+ years of consulting and expert witness experience in the following areas: Construction; Underground Construction; Tunneling, Mining & Mills; Risk Assessment; CAL/OSHA; IIPP, MSHA, NEC, NFPA, NRC Regs.; Safety Training. **Degrees/licenses:** MS; BS; CRSP; CSHM; CSP; WSO-CSE/CSM/CSS; Lic. PI; CIH; EMT.

See primary listing under ACCIDENT PREVENTION & SAFETY: General

Noise/Vibration

Jack E. Randorff, PhD, PE, FASA
Principal-in-Charge
Randorff and Associates, Inc.
11 West Canyon View Drive
Ransom Canyon, TX 79366
Tel: (806) 829-2521
Fax: (806) 829-2527

Specialties: Environmental noise assessments; sound level survey; train horn loudness assessments; employee hearing damage-risk assessments; vibration assessments; highway noise assessment; aircraft/airport noise assessment; architectural sound isolation assessments; industrial noise assessments; testimony - plaintiffs & defendants; clients - major companies, federal agencies, state agencies, local municipalities, private industry, schools, universities, national architectural/engineering firms; National Council of Acoustical Consultants, President (1992-1994), Vice President - membership (1998-2002), Vice President - finance (2002-2004); Fellow - Acoustical Society of America, American Institute of Physics; President - Engineers Council of Houston (1985-1986), Science Engineering Fair of Houston (1986-1988). **Degrees/licenses:** BS, MS, PhD, PE (Texas).

See primary listing under ACOUSTICS: General

Parking

Carl Walker, PE
Consultant
CW Consulting, LLC
2429 Highpointe Drive
Kalamazoo, MI 49008-2074
Tel: (269) 344-0803
Fax: (269) 344-0803 (call ahead)

Specialties: Parking Consulting - Structural Engineering; Precast Prestressed Concrete, Post-Tensioned Concrete, Durability, Security, Operations, Slip/Trip & Falls. American Concrete Institute, Precast Prestressed Concrete Institute, Post-Tensioning Institute, National Parking Association, International Parking

(Listing continued on next page)

Parking *(cont.)*

Carl Walker (cont.)
Institute, Parking Consultants Council. University of Michigan Adjunct Professor. **Degrees/licenses:** BSCE, MSCE, PE 12 states.

Petroleum

Ely and Associates, Inc.
John W. Ely
President
14343-G Torrey Chase Blvd.
Houston, TX 77014-1630
Tel: (281) 580-4646
Fax: (281) 580-3999
E-mail: elyfracs@sbcglobal.net
Web Site: http://www.elyfrac.com

Specialties: All aspects of petroleum engineering with specialties in stimulation, design and implementation. Over 60 publications to books including "Engineer's Guide to Stimulation." Member of Society of Petroleum Engineers, American Chemical Society, Fellow of American Institute of Chemists. Our company includes personnel with a multitude of training and experience including PhD in chemistry, reservoir engineering and a particularly deep understanding of the chemistry of stimulation fluids and their effect on formations, and stimulation techniques and processes. Testimony in more than 25 cases involving service company pumping operations and reservoir damage.

Gaffney, Cline & Associates
1360 Post Oak Blvd., Ste 2500
Houston, TX 77056
Tel: (713) 850-9955
Fax: (713) 850-9966
E-mail: gcah@gaffney-cline.com
Web Site: http://www.gaffney-cline.com

Specialties: Worldwide Oil and Gas Industry Technical and Management Consulting, including: Oil and gas reserves certification and valuation, Mineral property appraisal, Exploration property appraisal, Asset and business valuations, Transaction assistance, Gas processing plants, Pipeline evaluations, Oil & gas field development planning and optimization, Review and audit of operating practices, Gas market assessments, International business development planning and negotiation support, Litigation and dispute resolution support, Oil & gas contract analysis, Petroleum contract and economic modeling. Offices in UK, Houston, Singapore, Buenos Aires, Sydney, Moscow. **Degrees/licenses:** PhD, MSc, MBA, PE, BSc, CPG.

Robert C. Herr, III
Petroleum Engineer
P. O. Box 885
Mt. Vernon, IL 62864
Tel: (618) 244-5541
(618) 237-7101 (Cell)
E-mail: bobherr@mvn.net

Specialties: 35 years Petroleum Engineering and oilfield operations experience. Property evaluations for estates, divorce and business dissolution. Production and reservoir engineering. Arbitration and dispute resolution. Casualty loss and worker's compensation claim consulting. Drilling, completion, workover and production operations accident analysis. **Degrees/licenses:** BSME; Lic P. E., OK # 10271, IL # 062-039059.

James G. Speight, PhD, DSc
Consultant
2476 Overland Road
Laramie, WY 82070-4808
Tel: (307) 745-6069
Fax: (307) 721-3128
E-mail: jamessp8@aol.com
Web Site:
http://www.drjamesspeight.qpg.com

Specialties: More than 35 years experience with fossil fuels, especially petroleum technology, coal, and natural gas. See web page for more details. **Degrees/licenses:** PhD, DSc.

Petroleum Refining

James G. Speight, PhD, DSc

Consultant
2476 Overland Road
Laramie, WY 82070-4808
Tel: (307) 745-6069
Fax: (307) 721-3128
E-mail: jamessp8@aol.com
Web Site:
http://www.drjamesspeight.qpg.com

Specialties: More than 35 years experience with fossil fuels, especially petroleum technology, coal, and natural gas. See web page for more details. **Degrees/licenses:** PhD, DSc.

See primary listing under ENGINEERING: Petroleum

Pipelines

Douglas B. Chisholm

D.B. Chisholm Associates, Inc.
38074 Stevens Rd.
Lovettsville, VA 20180
Tel: (540) 822-4370
Fax: (540) 822-4371
E-mail: doug@dbchisholm.org
Web Site: http://www.dbchisholm.com

Specialties: D.B. Chisholm Assoc., Inc. specializes in Mechanical Engineering/Structural Engineering, Design and Failure Analysis of products and systems ranging from Automotive and Aircraft components, Pipelines & Pressure Vessels; Our firm can perform a broad range of Metallurgical Failure Analyses and Accident Reconstruction of large petroleum, chemical, industrial plant accidents, fuel tank farm fires, pipeline leaks, ruptures (both buried and under water) and manufacturing facility accidents; Our principal, Dr. Chisholm, PE, has over 30 years of Failure Analysis experience and has authored more than 200 publications and client reports. **Degrees/licenses:** BME, MEM, DSc, PE.

See primary listing under FAILURE ANALYSIS: General

Plastics

Ganstech Associates, LLC

Leo Gans
President
1044 East Lawn Court
Teaneck, NJ 07666
Tel: (201) 833-1529
Fax: (201) 833-0807
E-mail: LeoGans@aol.com

Specialties: Plastic Extrusion/Corporate Management - Former CEO international multiplant plastic extrusion manufacturer; Intimate familiarity with precision tubing, cast & blown film, extruded profiles, corrugated hose, compounding, cross-head & coextrusion; Supplied medical device, writing instrument, packaging, automotive, swimming pool, appliance and other industries; Operation of private/public manufacturers - personnel, commercial and technical issues; Served on corporate Boards of Directors; Quality matters/ISO 9000/Clean room; Patent development, licensing, & litigation; Product design, compound selection, & process development; Instructor plastic extrusion, manufacturing technology, and quality; Extrusion product patents & publications; Expert witness and consultant. **Degrees/licenses:** BS/MS Chemical Engineering, Licensed Prof. Engr. (PE).

Plastic Technologies, Inc.

Thomas E. Brady, PhD
President, CEO & Founder
1440 Timberwolf Drive
Holland, OH 43528-0964
Tel: (419) 867-5400
Fax: (419) 867-7700
E-mail: info@plastictechnologies.com or
t.brady@plastictechnologies.com
Web Site:
http://www.plastictechnologies.com

Specialties: Plastic packaging, containers, closures, processing, orientation, blow molding, injection molding, recycling, design, testing, failure analysis, plastic materials analysis, PET, PVC, PE, PP. Legal: patents, litigation, licensing, technology transfer, court

(Listing continued on next page)

Plastics *(cont.)*

Plastic Technologies, Inc. (cont.)

experience. Business: 30 years experience, patents, publications, R&D, manufacturing, business development; small business start up, operations, customer service. Personal: VP of Technology at Fortune 100 Company, Founder and President of leading PET R&D company and world class recycling company, Entrepreneur of the Year 1989, Small Business Man of the Year 1996, Amer. Management Award 1995, Ohio Technology Board. **Degrees/licenses:** BS, MS Dartmouth; PhD Univ. of Michigan.

See primary listing under PACKAGING: Plastic Containers

Plumbing

Ivey Engineering, Inc.
HVAC, Plumbing, Piping
& Fire Sprinkler Experts
6390 Greenwich Drive, Ste. 240
San Diego, CA 92122
Tel: (858) 587-2874
Fax: (858) 587-6749
E-mail: info@iveyengineering.com
Web Site: http://www.iveyengineering.com

Specialties: Ivey Engineering is a forensic engineering, failure analysis and construction claims consulting firm specializing in HVAC, plumbing, fire sprinkler and process piping systems. The staff is comprised of professional engineers, former construction executives and service and repair professionals. Clients include contractors, architectural and engineering firms, facility owners, law firms and insurance companies. The experts have managed over 1,000 construction projects, designed over 1,000 projects, estimated and bid over 3,000 projects, prepared and negotiated over 10,000 change orders and prepared or defended over 50 construction claims. For more information go to www.iveyengineering.com. **Degrees/licenses:** PEs in 10 States, ICBO Cert. Inspectors, BSMEs; Contractors two states.

See primary listing under CONSTRUCTION: Mechanical/Plumbing

Edward Saltzberg
President
Edward Saltzberg & Associates
14733 Oxnard Street
Van Nuys, CA 91411
Tel: (818) 994-2613
(323) 873-4752
Fax: (818) 782-7792
E-mail: ed@esaltzberg.com
Web Site: http://esaltzberg.com

Specialties: Nationally recognized mechanical engineer with over 50 years experience with plumbing, piping, HVAC, and fire protection for all types of projects. Registered mechanical engineer in approximately 16 states, as well as licensed plumber. Active in numerous technical societies, involved with code writing authority, has taught plumbing and mechanical engineering, and has designed and specified all types of plumbing and mechanical systems. Worked with plaintiffs or defendants on over 300 cases. Excellent credentials, CV, and references. In-house capability for preparing court presentation exhibits and meeting all your Expert Witness needs. **Degrees/licenses:** BSME, PE, FP, CIPE, CEM & PIPE.

Pressure Regulators

Robert W. Lindner, PE
President
Lindner Consulting Services, Inc.
7 Westmount Drive
Livingston, NJ 07039-4212
Tel: (973) 740-1319
Fax: (973) 740-1319
E-mail: boblindner@aol.com

Specialties: Natural Gas Industry: Transmission, Distribution and Operations; Pressure Regulators: Appliance, House Service, Commercial/Industrial, Distribution, M&R Station, High Pressure, Low Pressure, Installation & Design/Maintenance; Safety Relief Valves; Accident/Failure Analysis, Expert Witness Report/Testimony. Over 44 years engineering expertise in the application, operation, maintenance and design of all types of pressure regulator installations. Over 34 years engineering experience in process control and control valves. Lectured on pressure regulators at numerous seminars and gas utility training sessions. Career includes management & engineering experience plus leadership positions in national professional organizations. **Degrees/licenses:** BS, MS, PE.

See primary listing under ACCIDENT RECONSTRUCTION: Pressure Regulators

Pressure Vessels

A. Henry Studebaker, PE
Boiler Expert & Consultant
2946 Windsor Drive
Saint Joseph, MI 49085-9484
Tel: (269) 428-1709
Fax: (269) 429-8409
E-mail: Henrynavy@aol.com

Specialties: Litigation Support; Expert Witness Testimony; Casualty and Failure Analysis; Design, Code and Construction Review; Construction Dispute; Claim Evaluation. Principal has spent the major portion of lifetime career in matters dealing with boilers and pressure vessels. Boilers include residential, commercial, industrial and utility service of firetube and watertube types utilizing all types of fuels. Also, low, medium and high temperature water generators and cogeneration plants. **Degrees/licenses:** BSME, Purdue University; MBA, The University of Chicago.

See primary listing under ENGINEERING: Boilers & Power Plants

Product Liability

Frederick C. Kucklick
President
IMT Consulting, Inc.
21274 Sail Bay Drive
Cassopolis, MI 49031
Tel: (269) 445-8826
E-mail: kucklick@imtcusa.com
Web Site: http://www.imtcusa.com

Specialties: Engineering, Management and Litigation Support - Industrial Machinery and Complex Manufacturing Issues. My expertise is based on a mechanical engineering degree and over 25 years' ownership, top management, international sales, field startup, troubleshooting & installation, design engineering and project management positions with automotive component and heavy industrial machinery manufacturing companies in US and Europe. Cases handled include breaches of contracts (manufacturing production equipment and lines, vehicle components, failed joint venture), products liabilities (machine tools), trade secrets (machine designs, machine parts), bankruptcy administrative and transportation damage claims involving machine tools. **Degrees/licenses:** BSME.

See primary listing under MACHINERY: Industrial Manufacturing

James M. Miller, PE, PhD
President
Miller Engineering Associates, Inc.
2392 Fuller Court
Ann Arbor, MI 48105
Tel: (734) 662-6822
Fax: (734) 747-9712
E-mail: jmiller@millerengineering.com
Web Site:
http://www.millerengineering.com

Specialties: Mechanical Design Safety: Power Tools & Machine Guarding; OSHA/ANSI/ASTM Compliance; Warnings, Labels, Instructions & User Manuals: Health Hazard Warnings; Design of User Manuals & Warnings; Consumer Product Safety: Human Factors & Ergonomics, Slips, Falls-Premise,

(Listing continued on next page)

Product Liability *(cont.)*

James M. Miller (cont.)
Vehicle, Ladder; Child, Home Appliances, Furniture; Vehicles: Auto, Truck, ATV, Boat, Jet Ski, Snowmobile; Seat Belts & Air Bags; Chemical, Fire, Environmental & Waste Disposal: Fires & Explosions-Vapors/Electrical/ Chemical; Chemical Labeling Requirements; MSDS; Groundwater & Soil Contamination; Agricultural & Construction Safety: Tractor, Implement, Harvester & Grain Storage; Pesticides, Herbicides, Fungicides; Nursing Malpractice; Nursing Management. **Degrees/ licenses:** James Miller, PE, PhD; Bradley Cook, PE; Rebecca Lehto, PhD, RN, OCN.

See primary listing under ACCIDENT PREVENTION & SAFETY: General

Ronald L. Spear

President
R.L. Spear & Associates, Inc.
5249 Killdeer Place
Rockford, IL 61114-7083
Tel: (815) 282-9239
(815) 282-9238
Fax: (815) 282-9248
E-mail: SpearAssociates@aol.com

Specialties: Engineering advisor providing expert consultation and litigation support on agricultural tractors, asphalt paving equipment, forklift trucks, and other material handling and heavy construction equipment. Services provided include review of—vehicle design for standard and code compliance (ANSI, ASME, OSHA, SAE, ASAE), operator training, safe use and application, accident investigation, product liability, manufacturing and/or quality control deficiencies, and dealer or distributor performance in sales and service. Thirty-two years management experience within various engineering development and product support departments of a major manufacturer. **Degrees/licenses:** BSME.

Twomey Safety Engineering

Richard E. Twomey, CSP
147 Grassy Hill Road
East Lyme, CT 06333
Tel: (860) 442-8340
(860) 867-7511
Fax: (860) 444-1602
E-mail: rettse@snet.net
Web Site: http://www.twomeysafety.com

Specialties: OSHA compliance, general and products liability, slips and falls, accident reconstruction, safety audits. Ergonomics: risk assessments, work-site analysis, accident investigations, ergonomic program development and equipment. Industrial Hygiene: OSHA compliance - indoor air quality, industrial air contaminants, noise and personal protective equipment. Safety Engineering: OSHA compliance - chemical process safety management, control of hazardous energy (lockout-tagout), electrical, fire protection and life safety, machine guarding, walking/working surfaces, vehicles and construction safety standards. Products Liability: Safety standards - boiler and pressure vessel, chemical containers and labeling, elevators, equipment and machine tools, and vehicles. DEGREES/LICENSES: BS, Marine Engineer; BS, Mechanical Engineer; MS, Occupational Safety & Health; Certified Safety Professional. **Degrees/ licenses:** See above.

See primary listing under ENGINEERING: Safety

Project Planning & Management

Ronald D. Ostermiller, PE

President
Quad Consulting, Inc.
1500 S. Dairy Ashford, Ste. 125
Houston, TX 77077
Tel: (281) 679-1406
Fax: (281) 679-1409
E-mail: oquad@ev1.net

Specialties: Professional Chemical Engineers competent and experienced in the refining, petrochemical, chemical, polymer/plastics, and oil/gas industries. Expert witness experienced in the fields of accident/incident investigation/litigation as well as a broad range of technical/commercial issues. Expert in strategic planning, project development, financial analysis, and risk assessment. Extensive experience in the areas of conceptual planning, project direction/management, process design, construction and construction management, plant start-up and plant operations/maintenance. We serve the process industries, the legal profession, the insurance industry, and the financial community. **Degrees/licenses:** BSChE Univ. of Colorado 1961; PE (TX, ID, LA, AL).

See primary listing under ENGINEERING: Chemical

Quality Assurance

AINSLIE

Alan Broadwin
Principal
27 Pine Ridge Road
Larchmont, NY 10538-2616
Tel: (914) 833-2649
Fax: (914) 833-5037
E-mail: broadwin@ainslie.com
Web Site:
http://www.lawinfo.com/biz/ainslie

Specialties: Design and litigation consultant; Patent and Technology evaluation; Regulatory Compliance Assessment of ISO and GMP Quality Systems; Evaluation of adequacy of medical devices and disposables; Assistance in discovery and depositions as fact or expert witness; Engineering and due diligence investigations; Surgeon/hospital interface; Review of clinical/technical reports. **Degrees/licenses:** BA, BSME Columbia; MSIE Stevens; ASQ CQA; RAB cert. auditor; RAC.

See primary listing under MEDICINE & HEALTH: Medical Devices, Equip.

Railway Civil

Ronald H. Dunn, PE, FASCE

President
R.H. Dunn & Associates, Inc.
112 Lely
Williamsburg, VA 23188
Tel: (757) 253-1453
Fax: (757) 253-1162
E-mail: rhdunninc@tni.net

Specialties: Professional Engineer with 40 years experience in design, construction, maintenance and operation of railroads/rail transit systems; personally involved in major projects of 18 railroads/17 rail transit properties in 45+ states, DC and 6 provinces. Railway consulting/forensic engineering services include investigations of track failures, derailments, crossing accidents, construction claims, track construction/maintenance problems, and technical input/expert witness testimony for plaintiffs or defendants, in wrongful death, personal injury and FELA claims. COURT EXPERIENCE: Federal, State, ICC, Surface Transportation Board, Army Corps of Engineers - BCA, AAA, and Queen's Bench, Canada. **Degrees/licenses:** BS Engr., Johns Hopkins Univ.; PE; Fellow ASCE, NAFE, ITE, AREMA.

See primary listing under ACCIDENT RECONSTRUCTION: Railroads

Safety

A. William Breyer III, CHCM

Principal Consultant
Safety Consulting Services
178 Martesia Way
Indian Harbour Beach, FL 32937-3573
Tel: (321) 777-8599
E-mail: wbreyer@cfl.rr.com

Specialties: Occupational/Industrial Safety; Accident Investigations; OSHA Standards; Slips, Falls & Trips; Building Design Safety; Machine Guarding; National Fire Codes; National Electrical Code (NEC); NFPA Life Safety Code/NFPA #101; Plaintiff & Defense

(Listing continued on next page)

Safety *(cont.)*

A. William Breyer III (cont.)
Strategies; Job Hazard Analyses; "In-the-Home" Accidents; Construction Safety; Safety Inspections/Techniques; Accident Prevention; Walking/Working Surfaces; Litigation Consulting; Personal Injury Investigations & Reconstruction; Fall Protection; Personal Protective Equipment; Safety Program Evaluation; Risk Assessment of Processes, Plants & Facilities; Material Handling Safety; Workplace safety; Electrical/Mechanical Design Safety. DEGREES/LICENSES: BA; CHCM-#143-Master Level; NFPA Mem.: Arch., Engrs. & Bldg. Officials Section. **Degrees/licenses:** See above. Cirriculum Vitae/Consulting Resume Provided Upon Request.

See primary listing under ACCIDENT RECONSTRUCTION: General

Gary L. Buffington

President/CEO
American Safety Consulting, Inc.
P. O. Box 71017
Los Angeles, CA 90071
Tel: (661) 298-0006
(888) 828-1044
Fax: (661) 298-0311
E-mail: gbuff46@yahoo.com

Specialties: Safety Expert with 30+ years of consulting and expert witness experience in the following areas: Construction; Underground Construction; Tunneling, Mining & Mills; Risk Assessment; CAL/OSHA; IIPP, MSHA, NEC, NFPA, NRC Regs.; Safety Training. **Degrees/licenses:** MS; BS; CRSP; CSHM; CSP; WSO-CSE/CSM/CSS; Lic. PI; CIH; EMT.

See primary listing under ACCIDENT PREVENTION & SAFETY: General

John P. Coniglio, PhD, CSP, CHMM

Exec. VP - OPS
Occupational Safety
& Environmental Assoc., Inc.
3748 So. Park Ave.
Blasdell, NY 14219-1802
Tel: (716) 821-0091
Fax: (716) 821-0232
E-mail: johnconiglio@osea.com or
experts@osea.com
Web Site: http://johnconiglio.com

Specialties: Occupational safety & health specialist with 30 years experience working in heavy industry, process chemical, & construction. Testified in Federal, state and various regulatory courts and venues. Frequently called upon for NYS Labor Law and Federal OSHA matters. Areas of expertise include: Accident Investigation and Reconstruction, Indoor Air/Industrial Hygiene, Toxic Substances Control, Process Chemical, Construction, Demolition, Heavy Equipment, Machine Guarding, Excavation, Flammable/Combustible Materials, Fumes & Dusts, Confined Spaces, Fall Protection, Noise, Lockout/Tagout, Slip & Falls, Scaffold, Ladder Stairs, Competent Person, Overhead Cranes, Man Lifts, Industrial Practices, Process Safety. **Degrees/licenses:** AAS(2), BS, MS, PhD, CSP, CHMM, RPIH, CHCM, COHC.

CRAFT Forensic Services

Bradley D. Closson
180 Otay Lakes Road, Suite 109
Bonita, CA 91902
Tel: (619) 737-9563
Fax: (619) 737-9564
E-mail: bclosson@craftforensic.com
Web Site: http://www.craftforensic.com

Specialties: Crane, rigging, aerial devices, forklift accident investigation and reconstruction. All environments and jurisdictions. Extensive practical operation experience. Member ASME B30, SAE, ASCE, ASSE, ASNE, SAME, ACRP and CCAA. Previously accepted as expert in federal and numerous state jurisdictions. Active on state and federal advisory boards relevant to material handling safety, have trained equipment operators and riggers in all aspects of equipment and environmental safety, have trained equipment managers in operation safety. Speak at industry meetings on related safety issues. Perform material handling safety calculations and analysis as well as equipment condition inspections. **Degrees/licenses:** BS; California Crane, Nevada Crane, Maritime Crane Inspector.

See primary listing under ACCIDENT RECONSTRUCTION: Lifting Equipment

ForensisGroup, Inc.

Mercy Steenwyk
3452 E. Foothill Blvd., Ste. 1160
Pasadena, CA 91107
Tel: (626) 795-5000
(800) 555-5422
Fax: (626) 795-1950
E-mail: experts@forensisgroup.com
Web Site: http://forensisgroup.com

Specialties: Thousands of our clients have gained the technical advantage and the edge in their cases from our multidisciplined group of experts in hundreds of disciplines. We have some of the best and the brightest at competitive rates backed by 14 years of excellent track record and the support of our trained staff. We assist you until you have the right expert. Some of our areas of expertise are: Construction, Safety, Engineering, Product Liability, Accident Reconstruction, Automotive, Environmental, Slip & Fall, Appraisal, Medical and other scientific disciplines. Unsurpassed standards. Clients actively evaluate our experts. **Degrees/licenses:** PE, GC, CSP, PhD, MD, GC, CIH, AIA.

See primary listing under ACCIDENT PREVENTION & SAFETY: General

John Forester

7585 Church St.
Lemon Grove, CA 91945-2306
Tel: (619) 644-5481
E-mail: forester@johnforester.com
Web Site: http://www.johnforester.com

Specialties: Bicycles; Bicycle traffic engineering; Bikeways; Bike paths; Bicyclist performance. Affiliation: Independent Consultant. **Degrees/licenses:** MS; PE.

See primary listing under ENGINEERING: Civil

Vincent A. Gallagher

Safety Expert
Safety Research, Inc.
739 White Horse Pike, Ste. 3
Audubon, NJ 08106
Tel: (856) 547-4884
Fax: (856) 547-5551
E-mail: safety@snip.net
Web Site:
http://www.safetyresearchinc.com

Specialties: Former OSHA official. Served as safety expert for United Nations. Has consulted for major corporations and unions; Evaluated hazards related to hundreds of construction sites and manufacturing environments; Expert in construction safety management, fall hazard control, scaffolds, trench and excavations. Taught in ten colleges and universities; Received ten awards from OSHA and one from the United Nations. Certified hazard control manager and certified health and safety manager. **Degrees/licenses:** Masters Degree, Center for Safety, New York University.

See primary listing under CONSTRUCTION: Safety Engineering

J. Terrence Grisim, CSP, CDS, CPSM, ARM

President
Safety Management Consultants, Inc.
636 South Washington Street
Elmhurst, IL 60126-4347
Tel: (800) 726-1718
(630) 279-9499
Fax: (630) 279-9498
E-mail: jtgrisim@aol.com

Specialties: Premises Safety and Liability: retail store safety, retail display safety, slips/trips and falls, falling merchandise/top stock accidents, negligent maintenance, negligent method of operation; Transportation, Warehousing and Distribution: fleet safety, motor vehicle/fleet operations, forklifts, loading docks, warehouse safety, material handling DOT compliance, negligent entrustment/retention; Product Safety: product safety evaluation, product design review/hazard analysis, warning label development, product related

(Listing continued on next page)

Safety *(cont.)*

J. Terrence Grisim (cont.)
literature and video, machine guarding; Automotive Service: automotive lifts, shop safety; Workplace Safety and Health: workplace accidents, OSHA compliance and citation issues. **Degrees/licenses:** BGS Aviation Engr. Technology, Psych & Sociology, Texas Field Safety Rep.

See primary listing under ACCIDENT PREVENTION & SAFETY: General

George S. Kennedy, CSP

Kennedy Safety Services, Inc.
137 Ruhle Road
Ballston Spa, NY 12020
Tel: (518) 885-2560
Fax: (518) 884-8756
E-mail: kssinc@aol.com

Specialties: Accident and safety specialist; Litigation consulting; Safety training and education issues; Safety management; Personal injury investigation; Accident investigation and reconstruction; OSHA compliance and regulations; Construction and industrial safety and health issues: e.g., trenching, excavation, confined space entry, stairways, scaffolds, ladders, slips, falls, fall protection, electrical hazards, materials handling, loading docks, forklifts, tools, equipment, machine guarding, lockout/tagout, personal protective equipment, hazard communication. Certified Safety Professional, BS in Civil Engineering with 27 years safety and health experience. **Degrees/licenses:** CSP, CSHM, CHSP, BSCE, OSHA Instructor.

See primary listing under ACCIDENT PREVENTION & SAFETY: General

Pro/Consul Technical and Medical Experts

1945 Palo Verde Ave., Suite 200
Long Beach, CA 90815-3443
Tel: (800) 392-1119
(562) 799-0116
Fax: (562) 799-8821
E-mail: eexperts@msn.com
Web Site: http://www.expertinfo.com

Specialties: RIGHT EXPERT RIGHT AWAY!® 15,000 experts in 7,000 fields. Listed and recommended by the A. M. Best Company. Full-time research staff. We welcome your RUSH cases! TECHNICAL: Fast inspections. Categories from Accident Reconstruction to Zoology, also including appraisal, economics, employment, human factors, insurance, premises liability, security, and many more. MEDICAL: IME's. Inexpensive insurance medical records reviews by MDs. Categories from Addiction Medicine to Zooplasty, including board certified physicians in all fields, dentistry, geriatrics, neuropsychology, neurosurgery, nursing, orthopedics, psychiatry and many more. Reasonable fees. Free initial consultation. Free resume binder. Free CLE classes. **Degrees/licenses:** MD, PhD, DDS, DVM, DO, DPM, PE, CPA, ME, CE, CRC, MAI, et al.

See primary listing under ACCIDENT RECONSTRUCTION: General

Safety Consulting Engineers, Inc.

C. James Dahn
Registered Professional Engineer
2131 Hammond Drive
Schaumburg, IL 60173
Tel: (847) 925-8100
Fax: (847) 925-8120
E-mail: sceinc@sceinc.com
Web Site: http://www.sceinc.com

Specialties: Consulting, research & testing for fire and explosion hazards involving chemical, propellant, pyrotechnic and explosives manufacturing. Testing includes dust explosibility, electrostatics, thermal stability and mechanical sensitivity. Outdoor test site available for large-scale processing and testing. **Degrees/licenses:** BS Aeronautical Engineering.

See primary listing under ACCIDENT RECONSTRUCTION: Analysis

Safety Management Associates

Neil R. Temple, PE, CSP
Principal Consultant
11300 Lilting Lane
Fairfax Station, VA 22039-1718
Tel: (703) 978-3000
(703) 475-8590
Fax: (703) 978-3000 #51
E-mail: smasafety@compuserve.com
Web Site: http://www.sma-safety.com

Specialties: Accident causal determination, product design safety analysis, slip and fall dynamics, stair design and code compliance, walking surface characteristics and measurement, warning and instruction adequacy, electrical safety, machine guarding, building and safety code compliance. Scope of Services: Forensic safety analysis, accident investigation and reconstruction, product safety testing. Mr. Temple is a Registered Professional Engineer in Safety (PE) and a Board Certified Safety Professional (CSP) in Comprehensive Practice. He has over 30 years of diverse safety engineering, human factors and environmental management experience and is certified by three additional competency boards. **Degrees/licenses:** BS (VA Tech.), PE (Safety), CSP, CPSM, CHCM, CHSP.

Capt. Hugh M. Stephens, CSP, PE

President
Nautical Holdings Corp.
464 Main St., Suite 307
Port Washington, NY 11050
Tel: (516) 944-9600 (Winter)
(207) 622-9409 (Summer)
(504) 812-3786 (Cell)
E-mail: stephenssos2@aol.com

Specialties: Commercial merchant vessels, including supply, ROV and "frac" boats and ferries, Dynamic Positioning/Recreational Boating/Motion picture accident/Personal injury investigation. Collisions, Marine tankers, Confined space/Rescue/Slips/Falls, Marina casualties. Pres./Founder Marine Safety Engineering Firm. Positions in steamship industry: V.P. Operations, Marine Mgr., Marine Supt., Port Captain. Dredging & Repair Supt. Yacht Broker/Manager. Chartering Supervisor, Universal Marine Executive, Kevin Costner's feature film "Waterworld." Vice President No. Atl., Council American Master Mariners. Member Natl. Cargo Bureau, Commodore, Cobbosseecontee Yacht Club, Manchester, ME, Standing Committee Marine Society - NY. Certified Safety Professional, Professional Engineer - Safety Engineering (CA). **Degrees/licenses:** USCG Unlimited Ocean Master & First Class Pilot, Radar Operator, STCW95, GMDSS.

See primary listing under MARITIME & ADMIRALTY: Consulting

Twomey Safety Engineering

Richard E. Twomey, CSP
147 Grassy Hill Road
East Lyme, CT 06333
Tel: (860) 442-8340
(860) 867-7511
Fax: (860) 444-1602
E-mail: rettse@snet.net
Web Site: http://www.twomeysafety.com

Specialties: OSHA compliance, general and products liability, slips and falls, accident reconstruction, safety audits. Ergonomics: risk assessments, work-site analysis, accident investigations, ergonomic program development and equipment. Industrial Hygiene: OSHA compliance - indoor air quality, industrial air contaminants, noise and personal protective equipment. Safety Engineering: OSHA compliance - chemical process safety management, control of hazardous energy (lockout-tagout), electrical, fire protection and life safety, machine guarding, walking/working surfaces, vehicles and construction safety standards. Products Liability: Safety standards - boiler and pressure vessel, chemical containers and labeling, elevators, equipment and machine tools, and vehicles. DEGREES/LICENSES: BS, Marine Engineer; BS, Mechanical Engineer; MS, Occupational Safety & Health; Certified Safety Professional. **Degrees/licenses:** See above.

Structural

Heino Ainso, PE, PhD

Chief Engineer
Ainso & Associates, Inc.
61 Highbrook Ave.
Pelham, NY 10803
Tel: (914) 738-6323
Fax: (914) 738-6323
E-mail: heinoainso@aol.com

Specialties: Forensic investigations, failure analysis, damages quantification, building code compliance verification, preparation and analysis of construction claims, documentation, expert testimony. Member: Am Soc. of Civil Engineers, Am Conc. Institute; Published papers on shell theory and structural analysis. **Degrees/licenses:** BME, MME, PhD in Applied Mechanics; PE in NY and NJ.
See primary listing under CONSTRUCTION: Building Failures

Tore O. Arnesen, PE

President
Arnesen & Associates, Inc.
1330 Bellaire St.
Broomfield, CO 80020-1327
Tel: (303) 465-5806
Fax: (303) 438-1800
E-mail: Tore@Arnesen.us

Specialties: Structural and Architectural (Civil) Engineer with thirty years experience: forensic investigations and repairs of damaged structures and buildings; concrete restoration; expert witness testimony; structural assessments for damage due to natural disasters or fire; commercial, institutional & industrial projects; water projects such as treatment plants, storage or containment structures & canal structures. Published over twenty articles & technical standards; listed in Marquis' "Who's Who in Science and Engineering." Membership in American Society of Civil Engineers, American Concrete Institute, SEI/ASCE-condition assessment and rehab of buildings committee. Co-author of Civil Engineering Project Peer Review, Air Supported Structure and Tension Fabric Structure Standards. **Degrees/licenses:** MSCE; PE - CO, WY & NE.

Dr. Fari Barzegar, PE

Principal
Habitat Engineering & Forensics
446 17th Street, Suite 300
Oakland, CA 94612
Tel: (510) 891-0300
(510) 717-3600 (mobile)
Fax: (510) 891-0333
E-mail: Fari@HabitatEngineering.com
Web Site:
http://www.HabitatEngineering.com

Specialties: Building Design & Construction (Residential, Commercial, Industrial and Institutional); Seismic Resistant Design; Code Compliance; Construction Defects and Accidents; Repair & Retrofit Cost Estimates; Performance Evaluation of Bridges, Water Treatment and Sanitary Structures, Pavements, Retaining Walls, Underground Conduits and Pipelines; Diagnostic & Failure Investigations; Concrete and Repair Materials; Analysis of Damage due to Vibration, Blast, Impact, Wind and Earthquake; Finite Element Analysis of Structural/Mechanical Components; 21 years of experience in Consulting, Research and Teaching; 43 publications; Reviewer of Technical Articles for Prestigious Journals; Member: ASCE, SEAONC, ACI, EERI, AISC, ICC, FEWA. **Degrees/licenses:** BS, MS, PhD, Reg. Prof. Engr. & Bldg. Contractor (CA).

Carr & Associates Engineers, Inc.

Ben F. Carr, Jr., PE, RLS (President)
Bart Carr, RLS (Vice President)
2052 Oak Mountain Drive
Pelham, AL 35124
Tel: (205) 664-8498
Fax: (205) 664-9685
E-mail:
CarrAsso@aol.com or caebfcj@aol.com

Specialties: Carr & Associates, a thirty person civil/structural and surveying firm, established 1974, with civil, structural, environmental, and mechanical engineers, and surveyors. Approximately eighty percent of our work load is design, so that our forensic engineering is "real world" and not theory. The firm's engineers have investigated over 500 structural failures and testified in depositions and court numerous times for defense and plaintiffs. The firm has structural computer software in house. Our surveying capabilities assure accurate, useful site maps, where appropriate. **Degrees/ licenses:** BCE, MS, PE (AL, MS, TN, SC, GA, FL), RLS (AL, FL, MS, TN, SC).

See primary listing under ACCIDENT RECONSTRUCTION: General

Dr. W. Gene Corley

Senior Vice President
CTL Group
5400 Old Orchard Road
Skokie, IL 60077-1030
Tel: (847) 965-7500
Fax: (847) 965-6541
E-mail: gcorley@ctlgroup.com
Web Site: http://www.ctlgroup.com

Specialties: Expert witness testimony/litigation support in construction matters, structural/architectural engineering, and materials technology; Analysis of structural failures, collapse, buckling, cracking, vibrations, wind load, deformations, earthquakes, fire damage, and construction irregularities; Design methodology and code review; Forensic materials investigations; Structural documents, evaluation; In-house laboratory analysis; Report preparation; Color graphics, animated presentations; Post-tensioned concrete slabs; Reinforced concrete deflections/failures; Masonry; Explosion. Memberships include ASCE, ACI, NSPE, PCI, National Academy of Engineering. Numerous court appearances. Over 160 technical papers published. **Degrees/licenses:** BS, MS, PhD - Civil/Struct. Engr. PE in 22 States.

See primary listing under ENGINEERING: Forensic

Engineering Associate Services

Michael B. Plunkett, PE
President
P.O. Box 5420
Wakefield, RI 02880-5420
Tel: (401) 783-1591
(401) 935-6557 (Cell)
Fax: (801) 729-0611
E-mail: eas302@aol.com
Web Site: http://www.engineeringassociateservices.com

Specialties: Engineering Associate Services has been in the Engineering Consultant business for over 25 years and its key consultants have over 30 years of experience in failure analysis, product liability, pressure vessel & boiler analysis and evaluation of mechanical and structural components. Specializing in: seismic, pipelines, construction claims, product failure, product related injuries, design & construction, industrial accidents, mechanical/structural evaluation, patent infringement, failure analysis, power plants - piping - valves - tanks. **Degrees/licenses:** BSME, MSME, PE in numerous States.

See primary listing under ENGINEERING: Mechanical

Structural *(cont.)*

Josephson-Werdowatz & Associates, Inc.

Carl H. Josephson, SE
Principal Structural Engineer
6370 Lusk Blvd., Ste. F200
San Diego, CA 92121-2753
Tel: (858) 558-2181
Fax: (858) 558-2188
E-mail: cjosephson@jwa-se.com
Web Site: http://www.jwa-se.com

6900 E. Camelback Rd., Ste. 522
Scottsdale, AZ 85251-2442
Tel: (480) 945-5337
Fax: (480) 945-5499

2110 East Flamingo Rd., Ste. 203
Las Vegas, NV 89119-5192
Tel: (702) 733-6500
Fax: (702) 733-6555

Specialties: Construction defect investigations/evaluations; Structural design & analysis; Wood frame, steel, masonry & concrete structures; Building code review & analysis; Computer presentations & animations; Alternative dispute resolution. Carl Josephson and Dan Werdowatz of Josephson-Werdowatz & Associates (JW&A) have been retained on over 500 cases as expert witnesses for construction litigation. JW&A works as both plaintiff and defense experts for a wide range of clients, and has been jointly retained on a number of cases by both plaintiff and defendant. JW&A strives for a reasoned, accurate and practical solution to construction litigation problems. DEGREES/LICENSES: Mr. Josephson: BSCE (Structures), PE/SE (CA, AZ, ID, NV & WA); PE (UT, CO, FL, & NM). Mr. Werdowatz: BSCE, MS (Structures), PE/SE (CA, WA, AZ, OR, NV & HI); PE (CO & TX). **Degrees/licenses:** BSCE, MS, PE, SE (See above).

Robert C. Peters

Owner
RCP Engineering
11 Kenny Drive
Mohnton, PA 19540
Tel: (610) 775-2003
Fax: (610) 775-7044
E-mail: rcpengineering@verizon.net

Specialties: Member National Electrical Safety Code Subcommittee 5. Wood pole expert, overhead power lines, transmission line routing, overhead line failures, high voltage, steel towers and steel poles. Senior member IEEE, Life member ASCE. ANSI 05 wood standards, power line electric magnetic fields (EMF), clearances and safety of overhead electric power lines. Chairman IEEE Overhead Line Structural Material and Hardware Working Group. **Degrees/licenses:** BSCE, MSCE, Professional Engineer in 16 states.
See primary listing under ENGINEERING: Electrical Utility

Raths, Raths & Johnson, Inc.

Otto C. "Chuck" Guedelhoefer
Senior Principal
835 Midway Drive
Willowbrook, IL 60527
Tel: (630) 325-6160
Fax: (630) 325-2866
E-mail: ocguedelhoefer@rrj.com
Web Site: http://www.rrj.com

Specialties: Forensic Engineering; Failure Analysis; Structural Problem Analysis; Construction Problem Resolution; Extensive Expert Witness Testimony: State and Federal Courts; Performance Evaluation; Structural Repair Design; Material Evaluation & Testing; Full Scale Testing; Mock-up Testing; Models for Courtroom Exhibits; Presentation Graphics; Condition Assessment and Repair of Distressed or Aged Structures. Managed investigations of disputes involving a variety of complaints and assisted a diverse set of clients. Licensed Structural Engineer in Illinois; Professional Engineer in 17 states. Contributed articles to many technical and industry publications and lectured on various facets of engineering practice. **Degrees/licenses:** BSCE, MSCE Structures, PE, SE.

Zallen Engineering

Rubin M. Zallen
Principal
1101 Worcester Road
Framingham, MA 01701
Tel: (508) 875-1360
Fax: (508) 875-1369
E-mail: rmzallen@zallenengineering.com
Web Site:
http://www.zallenengineering.com

Specialties: STRUCTURAL FAILURES, PROBLEM STRUCTURES and CONSTRUCTION: Structural engineering, forensic engineering, earthquake engineering, and construction engineering for buildings, bridges, and special structures. Investigation of structural failures and problem structures; recommendations and design for reconstruction and repair; investigation and consulting on construction problems, claims, and procedures; consulting on earthquake analysis and design; structural design review; consulting in structural engineering; technical assistance to attorneys; expert testimony. Keywords: seismic; wind; civil; analysis; test; failure; foundation; settlement; pile; caisson; underpinning; shoring; steel; metal; welding; concrete; prestressing; post-tensioning; masonry; wood; timber; plastic; code; inspection; defects; dynamic. **Degrees/licenses:** PE, SE, MS, B of CE.

Structural, Civil, Consulting

James J. Mallett, PE, PA

Civil/Structural Consulting Engineer
416 N. Baylen St.
Pensacola, FL 32501
Tel: (850) 438-7794
Fax: (850) 438-7839
E-mail: malletteng@mallett-eng.com

Specialties: Civil/Structural Construction Documents, Reports, Investigations, Limited Litigation. Professional Organizations: FES, NSPE, AWS, PCI, ACI, ASCE, CRSI, AISC, SBCCI, and AIA. **Degrees/licenses:** BCE, MSCE, MBA - Registered AL, FL, GA, KY, LA, MS, SC, TN.

See primary listing under ENGINEERING: Civil, Structural, Consulting

Water (drinking)/Sewers

Helmer Engineering, Inc.

Ray G. Helmer, PE
9314 Bankside
Houston, TX 77031
Tel: (713) 777-7611
Fax: (713) 774-6881
E-mail: HelmerEng@Houston.RR.com
Web Site:
http://www.helmer-engineering.com

Specialties: Civil engineering; Hydraulics, hydrology; Drainage, flooding, stormwater management; Sanitary engineering; Sewer lines, pump stations, wastewater treatment plants; Sewer overflows; Water lines, pump stations, water treatment plants, Water Disinfection Byproducts (DBPs); plumbing; Firewater pressure, volume, adequacy; Tornado, hurricane, earthquake damage; Highway geometry, intersections, street engineering, grading, earthwork; Sight distance; Transportation/traffic engineering; Traffic accidents; Traffic signals, signs; Pavement marking, highway lighting; Train, automobile, bicycle, pedestrian accidents; Traffic accident expert testimony involving city, county, state DOTs; Construction accidents; Structures; Foundation failure, structural damage, water intrusion; Engineered product liability/defects; FAA standards; Airport pavement, lighting, signing; Soil expansion, contraction, settlement. **Degrees/licenses:** BS (Civil Engineering); Registered Professional Engineer.

See primary listing under ENGINEERING: Water Resources

Water Resources

Helmer Engineering, Inc.

Ray G. Helmer, PE
9314 Bankside
Houston, TX 77031
Tel: (713) 777-7611
Fax: (713) 774-6881
E-mail: HelmerEng@Houston.RR.com
Web Site:
http://www.helmer-engineering.com

Specialties: Civil engineering; Hydraulics, hydrology; Drainage, flooding, stormwater management; Sanitary engineering; Sewer lines, pump stations, wastewater treatment plants; Sewer overflows; Water lines, pump stations, water treatment plants, Water Disinfection Byproducts (DBPs); plumbing; Firewater pressure, volume, adequacy; Tornado, hurricane, earthquake damage; Highway geometry, intersections, street engineering, grading, earthwork; Sight distance; Transportation/traffic engineering; Traffic accidents; Traffic signals, signs; Pavement marking, highway lighting; Train, automobile, bicycle, pedestrian accidents; Traffic accident expert testimony involving city, county, state DOTs; Construction accidents; Structures; Foundation failure, structural damage, water intrusion; Engineered product liability/defects; FAA standards; Airport pavement, lighting, signing; Soil expansion, contraction, settlement. **Degrees/licenses:** BS (Civil Engineering); Registered Professional Engineer.

WEST Consultants, Inc.

Jeffrey B. Bradley, PhD, PE
President
2601 25th Street SE, #450
Salem, OR 97302
Tel: (425) 646-8806
(858) 487-9378
(480) 345-2155
Fax: (503) 485-5491
Web Site: http://www.westconsultants.com

Specialties: Registered Professional Engineer five states. Nationally recognized expert with 29 years experience hydraulics, hydrology and sedimentation. Lectured in many short courses, including Bridge Scour and HEC-RAS for ASCE. Written over 100 professional papers and reports. Editor of the books, "The Physics of Sediment Transport by Wind and Water: A Collection of Hallmark Papers" by R. A. Bagnold and "Gravel Bed Rivers and the Environment." Past chair ASCE Water Resources Engineering Division, and Sedimentation Committee. Past President of the ASCE Environmental and Water Resources Institute. President of ASCE's American Academy of Water Resources Engineers. **Degrees/licenses:** BSCE, MSCE, PhD Hydraulics.

See primary listing under ENGINEERING: Flood/ Hydraulic

ENVIRONMENTAL

General

Richard A. Baker, CPS, CEM, CELC, ACD

President
Baker Environmental Consulting, Inc.
7941 Westgate Street
Lenexa, KS 66215-2636
Tel: (913) 541-0220
Fax: (913) 541-0457
E-mail: ThePbMan@aol.com
Web Site:
http://www.bakerenvironmental.com

Specialties: Over 29 years of expert experience and technical expertise in all phases of the lead-based paint hazard inspection, risk assessment and abatement industry; Plaintiff expert witness; Environmental litigation support. Authored, co-authored and peer reviewed numerous state, local and federal regulations governing lead-based paint; Authored technical articles and guidance manuals for lead-based paint testing and lead-based paint hazard control issues. Provides environmental training for state agencies, attorneys, contractors, local agencies, federal agencies and universities. Received numerous awards for commitment and dedication to environmental excellence. Has been listed in top 50 of lead-based paint industry experts and environmental Who's Who. **Degrees/licenses:** Lic. Lead Insp., Risk

Assessor, Abatement Project Designer/Abatement Supervisor.

See primary listing under ENVIRONMENTAL: Lead Poisoning

ForensisGroup, Inc.

Mercy Steenwyk
3452 E. Foothill Blvd., Ste. 1160
Pasadena, CA 91107
Tel: (626) 795-5000
(800) 555-5422
Fax: (626) 795-1950
E-mail: experts@forensisgroup.com
Web Site: http://forensisgroup.com

Specialties: Thousands of our clients have gained the technical advantage and the edge in their cases from our multidisciplined group of experts in hundreds of disciplines. We have some of the best and the brightest at competitive rates backed by 14 years of excellent track record and the support of our trained staff. We assist you until you have the right expert. Some of our areas of expertise are: Construction, Safety, Engineering, Product Liability, Accident Reconstruction, Automotive, Environmental, Slip & Fall, Appraisal, Medical and other scientific disciplines. Unsurpassed standards. Clients actively evaluate our experts. **Degrees/licenses:** PE, GC, CSP, PhD, MD, GC, CIH, AIA.

See primary listing under ACCIDENT PREVENTION & SAFETY: General

Alberto A. Gutierrez, RG

President
GEOLEX, Inc.
500 Marquette Ave. NW, Ste. 1350
Albuquerque, NM 87102
Tel: (505) 842-8000
Fax: (505) 842-7380
E-mail: aag@geolex.com
Web Site: http://www.geolex.com

Specialties: Environmental litigation support; Hydrogeology; Contaminant fate and transport modeling; Hazardous waste management; Site investigation and remediation; RCRA and Superfund cost allocation/analysis; Forensic geochemistry and source identification of soil and groundwater contamination; Aerial photography interpretation/waste management practice documentation; Environmental liability assessment and forensic accounting; Asset evaluation for corporate mergers and acquisitions. Registered professional geologist with AIPG and in 18 states. Extensive expert witness experience in state and federal court and hearings before regulatory bodies. Former chairman of New Mexico Environmental Improvement Board. Former Commissioner, NM Water Quality Control Commission. Extensively published. **Degrees/licenses:** BS Geomorphology (magna cum laude); MS (cum laude); RG, CPG, REA.

Kenneth T. Kim, MD

Allergy, Asthma & Respiratory Care Medical Center
2600 Redondo Ave., #400
Long Beach, CA 90806-2330
Tel: (562) 997-7888
Fax: (562) 997-8884
E-mail: andrean@wcctrials.com
Web Site: http://www.allergy-asthma.info

Specialties: Expert reviewer & witness, QME, WC, pediatric and adult asthma, atopic dermatitis, eczema, hives, chronic cough, food/drug allergy, insect stings, mold allergy, latex allergy, sick building syndrome, disability evaluations, occupational latex allergy, disability evaluations for occupational asthma. **Degrees/licenses:** MD Harvard; Assistant Clinical Professor, UCLA, UCI.

See primary listing under MEDICINE & HEALTH: Allergy/Immunology

James M. Miller, PE, PhD

President
Miller Engineering Associates, Inc.
2392 Fuller Court
Ann Arbor, MI 48105
Tel: (734) 662-6822
Fax: (734) 747-9712
E-mail: jmiller@millerengineering.com
Web Site: www.millerengineering.com

Specialties: Chemical, Fire, Environmental & Waste Disposal: Fires & Explosions-Vapors/Electrical/Chemical; Chemical Label-

(Listing continued on next page)

General *(cont.)*

James M. Miller (cont.)

ing Requirements; MSDS; Groundwater & Soil Contamination; Mechanical Design Safety: Power Tools & Machine Guarding; OSHA/ANSI/ASTM Compliance; Warnings, Labels, Instructions & User Manuals: Health Hazard Warnings; Design of User Manuals & Warnings; Consumer Product Safety: Human Factors & Ergonomics, Slips, Falls-Premise, Vehicle, Ladder; Child, Home Appliances, Furniture; Vehicles: Auto, Truck, ATV, Boat, Jet Ski, Snowmobile; Seat Belts & Air Bags; Agricultural & Construction Safety: Tractor, Implement, Harvester & Grain Storage; Pesticides, Herbicides, Fungicides; Nursing Malpractice; Nursing Management. **Degrees/ licenses:** James Miller, PE, PhD; Bradley Cook, PE; Rebecca Lehto, PhD, RN, OCN.

See primary listing under ACCIDENT PREVENTION & SAFETY: General

John J. Oransky, PE, CIH, CSP, DEE, DABFET

Founder
Oransky Engineering & Consulting
374 West Ridge Street
Lansford, PA 18232
Tel: (570) 645-3582
Fax: (570) 645-4533

Specialties: Significant experience in hazardous and solid waste management, hazardous materials control, engineering studies and evaluations, industrial ventilation, safety and environmental audits, storage tank inspection, evaluation and certification, process development, design and optimization, air pollution system evaluation and design, wastewater system characterization and design, permit application assistance, technical training, environmental and safety program development and upgrade, waste minimization engineering, process modification assistance, industrial hygiene, material reuse and chemical substitution studies. Member of the American College of Forensic Examiners. **Degrees/ licenses:** BSCHE, MSCHE, PE, CIH, CSP, DEE, DABFET.

Aboveground Storage Tanks

Clement Mesavage, Jr.

Midstream Farm, LLC
3117 Stone Arbor Lane, Suite 1133
Glen Allen, VA 23050
Tel: (804) 262-6552
Fax: (804) 262-6555
E-mail: usaclem@erols.com
Web Site: http://www.usaclem.com

Specialties: Located near Washington, D. C. Over 25 years of consulting experience in environmental, health, safety, fire, explosion, variance, and facility security matters associated with petroleum & chemical storage and transfer; Completed work at over 500 bulk liquid, aboveground tank terminals ("tank farms") in 43 states; Has provided services to proprietary and for-hire terminal operators, private and government pipeline operators, the military, manufacturers, municipalities, and port authorities. Current services include performing due diligence site assessments, audits, permitting, and serving as expert witness concerning industry practices, equipment design, and regulatory and facility security matters. Please refer to website for additional information. **Degrees/licenses:** BSCE, MSCE, MPA, REA.

Aerial Photo Analysis & Mapping

Ebert & Associates, Inc.

Dr. James I. Ebert
Chief Scientist
3700 Rio Grande Blvd. NW, Ste. 3
Albuquerque, NM 87107
Tel: (505) 344-2345
(866) 503-9776 Toll Free
Fax: (505) 344-2444
E-mail: jebert@ebert.com
Web Site: http://www.ebert.com

Specialties: We specialize in developing and supporting legal arguments based on spatial and other data derived from photographs and maps through scientific analyses and expert witness testimony. Historic aerial photointerpretation, photo analysis, digital mapping, geographic information systems - GIS - database compilation and analysis, and subsurface contaminant modeling at Superfund, waste disposal, and other sites involved in environmental, land rights, and water rights litigation. Photo interpretation, photogrammetry, and 3-dimensional measurement and mapping from scene and evidence photographs and video for reconstruction of accident, fire, explosion, crime and other scenes in forensic cases. **Degrees/licenses:** BA, MA, PhD, Certified Photogrammetrist (ASPRS).

Analytical Labs

ZymaX Forensics

Alan Jeffrey, PhD
Senior Geochemist
71 Zaca Lane
San Luis Obispo, CA 93401-7300
Tel: (800) 644-4696 ext.327
Fax: (805) 544-8226
E-mail: forensics@zymax.net
Web Site: http://www.zymax.net/327

Specialties: Environmental forensics and geochemistry consulting, litigation support and expert witness testimony. Specialties: petroleum hydrocarbon analysis, gas geochemistry, biomarkers, PNA's, PCB's, oxygenates, fuel ID, mixing ratios, age dating, metal analysis by ICP/MS, inorganic and wet chemistry, stable isotope analysis, hydrology. Developed analyses allow us to: identify the types of product which have been released, distinguish between similar products from different sources, estimate the mixing ratios of different products, estimate the age of the product, assign probable responsibility for sources of the contamination, and give expert witness testimony. **Degrees/licenses:** PhD in Chemical Oceanography.

Asbestos Consulting

Brian E. Galligan

Owner/President
Triad Environmental Consulting, Inc.
309 3rd Avenue
Huntington, WV 25704
Tel: (304) 523-2195
Fax: (304) 523-2197
E-mail: duxster@earthlink.net

Specialties: OH, WV, VA & KY Asbestos Inspector; WV Asbestos Supervisor; WV Air Clearance. KY, OH, WV Project Design; VA Inspector/Mgmt. Planner; WV Lead Inspector/Risk Assessor. **Degrees/licenses:** Asbestos Inspector, Supr. Proj. Design, Air Clear; Lead Insp..

Jon J. Pina, MS, CSP

Safety, Health
& Environmental Professional
Evergreen Environmental Health
& Safety, Inc.
368 Rt. 110 Hwy.
Indiana, PA 15701
Tel: (724) 349-7029
Fax: (724) 349-3540
E-mail: jpina@adelphia.net

Specialties: Over 31 years experience; safety, industrial hygiene, environmental, PA state OSHA consultant, construction management, "hands-on" industrial and chemical operations; slip, trip, and falls; demolition; asbestos identification, abatement, disposal, final clearance, AHERA, NESHAPS, TSCA; asbestos training; environmental surveys/Phase I & II environmental assessments; hazardous waste site remediation; RCRA, CERCLA; mixed wastes, etc.; drum, soil, water, and air sampling; excavation, utility location/isolation, tank cleaning, boilers, confined space, fall protection, electrical hazards; emergency response; safety professor; professionally published, owns collection of asbestos samples. Demolished many steel, coke, and chemical facilities after managing asbestos abatement. **Degrees/licenses:** MS Safety Sci; MS Geol;

(Listing continued on next page)

Asbestos Consulting *(cont.)*

Jon J. Pina (cont.)
BS Geosci Ed.; Cert Safety Prof; Cert Prof Instructor.

See primary listing under ACCIDENT PREVENTION & SAFETY: General

Bioremediation

W. Edward Montz, Jr., PhD

Indoor Air Solutions, Inc.
1200 E. High St., Ste. 301
Pottstown, PA 19464
Tel: (610) 323-8818
Fax: (610) 323-8839
E-mail: wem@stachybotrys.com
Web Site: http://moldabatement.com

Specialties: Indoor Air Solutions, Inc. specializes in indoor air quality testing, surveys and inspections for residences, commercial offices, hospitals and public buildings. We provide litigation support services for both plaintiffs and defendants. The abatement division specializes in decontaminating mold-contaminated buildings. **Degrees/licenses:** PhD, CIAQP.

See primary listing under ENVIRONMENTAL: Indoor Air Quality

Consulting

Richard A. Baker, CPS, CEM, CELC, ACD

President
Baker Environmental Consulting, Inc.
7941 Westgate Street
Lenexa, KS 66215-2636
Tel: (913) 541-0220
Fax: (913) 541-0457
E-mail: ThePbMan@aol.com
Web Site:
http://www.bakerenvironmental.com

Specialties: Over 29 years of expert experience and technical expertise in all phases of the lead-based paint hazard inspection, risk assessment and abatement industry; Plaintiff expert witness; Environmental litigation support. Authored, co-authored and peer reviewed numerous state, local and federal regulations governing lead-based paint; Authored technical articles and guidance manuals for lead-based paint testing and lead-based paint hazard control issues. Provides environmental training for state agencies, attorneys, contractors, local agencies, federal agencies and universities. Received numerous awards for commitment and dedication to environmental excellence. Has been listed in top 50 of lead-based paint industry experts and environmental Who's Who. **Degrees/licenses:** Lic. Lead Insp., Risk Assessor, Abatement Project Designer/Abatement Supervisor.

See primary listing under ENVIRONMENTAL: Lead Poisoning

Princeton-Somerset Group, Inc.

Dennis M. Stainken, PhD
Principal
4 Carroll Drive
Hillsborough, NJ 08844
Tel: (908) 369-6890
(800) 597-8836
Fax: (908) 369-6881
E-mail: prinsomgrp@aol.com

Specialties: Expert Witness, Property Damage/Contamination & Remediation, Regulatory Agency Negotiations, Health Effects Evaluation, Gasoline & Oil Contamination Issues, Assessments, Audits, Oversight, Environmental Toxicology, Chemistry, Ecological Services, Risk Assessments, Wetlands, Remediation, Regulatory Issues, Natural Resource Damage, Water Quality, Industrial Services, Waste Water, Site Assessments and Property Transfer Assessments - Phase I, II, & III. Services nationwide, 30+ years of industrial & government experience in Pollution Control & Hazardous Water Projects. Extensive experience in environmental enforcement under NPDES, CERCLA, RCRA, SDWA and CWA. Former Regulator, Professor, Consultant. 75+ publications. National expert in Environmental Toxicology, fate/effects of pollutants. **Degrees/licenses:** BS, MS, PhD, NJ Lic. UST, Calif. REA; Diplomate, Am. Bd. Foren. Exam., CSE, PWS.

Engineering

The Whitman Companies, Inc.

Barry Skoultchi, PE
116 Tices Lane, Unit B-1
East Brunswick, NJ 08816-2014
Tel: (732) 390-5858
Fax: (732) 390-9496
E-mail: bskoultchi@whitmanco.com
Web Site: http://www.whitmanco.com

Specialties: Environmental Compliance; Ground Water; Wetland and Ecological Assessments; Urban Industrial Brownfields Restoration; Insurance and Predecessor Liability; USTs; Site Assessments; Indoor Air Quality; Asbestos Management; Mold Assessments. Expert Reports and Testimony. **Degrees/licenses:** PhD, PE, CIH, AST.

Environmental Assessment/ Impact Studies

Edward C. Keller Jr.

Professor of Biology
West Virginia University
236 Grand St.
Morgantown, WV 26505
Tel: (304) 292-4554
Fax: (304) 293-6363
E-mail: ekeller@wvu.edu
Web Site:
http://www.us.wvu.edu/~scidis/keller/

Specialties: Litigative & regulatory statistics; Ecological data handling techniques; Sampling design. **Degrees/licenses:** PhD, ScD, FAAAS.

See primary listing under STATISTICS: General

Forensics

ZymaX Forensics

Alan Jeffrey, PhD
Senior Geochemist
71 Zaca Lane
San Luis Obispo, CA 93401-7300
Tel: (800) 644-4696 ext.327
Fax: (805) 544-8226
E-mail: forensics@zymax.net
Web Site: http://www.zymax.net/327

Specialties: Environmental and geochemical laboratory and consulting company supporting attorneys, insurance companies and environmental consultants in assessment, remediation and litigation of spills in the environment. Specialized in environmental forensics. Analytical testing of petroleum related and other organic and inorganic spills. Consultants with specialized geochemical expertise in interpretation of analytical data. Product identification determines the responsible parties. Who did it? What was spilled? Estimate mixing ratios. Estimate how much was spilled. Estimate when it was spilled. We often perform expert testimony about our findings during discovery or at trial. **Degrees/licenses:** PhD in Chemical Oceanography.

See primary listing under ENVIRONMENTAL: Analytical Labs

Groundwater Pollution

Nicholas Albergo

Chairman & CEO
HSA Environmental
4019 East Fowler Avenue
Tampa, FL 33617
Tel: (813) 971-3882
Fax: (813) 971-1862
E-mail: nalbergo@hsa-env.com
Web Site: http://www.hsa-env.com

Specialties: Groundwater remediation, soil and water quality evaluations, contamination assessment, degradation and migration analysis, contaminant modeling, industrial wastewater treatment design, hazardous waste

(Listing continued on next page)

Groundwater Pollution *(cont.)*

Nicholas Albergo (cont.)
management, disposal and remedial strategy. Prior testimony includes cases involving difficult or unusual hazardous wastes, advanced hydrogeology, landfill gas and leachate assessment, geochemistry, water quality impact analysis, water resource management, and sensitive regulatory compliance issues. Has chaired several major scientific conferences, and has over 150 technical publications. Internationally recognized in the area of contamination assessment and remedial strategies associated with chlorinated solvents and other dense nonaqueous-phase liquids. **Degrees/licenses:** BSES, MSCE, PhDc, DEE, PE, REP.
See primary listing under ENGINEERING: Groundwater Remediation

David R. Hargis, PhD, RG

Principal Hydrogeologist
Hargis + Associates, Inc.
2365 Northside Dr., #C100
San Diego, CA 92108-2709
Tel: (619) 521-0165
Fax: (619) 521-8580
E-mail: drhargis@hargis.com
Web Site: http://www.hargis.com

Specialties: Hydrology/Hydrogeology; Contaminant Fate and Transport; Source Evaluation and Timing; Groundwater Modeling; Contaminant Transport Modeling; Groundwater and Soil Remediation; Litigation Support; Expert Witness Testimony; Cost Allocation Analysis; Water Resources Exploration, Design and Development. Provides expert witness testimony, technical counsel, litigation support concerning hydrological conditions and assessment of soil/groundwater contamination at complex industrial, commercial, or Superfund sites. Also provides technical support for PRP identification, cost allocation, negotiations with USEPA and state agencies involving site cleanup levels and approval of RI/FS/RD/RA documents, cost recovery issues, and toxic tort litigation. **Degrees/licenses:** PhD, MS, BS, Registered Geologist (CA, AZ, VA & TX).
See primary listing under GEOLOGY/ HYDROLOGY: Groundwater & Hydrogeology

Hazardous Materials

Edward W. Funk, PhD

EWF Consulting
676 DeTamble Ave.
Highland Park, IL 60035
Tel: (847) 433-5659
Fax: (847) 433-2837
E-mail: ewf@ewfconsulting.net
Web Site: http://www.ewfconsulting.net

Specialties: Chemical processes and products, polymers, resins, membranes, films, composites, coatings, plastic products, industrial chemicals, consumer chemicals, solvents, vapor and water emissions. Experience in cases involving patent infringement, chemical accidents, product liability, and environmental issues. Dr. Funk has 20 years industrial experience with Exxon and Honeywell and is also a Professor of Chemical Engineering at University of Illinois. He is the author of 6 U.S. patents and 70 technical publications. He has been a consultant to numerous chemical companies, law firms, and national laboratories. **Degrees/licenses:** BS, Yale; PhD, University of California, Berkeley.

See primary listing under CHEMISTRY/ CHEMICALS: Polymers

Hazardous Waste

Nicholas Albergo

Chairman & CEO
HSA Environmental
4019 East Fowler Avenue
Tampa, FL 33617
Tel: (813) 971-3882
Fax: (813) 971-1862
E-mail: nalbergo@hsa-env.com
Web Site: http://www.hsa-env.com

Specialties: Groundwater remediation, soil and water quality evaluations, contamination assessment, degradation and migration analysis, contaminant modeling, industrial wastewater treatment design, hazardous waste management, disposal and remedial strategy. Prior testimony includes cases involving difficult or unusual hazardous wastes, advanced hydrogeology, landfill gas and leachate assessment, geochemistry, water quality impact analysis, water resource management, and sensitive regulatory compliance issues. Has chaired several major scientific conferences, and has over 150 technical publications. Internationally recognized in the area of contamination assessment and remedial strategies associated with chlorinated solvents and other dense nonaqueous-phase liquids. **Degrees/licenses:** BSES, MSCE, PhDc, DEE, PE, REP.

See primary listing under ENGINEERING: Groundwater Remediation

Theodore O. Meiggs

President, Senior Consultant
Meiggs Environmental Consultants, Inc.
14250 Braun Rd.
Golden, CO 80401
Tel: (303) 278-7452
Fax: (303) 278-7478
E-mail: profinder1@comcast.net

Specialties: Air, water, wastewater, soil & hazardous waste testing, and investigations; Hazardous waste characterization including corrosive & reactive wastes; EPA enforcement practice; Environmental crime investigations; Environmental testing regulations; Analytical data quality evaluations; Analytical laboratory evaluations & management; Expert witness referrals. **Degrees/licenses:** PhD (Physical Organic Chemistry).

Alan D. Zunkel, D.Sc., PE

President
A.D. Zunkel Consultants Inc.
8020 NE 71st Loop
Vancouver, WA 98662
Tel: (360) 896-5301
Fax: (360) 896-2180
E-mail: DZunkel@aol.com

Specialties: Historical and modern minerals processing and extraction metallurgy of primary and secondary zinc, lead, copper, precious metals, cadmium, arsenic and by products. Extensive investigation, research, deposition and expert witness testimony in state and federal environmental cases. BS, Missouri School of Mines; MS and D.Sc., Colorado School of Mines. Past president, TMS of AIME; Fellow, IMM; Member: CIM, SME of AIME, AISE, MMSA. Over 30 publications in extraction metallurgy. **Degrees/licenses:** BS, MS, D.Sc., PE, Chartered Engineer (UK).

See primary listing under ENGINEERING: Metallurgical

Health & Safety

Richard A. Baker, CPS, CEM, CELC, ACD

President
Baker Environmental Consulting, Inc.
7941 Westgate Street
Lenexa, KS 66215-2636
Tel: (913) 541-0220
Fax: (913) 541-0457
E-mail: ThePbMan@aol.com
Web Site:
http://www.bakerenvironmental.com

Specialties: Over 29 years of expert experience and technical expertise in all phases of the lead-based paint hazard inspection, risk assessment and abatement industry; Plaintiff expert witness; Environmental litigation support. Authored, co-authored and peer reviewed numerous state, local and federal regulations governing lead-based paint; Authored technical articles and guidance manuals for lead-based paint testing and lead-based paint hazard control issues. Provides environmental training for state agencies, attorneys, contractors, local agencies, federal agencies and universities. Received numerous awards for commitment and dedication to environmental excellence. Has been listed in top 50 of lead-based paint industry experts and environmental Who's Who. **Degrees/licenses:** Lic. Lead Insp., Risk Assessor, Abatement Project Designer/Abatement Supervisor.

See primary listing under ENVIRONMENTAL: Lead Poisoning

Indoor Air Quality

Richard M. Lynch, PhD, CIH
President
Environmental Safety Management Corp.
21 E Scott Street
Riverside, NJ 08075
Tel: (856) 764-3557
Fax: (856) 764-3558
E-mail: rlynch@esmcorp.com
Web Site: http://www.esmcorp.com

Specialties: Indoor Air Quality, Mold, Ergonomics, Workers Compensation, Chemical Exposure Modeling, OSHA Compliance, Carpal Tunnel Syndrome, Back Injury, Industrial Hygiene, Safety. **Degrees/licenses:** PhD, MS, Certified Industrial Hygienist.

See primary listing under ACCIDENT PREVENTION & SAFETY: Industrial Hygiene

W. Edward Montz, Jr., PhD
Indoor Air Solutions, Inc.
1200 E. High St., Ste. 301
Pottstown, PA 19464
Tel: (610) 323-8818
Fax: (610) 323-8839
E-mail: wem@stachybotrys.com
Web Site: http://moldabatement.com

Specialties: Indoor Air Solutions, Inc. specializes in indoor air quality testing, surveys and inspections for residences, commercial offices, hospitals and public buildings. We provide litigation support services for both plaintiffs and defendants. The abatement division specializes in decontaminating mold-contaminated buildings. **Degrees/licenses:** PhD, CIAQP.

Investigation

Theodore O. Meiggs
President, Senior Consultant
Meiggs Environmental Consultants, Inc.
14250 Braun Rd.
Golden, CO 80401
Tel: (303) 278-7452
Fax: (303) 278-7478
E-mail: profinder1@comcast.net

Specialties: Air, water, wastewater, soil & hazardous waste testing, and investigations; Hazardous waste characterization including corrosive & reactive wastes; EPA enforcement practice; Environmental crime investigations; Environmental testing regulations; Analytical data quality evaluations; Analytical laboratory evaluations & management; Expert witness referrals. **Degrees/licenses:** PhD (Physical Organic Chemistry).

See primary listing under ENVIRONMENTAL: Hazardous Waste

Lead Poisoning

Richard A. Baker, CPS, CEM, CELC, ACD
President
Baker Environmental Consulting, Inc.
7941 Westgate Street
Lenexa, KS 66215-2636
Tel: (913) 541-0220
Fax: (913) 541-0457
E-mail: ThePbMan@aol.com
Web Site:
http://www.bakerenvironmental.com

Specialties: Over 29 years of expert experience and technical expertise in all phases of the lead-based paint hazard inspection, risk assessment and abatement industry; Plaintiff expert witness; Environmental litigation support. Authored, co-authored and peer reviewed numerous state, local and federal regulations governing lead-based paint; Authored technical articles and guidance manuals for lead-based paint testing and lead-based paint hazard control issues. Provides environmental training for state agencies, attorneys, contractors, local agencies, federal agencies and universities. Received numerous awards for commitment and dedication to environmental excellence. Has been listed in top 50 of lead-based paint industry experts and environmental Who's Who. **Degrees/licenses:** Lic. Lead Insp., Risk Assessor, Abatement Project Designer/Abatement Supervisor.

Rudy Von Burg, PhD

Principal
EnTox & Associates
230 Castro St.
Point Richmond, CA 94801
Tel: (510) 235-2969
(925) 288-2366
(415) 637-2402
Fax: (510) 235-2969
E-mail: rvonburg@entoxandassociates.com
Web Site: http://entoxandassociates.com

Specialties: Occupational & environmental toxicology Litigation Support and Expert Witness, petroleum products, pesticides, carbon monoxide, pharmaceutical agents, metals, asbestos, lead, indoor air, mold, household chemicals. OSHA training, plan preparation and compliance audits, worker protection, compensation claims. Board certified in Toxicology, Certified Industrial Hygiene, AHERA certified, Cal OSHA certified for asbestos, California certified for lead inspection and monitoring. **Degrees/licenses:** PhD, DABT, CIH, CEI, AHERA, CAC, CLI.

See primary listing under ENVIRONMENTAL: Toxicology

Noise & Vibration

Jack E. Randorff, PhD, PE, FASA

Principal-in-Charge
Randorff and Associates, Inc.
11 West Canyon View Drive
Ransom Canyon, TX 79366
Tel: (806) 829-2521
Fax: (806) 829-2527

Specialties: Environmental noise assessments; sound level survey; train horn loudness assessments; employee hearing damage-risk assessments; vibration assessments; highway noise assessment; aircraft/airport noise assessment; architectural sound isolation assessments; industrial noise assessments; testimony - plaintiffs & defendants; clients - major companies, federal agencies, state agencies, local municipalities, private industry, schools, universities, national architectural/engineering firms; National Council of Acoustical Consultants, President (1992-1994), Vice President - membership (1998-2002), Vice President - finance (2002-2004); Fellow - Acoustical Society of America, American Institute of Physics; President - Engineers Council of Houston (1985-1986), Science Engineering Fair of Houston (1986-1988). **Degrees/licenses:** BS, MS, PhD, PE (Texas).

See primary listing under ACOUSTICS: General

Petroleum

James G. Speight, PhD, DSc

Consultant
2476 Overland Road
Laramie, WY 82070-4808
Tel: (307) 745-6069
Fax: (307) 721-3128
E-mail: jamessp8@aol.com
Web Site:
http://www.drjamesspeight.qpg.com

Specialties: More than 35 years experience with fossil fuels, especially petroleum technology, coal, and natural gas. See web page for more details. **Degrees/licenses:** PhD, DSc.

See primary listing under ENGINEERING: Petroleum

ZymaX Forensics

Alan Jeffrey, PhD
Senior Geochemist
71 Zaca Lane
San Luis Obispo, CA 93401-7300
Tel: (800) 644-4696 ext.327
Fax: (805) 544-8226
E-mail: forensics@zymax.net
Web Site: http://www.zymax.net/327

Specialties: Environmental and geochemical laboratory and consulting company supporting

(Listing continued on next page)

Petroleum *(cont.)*

ZymaX Forensics (cont.)
attorneys, insurance companies and environmental consultants in assessment, remediation and litigation of spills in the environment. Specialized in environmental forensics. Analytical testing of petroleum related and other organic and inorganic spills. Consultants with specialized geochemical expertise in interpretation of analytical data. Product identification determines the responsible parties. Who did it? What was spilled? Estimate mixing ratios. Estimate how much was spilled. Estimate when it was spilled. We often perform expert testimony about our findings during discovery or at trial. **Degrees/licenses:** PhD in Chemical Oceanography.

See primary listing under ENVIRONMENTAL: Analytical Labs

Pollution (Air, Soil, Water)

Professional Analytical and Consulting Services, Inc. (PACS)

Henry G. Nowicki, PhD, MBA
President and Senior Consultant
409 Meade Drive
Coraopolis, PA 15108
Tel: (724) 457-6576
(800) 367-2587
Fax: (724) 457-1214
E-mail: hnpacs@aol.com
Web Site: http://www.pacslabs.com

Specialties: Data quality, toxicology, safety, risk assessments (carbon monoxide), evaluations for air, soil, water analysis; multi-disciplinary team; Computer experts, modeling and statistics. Thirty years experience working with lawyers to prepare winning strategies and expert testimony. Regulatory drinking water & wastewater experts. Provided services for Love Canal, Everglades, Phoenix drinking water chemicals (PAHs, THMs, haloacetic acids, arsenic, etc.) and health, patent infringement, and other cases. Short training courses (57 available) on environmental science subjects. Third-party independent laboratory testing for major organic and inorganic instrumental techniques and wet chemistry techniques. Microscope XRD and SEM laboratory images for failure analysis. Sponsors annual conferences, in addition to courses and laboratory testing. DEP Asbestos. Offices in Pittsburgh, PA; Orlando, FL; St. Louis, MO. **Degrees/licenses:** BS, MA, PhD, MBA, PE; ACS, ASCC, ASQC, AWWA, WQA, SSP, SACP, IACMA, EPA Arsenic.

Scrap Tire Processing

George M. Mallan, PhD

Owner
Mallan Associates, Inc.
405 Old Westport Rd.
P.O. Box 70523
North Dartmouth, MA 02747
Tel: (508) 994-3328
Fax: (508) 991-8068
E-mail: GMMallan@hotmail.com

Specialties: Waste-to-energy design and operations; Scrap tire processing and molding of resultant crumb rubber product; solid waste recycling. 25 years of managerial experience in heading resource recovery efforts of both multi-billion dollar corporations and entrepreneurial start-up firms. After stepping down as CEO of a start-up firm that successfully financed a $336 million waste-to-energy facility, established consulting firm in 1986. Served 10 clients as expert witness testifying in arbitration and State court settings. Numerous references cite exceptionally strong performance under cross-examination. **Degrees/licenses:** PhD, Chem. Engr., Univ. of Southern California.

See primary listing under ENVIRONMENTAL: Solid Waste

Solid Waste

George M. Mallan, PhD

Owner
Mallan Associates, Inc.
405 Old Westport Rd.
P.O. Box 70523
North Dartmouth, MA 02747
Tel: (508) 994-3328
Fax: (508) 991-8068
E-mail: GMMallan@hotmail.com

Specialties: Waste-to-energy design and operations; Scrap tire processing and molding of resultant crumb rubber product; solid waste recycling. 25 years of managerial experience in heading resource recovery efforts of both multi-billion dollar corporations and entrepreneurial start-up firms. After stepping down as CEO of a start-up firm that successfully financed a $336 million waste-to-energy facility, established consulting firm in 1986. Served 10 clients as expert witness testifying in arbitration and State court settings. Numerous references cite exceptionally strong performance under cross-examination. **Degrees/licenses:** PhD, Chem. Engr., Univ. of Southern California.

Testing & Measurement

A. Dallas Wait

Principal/Environmental Chemist
Gradient Corporation
20 University Rd.
Cambridge, MA 02138-5756
Tel: (617) 395-5000
Fax: (617) 395-5001
E-mail: dwait@gradientcorp.com
Web Site: http//www.gradientcorp.com

Specialties: Environmental chemistry; Petroleum & PCB chemistry; Analytical chemistry; Forensic chemistry; Chemical fingerprinting; Product characterization; Quality assurance; Data usability & integrity; Method design & evaluation; Lab fraud investigations; Historical analytical chemistry practices; Regulatory comment; Agency negotiations; Sampling techniques; Laboratory auditing & management. **Degrees/licenses:** PhD (Organic Chemistry); BS (Chemistry).

See primary listing under CHEMISTRY/ CHEMICALS: Environmental Chemistry

Toxicology

John D. Bogden, PhD

Professor
UMDNJ - New Jersey Medical School
Department of Preventive Medicine
& Community Health
185 South Orange Avenue
P.O. Box 1709
Newark, NJ 07101-1709
Tel: (973) 972-5432
Fax: (973) 972-7625
E-mail: bogden@umdnj.edu

Specialties: Toxicology & Nutrition Consultant; Specialty is Mineral and Trace Element Nutrition & Toxicology: lead poisoning, cadmium toxicity, chromium toxicity, mercury poisoning, overdoses of minerals and trace elements, vitamin and mineral supplements, air, soil and water pollutants, environmental toxins, occupational medicine, analyses of body tissues and fluids; Expert reports, deposition and court testimony experience; More than 100 publications in leading medical, nutrition, and toxicology journals. **Degrees/licenses:** MS, PhD, FACN, CNS.

Alan Buchwald, MD Inc.

Alan Buchwald, MD
P.O. Box 2009
Santa Cruz, CA 95063
Tel: (831) 761-0260
Fax: (831) 761-0260
E-mail: albuchwald955@pol.net
Web Site: http://doctor.medscape.com/alanbuchwaldmd

Specialties: Medical toxicology; Poisoning; Overdose; Envenomation; Industrial/occupational; Environmental, Hazardous materials; Agricultural; Food toxicology; Indoor air problems; Fellow American Academy of Emergency Medicine; Board Certified

(Listing continued on next page)

Toxicology *(cont.)*

Alan Buchwald, MD Inc. (cont.)
- American Board of Emergency Medicine and American Board of Medical Toxicology; Subspecialty Certification in Medical Toxicology, ABEM; Medical Director - Occupational Health Center, Dominican Santa Cruz Hospital; Affiliations - American Academy of Clinical Toxicology, American College of Occupational and Environmental Medicine, British Toxicology Society, Royal Society of Medicine (London), Aerospace Medicine Association (Space Medicine Branch); Categories - General consulting, personal injury, Workers' Compensation. **Degrees/licenses:** BA, MS, MD, ACMT, QME.

See primary listing under MEDICINE & HEALTH: Toxicology

Dermigen, Inc.

Earl F. Walborg, Jr., PhD
President
912 A Garwood St.
P.O. Box 727
Smithville, TX 78957
Tel: (512) 237-5357
Fax: (512) 237-5363
E-mail: ewalborg@dermigen.com
Web Site: http://www.dermigen.com

Specialties: Earl F. Walborg, Jr., PhD, President of Dermigen, Inc., coordinates the consulting services of scientific experts with a broad range of expertise in toxicology. Dermigen consultants are drawn from academia, contacts resulting from Dr. Walborg's research career with M.D. Anderson Cancer Center (1965-1985), and his more recent involvement in consulting and management of toxicological research. Dermigen consultants possess particular expertise in the carcinogenic potential of pesticides, petrochemicals, specialty organic chemicals, pharmaceuticals and electromagnetic fields. Consulting services include the preparation of position papers on the relevant science and expert testimony. **Degrees/licenses:** PhD.

H.M. Mehendale

The University of Louisiana at Monroe
College of Health Sciences
Department of Toxicology
Monroe, LA 71209-0495
Tel: (318) 342-1691
Fax: (318) 342-1686
E-mail: mehendale@ulm.edu
Web Site: http://www.ulm.edu/pharmacy/mehendale/default.htm

Specialties: Toxicology; Chemical toxicology; Pesticides, solvents, other industrial chemicals; Cancer; Regulatory affairs; Occupational or accidental exposures and short- or long-term hazards; Hazardous wastes; Forensic Toxicological analysis of extraneous evidence; Body fluids and tissues, drugs, and intoxicants; Exposure to single or combinations of chemicals; Extensive experience in toxicological data interpretations; Board certified by American Board of Toxicology; Fellow, Academy of Toxicological Sciences; Published over 250 original research papers, review articles and book chapters. **Degrees/licenses:** BS, MS, PhD, D-ABT, F-ATS.

See primary listing under MEDICINE & HEALTH: Toxicology

Harry A. Milman, PhD

Expert in Toxicology,
Carcinogenesis, Pharmacology,
and "Pharmacy Standard of Care"
ToxNetwork.com
14317 Bauer Drive
Rockville, MD 20853
Tel: (301) 871-6715
Fax: (301) 871-5586
E-mail: hmilman@toxnetwork.com
Web Site: http://www.toxnetwork.com

Specialties: Toxicology, carcinogens, drugs, and "Pharmacy Standard of Care." 35+ years experience in toxicology, carcinogenesis, pharmacology, and pharmacy as a Consultant/Expert Witness (since 1998), at the National Cancer Institute/NIH (10 years), at the Environmental Protection Agency (18 years), and as a licensed pharmacist (35 years). Published 5 books, >70 papers, and numerous governmental reports in toxicology and carcinogenesis. Litigation experience includes deposition and jury trial testimony; occupational cancer/toxicology; medical malpractice; product liability; carcinogens; toxic chemicals; sewer gas; DUI; morphine intoxication; and "Pharmacy Standard of Care." Member Society of Toxicology, ASPET, AGT. **Degrees/licenses:** BS, MS, PhD (Pharmacology - 1978).

Richard A. Parent, PhD, DABT, FATS, RAC, ERT

Consulting Toxicologist & President
Consultox Limited
P.O. Box 1239
Damariscotta, ME 04543
Tel: (207) 563-2300
Fax: (207) 563-8990
E-mail: rparent@consultox.com
Web Site: http://www.consultox.com

Specialties: Dr. Parent has been actively involved in litigation support for both plaintiff and defense since 1984. His credentials have been accepted in all local, state, and federal courts in which he has testified. He is doubly board certified in Toxicology (DABT, FATS), is a recognized expert toxicologist in Europe (ERT), and has published over 85 scientific studies in the peer-reviewed literature. Recent activities have involved vinyl chloride, pesticides, lindane, PCBs, dioxins, PPA, creosote, health surveys, ephedrine, welding fumes, tobacco smoke, metals, Fen-Phen, alcohol defense, benzene, diesel fumes, trichloroethylene, technical management of complex toxic tort litigation and health assessment through personal sampling. **Degrees/licenses:** PhD, DABT, FATS, RAC, ERT (Europe).

See primary listing under MEDICINE & HEALTH: Toxicology

Princeton-Somerset Group, Inc.

Dennis M. Stainken, PhD
Principal
4 Carroll Drive
Hillsborough, NJ 08844
Tel: (908) 369-6890
(800) 597-8836
Fax: (908) 369-6881
E-mail: prinsomgrp@aol.com

Specialties: Expert Witness, Toxicology, Health Issues, Chemical Exposure, Mold Issues, Worker Exposure, Contamination Issues, Causation Assessment, Property Damage/Contamination & Remediation, Sewage, Gasoline & Oil Issues & Age Determination, Chemicals/Products, Risk Assessment, Indoor Air Quality/Health Effects, Toxic Tort Causation or Defense, Chemistry, Site Assessment, Regulatory Issues, Environmental Toxicology; Environmental Issues, Wetland/Ecological. Services nationwide, 30+ years of industrial & government experience in pollution under NPDES, CERCLA, RCRA, SDWA & CWA. Former Regulator, Professor, Consultant. 75+ publication. National expert in Environmental Toxicology, Fate & Effect of Pollutants. Board Certified Medical Investigator - IV. **Degrees/licenses:** BS, MS, PhD, NJ Lic. UST, Calif. REA; Diplomate, Am. Bd. Foren. Exam., CSE, PWS.

See primary listing under ENVIRONMENTAL: Consulting

Rudy Von Burg, PhD

Principal
EnTox & Associates
230 Castro St.
Point Richmond, CA 94801
Tel: (510) 235-2969
(925) 288-2366
(415) 637-2402
Fax: (510) 235-2969
E-mail: rvonburg@entoxandassociates.com
Web Site: http://entoxandassociates.com

Specialties: Adult Psychiatry; Geriatric Psychiatry; Standard of care for psychiatric units, hospitals, geriatric psych. units, managed care companies, psychiatrists; Analyze interactions

(Listing continued on next page)

Toxicology *(cont.)*

Rudy Von Burg, PhD (cont.)
psychiatric, medical, side effects, substance abuse, intoxication issues; Psychopharmacology; Explain clinical issues for case presentation; private practice of psychiatry, Medical Director of psych. HMO, and psychiatric hospital and Geriatric Psych. Unit; Excellent reputation, teacher, communicator. Associate Professor of Psychiatry. **Degrees/licenses:** PhD, DABT, CIH, CEI, AHERA, CAC, CLI.

EXPERT WITNESS REFERRALS

General

Kevin Gohar, MD

Orthopaedic Surgeon including back surgery
1158 26th St., #537
Santa Monica, CA 90403
Tel: (310) 729-5839
(818) 710-9005
Fax: (818) 710-9006

Specialties: Orthopaedic Surgeon including back surgery, Sport Medicine. Board Certified Member American College of Sport Medicine, California Orthopaedic Association, Fellow Cerebral Palsy. **Degrees/licenses:** MD.

IPEC

Institute for Products, Engineering & Construction
A Consortium of Engineers, Construction & Safety Professionals
34522 N. Scottsdale Rd., Ste. D-8 #160
Scottsdale, AZ 85262
Tel: (888) 212-1155
Fax: (888) 414-1155
E-mail: ipec@forensicengineers.com
Web Site: http://www.forensicengineers.com

666 Fifth Ave., #122
New York, NY 10103
Tel: (212) 315-9523

1429 G St. NW, #415
Washington, DC 20005
Tel: (202) 822-9660

231 North Ave. West, #134
Westfield, NJ 07090
Tel: (908) 233-2973

1920 Abrams Pkwy., #95
Dallas, TX 75214
Tel: (214) 827-9892

Specialties: Product Liability; Construction Defects & Delays; Vehicle & Equipment Accidents & Design & Manufacture; Corrosion; Metallurgy; Recreation Facilities; Jogging Trails; Bleachers; Carnival Rides, Amusement Rides; Fires; Explosions; Portable Heaters; Ladders; Scaffolds; Construction Equipment; Agricultural Equipment; Appliances; Plastic Pipe; Plastic Products; Windows; Doors; Forklifts; Backhoes; Bulldozers; Exercise Equipment; Construction & Heavy Equipment; Trucks, Buses, Subways; Seatbelts; Airbags; Overhead Electric Lines; Valves; Trenches; Excavation; Utility Company Standard Practice; OSHA; Facility Maintenance; Energy; Fiber Optics; Oil Spills; Underground Tanks; Leaks; Lease Closeouts; HOAs; Warnings & Labels; Guards, Foundations, Bridges, Tunnels; Shock, Electrocution, Light Fixtures. Contact: Ned Howell. **Degrees/licenses:** Engineers: Auto, Constr, Mech, Elec, Struct, Civil, Chem, Safety, Arch, Aero.
See primary listing under CONSTRUCTION: General

Pro/Consul Technical and Medical Experts

1945 Palo Verde Ave., Suite 200
Long Beach, CA 90815-3443
Tel: (800) 392-1119
(562) 799-0116
Fax: (562) 799-8821
E-mail: eexperts@msn.com
Web Site: http://www.expertinfo.com

Specialties: RIGHT EXPERT RIGHT AWAY!® 15,000 experts in 7,000 fields. Listed and recommended by the A. M. Best Company. Full-time research staff. We welcome your RUSH cases! TECHNICAL: Fast inspections. Categories from Accident Reconstruction to Zoology, also including appraisal, economics, employment, human factors, insurance, premises liability, security, and many more. MEDICAL: IME's. Inexpensive insurance medical records reviews by MDs. Categories from Addiction Medicine to Zooplasty, including board certified physicians in all fields, dentistry, geriatrics, neuropsychology, neurosurgery, nursing, orthopedics, psychiatry and many more. Reasonable fees. Free initial consultation. Free resume binder. Free CLE classes. **Degrees/licenses:** MD, PhD, DDS, DVM, DO, DPM, PE, CPA, ME, CE, CRC, MAI, et al.

See primary listing under ACCIDENT RECONSTRUCTION: General

TASA

(Technical Advisory Service for Attorneys)
1166 DeKalb Pike
Blue Bell, PA 19422-1853
Tel: (800) 523-2319
Fax: (800) 329-8272
E-mail: experts@tasanet.com
Web Site: http://www.tasanet.com

Specialties: WE HAVE YOUR EXPERT® TASA's experienced referral advisors introduce you to top-caliber Local, Regional, and National Experts for Consulting, Testifying, and ADR, in more than 10,000 technical and scientific disciplines. Categories include Accident Analysis; Architecture; Automotive; Computers; Construction; Economics; Employment; Engineering; Environment; Finance; Insurance; Intellectual Property; Medicine (more than 900 healthcare fields available through TASAmed, also a TASA Group division); Product Liability; Recreation; Safety; Toxicology; and Thousands More. SERVICES INCLUDE prompt customized searches, referrals, resumes, and your initial interviews with experts. Over 44 years of referral experience. Exceptional, personal service. **Degrees/licenses:** All prof. degrees, licenses, certifications represented.

Toxicology Consultants Roundtable

John A. Budny, PhD
Director, Publicity
Tel: (818) 706-2410
Web Site: http://lawinfo.com/biz/toxicology/index.html

Specialties: Call for a nationwide FREE LIST OF EXPERIENCED TOXICOLOGY EXPERTS; Contact them directly; No fee. **Degrees/licenses:** Over 50 PhD's, MD's & DVM's + Board Certifications.

See primary listing under MEDICINE & HEALTH: Toxicology

Ralph S. Welsh, PhD, ABPP

Clinical Psychologist
P.O. Box 720
Georgetown, CT 06829-0720
Tel: (203) 743-1724
(203) 417-4330 (Cell)
Fax: (203) 938-9179
E-mail: rswelsh@mail.com

152 Deer Hill Ave.
Danbury, CT 06810

Specialties: Family, emigration, and personal injury law. Over 20 years of experience psychologically evaluating individuals for the state, the federal government, and for private attorneys. Thousands of hours on the stand providing expert testimony. Am particularly adept with emigration problems. Have written extensively in the area of child maltreatment and delinquency and recently received an award from the Connecticut Psychological Association for outstanding achievement in

(Listing continued on next page)

General *(cont.)*

Ralph S. Welsh (cont.)
professional psychology. Have taught at two major universities. Work well with MDs. Will travel as needed. **Degrees/licenses:** BS, MS, PhD, ABPP, DBFE, Lic. State of CT.

See primary listing under MEDICINE & HEALTH: Psychology

Medical

Chisolm Legal Nurse Consulting

Daniel Chisolm, RN, BSN
Certified Legal Nurse Consultant
11 Wayside Road
Asheville, NC 28805
Tel: (828) 236-0031
Fax: (828) 236-0031
E-mail: ncexpertnurse@yahoo.com
Web Site: http://www.ncexpertnurse.com

Specialties: Daniel W. Chisolm is a Registered Nurse with over 10 years experience in Critical Care, ICU, MICU, Recovery Room, ER, and general nursing. He is actively practicing bedside nursing. Mr. Chisolm is experienced with all nursing issues. He is also working with patients on ventilators, cardiac monitors, feeding tubes, IV therapy, arterial lines, respiratory failure and cardiac arrest. Experience includes care to cardiology, respiratory, renal, neurological and hepatic patients. Services include providing expert testimony, screening cases for merit, analyzing medical records for deviations from standards of care, nursing research. **Degrees/licenses:** Registered Nurse, Certified Legal Nurse Consultant.

See primary listing under MEDICAL-LEGAL: Nursing Malpractice

Kevin Gohar, MD

Orthopaedic Surgeon including back surgery
1158 26th St., #537
Santa Monica, CA 90403
Tel: (310) 729-5839
(818) 710-9005
Fax: (818) 710-9006

Specialties: Orthopaedic Surgeon including back surgery, Sport Medicine. Board Certified Member American College of Sport Medicine, California Orthopaedic Association, Fellow Cerebral Palsy. **Degrees/licenses:** MD.

See primary listing under EXPERT WITNESS REFERRALS: General

Manhattan Ophthalmology Associates

Spencer E. Sherman, MD
President & Medical Director
166 East 63rd Street
New York, NY 10021
Tel: (212) 753-8300
Fax: (212) 752-4285
E-mail: sesmdpc@aol.com
Web Site: http://www.nyeyelaser.com

Specialties: AB Princeton University - cum laude, 1958; MD Columbia College of Surgeons, 1962; Specializing in: cataract, glaucoma, refractive surgery, contact lenses; Residency 1965-68, Mt. Sinai Hospital NY (Ophthalmology); Attending surgeon: Mt. Sinai, Lenox Hill, Manhattan Eye & Ear, NY Eye & Ear (all in NY). Honors: honor award & service award (AAO), Sigma Xi (Princeton), named Top Doctors in U.S., Best Doctor in NY; Who's Who in America. Fellow of: American & International College of Surgeons; American Academy of Ophthalmology; International Society of Refractive Surgeons; New York Society of Ophthalmology, AMA. **Degrees/licenses:** MD, Lic. in NY, FL, CA & NJ.

See primary listing under MEDICINE & HEALTH: Ophthalmology

TASAmed

A Division of The TASA Group
1166 DeKalb Pike
Blue Bell, PA 19422-1853
Tel: (800) 659-8464
Fax: (800) 850-8272
E-mail: tasamed@tasanet.com
Web Site: http://www.tasanet.com

Specialties: FIND THE MEDICAL EXPERT YOU NEED with TASAmed, a co-division of TASA, North America's foremost Expert Referral Service. Thousands of top-caliber Local and National specialists for case review, IME's, consulting, and testifying in over 900 medical fields. Categories of expertise include Anesthesiology; Cardiology; Cosmetic Surgery; Dentistry; Elder Abuse; Emergency Care; Environmental Medicine; Forensic Pathology; Geriatrics; Nephrology; Obstetrics; Occupational Medicine; Oncology; Pediatrics; Psychiatry; Pulmonology; Radiology; Sports Medicine; Surgery; & More. SERVICES INCLUDE prompt customized searches, referrals, resumes, and your initial interview calls with experts. Exceptional personal service for over 44 years. **Degrees/licenses:** All prof. degrees, licenses, certifications represented.

See primary listing under EXPERT WITNESS REFERRALS: General

Technical/Scientific

W. Edward Montz, Jr., PhD

Indoor Air Solutions, Inc.
1200 E. High St., Ste. 301
Pottstown, PA 19464
Tel: (610) 323-8818
Fax: (610) 323-8839
E-mail: wem@stachybotrys.com
Web Site: http://moldabatement.com

Specialties: Indoor Air Solutions, Inc. specializes in indoor air quality testing, surveys and inspections for residences, commercial offices, hospitals and public buildings. We provide litigation support services for both plaintiffs and defendants. The abatement division specializes in decontaminating mold-contaminated buildings. **Degrees/licenses:** PhD, CIAQP.

See primary listing under ENVIRONMENTAL: Indoor Air Quality

Professional Analytical and Consulting Services, Inc. (PACS)

Henry G. Nowicki, PhD, MBA
President and Senior Consultant
409 Meade Drive
Coraopolis, PA 15108
Tel: (724) 457-6576
(800) 367-2587
Fax: (724) 457-1214
E-mail: hnpacs@aol.com
Web Site: http://www.pacslabs.com

Specialties: Data quality analysis; activated carbon; mass spectrometry; atomic spectrometry; quality assurance; computer experts; statistics; modeling; chemicals; pollution; drinking/waste water; toxicology; chemistry/biochemistry; clinical; risk assessment; pesticides; alcohol; drugs; forensic sciences; failure analysis; health/safety; industrial hygiene; product liability; property assessment; air/water quality; certified in asbestos and mold inspections; permitting; labeling; audits. PACS provides: laboratory testing, short courses; conferences. Courses: spectroscopy; chromatography, quality, environmental; activated carbons. Conferences: Environmental Sampling & Field Analysis; International Activated Carbon, Quality Issues, Endocrine Disrupters. Industrial & government clients. Federal, State & military courts, including Love Canal & Florida Everglades. DEP-PA drinking and waste water. Offices in Pittsburgh, PA; Orlando, FL; St. Louis, MO. **Degrees/licenses:** BS, MA, PhD, MBA, PE; ACS, ASCC, ASQC, AWWA, WQA, SSP, SACP, IACMA, EPA Arsenic.

See primary listing under ENVIRONMENTAL: Pollution (Air, Soil, Water)

FAILURE ANALYSIS

General

Automotive Engineering Consultants, Inc.

Donald B.H. Jeffers, PE
Principal Consultant
P.O. Box 7391
Ann Arbor, MI 48107-7391
Tel: (734) 994-0494
(800) 924-0494
Fax: (734) 994-0494
E-mail:
donjeffers@automotive-engineers.com
Web Site:
http://www.automotive-engineers.com

Specialties: Engineering audits of truck and automobile design, materials, manufacturing processes and maintenance to determine contribution to component and system failure, including the evaluation of philosophical aspects of design in relation to user safety. Analytic techniques including fracture analysis, materials testing, mathematical calculations, computer analyses, construction of empirical models of mechanical, electrical and other systems and the setup and testing of flawed vehicles. Brakes; Wheels; Tires; Steering; Vehicle and Component Structural Failure; Crashworthiness; Seat Belts; Engines; Transmissions; Fuel System Fires; Electrical Fires; Cruise Controls; Computer Controls. Computerized vehicular accident reconstruction. **Degrees/licenses:** University of Michigan BSE(ME), MSE(ME), PE.

See primary listing under ENGINEERING: Automotive

Chemical Accident Reconstruction Services, Inc.

Michael Fox, PhD
Founder
9121 E. Tanque Verde Rd., #105
Tucson, AZ 85749-8391
Tel: (800) 645-3369
Fax: (520) 749-0861
E-mail: services@chemaxx.com
Web Site: http://www.chemaxx.com

Specialties: Complex industrial chemical accidents, fires and explosions as well as chemical-related consumer product injuries. The founder of the company has his PhD in Physical Chemistry, is a Certified Fire & Explosion Investigator and Certified or Accredited in Hazardous Chemicals, OSHA Process Hazard Analysis Team Leader, DOT Hazardous Materials, Corrosion, Metallurgy, Failure Analysis and Aerosols. Other specialties include: Propane, plastics, water chemistry, skin burns, acids, alkalis, carbon monoxide, flammable liquids, gasoline, scanning microscopy, MSDSs, natural gas, solvents, warning labels, PEX, welding, construction, chemical packaging & transport. For more specialties see web site. **Degrees/licenses:** PhD, Physical Chemistry; See certifications above.

See primary listing under CHEMISTRY/ CHEMICALS: General

Douglas B. Chisholm

D.B. Chisholm Associates, Inc.
38074 Stevens Rd.
Lovettsville, VA 20180
Tel: (540) 822-4370
Fax: (540) 822-4371
E-mail: doug@dbchisholm.org
Web Site: http://www.dbchisholm.com

Specialties: D.B. Chisholm Assoc., Inc. specializes in Mechanical Engineering/Structural Engineering, Design and Failure Analysis of products and systems ranging from Automotive and Aircraft components, Pipelines & Pressure Vessels; Our firm can perform a broad range of Metallurgical Failure Analyses and Accident Reconstruction of large petroleum, chemical, industrial plant accidents, fuel tank farm fires, pipeline leaks, ruptures (both buried and under water) and manufacturing facility accidents; Our principal, Dr. Chisholm, PE, has over 30 years of Failure Analysis experience and has authored more than 200 publications and client reports. **Degrees/licenses:** BME, MEM, DSc, PE.

C. Michael Dickinson

President, Principal Engineer
Dickinson & Associates, Inc.
608-G Matthews-Mint Hill Rd. (28105)
P.O. Box 3093
Matthews, NC 28106-3093
Tel: (704) 847-4040
Fax: (704) 847-0788
E-mail:
mdickinson@dickinson-associates.com
Web Site:
http://www.dickinson-associates.com

Specialties: Mechanical system component design and failure analysis; machinery and equipment accident reconstruction and failure analysis; facility and equipment safety compliance evaluations; machine design, reliability and risk analysis; machine guarding and safety, textile-processing equipment; manlifts, material handling equipment including conveyors, forklifts, boom trucks; consumer products; vehicle accident reconstruction; computer-assisted vehicle dynamics and collision analysis; vision and visibility analysis. **Degrees/ licenses:** MSME, PE.

See primary listing under ACCIDENT RECONSTRUCTION: General

Engel Metallurgical Ltd.

Lester B. Engel,
PE, CEO/Metallurgical Engineer
James A. Brusso,
PhD, PE, Metallurgical Engineer
P.O. Box 6100
St. Cloud, MN 56302
Tel: (320) 253-7968
(800) 258-7968
Fax: (320) 253-7917
E-mail: info@engelmet.com
Web Site: http://www.engelmet.com

Specialties: Failure Analysis; Product Liability; Materials Evaluation; Trial Experience; Corrosion Testing; Product Development; Mechanical and Chemical Testing; Product Failure Simulations; Fracture Evaluations; Microstructural Studies; Scanning Electron Microscopy; Photographic Documentation; Product Design Evaluation; Specifications. Over 40 years experience as metallurgical engineers. Twenty years as a consulting and testing firm to a broad range of manufacturing, insurance and legal clientele. Extensive gas turbine, bearing, and steel products experience. ISO 17025 accredited. **Degrees/licenses:** MS, PhD, Metallurgical Engineering, Professional Engineer (PE).

See primary listing under ENGINEERING: Metallurgical

ForensisGroup, Inc.

Mercy Steenwyk
3452 E. Foothill Blvd., Ste. 1160
Pasadena, CA 91107
Tel: (626) 795-5000
(800) 555-5422
Fax: (626) 795-1950
E-mail: experts@forensisgroup.com
Web Site: http://forensisgroup.com

Specialties: Thousands of our clients have gained the technical advantage and the edge in their cases from our multidisciplined group of experts in hundreds of disciplines. We have some of the best and the brightest at competitive rates backed by 14 years of excellent track record and the support of our trained staff. We assist you until you have the right expert. Some of our areas of expertise are: Construction, Safety, Engineering, Product Liability, Accident Reconstruction, Automotive, Environmental, Slip & Fall, Appraisal, Medical and other scientific disciplines. Unsurpassed standards. Clients actively evaluate our experts. **Degrees/licenses:** PE, GC, CSP, PhD, MD, GC, CIH, AIA.

See primary listing under ACCIDENT PREVENTION & SAFETY: General

General *(cont.)*

IPEC

Institute for Products, Engineering & Construction
A Consortium of Engineers, Construction & Safety Professionals
34522 N. Scottsdale Rd., Ste. D-8 #160
Scottsdale, AZ 85262
Tel: (888) 212-1155
Fax: (888) 414-1155
E-mail: ipec@forensicengineers.com
Web Site: http://www.forensicengineers.com

666 Fifth Ave., #122
New York, NY 10103
Tel: (212) 315-9523

1429 G St. NW, #415
Washington, DC 20005
Tel: (202) 822-9660

231 North Ave. West, #134
Westfield, NJ 07090
Tel: (908) 233-2973

1920 Abrams Pkwy., #95
Dallas, TX 75214
Tel: (214) 827-9892

Specialties: Product Liability; Construction Defects; Vehicle & Equipment Design & Construction; Metallurgy; Welds, Valves; Recreation Facilities; Jogging Trails; Bleachers; Carnival Rides; Roller Coasters; Fires; Explosions; Portable Heaters; Ladders; Scaffolds; Construction Equipment; Agricultural Equipment; Appliances; Plastic Pipe; Plastic Products; Windows; Doors; Backhoes; Bulldozers; Exercise Equipment; Propane; Punch Presses; Bungee Cords; Pneumatic Tools; Electric Tools; Fire Trucks; Fuses; Water Heaters; Corrosion; Seatbelts; Airbags; Transmissions; Interlocks; Guards; Foundations; Saws; Grinders; Mixers; Printing Presses; Utility Poles; Shock; Electrocution; Light Fixtures; Electric Systems; Plastics; Telecommunications. Contact: Ned Howell. **Degrees/ licenses:** Engineers: Auto, Constr, Mech, Elec, Struct, Civil, Chem, Safety, Arch, Aero.

See primary listing under CONSTRUCTION: General

R. Craig Jerner, PhD, PE

President
J.E.I. Metallurgical, Inc.
7703 Queens Ferry Lane
Dallas, TX 75248
Tel: (972) 934-0493
Fax: (972) 233-5909
E-mail: r.c.jerner@metallurgist.com
Web Site: http://www.metallurgist.com

Specialties: 35+ years experience conducting failure analysis, accident investigations, and metallurgical engineering. Expert testimony and litigation support in 65+ trials, 225 depositions, and 1,000+ failure investigations. EXPERTISE: Accident investigation & reconstruction; failure analysis; consumer & industrial products; vehicular & heavy equipment; gas, oil & tubular products; corrosion; welding design; testing and evaluation; micro/macro photography. HONORS: "Who's Who in Science & Engineering," "Who's Who in Executives & Professionals," The Sigma Xi Society. Professor (Tenured) University of Oklahoma 1965-78. Registered consultant OSHA, U. S. Dept. of Defense, U. S. Coast Guard, and NTSB. Registered Professional Engineer in Texas and Oklahoma. **Degrees/ licenses:** PhD, Metallurgy; MS & BS, Metallurgical Engineering.

See primary listing under ACCIDENT RECONSTRUCTION: General

Robert W. Lindner, PE

President
Lindner Consulting Services, Inc.
7 Westmount Drive
Livingston, NJ 07039-4212
Tel: (973) 740-1319
Fax: (973) 740-1319
E-mail: boblindner@aol.com

Specialties: Natural Gas Industry: Transmission, Distribution and Operations; Pressure Regulators: Appliance, House Service, Commercial/Industrial, Distribution, M&R Station, High Pressure, Low Pressure, Installation & Design/Maintenance; Safety Relief Valves; Accident/Failure Analysis, Expert Witness Report/Testimony. Over 44 years engineering expertise in the application, operation, maintenance and design of all types of pressure regulator installations. Over 34 years engineering experience in process control and control valves. Lectured on pressure regulators at numerous seminars and gas utility training sessions. Career includes management & engineering experience plus leadership positions in national professional organizations. **Degrees/licenses:** BS, MS, PE.

See primary listing under ACCIDENT RECONSTRUCTION: Pressure Regulators

Materials Evaluation and Engineering, Inc.

Larry D. Hanke, PE
Principal Engineer
13805 1st Ave. N., Ste. 400
Plymouth, MN 55441-5447
Tel: (763) 449-8870
(888) 349-8870
Fax: (763) 449-8699
E-mail: hanke@mee-inc.com
Web Site: http://www.mee-inc.com

Specialties: Failure analysis of metal, plastic, paints, coatings including: medical devices, consumer products, vehicles, industrial machines, industrial systems, tanks, pipelines. Expert in materials behavior; fracture; corrosion; wear; environmental degradation. Comprehensive laboratory: light and scanning electron microscopy; mechanical tests; chemical analysis; surface analysis. Experienced with insurance cases and testimony for deposition and trial. Excellent communications, written and verbal, to clearly explain complex technical issues in layman terms. Twenty years experience as a failure analyst and expert witness. **Degrees/licenses:** BS Met. E, PE.

James M. Miller, PE, PhD

President
Miller Engineering Associates, Inc.
2392 Fuller Court
Ann Arbor, MI 48105
Tel: (734) 662-6822
Fax: (734) 747-9712
E-mail: jmiller@millerengineering.com
Web Site:
http://www.millerengineering.com

Specialties: Mechanical Design Safety: Power Tools & Machine Guarding; OSHA/ANSI/ASTM Compliance; Warnings, Labels, Instructions & User Manuals: Health Hazard Warnings; Design of User Manuals & Warnings; Consumer Product Safety: Human Factors & Ergonomics, Slips, Falls-Premise, Vehicle, Ladder; Child, Home Appliances, Furniture; Vehicles: Auto, Truck, ATV, Boat, Jet Ski, Snowmobile; Seat Belts & Air Bags; Chemical, Fire, Environmental & Waste Disposal: Fires & Explosions-Vapors/Electrical/Chemical; Chemical Labeling Requirements; MSDS; Groundwater & Soil Contamination; Agricultural & Construction Safety: Tractor, Implement, Harvester & Grain Storage; Pesticides, Herbicides, Fungicides; Nursing Malpractice; Nursing Management. **Degrees/licenses:** James Miller, PE, PhD; Bradley Cook, PE; Rebecca Lehto, PhD, RN, OCN.

See primary listing under ACCIDENT PREVENTION & SAFETY: General

Packer Engineering

Penny Rusch
Director of Business Development
1950 N. Washington St.
Naperville, IL 60563
Tel: (800) 323-0114
Fax: (630) 505-1986
E-mail: peinfo@packereng.com
Web Site: http://www.packereng.com

Specialties: Packer Engineering, a multidisciplinary engineering consulting company, provides expertise in the areas of failure analysis, accident investigation & reconstruction, cause & origin investigations, research & development, risk mitigation, and custom &

(Listing continued on next page)

General *(cont.)*

Packer Engineering (cont.)
routine testing. Packer offers a wide range of services in the following areas: Aviation, Biomechanical/Biomedical, Construction Technology, Chemical, Fire & Explosions, Electrical, Human Factors, Ergonomics, Machinery & Equipment, Materials, Occupational Safety, Product & Process Safety, System Failure Analysis & Recovery, Technology Assessment & Intellectual Property, and Transportation Systems. Our emergency response team is available 24 hours, 7 days a week.

See primary listing under ENGINEERING: Consulting

RJ Lee Group, Inc.

5 Nationwide locations:
CA, NY, PA, VA, WA
Keith Rickabaugh
Director of Sales and Marketing
350 Hochberg Road
Monroeville, PA 15146
Tel: (800) 860-1775
(724) 325-1776
Fax: (724) 733-1799
E-mail: krickabaugh@rjlg.com
Web Site: http://www.rjlg.com

Specialties: COMPANY INFORMATION: Independent laboratory and consulting group specializing in application of instrumental techniques to solve problems. Over 250 employees and 20 years litigation support experience. FAILURE ANALYSIS: materials, metals, polymers, and ceramics. CONSTRUCTION MATERIALS/DEFECT IDENTIFICATION: concrete and cement, aggregates, and fill materials. FORENSICS: gun shot residue, hair, fiber, and other trace evidence. ENVIRONMENTAL: disaster/impact assessment and remediation, receptor modeling, particulate characterization, air and dust analysis, and diesel particulate characterization. EXPANDED SERVICES: auger spectroscopy (AES), optical and electron microscopy (SEM & TEM), inorganic chemistry (AA/ICP & X-ray diffraction), organic chemistry (GC-ECD, GC-FID, GC/MS, FTIR & HPLC), thermal analysis (TGA, DSC, DTA), industrial hygiene, asbestos, silica, method development, product testing, software development, x-ray photoelectron spectroscopy, x-ray diffraction, and x-ray fluorescence (XPS, XRD, XRF). **Degrees/licenses:** BS, CIH, CSP, MA, MBA, MS, MSFS, PE, PhD; AIHA & NVLAP + Other Accred.

SEAL Laboratories

Arun Kumar, PhD
250 North Nash Street
El Segundo, CA 90245
Tel: (310) 322-2011
Fax: (310) 322-2243
E-mail: akumar@seallabs.com
Web Site: http://www.seallabs.com

Specialties: Fully equipped failure analysis laboratory with qualified PhD Metallurgists and Chemists, available to perform failure analysis and to determine cause of failures of aircraft and automobile components, machineries, tools, medical devices, implants, etc.; Experienced staff for product liability and patent infringement litigation support, to act as expert witness and for trial testimony; 1 mile from Los Angeles International Airport. **Degrees/licenses:** PhD.

Seasoned Engineering Consultants, Inc.

C. Michael Neal, PE
President
500 N. Shoreline Blvd., Ste. 709 (78471)
P.O. Box 4276
Corpus Christi, TX 78469-4276
Tel: (361) 887-9388
Fax: (361) 881-9899
E-mail: sec_inc@msn.com

Specialties: Experienced professional engineers and architects, qualified technicians and dedicated staff performing forensic investigations for the legal, insurance, real estate, industry and private businesses in the areas of: industrial and commercial accidents; vehicle accidents; product and equipment failure analysis (vehicle, appliances, tools, machinery, equipment, firearms, industrial, commercial, oil field, marine, residential); piping/piping components/pressure vessel design/failure analysis; fire cause and origin;

foundation distress; slip, trip & fall/building code compliance/ADA compliance/premises liability; catastrophe and storm damage evaluations; demonstrative exhibits; expert witness report/testimony; litigation support. **Degrees/ licenses:** BSME, MSME, BSEE, BSA, MSA / PADI, PE & RA in Texas.

See primary listing under ACCIDENT RECONSTRUCTION: General

TASA

(Technical Advisory Service for Attorneys)
1166 DeKalb Pike
Blue Bell, PA 19422-1853
Tel: (800) 523-2319
Fax: (800) 329-8272
E-mail: experts@tasanet.com
Web Site: http://www.tasanet.com

Specialties: Save search time! Contact TASA first. Benefit from 44 years of referral expertise. We assess your needs and refer experienced Local, Regional, or National professionals for Consulting, Testifying, and ADR in failure analysis specialties including Air Bags; Appliances; Chemicals; Conveyers; Corrosion; Elevators; Engineering; Escalators; Explosions; Fires; Fork Lifts; Human Factors; Industrial Injuries and Accidents; Labeling; Ladders; Machine Product Liability; Manufacturing Defects; Metals; Plastics; Premises Liability; Safety Guarding; Shocks; Tire Design; Tools; Much More. SERVICES INCLUDE prompt customized searches, referrals, resumes, and your initial interview calls with experts. Exceptional personal service. **Degrees/licenses:** All prof. degrees, licenses, certifications represented.

See primary listing under EXPERT WITNESS REFERRALS: General

Thielsch Engineering, Inc.

Ara Nalbandian, PE, Vice President
Bob Basile, PE
Florence Cone
195 Frances Avenue
Cranston, RI 02910
Tel: (401) 467-6454
Fax: (401) 467-2398
E-mail: nalbandiana@thielsch.com
Web Site: http://www.thielsch.com

Specialties: Failure analyses and forensic investigations of equipment and products in many different industries including power generation, pulp and paper, petroleum and chemical, process industries, mining, manufacturing, transportation, electronics, medical devices, failures or condition assessments of vessel, piping, bridges, building structures, electrical components/systems, pumps, water transmission, fire protection piping, compressors and other rotating equipment. Extensive laboratory testing facilities include full spectrum analyses, metallurgical, mechanical, chemical , analytical, bacteriological, environmental, structural and corrosion testing services. Registered Professional Engineers in Rhode Island, Massachusetts, Maine, New Jersey, Georgia, Florida, Indiana and California. **Degrees/licenses:** BS, PE, BS Mech. Engr. MS (RI, MA, ME, NJ, GA, FL, IN & CA).

See primary listing under ENGINEERING: Consulting

Automotive/Vehicular

John C. Glennon, Chartered

6917 W. 76th Street
Overland Park, KS 66204
Tel: (913) 383-3856
Fax: (913) 383-2277
E-mail: experts@johncglennon.com
Web Site: http://www.johncglennon.com

Specialties: Motor Vehicle Accident Investigation; Accident Reconstruction; Vehicle Crush Analysis; Vehicular Mechanical and Structural Failure Analysis for Automobiles, Trucks, and Motorcycles; Testing Capabilities for Air Brakes, Hydraulic Brakes, Suspension

(Listing continued on next page)

Automotive/Vehicular *(cont.)*

John C. Glennon, Chartered (cont.)
Systems, Steering Systems, Tires, and Wheels; Determination if Proper Maintenance and Repair Procedures were Followed; Identification of Previous Body Structural Damage; Motor Carrier Safety and Compliance; Commercial Driver Responsibilities and Qualifications; Commercial Driver Hours of Service and Daily Logs; Proper Load Securement Procedures; Fleet Maintenance Requirements; Computer Animation; Forensic Mapping; Photo Modeling; Downloading of Crash Data Retrieval Systems (Automobile "BLACK BOX"). **Degrees/licenses:** D. Engr., PE, BS Automotive Technology, ASE Cert., CDL.

See primary listing under ACCIDENT RECONSTRUCTION: General

William D. Guentzler

President
Forensics International
10298 Hawley Road
El Cajon, CA 92021
Tel: (619) 390-9081
Fax: (619) 390-9086
E-mail: forensicsintl@msn.com

Specialties: Thirty six years as university professor, twenty five years as forensic examiner. Failure analysis of automotive, truck, ATV/ ATC, motorcycle, golf cart and recreational vehicles; Specialist in braking systems, cooling systems, steering, suspension, fuel systems including gas, diesel, propane, CNG, LNG, and electric; Vehicle fire cause and origin and tires. **Degrees/licenses:** BS, MA, PhD.

Construction

The Nielsen-Wurster Group, Inc.

Patricia Galloway, CEO
Kris R. Nielsen, Chairman
Reza Nikain, President
Jack L. Dignum, Senior VP
345 Wall Street
Princeton, NJ 08540
Tel: (609) 497-7300
Fax: (609) 497-3412
E-mail: njnwg@aol.com
Web Site: http://www.nielsen-wurster.com

Specialties: Dispute resolution; Litigation support; Schedule delay analyses; Geotechnical evaluations; Forensic investigations; Damage Quantification; Arbitration, mediation and dispute review boards; Management consulting; Audits; Risk Evaluations; Training seminars; Risk management; Project planning; Project execution; Risk assessments; Trend evaluations; Risk reduction strategies; Systems implementation; Services worldwide; Licensed professional engineers in all states; CPAs, Project management professionals; Extensive experience in project management and project controls. Authored numerous professional papers on Project Management, Risk Management and Analysis of Project Delay. Serving private and public companies throughout the power, building, transportation, infrastructure, telecommunications and process industries. **Degrees/licenses:** MSCE, BSCE, MBA, PE, PMP, P.Eng., CCE, PSP, C.Eng., JD, CPA, F.ICE.

See primary listing under CONSTRUCTION: Consulting

WWCOT

Dean Vlahos, AIA, NCARB, CCCA
David Sakaguchi, AIA
3130 Wilshire Blvd., 6th Floor
Santa Monica, CA 90403
Tel: (310) 828-0040
Fax: (310) 453-9432
Web Site: http://www.wwcot.com

Specialties: On site observations; destructive investigations; analysis; research; expert testimony on design, building codes, general construction defects and repair methods. **Degrees/licenses:** AIA, NCARB, CCCA, LEEO.

See primary listing under ARCHITECTURE: General

Industrial/Manufacturing

Metallurgy/Materials Consulting

David J. Dunn
Metallurgical Consultant
930 Mountain View Drive
Leadville, CO 80461
Tel: (719) 486-0838
Fax: (719) 486-3244
E-mail: glendavedunn@aol.com

Specialties: Failure Analysis, on-site investigation, materials testing, materials specification, warranty investigations; pertaining to steel and cast iron subjected to wear, fracture, and corrosion; Emphasis on alloys used in mining, earth moving, mineral processing. Forty years continuous experience serving clients worldwide. Read, write, speak Spanish. Travel anywhere. Metallurgical Engineering Degree, Colorado School of Mines, 1959. **Degrees/licenses:** Metallurgical Engr. Deg., Colorado School of Mines, 1959.

See primary listing under MATERIALS SCIENCE: General

Materials

Anamet, Inc.

Kenneth R. Pytlewski
Director of Engineering and Laboratories
26102 Eden Landing Rd., Ste. 3
Hayward, CA 94545
Tel: (800) 377-7768
Fax: (510) 887-8427
E-mail: info@anametinc.com
Web Site: http://www.anametinc.com

Specialties: Engineers in most major disciplines. Professional engineers with extensive experience as experts for litigation support. On-site laboratory capabilities include, but not limited to, inorganic chemical analysis, mechanical testing and metallurgical evaluation including mechanical and materials failure analysis. **Degrees/licenses:** BS, MS, PE.

See primary listing under ENGINEERING: Failure Analysis

Calcoast Labs / DL Labs, Inc.

D. Patrick Fairley, Pres. - Lab Director
Antoine Chamsi, VP Materials Chemistry
Thomas Sliva, VP - Tech. Direc. (DL Labs)
4072 Watts Street
Emeryville, CA 94608
Tel: (510) 652-2979
Fax: (510) 652-3085
E-mail: ccoastlabs@aol.com
or dllabs@aol.com
Web Site: http://www.calcoastlabs.com
or http://www.dllabs.com

DL Labs, Inc.
74 Kent Street
Brooklyn, NY 11222
Tel: (718) 383-5080
Fax: (718) 383-7445

Specialties: Calcoast Labs, Inc. of Emeryville, California, has acquired DL Labs of New York City, formerly David Litter Laboratories. The acquisition makes Calcoast/DL Labs one of the largest independent paint, coatings, sealant & materials testing laboratories in North America. The California/New York locations also provide for universal coverage of our domestic and foreign client base. We provide analytical & expert services to the legal community. DL Labs is accredited by NVLAP (Code 100252-0), CGSB, ISO/IEC25. Calcoast Labs is accredited by DEA & Los Angeles Department of Building & Safety. **Degrees/licenses:** BS, MS, PhD.

Materials *(cont.)*

Chemir Analytical Services

Shri Thanedar, PhD
CEO
2672 Metro Blvd.
Maryland Heights, MO 63043
Tel: (800) 659-7659
Fax: (314) 291-6630
E-mail: info@chemir.com
Web Site: http://www.chemir.com

Specialties: Materials Identification - identify and quantify components in an unknown sample; Deformulation - reverse engineering of a product; Failure Analysis - material and product failures; Comparative Analysis - product contamination and "good vs. bad" product comparison. Experienced in the chemical analysis of polymers, plastics, paints, coatings, drugs, adhesives and rubbers. Recent cases include patent infringement; product liability and failure; arson investigation; insurance claim validation. Experienced PhD chemists available for consultation including expert witness and testimony to back up laboratory data. In business since 1959.

See primary listing under CHEMISTRY/ CHEMICALS: General

Dedicated Roof and Hydro-Solutions

David R. Hawn, RRC, CEM
President
6500 Harvest Mill Ct.
Centreville, VA 20121-4819
Tel: (703) 266-6638
Fax: (703) 266-1660
E-mail: drhawn@worldnet.att.net
Web Site: http://www.drhroofsolutions.com

Specialties: Roof and waterproofing forensic investigations and failure analysis; warranty issues; insurance issues; construction issues; wind; hail; and water entry damage. All roof and waterproofing types: low slope, steep slope, plaza decks, and sub-grade systems. All building types: commercial, industrial, institutional, and multi-residential. Experienced on a nationwide and international basis. Roof and waterproofing consultation services provided since 1982. Expert testimony provided over the last 16 years on numerous occasions. Serves on the Ethics and "Interface" peer review committees of the Roof Consultants Institute (RCI). **Degrees/licenses:** BSConE, Iowa State Univ.; Reg. Roof Consultant (RRC), Cert. Energy Mgr. (CEM).

See primary listing under CONSTRUCTION: Roofing/Waterproofing

Richard F. Lynch, PhD

Lynch & Associates, Inc.
377 Sicomac Avenue
Wyckoff, NJ 07481-2128
Tel: (201) 891-8399
Fax: (201) 891-8398
E-mail: richardflynch@aol.com
Web Site: http://www.JurisPro.com/mem/RichardFLynch

Specialties: Expert witness in nonferrous and steel metallurgy including failure analysis. Metallurgical failure investigation/test interpretation for legal profession. Effective court testimony. Specialties in fracture and corrosion failure of nonferrous metal and steel, structural materials and fabricated products. Zinc, aluminum, brass/bronze and galvanized steel expert. Extensive background in nonferrous castings/ wrought products including manufacture and performance. Expert in surface preparation, metal pretreatments and painting of galvanized steel including white rust formation and paint failure. Experienced in writing and interpreting standards and specifications for bare, painted and galvanized steel, and nonferrous products. ASTM Fellow. **Degrees/licenses:** PhD, MS & BS in Metallurgy & Materials Science, Lehigh University.

See primary listing under ENGINEERING: Metallurgical

Read Consulting, LLC

1435 Fulton Rd.
Santa Rosa, CA 95403
Tel: (707) 544-2374
E-mail: lread@sonic.net
Web Site: http://www.readconsulting.com

Specialties: Glass failure; Patent expertise; Plastic failures; Fatigue; Rubber Failures; Metallurgy; Corrosion; Manufacturing processes; Failure analysis; Product liability; Quality control; Product failure analysis; Wood failures; Wire Cable failures; Electrical connections, Tempered glass; Vacuum coating; Thin Film coating; Product design; Accident reconstruction; Bottle failures; Window failures; Manufacturing qualification testing; Food safety; Food processing; Canning. **Degrees/licenses:** PhD, PE.

See primary listing under MATERIALS SCIENCE: General

Mechanical

Steven B. Kushnick, PE, Inc.

Steven B. Kushnick, PE
Principal Engineer
P.O. Box 670084
Marietta, GA 30066-0119
Tel: (770) 591-1720
Fax: (770) 591-7996
E-mail: sbk@sbkushnick.com
Web Site: http://www.sbkushnick.com

Specialties: Failure analysis, durability assessment, mechanical design, and performance analysis and optimization of turbines, turbine engines, turbocompressors, reciprocating compressors, expanders, and ancillary equipment including diesel engines; Analyze equipment failures to determine cause and recommend preventive action; Reverse-engineer hardware for users and manufacturers; Assess hardware durability; Develop component inspections and repairs; Analyze stress, creep, fatigue, vibration, heat transfer, temperature, pressure, and flow. Experienced expert witness, expert consultant, and third-party engineering consultant. Access to metallurgical laboratory. Two patents in the field of turbine engines. **Degrees/licenses:** BSME, PE.

See primary listing under ENGINEERING: Mechanical

Packaging

Richard P. Muny

President
Chemsultants International, Inc.
9349 Hamilton Drive
Mentor, OH 44060
Tel: (440) 352-0218
Fax: (440) 352-8572
E-mail: rmuny@chemsultants.com
Web Site: http://www.chemsultants.com

Specialties: Adhesives, sealants and coatings of all types: Epoxies, Acrylics, Urethanes, Natural Rubber, Styrene Butadiene, Polyvinyl Acetates & others; Pressure Sensitive, Heat seal and Contact Adhesives: Water-based, Hotmelt, 100% solids and solvent adhesives; Thermal and UV drying and curing; Extensive laboratory and coating facility: activities include benchmarking, quality evaluation, physical and analytical testing; product formulation, development, litigation support and expert witness. Markets include PSA tapes and labels, graphic arts, medical, electronics, consumer products, automotive and industrial coatings. **Degrees/licenses:** Ten degreed chemists and engineers; A2LA laboratory accreditation.

See primary listing under CHEMISTRY/ CHEMICALS: Adhesives

Piping Systems

Robert D. Hookway

President/Sr. Consultant
Hookway Engineering PC
115 Kristin Drive
Chelmsford, MA 01824
Tel: (978) 256-4852
Fax: (978) 244-0392
E-mail: hookwayeng@comcast.net

Specialties: EXPERT CATEGORY: PIPING SYSTEMS. Design, analysis and evaluation of piping systems, pressure vessels and structures considering temperature (1400F to -320F), pressure, earthquake etc, loadings. Condition assessment - piping installation and equipment in consideration of fatigue, corrosion,

(Listing continued on next page)

Piping Systems *(cont.)*

Robert D. Hookway (cont.)

load capacity and demand. Failure analysis. Litigation support. Registered professional engineer. Service to the power generation, petroleum and process industries. Member of ASME B31.3 Process Piping Main Committee and past member of ASME Section III (ASME Boiler and Pressure Vessel Code) Working Group on Piping and Special Working Group on Seismic Design Rules. **Degrees/licenses:** BS, MS Mech. Eng.; P.E. MA, VA.

See primary listing under ENGINEERING: Design

Protective Coatings

Calcoast Labs / DL Labs, Inc.

D. Patrick Fairley, Pres. - Lab Director
Antoine Chamsi, VP Materials Chemistry
Thomas Sliva, VP - Tech. Direc. (DL Labs)
4072 Watts Street
Emeryville, CA 94608
Tel: (510) 652-2979
Fax: (510) 652-3085
E-mail:
ccoastlabs@aol.com or dllabs@aol.com
Web Site: http://www.calcoastlabs.com or
http://www.dllabs.com

DL Labs, Inc.
74 Kent Street
Brooklyn, NY 11222
Tel: (718) 383-5080
Fax: (718) 383-7445

Specialties: Calcoast Labs, Inc. of Emeryville, California, has acquired DL Labs of New York City, formerly David Litter Laboratories. The acquisition makes Calcoast/DL Labs one of the largest independent paint, coatings, sealant & materials testing laboratories in North America. The California/New York locations also provide for universal coverage of our domestic and foreign client base. We provide analytical & expert services to the legal community. DL Labs is accredited by NVLAP (Code 100252-0), CGSB, ISO/IEC25. Calcoast Labs is accredited by DEA & Los Angeles Department of Building & Safety. **Degrees/licenses:** BS, MS, PhD.

See primary listing under FAILURE ANALYSIS: Materials

Consolidated Research, Inc.

Darlene R. Brezinski, PhD
President
P.O. Box 2190
Kingsford, MI 49802
Tel: (906) 779-9498
Fax: (906) 779-9787
E-mail: darpaint@aol.com

Specialties: Consolidated Research is a technical consulting firm for the paint and coatings industry. Staff have career backgrounds with firms within the industry. These include raw materials suppliers, coatings manufacturers and end-use applicators. We offer expertise in paint, polymers, pigments, additives, failure analysis, liability, toxic issues, patent infringement, analysis and identification of paint, and expert witness services. **Degrees/licenses:** PhD, DABFE, FACFE.

See primary listing under CHEMISTRY/ CHEMICALS: Paints & Coatings

Structural

Tore O. Arnesen, PE

President
Arnesen & Associates, Inc.
1330 Bellaire St.
Broomfield, CO 80020-1327
Tel: (303) 465-5806
Fax: (303) 438-1800
E-mail: Tore@Arnesen.us

Specialties: Structural and Architectural (Civil) Engineer with thirty years experience: forensic investigations and repairs of damaged structures and buildings; concrete restoration; expert witness testimony; structural assessments for damage due to natural disasters or fire; commercial, institutional & industrial projects; water projects such as treatment plants, storage or containment structures & canal structures. Published over twenty articles & technical standards; listed in

Marquis' "Who's Who in Science and Engineering." Membership in American Society of Civil Engineers, American Concrete Institute, SEI/ASCE-condition assessment and rehab of buildings committee. Co-author of Civil Engineering Project Peer Review, Air Supported Structure and Tension Fabric Structure Standards. **Degrees/licenses:** MSCE; PE - CO, WY & NE.

See primary listing under ENGINEERING: Structural

Vincent A. Ettari, PE

CEO: NY City Expeditor
Vincent A. Ettari, PE, PC
1065 Spillway Road
Shrub Oak, NY 10588
Tel: (914) 245-6320
Fax: (914) 245-6335
E-mail: ettari@ettari.com
Web Site: http://www.ettari.com

Specialties: Sanitary Waste Systems; Septic Systems; Water Supply Systems; Storm Drainage Systems; Flood Plain Analysis; Site Planning; Land Development; Subdivisions; Sitework; Parking Lots; Rock Cuts and Blasting; Soils and Slope Analyses; Geotechnical Engineering; Retaining Walls; Wetlands Issues; Groundwater Issues; Marine and Marinas; Dredging; Design of Small Dams, Retaining Walls, and Underground Chambers; Structural Design of Houses and Commercial Buildings; Building Codes Issues; Building Failures; Failure Analysis; Concrete, Steel, and Wood Design (member: ACI, AISC, AWC); Fire Protection (member NFPA); Supervision of Construction Sites; Slip, Trip and Fall; Personal Injury Investigations; House Inspections. **Degrees/licenses:** West. Co. Mun. Plan. Fed. Fallout Shelter Tech. (FEMA); Water Sys. Op. (NYSDOH).

See primary listing under ENGINEERING: Civil

Carl Walker, PE

Consultant
CW Consulting, LLC
2429 Highpointe Drive
Kalamazoo, MI 49008-2074
Tel: (269) 344-0803
Fax: (269) 344-0803 (call ahead)

Specialties: Parking Consulting - Structural Engineering; Precast Prestressed Concrete, Post-Tensioned Concrete, Durability, Security, Operations, Slip/Trip & Falls. American Concrete Institute, Precast Prestressed Concrete Institute, Post-Tensioning Institute, National Parking Association, International Parking Institute, Parking Consultants Council. University of Michigan Adjunct Professor. **Degrees/licenses:** BSCE, MSCE, PE 12 states.

See primary listing under ENGINEERING: Parking

Tires & Rims

John C. Glennon, Chartered

6917 W. 76th Street
Overland Park, KS 66204
Tel: (913) 383-3856
Fax: (913) 383-2277
E-mail: experts@johncglennon.com
Web Site: http://www.johncglennon.com

Specialties: Motor Vehicle Accident Investigation; Accident Reconstruction; Vehicle Crush Analysis; Vehicular Mechanical and Structural Failure Analysis for Automobiles, Trucks, and Motorcycles; Testing Capabilities for Air Brakes, Hydraulic Brakes, Suspension Systems, Steering Systems, Tires, and Wheels; Determination if Proper Maintenance and Repair Procedures were Followed; Identification of Previous Body Structural Damage; Motor Carrier Safety and Compliance; Commercial Driver Responsibilities and Qualifications; Commercial Driver Hours of Service and Daily Logs; Proper Load Securement Procedures; Fleet Maintenance Requirements; Computer Animation; Forensic Mapping; Photo Modeling; Downloading of Crash Data Retrieval Systems (Automobile "BLACK

(Listing continued on next page)

Tires & Rims *(cont.)*

John C. Glennon, Chartered (cont.)
BOX"). **Degrees/licenses:** D. Engr., PE, BS Automotive Technology, ASE Cert., CDL.

See primary listing under ACCIDENT RECONSTRUCTION: General

FINANCE

General

B & F Experts, Inc.

Financial Institutions, Business,
Mortgage, Finance, Banking
J. F. "Chip" Morrow
Principal
Nationwide from San Antonio, TX
Tel: (866) 365-7212 (Toll Free)
Fax: (866) 869-4062 (Toll Free)
E-mail: jfmorrow@earthlink.net
Web Site: http://www.jfmorrow.com

Specialties: 35+ years management for financial institutions and business. 31+ years bank and mortgage lending experience funding 10+ billion. 18+ years President, CEO &/or Director. 7+ years mortgage company director and 22+ years mortgage lending. 15+ years leadership in state/national financial trade associations. 150+ nationwide cases: approximately 50% defendants and 50% plaintiffs. 40% cases for financial institutions, 40% against and 20% non-financial institution. Prepared court presentations, court testimonies, reports, declarations, findings, affidavits and other for Federal, bankruptcy and state courts. Cases involving financial institutions, businesses, lending, mortgage, lender liability, D/O, checks, operations and others.

Fulcrum Financial Inquiry

David Nolte
Principal
1000 Wilshire Blvd., Ste. 1650
Los Angeles, CA 90017
Tel: (213) 787-4111
(213) 787-4100
Fax: (213) 787-4141
E-mail: dnolte@fulcruminquiry.com
Web Site: http://www.fulcruminquiry.com

Specialties: Our analysis and research combined with unique presentation techniques have resulted in an unequaled track record in successful court cases and client recoveries. Our personnel are full time and fully focused on the services we provide. We thoughtfully incorporate technology into our work to provide great results at a more reasonable cost. Our expertise encompasses damages analysis, lost profit studies, business & intangible asset valuations, fraud investigations, statistics, forensic economic analysis, royalty audits, strategic & market assessments, competitive surveys, analysis of computerized data including computer forensics, and a wide range of other financial advisory services. **Degrees/ licenses:** CPA, ASA, CMA, MBA, CFA.

See primary listing under ACCOUNTING: General

Michael D. Haslam

AFS Risk Management Services
3540 Simsbury Court
Carlsbad, CA 92008
Tel: (760) 729-8457
Fax: (760) 729-8581
E-mail: BLCexpert@aol.com

Specialties: Auto Industry expert with 40+ years of consulting and expert witness experience in the following areas: Auto Financing/ Leasing; Regulation Z & M; FCRA; ECOA; FDCPA; UCC; Portfolio Management; Lender Due Diligence; Repossessions/Asset Disposal; Consumer/Commercial Transactions.

See primary listing under AUTOMOTIVE: General

Market Consulting Corporation

Tel: (888) 397-9867
E-mail: marktcon@ix.netcom.com
Web Site:
http://www.market-consulting.com

Specialties: Broker/Customer disputes: stocks and bonds; options, commodity futures, currency trading; derivatives including swaps; limited partnerships, hedge funds and managed futures, e.g., suitability, churning, unauthorized trading, lack of supervision, spreading and hedging, due diligence, marketing. Other areas: asset management, pension investments; securities and futures tax matters including IRS examinations, appeals, US Tax Court appearances. Services: consultation, statistical and damage analysis, arbitration, mediation, court testimony. Consultants to NYSE, Options Clearing Corporation, CBOT, CME, COMEX, TIAA/CREF, banks, other major clients. Member: Compliance and Legal Division, Securities Industry Association. 20 years experience nationwide-plaintiffs/claimants, defendants/respondents. **Degrees/licenses:** ScD (MIT). Arbitrator NASD, NYSE, AAA, NFA. Mediator with NASD training.

See primary listing under FINANCE: Commodity Futures & Options

Arbitration

Ronald C. Peters & Associates, Inc.

Ronald C. Peters
President
6447 W. Cermak Rd.
Berwyn, IL 60402-2311
Tel: (708) 656-7788
Fax: (708) 749-7788
E-mail: hedge4@sbcglobal.net
Web Site: http://www.expertwitnessron.com

Specialties: Arbitration & Mediation; Investments, Securities; D & O Liability; Commodity trading; Unauthorized trading; NASD Arbitrator; Futures; Options; Hedging; Bonds; Futures trading activity analysis; Financial forecasting; Financial modeling; Asset & Liability management; Financial & investment management; Portfolio advisory; Corporate finance; Investment analysis; Banking; Savings & Loans; FHLB, FDIC cases. **Degrees/licenses:** CPA; CFTC Registered Commodity Trading Advisor; CTA.

See primary listing under FINANCE: Securities

Peter J. Pfeffer

605 Woodhaven Dr.
Mundelein (metro Chicago), IL 60060-1530
Tel: (847) 837-0791
Fax: (847) 970-6383
E-mail: barlowe@interaccess.com
Web Site: http://firms.findlaw.com/pfeffer

Specialties: Securities fraud examiner, case evaluation, arbitration panelist selection, derivatives (incl. commodities), defense and plaintiff, domestic and foreign, portfolio evaluation, written opinion, damage assessment, supervision, turn-over evaluation, suitability, investment advisors, discretionary accounts, securities valuation, registered employee/brokerage firm disputes. Thirty years experience in securities industry, AE through EVP of major firm (see Web site). Expert witness or arbitrator, exchange, NASD, AAA, NFA, appellate panelist, federal reparations proceedings, federal and state jury and bench trials. **Degrees/licenses:** See Web Site.

See primary listing under FINANCE: Securities

Automotive

J.A. "Doc" Watson

P.O. Box 758
Humble, TX 77347
Tel: (281) 540-8257
Fax: (281) 446-5212
E-mail: theautoexpert@aol.com
Web Site: http://www.theautoexpert.com

Specialties: Automotive consumer fraud, deceptive trade practices. Opinions, depositions and testimony which have led to successful solutions in mediation, arbitration, pre-trial settlements and trials. Ten+ years' experience expert witness plaintiff and defense. Expertise - sales and finance tactics, leasing, diminished value, rebates, curbstoning, odometers,

(Listing continued on next page)

Automotive *(cont.)*

J. A. "Doc" Watson (cont.)
repossession, salvage, credit procedures, vehicle appraisals, mechanical and body repair fraud, previous damage, trucks, lemon law, title kiting, program cars, bad credit, service contracts, life and accident & health policies, auto auctions, wholesaling, manufacturers' warranties, lender fraud, flood damage, class action, personal injury. 40+ years automotive employment history.

See primary listing under APPRAISAL & VALUATION: Vehicles

Bankruptcy

B & F Experts, Inc.

Financial Institutions, Business,
Mortgage, Finance, Banking
J. F. "Chip" Morrow
Principal
Nationwide from San Antonio, TX
Tel: (866) 365-7212 (Toll Free)
Fax: (866) 869-4062 (Toll Free)
E-mail: jfmorrow@earthlink.net
Web Site: http://www.jfmorrow.com

Specialties: 35+ years management for financial institutions and business. 31+ years bank and mortgage lending experience funding 10+ billion. 18+ years President, CEO &/or Director. 7+ years mortgage company director and 22+ years mortgage lending. 15+ years leadership in state/national financial trade associations. 150+ nationwide cases: approximately 50% defendants and 50% plaintiffs. 40% cases for financial institutions, 40% against and 20% non-financial institution. Prepared court presentations, court testimonies, reports, declarations, findings, affidavits and other for Federal, bankruptcy and state courts. Cases involving financial institutions, businesses, lending, mortgage, lender liability, D/O, checks, operations and others.

See primary listing under FINANCE: General

Business Valuations

Anderson Economic Group, LLC

Patrick L. Anderson
Principal
260 East Saginaw Street
East Lansing, MI 48823
Tel: (517) 333-6984
Fax: (517) 333-7058
E-mail: webmaster@AndersonEconomicGroup.com
Web Site: http://www.AndersonEconomicGroup.com

Specialties: AEG economists and CPAs provide expert testimony regarding business valuation and lost earnings, for privately-held and publicly-traded companies. We use one or more of the three traditional approaches to business valuation, as well as newer techniques incorporating uncertainty and growth options. We perform the industry, market, and economic analyses required for proper valuation, as well as review financial statements. Our reports are both technically sound and well-summarized. Principal Patrick Anderson is the award-winning author of over 90 published articles and the book "Business Economics and Finance.". **Degrees/licenses:** CVs & publication list available upon request.

See primary listing under ECONOMICS: General

Check Fraud

Gene Cooney

Managing Director
CCI Consulting
4371 Winters Chapel Road, #1411
Atlanta, GA 30360
Tel: (770) 242-3569
E-mail: cciconsulting@comcast.net
Web Site:
http://www.consultcci.com/litigation.html

Specialties: Held senior positions at two of the 50 largest financial institutions in America. Consultant to financial services organizations with assets ranging from $250 million to over $300 billion. As primary expert, $130 million fraud and $53 million embezzlement cases were resolved in clients' favor during 2004. Over 30 years hands-on experience with virtually all check, deposit, cash management/treasury management and loan accounting products and services to include transactions, accounts, maintenance, exceptions, workflows, hardware, software, policies, procedures, processing standards and ANSI banking standards. No geographic restrictions. No case is too small. **Degrees/ licenses:** BSBA, M Adm, Stonier Graduate School of Banking.

See primary listing under FINANCE: Commercial Banking

Catherine A. Ghiglieri

President
Ghiglieri & Company
2300 Cypress Point West
Austin, TX 78746
Tel: (512) 329-5101
Fax: (512) 329-5166
E-mail: cathy@ghiglieri.com
Web Site: http://www.ghiglieri.com

Specialties: Bank regulatory practices; banking industry standards; deposit account procedures; banking practices and procedures; commercial and real estate lending practices; directors and officers duties and responsibilities; fraud detection procedures; loan review. University of Notre Dame, BBA in Finance; Georgia State University, JD. Former Texas Banking Commissioner and eighteen-year veteran with Comptroller of the Currency. Experienced expert witness. **Degrees/ licenses:** BBA, JD; Member: State Bar of Georgia, DC Bar.

See primary listing under FINANCE: Commercial Banking

Pat McElroy, Jr.

President
McElroy Consulting and Litigation Services
4041 W. Wheatland, Ste. 156-383
Dallas, TX 75237
Tel: (972) 780-7883
Fax: (972) 296-4298
E-mail: pmcelroy@bankdoctor.com

Specialties: Banking industry standards; Lending related matters; Checking and deposit procedures; Fidelity bond claims; Lender liability; Fraud, Bank regulations; Director and officer liability; Policies and procedures. BBA Texas Christian University. Former Federal Reserve Bank Examiner. Currently, consultant to numerous financial institutions. Instructor: Bank Administration Institute, American Institute of Banking. Author of problem loan seminar for Comptroller of the Currency bank examiners. Publications: various articles. 30+ years experience in banking. Previous clients include FDIC, U.S. Trustee, Texas Attorney General's Office, numerous banks and individuals. Courtroom seasoned and high profile case experience. **Degrees/licenses:** BBA.

See primary listing under FINANCE: Commercial Banking

Commercial Banking

Advisors/Experts @ MCS Associates

Norman Katz
Managing Partner
18881 Von Karman Ave., Ste. 1175
Irvine, CA 92612-1569
Tel: (949) 263-8700
Fax: (949) 263-0770
E-mail: info@mcsassociates.com
Web Site: http://www.mcsassociates.com

Specialties: Nationally recognized banking, financial services, real estate consulting group; Experienced expert witnesses and consultants include bankers, lenders, insurance managers, brokers, agents, economists, securities brokers, trust fiduciaries, appraisers, accountants. Expertise: Bank operations, check fraud; Lending policies, procedures; Loan admin-

(Listing continued on next page)

Commercial Banking *(cont.)*

Advisors/Experts @ MCS Associates (cont.)
istration, foreclosures, bankruptcy; Lender liability; D&O Liability; Insurance (Life, Disability, Property & Casualty, Reinsurance, Surplus) underwriting, claims handling, bad faith; Broker duties, agency management; Title insurance & escrow; R/E brokerage, leasing, property management, appraisal, development, construction defects; Business valuation, lost profits, damages assessment; Forensic accounting; Securities brokerage, trading, investment suitability; Economic & statistical analysis. **Degrees/licenses:** MBA, PhD, CPA, CLU, CPCU, CFP, CFA, CREA, MAI, ASA.

B & F Experts, Inc.

Financial Institutions, Business,
Mortgage, Finance, Banking
J. F. "Chip" Morrow
Principal
Nationwide from San Antonio, TX
Tel: (866) 365-7212 (Toll Free)
Fax: (866) 869-4062 (Toll Free)
E-mail: jfmorrow@earthlink.net
Web Site: http://www.jfmorrow.com

Specialties: 35+ years management for financial institutions and business. 31+ years bank and mortgage lending experience funding 10+ billion. 18+ years President, CEO &/or Director. 7+ years mortgage company director and 22+ years mortgage lending. 15+ years leadership in state/national financial trade associations. 150+ nationwide cases: approximately 50% defendants and 50% plaintiffs. 40% cases for financial institutions, 40% against and 20% non-financial institution. Prepared court presentations, court testimonies, reports, declarations, findings, affidavits and other for Federal, bankruptcy and state courts. Cases involving financial institutions, businesses, lending, mortgage, lender liability, D/O, checks, operations and others.

See primary listing under FINANCE: General

Gene Cooney

Managing Director
CCI Consulting
4371 Winters Chapel Road, #1411
Atlanta, GA 30360
Tel: (770) 242-3569
E-mail: cciconsulting@comcast.net
Web Site:
http://www.consultcci.com/litigation.html

Specialties: Held senior positions at two of the 50 largest financial institutions in America. Consultant to financial services organizations with assets ranging from $250 million to over $300 billion. As primary expert, $130 million fraud and $53 million embezzlement cases were resolved in clients' favor during 2004. Over 30 years hands-on experience with virtually all check, deposit, cash management/treasury management and loan accounting products and services to include transactions, accounts, maintenance, exceptions, workflows, hardware, software, policies, procedures, processing standards and ANSI banking standards. No geographic restrictions. No case is too small. **Degrees/licenses:** BSBA, M Adm, Stonier Graduate School of Banking.

Richard E. Dressel

Bank Operations Consultant
962 Kennett Way
West Chester, PA 19380
Tel: (610) 344-0809
Fax: (610) 344-0769
E-mail: redxsvp@aol.com

Specialties: Thirty three years of Bank Operations experience. Credible analysis and persuasive testimony on banking policies and industry practices. Expertise includes Demand Deposit/checking account processing; check payment, exception handling, fraud detection, overdrafts, NSF checks, signature verification and statement rendering. Was SVP - Deposit Accounting Services for CoreStates Bank in Philadelphia, now Wachovia. Since 1995 have served as independent consultant providing litigation support and expert witness services. **Degrees/licenses:** BS, Stonier Graduate School of Banking.

See primary listing under LITIGATION SUPPORT: Check Fraud, Bank Operations

Samuel K. Freshman, BA, JD

President
Standard Management Company
6151 W. Century Blvd., Suite 300
Los Angeles, CA 90045
Tel: (310) 410-2300
Fax: (310) 410-2919
E-mail:
sfreshman@standardmanagement.com

Specialties: Attorney, Real Estate Broker, Banker, Professor, Legal Malpractice, Arbitration, Brokerage, Malpractice, Leases, Syndication, Construction, Property Management, Finance, Due Diligence, Conflict of Interest, Title Insurance, Banking, Escrow. 32 years State & Federal Courts. 29 articles. Mediator, Fiduciary Duties, Lease Inerpretation, Banking Title Company President. **Degrees/licenses:** BA, JD, California Bar, U. S. Supreme Court & District Court, U. S. Tax Court.

See primary listing under REAL ESTATE: General

Catherine A. Ghiglieri

President
Ghiglieri & Company
2300 Cypress Point West
Austin, TX 78746
Tel: (512) 329-5101
Fax: (512) 329-5166
E-mail: cathy@ghiglieri.com
Web Site: http://www.ghiglieri.com

Specialties: Bank regulatory practices; banking industry standards; deposit account procedures; banking practices and procedures; commercial and real estate lending practices; directors and officers duties and responsibilities; fraud detection procedures; loan review. University of Notre Dame, BBA in Finance; Georgia State University, JD. Former Texas Banking Commissioner and eighteen-year veteran with Comptroller of the Currency. Experienced expert witness. **Degrees/ licenses:** BBA, JD; Member: State Bar of Georgia, DC Bar.

JRB Associates

John R. Britt
24208 Heritage Lane
Newhall, CA 91321-3536
Tel: (661) 255-0090
Fax: (661) 255-0091
E-mail: jrbassoc@earthlink.net
Web Site: http://www.bankingexpert.com

Specialties: Lender liability; Credit; Loan review and analysis; Bank operations; New accounts; Deposit and check fraud; Code of conduct; Branch administration; Board of Directors; Personnel; Previous experience as senior executive of major bank and President and CEO of two independent banks; Claremont McKenna College, BA, Business and Economics; Graduate, Pacific Coast Banking School, University of Washington; Deposition and trial experience since 1989; Board Certified Forensic Examiner and Fellow, American Board of Forensic Examiners. Forty years experience in the financial services industry. **Degrees/licenses:** BA: Business & Economics.

Pat McElroy, Jr.

President
McElroy Consulting and Litigation Services
4041 W. Wheatland, Ste. 156-383
Dallas, TX 75237
Tel: (972) 780-7883
Fax: (972) 296-4298
E-mail: pmcelroy@bankdoctor.com

Specialties: Banking industry standards; Lending related matters; Checking and deposit procedures; Fidelity bond claims; Lender liability; Fraud, Bank regulations; Director and officer liability; Policies and procedures. BBA Texas Christian University. Former Federal Reserve Bank Examiner. Currently, consultant to numerous financial institutions. Instructor: Bank Administration Institute, American Institute of Banking. Author of problem loan seminar for Comptroller of the Currency bank examiners. Publications: various articles. 30+ years experience in banking. Previous clients include FDIC, U.S. Trustee, Texas Attorney General's Office, numerous banks and individuals. Courtroom seasoned and high profile case experience. **Degrees/licenses:** BBA.

Commercial Banking *(cont.)*

Thomas A. Tarter

Andela Consulting Group, Inc.
15250 Ventura Blvd., Ste. 610
Sherman Oaks, CA 91403-3218
Tel: (818) 380-3102
(818) 368-1068
Fax: (818) 501-5412
E-mail: ttarter@earthlink.net
Web Site:
http://www.commercepartners.org

Specialties: Banking, bankruptcy - interest rate & plan feasibility opinions, business litigation support, checking account disputes, embezzlement, forgeries, credit card fraud, credit damages, debt restructure, lender liability, loan policy & practices, bank management & operating controls, trade and standby letters of credit, guarantees, consumer lending, real estate & construction lending, credit facility disputes, shareholder & insider loan transactions, note valuations, expert referral service; Bank founder, director & CEO; financial and management advisor; 25+ years experience. Experience: over 500 cases - State, Federal & Bankruptcy Court. Clients: individuals, businesses, banks, government agencies, financial institutions. **Degrees/licenses:** BS, MBA.

Commodity Futures & Options

Market Consulting Corporation

Tel: (888) 397-9867
E-mail: marktcon@ix.netcom.com
Web Site:
http://www.market-consulting.com

Specialties: Broker/Customer disputes: stocks and bonds; options, commodity futures, currency trading; derivatives including swaps; limited partnerships, hedge funds and managed futures, e.g., suitability, churning, unauthorized trading, lack of supervision, spreading and hedging, due diligence, marketing. Other areas: asset management, pension investments; securities and futures tax matters including IRS examinations, appeals, US Tax Court appearances. Services: consultation, statistical and damage analysis, arbitration, mediation, court testimony. Consultants to NYSE, Options Clearing Corporation, CBOT, CME, COMEX, TIAA/CREF, banks, other major clients. Member: Compliance and Legal Division, Securities Industry Association. 20 years experience nationwide-plaintiffs/claimants, defendants/respondents. **Degrees/licenses:** ScD (MIT). Arbitrator NASD, NYSE, AAA, NFA. Mediator with NASD training.

Peter J. Pfeffer

605 Woodhaven Dr.
Mundelein (metro Chicago), IL 60060-1530
Tel: (847) 837-0791
Fax: (847) 970-6383
E-mail: barlowe@interaccess.com
Web Site: http://firms.findlaw.com/pfeffer

Specialties: Securities fraud examiner, case evaluation, arbitration panelist selection, derivatives (incl. commodities), defense and plaintiff, domestic and foreign, portfolio evaluation, written opinion, damage assessment, supervision, turn-over evaluation, suitability, investment advisors, discretionary accounts, securities valuation, registered employee/brokerage firm disputes. Thirty years experience in securities industry, AE through EVP of major firm (see Web site). Expert witness or arbitrator, exchange, NASD, AAA, NFA, appellate panelist, federal reparations proceedings, federal and state jury and bench trials. **Degrees/licenses:** See Web Site.

See primary listing under FINANCE: Securities

Due Diligence & Selling Away

Stuart A. Ober, AIFA®
President
Securities Investigations, Inc.
2626 Route 212
P.O. Box 888
Woodstock, NY 12498
Tel: (845) 679-2300
Fax: (845) 679-2301
E-mail: ober@hvc.rr.com
Web Site: http://www.duediligencefirm.com

Specialties: Expert in Securities Litigation/Arbitration (30 years experience - clients include U.S. Treasury Dept., plaintiffs/defendants): selling away; fiduciary responsibility; fraud; churning; misrepresentations/omissions; due diligence; supervision failure; damages calculations; supervision/compliance; partnership analysis; economic evaluations; publishing; work-life expectancy; personal injury/wrongful death. Arbitrator: NASD (Chairperson); NYSE; NFA; AAA. Member: ICFP Standards Board - established standards: Investor suitability, real estate, oil/gas, mutual funds, life insurance (chairperson), equipment leasing. SEC Registered Investment Advisor. Advisory Board, "Personal Financial Planning," Author, EVERYBODY'S GUIDE - TAX SHELTERS, training manuals, articles, investment newsletter. Quoted: New York Times, Wall Street Journal, Forbes, Money. Accredited investment fiduciary auditor, Katz Graduate School of Business, University of Pittsburgh. **Degrees/licenses:** BA Wesleyan; License, Sorbonne, U. of Paris; MBA Program, CUNY.

See primary listing under FINANCE: Securities

Securities

Thomas C. Grzymala, CFP®, AIFA®
Principal
Forensic Analytics LLC
3506 Glasgow Lane
Keswick, VA 22947-2748
Tel: (434) 293-8882
Fax: (434) 293-9931
E-mail: tom@fa-llc.net

Specialties: Experienced fee-only Certified Financial Planner (CFP) and investment manager; SEC-Registered Investment Advisor; prepare, consult and testify as expert witness in litigation and securities arbitration involving suitability, churning, breach of (trustee) fiduciary duty, damage calculations, trial exhibits preparation, due diligence, professional malpractice, general financial analysis and litigation support. Member: Financial Planning Association, National Association of Personal Financial Advisors, American Bar Association. BS, U.S. Naval Academy; MPA, The American University. **Degrees/licenses:** BS; MPA; CFP; NASD Series 65; AIFA.

Market Consulting Corporation
Tel: (888) 397-9867
E-mail: marktcon@ix.netcom.com
Web Site:
http://www.market-consulting.com

Specialties: Broker/Customer disputes: stocks and bonds; options, commodity futures, currency trading; derivatives including swaps; limited partnerships, hedge funds and managed futures, e.g., suitability, churning, unauthorized trading, lack of supervision, spreading and hedging, due diligence, marketing. Other areas: asset management, pension investments; securities and futures tax matters including IRS examinations, appeals, US Tax Court appearances. Services: consultation, statistical and damage analysis, arbitration, mediation, court testimony. Consultants to NYSE, Options Clearing Corporation, CBOT, CME, COMEX, TIAA/CREF, banks, other major clients. Member: Compliance and Legal Division, Securities Industry Association. 20 years

(Listing continued on next page)

Securities *(cont.)*

Market Consulting Corporation (cont.) experience nationwide-plaintiffs/claimants, defendants/respondents. **Degrees/licenses:** ScD (MIT). Arbitrator NASD, NYSE, AAA, NFA. Mediator with NASD training.

See primary listing under FINANCE: Commodity Futures & Options

Stuart A. Ober, AIFA®

President
Securities Investigations, Inc.
2626 Route 212
P.O. Box 888
Woodstock, NY 12498
Tel: (845) 679-2300
Fax: (845) 679-2301
E-mail: ober@hvc.rr.com
Web Site: http://www.duediligencefirm.com

Specialties: Expert in Securities Litigation/Arbitration (30 years experience - clients include U.S. Treasury Dept., plaintiffs/defendants): selling away; fiduciary responsibility; fraud; churning; misrepresentations/omissions; due diligence; supervision failure; damages calculations; supervision/compliance; partnership analysis; economic evaluations; publishing; work-life expectancy; personal injury/wrongful death. Arbitrator: NASD (Chairperson); NYSE; NFA; AAA. Member: ICFP Standards Board - established standards: Investor suitability, real estate, oil/gas, mutual funds, life insurance (chairperson), equipment leasing. SEC Registered Investment Advisor. Advisory Board, "Personal Financial Planning," Author, EVERYBODY'S GUIDE - TAX SHELTERS, training manuals, articles, investment newsletter. Quoted: New York Times, Wall Street Journal, Forbes, Money. Accredited investment fiduciary auditor, Katz Graduate School of Business, University of Pittsburgh. **Degrees/licenses:** BA Wesleyan; License, Sorbonne, U. of Paris; MBA Program, CUNY.

Ronald C. Peters & Associates, Inc.

Ronald C. Peters
President
6447 W. Cermak Rd.
Berwyn, IL 60402-2311
Tel: (708) 656-7788
Fax: (708) 749-7788
E-mail: hedge4@sbcglobal.net
Web Site: http://www.expertwitnessron.com

Specialties: Securities; Investments; Trading Activity Analysis; Banks; Savings & Loans; Compliance (financial institutions); Accounting & auditing; Gap management; Financial & investment management; Directors & Officers liability; FHLB, FDIC cases; Check kiting; Wire transfers; Lender liability; Due diligence; Financial forecasting; Fixed income; Investments; Financial modeling; Portfolio advisory; Corporate finance; CTA; Supervision; Suitability; Churning; Cash management; Expert Witness banking; Expert Witness securities; Expert Witness supervision, Expert Witness suitability; Expert Witness churning; Fixed income securities; Commodity futures; Damage determination; Damage limitation; Fire loss. **Degrees/licenses:** CPA; CFTC Registered Commodity Trading Advisor; CTA.

Peter J. Pfeffer

605 Woodhaven Dr.
Mundelein (metro Chicago), IL 60060-1530
Tel: (847) 837-0791
Fax: (847) 970-6383
E-mail: barlowe@interaccess.com
Web Site: http://firms.findlaw.com/pfeffer

Specialties: Securities fraud examiner, case evaluation, arbitration panelist selection, derivatives (incl. commodities), defense and plaintiff, domestic and foreign, portfolio evaluation, written opinion, damage assessment, supervision, turn-over evaluation, suitability, investment advisors, discretionary accounts, securities valuation, registered employee/brokerage firm disputes. Thirty years experience in securities industry, AE through EVP of major firm (see Web site). Expert witness or arbitrator, exchange, NASD, AAA, NFA, appellate panelist, federal reparations proceedings, federal and state jury and bench trials. **Degrees/licenses:** See Web Site.

FIREARMS & BALLISTICS

General

John H. Dillon, Jr.
Forensic Consultant
7007 Trails End Road
Manassas, VA 20112-3602
Tel: (703) 791-5559
Fax: (703) 791-6712
E-mail: jhdillonjr@aol.com

Specialties: Ballistics; Microscopic Examinations of Bullets, Cartridge Cases, Shotshells; Firearms Operability, Accidental Discharges, Trigger Pull Analyses; Shooting Reconstruction; Gunshot Residues; Muzzle-to-Victim Distance Determinations; Shotgun Shooting Distance Determinations; Ejection Pattern Testing; Crime Scene Documentation and Laboratory Procedures Review. Court Qualified, 24 States, 12 Federal Courts. U.S. Naval Academy, BS; University of Virginia, MEd; Numerous articles in forensic journals. Retired FBI Agent, former Chief FBI Ballistics Unit. Member, American Academy of Forensic Sciences, Association for Crime Scene Reconstruction and Mid-Atlantic Association of Forensic Scientists. Distinguished/Life Member and Past President, Association of Firearm and Toolmark Examiners. Consultant, Forensic Technology, Inc. Consultant, The Academy Group. **Degrees/licenses:** BS, MEd, D-ABFE, FBI Lab Certified Ballistics & Toolmarks.

Richard N. Ernest
Forensic Consultant
7413 Arcadia Trail
Fort Worth, TX 76137
Tel: (817) 228-6526
Fax: (817) 498-6375
E-mail: rernest@e-gunlab.com
Web Site: http://www.e-gunlab.com

Specialties: Ballistics; Shooting Scene Reconstructions; Accidental Shootings; Firearms Examination; Microscopic Examination of Bullets, Cartridge Cases & Shotshells; Toolmark Examination; Trigger Pull Analysis; Ejection Pattern Testing; Gunshot Residues Consulting & Distance Determinations; Crime Scene Reconstructions; General Criminalistics Examinations including hair, fibers, tire tracks, shoe prints, lamp filament examinations; Forensic Casework Review. Extensive courtroom testimony experience. Testified over 1,000 times in several states & in Federal courts. Distinguished Member of Association of Firearms & Toolmarks Examiners, American Academy of Forensic Sciences, Charter Member of Association for Crime Scene Reconstruction, International Wound Ballistics Association. **Degrees/licenses:** BS- Univ. of GA, AFTE, AAFS, SAFS, SWAFS, ACSR & IWBA.

Jon J. Nordby, PhD, D-ABMDI
Consultant in Forensic Science
& Forensic Medicine
Final Analysis Forensics
3532 Soundview Dr. West
University Place, WA 98466-1426
Tel: (253) 627-2739
Fax: (253) 627-0350
E-mail: finalanalysis@comcast.net
Web Site:
http://www.finalanalysisforensics.com

Specialties: Death, medical investigation: cause, manner of death, investigation of scenes, mass disasters; Criminalistics: trace evidence, organic/inorganic identifications, comparisons, ballistics; Scene investigation: bloodstain pattern analysis, evidence collection, event reconstruction; Scientific evidence: chain of custody; recognition/col-

(Listing continued on next page)

General *(cont.)*

Jon J. Nordby (cont.)

lection issues, limitations/scope of sciences applied, assess omissions, opinions, expert testimony; Fellow, American Academy of Forensic Sciences; Member, Canadian Society of Forensic Sciences, International Association of Bloodstain Pattern Analysts, & Association of Crime Scene Reconstruction; Founding member, Dept. of Homeland Security, DMORT; Deployments: WTC investigation, NYC, 2001; Member SWGSTAIN, FBI Scientific Working Group in bloodstain pattern analysis. **Degrees/licenses:** MA, PhD; Diplomat, Amer. Bd. of Medicolegal Death Investigators, Registry #412.

See primary listing under LITIGATION SUPPORT: Forensic Science

FOOD FACILITIES

Consulting

Edwin L. Fellerman

CEO
Sales & Design Associates, Inc.
51 Cooper Lane
Rivervale, NJ 07675
Tel: (201) 666-1475
Fax: (201) 666-6864
E-mail: efellerman@aol.com or
info@fdsvcequipconsult.com
Web Site:
http://www.fdsvcequipconsult.com

Specialties: Designed, sold, purchased, supplied and financed millions of dollars in construction of hotels, restaurants, cafeterias, fast food and food service establishments. Supervised construction and coordinated all trades, plumbing, electrical, masonry, carpentry, heating, ventilating, air conditioning (HVAC), Decorating, contract furnishing and food and beverage service equipment nationally and internationally since 1946. **Degrees/licenses:** ASID, IBD, AAC, FSC.

FRANCHISING

General

Anderson Economic Group, LLC

Patrick L. Anderson
Principal
260 East Saginaw Street
East Lansing, MI 48823
Tel: (517) 333-6984
Fax: (517) 333-7058
E-mail: webmaster@AndersonEconomicGroup.com
Web Site: http://www.AndersonEconomicGroup.com

Specialties: AEG economists and CPAs have particular expertise in franchised industries, including automotive; beer, wine, and spirits; rental cars; retail; hospitality; and other distribution systems in which retailers are separate from the manufacturer. Our experts provide testimony regarding reductions in earnings; value of lost of franchise or distribution rights; "good cause" or other grounds for termination; encroachment of trade area; cannibalization of sales; sales quotas or allocation of product; and related topics. AEG Principal Patrick Anderson is the author of over 90 published articles and the book "Business Economics and Finance.". **Degrees/licenses:** CVs & publication list available upon request.

See primary listing under ECONOMICS: General

R. Britton Colbert, CHA

P.O. Box 868
Ligonier (Pittsburgh), PA 15658-0868
Tel: (724) 238-5180
Fax: (724) 238-5188
E-mail: britt@colberthotelconsulting.com
Web Site:
http://www.colberthotelconsulting.com

Specialties: Hotel expert regarding hotel operating standards. Hotel franchise experience with brand standards, inspections, Franchisor-Franchisee relationships, impact, financial and operational qualifications, financing and independent contractor status. Assist in interrogatories and discovery procedures. 30-yr. experience, with multi-unit operational responsibility for hotel portfolio nationwide as EVP operations. Plaintiff and defense experience. Former partner at L&H. Court appointed hotel expert in CA. University of Denver, Hotel School, CHA Certification by American Hotel & Lodging Association. **Degrees/licenses:** BSBA, CHA (Cert. Hotel Admin.); Real Estate Lic. PA, CA.

See primary listing under HOTEL/RESTAURANT INDUSTRY: General

Leon Gottlieb

USA-International Restaurant,
Hotel & Franchise Consultant
Est. 1969
4601 Sendero Place
Tarzana, CA 91356-4821
U.S.A.
Tel: (818) 757-1131
Fax: (818) 757-1816
E-mail: LGottlieb@aol.com
Web Site: http://hometown.aol.com/lgottlieb/myhomepage/business.html

Specialties: USA-International Consultant-expert on industry standards, franchising, fast food, restaurants, management, operations of all types, hotels, retail, service industries, advertising, promotion, sales, multi-level marketing, convenience stores, food courts, shopping malls, food manufacturing, distribution, brokerage, licensing agreements, training manuals, security, safety, injury, construction, equipment, site selection, encroachment, turnaround problems, profit & loss damage assessment. Former partner IHOP, V.P. National Franchise & Restaurant Operations, Director to USA Chains, Who's Who in America, Columnist, Author, AAA & Superior Court Arbitrator with substantial court, deposition and expert witness experience. **Degrees/licenses:** UCLA Instructor; Certified ServSafe National Food Safety Program.

See primary listing under HOTEL/RESTAURANT INDUSTRY: General

THE HOTEL EXPERTS

Stephen P. Stearns, Partner (FL)
Skip Stearns, Partner (NH)
258 E. Tall Oaks Circle
Palm Beach Gardens, FL 33410
Tel: (561) 775-4990
Fax: (561) 622-9223
E-mail: stevest50@aol.com or
SaltRiverFarm@yahoo.com
Web Site: http://expert.expertpages.com/thehotelexperts

Additional Office Location
P.O. Box 113
Stratham, NH 03885-0113
Tel: (603) 778-0110
Fax: (603) 778-0333

Specialties: Steve and Skip Stearns have 70+ years combined hotel management experience. Steve was senior operating officer at major resorts and convention hotels. He's currently Senior Vice President with Richey International providing service, operating and product standards evaluations for hotels, casinos and resorts worldwide. Most of Skip's career was spent as a corporate marketing and franchising officer. He now has a consulting practice. Expert witness experience includes financial statement interpretation, contract disputes, mismanagement, personal injuries and wrongful deaths. THE HOTEL EXPERTS has 10+ years of witness experience representing plaintiffs and defendants. **Degrees/licenses:** Steve Stearns: BS Purdue Univ.; Skip Stearns: BA Univ. of Massachusetts.

See primary listing under HOTEL/RESTAURANT INDUSTRY: General

Automotive

The Fontana Group, Inc.
Ernest H. Manuel, Jr., PhD, President
Joseph F. Roesner, Vice President
3509 N. Campbell Ave.
Tucson, AZ 85719
Tel: (520) 325-9800
Fax: (520) 325-9847
E-mail: tfgi@fontanagroup.com
Web Site: http://www.fontanagroup.com

Specialties: Marketing and economic impact studies in automotive retailing; Largest specialist with state and federal litigation experience (since 1973) in terminations, relocations, new dealerships, allocation systems, business valuations and economic damages; All linemakes; US and Canada. Outstanding references. **Degrees/licenses:** PhD, DBA, MBA, CMA.

See primary listing under ECONOMICS: Economic Losses/Damages

GEOLOGY

Economic & Mineral Geology

Joseph G. Wargo
Consultant - Geology, Mineral Exploration
21 Birchwood Place
Moraga, CA 94556
Tel: (925) 376-1091
Fax: (925) 376-0959
E-mail: jwargo@aol.com

Specialties: Geology; Mineral property exploration; Economic geology; Negotiations; Evaluation of geologic and exploration data; Expert testimony; Mining history. "Qualified Person" per Canada NI 43-101. **Degrees/licenses:** PhD; Registered Geologist (CA #328); Certified Professional Geologist (#54).

GEOLOGY/ HYDROLOGY

General

Environmental Geology Services
Marc Seeley, CEG, REA-II
1695 Willowside Road
Santa Rosa, CA 95401
Tel: (707) 528-0810
Fax: (707) 528-1956
E-mail: egs@ap.net

Specialties: 25+ years experience; Engineering geology, hazardous materials, environmental assessments; Causation and failure analysis, peer review, expert consulting; Civil Trial Science Panelist, 30+ depositions, contract management; Fault studies, earth movement and landslide investigations, air photo interpretation, underground storage tank investigations, ground water investigations and remediation; Land development/planning studies. Registered Geologist (CA, OR, ID), Certified Engineering Geologist (OR), Certified Environmental Manager (NV), Registered Environmental Assessor II (CA). **Degrees/ licenses:** BA, MS Geology. See above for certifications.

See primary listing under ENGINEERING: Geotechnical

Alberto A. Gutierrez, RG
President
GEOLEX, Inc.
500 Marquette Ave. NW, Ste. 1350
Albuquerque, NM 87102
Tel: (505) 842-8000
Fax: (505) 842-7380
E-mail: aag@geolex.com
Web Site: http://www.geolex.com

Specialties: Environmental litigation support; Hydrogeology; Contaminant fate and transport modeling; Hazardous waste management; Site investigation and remediation; RCRA and Superfund cost allocation/analysis; Forensic geochemistry and source identification of soil and groundwater contamination; Aerial photography interpretation/waste management practice documentation; Environmental liability assessment and forensic accounting; Asset evaluation for corporate mergers and acquisitions. Registered professional geologist with AIPG and in 18 states. Extensive expert witness experience in state and federal court and hearings before regulatory bodies. Former chairman of New Mexico Environmental Improvement Board. Former Commissioner, NM Water Quality Control Commission. Extensively published. **Degrees/licenses:** BS Geomorphology (magna cum laude); MS (cum laude); RG, CPG, REA.

See primary listing under ENVIRONMENTAL: General

Water Resources Consulting Services

Rick Van Bruggen, MS, PE
President
P.O. Box 19
Guerneville, CA 95446
Tel: (800) 776-3070 (Toll Free)
(707) 604-0050 (Office)
Fax: (707) 604-0051
E-mail: rvb@waterengr.com
Web Site: http://www.hydrologyexpert.com

Specialties: Mr. Van Bruggen has twenty-four years of engineering experience specializing in the use of systems engineering and modeling techniques to define and evaluate surface water resource systems, forensic hydrology and hydraulics, and alternative flood control measures. He has performed numerous studies of watershed hydrology, floodplain and storm drain system hydraulics, reservoir and flood control operations, and the hydraulics behind drownings. He is a founding Board Member and the San Francisco Chapter President of the Forensic Expert Witness Association, reflecting his considerable experience testifying as an expert in Water Resources Engineering. **Degrees/licenses:** BSCE, MSCE, PE (CA, AZ, NV).

See primary listing under ENGINEERING: Flood/Hydraulic

William B. Wigginton, RG, CEG, CHG

Geolex, Inc.
P.O. Box 374
Aptos, CA 95001
Tel: (831) 662-0609
Fax: (831) 662-0609
E-mail: wwigginton@aol.com

Specialties: Landslide identification and repair; Foundation failure; Construction failure analysis; Groundwater resources and studies; Soil testing; Roadway construction and failure investigations; Insurance causation studies. **Degrees/licenses:** MS Geology, RG (CA), CEG (CA), Cert. Hydrogeologist (CA).

Groundwater & Hydrogeology

David R. Hargis, PhD, RG

Principal Hydrogeologist
Hargis + Associates, Inc.
2365 Northside Dr., #C100
San Diego, CA 92108-2709
Tel: (619) 521-0165
Fax: (619) 521-8580
E-mail: drhargis@hargis.com
Web Site: http://www.hargis.com

Specialties: Hydrology/Hydrogeology; Contaminant Fate and Transport; Source Evaluation and Timing; Groundwater Modeling; Contaminant Transport Modeling; Groundwater and Soil Remediation; Litigation Support; Expert Witness Testimony; Cost Allocation Analysis; Water Resources Exploration, Design and Development. Provides expert witness testimony, technical counsel, litigation support concerning hydrological conditions and assessment of soil/groundwater contamination at complex industrial, commercial, or Superfund sites. Also provides technical support for PRP identification, cost allocation, negotiations with USEPA and state agencies involving site cleanup levels and approval of RI/FS/RD/RA documents, cost recovery issues, and toxic tort litigation. **Degrees/licenses:** PhD, MS, BS, Registered Geologist (CA, AZ, VA & TX).

GRAPHIC ARTS/ PRINTING

General

Philip K. Ruggles
Printing Management Services
PO Box 46
San Luis Obispo, CA 93406
Tel: (805) 543-5968
Fax: (805) 543-9579
E-mail: pruggles@charter.net

Specialties: Litigation/consulting services for printing, publishing & allied graphic imaging industries; Damage evaluation for insurance; Quality systems; Safety issues; Training; Extensive knowledge of graphic arts business practices & manufacturing methods; Print estimating & costing methods; Evaluation of marketing, selling & pricing for traditional & digital products & services; Computer management systems for print manufacturing & printing company operation; Print production workflow; Prepress, litho sheetfed & web print production; Postpress production; Distribution of printed goods; Digital print production; Affiliation: Distinguished Emeritus Professor, California Polytechnic State University (Graphic Communication/Printing Management); Textbook author. **Degrees/licenses:** BS; MS.

HAZARDOUS MATERIALS

General

John Badger, CTL
508 Cushing Rd.
Newmarket, NH 03857-1738
Tel: (603) 292-5977
(203) 981-7219 (Cell)
E-mail: jbadger.1@comcast.net
Web Site: http://www.badgerconsulting.com

Specialties: Industrial Transportation, Distribution & Logistics specializing in Chemical Industry including Standards of Practice; Private Rail Fleet Management, Tankcar Design, Linings, Procurement, Operating Practices & Maintenance; Tanktruck, Tankcar Release Analysis, Investigation: Railroad Operating Practices, Procedures, Car Handling; Hazardous Materials Expertise, 49CFR FMCS Regulations/HAZMAT Compliance; Private Truck Fleet Operations; Freight Payment Analysis, Transaction Audit, Fraudulent Payment; Loss & Damage Analysis, Claim Management. Executive Consultant CG Ernst & Young, Genesis Solutions, RAS Associates, Daniel Penn Associates, etc. in all areas of supply chain. Former VP - Logistics, Olin Corporation; Former Chairman, CMA Distribution Committee; STB Rail Arbitrator. **Degrees/ licenses:** BS, MA, ASTL-CTL, ATLLP, ICC/ STB Practitioner.

See primary listing under TRANSPORTATION: General

Chemical Accident Reconstruction Services, Inc.

Michael Fox, PhD
Founder
9121 E. Tanque Verde Rd., #105
Tucson, AZ 85749-8391
Tel: (800) 645-3369
Fax: (520) 749-0861
E-mail: services@chemaxx.com
Web Site: http://www.chemaxx.com

Specialties: Complex industrial chemical accidents, fires and explosions as well as chemical-related consumer product injuries. The founder of the company has his PhD in Physical Chemistry, is a Certified Fire & Explosion Investigator and Certified or Accredited in Hazardous Chemicals, OSHA Process Hazard Analysis Team Leader, DOT Hazardous Materials, Corrosion, Metallurgy, Failure Analysis and Aerosols. Other specialties include: Propane, plastics, water chemistry, skin burns, acids, alkalis, carbon monoxide, flammable liquids, gasoline, scanning microscopy, MSDSs, natural gas, solvents, warning labels, PEX, welding, construction, chemical packaging & transport. For more specialties see web site. **Degrees/licenses:** PhD, Physical Chemistry; See certifications above.

See primary listing under CHEMISTRY/ CHEMICALS: General

Merlyn Robert "Bob" Wilson

Transportation Safety, Inc.
Sacramento Office
2377 Gold Meadow Way, Suite 100
Gold River, CA 95670
Tel: (916) 526-2845
Fax: (916) 631-1515
E-mail: Bob-Wilson@msn.com
Web Site: http://www.transafetyinc.com

Los Angeles Office
13104 Philadelphia St., Suite 218
Whittier, CA 90601
Tel: (562) 698-0040
Fax: (562) 698-0139

Specialties: Diesel Engine Electronic Control Modules; Black Box Downloads; Tachograph Analysis; Hydraulic & Air Brakes Systems; Driver's Hours of Service and Log Books; Commercial Driver Qualification; Preventative Maintenance Inspections; Driver Pre-trip Inspections; Loading, Unloading and Cargo Securement; Hazardous Materials; Off-Tracking or Trailer Cheat; Out of Service Criteria; Permit Loads; Transport of Intermodal Freight Containers. Mr. Wilson is certified through "ASE" as a truck technician specializing in hydraulic and air brake equipped trucks and buses. Past instructor for the Federal Transit Administration, University of California at Riverside, and the Northern California Public Safety Training & Education Center through Sacramento City College. Licensed forklift driver. **Degrees/licenses:** BS; AA (Admin. of Justice); Licensed private investigator, CA 13828.

See primary listing under ACCIDENT PREVENTION & SAFETY: Trucks, Buses & Forklifts

HOTEL/RESTAURANT INDUSTRY

General

R. Britton Colbert, CHA

P.O. Box 868
Ligonier (Pittsburgh), PA 15658-0868
Tel: (724) 238-5180
Fax: (724) 238-5188
E-mail: britt@colberthotelconsulting.com
Web Site:
http://www.colberthotelconsulting.com

Specialties: Hotel expert in operating and reporting standards; issues regarding franchising, security, cash-flow, wrongful termination, premise liability, personal injury, assault and wrongful death claims, mismanagement, negligent hiring/retention, acquisition & financing due diligence. Assist in interrogatories and discovery procedures. 30-yr. experience, with multi-unit operational responsibility for hotel portfolio nationwide as EVP operations. Plaintiff and defense experience. Former partner at L&H. Court appointed hotel expert in

(Listing continued on next page)

General *(cont.)*

R. Britton Colbert (cont.)
CA. University of Denver, Hotel School, CHA Certification by American Hotel & Lodging Association. **Degrees/licenses:** BSBA, CHA (Cert. Hotel Admin.); Real Estate Lic. PA, CA.

Edwin L. Fellerman

CEO
Sales & Design Associates, Inc.
51 Cooper Lane
Rivervale, NJ 07675
Tel: (201) 666-1475
Fax: (201) 666-6864
E-mail: efellerman@aol.com or
info@fdsvcequipconsult.com
Web Site:
http://www.fdsvcequipconsult.com

Specialties: Designed, sold, purchased, supplied and financed millions of dollars in construction of hotels, restaurants, cafeterias, fast food and food service establishments. Supervised construction and coordinated all trades, plumbing, electrical, masonry, carpentry, heating, ventilating, air conditioning (HVAC), Decorating, contract furnishing and food and beverage service equipment nationally and internationally since 1946. **Degrees/licenses:** ASID, IBD, AAC, FSC.

See primary listing under FOOD FACILITIES: Consulting

Leon Gottlieb

USA-International Restaurant,
Hotel & Franchise Consultant
Est. 1969
4601 Sendero Place
Tarzana, CA 91356-4821
U.S.A.
Tel: (818) 757-1131
Fax: (818) 757-1816
E-mail: LGottlieb@aol.com
Web Site: http://hometown.aol.com/lgottlieb/myhomepage/business.html

Specialties: USA-International Consultant-expert on industry standards, franchising, fast food, restaurants, management, operations of all types, hotels, retail, service industries, advertising, promotion, sales, multi-level marketing, convenience stores, food courts, shopping malls, food manufacturing, distribution, brokerage, licensing agreements, training manuals, security, safety, injury, construction, equipment, site selection, encroachment, turnaround problems, profit & loss damage assessment. Former partner IHOP, V.P. National Franchise & Restaurant Operations, Director to USA Chains, Who's Who in America, Columnist, Author, AAA & Superior Court Arbitrator with substantial court, deposition and expert witness experience. **Degrees/licenses:** UCLA Instructor; Certified ServSafe National Food Safety Program.

THE HOTEL EXPERTS

Stephen P. Stearns, Partner (FL)
Skip Stearns, Partner (NH)
258 E. Tall Oaks Circle
Palm Beach Gardens, FL 33410
Tel: (561) 775-4990
Fax: (561) 622-9223
E-mail: stevest50@aol.com or
SaltRiverFarm@yahoo.com
Web Site: http://expert.expertpages.com/thehotelexperts

Additional Office Location
P.O. Box 113
Stratham, NH 03885-0113
Tel: (603) 778-0110
Fax: (603) 778-0333

Specialties: Steve and Skip Stearns have 70+ years combined hotel management experience. Steve was senior operating officer at major resorts and convention hotels. He's currently Senior Vice President with Richey International providing service, operating and product standards evaluations for hotels, casinos and resorts worldwide. Most of Skip's career was spent as a corporate marketing and franchising officer. He now has a consulting practice. Expert witness experience includes financial statement interpretation, contract disputes, mismanagement, personal injuries and wrongful deaths. THE HOTEL EXPERTS has 10+ years of witness experience representing plaintiffs and defendants. **Degrees/licenses:**

Steve Stearns: BS Purdue Univ.; Skip Stearns: BA Univ. of Massachusetts.

R. Maurice Robinson, ISHC, CRE, ASA

President
Maurice Robinson & Associates, LLC
880 Apollo St. #125
El Segundo, CA 90245
Tel: (310) 640-9656
Fax: (310) 640-9276
E-mail: Maurice@MauriceRobinson.com
Web Site: http://www.mauricerobinson.com

Specialties: CRE, ASA, ISHC, trained arbitrator & mediator, certified appraiser. Recipient of top award for real estate consultants and appraisers for valuing the Grand Canyon National Park in 2000. Hotel and real estate industry business issues expert with 25 years consulting experience resolving disputes between owner-operator, borrower-lender and franchisee-franchisor. Fluent in ground & building leases; management contracts; franchise agreements; partnership & JV agreements; concession contracts; development agreements and loan docs. Expert witness testimony; damage calculations; lost profits analysis; deal structuring; workouts; bankruptcy; new development planning; market demand assessment; acquisition due diligence; and economic, market, financial & investment analysis. **Degrees/licenses:** MPA; BA Economics; State Certified General Real Estate Appraiser.

See primary listing under APPRAISAL & VALUATION: Personal Property

Jeffrey D. Schaffer

232 W. Kenilworth Street
New Orleans, LA 70124
Tel: (504) 482-8051
Fax: (504) 280-3189
E-mail: jschaffe@uno.edu

Specialties: Hotel & motel operations; Restaurant; Foodservice operations; Bar operations; Tourism operations; Sanitation; Safety; Contracts; Franchising; Training; Dram Shop Issues. Affiliation: School of Hotel, Restaurant & Tourism Administration, College of Business Administration, University of New Orleans (Professor). Degrees and Licenses: BA (Hotel, Restaurant & Institutional Management); CHA (Certified Hotel Administrator, American Hotel & Motel Association); FMP (Foodservice Management Professional, National Restaurant Association). **Degrees/ licenses:** PhD (Business Policy/Strategic Management); MBA (Finance).

HUMAN FACTORS

General

Mark S. Sanders, PhD, CHFP

Professor Emeritus, CSU Northridge
17060 Rancho Street
Encino, CA 91316
Tel: (818) 784-7041
Fax: (818) 784-4453

Specialties: Human Factors specialist with extensive consulting and expert witness experience in the following: Human Factors; Perception; Information Processing; Reaction Time; Risk Perception; Decision Making; Behavioral Expectations; Slips/Trips/Falls; Warning Effectiveness; Driver Performance; Product Safety. 1000+ cases and 150+ court appearances. 90+ Human Factors textbooks. Professor Emeritus, CSU Northridge; Senior Staff Scientist, Essex Corporation. Fellow and Past President, Human Factors & Ergonomics Society; Member, Society of Automotive Engineers; Ergonomics Society; Illuminating Engineer Society; National Safety Council. **Degrees/licenses:** PhD & MS Human Factors, Purdue University; Certified Human Factors Professional.

See primary listing under ACCIDENT RECONSTRUCTION: Slip & Fall

IDENTIFICATION

General

Forensic Analytical

Celia Hartnett
Laboratory Director
3777 Depot Road, Ste. 409
Hayward, CA 94545-2761
Tel: (800) 827-3274 ext. 148
(510) 887-8828 ext. 148
Fax: (510) 887-4451
E-mail: cchartnett@forensica.com
Web Site: http://www.forensica.com

Specialties: Extensive experience in the following areas: Blood spatter analysis; Crime scene reconstruction; Criminalistics; DNA typing; Identification (gunshot residue, firearms, bullets, cartridge cases, hairs, fibers, glass, plastics, polymers, paints); Trace evidence analysis. **Degrees/licenses:** MCrim, MPH, PhD, DCrim..

Eyewitness

Martin Blinder, MD

Assistant Clinical Professor, Psychiatry
50 Idalia Road
San Anselmo, CA 94960
Tel: (415) 453-8920

Specialties: Extensive experience with nationwide court appearances in the following areas: Criminal responsibility; Eye witness identification; Head injuries; Malingering; Psychiatric malpractice; Sexual harassment/molestation; Testamentary capacity and undue influence; Wrongful termination. Professional Experience: (Adjunct) Assistant Professor of Law, Hastings; Supervising Psychiatrist, Inpatient Psychiatric Service, UC Hospital; Psychiatric Consultant; FAA, U. S. Department of Justice, USPHS, U. S. Postal Service, Government of New Zealand; Qualified Medical Examiner, CA Department of Industrial Relations. Fellow, APA. Professional Societies: AMA, CMA, NCPS. More than 100 publications, including 6 books. **Degrees/licenses:** BA, Cornell University; MD, Chicago Medical School; Lic. (CA, GA, HI, KY).

Human Factors Consultants

Ralph N. Haber, Ph.D., Partner
Lyn Haber, Ph.D., Partner
313 Ridge View Drive
Swall Meadows, CA 93514
Tel: (760) 387-2458
Fax: (760) 387-2459
E-mail: Haberhfc@telis.org
Web Site:
http://www.humanfactorsconsultants.com

Specialties: Pretrial consultation and expert testimony on eyewitness perception and identification; fingerprint science; memory; language; and human factors of safety and accidents. (1) Eyewitness accuracy: effects of conditions of observation, intervening events, police procedures, lineup identifications, and earlier testimony. (2) Fingerprint science: accuracy of fingerprint comparisons; evaluation of comparison methods and laboratory procedures; underlying scientific assumptions and evidence; training and proficiency of examiners. (3) Memory: accuracy of recall by adults and by children, including recovery of memory. (4) Language: children and adults' comprehension; verbal and non-verbal harassment; factors of verbal interviewing that may alter memory; assessment of language disabilities. (5) Human factors: product safety; analyses of transportation, industrial and residential accidents in which equipment failure, human reaction/decision time, training adequacy, attention, error and warning signage may be implemented. Together, we have 45 years courtroom experience, 70 years research, 12 books, 250 published scientific articles. **Degrees/licenses:** PhD exptl psych; exptl linguistics; CCCSLP.

Fingerprints

Human Factors Consultants

Ralph N. Haber, Ph.D., Partner
Lyn Haber, Ph.D., Partner
313 Ridge View Drive
Swall Meadows, CA 93514
Tel: (760) 387-2458
Fax: (760) 387-2459
E-mail: Haberhfc@telis.org
Web Site:
http://www.humanfactorsconsultants.com

Specialties: Pretrial consultation and expert testimony on eyewitness perception and identification; fingerprint science; memory; language; and human factors of safety and accidents. (1) Eyewitness accuracy: effects of conditions of observation, intervening events, police procedures, lineup identifications, and earlier testimony. (2) Fingerprint science: accuracy of fingerprint comparisons; evaluation of comparison methods and laboratory procedures; underlying scientific assumptions and evidence; training and proficiency of examiners. (3) Memory: accuracy of recall by adults and by children, including recovery of memory. (4) Language: children and adults' comprehension; verbal and non-verbal harassment; factors of verbal interviewing that may alter memory; assessment of language disabilities. (5) Human factors: product safety; analyses of transportation, industrial and residential accidents in which equipment failure, human reaction/decision time, training adequacy, attention, error and warning signage may be implemented. Together, we have 45 years courtroom experience, 70 years research, 12 books, 250 published scientific articles. **Degrees/licenses:** PhD exptl psych; exptl linguistics; CCCSLP.

See primary listing under IDENTIFICATION: Eyewitness

Memory

Human Factors Consultants

Ralph N. Haber, Ph.D., Partner
Lyn Haber, Ph.D., Partner
313 Ridge View Drive
Swall Meadows, CA 93514
Tel: (760) 387-2458
Fax: (760) 387-2459
E-mail: Haberhfc@telis.org
Web Site:
http://www.humanfactorsconsultants.com

Specialties: Pretrial consultation and expert testimony on eyewitness perception and identification; fingerprint science; memory; language; and human factors of safety and accidents. (1) Eyewitness accuracy: effects of conditions of observation, intervening events, police procedures, lineup identifications, and earlier testimony. (2) Fingerprint science: accuracy of fingerprint comparisons; evaluation of comparison methods and laboratory procedures; underlying scientific assumptions and evidence; training and proficiency of examiners. (3) Memory: accuracy of recall by adults and by children, including recovery of memory. (4) Language: children and adults' comprehension; verbal and non-verbal harassment; factors of verbal interviewing that may alter memory; assessment of language disabilities. (5) Human factors: product safety; analyses of transportation, industrial and residential accidents in which equipment failure, human reaction/decision time, training adequacy, attention, error and warning signage may be implemented. Together, we have 45 years courtroom experience, 70 years research, 12 books, 250 published scientific articles. **Degrees/licenses:** PhD exptl psych; exptl linguistics; CCCSLP.

See primary listing under IDENTIFICATION: Eyewitness

Microscopy/DNA

Forensic Analytical

Celia Hartnett
Laboratory Director
3777 Depot Road, Ste. 409
Hayward, CA 94545-2761
Tel: (800) 827-3274 ext. 148
(510) 887-8828 ext. 148
Fax: (510) 887-4451
E-mail: cchartnett@forensica.com
Web Site: http://www.forensica.com

Specialties: Extensive experience in the following areas: Blood spatter analysis; Crime scene reconstruction; Criminalistics; DNA typing; Identification (gunshot residue, firearms, bullets, cartridge cases, hairs, fibers, glass, plastics, polymers, paints); Trace evidence analysis. **Degrees/licenses:** MCrim, MPH, PhD, DCrim..

See primary listing under IDENTIFICATION: General

Technical Associates, Inc.

Marc Scott Taylor
4125 Market Street, Ste. 3
Ventura, CA 93003
Tel: (805) 677-2155
Fax: (805) 676-1638
E-mail: info@tai-labs.com
Web Site: http://www.tai-labs.com

Specialties: Criminalistics firm with extensive experience in the following areas: Criminalistics & DNA Analysis; PCR & RFLP Consultation and Testing; Crime Scene Reconstruction; Gunshot Residue; Toolmarks; Shoeprints; Tiretracks; Firearms; Blood Splatter. Extremely sensitive testing of all types of forensic samples. **Degrees/licenses:** BS Zoology; MS.

See primary listing under CRIMINALISTICS/ CRIMINOLOGY: General

Tape-Recorded Evidence/ Tapes

Audio Forensic Center

Durand R. Begault, PhD
130 Sutter Street, Ste. 500
San Francisco, CA 94104
Tel: (800) 257-7706 (Ext. 261)
Fax: (415) 397-0454
E-mail: dbegault@cmsalter.com
Web Site: http://www.audioforensics.com

Specialties: Acoustics; audibility; audio demonstrations; audio and video tape enhancement; voice identification and elimination; audio tape authentication; intellectual property and patent claims; acoustical compliance; acoustical gunshot analysis; transcripts from noisy tapes. **Degrees/licenses:** BA UC - Santa Cruz; MFA Mills College, Oakland, CA; PhD UC - San Diego.

See primary listing under AUDIO/VIDEO EVIDENCE: General

Testing Labs

Laboratory Corporation of America

1912 Alexander Dr.
Research Triangle Park, NC 27709
Tel: (800) 533-0567, Dept. 6
Fax: (919) 361-7737
E-mail: ForensicIdentity@labcorp.com
Web Site: http://www.labcorp.com

Specialties: Independent DNA testing; Criminal DNA case review, consulting, expert witness testimony. Experienced personnel, 3500+ cases completed. Hundreds of courtroom testimonies for prosecution and/or defense. ASCLD/LAB, CAP and New York State Department of Health accredited.

See primary listing under LITIGATION SUPPORT: Forensic Science

INSURANCE

General

Advisors/Experts @ MCS Associates

Norman Katz
Managing Partner
18881 Von Karman Ave., Ste. 1175
Irvine, CA 92612-1569
Tel: (949) 263-8700
Fax: (949) 263-0770
E-mail: info@mcsassociates.com
Web Site: http://www.mcsassociates.com

Specialties: Nationally recognized banking, financial services, real estate consulting group; Experienced expert witnesses and consultants include bankers, lenders, insurance managers, brokers, agents, economists, securities brokers, trust fiduciaries, appraisers, accountants. Expertise: Bank operations, check fraud; Lending policies, procedures; Loan administration, foreclosures, bankruptcy; Lender liability; D&O Liability; Insurance (Life, Disability, Property & Casualty, Reinsurance, Surplus) underwriting, claims handling, bad faith; Broker duties, agency management; Title insurance & escrow; R/E brokerage, leasing, property management, appraisal, development, construction defects; Business valuation, lost profits, damages assessment; Forensic accounting; Securities brokerage, trading, investment suitability; Economic & statistical analysis. **Degrees/licenses:** MBA, PhD, CPA, CLU, CPCU, CFP, CFA, CREA, MAI, ASA.

See primary listing under FINANCE: Commercial Banking

Martin J. Calpin, CPCU

14 Slab Branch Court
Evesham, NJ 08053
Tel: (856) 753-8353
Fax: (856) 753-8517
E-mail: mjcalpin@comcast.net

Specialties: Standard and Surplus Lines Commercial Casualty both Primary and Excess including Umbrellas; MGA and Brokerage Agreements; Underwriting Authorities; Insurance Business Practices; Corporate Management and Governance; Book of Business Development. Full professional and educational history is listed in "Who's Who in Insurance and Risk Management". **Degrees/licenses:** BS, CPCU, NJ Ins. Prod. License - P&C, Health, Surplus Lines.

Joseph H. Dabrowski, PE

President
Visionary, LLC
7250 Ledgewood Drive
(Greater Cleveland)
Kirtland, OH 44094
Tel: (440) 256-9274
(440) 477-6566 (Mobile)
Fax: (440) 256-9274
E-mail: joseph_dabrowski@sbcglobal.net

Specialties: Property/Casualty Insurance; Construction-Related Litigation Support and Expert Testimony; Forensic Investigations; Bad Faith; Risk Management; Construction Claim preparation or defense, analysis and resolution; Dispute Resolution Board participation; Defaulted or terminated contractor assessment and bond claim issues; Schedule Delay & Impact Analysis; Professional Liability; 27 years of service to the Construction, Insurance, Legal and Surety Industries. **Degrees/licenses:** BSME; MBA; Professional Engineer (Ohio); AAA Commercial Arbitrator.

Phil C. Gallagher

President
Phil C. Gallagher Associates, Inc.
2500 NW 79th Ave., Ste. 101
Miami, FL 33122
Tel: (305) 714-4416
(800) 240-5359
(305) 343-0229 (Cellular)
Fax: (305) 757-2681
E-mail: pcga@bellsouth.net
Web Site: http://member.expertpages.com/pcgallagher

Specialties: Expert Witness/Litigation Consultant as to customs and practices in the

(Listing continued on next page)

General *(cont.)*

Phil C. Gallagher (cont.)
insurance industry; Insurance company and agency disputes; Agency and brokerage agreement interpretations; Policy interpretations; Professional liability defenses for agents and brokers; Managing agency evaluations for divorce, estate taxes; and Acquisition/merger of many insurance agencies. Over 500 engagements in various courts in 30 states, District of Columbia, Bahamas and the Virgin Islands for plaintiff and defendant.

Frank E. Raab

Former President & CEO
Insurance Co. of North America
& Allianz Insurance Co.
1280 Monte Cielo Dr.
Beverly Hills, CA 90210
Tel: (310) 273-9258
Fax: (310) 276-1026
E-mail: apoli22otto@daarnewman.com
Web Site: http://www.FrankRaab.com

Specialties: Consulting, Arbitration, Mediation, Expert Witness; Management, Coverages, Underwriting, Claims, Agency Relations, Bad Faith, Business Interruption, Umbrellas, Reinsurance, Surplus Lines (Company & Brokerage), Risk Management, Forming Insurance Cos. & Captives, Self Insurance. Past National President CPCU. Rear Admiral USNR. BS Univ. of Calif. **Degrees/licenses:** CPCU, ARM, Calif. Insur. Agent.
See primary listing under INSURANCE: Property & Casualty

Robert Hughes Associates, Inc.

John R. Oakley
President
508 Twilight Trl., #200
Richardson, TX 75080-8100
Tel: (972) 980-0088
Fax: (972) 233-1548
E-mail: joakley@roberthughes.com
Web Site: http://www.roberthughes.com

Specialties: Property/Casualty Insurance; Life/Health Insurance; Medicare/Medicaid; Lloyd's of London; Claims Handling; Bad Faith; Policy Analysis; Policy Interpretation; Insurance Archaeology; Insurance Laws; Agency Management & Practices; Industry Standards & Practices; Reinsurance; Risk Management; Underwriting; Self-Insurance; Excess & Surplus Lines; Insurance Fraud; Professional Liability; Decision Analysis; Workers' Compensation; Contracts & Treaties; Actuarial Analysis; Statistical Forecasting. Retained in more than 800 cases. **Degrees/ licenses:** CPCU, ARM, PhD, FCAS, MAAA, ChFC, CLU, CFP, CPA, CIC, MBA, ACFE, RPLU.

RWL GROUP

Robert W. Lazarus
President/Senior Consultant
300 N. Coit Rd., #810
Richardson, TX 75080-5456
Tel: (972) 907-9095
Fax: (972) 907-9198
E-mail: rwlgroup@rwlgroup.com
Web Site: http://www.rwlgroup.com

Specialties: We are independent risk management, insurance, workers compensation, and employee benefits consultants. No insurance sales or affiliations. We have extensive experience providing expert testimony, litigation support, and advice to clients/attorneys for all lines of personal and commercial insurance. We are also experienced in dispute resolution involving insurance costs and coverages; agent/insurer duties to policyholder; bad faith; loss-sensitive rating; premium audits; experience modification, etc. Our professional staff includes MBAs, CPCUs, FLMIs, CPAs and ARMs. We are also members of the Society of Risk Management Consultants, which maintains high ethical standards for the industry. **Degrees/licenses:** MBA, ARM, CPCU, FLMI, CPA.

Adjusting

JBK Consultants

Joel B. Kipphut, RPA
President
309 Lakeside Drive
Southampton, PA 18966
Tel: (215) 396-8700
Fax: (215) 396-8704
E-mail: jbkipphut@broadviewnet.net
Web Site: http://kipphutassoc.com

Specialties: Over thirty years experience in adjusting first party property claims, Registered Professional Adjuster, Member NAIIA, Loss Executives Association, Insurance Society of Philadelphia; Coverage disputes; Coverage analysis, good/bad faith issues; Appraiser/umpire. BA, The Citadel. **Degrees/licenses:** BA, RPA, Licensed in Delaware.

See primary listing under INSURANCE: Bad Faith

Bad Faith

JBK Consultants

Joel B. Kipphut, RPA
President
309 Lakeside Drive
Southampton, PA 18966
Tel: (215) 396-8700
Fax: (215) 396-8704
E-mail: jbkipphut@broadviewnet.net
Web Site: http://kipphutassoc.com

Specialties: Over thirty years experience in adjusting first party property claims, Registered Professional Adjuster, Member NAIIA, Loss Executives Association, Insurance Society of Philadelphia; Coverage disputes; Coverage analysis, good/bad faith issues; Appraiser/umpire. BA, The Citadel. **Degrees/licenses:** BA, RPA, Licensed in Delaware.

Michael B. Levitt

Insurance Agent
M.B. Levitt Consulting, Inc.
9941 Middle Mill Dr.
Owings Mills, MD 21117
Tel: (410) 356-6111
Fax: (410) 356-6111
E-mail: mlevitt1@comcast.net

Specialties: Ten years experience as a bodily injuries claim specialist. Duties included liability determination, negotiating with claimants' attorneys as well as unrepresented claimants, scene investigations and all areas of preparation in anticipation of trial. 23 years experience as a licensed insurance agent. Duties included the daily operation of a multi-line insurance agency, including training and supervising staff in best insurance practices and dealing with the public on a daily basis. Experience testifying as a company representative and as an expert witness, reviewing depositions of opposing witnesses and preparing evaluations. **Degrees/licenses:** JD; Lic. Reg. Rep.; Lic. to Sell/Serv. Prop., Casualty, Life & Health Insurance.

M & Z Claims Service, Inc.

Frank T. Zeigon, RPA, CCLA
President
18032-C Lemon Drive
PMB 164
Yorba Linda, CA 92886-3386
Tel: (714) 777-4462
Fax: (714) 777-4507
E-mail: frank@insuranceclaimsexpert.com
Web Site:
http://www.insuranceclaimsexpert.com

Specialties: Frank has 37+ years claims experience. Specialist in claim handling custom and practice, claim adjusting, coverage interpretation, S.I.U. practices and auditing procedures. Services include complex claim handling issues; claim community standards; serving as an expert witness, appraiser, umpire, mediator and other claim handling and adjusting services. Frank has worked at branch, regional, zone and home office levels. He has multi-line experience in auto, general liability and property claims. **Degrees/licenses:** Reg. Prof. Adjuster, Casualty Claims Law Assoc., CA Independent Adjusters Lic.

Bad Faith *(cont.)*

Clinton E. Miller, JD, BCFE

President
Clinton E. Miller, JD, BCFE
502 Park Ave.
San Jose, CA 95110
Tel: (408) 279-1034
Fax: (408) 279-3562
E-mail: cemcom@comcast.net
Web Site:
http://www.quickpage.com/m/millerjd

Specialties: Thirty three years experience in Claims Adjusting; Consulting; Expert Witness; Author, Lecturer; Customs and Practices of the insurance industry; Coverage Analysis; Coverage Disputes; Good Faith - Bad Faith issues; Duty to Defend, Arson Cases; Auto, Homeowner Policies; Col. Policies; E & O claims; Agents, Brokers Duties; Lapse of Policy issues; Flood Claims; Life, Health, Disability Claims; Underwriting Practices and Procedures. **Degrees/licenses:** AA, BS, JD, BCFE.

Robert Hughes Associates, Inc.

John R. Oakley
President
508 Twilight Trl., #200
Richardson, TX 75080-8100
Tel: (972) 980-0088
Fax: (972) 233-1548
E-mail: joakley@roberthughes.com
Web Site: http://www.roberthughes.com

Specialties: Property/Casualty Insurance; Life/Health Insurance; Medicare/Medicaid; Lloyd's of London; Claims Handling; Bad Faith; Policy Analysis; Policy Interpretation; Insurance Archaeology; Insurance Laws; Agency Management & Practices; Industry Standards & Practices; Reinsurance; Risk Management; Underwriting; Self-Insurance; Excess & Surplus Lines; Insurance Fraud; Professional Liability; Decision Analysis; Workers' Compensation; Contracts & Treaties; Actuarial Analysis; Statistical Forecasting. Retained in more than 800 cases. **Degrees/licenses:** CPCU, ARM, PhD, FCAS, MAAA, ChFC, CLU, CFP, CPA, CIC, MBA, ACFE, RPLU.

See primary listing under INSURANCE: General

Peter N. Rogers, JD

Senior Partner
Rogers, Booker & Trevino, PC
901 Waterfall Way, #105
Richardson, TX 75080
Tel: (972) 644-1111
Fax: (972) 644-7600
E-mail: Peter@workerscomppubs.com
Web Site:
http://www.workerscomppubs.com

Specialties: Workers' compensation in Texas. Mr. Rogers is a retired Air Force Colonel who served 23 years as a judge advocate. After retiring from the Air Force in 1991, Mr. Rogers became an Administrative Law Judge in workers' compensation courts in Dallas, Texas. After entering private practice in 1995, Mr. Rogers built a successful workers' compensation law firm. He is a published author of workers' compensation handbooks, has developed and lectured in over 50 continuing legal education courses on workers' compensation topics, and has provided expert opinions and/or deposition testimony in over 30 cases involving workers' compensation in Texas. **Degrees/licenses:** BA, JD, Board Certified - Workers' Compensation - TBLS.

See primary listing under EMPLOYMENT: Workers' Compensation

Gordon K. Rose, CLU, CHFC

Insurance Education Consultant
735 Virginia Rail
Kiawah Island, SC 29455-5909
Tel: (843) 768-6669
Fax: (843) 768-0344
E-mail: gkroseclu@aol.com

Specialties: CLU and CHFC Professional Designations; Instructed CLU - CHFC, 30+ years; Vice President of the American College, 20 years; Columbus Mutual Life Home Office, 6 years; New York Life, 12 years (Agent, Recruiter, Trainer, Home Office); Past President of Society of Insurance Trainers and Educators (National Organization); Deposition and/or Court Testimony 25+ times. **Degrees/licenses:** BS Penn State 1950, CLU 1957, Mgt. Degree Am. College 1959, CHFC 1983.

See primary listing under INSURANCE: Life, Health & Disability

William J. Warfel

Prof. of Insurance & Risk Management
Indiana State University
Insurance and Risk Mgt. Program
College of Business
Terre Haute, IN 47809
Tel: (812) 237-2122
Fax: (812) 237-4374

Specialties: Specialize in personal and commercial, property/casualty coverage analysis, bad faith, and agent/broker liability issues. Have been retained in a number of cases by attorneys who represent policyholders, insurers, and third parties. Widely published in applied, professional journals. **Degrees/licenses:** PhD, CPCU, CLU.

See primary listing under INSURANCE: Coverage Analysis

Claims Handling

Clinton E. Miller, JD, BCFE

President
Clinton E. Miller, JD, BCFE
502 Park Ave.
San Jose, CA 95110
Tel: (408) 279-1034
Fax: (408) 279-3562
E-mail: cemcom@comcast.net
Web Site:
http://www.quickpage.com/m/millerjd

Specialties: Thirty three years experience in Claims Adjusting; Consulting; Expert Witness; Author, Lecturer; Customs and Practices of the insurance industry; Coverage Analysis; Coverage Disputes; Good Faith - Bad Faith issues; Duty to Defend, Arson Cases; Auto, Homeowner Policies; Col. Policies; E & O claims; Agents, Brokers Duties; Lapse of Policy issues; Flood Claims; Life, Health, Disability Claims; Underwriting Practices and Procedures. **Degrees/licenses:** AA, BS, JD, BCFE.

See primary listing under INSURANCE: Bad Faith

Claims Investigation

Donald J. Imbordino

President
Imbordino Polygraph Examinations, LLC
3330 Cobb Pkwy., Ste. 17 - Box 359
Acworth, GA 30101
Tel: (678) 986-9600
Fax: (678) 574-6723
E-mail: dimbordino@earthlink.net
Web Site:
http://www.ImbordinoPolygraph.com

Specialties: Former federal polygraph supervisor with over 16 years of federal polygraph experience. (U.S. Department of Justice - Retired in 2003). Former Police Officer/Investigator. Adjunct Faculty Member with the Department of Defense Polygraph Institute. Director of Computerized Polygraph Training, Texas Department of Public Safety Polygraph School. Utilizes only state-of-the-art computerized polygraph systems. American Association of Police Polygraphists (AAPP) - Vice President. American Polygraph Association (APA) - Full Member. Georgia Polygraph Association (GPA) - Past Vice President. Mr. Imbordino's professional goal is to provide his clients with accurate results they can rely on. Every polygraph examination is administered in a discreet and professional manner. **Degrees/licenses:** BS- Behavioral Science, Certified Examiner - AAPP.

See primary listing under LITIGATION SUPPORT: Polygraph/Lie Detection

Claims Investigation *(cont.)*

Michael B. Levitt

Insurance Agent
M.B. Levitt Consulting, Inc.
9941 Middle Mill Dr.
Owings Mills, MD 21117
Tel: (410) 356-6111
Fax: (410) 356-6111
E-mail: mlevitt1@comcast.net

Specialties: Ten years experience as a bodily injuries claim specialist. Duties included liability determination, negotiating with claimants' attorneys as well as unrepresented claimants, scene investigations and all areas of preparation in anticipation of trial. 23 years experience as a licensed insurance agent. Duties included the daily operation of a multi-line insurance agency, including training and supervising staff in best insurance practices and dealing with the public on a daily basis. Experience testifying as a company representative and as an expert witness, reviewing depositions of opposing witnesses and preparing evaluations. **Degrees/licenses:** JD; Lic. Reg. Rep.; Lic. to Sell/Serv. Prop., Casualty, Life & Health Insurance.

See primary listing under INSURANCE: Bad Faith

Evan S. Rost, DC

1 Madelyne Place
Fair Lawn, NJ 07410
Tel: (201) 791-0004
Fax: (201) 791-0045
E-mail: doc@expertchiropractor.com
Web Site:
http://www.expertchiropractor.com

Specialties: Chiropractic; Chiropractic Medicine; Forensic Examiner. Member, American College of Forensic Examiners #14745; Member, National Forensic Center, Certified Chiropractic Peer Reviewer and Independent Examiner, Certified Chiropractic Insurance Consultant, both certifications by Texas Chiropractic College; Diplomate, American Board of Disability Analysts; Diplomate, American Academy of Certified Consultants and Experts; Diplomate, American Academy of Experts in Traumatic Stress; Cleveland Chiropractic College 1983. Membership: American Pain Society, Headache Cooperative of New England, Inc., Florida Chiropractic Association, Indiana State Chiropractic Association, Northern New Jersey Chiropractic Society, New York State Chiropractic Association. **Degrees/licenses:** DC, CCIC, ACD, DABDA, FAAIM; Lic.: NJ, NY, FL, RI, IN.

See primary listing under MEDICINE & HEALTH: Chiropractic Medicine

Claims Practices

Phil C. Gallagher

President
Phil C. Gallagher Associates, Inc.
2500 NW 79th Ave., Ste. 101
Miami, FL 33122
Tel: (305) 714-4416
(800) 240-5359
(305) 343-0229 (Cellular)
Fax: (305) 757-2681
E-mail: pcga@bellsouth.net
Web Site: http://member.expertpages.com/pcgallagher

Specialties: Expert Witness/Litigation Consultant as to customs and practices in the insurance industry; Insurance company and agency disputes; Agency and brokerage agreement interpretations; Policy interpretations; Professional liability defenses for agents and brokers; Managing agency evaluations for divorce, estate taxes; and Acquisition/merger of many insurance agencies. Over 500 engagements in various courts in 30 states, District of Columbia, Bahamas and the Virgin Islands for plaintiff and defendant.

See primary listing under INSURANCE: General

Gerald "Gerry" Katz, MSPA, RHU, ALHC, DABFE
President & Founder
Disability Income Concepts, Inc.
P.O. Box 266257
Weston, FL 33326
Tel: (877) 776-3948
Fax: (954) 217-8241
E-mail: disability@disabilityconcepts.com
Web Site: http://www.disabilityconcepts.com

Specialties: My services as a disability claims consultant or expert witness are available throughout the U.S. Over 38 years marketing & designing disability insurance products. Instructor and Provider of qualified Continuing Education courses on disability subjects. Produced $10 million+ of individual disability & long term care insurance premiums during sales career. Helped major DI carrier design entire portfolio of disability insurance products. Awarded Harold R. Gordon Memorial Award for "Health Insurance Industry Person of the Year" - 1997, by the National Association of Health Underwriters. No charge for initial phone consultation. **Degrees/licenses:** 2-18 Life, Health, Disability - FL.

See primary listing under INSURANCE: Life, Health & Disability

Robert Hughes Associates, Inc.
John R. Oakley
President
508 Twilight Trl., #200
Richardson, TX 75080-8100
Tel: (972) 980-0088
Fax: (972) 233-1548
E-mail: joakley@roberthughes.com
Web Site: http://www.roberthughes.com

Specialties: Property/Casualty Insurance; Life/Health Insurance; Medicare/Medicaid; Lloyd's of London; Claims Handling; Bad Faith; Policy Analysis; Policy Interpretation; Insurance Archaeology; Insurance Laws; Agency Management & Practices; Industry Standards & Practices; Reinsurance; Risk Management; Underwriting; Self-Insurance; Excess & Surplus Lines; Insurance Fraud; Professional Liability; Decision Analysis; Workers' Compensation; Contracts & Treaties; Actuarial Analysis; Statistical Forecasting. Retained in more than 800 cases. **Degrees/licenses:** CPCU, ARM, PhD, FCAS, MAAA, ChFC, CLU, CFP, CPA, CIC, MBA, ACFE, RPLU.

See primary listing under INSURANCE: General

Coverage Analysis

JBK Consultants
Joel B. Kipphut, RPA
President
309 Lakeside Drive
Southampton, PA 18966
Tel: (215) 396-8700
Fax: (215) 396-8704
E-mail: jbkipphut@broadviewnet.net
Web Site: http://kipphutassoc.com

Specialties: Over thirty years experience in adjusting first party property claims, Registered Professional Adjuster, Member NAIIA, Loss Executives Association, Insurance Society of Philadelphia; Coverage disputes; Coverage analysis, good/bad faith issues; Appraiser/umpire. BA, The Citadel. **Degrees/licenses:** BA, RPA, Licensed in Delaware.

See primary listing under INSURANCE: Bad Faith

Maurice Lieberman, CLU, ChFC, RHU, LUTCF
Owner
Expert Witness & Consulting Services
1866 Claire Court
Concord, CA 94519
Tel: (925) 685-5444 (Office)
(925) 768-4888 (Cell)
Fax: (925) 687-3444
E-mail: mlieberman@sbcglobal.net

Specialties: Consults with attorneys and assists counsel in trial preparation regarding issues of life insurance and annuity coverage analysis, coverage disputes, & company practices. Expert level knowledge of life insurance products and services. A strong understanding of the legal aspects of the industry including contracts, regulations, compliance, and the

(Listing continued on next page)

Coverage Analysis *(cont.)*

Maurice Lieberman (cont.)
application of best practice principles, and life insurance underwriting procedures. A successful track record working with a professional insurance sales force including all areas of the career and direct distribution system. Developed and edited training programs & insurance licensing courses for insurance companies and private schools. Mr. Lieberman provides high quality service and insurance/investment advice to clients in all walks of life. Member: National Association of Insurance & Financial Advisors, Society of Financial Service Professionals, and The American College of Forensic Examiners International. **Degrees/licenses:** CLU, ChFC, RHU, LUTCF, CA L & D Ins. Lic., NASD Series 6 & 63 Registered Rep.

See primary listing under INSURANCE: Life, Health & Disability

Robert Hughes Associates, Inc.

John R. Oakley
President
508 Twilight Trl., #200
Richardson, TX 75080-8100
Tel: (972) 980-0088
Fax: (972) 233-1548
E-mail: joakley@roberthughes.com
Web Site: http://www.roberthughes.com

Specialties: Property/Casualty Insurance; Life/Health Insurance; Medicare/Medicaid; Lloyd's of London; Claims Handling; Bad Faith; Policy Analysis; Policy Interpretation; Insurance Archaeology; Insurance Laws; Agency Management & Practices; Industry Standards & Practices; Reinsurance; Risk Management; Underwriting; Self-Insurance; Excess & Surplus Lines; Insurance Fraud; Professional Liability; Decision Analysis; Workers' Compensation; Contracts & Treaties; Actuarial Analysis; Statistical Forecasting. Retained in more than 800 cases. **Degrees/licenses:** CPCU, ARM, PhD, FCAS, MAAA, ChFC, CLU, CFP, CPA, CIC, MBA, ACFE, RPLU.

See primary listing under INSURANCE: General

William J. Warfel

Prof. of Insurance & Risk Management
Indiana State University
Insurance and Risk Mgt. Program
College of Business
Terre Haute, IN 47809
Tel: (812) 237-2122
Fax: (812) 237-4374

Specialties: Specialize in personal and commercial, property/casualty coverage analysis, bad faith, and agent/broker liability issues. Have been retained in a number of cases by attorneys who represent policyholders, insurers, and third parties. Widely published in applied, professional journals. **Degrees/licenses:** PhD, CPCU, CLU.

Excess & Surplus Lines

Martin J. Calpin, CPCU

14 Slab Branch Court
Evesham, NJ 08053
Tel: (856) 753-8353
Fax: (856) 753-8517
E-mail: mjcalpin@comcast.net

Specialties: Standard and Surplus Lines Commercial Casualty both Primary and Excess including Umbrellas; MGA and Brokerage Agreements; Underwriting Authorities; Insurance Business Practices; Corporate Management and Governance; Book of Business Development. Full professional and educational history is listed in "Who's Who in Insurance and Risk Management." **Degrees/licenses:** BS, CPCU, NJ Ins. Prod. License - P&C, Health, Surplus Lines.

See primary listing under INSURANCE: General

Life, Health & Disability

Gerald "Gerry" Katz, MSPA, RHU, ALHC, DABFE

President & Founder
Disability Income Concepts, Inc.
P.O. Box 266257
Weston, FL 33326
Tel: (877) 776-3948
Fax: (954) 217-8241
E-mail: disability@disabilityconcepts.com
Web Site:
http://www.disabilityconcepts.com

Specialties: My services as a disability claims consultant or expert witness are available throughout the U.S. Over 38 years marketing & designing disability insurance products. Instructor and Provider of qualified Continuing Education courses on disability subjects. Produced $10 million+ of individual disability & long term care insurance premiums during sales career. Helped major DI carrier design entire portfolio of disability insurance products. Awarded Harold R. Gordon Memorial Award for "Health Insurance Industry Person of the Year" - 1997, by the National Association of Health Underwriters. No charge for initial phone consultation. **Degrees/licenses:** 2-18 Life, Health, Disability - FL.

Maurice Lieberman, CLU, ChFC, RHU, LUTCF

Owner
Expert Witness & Consulting Services
1866 Claire Court
Concord, CA 94519
Tel: (925) 685-5444 (Office)
(925) 768-4888 (Cell)
Fax: (925) 687-3444
E-mail: mlieberman@sbcglobal.net

Specialties: Consults with attorneys and assists counsel in trial preparation regarding issues of life insurance and annuity coverage analysis, coverage disputes, & company practices. Expert level knowledge of life insurance products and services. A strong understanding of the legal aspects of the industry including contracts, regulations, compliance, and the application of best practice principles, and life insurance underwriting procedures. A successful track record working with a professional insurance sales force including all areas of the career and direct distribution system. Developed and edited training programs & insurance licensing courses for insurance companies and private schools. Mr. Lieberman provides high quality service and insurance/investment advice to clients in all walks of life. Member: National Association of Insurance & Financial Advisors, Society of Financial Service Professionals, and The American College of Forensic Examiners International. **Degrees/licenses:** CLU, ChFC, RHU, LUTCF, CA L & D Ins. Lic., NASD Series 6 & 63 Registered Rep.

Gordon K. Rose, CLU, CHFC

Insurance Education Consultant
735 Virginia Rail
Kiawah Island, SC 29455-5909
Tel: (843) 768-6669
Fax: (843) 768-0344
E-mail: gkroseclu@aol.com

Specialties: CLU and CHFC Professional Designations; Instructed CLU - CHFC, 30+ years; Vice President of the American College, 20 years; Columbus Mutual Life Home Office, 6 years; New York Life, 12 years (Agent, Recruiter, Trainer, Home Office); Past President of Society of Insurance Trainers and Educators (National Organization); Deposition and/or Court Testimony 25+ times. **Degrees/ licenses:** BS Penn State 1950, CLU 1957, Mgt. Degree Am. College 1959, CHFC 1983.

Marine

Trident Marine Safety Associates

Henry S. Woods III
16850 Saturn Lane, #100
Houston, TX 77058
Tel: (281) 486-4552
Fax: (281) 486-9295
E-mail: hsw123@earthlink.net
Web Site:
http://www.tridentmarinesafety.com

P.O. Box 435
East Boothbay, ME 04544
Tel: (800) 580-BUOY

Specialties: Claims adjudication; claims investigation;, claims adjusting in damage, theft, and accident situations; litigation support; expert witness work in boating and commercial marine applications and situations; post-accident inspections and damage assessments; boat value appraisals; boat condition/use surveys and reports. **Degrees/licenses:** BS, MS.

See primary listing under ACCIDENT RECONSTRUCTION: Marine

Property & Casualty

M & Z Claims Service, Inc.

Frank T. Zeigon, RPA, CCLA
President
18032-C Lemon Drive
PMB 164
Yorba Linda, CA 92886-3386
Tel: (714) 777-4462
Fax: (714) 777-4507
E-mail: frank@insuranceclaimsexpert.com
Web Site:
http://www.insuranceclaimsexpert.com

Specialties: Frank has 37+ years claims experience. Specialist in claim handling custom and practice, claim adjusting, coverage interpretation, S.I.U. practices and auditing procedures. Services include complex claim handling issues; claim community standards; serving as an expert witness, appraiser, umpire, mediator and other claim handling and adjusting services. Frank has worked at branch, regional, zone and home office levels. He has multi-line experience in auto, general liability and property claims. **Degrees/licenses:** Reg. Prof. Adjuster, Casualty Claims Law Assoc., CA Independent Adjusters Lic.

See primary listing under INSURANCE: Bad Faith

Matson, Driscoll & Damico

John A. Damico, PC, CPA
Managing Partner
750 Hammond Dr. NE, Bldg. 14
Atlanta, GA 30328
Tel: (404) 252-0085
Fax: (404) 255-0673
E-mail: jdamico@mdd.net
Web Site: http://www.mdd.net

Specialties: Matson, Driscoll, and Damico is an international forensic accounting and consulting firm with a specialty in property, casualty and surety insurance claims. There are currently 28 MD&D offices across the world. MD&D's analysis and verification of the facts and reporting pave the way for prompt and equitable resolutions of each case. Skill, proven expertise and total dedication to this special area of accounting are the characteristics that separate MD&D professionals from other accountants. Professional excellence in all aspects of forensic insurance claims accounting is the distinguishing hallmark of the firm. For more information, visit www.mdd.net. **Degrees/licenses:** The firm: BA, MBA, CFE, CPA, CMA, CVA, MCP.

See primary listing under ACCOUNTING: Business Interruption/Lost Profits

Frank E. Raab

Former President & CEO
Insurance Co. of North America
& Allianz Insurance Co.
1280 Monte Cielo Dr.
Beverly Hills, CA 90210
Tel: (310) 273-9258
Fax: (310) 276-1026
E-mail: apoli22otto@daarnewman.com
Web Site: http://www.FrankRaab.com

Specialties: Consulting, Arbitration, Mediation, Expert Witness; Management, Coverages, Underwriting, Claims, Agency Relations,

Bad Faith, Business Interruption, Umbrellas, Reinsurance, Surplus Lines (Company & Brokerage), Risk Management, Forming Insurance Cos. & Captives, Self Insurance. Past National President CPCU. Rear Admiral USNR. BS Univ. of Calif. **Degrees/licenses:** CPCU, ARM, Calif. Insur. Agent.

William J. Warfel

Prof. of Insurance & Risk Management
Indiana State University
Insurance and Risk Mgt. Program
College of Business
Terre Haute, IN 47809
Tel: (812) 237-2122
Fax: (812) 237-4374

Specialties: Specialize in personal and commercial, property/casualty coverage analysis, bad faith, and agent/broker liability issues. Have been retained in a number of cases by attorneys who represent policyholders, insurers, and third parties. Widely published in applied, professional journals. **Degrees/licenses:** PhD, CPCU, CLU.

See primary listing under INSURANCE: Coverage Analysis

Surety

Matson, Driscoll & Damico

John A. Damico, PC, CPA
Managing Partner
750 Hammond Dr. NE, Bldg. 14
Atlanta, GA 30328
Tel: (404) 252-0085
Fax: (404) 255-0673
E-mail: jdamico@mdd.net
Web Site: http://www.mdd.net

Specialties: Matson, Driscoll, and Damico is an international forensic accounting and consulting firm with a specialty in surety insurance claims. There are currently 28 MD&D offices across the world. MD&D's analysis and verification of the facts and reporting pave the way for prompt and equitable resolutions of each case. Skill, proven expertise and total dedication to this special area of accounting are the characteristics that separate MD&D professionals from other accountants. Professional excellence in forensic surety insurance claims accounting is the distinguishing hallmark of the firm. For more information, visit www.mdd.net. **Degrees/licenses:** The firm: BA, MBA, CFE, CPA, CMA, CVA, MCP.

See primary listing under ACCOUNTING: Business Interruption/Lost Profits

Underwriting

Clinton E. Miller, JD, BCFE

President
Clinton E. Miller, JD, BCFE
502 Park Ave.
San Jose, CA 95110
Tel: (408) 279-1034
Fax: (408) 279-3562
E-mail: cemcom@comcast.net
Web Site:
http://www.quickpage.com/m/millerjd

Specialties: Thirty three years experience in Claims Adjusting; Consulting; Expert Witness; Author, Lecturer; Customs and Practices of the insurance industry; Coverage Analysis; Coverage Disputes; Good Faith - Bad Faith issues; Duty to Defend, Arson Cases; Auto, Homeowner Policies; Col. Policies; E & O claims; Agents, Brokers Duties; Lapse of Policy issues; Flood Claims; Life, Health, Disability Claims; Underwriting Practices and Procedures. **Degrees/licenses:** AA, BS, JD, BCFE.

See primary listing under INSURANCE: Bad Faith

Robert Hughes Associates, Inc.

John R. Oakley
President
508 Twilight Trl., #200
Richardson, TX 75080-8100
Tel: (972) 980-0088
Fax: (972) 233-1548
E-mail: joakley@roberthughes.com
Web Site: http://www.roberthughes.com

Specialties: Property/Casualty Insurance; Life/Health Insurance; Medicare/Medicaid; Lloyd's of London; Claims Handling; Bad

(Listing continued on next page)

Underwriting *(cont.)*

Robert Hughes Associates, Inc. (cont.)
Faith; Policy Analysis; Policy Interpretation; Insurance Archaeology; Insurance Laws; Agency Management & Practices; Industry Standards & Practices; Reinsurance; Risk Management; Underwriting; Self-Insurance; Excess & Surplus Lines; Insurance Fraud; Professional Liability; Decision Analysis; Workers' Compensation; Contracts & Treaties; Actuarial Analysis; Statistical Forecasting. Retained in more than 800 cases. **Degrees/ licenses:** CPCU, ARM, PhD, FCAS, MAAA, ChFC, CLU, CFP, CPA, CIC, MBA, ACFE, RPLU.

See primary listing under INSURANCE: General

INTELLECTUAL PROPERTY

General

Delos Research Group

W.M. vanCleemput, PhD
President
333 Maude Avenue
Sunnyvale, CA 94085
Tel: (408) 733-8000
Fax: (408) 733-8008
E-mail: wmvc@acm.org
Web Site: http://www.delosresearch.com

Specialties: Technical Expertise: Computer engineering, emphasis on software, computer architecture, computer-aided design, hardware testing, software development methodology, management of large software development projects; Ex Stanford University faculty; Founder of several software companies. Functional Expertise: Prior art searches, patent validity searches, database searches, patent claim analysis, copyright and trade secret issues, expert witness testimonial, discovery phase investigations, deposition assistance, patent portfolio evaluation, contract disputes, intellectual property protection: audits, creation of policies and procedures. Special Areas: European prior art searches; Extensive collection of software prior art. **Degrees/ licenses:** PhD.

See primary listing under COMPUTERS/ SOFTWARE: General

John C. Donovan

President
Telecom Visions, Inc.
11 Osborne Rd.
Garden City, NY 11530
Tel: (516) 739-3565
Fax: (516) 739-0181
E-mail: donovan@speakeasy.org
Web Site: http://telecomexpertwitness.com

Specialties: Nationally recognized telecommunications expert witness before FCC and 44 jurisdictions throughout USA. 40 personal appearances; 60 affidavits, expert reports, and prefiled testimony. Dozens of lawyers as references. See website for 14-page CV. Expert in telephone industry planning, engineering, construction, customer service, operating support systems, field operations, and many other skill-sets as indicated at www.telecomexpertwitness.com. Experienced with pricing and estimating telecommunications construction, cable damage assessment and litigation, class action lawsuits against major regional telephone companies, investment due diligence investigations, patent infringement lawsuits, and other telecommunications projects. **Degrees/licenses:** BSEE - West Point, MBA - Purdue, Mgt. Dev.- Penn State.

See primary listing under COMMUNICATIONS/ TELECOMMUNICATIONS: General

Fulcrum Financial Inquiry

David Nolte
Principal
1000 Wilshire Blvd., Ste. 1650
Los Angeles, CA 90017
Tel: (213) 787-4111
(213) 787-4100
Fax: (213) 787-4141
E-mail: dnolte@fulcruminquiry.com
Web Site: http://www.fulcruminquiry.com

Specialties: Our analysis and research combined with unique presentation techniques have resulted in an unequaled track record in successful court cases and client recoveries. Our personnel are full time and fully focused on the services we provide. We thoughtfully incorporate technology into our work to provide great results at a more reasonable cost. Our expertise encompasses damages analysis, lost profit studies, business & intangible asset valuations, fraud investigations, statistics, forensic economic analysis, royalty audits, strategic & market assessments, competitive surveys, analysis of computerized data including computer forensics, and a wide range of other financial advisory services. **Degrees/licenses:** CPA, ASA, CMA, MBA, CFA.

See primary listing under ACCOUNTING: General

Matson, Driscoll & Damico

John A. Damico, PC, CPA
Managing Partner
750 Hammond Dr. NE, Bldg. 14
Atlanta, GA 30328
Tel: (404) 252-0085
Fax: (404) 255-0673
E-mail: jdamico@mdd.net
Web Site: http://www.mdd.net

Specialties: Matson, Driscoll, and Damico is an international forensic accounting and consulting firm with a specialty in intellectual property and patent infringement cases. There are currently 28 MD&D offices across the world. MD&D's analysis and verification of the facts and reporting pave the way for prompt and equitable resolutions of each case. Skill, proven expertise and total dedication to this special area of accounting are the characteristics that separate MD&D professionals from other accountants. Professional excellence in forensic and insurance claims accounting is the distinguishing hallmark of the firm. For more information, visit www.mdd.net. **Degrees/licenses:** The firm: BA, MBA, CFE, CPA, CMA, CVA, MCP.

See primary listing under ACCOUNTING: Business Interruption/Lost Profits

TASA

(Technical Advisory Service for Attorneys)
1166 DeKalb Pike
Blue Bell, PA 19422-1853
Tel: (800) 523-2319
Fax: (800) 329-8272
E-mail: experts@tasanet.com
Web Site: http://www.tasanet.com

Specialties: Save search time! Contact TASA first. Benefit from 44 years of referral expertise. We assess your needs and refer experienced Local, Regional, or National professionals in IP expertise areas you require for Consulting and Litigation, including Art & Music Valuation; Chemical & Material Analysis; Competition; Contracts; Copyrights; Damages; Electronics; Film; Interference; Internet Privacy; Lost Profits; Materials Identification; Packaging; Patents; Photography; Plagiarism; Product Development; Royalties; Software & Technology Licensing; Trade Dress; Trademarks; Trade Secrets; Valuations; and More. SERVICES INCLUDE prompt customized searches, referrals, resumes, and your initial interview calls with experts. Exceptional personal service. **Degrees/licenses:** All prof. degrees, licenses, certifications represented.

See primary listing under EXPERT WITNESS REFERRALS: General

Copyright

The Chatham Group

Jerry A. Klein
President
101 First Street, Ste. 477
Los Altos, CA 94022
Tel: (650) 948-1243
Fax: (650) 949-0534
E-mail: jaklein@chathamlaw.com
Web Site: http://www.chathamlaw.com

Specialties: Silicon Valley based consulting organization specializing in litigation support services for intellectual property litigation matters in state, federal and international proceedings. Our group consists of senior scientists, engineers, managers and experts in the fields of: Electronics, Semiconductors, Computer Hardware and Software, Telecommunications, Office Automation, Communications, Medical Electronics, Biotechnology, Materials, Manufacturing Processes, Industry Custom and Practice, Marketing. Expert witnesses, technical consulting, tutorials, discovery assistance, trial aids, market studies, patent portfolio strategy, damage determinations, investment banking and venture capital due diligence, witness location, prior art search and evaluation for domestic and international matters. **Degrees/licenses:** BSME, Patent Agent, PhDs in Computer Science, etc.

See primary listing under INTELLECTUAL PROPERTY: Patent Infringement

Patent Infringement

AINSLIE

Alan Broadwin
Principal
27 Pine Ridge Road
Larchmont, NY 10538-2616
Tel: (914) 833-2649
Fax: (914) 833-5037
E-mail: broadwin@ainslie.com
Web Site:
http://www.lawinfo.com/biz/ainslie

Specialties: Design and litigation consultant; Patent and Technology evaluation; Regulatory Compliance Assessment of ISO and GMP Quality Systems; Evaluation of adequacy of medical devices and disposables; Assistance in discovery and depositions as fact or expert witness; Engineering and due diligence investigations; Surgeon/hospital interface; Review of clinical/technical reports. **Degrees/licenses:** BA, BSME Columbia; MSIE Stevens; ASQ CQA; RAB cert. auditor; RAC.

See primary listing under MEDICINE & HEALTH: Medical Devices, Equip.

Berg Software Design

Brian A. Berg
President
14500 Big Basin Way, Ste. F
Saratoga, CA 95070
Tel: (408) 741-5010
Fax: (408) 741-5234
E-mail: bberg@bswd.com
Web Site: http://www.bswd.com

Specialties: Computer software and firmware; Device drivers; Real-time software; SCSI; ATAPI/IDE; Fibre Channel; Storage devices: optical storage (WORM, rewritable, M-O, CD-ROM, jukeboxes); Windows, UNIX, Silicon Graphics (SGI) IRIX, embedded operating systems; Software comparison; Patent infringement investigation. Books: "Software for Optical Storage," "Rewritable Optical Storage Technology." Articles: "SCSI: An Integrator's Resource Guide," and eight others. Professional Affiliations: IEEE, ACM, CPSR, IDEMA, PATCA. Conference chair, speaker and session chair: Asilomar Microcomputer Workshop; Conference speaker, session chair, and conference advisory board member: Storage Area Networks (SAN) Conference and Server Blade Summit. **Degrees/licenses:** BS Mathematics.

See primary listing under COMPUTERS/ SOFTWARE: General

The Chatham Group

Jerry A. Klein
President
101 First Street, Ste. 477
Los Altos, CA 94022
Tel: (650) 948-1243
Fax: (650) 949-0534
E-mail: jaklein@chathamlaw.com
Web Site: http://www.chathamlaw.com

Specialties: Silicon Valley based consulting organization specializing in litigation support services for intellectual property litigation matters in state, federal and international proceedings. Our group consists of senior scientists, engineers, managers and experts in the fields of: Electronics, Semiconductors, Computer Hardware and Software, Telecommunications, Office Automation, Communications, Medical Electronics, Biotechnology, Materials, Manufacturing Processes, Industry Custom and Practice, Marketing. Expert witnesses, technical consulting, tutorials, discovery assistance, trial aids, market studies, patent portfolio strategy, damage determinations, investment banking and venture capital due diligence, witness location, prior art search and evaluation for domestic and international matters. **Degrees/licenses:** BSME, Patent Agent, PhDs in Computer Science, etc.

Chemir Analytical Services

Shri Thanedar, PhD
CEO
2672 Metro Blvd.
Maryland Heights, MO 63043
Tel: (800) 659-7659
Fax: (314) 291-6630
E-mail: info@chemir.com
Web Site: http://www.chemir.com

Specialties: Materials Identification - identify and quantify components in an unknown sample; Deformulation - reverse engineering of a product; Failure Analysis - material and product failures; Comparative Analysis - product contamination and "good vs. bad" product comparison. Experienced in the chemical analysis of polymers, plastics, pharmaceuticals, medical devices, paints, coatings, drugs, adhesives and rubbers. Recent cases include trade secret infringement; product failure; patent disputes. Experienced PhD chemists available for consultation including expert witness and testimony to back up laboratory data. In business since 1959.

See primary listing under CHEMISTRY/ CHEMICALS: General

L.A. Geddes

Forensic Engineer
400 North River Rd., Ste. 701
West Lafayette, IN 47906
Tel: (765) 743-1941
(765) 494-2997
Fax: (765) 494-1193
E-mail: geddes@ecn.purdue.edu

Specialties: Electrical engineer, physiologist, biomedical engineer, certified clinical engineer, professional engineer (Texas license 10170). Author of "Medical Device Accidents" (Lawyers & Judges Publ., Inc. Tucson, Arizona) and over 750 scientific publications and 20 books. Holds 22 U.S. and foreign patents. Fellow IEEE, AAAS, American College of Cardiology, Royal Society of Medicine. Numerous scientific and teaching awards. Expert witness in over 100 lawsuits, depositions and 6 court cases. **Degrees/licenses:** ME, PhD, DSc, Texas License 10170.

See primary listing under MEDICINE & HEALTH: Medical Devices, Equip.

Jack Goldberg

President
Metrionix, Inc.
9340 Carmel Mountain Rd., Ste. E
San Diego, CA 92129-2161
Tel: (858) 780-9311
Fax: (858) 780-9312
E-mail: info@metrionix.com
Web Site: http://www.metrionix.com

Specialties: Metrionix, Inc. provides expert witness, consulting and design services with expertise in medical and scientific instruments, audio and acoustics. Mr. Goldberg has 30 years of engineering experience and has served as an expert in patent litigation, trade secrets, criminal earwitness, failure analysis, and product liability, many cases involving medi-

(Listing continued on next page)

Patent Infringement *(cont.)*

Jack Goldberg (cont.)
cal instruments. Detailed knowledge includes circuit and system design, measurement and control, embedded software, signal processing, vital signs, infusion pumps and hearing. Trial experience includes testimony for plaintiff in medical instrument patent case which successfully led to award exceeding $100M. **Degrees/licenses:** MIT: MS and BS Elec Eng & Comp Sci; Sr. member IEEE.

See primary listing under MEDICINE & HEALTH: Medical Devices, Equip.

Matson, Driscoll & Damico

John A. Damico, PC, CPA
Managing Partner
750 Hammond Dr. NE, Bldg. 14
Atlanta, GA 30328
Tel: (404) 252-0085
Fax: (404) 255-0673
E-mail: jdamico@mdd.net
Web Site: http://www.mdd.net

Specialties: Matson, Driscoll, and Damico is an international forensic accounting and consulting firm with a specialty in intellectual property and patent infringement cases. There are currently 28 MD&D offices across the world. MD&D's analysis and verification of the facts and reporting pave the way for prompt and equitable resolutions of each case. Skill, proven expertise and total dedication to this special area of accounting are the characteristics that separate MD&D professionals from other accountants. Professional excellence in forensic and insurance claims accounting is the distinguishing hallmark of the firm. For more information, visit www.mdd.net. **Degrees/licenses:** The firm: BA, MBA, CFE, CPA, CMA, CVA, MCP.

See primary listing under ACCOUNTING: Business Interruption/Lost Profits

R.F. Schiffmann Associates, Inc.

Robert F. Schiffmann
President
149 West 88 Street
New York, NY 10024-2401
Tel: (212) 362-7021
Fax: (212) 769-4630
E-mail: microwaves@juno.com
Web Site:
http://www.microwaveinnovations.com

Specialties: Microwave Heating; Microwave Ovens; Microwave Foods; Microwave Packaging; Microwave Cookware; Microwave oven accidents and injuries; Microwave fires; Microwave patents and infringement; Industrial Microwave Processing Systems. Independent consultant since 1971; Contract R&D Laboratory; Teach two international courses on Microwave Technology annually; Lecture worldwide on Microwave Technology; Fellow of the International Microwave Power Institute (IMPI); Past Chairman, President & Board member of IMPI for 18 years; Over 30 U.S. patents; Scientific Lecturer on Microwave Technology for Institute of Food Technologists; Extensive Expert Witness Testimony. **Degrees/licenses:** BS, MS, FIMPI.

See primary listing under ACCIDENT RECONSTRUCTION: Microwave Heating

Neil Sheehan

Consulting Engineer, Medical Products
One Southgate Street
Atherton, CA 94027
Tel: (650) 363-0913
Fax: (650) 363-0923
E-mail: neiljs@aol.com

Specialties: Thirty years of experience in all aspects of medical device design and development from individual contributor to Vice President of Engineering and Manufacturing; Emphasis on disposables and associated hardware of all kinds (intravenous systems and components, surgical devices, catheters, hemodialysis, electrodes, pipettors, breathing circuits, connector systems, et al.) including manufacturing processes; Thirty-six patents; Experienced successful expert witness in major patent infringement suits; Also numerous favorable product liability and contract cases;

Demonstrative evidence and litigation graphics; Excellent, likable courtroom presence; Education: Villanova Univ.; Harvard Univ. (Grad. School); University of Calif., Berkeley (Pre-Med). **Degrees/licenses:** BSME, Summa Cum Laude, Alumni Achiev. Award; Sr. Member SPE.

See primary listing under MEDICINE & HEALTH: Medical Devices, Equip.

INTERNET

Email/SPAM

Richard Van Leer, PhD

President/Master Data Analyst
ENTERPRIT.COM CORP
15841 Pines Blvd., #400
Pembroke Pines, FL 33027
Tel: (954) 450-0745
Fax: (954) 450-3065
E-mail: rvl@enterprit.com
Web Site: http://www.enterprit.com

Specialties: Dr. Van Leer has been providing technical expertise to industry leaders, fortune 500 companies, manufacturers world-wide and the legal profession on most areas of Information Technology for 38 years. Currently he is prominently situated in the nation's highest-profile Email and SPAM litigations. His company, Enterprit.com Corporation provides the extensive data analysis that makes the difference in winning the case, and defending/prosecuting it. Dr. Van Leer consults routinely on the Internet and intranets to corporate executives and attorneys between speaking engagements around the country. **Degrees/licenses:** Msc, PhD Information Technology.

Information Systems

Richard Van Leer, PhD

President/Master Data Analyst
ENTERPRIT.COM CORP
15841 Pines Blvd., #400
Pembroke Pines, FL 33027
Tel: (954) 450-0745
Fax: (954) 450-3065
E-mail: rvl@enterprit.com
Web Site: http://www.enterprit.com

Specialties: Dr. Van Leer has been providing technical expertise to industry leaders, fortune 500 companies, manufacturers world-wide and the legal profession on most areas of Information Technology for 38 years. Currently he is prominently situated in the nation's highest-profile Email and SPAM litigations. His company, Enterprit.com Corporation provides the extensive data analysis that makes the difference in winning the case, and defending/prosecuting it. Dr. Van Leer consults routinely on the Internet and intranets to corporate executives and attorneys between speaking engagements around the country. **Degrees/licenses:** Msc, PhD Information Technology.

See primary listing under INTERNET: Email/SPAM

INVESTIGATION

General

Specialized Investigations

Richard Harer
14530 Delano Street
Van Nuys, CA 91411
Tel: (818) 909-9607
Fax: (818) 782-3012
E-mail: si@specialpi.com
Web Site: http://www.specialpi.com

Specialties: Investigations firm with 22+ years consulting and expert witness experience involving the following types of cases: Insurance Fraud; Worker's Compensation;

(Listing continued on next page)

General *(cont.)*

Specialized Investigations (cont.)

Employment/Labor Law; Healthcare Fraud; Civil & Criminal Cases; Surveillance; Background Checks & Locates; Asset Searches & Financial Backgrounds; Trial Preparation. Bilingual Spanish/Korean investigators. **Degrees/licenses:** Private Investigator (CA #9869); CFE; CPI; CPII.

Death

Jon J. Nordby, PhD, D-ABMDI

Consultant in Forensic Science
& Forensic Medicine
Final Analysis Forensics
3532 Soundview Dr. West
University Place, WA 98466-1426
Tel: (253) 627-2739
Fax: (253) 627-0350
E-mail: finalanalysis@comcast.net
Web Site:
http://www.finalanalysisforensics.com

Specialties: Death, medical investigation; Criminalistics: trace evidence, organic/inorganic identifications, comparisons, ballistics; Scene investigation: bloodstain pattern analysis, evidence collection, event reconstruction; Scientific evidence: chain of custody; recognition/collection issues, limitations/scope of sciences applied, assess omissions, opinions, expert testimony; Fellow, American Academy of Forensic Sciences; Member, Canadian Society of Forensic Sciences, International Association of Bloodstain Pattern Analysts, & Association of Crime Scene Reconstruction; Founding member, Dept. of Homeland Security, DMORT; Deployments: WTC investigation, NYC, 2001; Member SWGSTAIN, FBI Scientific Working Group in bloodstain pattern analysis. **Degrees/licenses:** MA, PhD; Diplomat, Amer. Bd. of Medicolegal Death Investigators, Registry #412.

See primary listing under LITIGATION SUPPORT: Forensic Science

LAND PLANNING & ZONING

General

Petru Corporation

Timothy B. Truwe
President
250 S. Hallock Drive, Suite 100
Santa Paula, CA 93060
Tel: (805) 933-1389
Fax: (805) 933-1380

Specialties: Title, resource, and land consulting company with extensive consulting and expert witness experience in the following areas: Title Research; Title Engineering; Oil, Gas, Mineral & Geothermal; Regulatory Compliance; Due Diligence; Water Rights; Subdivision Map Act; Rights-of-Way; Title Insurance. Petru Corporation has provided its services on multi-million dollar projects and complex litigation. **Degrees/licenses:** Reg. Land Professional; Reg. Environmental Assessor.

See primary listing under REAL ESTATE: Title

Robert W. Thorpe, AICP

President
R.W. Thorpe & Associates, Inc.
(Seattle/Anchorage/Denver/Winthrop)
705 2nd Ave., Ste. 710, Hoge Bldg.
Seattle, WA 98104
Tel: (206) 624-6239
Fax: (206) 625-0930
E-mail: rwta@rwta.com
Web Site: http://www.rwta.com

Specialties: Expert Witness, Courts, Quasi-judicial; Highest & Best Use, Land Use, Zoning; Development Permits; Instructor at Universities, Community Colleges & NAHB: Land Economics/Planning; Masters degrees in Urban Planning & Urban Development. **Degrees/licenses:** AICP, BS Business &

Economics, M-Urb.Dev/Urb. Plng, NAHB, College & Univ. Inst.

See primary listing under APPRAISAL & VALUATION: Real Estate

LANGUAGE

General

Human Factors Consultants

Ralph N. Haber, Ph.D., Partner
Lyn Haber, Ph.D., Partner
313 Ridge View Drive
Swall Meadows, CA 93514
Tel: (760) 387-2458
Fax: (760) 387-2459
E-mail: Haberhfc@telis.org
Web Site:
http://www.humanfactorsconsultants.com

Specialties: Pretrial consultation and expert testimony on eyewitness perception and identification; fingerprint science; memory; language; and human factors of safety and accidents. (1) Eyewitness accuracy: effects of conditions of observation, intervening events, police procedures, lineup identifications, and earlier testimony. (2) Fingerprint science: accuracy of fingerprint comparisons; evaluation of comparison methods and laboratory procedures; underlying scientific assumptions and evidence; training and proficiency of examiners. (3) Memory: accuracy of recall by adults and by children, including recovery of memory. (4) Language: children and adults' comprehension; verbal and non-verbal harassment; factors of verbal interviewing that may alter memory; assessment of language disabilities. (5) Human factors: product safety; analyses of transportation, industrial and residential accidents in which equipment failure, human reaction/decision time, training adequacy, attention, error and warning signage may be implemented. Together, we have 45 years courtroom experience, 70 years research, 12 books, 250 published scientific articles. **Degrees/licenses:** PhD exptl psych; exptl linguistics; CCCSLP.

See primary listing under IDENTIFICATION: Eyewitness

LAW ENFORCEMENT

General

John T. Dorsey

Principal
Dorsey-Pages LLC
P.O. Box 760397
Lathrup Village, MI 48076
Tel: (248) 642-2420
Fax: (248) 642-7475
E-mail: jtdorsey@dorsey-pages.com
Web Site: http://Dorsey-Pages.com

Specialties: Governmental Systems Expert. Served as Expert Witness and developed Expert Reports and Rebuttal in Federal and State cases involving Public Safety Computer Aided Dispatch and Records Management Systems. General expertise in: Systems Development, EDP/MIS Systems, Data Networking, EDP/MIS Audit, Equipment Evaluation and Selection, Financial Information and Reporting, Information Technology Strategic Planning, Records Management, Computer Contracts, Courts and Criminal Justice System. Thirty years of computer industry and consulting experience; awarded ICCP's CDP (Certificate in Data Processing), 1978. Twenty five years of management consulting experience; awarded IMC's CMC (Certified Management Consultant), 1986. **Degrees/licenses:** BS, Math - UD (1968); MBA Wash. U (1973); CMC; CDP.

See primary listing under COMPUTERS/SOFTWARE: General

Glenn A. Marin

Vice President
IXP Corp.
8256 Enramada Ave.
Whittier, CA 90605
Tel: (562) 696-1286
Fax: (562) 693-5002
E-mail: glennm8256@aol.com

Specialties: Public Safety Systems (EMS, fire, police): Computer Aided Dispatch, Records Management, Mobile Data Terminal

(Listing continued on next page)

General *(cont.)*

Glenn A. Marin (cont.)
Systems; Two-way mobile radio: design and operational use parameters; Emergency Dispatching: practices and operations; Staffing, working environment, facility requirements; Jail Systems: computer support requirements, inmate housing analysis; Court Master for Jail overcrowding; Computer simulation analysis of radio systems channel loading, fire move-up analysis, dispatch staffing requirements. Retired Police Lieutenant. 22 years serving hundreds of public safety clients from small to very large. International experience. Extensive expert witness cases in Federal and State Courts. **Degrees/licenses:** BS, CSU - LA (1966); MPA, USC (1972); Grad. work, Comp. Sci., UC - Fullerton.

Frank H. Saunders

Owner
Frank Saunders & Associates
PO Box 1730
Capitola, CA 95010
Tel: (831) 462-4851
(800) 526-5177, Ext. 820
Fax: (831) 462-3813
E-mail: fhs8686@aol.com
Web Site:
http://wwwexpertwitness.com/saunders

Specialties: Law enforcement: Practices & procedures; Wrongful deaths; Use of deadly & non-lethal force: batons, mace, o.c. spray, handcuffs, flash-bang devices, bean-bag rounds, tazers, stun-guns, handling of mentally ill, tactical deployment, control holds (including carotid restraint); Excessive force or police brutality; Cord cuffing (hog tying); Positional asphyxia; Negligent hiring, retention & training; High speed pursuit conduct; Failure to protect; Jail procedures & prisoner safety; Barricaded suspects; Hostage protection; Crime scene investigations; Officer safety; Reaction & control of drug and/or alcohol intoxicants; Internal affairs & related agency investigations; Security: Event & crowd control; Store agent or citizen arrest procedures; Private guard security for location & transportation means or procedures; Building safety; Industrial & internal theft security; Use of canine or guard dog security & procedures; Court qualified 400+ times in 18 states and New Zealand. Licensed Private Investigator (CA); Certified Field Training Officer (FTO); Medal of Valor Recipient. **Degrees/licenses:** Los Angeles Police Department Academy Graduate.

Sullivan & Associates International

John L. Sullivan, LVMPD Dep. Chief (Ret.)
President
P.O. Box 36147
Las Vegas, NV 89133
Tel: (702) 255-0123
E-mail: johnlsai@ix.netcom.com
Web Site: http://jlsai.com

Specialties: Retired from LVMPD as Deputy Chief, Chief of Detectives after a 34-year police career. Provides expert witness testimony and litigation consultation on Law Enforcement related issues, i.e., Use of Force , Less than Lethal Force, Policies and Procedures, Arrest Tactics, Internal Affairs, Criminal Investigations, Vehicle Pursuits, Supervision and Training. Supervised the investigations of over 100 officer involved deadly force cases. For approximately 30 years, taught basic and in-service POST and law enforcement academy classes to federal, state and local officers. Taught university Criminal Justice classes for over 23 years. **Degrees/licenses:** BA & Graduate Studies; FBI N/A Academy.

Emergency Vehicles

Thomas M. Walton

Thomas Walton - Expert Witness/Consultant
P. O. Box 3365
Barrington, IL 60011-3365
Tel: (847) 304-0285
Fax: (847) 304-0308
E-mail: marine2@comcast.net
Web Site: http://www.jmarshassoc.com

Specialties: Deputy Chief, Chicago Police Department, (Retired) with over 30 years experience in police operations, training and supervision. Highly experienced Expert in Police Standards, Procedures, Training and Supervision including but not limited to: Vehicle Pursuits; Emergency Response Driving;

Search and Seizure; Investigative Detentions; Patrol/Investigative Procedures; Use of Force; Suicides in Police Custody; Sexual Harassment; Domestic Violence; First Aid; Swat Operations; Raids; Positional Asphyxia; Caring for Injured Parties; Felony Vehicle Stops; Road Blocks; Search Warrants; Private Security; Use of Pepper Spray; Field Sobriety Tests, ADA. Qualified Expert in Federal and State Courts. Retained in twenty states. **Degrees/licenses:** BA, MS; CPI (ILETSB), CPO.

See primary listing under LAW ENFORCEMENT: Police Practices/Procedures

Informants

Michael Levine

Litigation & Trial Consultant
P.O. Box 533
Stone Ridge, NY 12484
Tel: (845) 687-9642
Fax: (845) 687-4916
E-mail: expert53@aol.com
Web Site:
http://www.expertwitnessradio.org

Specialties: Take advantage of a free consultation with a veteran of 39 years of REAL courtroom experience (civil and criminal). Highly decorated retired federal agent, best-selling author, police instructor, trial consultant, with supervisory service in DEA, Customs, BATF, IRS & FBI/DEA Task Force. Expert testimony accepted on 250+ occasions (Fed/State/Civil/Criminal). Areas include: NARCOTICS, TITLE III, RICO, USE OF FORCE, INFORMANTS, INVESTIGATIVE (due diligence), UNDERCOVER, SMUGGLING, BLIND MULES, CONSPIRACY, ASSET FORFEITURES and more. Publications include NY Times and national best-sellers "Deep Cover," "The Big White Lie," and "Fight Back" (community anti-drug plan recommended by the Clinton Administration). Full Service Trial Consulting.

See primary listing under LAW ENFORCEMENT: Police Practices/Procedures

Michael D. Lyman, PhD

Expert in Criminal & Civil Litigation
4613 Villa Wood Ct.
Columbia, MO 65203
Tel: (573) 875-7472
(573) 999-1790 (Cell)
Fax: (573) 256-5067
E-mail: michaellyman@mac.com
Web Site: http://www.policeexpert.net

Specialties: Nationally recognized police expert with thirty years as criminal investigator, police trainer and criminal justice educator. Dr. Lyman specializes in the area of police procedure and has an 18-year publishing record. His peer-reviewed publications and books are widely used by many of the nation's most prestigious colleges and universities. His publications have also been adopted by law enforcement agencies as procedural training guides. Expert witness, trial preparation and consultation services available. Areas of expertise include use of force, investigative procedures, police supervision, and related matters. Will consider cases for both plaintiff and defense. **Degrees/licenses:** PhD, MS, BS.

See primary listing under LAW ENFORCEMENT: Police Practices/Procedures

Interview & Interrogation

Jack Trimarco

President
Jack Trimarco & Assoc.
Polygraph/Investigations, Inc.
9454 Wilshire Blvd., 6th Fl.
Beverly Hills, CA 90212-2900
Tel: (310) 247-2637
Fax: (760) 777-1836
E-mail: jtrimarco@aol.com
Web Site: http://www.jacktrimarco.com

Specialties: Host of Court TV's "Fake Out." Former manager of the Federal Bureau of Investigation's Polygraph Program in Los Angeles. Former Inspector General Polygraph Program - Department of Energy; Nationally known and respected Polygraph Expert. I have the credentials you would want when you

(Listing continued on next page)

Interview & Interrogation
(cont.)

Jack Trimarco (cont.)
have a client polygraphed, a case reviewed, a motion made regarding polygraph, or an in-depth professional investigation. My unique background allows me to bring the highest levels of service and expertise to any polygraph situation. **Degrees/licenses:** BS Psychology; Certified APA, AAPP, CAPE, AAFE.

See primary listing under LITIGATION SUPPORT: Polygraph/Lie Detection

Police Practices/Procedures

ECJM Consultants, Inc.
Edward Mamet, CPP, CFE
Captain, New York City Police Dept. (Ret.)
P.O. Box 1559
Cooper Station
New York, NY 10276
Tel: (212) 475-8215
Fax: (646) 349-3238
E-mail: ecjm2@msn.com
Web Site:
http://member.expertpages.com/edmamet

Specialties: Retired New York City Police Department Captain Edward Mamet founded ECJM Consultants Inc. after completing forty years service. His group provides high quality police and security related issues. ECJM Consultants Inc. specializes in law enforcement and security liability matters, supporting both plaintiff and defense attorneys. ECJM consultants are retired New York City Police Department command level officers whose combined experience exceeds 125 years in law enforcement and security. Law enforcement areas include negligent investigation, excessive force, in-custody death, high speed chases, false arrest, police misconduct, negligent hiring, training, supervision and retention. **Degrees/licenses:** AAS, Police Science; BS, Criminal Justice; MPA.

William T. "Bill" Gaut
9063 Autumn Haze Dr.
Naples, FL 34109-1501
Tel: (239) 593-8033
Fax: (239) 593-8033
E-mail: WTGaut@aol.com
Web Site: http://www.wtgaut.com

Specialties: Case Review and Expert Opinion in the areas of: Wrongful Death; Criminal Case Review; Security Industry Consultation; Security Management; Security Guard Training; Security Guard Operations; Premise Liability; Foreseeability Expectations; Police Management and Procedures; and Litigation Support. Thirty (30) years extensive experience in the fields of Criminal and Civil Investigation, Courtroom Testimony, Security Management and Training Standards, and Litigation Support. SEE WEB SITE FOR DETAILS: Criminal Justice College Professor, Captain of Detectives (135), Lead Homicide Detective, Certified Security Instructor, District Attorney Special Services Director, Multi-State Approved Security Training School Owner, and Corporate CEO. **Degrees/licenses:** AA-Cr Jus; BS-Cr Jus; MS- Pub & Priv Adm (MPA/MBA).

See primary listing under SECURITY: Premises Liability

Richard W. Kobetz
Executive Protection Institute
P.O. Box 802
Berryville, VA 22611-0802
Tel: (540) 554-2540
Fax: (540) 554-2558
E-mail: rwk@crosslink.com
Web Site:
http://www.personalprotection.com

Specialties: Police conduct, operations, practices, procedures, supervision, training, vehicle pursuit, proper use of force; Practical working experience from patrolman through Chief of Police & Assistant Director of International Association of Chiefs of Police (IACP). **Degrees/licenses:** MS, MPA, DPA, CST, PPS.

Michael Levine

Litigation & Trial Consultant
P.O. Box 533
Stone Ridge, NY 12484
Tel: (845) 687-9642
Fax: (845) 687-4916
E-mail: expert53@aol.com
Web Site:
http://www.expertwitnessradio.org

Specialties: Take advantage of a free consultation with a veteran of 39 years of REAL courtroom experience (civil and criminal). Highly decorated retired federal agent, best-selling author, police instructor, trial consultant, with supervisory service in DEA, Customs, BATF, IRS & FBI/DEA Task Force. Expert testimony accepted on 250+ occasions (Fed/State/Civil/Criminal). Areas include: NARCOTICS, TITLE III, RICO, USE OF FORCE, INFORMANTS, INVESTIGATIVE (due diligence), UNDERCOVER, SMUGGLING, BLIND MULES, CONSPIRACY, ASSET FORFEITURES and more. Publications include NY Times and national best-sellers "Deep Cover," "The Big White Lie," and "Fight Back" (community anti-drug plan recommended by the Clinton Administration). Full Service Trial Consulting.

Michael D. Lyman, PhD

Expert in Criminal & Civil Litigation
4613 Villa Wood Ct.
Columbia, MO 65203
Tel: (573) 875-7472
(573) 999-1790 (Cell)
Fax: (573) 256-5067
E-mail: michaellyman@mac.com
Web Site: http://www.policeexpert.net

Specialties: Nationally recognized police expert with thirty years as criminal investigator, police trainer and criminal justice educator. Dr. Lyman specializes in the area of police procedure and has an 18-year publishing record. His peer-reviewed publications and books are widely used by many of the nation's most prestigious colleges and universities. His publications have also been adopted by law enforcement agencies as procedural training guides. Expert witness, trial preparation and consultation services available. Areas of expertise include use of force, investigative procedures, police supervision, and related matters. Will consider cases for both plaintiff and defense. **Degrees/licenses:** PhD, MS, BS.

Robinette & Associates, Inc.

Fred G. Robinette III
President
P.O. Box 340
Cartersville, GA 30120
Tel: (770) 383-8933
Fax: (770) 383-9676
E-mail: frobinette@msn.com

Specialties: Special Agent, FBI, retired; Chairman, Georgia Committee on Civil Rights under Color of Law. Publication: Excessive Force Incidents - An Ounce of Prevention, A Handbook for Law Enforcement Executives. Noted lecturer on 42, USC, 1983 litigation. Robinette & Associates is a group of exceptionally credentialed active and retired law enforcement/corrections professionals, nationally recognized for the competence and integrity of its experts. All aspects of police operations and standards, use of force and deadly force, pursuits, less lethal weaponry, detention/correction facility operations and standards, as well as 911 communications, polygraph, and internal investigations, and training.

Thomas M. Walton

Thomas Walton - Expert Witness/Consultant
P. O. Box 3365
Barrington, IL 60011-3365
Tel: (847) 304-0285
Fax: (847) 304-0308
E-mail: marine2@comcast.net
Web Site: http://www.jmarshassoc.com

Specialties: Deputy Chief, Chicago Police Department, (Retired) with over 30 years experience in police operations, training and supervision. Highly experienced Expert in Police Standards, Procedures, Training and Supervision including but not limited to: Vehicle Pursuits; Emergency Response Driving; Search and Seizure; Investigative Detentions; Patrol/Investigative Procedures; Use of Force;

(Listing continued on next page)

Police Practices/Procedures
(cont.)

Thomas M. Walton (cont.)
Suicides in Police Custody; Sexual Harassment; Domestic Violence; First Aid; Swat Operations; Raids; Positional Asphyxia; Caring for Injured Parties; Felony Vehicle Stops; Road Blocks; Search Warrants; Private Security; Use of Pepper Spray; Field Sobriety Tests, ADA. Qualified Expert in Federal and State Courts. Retained in twenty states. **Degrees/licenses:** BA, MS; CPI (ILETSB), CPO.

Prison/Corrections Practices

Robinette & Associates, Inc.

Fred G. Robinette III
President
P.O. Box 340
Cartersville, GA 30120
Tel: (770) 383-8933
Fax: (770) 383-9676
E-mail: frobinette@msn.com

Specialties: Special Agent, FBI, retired; Chairman, Georgia Committee on Civil Rights under Color of Law. Publication: Excessive Force Incidents - An Ounce of Prevention, A Handbook for Law Enforcement Executives. Noted lecturer on 42, USC, 1983 litigation. Robinette & Associates is a group of exceptionally credentialed active and retired law enforcement/corrections professionals, nationally recognized for the competence and integrity of its experts. All aspects of police operations and standards, use of force and deadly force, pursuits, less lethal weaponry, detention/correction facility operations and standards, as well as 911 communications, polygraph, and internal investigations, and training.

See primary listing under LAW ENFORCEMENT: Police Practices/Procedures

Use of Force, Police Misconduct

Michael Levine

Litigation & Trial Consultant
P.O. Box 533
Stone Ridge, NY 12484
Tel: (845) 687-9642
Fax: (845) 687-4916
E-mail: expert53@aol.com
Web Site:
http://www.expertwitnessradio.org

Specialties: Take advantage of a free consultation with a veteran of 39 years of REAL courtroom experience (civil and criminal). Highly decorated retired federal agent, best-selling author, police instructor, trial consultant, with supervisory service in DEA, Customs, BATF, IRS & FBI/DEA Task Force. Expert testimony accepted on 250+ occasions (Fed/State/Civil/Criminal). Areas include: NARCOTICS, TITLE III, RICO, USE OF FORCE, INFORMANTS, INVESTIGATIVE (due diligence), UNDERCOVER, SMUGGLING, BLIND MULES, CONSPIRACY, ASSET FORFEITURES and more. Publications include NY Times and national best-sellers "Deep Cover," "The Big White Lie," and "Fight Back" (community anti-drug plan recommended by the Clinton Administration). Full Service Trial Consulting.

See primary listing under LAW ENFORCEMENT: Police Practices/Procedures

Michael D. Lyman, PhD

Expert in Criminal & Civil Litigation
4613 Villa Wood Ct.
Columbia, MO 65203
Tel: (573) 875-7472
(573) 999-1790 (Cell)
Fax: (573) 256-5067
E-mail: michaellyman@mac.com
Web Site: http://www.policeexpert.net

Specialties: Nationally recognized police expert with thirty years as criminal investigator, police trainer and criminal justice educator. Dr. Lyman specializes in the area of police procedure and has an 18-year publishing record. His peer-reviewed publications and books are widely used by many of the nation's most prestigious colleges and universities. His publications have also been adopted by law enforcement agencies as procedural training guides. Expert witness, trial preparation and consultation services available. Areas of expertise include use of force, investigative procedures, police supervision, and related matters. Will consider cases for both plaintiff and defense. **Degrees/licenses:** PhD, MS, BS.

See primary listing under LAW ENFORCEMENT: Police Practices/Procedures

James F. Marsh

Marsh and Associates
98 Shenandoah Dr.
Galena, IL 61036-9346
Tel: (815) 858-2534
(866) 858-2534 (Toll free)
Fax: (815) 858-2534
E-mail: jmarsh7618@aol.com or
jmarsh@jmarsh.com
Web Site: http://jmarshassoc.com

Specialties: Police misconduct cases. We are training and liability experts with many years experience. Marsh and Associates are State and Federal Court Qualified Experts. James F. Marsh, MS and consulting associate Thomas M. Walton, MS specialize in the following: Use of Force Analysis, Firearms Training, Vehicle Pursuits, Emergency Driving, Roadblocks and Stops, Police Policies, Procedures, Training and Supervision, Search and Seizure, Probable Cause, Warrantless Entries, Arrest and Control Procedures, Raid Tactics, Riot Control Procedures, Policy and Standards, lock-up and Jail Procedures, In-Custody Suicides, Domestic Violence. **Degrees/licenses:** MS degree & Certified Law Enforcement Trainer.

Sullivan & Associates International

John L. Sullivan, LVMPD Dep. Chief (Ret.)
President
P.O. Box 36147
Las Vegas, NV 89133
Tel: (702) 255-0123
E-mail: johnlsai@ix.netcom.com
Web Site: http://jlsai.com

Specialties: Retired from LVMPD as Deputy Chief, Chief of Detectives after a 34-year police career. Provides expert witness testimony and litigation consultation on Law Enforcement related issues, i.e., Use of Force , Less than Lethal Force, Policies and Procedures, Arrest Tactics, Internal Affairs, Criminal Investigations, Vehicle Pursuits, Supervision and Training. Supervised the investigations of over 100 officer involved deadly force cases. For approximately 30 years, taught basic and in-service POST and law enforcement academy classes to federal, state and local officers. Taught university Criminal Justice classes for over 23 years. **Degrees/licenses:** BA & Graduate Studies; FBI N/A Academy.

See primary listing under LAW ENFORCEMENT: General

LAW/LEGAL

Family Law

Howard Goldfarb, MA, CRC

Vocational Rehabilitation Consultant
Goldfarb and Associates
1101 Fremont Avenue, Suite 103
South Pasadena, CA 91030
Tel: (626) 441-9687
Fax: (626) 799-8736
E-mail: goldfarbassociates@yahoo.com

Specialties: Twenty years of experience providing expert witness testimony as a vocational rehabilitation and employability consultant. Involved with personal injury, third party litigation and marriage dissolution matters.

(Listing continued on next page)

Family Law *(cont.)*

Howard Goldfarb (cont.)
Evaluate long-term disability and ERISA cases. Testify as a Vocational Expert for the Social Security Administration. Certified to provide counseling services to injured workers through the U. S. Department of Labor, Office of Workers Compensation programs. Independent Vocational Evaluator. Instructor at the California State University, Los Angeles. Administer and interpret vocational testing. **Degrees/licenses:** MA, New York University; Certified Rehabilitation Counselor.

See primary listing under EMPLOYMENT: Vocational Rehabilitation

LITIGATION SUPPORT

General

Arnold D. Brown

Principal
Brown CPA Group, Ltd.
Northbrook Office Court
666 Dundee Rd., Suite 1603
Northbrook, IL 60062-2737
Tel: (847) 509-4100
Fax: (847) 509-1040
E-mail: arnieb@browncpagroup.com
Web Site: http://www.browncpagroup.com

Specialties: Forensic accounting; Business valuations; Estate & gift tax valuations; Malpractice claims; Damage claims; Shareholder disputes; Stock options; Analysis of documents & structuring of divorce settlements; Trial strategy; Expert testimony; Deposition & cross examination assistance to counsel. **Degrees/licenses:** BBA; CPA; CVA.

Joseph H. Dabrowski, PE

President
Visionary, LLC
7250 Ledgewood Drive
(Greater Cleveland)
Kirtland, OH 44094
Tel: (440) 256-9274
(440) 477-6566 (Mobile)
Fax: (440) 256-9274
E-mail: joseph_dabrowski@sbcglobal.net

Specialties: Property/Casualty Insurance; Construction-Related Litigation Support and Expert Testimony; Forensic Investigations; Bad Faith; Risk Management; Construction Claim preparation or defense, analysis and resolution; Dispute Resolution Board participation; Defaulted or terminated contractor assessment and bond claim issues; Schedule Delay & Impact Analysis; Professional Liability; 27 years of service to the Construction, Insurance, Legal and Surety Industries. **Degrees/licenses:** BSME; MBA; Professional Engineer (Ohio); AAA Commercial Arbitrator.

See primary listing under INSURANCE: General

Thomas C. Grzymala, CFP®, AIFA®

Principal
Forensic Analytics LLC
3506 Glasgow Lane
Keswick, VA 22947-2748
Tel: (434) 293-8882
Fax: (434) 293-9931
E-mail: tom@fa-llc.net

Specialties: Experienced fee-only Certified Financial Planner (CFP) and investment manager; SEC-Registered Investment Advisor; prepare, consult and testify as expert witness in litigation and securities arbitration involving suitability, churning, breach of (trustee) fiduciary duty, damage calculations, trial exhibits preparation, due diligence, professional malpractice, general financial analysis and litigation support. Member: Financial Planning Association, National Association of Personal Financial Advisors, American Bar Association. BS, U.S. Naval Academy; MPA, The American University. **Degrees/licenses:** BS; MPA; CFP; NASD Series 65; AIFA.

See primary listing under FINANCE: Securities

Philip Kroeze, AIA

Principal
Consulting Architectural Services
19 Summerside
Coto de Caza, CA 92679
Tel: (949) 589-0554
Fax: (949) 589-4351
E-mail: kroeze@cox.net
Web Site:
http://www.jurispro.com/mem/kroeze

Specialties: Licensed Architect (CA); Member: American Institute of Architects (AIA), Construction Specifications Institute (CSI), International Congress of Building Officials (ICBO), National Council of Architectural Registration Boards (NCARB). Architectural/Engineering standard of care; moisture intrusion; construction documents. 35+ years experience in design, working drawings, specifications, construction; litigation support; single & multi-family residential, commercial, offices; personal injury; ADA compliance; UBC types I-V; wood, steel & concrete structures; models, charts, renderings, & other exhibits; photographs. **Degrees/licenses:** Licensed Architect (CA); Bachelor of Architecture; US Army Corps of Engineers.

See primary listing under ARCHITECTURE: General

Legier & Materne, apac

Consultants and CPAs
William R. Legier, CPA, CFE
Managing Director
Energy Centre
1100 Poydras St., 34th Floor
New Orleans, LA 70163
Tel: (504) 561-0020
Fax: (504) 561-0023
E-mail: legier@lmcpa.com
Web Site: http://www.lmcpa.com

Specialties: Certified Public Accountant; Certified Fraud Examiner; Extensive Testifying in Federal and State Courts for leading national law firms and Fortune 500 companies in areas including accounting, calculating and refuting financial damages including lost profits, fraud detection and recovery, mismanagement, appointment of receiver, business valuations, shareholder disputes, evidence of ownership, identification of hidden assets, corporate veil piercing, analysis and explanation of complex financial transactions, bankruptcies, forensic accounting, accounting malpractice, marital dissolutions, document control, advanced automated graphic design and display techniques. **Degrees/licenses:** CPA, CFE.
See primary listing under ACCOUNTING: General

David Ostrove, Attorney-CPA

5757 Wilshire Blvd., Ste. 535
Los Angeles, CA 90036-3600
Tel: (323) 939-3400
Fax: (323) 939-3500
E-mail: dostrove@comcast.net
Web Site:
http://www.lawyers.com/ok&olaw

Specialties: Special master, arbitrator, mediator, law school professor, author, lecturer; Forensic accounting; Experienced witness 40+ years; Accounting malpractice; Lawyer malpractice; Litigation support; Books, records & accounting issues; Consulting & evaluation; Damages assessment and computations; Tax issues; Breach of fiduciary duties; Real estate transactions; Malpractice arising out of probate, wills, trusts; Leveraged buyouts; Exchanges of properties; Corporate transactions; Reasonable value of services; Business valuation; Financial statement analysis; Wrongful discharge; Tax preparer negligence; Case review, analysis and consulting; 50 years combined history in the professions of accounting and law. **Degrees/licenses:** JD, CPA.
See primary listing under ACCOUNTING: General

Packer Engineering

Penny Rusch
Director of Business Development
1950 N. Washington St.
Naperville, IL 60563
Tel: (800) 323-0114
Fax: (630) 505-1986
E-mail: peinfo@packereng.com
Web Site: http://www.packereng.com

Specialties: Packer Engineering, a multi-disciplinary engineering consulting company,

(Listing continued on next page)

General *(cont.)*

Packer Engineering (cont.)
provides expertise in the areas of failure analysis, accident investigation & reconstruction, cause & origin investigations, research & development, risk mitigation, and custom & routine testing. Packer offers a wide range of services in the following areas: Aviation, Biomechanical/Biomedical, Construction Technology, Chemical, Fire & Explosions, Electrical, Human Factors, Ergonomics, Machinery & Equipment, Materials, Occupational Safety, Product & Process Safety, System Failure Analysis & Recovery, Technology Assessment & Intellectual Property, and Transportation Systems. Our emergency response team is available 24 hours, 7 days a week.

See primary listing under ENGINEERING: Consulting

Peter J. Pfeffer

605 Woodhaven Dr.
Mundelein (metro Chicago), IL 60060-1530
Tel: (847) 837-0791
Fax: (847) 970-6383
E-mail: barlowe@interaccess.com
Web Site: http://firms.findlaw.com/pfeffer

Specialties: Securities fraud examiner, case evaluation, arbitration panelist selection, derivatives (incl. commodities), defense and plaintiff, domestic and foreign, portfolio evaluation, written opinion, damage assessment, supervision, turn-over evaluation, suitability, investment advisors, discretionary accounts, securities valuation, registered employee/brokerage firm disputes. Thirty years experience in securities industry, AE through EVP of major firm (see Web site). Expert witness or arbitrator, exchange, NASD, AAA, NFA, appellate panelist, federal reparations proceedings, federal and state jury and bench trials. **Degrees/licenses:** See Web Site.

See primary listing under FINANCE: Securities

RWL GROUP

Robert W. Lazarus
President/Senior Consultant
300 N. Coit Rd., #810
Richardson, TX 75080-5456
Tel: (972) 907-9095
Fax: (972) 907-9198
E-mail: rwlgroup@rwlgroup.com
Web Site: http://www.rwlgroup.com

Specialties: We are independent risk management, insurance, workers compensation, and employee benefits consultants. No insurance sales or affiliations. We have extensive experience providing expert testimony, litigation support, and advice to clients/attorneys for all lines of personal and commercial insurance. We are also experienced in dispute resolution involving insurance costs and coverages; agent/insurer duties to policyholder; bad faith; loss-sensitive rating; premium audits; experience modification, etc. Our professional staff includes MBAs, CPCUs, FLMIs, CPAs and ARMs. We are also members of the Society of Risk Management Consultants, which maintains high ethical standards for the industry. **Degrees/licenses:** MBA, ARM, CPCU, FLMI, CPA.

See primary listing under INSURANCE: General

Thielsch Engineering, Inc.

Ara Nalbandian, PE, Vice President
Bob Basile, PE
Florence Cone
195 Frances Avenue
Cranston, RI 02910
Tel: (401) 467-6454
Fax: (401) 467-2398
E-mail: nalbandiana@thielsch.com
Web Site: http://www.thielsch.com

Specialties: Failure analyses and forensic investigations of equipment and products in many different industries including power generation, pulp and paper, petroleum and chemical, process industries, mining, manufacturing, transportation, electronics, medical devices, failures or condition assessments of vessel, piping, bridges, building structures, electrical components/systems, pumps, water transmission, fire protection piping, compressors and other rotating equipment. Extensive laboratory testing facilities include full spectrum analyses, metallurgical, mechanical, chemical , analytical, bacteriological, environmental, structural and corrosion testing services. Registered Professional Engineers in Rhode Island, Massachusetts, Maine, New Jersey, Georgia, Florida, Indiana and California. **Degrees/licenses:** BS, PE, BS Mech. Engr. MS (RI, MA, ME, NJ, GA, FL, IN & CA).

See primary listing under ENGINEERING: Consulting

Arson Investigation

John Michael Agosti & Associates, Inc.

John Michael Agosti
Fire Analyst & Consultant
23808 N. Overhill
Lake Zurich, IL 60047
Tel: (847) 682-6793
Fax: (847) 540-6297
E-mail: johnagosti@earthlink.net
Web Site: http://www.arsonexpert.com

Specialties: Fire Cause & Origin; Arson Defense; Fire Related Injury/Death Cases; Vehicle Fires; Explosion & Gas Fires; Building & Fire Code Research; Fire Department Operations; Fire Department Management/ Labor Consulting. Over 28 years of fire dept. experience blended with 10 years of private investigations for insurance companies, attorneys and as an expert witness. Over 1,400 fires investigated. Experienced in plaintiff/defense/criminal/civil cases. Qualified in state and federal courts. Free initial phone consultation. **Degrees/licenses:** Fire Science Degree, State Certified Fire Investigator.

See primary listing under ACCIDENT RECONSTRUCTION: Fires & Explosions

Brokerage & Banking

Thomas A. Tarter

Andela Consulting Group, Inc.
15250 Ventura Blvd., Ste. 610
Sherman Oaks, CA 91403-3218
Tel: (818) 380-3102
(818) 368-1068
Fax: (818) 501-5412
E-mail: ttarter@earthlink.net
Web Site:
http://www.commercepartners.org

Specialties: Banking, bankruptcy - interest rate & plan feasibility opinions, business litigation support, checking account disputes, embezzlement, forgeries, credit card fraud, credit damages, debt restructure, lender liability, loan policy & practices, bank management & operating controls, trade and standby letters of credit, guarantees, consumer lending, real estate & construction lending, credit facility disputes, shareholder & insider loan transactions, note valuations, expert referral service; Bank founder, director & CEO; financial and management advisor; 25+ years experience. Experience: over 500 cases - State, Federal & Bankruptcy Court. Clients: individuals, businesses, banks, government agencies, financial institutions. **Degrees/licenses:** BS, MBA.

See primary listing under FINANCE: Commercial Banking

Check Fraud, Bank Operations

Richard E. Dressel

Bank Operations Consultant
962 Kennett Way
West Chester, PA 19380
Tel: (610) 344-0809
Fax: (610) 344-0769
E-mail: redxsvp@aol.com

Specialties: Thirty three years of Bank Operations experience. Credible analysis and persuasive testimony on banking policies and industry practices. Expertise includes Demand Deposit/checking account processing; check

(Listing continued on next page)

Check Fraud, Bank Operations *(cont.)*

Richard E. Dressel (cont.)
payment, exception handling, fraud detection, overdrafts, NSF checks, signature verification and statement rendering. Was SVP - Deposit Accounting Services for CoreStates Bank in Philadelphia, now Wachovia. Since 1995 have served as independent consultant providing litigation support and expert witness services. **Degrees/licenses:** BS, Stonier Graduate School of Banking.

Expert Witness Preparation

James F. Marsh

Marsh and Associates
98 Shenandoah Dr.
Galena, IL 61036-9346
Tel: (815) 858-2534
(866) 858-2534 (Toll free)
Fax: (815) 858-2534
E-mail: jmarsh7618@aol.com or
jmarsh@jmarsh.com
Web Site: http://jmarshassoc.com

Specialties: Police misconduct cases. We are training and liability experts with many years experience. Marsh and Associates are State and Federal Court Qualified Experts. James F. Marsh, MS and consulting associate Thomas M. Walton, MS specialize in the following: Use of Force Analysis, Firearms Training, Vehicle Pursuits, Emergency Driving, Roadblocks and Stops, Police Policies, Procedures, Training and Supervision, Search and Seizure, Probable Cause, Warrantless Entries, Arrest and Control Procedures, Raid Tactics, Riot Control Procedures, Policy and Standards, lock-up and Jail Procedures, In-Custody Suicides, Domestic Violence. **Degrees/licenses:** MS degree & Certified Law Enforcement Trainer.

See primary listing under LAW ENFORCEMENT: Use of Force, Police Misconduct

Capt. Mitchell S. Stoller

President
MAREX
30021 Tomas St., Ste. 300
Rancho Santa Margarita, CA 92688
Tel: (949) 858-5475
Fax: (949) 858-5477
E-mail: marexco@aol.com

Specialties: Expert Witness to the marine industry. Experience in Federal and State court, judicial arbitration, mediation services, and represents both plaintiff and defense. Consultant to the United States Coast Guard. Captain Stoller is the President and founder of Marex, a marine consulting company designed to market the safety expertise that enabled him to become the youngest captain of Exxon Shipping Company, U.S.A. He also holds an outstanding tanker safety operational record both at the Company and as a Los Angeles Harbor Pilot. Capt. Stoller has written and/or consulted on Safety and procedural manuals for numerous shipping companies and has been retained in over 800 blue/brown water cases across the nation from jet skis to pleasure crafts to super tankers. **Degrees/licenses:** Unlimited Master Mariner's Lic., Extensive Pilotage Lic., BS Nautical Sci.

See primary listing under MARITIME & ADMIRALTY: General

Forensic Science

Zvi Herschman, MD

346 Wilson Street
West Hempstead, NY 11552
Tel: (516) 486-7384
Fax: (516) 486-2743
E-mail: hesh346@juno.com

Specialties: Medical Malpractice, Trace evidence, Toxicology, Computer Forensics, Crime scene reconstruction, Medical Fraud and Abuse Litigation, Pain Management, Accident Reconstruction, Criminalistics, Critical Care, Anesthesiology. Dr. Herschman is a practicing Anesthesiologist, Board Certified in Anesthesiology, Pain Management, Critical Care. Consultant in Toxicology for 15 years. PhD Candidate at John Jay College of

Criminal Justice - Trace Evidence, Toxicology, Medical Fraud and Abuse litigation. Well published, experienced with expert testimony and accident reconstruction. **Degrees/licenses:** MD, DABA.
See primary listing under MEDICINE & HEALTH: Pain Management

Human Factors Engineering Services

Ezra S. Krendel
211 Cornell Avenue
Swarthmore, PA 19081-1933
Tel: (610) 543-9107
Fax: (610) 543-9107
E-mail: krendel@wharton.upenn.edu

Specialties: Construction and Industrial Equipment, Workplace, Recreation, and Highway Safety; Vehicular Control; Visual Search; Perception and Behavior; Product Liability; Warnings; Slip and Fall; Human Performance Reliability and Error. 30 years experience in litigation about 60/40 plaintiff/defendant. Professor Emeritus of Statistics and Operations Research, and of Systems Engineering; Human Factors Engineering and Ergonomics, University of Pennsylvania. Formerly Technical Director, Franklin Institute Research Laboratories, Philadelphia, PA. Consultant To U.S. Departments of Defense, Air Force, Army, Navy, Justice, Transportation, and to Industry. Labor Arbitrator, Federal Mediation and Conciliation Service. Fellow: IEEE, HFES, APA, APS, AAAS. **Degrees/licenses:** ScM.
See primary listing under ACCIDENT PREVENTION & SAFETY: Human Factors

Laboratory Corporation of America

1912 Alexander Dr.
Research Triangle Park, NC 27709
Tel: (800) 533-0567, Dept. 6
Fax: (919) 361-7737
E-mail: ForensicIdentity@labcorp.com
Web Site: http://www.labcorp.com

Specialties: Independent DNA testing; Criminal DNA case review, consulting, expert witness testimony. Experienced personnel, 3500+ cases completed. Hundreds of courtroom testimonies for prosecution and/or defense. ASCLD/LAB, CAP and New York State Department of Health accredited.

Jon J. Nordby, PhD, D-ABMDI

Consultant in Forensic Science
& Forensic Medicine
Final Analysis Forensics
3532 Soundview Dr. West
University Place, WA 98466-1426
Tel: (253) 627-2739
Fax: (253) 627-0350
E-mail: finalanalysis@comcast.net
Web Site:
http://www.finalanalysisforensics.com

Specialties: Death, medical investigation; Criminalistics: trace evidence, organic/inorganic identifications, comparisons, ballistics; Scene investigation: bloodstain pattern analysis, evidence collection, event reconstruction; Scientific evidence: chain of custody; recognition/collection issues, limitations/scope of sciences applied, assess omissions, opinions, expert testimony; Fellow, American Academy of Forensic Sciences; Member, Canadian Society of Forensic Sciences, International Association of Bloodstain Pattern Analysts, & Association of Crime Scene Reconstruction; Founding member, Dept. of Homeland Security, DMORT; Deployments: WTC investigation, NYC, 2001; Member SWGSTAIN, FBI Scientific Working Group in bloodstain pattern analysis. **Degrees/licenses:** MA, PhD; Diplomat, Amer. Bd. of Medicolegal Death Investigators, Registry #412.

RJ Lee Group, Inc.

5 Nationwide locations:
CA, NY, PA, VA, WA
Keith Rickabaugh
Director of Sales and Marketing
350 Hochberg Road
Monroeville, PA 15146
Tel: (800) 860-1775
(724) 325-1776
Fax: (724) 733-1799
E-mail: krickabaugh@rjlg.com
Web Site: http://www.rjlg.com

Specialties: COMPANY INFORMATION: Independent laboratory and consulting group

(Listing continued on next page)

Forensic Science *(cont.)*

RJ Lee Group, Inc. (cont.)
specializing in application of instrumental techniques to solve problems. Over 250 employees and 20 years litigation support experience. FAILURE ANALYSIS: materials, metals, polymers, and ceramics. CONSTRUCTION MATERIALS/DEFECT IDENTIFICATION: concrete and cement, aggregates, and fill materials. FORENSICS: gun shot residue, hair, fiber, and other trace evidence. ENVIRONMENTAL: disaster/impact assessment and remediation, receptor modeling, particulate characterization, air and dust analysis, and diesel particulate characterization. EXPANDED SERVICES: auger spectroscopy (AES), optical and electron microscopy (SEM & TEM), inorganic chemistry (AA/ICP & X-ray diffraction), organic chemistry (GC-ECD, GC-FID, GC/MS, FTIR & HPLC), thermal analysis (TGA, DSC, DTA), industrial hygiene, asbestos, silica, method development, product testing, software development, x-ray photoelectron spectroscopy, x-ray diffraction, and x-ray fluorescence (XPS, XRD, XRF). **Degrees/licenses:** BS, CIH, CSP, MA, MBA, MS, MSFS, PE, PhD; AIHA & NVLAP + Other Accred.

See primary listing under FAILURE ANALYSIS: General

Forensic Support Services

AINSLIE

Alan Broadwin
Principal
27 Pine Ridge Road
Larchmont, NY 10538-2616
Tel: (914) 833-2649
Fax: (914) 833-5037
E-mail: broadwin@ainslie.com
Web Site:
http://www.lawinfo.com/biz/ainslie

Specialties: Design and litigation consultant; Patent and Technology evaluation; Regulatory Compliance Assessment of ISO and GMP Quality Systems; Evaluation of adequacy of medical devices and disposables; Assistance in discovery and depositions as fact or expert witness; Engineering and due diligence investigations; Surgeon/hospital interface; Review of clinical/technical reports. **Degrees/licenses:** BA, BSME Columbia; MSIE Stevens; ASQ CQA; RAB cert. auditor; RAC.

See primary listing under MEDICINE & HEALTH: Medical Devices, Equip.

Gangs

Dr. Lewis Yablonsky, PhD

Emeritus Professor of Criminology
California State University - Northridge
2311 4th St., Ste. 312
Santa Monica, CA 90405
Tel: (310) 450-3697
Fax: (310) 450-3697
E-mail: expertwitness@lewyablonsky.com
Web Site: http://www.lewyablonsky.com

Specialties: Former Director, Crime Prevention program for Security in NYC sponsored by Columbia Univ. and others. Author of 17 books including the textbooks: "Criminology" (Harper Collins, 1990), "Gangsters" (NYU Press, 1997), and "Gangs In Court" (Lawyers & Judges Publishers, 2005). Expert witness in over 150 cases involving gang behavior, substance abuse, violence, family violence, company security/liability and related criminal subjects. Expert witness for corporations on legal/financial responsibility when crimes occurred on their property. Participated as an E-W in courts: LA, NY, AZ, Fla., San Jose, San Diego, San Francisco, Orange, Riverside, Sacramento, U.S. Federal. For complete resume, contact Dr. Lewis Yablonsky or check website (see above). **Degrees/licenses:** PhD, NYU; Calif. Licensed Therapist (#21997).

See primary listing under CRIMINOLOGY: Gangs

Jury Trial Consultants

Molly M. Murphy

Trial Consultant - Mediator
1541 Ocean Ave., 2nd Floor
Santa Monica, CA 90401
Tel: (310) 458-7720
Fax: (310) 458-7298
E-mail: mickeyslaw@yahoo.com
Web Site:
http://www.jury-trialconsultant.com

Specialties: Trial Consultant and Mediator with extensive consulting and expert witness experience in the following areas: Theme Development, Trial/Evidence Strategy; Preparation of Expert/Lay Witnesses; Mock Trials; Voir Dire Strategy; Jury Questions and Questionnaires; Jury Selection; Jury Monitoring and Post-Trial Interviews; Elmo System for Trial Presentation.. **Degrees/licenses:** Dispute Resolution Masters Program; Pepperdine U. Law School Mediation Training.

See primary listing under ARBITRATION/ MEDIATION: General

Paints & Coatings

Calcoast Labs / DL Labs, Inc.

D. Patrick Fairley, Pres. - Lab Director
Antoine Chamsi, VP Materials Chemistry
Thomas Sliva, VP - Tech. Direc. (DL Labs)
4072 Watts Street
Emeryville, CA 94608
Tel: (510) 652-2979
Fax: (510) 652-3085
E-mail: ccoastlabs@aol.com or
dllabs@aol.com
Web Site: http://www.calcoastlabs.com or
http://www.dllabs.com

DL Labs, Inc.
74 Kent Street
Brooklyn, NY 11222
Tel: (718) 383-5080
Fax: (718) 383-7445

Specialties: Calcoast Labs, Inc. of Emeryville, California, has acquired DL Labs of New York City, formerly David Litter Laboratories. The acquisition makes Calcoast/DL Labs one of the largest independent paint, coatings, sealant & materials testing laboratories in North America. The California/New York locations also provide for universal coverage of our domestic and foreign client base. We provide analytical & expert services to the legal community. DL Labs is accredited by NVLAP (Code 100252-0), CGSB, ISO/IEC25. Calcoast Labs is accredited by DEA & Los Angeles Department of Building & Safety. **Degrees/licenses:** BS, MS, PhD.

See primary listing under FAILURE ANALYSIS: Materials

Consolidated Research, Inc.

Darlene R. Brezinski, PhD
President
P.O. Box 2190
Kingsford, MI 49802
Tel: (906) 779-9498
Fax: (906) 779-9787
E-mail: darpaint@aol.com

Specialties: Consolidated Research is a technical consulting firm for the paint and coatings industry. Staff have career backgrounds with firms within the industry. These include raw materials suppliers, coatings manufacturers and end-use applicators. We offer expertise in paint, polymers, pigments, additives, failure analysis, liability, toxic issues, patent infringement, analysis and identification of paint, and expert witness services. **Degrees/licenses:** PhD, DABFE, FACFE.

See primary listing under CHEMISTRY/ CHEMICALS: Paints & Coatings

Personal Injury

Milton Bailey

18 Bayfield Rd.
Wayland, MA 01778
Tel: (508) 653-9489
Fax: (508) 653-9489
E-mail: milbbbb@hotmail.com
Web Site: http://www.baileystc.com

Specialties: Slip, trip & fall; Walkways; Ramps; Shoes; Safety shoes; Sports; Recreation; Dance floors; Mats & carpets;; Handicapped; Stairs; Escalators; Playing surfaces; Accident reconstruction; Accident analysis; Material evaluation; Foot protection; Roller skating rinks; Human factors; Ergonomics; Bathtubs; Showers; Grates; Ladders; Scaffolds; Review experts' work (Daubert, Kumho, Lanigan). Affiliation: Independent Consultant; AAA Arbitrator. **Degrees/licenses:** MS.

See primary listing under ACCIDENT RECONSTRUCTION: Slip & Fall

Petroleum

Robert C. Herr, III

Petroleum Engineer
P. O. Box 885
Mt. Vernon, IL 62864
Tel: (618) 244-5541
(618) 237-7101 (Cell)
E-mail: bobherr@mvn.net

Specialties: 35 years Petroleum Engineering and oilfield operations experience. Property evaluations for estates, divorce and business dissolution. Production and reservoir engineering. Arbitration and dispute resolution. Casualty loss and worker's compensation claim consulting. Drilling, completion, workover and production operations accident analysis. **Degrees/licenses:** BSME; Lic P. E., OK # 10271, IL # 062-039059.

See primary listing under ENGINEERING: Petroleum

Clement Mesavage, Jr.

Midstream Farm, LLC
3117 Stone Arbor Lane, Suite 1133
Glen Allen, VA 23050
Tel: (804) 262-6552
Fax: (804) 262-6555
E-mail: usaclem@erols.com
Web Site: http://www.usaclem.com

Specialties: Located near Washington, D. C. Over 25 years of consulting experience in environmental, health, safety, fire, explosion, variance, and facility security matters associated with petroleum & chemical storage and transfer; Completed work at over 500 bulk liquid, aboveground tank terminals ("tank farms") in 43 states; Has provided services to proprietary and for-hire terminal operators, private and government pipeline operators, the military, manufacturers, municipalities, and port authorities. Current services include performing due diligence site assessments, audits, permitting, and serving as expert witness concerning industry practices, equipment design, and regulatory and facility security matters. Please refer to website for additional information. **Degrees/licenses:** BSCE, MSCE, MPA, REA.

See primary listing under ENVIRONMENTAL: Aboveground Storage Tanks

ZymaX Forensics

Alan Jeffrey, PhD
Senior Geochemist
71 Zaca Lane
San Luis Obispo, CA 93401-7300
Tel: (800) 644-4696 ext.327
Fax: (805) 544-8226
E-mail: forensics@zymax.net
Web Site: http://www.zymax.net/327

Specialties: Environmental forensics and geochemistry consulting, litigation support and expert witness testimony. Specialties: petroleum hydrocarbon analysis, gas geochemistry, biomarkers, PNA's, PCB's, oxygenates, fuel ID, mixing ratios, age dating, metal analysis by ICP/MS, inorganic and wet chemistry, stable isotope analysis, hydrology. Developed analyses allow us to: identify the types of product which have been released, distinguish between similar products from different sources, estimate the mixing ratios of different products, estimate the age of the product, assign probable responsibility for sources of the contamination, and give expert witness testimony. **Degrees/licenses:** PhD in Chemical Oceanography.

See primary listing under ENVIRONMENTAL: Analytical Labs

Petroleum Products

Jewitt & Associates Fuels Technology

Carlton H. Jewitt
President
17572 Plumera Ln.
Fort Myers, FL 33917
Tel: (239) 731-2124
Fax: (239) 731-2124
E-mail: chjewitt@strato.net

Specialties: Thirty nine year career in petroleum fuels technology and technical services. Professional experience includes management, research, environmental, health and safety. Managed fuels technical services group providing support throughout Ashland Petroleum Division to key operating groups including Supply and Distribution, Trucks and Terminals, Refinery Sales, Marine, Pipeline, Bulk Plants and retail operations of Ashland and SuperAmerica. Conventional, reformulated, racing gasolines; diesel, aviation and renewable fuels; fuel oils. Ashland Petroleum representative (1/81 - 9/95) to the Coordinating Research Council Oil/Auto Research Committee. Former Chairman (6/85 - 12/95) ASTM Diesel Fuels Subcommittee. Accomplished technical writer. **Degrees/licenses:** BS Chemistry; ASTM & SAE Fuels Technical Committees.

See primary listing under PRODUCT LIABILITY: Petroleum Products

Police

ECJM Consultants, Inc.

Edward Mamet, CPP, CFE
Captain, New York City Police Dept. (Ret.)
P.O. Box 1559
Cooper Station
New York, NY 10276
Tel: (212) 475-8215
Fax: (646) 349-3238
E-mail: ecjm2@msn.com
Web Site:
http://member.expertpages.com/edmamet

Specialties: Retired New York City Police Department Captain Edward Mamet founded ECJM Consultants Inc. after completing forty years service. His group provides high quality police and security related issues. ECJM Consultants Inc. specializes in law enforcement and security liability matters, supporting both plaintiff and defense attorneys. ECJM consultants are retired New York City Police Department command level officers whose combined experience exceeds 125 years in law enforcement and security. Law enforcement areas include negligent investigation, excessive force, in-custody death, high speed chases, false arrest, police misconduct, negligent hiring, training, supervision and retention. **Degrees/licenses:** AAS, Police Science; BS, Criminal Justice; MPA.

See primary listing under LAW ENFORCEMENT: Police Practices/Procedures

R. Paul McCauley, PhD, BCFE

4620 Lucerne Road
Indiana, PA 15701
Tel: (724) 349-9676
Fax: (724) 349-6477
E-mail: mccauley@iup.edu

Specialties: Security and police malpractice; Assist defense and plaintiff attorneys in premise (crime) liability and police operations cases; Adequacy of security, crime foreseeability, personnel hiring and training, security policies and procedures; Police use of force, pursuits, policies and procedures, police standards, off-duty police working as security, false arrest;

(Listing continued on next page)

Police *(cont.)*

R. Paul McCauley (cont.)

Former security manager and Police Captain; Fulbright Scholar - Australia - police and security interaction. **Degrees/licenses:** PhD, Board Certified Forensic Examiner.

Thomas M. Walton

Thomas Walton - Expert Witness/Consultant
P. O. Box 3365
Barrington, IL 60011-3365
Tel: (847) 304-0285
Fax: (847) 304-0308
E-mail: marine2@comcast.net
Web Site: http://www.jmarshassoc.com

Specialties: Deputy Chief, Chicago Police Department, (Retired) with over 30 years experience in police operations, training and supervision. Highly experienced Expert in Police Standards, Procedures, Training and Supervision including but not limited to: Vehicle Pursuits; Emergency Response Driving; Search and Seizure; Investigative Detentions; Patrol/Investigative Procedures; Use of Force; Suicides in Police Custody; Sexual Harassment; Domestic Violence; First Aid; Swat Operations; Raids; Positional Asphyxia; Caring for Injured Parties; Felony Vehicle Stops; Road Blocks; Search Warrants; Private Security; Use of Pepper Spray; Field Sobriety Tests, ADA. Qualified Expert in Federal and State Courts. Retained in twenty states. **Degrees/licenses:** BA, MS; CPI (ILETSB), CPO.

See primary listing under LAW ENFORCEMENT: Police Practices/Procedures

Polygraph/Lie Detection

Brunette & Associates

Leo L. Brunette
Certified voice stress Analyst
P O Box 590
La Center, WA 98629-0590
Tel: (360) 263-2209
(360) 910-4770
E-mail: diogeneswest@tds.net
Web Site: http://www.truthsearch.net

Specialties: Mr. Brunette has 44 years law enforcement experience in both public and private sectors as well as 27 in voice stress analysis where he has worked with all voice stress systems. He is both a Polygrapher and voice stress analyst certified by the ISSA College of Analysts and qualified instructor in voice stress analysis. Currently the Vice President of Training for the Diogenes Company, he designed the latest high speed computerized systems on the market today, currently used by many Government agencies in the USA and the free world. **Degrees/licenses:** ISSA, CFE, KofC, Nebraska VSA, Lic. #24 since 1984.

Donald J. Imbordino

President
Imbordino Polygraph Examinations, LLC
3330 Cobb Pkwy., Ste. 17 - Box 359
Acworth, GA 30101
Tel: (678) 986-9600
Fax: (678) 574-6723
E-mail: dimbordino@earthlink.net
Web Site:
http://www.ImbordinoPolygraph.com

Specialties: Former federal polygraph supervisor with over 16 years of federal polygraph experience. (U.S. Department of Justice - Retired in 2003). Former Police Officer/Investigator. Adjunct Faculty Member with the Department of Defense Polygraph Institute. Director of Computerized Polygraph Training, Texas Department of Public Safety Polygraph School. Utilizes only state-of-the-art computerized polygraph systems. American Association of Police Polygraphists (AAPP) - Vice President. American Polygraph Association (APA) - Full Member. Georgia Polygraph

Association (GPA) - Past Vice President. Mr. Imbordino's professional goal is to provide his clients with accurate results they can rely on. Every polygraph examination is administered in a discreet and professional manner. **Degrees/licenses:** BS- Behavioral Science, Certified Examiner - AAPP.

Jack Trimarco

President
Jack Trimarco & Assoc.
Polygraph/Investigations, Inc.
9454 Wilshire Blvd., 6th Fl.
Beverly Hills, CA 90212-2900
Tel: (310) 247-2637
Fax: (760) 777-1836
E-mail: jtrimarco@aol.com
Web Site: http://www.jacktrimarco.com

Specialties: Host of Court TV's "Fake Out." Former manager of the Federal Bureau of Investigation's Polygraph Program in Los Angeles. Former Inspector General Polygraph Program - Department of Energy; Nationally known and respected Polygraph Expert. I have the credentials you would want when you have a client polygraphed, a case reviewed, a motion made regarding polygraph, or an in-depth professional investigation. My unique background allows me to bring the highest levels of service and expertise to any polygraph situation. **Degrees/licenses:** BS Psychology; Certified APA, AAPP, CAPE, AAFE.

Questioned Documents

Moore Document Laboratory

David S. Moore, BS, MEd
9010 Barrhill Way
Fair Oaks, CA 95628
Tel: (800) 989-3205
Fax: (916) 989-9674
E-mail: dmoore@mooredocs.com
Web Site: http://www.mooredocs.com

Specialties: All aspects of Forensic Questioned Documents, including: Identification of Signatures, Handwriting & Handprinting; Typewriter & Business Machine identification; Ink & Paper examinations; Examinations for Alterations, Indentations and Obliterations; Photography for Court Demonstration; Fully Equipped Document Laboratory & Reference Materials; Expert Testimony in excess of 575 times in more than 20 states in Civil & Criminal Trials, Administrative Hearings, Arbitrations and Depositions; CV & fee schedule upon request; 25+ years experience; Full-time private practice; Formerly employed in Questioned Document labs of U.S. Army, U.S. Postal Inspection Service and California Department of Justice. **Degrees/licenses:** Certified by ABFDE since 1978.

Farrell C. Shiver

Shiver & Nelson Document
Investigation Laboratory, Inc.
1903 Lilac Ridge Drive
Woodstock, GA 30189
Tel: (770) 517-6008
Fax: (678) 494-9283
E-mail: shiver@documentlab.com
Web Site: http://www.documentlab.com

Specialties: Former Chief Document Examiner, U.S. Army Crime Lab, Certified by the American Board of Forensic Document Examiners, Treasurer of the American Society of Questioned Document Examiners, member of the Questioned Document Section of the American Academy of Forensic Sciences. Handwriting comparison and forgery detection; Detection and decipherment of alterations; Decipherment of faint, faded, altered or obliterated entries; Identification of typewriters, photocopiers and other office machines; Nondestructive ink examination; Detection and decipherment of indented writing impressions; Typical cases - medical malpractice (alteration of medical record), signatures on documents, anonymous letters. **Degrees/ licenses:** BS, MS, Diplomate - ABFDE.

See primary listing under DOCUMENT EXAMINATION: General

Securities Fraud

Forensic Accounting Consultants, PC

Victor C. Moore, CPA
President
2904 White Oak Drive
Houston, TX 77007
Tel: (713) 426-3444
Fax: (713) 426-3031
E-mail: vmoore@facpc.com
Web Site: http://www.facpc.com

Specialties: Litigation consulting, forensic accounting, expert witness testimony, class-action securities fraud, derivative actions, damages calculations, business valuation. Extensive experience: SEC reporting, banking, trusts, mortgage companies, real estate, sub-prime lending, oil & gas, fiduciary conduct, pension plans, regulatory & statutory accounting, auditing & accounting malpractice, high-tech manufacturing, utilities, state & municipal governments, lost profits claims. **Degrees/licenses:** Firm Members Hold CPA, MSA, MA Licenses/Degrees.

See primary listing under ACCOUNTING: Forensic Accounting

Security

John H. Christman, CPP

Principal
John H. Christman - Security Consultant
2055 Oxford Ave.
Cardiff, CA 92007
Tel: (760) 632-1979
E-mail: john@securityexpert.com
Web Site: http://www.SecurityExpert.com

Specialties: Analysis of security/loss prevention programs and operations; Consultation; Expert opinion and testimony for all civil litigation involving PI claims resulting from security operations including shoplifting, investigations, dishonest employee terminations, guard operations & premises liability. Over thirty years management experience (VP level) in security, including department stores, supermarkets and drug stores. Former federal & local law enforcement. Published author and lecturer at college/security seminar/conference level. Twelve years on National Retail Federation LP Board of Directors. Member: American Society for Industrial Security and International Association of Professional Security Consultants. **Degrees/licenses:** BA, CPP, Licensed Private Investigator (CA).

See primary listing under SECURITY: General

Dalton Affiliates

Dennis R. Dalton, PhD
2280 Country Lane
Auburn, CA 95603
Tel: (530) 889-0588
Fax: (530) 889-9162
E-mail: daltonaffiliates@direcway.com

Specialties: Security expert in Premises Liability and Guard Operations; Mkts: Retail, Finance, Property Management and Entertainment; Assistance in Case Preparation; Discovery, Interrogatories, Depositions and Testimony; Former Corporate Security Manager and Police Officer; Nationally Known Consultant; Extensively Published; Frequent Lecturer; Numerous Awards; Professional Associations: ASIS, IAPSC and AMA. **Degrees/licenses:** BS, MA, PhD.

See primary listing under SECURITY: General

Thomas G. Davis

President
Security Litigation Group, Inc.
6099 Riverside Dr., Suite 102
Dublin, OH 43017
Tel: (614) 793-1614
Fax: (614) 793-1965
E-mail: thomdavis@securitylitigation.com
Web Site: http://www.securitylitigation.com

Specialties: Wide range of premises security and safety issues, including adequate/inadequate security/safety; negligent hiring, supervision and retention; management/policy concerns; violent criminal acts; contract security company operations; and alcohol-related incidents. His areas of expertise include lodging facilities, residential communities, office buildings, nightclubs/bars, senior living/nursing homes, childcare activities, hospitals, banks, casinos, racetracks, shopping/strip malls, parking facilities, universities/colleges, transportation companies, and retail establishments. Thom Davis has been retained as an expert in more than 350 cases in 45 states and the Caribbean since 1990. He has conducted several thousand safety/security evaluations of various properties and has been involved in law enforcement and safety and security management since 1971. **Degrees/licenses:** Certified Hotel Administrator (CHA), Certified Lodging Security Director (CLSD).

See primary listing under SECURITY: General

Lance R. Foster, CPP, CFE

Security Consultant
Security Associates, Inc.
619 Riviera Dr.
Tampa, FL 33606
Tel: (813) 254-3654
Fax: (813) 251-2210
E-mail: seccon@aol.com
Web Site: http://www.seccon.com

Specialties: Security management; premises liability; negligent security; banks; apartments; parking facilities; guard operations; retail stores; hotels; office buildings; restaurants; ATMs; malls; commercial properties; casinos; security equipment; special events; fraud. Former homicide detective, bank director of security and college criminology instructor. Practicing consultant. Highly qualified and experienced. Editorial advisor and contributing author to Hospitality Law newsletter. Certified as a protection professional (CPP) and fraud examiner (CFE). **Degrees/licenses:** BS-Law Enforcement & Security; MEd-Education.

See primary listing under SECURITY: General

David L. Johnston, CPP, CFE

301 N. Harrison St., Ste. 114
Princeton, NJ 08540
Tel: (800) 578-0997
Fax: (856) 786-6777
E-mail: dljcpp@comcast.net
Web Site:
http://www.expertpages.com/cv/johnston

Specialties: Negligence/Forseeability/adequacy of Security Matters involving Business, Industry and Higher Education - Specializing in College & University Security Operations; Warehousing & Distribution Centers; Manufacturing Operations; Parking Garages & Lots; Retail Security & Shoplifting; Apartment & Multi-Family Dwellings; Office Buildings & High-Rise; White Collar Crime/Internal Frauds & Defalcations; Pre-Employment Screening; Adequacy of Security Training; Disaster Management/Business Continuity; Sexual Harassment Matters. Thirty years experience as Director in major corporations and universities. **Degrees/licenses:** BS, MA, CPP, CFE, CDRP, PTS, PEA.

See primary listing under SECURITY: Premises Liability

R. Paul McCauley, PhD, BCFE

4620 Lucerne Road
Indiana, PA 15701
Tel: (724) 349-9676
Fax: (724) 349-6477
E-mail: mccauley@iup.edu

Specialties: Security and police malpractice; Assist defense and plaintiff attorneys in premise (crime) liability and police operations cases; Adequacy of security, crime foreseeability, personnel hiring and training, security policies and procedures; Police use of force, pursuits, policies and procedures, police standards, off-duty police working as security, false arrest; Former security manager and Police Captain; Fulbright Scholar - Australia - police and security interaction. **Degrees/licenses:** PhD, Board Certified Forensic Examiner.

See primary listing under LITIGATION SUPPORT: Police

Weather

Climatological Consulting Corporation

Contact: Lee E. Branscome, PhD, CCM
7338 155th Place North
Palm Beach Gardens, FL 33418
Tel: (561) 744-4889
Fax: (561) 744-5098
E-mail: lbranscome@ccc-weather.com
Web Site: http://www.ccc-weather.com

Specialties: Climatological Consulting Corporation, headed by Dr. Lee E. Branscome, specializes in forensic meteorology and climatology with an emphasis on aviation and marine weather, severe storms and hurricanes, floods, fog, air quality, and weather satellite and radar analysis. A staff of meteorologists in the Palm Beach Gardens, FL office is complemented by a nationwide team of Associates. Testifying experts are Certified Consulting Meteorologists by the American Meteorological Society. **Degrees/licenses:** MSs, PhDs, CCMs. Resumes available on request.
See primary listing under METEOROLOGY/ CLIMATOLOGY: General

Compu-Weather Experts, Inc.

2566 Route 52
Hopewell Junction, NY 12533
Tel: (800) 825-4445
Fax: (800) 825-4441
E-mail: experts@compuweather.com
Web Site: http://www.compuweather.com

Specialties: Admiralty, tides, lighting conditions, pollution, lightning strike verification, slip and fall cases, severe weather, climate analysis; Services: Official weather records, Plain-English written reports, Depositions, Site visits, Expert testimony; A complete forensic meteorology and expert service with twenty (20) professional meteorologists on staff; We offer fast efficient service, the most extensive in-house archive of past-weather records, and experienced experts to answer your questions and testify in "plain-English;" Rush service available. **Degrees/licenses:** BA, BS, MA, MS, PhD, Consulting Meteorologists.
See primary listing under METEOROLOGY/ CLIMATOLOGY: General

Cox Weather Services

Robert B. Cox
Consulting Meteorologist
125 Frisbie Street
Middletown, CT 06457
Tel: (888) 248-9347
Fax: (888) 248-9347
E-mail: bob@coxweatherservices.com
Web Site:
http://www.coxweatherservices.com

Specialties: Forensic meteorology - determining past weather conditions for any U. S. location. Involved in over 700 cases since 1999. Expert witness testimony. Customized weather forecasting. Broadcast meteorologist. **Degrees/licenses:** BS, Meteorology.

Expert Weather Investigations (EWI)

Thomas E. Downs,V
Forensic Meteorologist
450 Seventh Ave., Ste. 1308
New York, NY 10123
Tel: (212) 594-3348
Fax: (212) 629-5825
E-mail: info@expertweather.com
Web Site: http://www.expertweather.com

Specialties: Specialists in acquiring and analyzing past weather records (Establish liability or non-liability); Comprehensive reports and graphics using the latest scientific methods (Utilize demonstrative evidence); Highly competent testimony from qualified and credentialed experts (Maximize recovery). Meteorological assistance with Personal Injury/Slip & Fall, Auto accidents, Claim investigations, Construction delays, Structure damage, Agricultural losses, Working conditions, Health concerns, Audibility & Illumination conditions, etc. Scientific analysis of Snow, Ice, Rain, Wind, Extreme Cold and Heat, Fog, Thunderstorms, Hurricanes, Sun Angle, Air Pollution. Background affiliations: New York State Climatologist's Office, Northeast Regional Climate Center (NCDC/NOAA). **Degrees/licenses:** CCM, PhD, BS, MS, AMS, NYAS, NCIM; Cornell, MIT, NYU, CCNY, NWS.

See primary listing under METEOROLOGY/ CLIMATOLOGY: General

Falconer Weather Information Service, LLC

Phillip D. Falconer, CCM
7 Via Maria Drive
Scotia, NY 12302
Tel: (800) 428-5621
Fax: (518) 399-5320
E-mail: pfalcone@nycap.rr.com
Web Site: http://www.wxscape.com/FWIS

Specialties: Acquisition and analysis of past weather records; Evaluation of weather conditions relating to accidents; Preparation of easy-to-read, interpretive reports on weather incidents anywhere within the United States. Official weather record certification and rush services available. Previously qualified as expert meteorologist by both education (BS, Penn State, 1971; MS, University of Wisconsin, 1973) and over twenty-five years of professional experience and training. Numerous technical and popular articles and presentations on weather topics. Professional member: American Meteorological Society; National Council of Industrial Meteorologists. AMS Certified Consulting Meteorologist (no. 411). **Degrees/licenses:** BS, MS, CCM.

See primary listing under METEOROLOGY/ CLIMATOLOGY: General

Forensic Meteorology Associates, Inc.

Walter A. Lyons, PhD, CCM
President
46050 Weld County Road 13
Ft. Collins, CO 80524
Tel: (970) 568-7664
Fax: (970) 482-8627
E-mail: walt.lyons@forensic-weather.com
Web Site: http://www.forensic-weather.com

Specialties: Litigation support and expert witness; Reconstruction of weather events including lightning strike verification; Severe weather impacts: Tornadoes, microbursts, hurricanes and winter storms; Coastal and mountain meteorology; Local scale weather systems and microclimates; Air pollution and related issues; Extensive in-house weather data archives and technical library for fast responses; Technical communication to lay audiences; Advanced computer graphics, simulation and visualization facilities; Video presentations; Nationwide service. Member: National Council of Industrial Meteorologists; 35 years experience in university and industrial research and television weathercasting. DEGREES/LICENSES: PhD (University of Chicago); Certified Consulting Meteorologist (No. 163); Fellow and 2005 President of the American Meteorological Society. **Degrees/ licenses:** PhD, CCM. See Above.

See primary listing under METEOROLOGY/ CLIMATOLOGY: General

MET Associates

David L. Mitchell, PhD
Managing Director & Consulting Forensic Meteorologist
P.O. Box 70
Dayton, TX 77535-0070
Tel: (936) 257-1633 (office)
(713) 301-0242 (mobile)
Fax: (936) 258-4237
E-mail: mitchelldl@metassociates.net
Web Site: http://www.metassociates.net

Specialties: Forensic Meteorology, Air Quality Modeling and Weather Event Reconstruction and Analysis for insurance claims; Litigation Support Services and Expert Witness Testimony in the areas of Toxic Tort, Air Pollution Modeling, Weather related events including flooding, wind damage and weather related losses. David L. Mitchell is an authority on the numerical modeling of geophysical data with a doctorate in Meteorology from Purdue University. Dr. Mitchell has over 25 years of technical modeling experience in industry and consulting. He is an expert on Atmospheric Fluid Dynamics, Air Dispersion Modeling and Air Pollution Meteorology. He holds Texas Board of Professional Geoscientists License No. 1330. **Degrees/licenses:** PhD, MS, Purdue University; BS, Baylor University; Cert. Prof. Geoscientist.

See primary listing under METEOROLOGY/ CLIMATOLOGY: General

Weather *(cont.)*

Murray & Trettel, Inc.
Mark T. Carroll
Vice President/Consulting Meteorologist
600 N 1st Bank Drive, Ste A
Palatine, IL 60067-8185
Tel: (847) 963-9000 Ext. 130
Fax: (847) 963-0199
E-mail: mt@weathercommand.com
Web Site:
http://www.weathercommand.com

Specialties: Since 1946. Sixteen full-time meteorologists. Forensic meteorology specialists. Written "plain-English" opinions, depositions, site visits and expert testimony on all weather related incidents including but not limited to slip and fall, aviation, rail, vehicle, wind damage, etc. Climatological studies. Lightning verification, radar and satellite analysis. Staff includes members of the American Meteorological Society (AMS), National Weather Association, Midwestern Regional Climate Center Advisory Panel, Northern Illinois University Advisory Panel, Nuclear Utility Meteorological Users Group, Illinois Association of Environmental Professionals. **Degrees/licenses:** MS, BS.

See primary listing under METEOROLOGY/ CLIMATOLOGY: General

MACHINERY

Industrial Manufacturing

Frederick C. Kucklick
President
IMT Consulting, Inc.
21274 Sail Bay Drive
Cassopolis, MI 49031
Tel: (269) 445-8826
E-mail: kucklick@imtcusa.com
Web Site: http://www.imtcusa.com

Specialties: Engineering, Management and Litigation Support - Industrial Machinery and Complex Manufacturing Issues. My expertise is based on a mechanical engineering degree and over 25 years' ownership, top management, international sales, field startup, troubleshooting & installation, design engineering and project management positions with automotive component and heavy industrial machinery manufacturing companies in US and Europe. Cases handled include breaches of contracts (manufacturing production equipment and lines, vehicle components, failed joint venture), products liabilities (machine tools), trade secrets (machine designs, machine parts), bankruptcy administrative and transportation damage claims involving machine tools. **Degrees/licenses:** BSME.

MANAGEMENT/ BUSINESS CONSULTING

General

William P. Anthony, PhD, SPHR
Professor of Management
The Carl De Santis Professor of
Business Administration
Florida State University
College of Business
Tallahassee, FL 32306-1110
Tel: (850) 644-7844
Fax: (850) 644-0588
E-mail: banthon@cob.fsu.edu
Web Site: http://garnet.acns.fsu.edu/
~banthon/

Specialties: Consulting, advice and testimony in numerous areas of management strategy development, downsizing, organization design and strategy. Have published extensively and am involved on the side of both plaintiff and defendants on various cases. Major strength is policy development and implementation. **Degrees/licenses:** PhD, MBA, SPHR.

See primary listing under EMPLOYMENT: General

William H. Drumm, CMC

President & CEO
Establish, Inc./
Herbert W. Davis and Company
2200 Fletcher Ave.
Fort Lee, NJ 07024-5005
Tel: (201) 944-5580
Fax: (201) 944-2044
E-mail: william.drumm@establishinc.com
Web Site: http://www.establishinc.com

Specialties: Logistics Audits and Benchmarks; Logistics Network Design; Computer Modeling; Warehousing; Layouts; Labor Standards; Materials Handling; Operations Analysis; Cost Reduction Programs; Warehouse Handling Systems; Integrated Logistics Planning Design and Implementation; Logistics Manufacturing Planning; Business Change Analysis, Design and Facilitation; Quick Response Programs; Computer-Based Information Systems; Operations Research; Transportation; Rate and Cost Reductions; Transit Time Analysis and Auditing; Organizational Audits; Purchasing; Customer Service Surveys, Standards, Audits, Comparisons, and Measurements; Corporate Planning and Development; Marketing and Manufacturing Management; Make-to-Order Production Systems; Production and Inventory Control Audits; Manufacturing Reporting Systems; Distribution Planning and Management. **Degrees/licenses:** BE, MMS, CMC.

ForensisGroup, Inc.

Mercy Steenwyk
3452 E. Foothill Blvd., Ste. 1160
Pasadena, CA 91107
Tel: (626) 795-5000
(800) 555-5422
Fax: (626) 795-1950
E-mail: experts@forensisgroup.com
Web Site: http://forensisgroup.com

Specialties: Thousands of our clients have gained the technical advantage and the edge in their cases from our multidisciplined group of experts in hundreds of disciplines. We have some of the best and the brightest at competitive rates backed by 14 years of excellent track record and the support of our trained staff. We assist you until you have the right expert. Some of our areas of expertise are: Construction, Safety, Engineering, Product Liability, Accident Reconstruction, Automotive, Environmental, Slip & Fall, Appraisal, Medical and other scientific disciplines. Unsurpassed standards. Clients actively evaluate our experts. **Degrees/licenses:** PE, GC, CSP, PhD, MD, GC, CIH, AIA.

See primary listing under ACCIDENT PREVENTION & SAFETY: General

Jeffrey D. Schaffer

232 W. Kenilworth Street
New Orleans, LA 70124
Tel: (504) 482-8051
Fax: (504) 280-3189
E-mail: jschaffe@uno.edu

Specialties: Hotel & motel operations; Restaurant; Foodservice operations; Bar operations; Tourism operations; Sanitation; Safety; Contracts; Franchising; Training; Dram Shop Issues. Affiliation: School of Hotel, Restaurant & Tourism Administration, College of Business Administration, University of New Orleans (Professor). Degrees and Licenses: BA (Hotel, Restaurant & Institutional Management); CHA (Certified Hotel Administrator, American Hotel & Motel Association); FMP (Foodservice Management Professional, National Restaurant Association). **Degrees/ licenses:** PhD (Business Policy/Strategic Management); MBA (Finance).

See primary listing under HOTEL/RESTAURANT INDUSTRY: General

Automotive

J.A. "Doc" Watson

P.O. Box 758
Humble, TX 77347
Tel: (281) 540-8257
Fax: (281) 446-5212
E-mail: theautoexpert@aol.com
Web Site: http://www.theautoexpert.com

Specialties: Automotive consumer fraud, deceptive trade practices. Opinions, depositions and testimony which have led to successful solutions in mediation, arbitration, pre-trial

(Listing continued on next page)

Automotive *(cont.)*

J. A. "Doc" Watson (cont.)

settlements and trials. Ten+ years' experience expert witness plaintiff and defense. Expertise - sales and finance tactics, leasing, diminished value, rebates, curbstoning, odometers, repossession, salvage, credit procedures, vehicle appraisals, mechanical and body repair fraud, previous damage, trucks, lemon law, title kiting, program cars, bad credit, service contracts, life and accident & health policies, auto auctions, wholesaling, manufacturers' warranties, lender fraud, flood damage, class action, personal injury. 40+ years automotive employment history.

See primary listing under APPRAISAL & VALUATION: Vehicles

Manufacturing, Indust. Engineering

Ganstech Associates, LLC

Leo Gans
President
1044 East Lawn Court
Teaneck, NJ 07666
Tel: (201) 833-1529
Fax: (201) 833-0807
E-mail: LeoGans@aol.com

Specialties: Plastic Extrusion/Corporate Management - Former CEO international multiplant plastic extrusion manufacturer; Intimate familiarity with precision tubing, cast & blown film, extruded profiles, corrugated hose, compounding, cross-head & coextrusion; Supplied medical device, writing instrument, packaging, automotive, swimming pool, appliance and other industries; Operation of private/public manufacturers - personnel, commercial and technical issues; Served on corporate Boards of Directors; Quality matters/ISO 9000/Clean room; Patent development, licensing, & litigation; Product design, compound selection, & process development; Instructor plastic extrusion, manufacturing technology, and quality; Extrusion product patents & publications; Expert witness and consultant. **Degrees/licenses:** BS/MS Chemical Engineering, Licensed Prof. Engr. (PE).

See primary listing under ENGINEERING: Plastics

MANUFACTURED HOUSING INDUSTRY

General

Dan M. Pate

President
Dan Pate Enterprises, Inc.
P.O. Box 691991
Tulsa, OK 74169-1991
Tel: (918) 234-2556
Fax: (918) 234-2556
E-mail: DanPateInc@aol.com

Specialties: Litigation, Arbitration, Mediation as Expert Witness in Manufactured Home (mobilehome) cases; Technical assistance for depositions; Inspections of factory-built homes; Investigation of transportation, foundation and installation issues; Inspections of delivery sites; Assessment of warranty repairs by industry standards; Certified manufactured housing appraisals. Thirty-year veteran of manufactured housing (mobilehome) industry as retailer, transporter, installer, inspector and consultant. Experienced in recovery and refurbishing of repossessed manufactured homes. State Licensed Mechanical Contractor, Certified Home Installation Technician, Specialized Training in installation per ANSI 225.1 code, Certified by National Society of Appraiser Specialists.

MARITIME & ADMIRALTY

General

Fisher Maritime Consulting Group

Dr. Kenneth W. Fisher
President
147 Columbia Tpke., #203
Florham Park, NJ 07932
Tel: (800) 732-3476
(973) 660-1116
Fax: (973) 660-1144
E-mail: email@fishermaritime.com
Web Site: http://www.fishermaritime.com

Specialties: Ships, Offshore, Workboats, Barges, Inland, Boating; Design, Construction, Conversion, Repair, Dismantling; Shipyard Site Contamination, Marinas, Asbestos, Personal Watercraft. We assist owners and shipyards in developing, asserting and rebutting ship construction, conversion and repair claims. We analyze operational casualties and personal injury claims including allegations of unseaworthiness, negligent vessel design or operations, product failures, collisions, explosions, improper construction and maintenance in boat and marine accidents. We provide analytical defensive support for marine equipment manufacturers, and we assist plaintiffs to establish a basis for recovery of losses stemming from manufacturers of defective products. **Degrees/licenses:** Naval Architects, MSc, PhD, USCG Licensed.

Don Green

Marine Consultant
KDON Marine Consulting
8876 Gulf Freeway, Ste. 120
Houston, TX 77017
Tel: (713) 944-0966
(800) 444-3926
(281) 414-1954
Fax: (713) 944-2546
E-mail: don@kdoncorp.com
Web Site: http://www.kdoncorp.com

Specialties: Nationally recognized maritime expert. Retired Coast Guard Commander. Marine accident reconstruction, marine investigations, Coast Guard rules and regulations, boating accidents, collisions, allisions, fires, personal injuries. Litigation support. Accepted as a marine safety expert in federal and state courts. **Degrees/licenses:** MA, BS, Master 1600 Tons Oceans; Second Mate.

Edward L. Guess, PE

Principal
Alpha Design & Engineering
2707 N. Xenophon Ave.
Tulsa, OK 74127
Tel: (918) 695-0618
Fax: (918) 582-9553
E-mail: eguess@galstar.com
Web Site:
http://www.guessengineering.com

Specialties: Heating, Ventilation, Air Conditioning (HVAC), Failure analysis, Pressure vessels, pumps and pumping systems, construction, lighting/illumination, pipelines, petroleum, noise, vibration, boat and system design, valves, fire protection, electrical systems-worked in the Power, Oil and Architectural/Engineering Industries. Services to Legal Profession include information for legal briefs investigations, research, depositions, court appearances, arbitration. **Degrees/licenses:** BSME, MSME, PE.

See primary listing under ENGINEERING: General

General *(cont.)*

Hector V. Pazos, PE

Ocean-Oil Expert Witness, Inc.
& Yachts Unlimited, Inc.
P.O. Box 47188
St. Petersburg, FL 33743-7188
Tel: (727) 347-2556
(504) 367-4072
Fax: (727) 343-9717 or (504) 367-3790
E-mail: Oceanoilpazos@cs.com or
Hectorpazos75597@aol.com
Web Site: http://www.siterrific.com/pazos

Specialties: Expert Witness; Maritime accident reconstruction; Personal injury; Slip and fall; Inclined and vertical ladders; Safety; Product liability; Design and latent defects; Structural and equipment failure; Fires and explosions; Power and sail pleasure boats; Passenger and cargo vessels; Offshore platforms; Drilling rigs; Pipelines; Barges and tugboats; Floating cranes; Container ships; Dredges; Fishing vessels; Noise and vibrations; Diving accidents; Human errors regarding vessel design, construction and operations; Marine surveying; Expert reports. Expert witness testimony provided in over 400 cases and analysis and/or investigation participation in over 1,200 cases. Boat owner and operator. **Degrees/licenses:** MS Naval Architect, Marine & Mechanical Engineer, PE.

Mike Russell, U.S. Coast Guard (Ret)

Turnaround Maritime Services
P.O. Box 580128
Houston, TX 77258-0128
Tel: (281) 326-3191
Fax: (281) 326-3191
E-mail: MRuss6@aol.com

Specialties: Code of Federal Regulations, Coast Guard policies & regulations, marine industry standards, tankship, towboat, barge, passenger, airboat, amphibious & barge fleeting operations; tankship & tank barge pollution prevention & safety. Case review of vessel, longshoreman & stevedore personal injuries, marine collisions, fires, explosions, groundings, sinkings, boating, offshore platform & drilling rig incidents. Eighteen years in marine safety. Enforced Coast Guard regulations as former Chief, Inspections & Investigations. Reviewed over 760 marine casualties & personal injuries. Former towboat company safety director. Accepted as an expert in both state & federal courts. **Degrees/licenses:** BS.

Alan M. Steinman, MD, MPH

Rear Admiral (Ret.), USCG/USPHS
1135 Harrington Place
DuPont, WA 98327
Tel: (253) 229-4088
Fax: (253) 964-3549
E-mail: asteinman@aol.com

Specialties: Drowning, hypothermia, sea survival, maritime medicine, water survival, protective clothing, cold water immersion, water rescue, safety investigation, life jackets, life rafts; past Surgeon General of the U.S. Coast Guard; developed cold water survival time charts for USCG; widely published in areas of sea survival and hypothermia; chapter on immersion hypothermia in leading textbook of emergency medicine; lectures in drowning, hypothermia and sea survival; Board Certified in Occupational Medicine; MD from Stanford University; post-graduate training at Mayo Clinic and University of Washington; experience as expert witness in both state and federal courts. **Degrees/licenses:** MD, MPH, FACPM.

See primary listing under MEDICINE & HEALTH: Occup./Environ. Medicine

Capt. Mitchell S. Stoller

President
MAREX
30021 Tomas St., Ste. 300
Rancho Santa Margarita, CA 92688
Tel: (949) 858-5475
Fax: (949) 858-5477
E-mail: marexco@aol.com

Specialties: Expert Witness to the marine industry. Experience in Federal and State court, judicial arbitration, mediation services, and represents both plaintiff and defense. Consultant to the United States Coast Guard. Captain Stoller is the President and founder of

Marex, a marine consulting company designed to market the safety expertise that enabled him to become the youngest captain of Exxon Shipping Company, U.S.A. He also holds an outstanding tanker safety operational record both at the Company and as a Los Angeles Harbor Pilot. Capt. Stoller has written and/or consulted on Safety and procedural manuals for numerous shipping companies and has been retained in over 800 blue/brown water cases across the nation from jet skis to pleasure crafts to super tankers. **Degrees/licenses:** Unlimited Master Mariner's Lic., Extensive Pilotage Lic., BS Nautical Sci.

Trident Marine Safety Associates

Henry S. Woods III
16850 Saturn Lane, #100
Houston, TX 77058
Tel: (281) 486-4552
Fax: (281) 486-9295
E-mail: hsw123@earthlink.net
Web Site:
http://www.tridentmarinesafety.com

P.O. Box 435
East Boothbay, ME 04544
Tel: (800) 580-BUOY

Specialties: Litigation support services for plaintiff and defense counsel and insurers in the following areas: Accident causation; Boating safety; Marine safety; Marine standards/codes/regulations; Rules of the Road ("right-of-way" issues); Collisions; Groundings; Hazards to navigation; Cargo loss/damage; Coast Guard regulations; Carbon monoxide poisoning; Jetski accidents; Water skiing accidents. **Degrees/licenses:** BS, MS.

See primary listing under ACCIDENT RECONSTRUCTION: Marine

Consulting

Capt. Hugh M. Stephens, CSP, PE

President
Nautical Holdings Corp.
464 Main St., Suite 307
Port Washington, NY 11050
Tel: (516) 944-9600 (Winter)
(207) 622-9409 (Summer)
(504) 812-3786 (Cell)
E-mail: stephenssos2@aol.com

Specialties: Commercial merchant vessels, including supply, ROV and "frac" boats and ferries, Dynamic Positioning/Recreational Boating/Motion picture accident/Personal injury investigation. Collisions, Marine tankers, Confined space/Rescue/Slips/Falls, Marina casualties. Pres./Founder Marine Safety Engineering Firm. Positions in steamship industry: V.P. Operations, Marine Mgr., Marine Supt., Port Captain. Dredging & Repair Supt. Yacht Broker/Manager. Chartering Supervisor, Universal Marine Executive, Kevin Costner's feature film "Waterworld." Vice President No. Atl., Council American Master Mariners. Member Natl. Cargo Bureau, Commodore, Cobbosseecontee Yacht Club, Manchester, ME, Standing Committee Marine Society - NY. Certified Safety Professional, Professional Engineer - Safety Engineering (CA). **Degrees/licenses:** USCG Unlimited Ocean Master & First Class Pilot, Radar Operator, STCW95, GMDSS.

Towboats & Barges

Mike Russell, U.S. Coast Guard (Ret)

Turnaround Maritime Services
P.O. Box 580128
Houston, TX 77258-0128
Tel: (281) 326-3191
Fax: (281) 326-3191
E-mail: MRuss6@aol.com

Specialties: Code of Federal Regulations, Coast Guard policies & regulations, marine industry standards, tankship, towboat, barge, passenger, airboat, amphibious & barge fleet-

(Listing continued on next page)

Towboats & Barges *(cont.)*

Mike Russell (cont.)
ing operations; tankship & tank barge pollution prevention & safety. Case review of vessel, longshoreman & stevedore personal injuries, marine collisions, fires, explosions, groundings, sinkings, boating, offshore platform & drilling rig incidents. Eighteen years in marine safety. Enforced Coast Guard regulations as former Chief, Inspections & Investigations. Reviewed over 760 marine casualties & personal injuries. Former towboat company safety director. Accepted as an expert in both state & federal courts. **Degrees/licenses:** BS.

See primary listing under MARITIME & ADMIRALTY: General

U.S. Coast Guard

Mike Russell, U.S. Coast Guard (Ret)
Turnaround Maritime Services
P.O. Box 580128
Houston, TX 77258-0128
Tel: (281) 326-3191
Fax: (281) 326-3191
E-mail: MRuss6@aol.com

Specialties: Code of Federal Regulations, Coast Guard policies & regulations, navigation Rules of the Road, marine industry standards, tankship, towboat, barge, passenger, airboat, amphibious & barge fleeting operations; tankship & tank barge pollution prevention & safety. Case review of vessel, longshoreman & stevedore personal injuries, marine collisions, fires, explosions, groundings, sinkings, boating, offshore platform & drilling rig incidents. Eighteen years in marine safety. Enforced Coast Guard regulations as former Chief, Inspections & Investigations. Reviewed over 760 marine casualties & personal injuries. Former towboat company safety director. Accepted as an expert in both state & federal courts. **Degrees/licenses:** BS.

See primary listing under MARITIME & ADMIRALTY: General

MARKETING

General

Robert A. Grayson, PhD
President
Grayson Associates
30728 Paseo Elegancia
San Juan Capistrano, CA 92675-5426
Tel: (949) 487-9970
Fax: (949) 487-9975
E-mail: bob@graysonassociates.com
Web Site:
http://www.marketingexpertwitness.com

136 East 56th Street
New York, NY 10022
Tel: (212) 688-6175

Specialties: Internationally known marketing consultant: 35 years experience, big and little companies, Fortune 500, advertising agency/marketing company experience, prof. Graduate School, author, publisher, lecturer. Specialty: consumer products, services. Expert testimony: advertising, promotion, trademark, packaging, acquisitions, all marketing mix. **Degrees/licenses:** MBA, PhD.

Performance Analysis Group, Inc.
Richard Shain, President
Pamela Shain, Managing Director
100 Wells Ave., Ste 202
Newton, MA 02459-3210
Tel: (617) 244-5700
Fax: (617) 527-2422
E-mail: richard@pag-adsave.com
Web Site: http://www.pag-adsave.com

Specialties: Determination of advertising and marketing effectiveness. Advertising/Media Auditing. Specializing in Spot TV, Network Television, Cable, Radio, Magazines, Newspapers; Evaluation of budgets and plans; Billing reconciliations, audience delivery evaluations; Customized analysis. A nationally recognized firm with a broad range of industry experience auditing many market leaders. Experience in many industries including pharmaceuticals, entertainment, automotive, financial, and fast foods. Legal references available. Principals are former senior level advertising and media executives at top advertising agencies and multi-national corporations with extensive industry knowledge. **Degrees/licenses:** BA - Math, BS - Economics, MBA - Marketing Program.

See primary listing under ADVERTISING: General

Manufacturers' Representative

Glen Balzer

President
New Era Consulting
11550 Magdalena Ave.
Los Altos, CA 94024
Tel: (650) 917-0703
Fax: (650) 618-8692
E-mail: glenbalzer@msn.com

Specialties: Representative agreements, manufacturers' representatives, distribution agreements, industrial distributors; Domestic and international marketing and sales; Integration and rationalization of merged and acquired companies; Mr. Balzer has been involved in all aspects of establishing, upgrading and managing marketing and sales organizations throughout America, Europe and Asia. Expert witness in deposition and arbitration testimony. Published as author regarding representative and distributor agreements. Director, Forensic Expert Witness Association. **Degrees/licenses:** BSEE, MBA.

MARKETING RESEARCH

General

Cogan Research Group

Dr. Sandra R. Cogan
President
3528 Torrance Blvd., Ste. 219
Torrance, CA 90503
Tel: (310) 316-4289
Fax: (310) 316-4939
E-mail: scogan@coganresearch.com
Web Site: http://coganresearch.com

Specialties: Conducts, critiques, and acts as an expert witness on surveys. Survey types: trademark; likelihood of confusion, secondary meaning, genericness, dilution; design patent infringement; misleading advertising; defamation of character; copyright infringement; and right of publicity. Has conducted over 150 surveys for trademark and unfair competition cases and testified in state and federal court. Taught Marketing at Loyola Marymount University, Cal State University Dominguez Hills, Pepperdine University; Taught Marketing Research at UCLA Extension. Teaches California State Bar accredited seminar, "Survey Research for Trademark Cases." **Degrees/ licenses:** BS, Marketing; MBA, Doctorate of Business Admin.

MATERIALS HANDLING

General

Frederick G. Heath

Principal
Heath and Associates
3316 Springcrest Drive
Louisville, KY 40241
Tel: (502) 425-2385
Fax: (502) 339-0729
E-mail: fgheath@bellsouth.net
Web Site: www.heathandassociates.com

Specialties: Expert services covering industrial machines, lifts, hoists, jacks, cranes and material handling equipment. Heath and Associates draws on 40 years of engineering, manufacturing and management experience to provide services relating to product safety analysis and planning, accident investigation and reconstruction, product design, documentation and cost reduction and quality assurance and manufacturing. Heath and Associates can assist in product evaluations, testing, compliance with applicable standards, compliance with applicable regulations (OSHA, EPA & DOT), adequacy of instructional materials and labeling, development of explanatory exhibits and preparation of evidence for trial. **Degrees/ licenses:** BSME, CHMM, CSS.

See primary listing under ACCIDENT RECONSTRUCTION: Lifting Equipment

Conveyors & Conveyor Systems

Loeffler Engineering Group

Frank J. Loeffler Jr.
Principal
20511 Haighland Lake Drive
Lago Vista, TX 78645-6633
Tel: (512) 267-8700
Fax: (512) 267-2547
E-mail: frank@loefflerengineering.com
Web Site: http://loefflerengineering.com

Specialties: Over 38 years experience with major belt conveyor and bulk materials handling systems suppliers. Includes systems for power generation, mining, aggregates, grain terminals, steel plants, aluminum plants, minerals processing, pulp & paper, ports, shipping terminals, cement plants and petroleum coke handling in oil refineries. Experience in legal services includes: forensic engineering, trial testimony, depositions and litigation support for cases involving personnel injury, product liability, restraint of trade and real estate asset appraisal. We have worked for the plaintiff and defense. Member Houston Materials Handling Society, CEMA, ASME Committee B20, SME. **Degrees/licenses:** BS Mech. Engr., Newark College of Engr.; Prof. Engineer (TX, LA, NJ, PA & AL).

Machine Guarding

Loeffler Engineering Group

Frank J. Loeffler Jr.
Principal
20511 Haighland Lake Drive
Lago Vista, TX 78645-6633
Tel: (512) 267-8700
Fax: (512) 267-2547
E-mail: frank@loefflerengineering.com
Web Site: http://loefflerengineering.com

Specialties: Over 38 years experience with major belt conveyor and bulk materials handling systems suppliers. Includes systems for power generation, mining, aggregates, grain terminals, steel plants, aluminum plants, minerals processing, pulp & paper, ports, shipping terminals, cement plants and petroleum coke handling in oil refineries. Experience in legal services includes: forensic engineering, trial testimony, depositions and litigation support for cases involving personnel injury, product liability, restraint of trade and real estate asset appraisal. We have worked for the plaintiff and defense. Member Houston Materials Handling Society, CEMA, ASME Committee B20, SME. **Degrees/licenses:** BS Mech. Engr., Newark College of Engr.; Prof. Engineer (TX, LA, NJ, PA & AL).

See primary listing under MATERIALS HANDLING: Conveyors & Conveyor Systems

MATERIALS SCIENCE

General

Metallurgy/Materials Consulting

David J. Dunn
Metallurgical Consultant
930 Mountain View Drive
Leadville, CO 80461
Tel: (719) 486-0838
Fax: (719) 486-3244
E-mail: glendavedunn@aol.com

Specialties: Failure Analysis, on-site investigation, materials testing, materials specification, warranty investigations; pertaining to steel and cast iron subjected to wear, fracture, and corrosion; Emphasis on alloys used in mining, earth moving, mineral processing. Forty years continuous experience serving clients worldwide. Read, write, speak Spanish. Travel anywhere. Metallurgical Engineering Degree, Colorado School of Mines, 1959. **Degrees/licenses:** Metallurgical Engr. Deg., Colorado School of Mines, 1959.

Read Consulting, LLC

1435 Fulton Rd.
Santa Rosa, CA 95403
Tel: (707) 544-2374
E-mail: lread@sonic.net
Web Site: http://www.readconsulting.com

Specialties: Glass failure; Patent expertise; Plastic failures; Fatigue; Rubber Failures; Metallurgy; Corrosion; Manufacturing processes; Failure analysis; Product liability; Quality control; Product failure analysis; Wood failures; Wire Cable failures; Electrical connections, Tempered glass; Vacuum coating; Thin Film coating; Product design; Accident reconstruction; Bottle failures; Window failures; Manufacturing qualification testing; Food safety; Food processing; Canning. **Degrees/licenses:** PhD, PE.

RJ Lee Group, Inc.

5 Nationwide locations:
CA, NY, PA, VA, WA
Keith Rickabaugh
Director of Sales and Marketing
350 Hochberg Road
Monroeville, PA 15146
Tel: (800) 860-1775
(724) 325-1776
Fax: (724) 733-1799
E-mail: krickabaugh@rjlg.com
Web Site: http://www.rjlg.com

Specialties: COMPANY INFORMATION: Independent laboratory and consulting group specializing in application of instrumental techniques to solve problems. Over 250 employees and 20 years litigation support experience. FAILURE ANALYSIS: materials, metals, polymers, and ceramics. CONSTRUCTION MATERIALS/DEFECT IDENTIFICATION: concrete and cement, aggregates, and fill materials. FORENSICS: gun shot residue, hair, fiber, and other trace evidence. ENVIRONMENTAL: disaster/impact assessment and remediation, receptor modeling, particulate characterization, air and dust analysis, and diesel particulate characterization. EXPANDED SERVICES: auger spectroscopy (AES), optical and electron microscopy (SEM & TEM), inorganic chemistry (AA/ICP & X-ray diffraction), organic chemistry (GC-ECD, GC-FID, GC/MS, FTIR & HPLC), thermal analysis (TGA, DSC, DTA), industrial hygiene, asbestos, silica, method development, product testing, software development, x-ray photoelectron spectroscopy, x-ray diffraction, and x-ray fluorescence (XPS, XRD, XRF). **Degrees/licenses:** BS, CIH, CSP, MA, MBA, MS, MSFS, PE, PhD; AIHA & NVLAP + Other Accred.

See primary listing under FAILURE ANALYSIS: General

Abrasives; Brick & Clay; Ceramics; Etc.

E. Dow Whitney

Vice President; Professor Emeritus
Materials Consultants, Inc.
University of Florida
2016 NW 18th Lane
Gainesville, FL 32605
Tel: (352) 846-3783
Fax: (352) 846-3355
E-mail: ewhit@mse.ufl.edu

Specialties: Failure analysis of glass & ceramic products including grinding wheels re: technical aspects of products liability litigation. Slip and fall litigation. **Degrees/licenses:** PhD; PE; Certified Manufacturing Engineer.

MEDICAL-LEGAL

General

Accredited Psychiatry & Medicine

Harvard Medical School Alumni
& Faculty Experts
Tel: (617) 492-8366
Fax: (617) 441-3195
E-mail: harold_bursztajn@hms.harvard.edu
Web Site: http://www.forensic-psych.com

Specialties: Psychiatry, Forensic Psychiatry, Legal Medicine & Analysis, Managed Care, Testamentary Capacity, Addiction, Product Liability, Neuropsychiatric, Medical Employment & Discrimination, Toxic Torts, Independent Medical Examinations & Testing, Professional Ethics, Expert Testimony, Custodial Issues, Criminal Justice & Public Safety, Diminished Capacity, PTSD. Plaintiff and defense expert with local and national references. Over twenty five years of service as a distinguished patient care-focused clinician and as senior clinical faculty at Harvard Medical School; Co-Director of the Program in Psychiatry and the Law and Associate Professor of Psychiatry at the Harvard Medical School. **Degrees/licenses:** BA, MD, Lic.: MA, NH, National Dual Medical Board Certification.

See primary listing under PSYCHIATRY: General

William D. Barnhart, MD, MBA, FACP, FACFE

Internal Medicine/Geriatrics
2625 Harlem Blvd.
Rockford, IL 61103
Tel: (815) 962-4299
Fax: (815) 965-8641
E-mail: wbarnh9400@aol.com
Web Site: www.dr-barnhart.yourmd.com

Specialties: Twenty years experience in medical malpractice, personal injury and Workers' Compensation - defense and plaintiff. Medical Educator and practitioner in internal medicine, primary care, preventive medicine, clinical ethics and clinical geriatrics. Active medical school faculty member. Extensive trial experience and skills in discovery and evidence depositions. Member - ASIM, AMA, ACLM, ASLME, ACFM, and other national organizations. Presenter nationally, in medical ethics and law for physicians. Fellow of the Institute of Medicine of Chicago, the American College of Physicians, and the American College of Forensic Examiners. **Degrees/licenses:** MD, MBA, FACP, BCME, BCFM, FACFE.

Robert G. Brueckner, MPH, LCHE

President
Health Care Administration
Legal Consultants
3131 Westberry Square, Ste. E
Joplin, MO 64804
Tel: (417) 623-5650
Fax: (417) 623-5650
E-mail: bbrueckner@earthlink.net
Web Site:
http://www.healthcarelegalconsulting.com

Specialties: Over 30 years experience in health care executive management, including CEO of two large nonprofit community/tertiary hospitals. Masters Degree in Public Health/Health Care Administration, UC - Berkeley. Plaintiff and Defense. Extensive experience in JCAHO; Operating Policies, Procedures, and Standards of Care; Physician Credentialing, Privileges, and Peer Review; Hospital and Medical Staff Bylaws, Rules and Regulations; Physician Contracts; Third-party Payor/Managed Care Relationships; EMTALA; Hospital/Physician Joint Ventures; Hospital/System Affiliations. Assistance in Case Screening for Merit; Identification of Issues; Case Development; Depositions; Trial Testimony. Life Diplomate, American College of Healthcare Executives. **Degrees/licenses:** BA, MPH, LCHE.

Andrew A. Dahl, MD, FACS

President
Ophthalmic Consultants
1 Gus Siko Rd.
Poughkeepsie, NY 12601
Tel: (845) 471-7808
Fax: (845) 471-7640
E-mail: AndrewDahl@pol.net
Web Site: www.andrewdahl.yourmd.com

Specialties: Alpha Omega Alpha Medical Honor Society. Former Faculty, Harvard Medical School. Twenty five years practice of Ophthalmology and Ophthalmic Surgery. Twenty-five years experience in forensic eye cases including medical malpractice and product liability. Medical record review and expert witness services. Chairman, Medical Society Peer Review Committee; Chairman, Institutional Review Board. **Degrees/licenses:** BA, MD, FACS, FAAO.

See primary listing under MEDICINE & HEALTH: Ophthalmology

Cadvan O. Griffiths Jr., MD, LLB, FCLM

11645 Wilshire Blvd., Ste. 600
Los Angeles, CA 90025-6807
Tel: (310) 477-5558
Fax: (310) 274-7564
E-mail: cadvan@aol.com
Web Site: http://www.plasticsurgery.org

Specialties: Medical-legal consultation and malpractice review related to cosmetic and reconstructive surgery; Head, neck, hands, and extremities; QME; IME; AME; Certified American Board of Plastic Surgery; Certified Medical Review Officer; Member International Society of Aesthetic Plastic Surgery; Society of Head and Neck Surgeons; American Society of Plastic and Reconstructive Surgeons; American Arbitration Association; Society of Surgical Oncologists; Assoc. member American Bar Association; Consumer Attorney's Assn. **Degrees/licenses:** MD, LLB, FCLM.

See primary listing under MEDICINE & HEALTH: Plastic & Reconstructive Surgery

Healthcare Litigation Support

PO Box 833
Petersham, MA 01366
Tel: (978) 724-0299
E-mail: pgeorge@healthcarelitigation.com
Web Site: www.healthcarelitigation.com

Specialties: A team of experts (not a referral service)-physicians, healthcare administrators, reimbursement specialists, health organization experts, health insurance experts, and other healthcare personnel-with broad, extensive experience and expertise in medical and administrative malpractice issues, physician practice operations, hospital management, health insurance and TPA issues, Medicare and Medicaid, medical billing and collections, fraud and abuse, managed care and other areas. Review case for merit, analyze medical and administrative events, identify causation, address standards of care, and articulate complex issues to triers of fact. Additional offices Toledo, Kansas City and Washington, D. C. **Degrees/licenses:** MD, JD, MPH; JD; PhD; BA.

General *(cont.)*

Kathleen M. Martin, RN, MSN, MPA, LNHA

368 White Oak Ridge Road
Short Hills, NJ 07078
Tel: (973) 912-9154
Fax: (973) 912-9702
E-mail: martgatt@yahoo.com
Web Site:
http://www.jurispro.com/KathleenMartin

Specialties: Long Term Care nursing; general nursing; geriatrics; assisted living; Nursing standards & documentation; JCAHO, ANA, and State Dept. of Health standards; wound care issues; falls; physical & chemical restraint; clinical & managerial experience; Cert. In Life Care Planning; expert testimony, deposition and trial experience over 16 years. Affiliation: Plaza Regency at Park Ridge, NJ. Administrator/Corporate Executive. Licensed LTC Administrator-NJ-5yrs. RN 27 years. **Degrees/licenses:** RN; MSN; MPA (Master in Public (Health Care) Admin).

See primary listing under MEDICINE & HEALTH: Nursing

Medstuff

William W. Filler, Jr., MD, FACOG
Gilbert J. Martinez, MD, JD
42525 Chaparral Dr.
Temecula, CA 92592-8955
Tel: (951) 303-1429
Fax: (951) 303-9357
E-mail: bfiller@medstuff.com
Web Site: http://www.medstuff.com

Specialties: Medstuff specializes in providing medical expert witnesses for plaintiff or defense, matching the right experts for your particular needs. William W. Filler, Jr., MD, FACOG: Expert in all related OB/Gyn matters; Board Certified. Gilbert J. Martinez, MD, JD: Board Certified Family Practitioner. See website at www.medstuff.com for details.

See primary listing under MEDICINE & HEALTH: General

David M. Priver, MD

Obstetrician & Gynecologist
OB/GYN Expert Witness Services
4282 Genesee Ave., Ste. 201
San Diego, CA 92117
Tel: (858) 268-7324
Fax: (858) 268-3894
E-mail: dpriver@aol.com
Web Site:
http://www.OBGynExpertWitness.com

Specialties: Pregnancy Care; Complications of Pregnancy; Abortion; Complications of Abortion; Gynecology; Pelvic Surgery; Laparoscopy; Ultrasound; Hormone Therapy. IAST President, San Diego County Medical Society, 1996-1997. 30 years in private practice of OB/Gyn. **Degrees/licenses:** BA, MD, FACOG.

See primary listing under MEDICINE & HEALTH: Obstetrics & Gynecology

Pro/Consul Technical and Medical Experts

1945 Palo Verde Ave., Suite 200
Long Beach, CA 90815-3443
Tel: (800) 392-1119
(562) 799-0116
Fax: (562) 799-8821
E-mail: eexperts@msn.com
Web Site: http://www.expertinfo.com

Specialties: RIGHT EXPERT RIGHT AWAY!® 15,000 experts in 7,000 fields. Listed and recommended by the A. M. Best Company. Full-time research staff. We welcome your RUSH cases! TECHNICAL: Fast inspections. Categories from Accident Reconstruction to Zoology, also including appraisal, economics, employment, human factors, insurance, premises liability, security, and many more. MEDICAL: IME's. Inexpensive insurance medical records reviews by MDs. Categories from Addiction Medicine to Zooplasty, including board certified physicians in all fields, dentistry, geriatrics, neuropsychology, neurosurgery, nursing, orthopedics, psychiatry and many more. Reasonable fees. Free initial consultation. Free resume binder. Free CLE classes. **Degrees/licenses:** MD,

PhD, DDS, DVM, DO, DPM, PE, CPA, ME, CE, CRC, MAI, et al.

See primary listing under ACCIDENT RECONSTRUCTION: General

Jerald H. Ratner, MD

9750 NW 33rd St., Ste. 211
Coral Springs, FL 33065
Tel: (954) 752-9450
Fax: (954) 752-9888

Specialties: Independent Medical Examinations, Malpractice, Competency, Malingering, Medical Records Review, Psychotropic Drug Reactions. Former Chairman of Psychiatry at two hospitals; Fellow, College of Physicians of Philadelphia; Board Certified in Psychiatry; Diplomate, American Board of Forensic Medicine; Diplomate, American Board of Forensic Examiners; Fellow, American Psychiatric Association. **Degrees/licenses:** MD, DABFM, DABFE, FCPP, DABPN, FAPA.

See primary listing under PSYCHIATRY: General

Jeffrey R. Richardson, MD, FACOG

3555 Loma Vista Rd., Ste. 115
Ventura, CA 93003
Tel: (805) 648-4425
Fax: (805) 648-4426
E-mail: jrr6004@cs.com
Web Site: http://member.expertpages.com/obgynxpertwitnes

Specialties: Twenty plus years experience in private practice of OB/Gyn, Primary Care, Infertility, Gyn Surgery, Gyn Cancers, High Risk Obstetrics, Office Practice, Cancer Screening, Teaching of Residents. **Degrees/licenses:** MD, FACOG, Board Certified OB/Gyn.

See primary listing under MEDICINE & HEALTH: Obstetrics & Gynecology

Kenneth A. Stein, MD

14312 Aitken Hill Court
Chesterfield (St. Louis), MO 63017
Tel: (314) 495-7009
Fax: (708) 585-3348
E-mail: kenny@er-md.com
Web Site: http://www.er-md.com

Specialties: Attending Staff Physician in Emergency Medicine and Critical Care at St. Anthony's Medical Center and Assistant Clinical Professor at St. Louis University Health Sciences Center, Department of Surgery/Emergency Medicine Division. Furnishes an unbiased opinion on medical malpractice and negligence, emergency medicine and internal medicine, for plaintiff or defense. Survey of case for merit, medical chart review and analysis, formulation of case strategy, preparation for opposing expert deposition and cross-examination, medical literature search, expert witness testimony. **Degrees/licenses:** MD, Board Certified in Internal Medicine.

See primary listing under MEDICINE & HEALTH: Emergency Medicine

TASAmed

A Division of The TASA Group
1166 DeKalb Pike
Blue Bell, PA 19422-1853
Tel: (800) 659-8464
Fax: (800) 850-8272
E-mail: tasamed@tasanet.com
Web Site: www.tasanet.com

Specialties: FIND THE MEDICAL EXPERT YOU NEED with TASAmed, a co-division of TASA, North America's foremost Expert Referral Service. Thousands of top-caliber Local and National specialists for case review, IME's, consulting, and testifying in over 900 medical fields. Categories of expertise include Anesthesiology; Cardiology; Cosmetic Surgery; Dentistry; Elder Abuse; Emergency Care; Environmental Medicine; Forensic Pathology; Geriatrics; Nephrology; Obstetrics; Occupational Medicine; Oncology; Pediatrics; Psychiatry; Pulmonology; Radiology; Sports Medicine; Surgery; & More. SERVICES INCLUDE prompt customized searches, refer-

(Listing continued on next page)

General *(cont.)*

TASAmed (cont.)
rals, resumes, and your initial interview calls with experts. Exceptional personal service for over 44 years. **Degrees/licenses:** All prof. degrees, licenses, certifications represented.
See primary listing under EXPERT WITNESS REFERRALS: General

Toxicology Consultants Roundtable

John A. Budny, PhD
Director, Publicity
Tel: (818) 706-2410
Web Site: http://lawinfo.com/biz/toxicology/index.html

Specialties: Call for a nationwide FREE LIST OF EXPERIENCED TOXICOLOGY EXPERTS; Contact them directly; No fee. **Degrees/licenses:** Over 50 PhD's, MD's & DVM's + Board Certifications.
See primary listing under MEDICINE & HEALTH: Toxicology

Robert Wagmeister, MD

2001 Santa Monica Blvd., #1170-W
Santa Monica, CA 90404
Tel: (310) 828-5626
Fax: (310) 828-2826
E-mail: rwagmd@aol.com

Specialties: Vascular Surgery: diseases, trauma, & surgery of the circulation, both arterial and venous. Includes carotid artery, aneurysms, bypass surgery, dialysis surgery, amputations, pulmonary embolus, spine access, phlebitis. Birthdate: May 16, 1949. MD, Tufts Medical School, 1974. Special Certification in Vascular Surgery given by American Board of Surgery. Memberships: Southern California Vascular Surgery Society; Society for Vascular Surgery; Society for Clinical Vascular Surgery; Peripheral Vascular Surgery Society. Extensive experience in medical malpractice cases; numerous cases each year; depositions; expert witness; court appearance as required. **Degrees/licenses:** MD, FACS.

See primary listing under MEDICINE & HEALTH: Vascular Surgery

Cancer/Oncology

Richard J. Cohen, MD, FACP

Consultant in Medical Oncology/Hematology
3838 California St., Ste. 707
San Francisco, CA 94118
Tel: (415) 668-0160
Fax: (415) 752-4635
E-mail: rcohen3@aol.com
Web Site: http://doctor.pol.net/rjcohen

Specialties: Board certified in Medical Oncology, Hematology and Internal Medicine. Clinical Professor of Medicine, Univ. of Calif. Med. Center, San Francisco. Special expertise in cancers of breast, colon, lung, lymphomas, melanoma, etc. Extensive experience as consultant and expert witness in Medical-Legal cases for both plaintiff and defense. **Degrees/licenses:** MD, Fellow of the American College of Physicians.

Capacity-Competence, Wills

Stephen Read, MD

2566 Overland Ave., Ste. 500B
Los Angeles, CA 90064
Tel: (310) 521-9747
Fax: (310) 521-8112
E-mail: readsmd@aol.com
Web Site: http://www.geriatricpsychiatrist.com

Specialties: Practicing psychiatrist for twenty years; qualified as medical psychiatric expert witness more than 300 cases in federal and multiple state courts; capacity, testamentary capacity, will contests; conservatorship, competence to testify; undue influence, elder abuse, financial abuse; skilled nursing homes; quality of care; psychotropic medications; dementia, Alzheimer's Disease, frontal lobe, stroke, vascular dementias, Parkinson's disease, hydrocephalus, depression, psychosis;

personal injury; Americans with Disability Act (ADA). Associate Clinical Professor UCLA, board certified: Psychiatry, Forensic Psychiatry, Geriatric Psychiatry; medical staff at UCLA Neuropsychiatric Hospital, Los Angeles VA and Air Force Base. **Degrees/licenses:** MD; Board Cert.: Psychiatry, Geriatric Psych., Forensic Psych.

See primary listing under MEDICINE & HEALTH: General

Chiropractic Malpractice

Evan S. Rost, DC

1 Madelyne Place
Fair Lawn, NJ 07410
Tel: (201) 791-0004
Fax: (201) 791-0045
E-mail: doc@expertchiropractor.com
Web Site:
http://www.expertchiropractor.com

Specialties: Chiropractic; Chiropractic Medicine; Forensic Examiner. Member, American College of Forensic Examiners #14745; Member, National Forensic Center, Certified Chiropractic Peer Reviewer and Independent Examiner, Certified Chiropractic Insurance Consultant, both certifications by Texas Chiropractic College; Diplomate, American Board of Disability Analysts; Diplomate, American Academy of Certified Consultants and Experts; Diplomate, American Academy of Experts in Traumatic Stress; Cleveland Chiropractic College 1983. Membership: American Pain Society, Headache Cooperative of New England, Inc., Florida Chiropractic Association, Indiana State Chiropractic Association, Northern New Jersey Chiropractic Society, New York State Chiropractic Association. **Degrees/licenses:** DC, CCIC, ACD, DABDA, FAAIM; Lic.: NJ, NY, FL, RI, IN.

See primary listing under MEDICINE & HEALTH: Chiropractic Medicine

Chiropractic Record Review

Evan S. Rost, DC

1 Madelyne Place
Fair Lawn, NJ 07410
Tel: (201) 791-0004
Fax: (201) 791-0045
E-mail: doc@expertchiropractor.com
Web Site:
http://www.expertchiropractor.com

Specialties: Chiropractic; Chiropractic Medicine; Forensic Examiner. Member, American College of Forensic Examiners #14745; Member, National Forensic Center, Certified Chiropractic Peer Reviewer and Independent Examiner, Certified Chiropractic Insurance Consultant, both certifications by Texas Chiropractic College; Diplomate, American Board of Disability Analysts; Diplomate, American Academy of Certified Consultants and Experts; Diplomate, American Academy of Experts in Traumatic Stress; Cleveland Chiropractic College 1983. Membership: American Pain Society, Headache Cooperative of New England, Inc., Florida Chiropractic Association, Indiana State Chiropractic Association, Northern New Jersey Chiropractic Society, New York State Chiropractic Association. **Degrees/licenses:** DC, CCIC, ACD, DABDA, FAAIM; Lic.: NJ, NY, FL, RI, IN.

See primary listing under MEDICINE & HEALTH: Chiropractic Medicine

Consulting

Chisolm Legal Nurse Consulting

Daniel Chisolm, RN, BSN
Certified Legal Nurse Consultant
11 Wayside Road
Asheville, NC 28805
Tel: (828) 236-0031
Fax: (828) 236-0031
E-mail: ncexpertnurse@yahoo.com
Web Site: http://www.ncexpertnurse.com

Specialties: Daniel W. Chisolm is a Registered Nurse with over 10 years experience in Critical Care, ICU, MICU, Recovery Room, ER, and general nursing. He is actively practicing bedside nursing. Mr. Chisolm is experienced with all nursing issues. He is also working with patients on ventilators, cardiac monitors, feeding tubes, IV therapy, arterial lines, respiratory failure and cardiac arrest. Experience includes care to cardiology, respiratory, renal, neurological and hepatic patients. Services include providing expert testimony, screening cases for merit, analyzing medical records for deviations from standards of care, nursing research. **Degrees/licenses:** Registered Nurse, Certified Legal Nurse Consultant.

See primary listing under MEDICAL-LEGAL: Nursing Malpractice

Ronald Citron, MD

4189 Silverado Trail
Calistoga, CA 94515-9610
Tel: (707) 942-5818
E-mail: rscitronmd@earthlink.net

Specialties: Causation analysis of missed cancer diagnosis. Diplomate, American Board of Internal Medicine; Diplomate, American Board of Medical Oncology; Diplomate, American Board of Forensic Examiners. **Degrees/licenses:** MD.

See primary listing under MEDICINE & HEALTH: Cancer/Oncology

Richard S. Goodman, MD, JD, FAAOS, ACLM

Physician & Attorney
Richard S. Goodman, MD, JD
285 East Main Street
Smithtown, NY 11787
Tel: (631) 724-2727
Fax: (631) 724-2729
E-mail: rsgmdesq@ipninet.com

Second Office
70 Glen Cove Rd., Ste. LL1
Roslyn Heights, NY 11577

Third Office
743 Columbia Turnpike
East Greenbush, NY 12061

Specialties: Orthopedics, Sport Injuries, Pediatric Orthopedics, Review of Medical Records, Standards of Care - Motor Vehicle Accidents, Personal Injuries. Consultant, Social Security Administration & New York State Retirement Board. MD, JD, License in NY & CA. Admitted NYS bar. Consultant, Long Island Jewish Medical Center & North Shore University Medical Center. Certified - American Board of Orthopaedic Surgery; Fellow - American Academy of Orthopaedic Surgery; Fellow - American College of Legal Medicine; Certified - New York State Workers' Compensation Board. **Degrees/licenses:** MD, JD, Med. Lic. NY & CA; Cert. NYS Work. Comp. Board; Admitted NY Bar.

See primary listing under MEDICINE & HEALTH: Orthopedics

Stephen Hubbard, MD

4490 Eagle Harbor Dr. NE
Bainbridge Island, WA 98110
Tel: (206) 855-8132
Fax: (206) 855-8139
E-mail: stehub@pol.net
Web Site: http://stephenhubbardmd.com

Specialties: Interventional cardiologist with experience in chart review, depositions, testimony. Expertise in myocardial infarction management, chest pain evaluation, angiography, angioplasty, pacemakers, medical management of hypertension, hyperlipidemia, CHF, CAD, arrhythmias. Graduate of UCSF

School of Medicine; board certified in Internal Medicine and Cardiovascular Disease. Fellow, American College of Cardiology. Recently retired from private practice and now Clinical Assoc. Professor at UW School of Medicine, attending at Harborview Medical Center. **Degrees/licenses:** MD, Lic. in WA; FACC; Boards: Int. Med., CV.

See primary listing under MEDICINE & HEALTH: Cardiology

Hospital Staff Issues

Mark W. Gordon, MD

Mark W. Gordon, MD, PA
2301 N. University Drive
Pembroke Pines, FL 33024
Tel: (954) 964-1490
Fax: (954) 963-3453
E-mail: drmark@dslx.net

Specialties: Litigation experience in hospital staff issues. Twenty-five years service on hospital committees from member to chairman. Activities include: Infection control, quality assurance, institutional review board, tissue, credentials and ethics, executive, and numerous ad hoc appointments. Have served in, and worked with, due process staff membership removal, defamation, privilege disputes, peer review. See other listings - Surgery, General & Medical/Hospital Malpractice. **Degrees/ licenses:** BS, MD.

See primary listing under MEDICAL-LEGAL: Medical/Hospital Malpractice

Legal Malpractice

Phillip Feldman

Law Offices of Phillip Feldman
15250 Ventura Blvd. Ste. 610
Sherman Oaks, CA 91403
Tel: (310) LEG-MALP (534-6257)
Fax: (818) 986-1757
E-mail: LegMalpExpert@aol.com
Web Site:
http://www.LegalMalpracticeExperts.com

Specialties: Thirty-seven years Malpractice, professional liability, ethics & professional responsibility; fee disputes; with experience on both sides of the bar. Hands-on experience in almost all transactional & trial lawyering underlying matters ("case within a case," causation issues) including over 25 years as a Judge Pro Temp & Attorney/Client Fee Dispute Arbitrator (accounting degree). Former State Bar Prosecutor, present Attorney Discipline & Ethics Defense counsel. Prolific national author & lecturer. Never disqualified or failed to qualify in any jurisdiction. Testimony, reports & consults have been used in almost all jurisdictions (state & federal) for twenty-three years. **Degrees/licenses:** BS, MBA, JD, Bd. Cert. Legal & Med. Malpractice, ABA, ABPLA, CA.

Life Care Planning

Leona H. Liberty, Ed.D., CRC, NCC, CLCP

Director
Capabilities Evaluation Center, Inc.
120 DeFreest Drive
Rensselaer Technology Park
Troy, NY 12180-7608
Tel: (518) 283-7148
Fax: (518) 283-7168
E-mail: T20@msn.com

Specialties: Address the employability and vocational potential, earnings capacity and other needs or losses of individuals who suffered personal injury through work, motor vehicle accidents, developmental or progressive diseases, or other conditions; the result of divorce, employment discrimination, or other separation from the workplace. The method to do the aforementioned includes face-to-face or hypothetical Vocational Evaluations, with testing, if permitted, to assess strengths and limitations for gainful or other employment; Labor Market Surveys to assess and determine pre-post employability opportunities and earnings capacity. Life Care Plans are developed that identify projected needs and costs for individuals who suffer catastrophic injuries. **Degrees/licenses:** Doctor of Education, Ed.D., CRC, NCC, CLCP.

See primary listing under EMPLOYMENT: Employability/Earning Capacity

Life Care Planning *(cont.)*

Life Management Services

a division of CERA, Inc.
Donna D. Archer, ORT/L, CLCP
Consultant
P. O. Box 11247
Pensacola, FL 32524-1247
Tel: (888) 476-7707 (Toll Free)
(850) 476-7707
Fax: (850) 995-9440
E-mail: darcher@cerainc.com
Web Site: http://www.lms.cerainc.com/

Specialties: Life Management Services is a division of CERA, Inc. CERA is a physician owned and operated consulting group providing medical malpractice support services including preparation of Life Care Plans. CERA's Life Care Planner is certified (CLCP) and has 30+ years experience in the field of rehabilitation. For a no-obligation consultation, please call Toll Free (888) 476-7707. **Degrees/licenses:** CLCP, OTR, MD, RN, CLNC.

Eugene E. Van de Bittner, PhD, CRC

President/Rehabilitation Consultant
Mirfak Associates, Inc.
577 Ygnacio Valley Road
Walnut Creek, CA 94596
Tel: (925) 296-0300
Fax: (925) 296-0301
E-mail: drgene@mirfak.com
Web Site: http://www.mirfak.com

Specialties: Rehabilitation consulting and expert witness services regarding employability, earning capacity, and life care needs and costs. Vocational rehabilitation evaluations, plan development, and monitoring. Return to work services to arrange modified or alternate employment through an interactive process. Evaluating the adequacy of job search efforts. Labor market research and job placement services. Life care planning and management. **Degrees/licenses:** Ph.D., Rehabilitation; M.Ed., Vocational Rehabilitation; CRC, CLCP, ABVE.

See primary listing under EMPLOYMENT: Employability/Earning Capacity

Medical Billing

Robert J. Bargar, MD, SM

137 Pine Ridge Road
Newton, MA 02468
Tel: (617) 527-5225
Fax: (617) 965-9355
E-mail: nelsonbargar@msn.com
Web Site: http://member.expertpages.com/robertbargar

Specialties: Quality Assurance and Utilization Review (Board Certified); Public Health/Preventive Medicine (Board Certified); Medical Management (Board Certified); Physician Billing and Fraud; Health Insurance Administration; Claims Review; Evaluation of medical care involving multiple providers of different specialties and the institutions at which they practice. Qualified as expert by U.S. Dept. of Labor & U.S. Dept. of Justice. Member American College of Physician Executives & National Association of Physician Broadcasters. **Degrees/licenses:** MD Tufts, SM & AB Harvard, Med. & Ins. Adv. Lic. MA.

See primary listing under MEDICAL-LEGAL: Medical/Hospital/HMO Malpractice

Medical Malpractice

Comprehensive Radiology Review, PLLC

A. Robert Tantleff, MD
57 Starling Court
East Hills, NY 11576
Tel: (516) 626-3688
Fax: (516) 626-6151
E-mail: artan@optonline.net
Web Site:
www.comprehensiveradiologyreview.com

Specialties: Board Certified Diagnostic Radiology/Radiographic Imaging (MRI, CAT Scan, Ultrasound, Nuclear Medicine, Angiography). Independent radiology review,

IME, peer review, second opinion radiology interpretation, medical record review. Workers' Compensation, personal injury, long-term disability, medical malpractice. No geographical limits. 30 years in medical practice. Testimony experience. Available to insurance companies, plaintiff and defense attorneys, physicians and hospitals. **Degrees/licenses:** MD Summa Cum Laude, State Univ. of NY, Downstate Med. Ctr.

See primary listing under MEDICINE & HEALTH: Radiology/Nuclear Medicine

Richard C. Davi, MD, FACS

Urologic Surgeon
Expert Witnessing & Litigation Consulting
1541 Brickell Ave., Ste. 3604
Miami, FL 33129
Tel: (305) 342-6262
Fax: (305) 854-9069
E-mail: docrich2@bellsouth.net

Specialties: Urologic Oncology, Infertility, Lithotripsy/Stone Disease, Vasectomy, Prostate Diseases, Bladder Diseases, Incontinence, Sexually Transmitted Diseases, Interstitial Cystitis, Female Urology, Pediatric Urology (limited). Georgetown University, Georgetown University School of Medicine, University of Miami Residency, New York State and Florida Board of Medicine, American Board of Urology, FACS. **Degrees/licenses:** MD (New York & FL), Amer. Board of Urology, FACS.

See primary listing under MEDICINE & HEALTH: Urology

Anthony R. DeSalvo, MD

1842 East Market St.
Warren, OH 44483
Tel: (330) 856-7212
Fax: (330) 856-6101
E-mail: Tony@DrDeSalvo.com
Web Site: http://www.DrDeSalvo.com

Specialties: Board Certified in Obstetrics and Gynecology, in full-time private practice, and a public speaker. Provides medical record and report review, medical literature search, peer review, second opinion, and expert witness testimony for attorneys in Medical Malpractice and Personal Injury, both plaintiff and defense. Issues addressed are general obstetrical and gynecological cases, high-risk obstetrics, cesarean section, prenatal care, miscarriage, traumatic birth injury, perinatal medicine, antenatal care, abortion problems, sterilization, contraception, menstrual disorders, menopause HRT, gynecological surgery, laser surgery, endometriosis, hysterectomy, hysteroscopy, bladder repair, and incontinence. **Degrees/licenses:** MD, FACOG, Board Certified Ob/Gyn.

See primary listing under MEDICINE & HEALTH: Obstetrics & Gynecology

John H. Harris, Jr., MD, DSc, FACR

Emeritus Professor of Radiology
University of Texas-Houston Med. School
200 Alta Vista Dr.
Sedona, AZ 86351-6910
Tel: (928) 284-9392
Fax: (928) 284-9170
E-mail: jhharris@myexcel.com

Specialties: Dr. Harris, as the principal author of the "Radiology of Emergency Medicine," 4th ed., and "Radiology of Acute Cervical Spine Trauma," 3rd ed., is an internationally recognized authority in Emergency Radiology with special interest in cervical spine injury; Experienced expert medical witness; Awarded 1st Gold Medal, American Society of Emergency Radiology; Awarded 2001 Gold Medal of the American College of Radiology; Associate, American Academy of Orthopedic Surgeons; Honorary Member, American College of Emergency Physicians; F (Hon.)-Royal Australasian College of Radiologists. **Degrees/licenses:** MD, DSc, D-ABR; F-ASER; F-ACR; Arizona & Texas Med. Lic.

See primary listing under MEDICINE & HEALTH: Radiology/Nuclear Medicine

Medical Malpractice *(cont.)*

Arlene F. Hoffman, DPM, PhD

California Pacific Medical Center
2100 Webster St., Ste. 202
San Francisco, CA 94115-2375
Tel: (415) 923-3535
Fax: (415) 923-3672

Specialties: Medical evaluation and treatment of podiatric injuries; Perioperative evaluation; Wound healing; Blood flow evaluation of the lower extremity; Use of pharmaceuticals and laboratory evaluation. PhD, Downstate Medical Center, SUNY; DPM, California College of Podiatric Medicine; Fellow, Stanford University College of Medicine. Previous/current positions: Professor; Chair, Exam Committee, American Board of Podiatric Orthopedics; Board Trustee, ABPOPPM, ASPM, ASPD, ASPA; Special Editor, "The Lower Extremity;" General Editor, "Journal of the American Podiatric Medical Association;" Editor, "Yearbook of Podiatric Medicine and Surgery." Recipient of the Meritorious Service Award, APMA. 35+ publications. **Degrees/licenses:** DPM, PhD.

See primary listing under MEDICINE & HEALTH: Podiatry

Perry Hookman, MD

Perry Hookman, MD, PA
5607 NW 24th Terrace
Boca Raton, FL 33496
Tel: (561) 241-8550
E-mail: hookman@hookman.com
Web Site: http://www.hookman.com

Specialties: Expert medical opinion from board certified physician in internal medicine and gastroenterology. Will review medical records, diagnoses & treatment of internal medicine and gastrointestinal diseases. In current active private medical practice & medical school teaching faculty. See publications on Dr. Hookman's website. **Degrees/licenses:** Perry Hookman, MD, FACP, FACG, FACPE.

Richard D. Kane, MD

Urologist/President
Wake Urological Assoc.
4301 Lake Boone Trail, Ste. 300
Raleigh, NC 27607
Tel: (919) 782-1255
Fax: (919) 782-6056
E-mail: wakeurol@aol.com

Specialties: Impotence; Incontinence; Renal and Ureteral Calculi; Prostate Cancer; Bladder Cancer; Penile Prosthesis complications and repairs; Surgical complications of prostate treatment; Testicular Torsion; Vasectomy complications. Northwestern University, MD; Duke University, General Surgery, Urology; Extensive expert witness testimony and/or case reviews; Private practice with appointment as clinical professor of Urology, University of North Carolina. **Degrees/licenses:** BS, MD, Board Certified.

See primary listing under MEDICINE & HEALTH: Urology

Henry W. Lahmeyer, MD

Clinical Professor of Psychiatry
Chicago Medical School
Two Northfield Plaza, Ste. 100
Northfield, IL 60093
Tel: (847) 446-3531
Fax: (847) 446-3573
E-mail: henry@lahmeyermd.com
Web Site: www.lahmeyermd.com

Specialties: Malpractice in areas of: psychopharmacology, suicide, depression & bipolar disorders, drug abuse, closed head injury, and wrongful death. Previously Professor at the University of Illinois and Northwestern University. Currently Clinical Profesor of Psychiatry, Chicago Medical School. Published over 70 articles and received over 40 research grants. Twenty five years of experience in forensic medicine. Maintains an active clinical and research practice. Testify for both plaintiff and defense. **Degrees/licenses:** BA, MD; Board Cert. in Psych, Sleep Med. & Forensic Psych.

See primary listing under MEDICINE & HEALTH: Psychiatry

David A. Libert, MD, FAAFP, PA

First Choice Medical Center
697 Maitland Ave., Ste. 1001
Altamonte Springs, FL 32701
Tel: (407) 539-2111
Fax: (407) 539-1211
E-mail: dlibert@earthlink.net
Web Site: http://www.fcmedcenter.com

Specialties: Dr. Libert has been a practicing physician since 1985; Has held positions of team physician, practicing physician and medical director at several area medical centers; Extensive experience in family practice and disability medicine. Plaintiff and defense Medical-Legal Services: Medical Record Review & Analysis; Identification of Standards of Care, Causation & Damage Issues; Definitions of Medical Terms & Procedures; Collaboration for Interrogatory Development; Expert Witness Deposition & Trial Testimony. MD University of Florida 1982; Diplomate American Board of Family Practice. **Degrees/licenses:** MD, FAAFP; Lic. in the State of Florida since 1983.

Stephen Morewitz, PhD & Associates

Tel: (312) 263-9160
(415) 252-0569
(818) 594-1587
E-mail: morewitz@earthlink.net
Web Site:
http://home.earthlink.net/~morewitz

Specialties: Assesses disability, quality of life losses, and sexual harassment/sexual assault. Also provides medical record and employment record reviews, technical research, and experts in other fields. Over 18 years experience. Professor, Dean, author or co-author of 5 books, including "Chronic Disease and Health Care" (forthcoming, 2005), "The Medical Malpractice Handbook," (1996), "Sexual Harassment & Social Change" (1996), and more than 70 other publications. Secured major federal research and training grants. Presented research papers at national and international conferences and reviewer of conference research papers. Management consultant. 2 Outstanding Scholar Book Awards, 2003 and 2004, American Public Health Association, Top Ten Injury Research Poster, "Who's Who in Medicine & Healthcare," and other honors. Offices in Buffalo Grove, IL, San Francisco & Tarzana, CA. **Degrees/licenses:** PhD, Certified Behavioral Scientist (CPSP).

See primary listing under EMPLOYMENT: Sexual Harassment

Edson O. Parker, MD

P. O. Box 29209
Las Vegas, NV 89126
Tel: (702) 499-9994
Fax: (702) 474-9420
E-mail: eoparker@aol.com
Web Site: http://www.eoparker.com

Specialties: Medical expert with over twenty years experience in all aspects of Pain Medicine, from medication management to very invasive therapies with injections, spinal cord stimulators, spinal infusion pumps and neurolytic procedures. MD from Vanderbilt University School of Medicine 1978. Board certified by the American Board of Anesthesiology in both Anesthesiology and Pain Medicine and Diplomate of the American Board of Pain Medicine. Clinical Professor of Surgery at the University of Nevada School of Medicine. Experienced in performing case reviews, IME's and depositions in a thoughtful and thorough manner, with insightful analysis and conclusions. Areas of expertise include pain management, pain medications, pain medicine and medical malpractice. CV available upon request. **Degrees/licenses:** MD, Board Cert. Anesthesiology & Pain Medicine.

See primary listing under MEDICINE & HEALTH: Pain Management

James L. Pearle, MD

President
Western Pulmonary Medical Group, Inc.
220 Laguna Road, Ste. 2
Fullerton, CA 92835-2523
Tel: (714) 446-7454
Fax: (714) 879-1049
E-mail: jpearlemd@hotmail.com

Specialties: Asbestosis and Occupational Lung Diseases with national experience and

(Listing continued on next page)

Medical Malpractice *(cont.)*

James L. Pearle, MD (cont.)
publications; Medical Malpractice, Sleep Disorders; Hospitalist, Pulmonary, Critical Care, and Internal Medicine. Hospital Medical Director, Hospital Chief of Staff, Director of Hospital Respiratory Therapy Department, President of Medical Group, Independent Medical Examiner, Principal Investigator for Clinical Trials, Experienced in Hyperbaric Medicine. Over one hundred depositions and trials. Board certified in Internal Medicine and Pulmonary Disease. Fellow, American College of Chest Physicians. Former Assistant Professor, UCLA School of Medicine and UC Irvine School of Medicine. **Degrees/licenses:** BA, MD.

See primary listing under MEDICINE & HEALTH: Pulmonary Medicine

C. Paul Sinkhorn, MD, FACOG

2642 Marley Drive
Riverside, CA 92506
Tel: (909) 241-2745
Fax: (951) 779-9189
E-mail: cpaulsinkhorn@earthlink.net
Web Site: http://www.expertdoc.net

Specialties: Board Cert Obstetrics/Gynecology; Clinical Assoc. Prof, OB/GYN, Univ. of Calif.-Riverside; Teaching Faculty Arrowhead Regional Medical Center (San Bernardino County); High-risk obstetrics; expert in laparoscopy, laser, cesarean, sterilization, contraception, infertility, hysteroscopy, hysterectomy, bladder repair, incontinence; Deposition/Trial experience; Tobacco and smoking liability; past-President Professional Liability Committee for Riverside County Medical Association; Peer reviewer and Hospital Medical Staff Surveyor for California Medical Association; American Association of Gyn. Laparoscopists; ACOG; AOA Honorary; Am. Soc. Forensic OB/GYNs (past president); approx 60-40 plaintiff/defense. **Degrees/licenses:** MD, FACOG; licensed CA & AR.

See primary listing under MEDICINE & HEALTH: Obstetrics & Gynecology

Ron Surowitz, DO

Board Certified Family Physician
Surowitz Consulting, Inc.
2185 Radnor Court
North Palm Beach, FL 33408
Tel: (561) 746-7826
(561) 746-7811
(561) 627-5952
Fax: (561) 744-1970
E-mail: rsurowitz1@aol.com

Specialties: Malpractice consulting and expert witness services; Evaluate standard of care for family and general practice; Expert diagnostic opinions; Board Certified in Osteopathic Family Practice; Past President of the Florida Osteopathic Medical Association; 33 years of practice experience; Plaintiff and defense review to evaluate medical malpractice; Rapid response; Thorough analysis of issues. **Degrees/licenses:** DO, FAOCFP / Florida, Missouri, Michigan, California.

See primary listing under MEDICINE & HEALTH: Family Medicine

Arthur Taub, MD, PhD, PC

Arthur Taub, MD, PhD
1 Bradley Road
Woodbridge, CT 06525
Tel: (203) 389-6046
Fax: (203) 389-6053
E-mail: atmd@ix.netcom.com

Specialties: Data analysis, examination of major abnormalities of the central, peripheral, and autonomic nervous systems, caused by aging, mechanical (e.g., automobile, railroad, aircraft, nautical, gunshot) or toxic e.g., hydrocarbons) trauma (personal injury), or medical malpractice (standard of care, cause in fact, and damages: physical, pain and suffering, cognitive/behavioral). More than two decades of close experience with the civil bar, and more recently, with the Public Defender (capital crimes). Full time Neurologic practice of complex matters of pain, cognition, and behavior. Clinical Full Professor (1975-2000), Yale University School of Medicine. **Degrees/licenses:** MD cum laude, Yale; PhD Neurophysiology, MIT.
See primary listing under MEDICINE & HEALTH: Neurology

Alan J. Zimmerman, MD
17 Eden Road
Lido Beach, NY 11561
Tel: (516) 431-5559
Fax: (309) 422-7208
E-mail: J40sailor@aol.com

Specialties: Orthopedic Surgery; Extensive Experience Expert Witness Testimony, Records Review; Personal Injury, Medical Malpractice, Plaintiff/Defense. Chief of Orthopedic Surgery, Long Beach Medical Center; Assist. Professor Clinical Orthopedic Surgery, State University of New York at Stony Brook, Adjunct Clinical Assistant Professor of Surgery, New York College of Osteopathic Medicine; Listed in "Best Doctors, NY Metro Area;" Board Certified American Board of Orthopedic Surgery; Fellow, American Academy of Orthopedic Surgeons. **Degrees/licenses:** BS Cum Laude; MD.

See primary listing under MEDICINE & HEALTH: Orthopedic Surgery

Medical Malpractice, Family Practice

Elliot D. Felman, MD
2336 Santa Monica Blvd., Ste. 208
Santa Monica, CA 90404
Tel: (310) 453-0033
Fax: (310) 453-2114
E-mail: drfelman@earthlink.net

Specialties: Board Certified Family Practice. In practice over 25 years. Experienced in both Plaintiff and Defense Review, Deposition and Trial Testimony for evaluation of Medical Malpractice. Evaluation of Standard of Care for Family Practice, General Practice & Internal Medicine. Clinical faculty, UCLA Medical School. **Degrees/licenses:** MD.

Medical Record Review

Burton Bentley II, MD, FAAEM
President
Emergency Medicine
Litigation Analysts, Inc.
5189 N. Marlin Canyon Place
Tucson, AZ 85750
Tel: (888) 335-3652
Fax: (520) 615-5413
E-mail: bentley@erexperts.com
Web Site: http://www.erexperts.com

Specialties: Immediate, cost-effective, impartial analysis of emergency medicine cases; Review of duty, breach, harm, and causation; Summary of medical records; Explanation of medical terms and processes; Strategic planning; Database searches referenced to your case; Provision of expert witness services by board-certified, actively practicing emergency physicians; Complete start-to-finish litigation support for both plaintiff and defense. **Degrees/licenses:** MD, ABEM, FAAEM.

See primary listing under MEDICINE & HEALTH: Emergency Medicine

Todd C. Case, MD, FACS
President
Todd C. Case, MD, PC
5881 N. Misty Ridge Dr.
Tucson, AZ 85718-3434
Tel: (520) 615-0597
Fax: (520) 615-0599
E-mail: tccaseworks@aol.com

Specialties: Complete start-to-finish cost-effective litigation support for plaintiff and defense; Impartial analysis; Reports summarizing medical records, explaining medical terms and procedures, and reviewing duty, breach, causation and damages; Strategic planning; Database searches; Expert witness services. Dr. Case is ABPS certified; Past Chief, plastic surgery (Tucson Medical Center); A former director of division of plastic surgery; Received prestigious national award for research; Authored and presented numerous papers; Invited lecturer (Italy, India). Actively practicing; Interests in facial , breast

(Listing continued on next page)

Medical Record Review
(cont.)

Todd C. Case, MD (cont.)

and body surgery, including cosmetic and laser procedures, and treatment for lymphedema. **Degrees/licenses:** MD, FACS, ABPS, AOA; Lic. AZ, CA, TX.

See primary listing under MEDICINE & HEALTH: Plastic & Reconstructive Surgery

CERA, Inc., Medical Legal Support Services

Timothy D. Brooks, MD
Medical Director
P. O. Box 11247
Pensacola, FL 32524-1247
Tel: (888) 476-7707 (Toll Free)
(850) 476-7707
Fax: (850) 995-9440
E-mail: info@cerainc.com
Web Site: http://www.cerainc.com/

Specialties: CERA, Inc. is a physician owned and operated consulting group providing medical malpractice case screening, expert witness identification, and preparation of Life Care Plans. CERA's staff of physicians and nurses can review your case and offer a preliminary opinion on merit. We also have experts available in all areas of medicine to review your case and offer a formal opinion on standard of care for plaintiff or defense. CERA's services are rapid, accurate and cost effective. For a no-obligation consultation, please call Toll Free (888) 476-7707. **Degrees/licenses:** MD, RN, CLNC, CLCP, OTR.

David A. Libert, MD, FAAFP, PA

First Choice Medical Center
697 Maitland Ave., Ste. 1001
Altamonte Springs, FL 32701
Tel: (407) 539-2111
Fax: (407) 539-1211
E-mail: dlibert@earthlink.net
Web Site: http://www.fcmedcenter.com

Specialties: Dr. Libert has been a practicing physician since 1985; Has held positions of team physician, practicing physician and medical director at several area medical centers; Extensive experience in family practice and disability medicine. Plaintiff and defense Medical-Legal Services: Medical Record Review & Analysis; Identification of Standards of Care, Causation & Damage Issues; Definitions of Medical Terms & Procedures; Collaboration for Interrogatory Development; Expert Witness Deposition & Trial Testimony. MD University of Florida 1982; Diplomate American Board of Family Practice. **Degrees/ licenses:** MD, FAAFP; Lic. in the State of Florida since 1983.

See primary listing under MEDICAL-LEGAL: Medical Malpractice

Steven Richeimer, MD

Director
USC Pain Center
137 N. Larchment Blvd., #448
Los Angeles, CA 90004
Tel: (323) 692-3611
Fax: (323) 935-0791
E-mail: steven@richeimer.com
Web Site: http://www.painlegal.com

Specialties: Psychiatry, Anesthesiology, and Pain Management: (1) Is there reasonable support for the claim of chronic pain? (2) Has appropriate treatment of the pain problem been provided? (3) Where can expert pain treatment be provided? (4) Is significant disability expected? (5) Did prior pain treatment meet community standards of care? Dr. Richeimer is the Director of the University of Southern California Pain Center. Triple board certifications in Psychiatry, Anesthesiology, and Pain Management; Trained at the UCSF, UCLA, and Harvard Medical Schools; Former Director of the UC Davis Pain Management Center. **Degrees/licenses:** MD, License: CA.

See primary listing under MEDICINE & HEALTH: Pain Management

Isabelle L. Richmond, MD, PhD

Neurosurgical Consultant
912 Cedar Meadow Drive
Nellysford, VA 22958
Tel: (434) 361-9392
Fax: (434) 361-1419
E-mail: irneuro@hotmail.com

Specialties: Personal Injury, Workers' Compensation, Medical Malpractice, Medical Billing Issues, Federal/Military case review. Strong academic/basic neuroscience background. 20 years+ clinical experience medical records review: causation, standard of care, peer review, credentialling. Timely, accurate, articulate reports/depositions facilitate resolution of medical issues. Certified mediator comfortable with alternative dispute resolution methods. MD Duke 1974; PhD neurobiology Cornell 1968; Residency UCSF 1979; ABNS Certified 1982; ATLS Instructor, Level I Trauma Center. Prof. Clinical Surgery USUHS (Col. USAR). Chairman Medical Costs Peer Review, Workers' Compensation Commission of Virginia, 1993-1999. **Degrees/licenses:** MD, PhD, FACS, ABNS Cert.; Med. Lic. in VA.

Sacramento Ear, Nose & Throat Surgical & Medical Group, Inc.

Jeffrey W. Dudley
CFO/Medical Group Administrator
3810 J Street
Sacramento, CA 95816
Tel: (916) 736-3399
Fax: (916) 736-9837
E-mail: jdudley@sacent.com
Web Site: http://www.sacent.com

Specialties: Twelve Board Certified, full-time practicing Otolaryngologists; Otology; Neurotology; Hearing Loss; Tinnitus; Audiology; Head and Neck Cancer; Endoscopic Sinus Surgery; Facial Plastic Surgery; Allergy; Voice Disorders; Sleep Disorders; Swallowing Disorders; Vertigo; Smell and Taste Disorders. **Degrees/licenses:** All Board Certified MDs.

See primary listing under MEDICINE & HEALTH: Otolaryngology

Anthony J. Scarcella, MD, JD

380 S. State Road 434
Suite 1004, #388
Altamonte Springs, FL 32714
Tel: (407) 616-7295
Fax: (407) 299-8735
E-mail: ascarcellamd@aol.com
Web Site: http://www.ermedicineexpert.com

Specialties: Board Certified Emergency Medicine with extensive experience in Medical Record Review for lawyers as well as insurance companies. Disability Analysis and Verification, Malpractice Consulting and Expert Witness Services. **Degrees/licenses:** MD Certified - American Board of Emergency Medicine.

See primary listing under MEDICINE & HEALTH: Emergency Medicine

C. Paul Sinkhorn, MD, FACOG

2642 Marley Drive
Riverside, CA 92506
Tel: (909) 241-2745
Fax: (951) 779-9189
E-mail: cpaulsinkhorn@earthlink.net
Web Site: http://www.expertdoc.net

Specialties: Board Cert Obstetrics/Gynecology; Clinical Assoc. Prof, OB/GYN, Univ. of Calif.-Riverside; Teaching Faculty Arrowhead Regional Medical Center (San Bernardino County); High-risk obstetrics; expert in laparoscopy, laser, cesarean, sterilization, contraception, infertility, hysteroscopy, hysterectomy, bladder repair, incontinence; Deposition/Trial experience; HMO liability; Tobacco and smoking liability; past-President Professional Liability Committee for Riverside County Medical Association; Peer reviewer and Hospital Medical Staff Surveyor for California Medical Association; American Association of Gyn. Laparoscopists; ACOG; AOA Honorary; Am. Soc. Forensic OB/GYNs (past president); approx 60-40 plaintiff/defense. **Degrees/licenses:** MD, FACOG; licensed CA & AR.

See primary listing under MEDICINE & HEALTH: Obstetrics & Gynecology

Medical Record Review
(cont.)

Alvin Stein, MD, FACS
President
Stein Orthopedic Assoc., PA
4101 NW 4th Street, Ste. 401
Plantation, FL 33317
Tel: (954) 581-8585
Fax: (954) 581-5580
E-mail: nobones@aol.com
Web Site: http://www.proloshot.com

Specialties: A board certified orthopedic surgeon and pain management specialist with extensive experience in chart review for standard of care issues, utilization issues, and worker compensation claims. ABQAURP certified. Available for IMEs or chart reviews, plaintiff or defense, for an honest evaluation. Over 35 years of experience in practice of medicine. Rapid response and thorough analysis of the issues in any case. Available to testify if needed. References available. **Degrees/licenses:** MD, FACS.

John Scott Stephens, MS, PT
Carolina Rehabilitation, Inc.
809 Inlet View Dr.
Wilmington, NC 28409-2106
Tel: (910) 385-7149 (Cellular)
(910) 285-1650 (Office)
Fax: (910) 285-1675
E-mail: rehabservi@aol.com

Specialties: Physical therapist with thirty plus years clinical experience. Developed private practice to 20 offices including supervision of physical therapists, occupational therapists and speech-language therapists. Patient population served includes age ranges from birth through geriatrics. Positions held include founding president of Federation of State Boards of Physical Therapy, 1986-90; President, Virginia Physical Therapy Association, 1990-92; Chair, Practice Committee for Orthopaedic Section of the American Physical Therapy Association (APTA), 1992-1997; Board of Directors of APTA, 1994-97. Candidate for APTA vice-president, 1997. Case review experience for plaintiffs, defendants and insurers. $300/hour plus expenses. **Degrees/licenses:** NC/VA licensed physical therapist, BA UVA, MS Duke.

See primary listing under MEDICINE & HEALTH: Physical Medicine/Rehabilitation

Janet Winikoff, MD, FACE
2021 Santa Monica Blvd., Ste. 325 E.
Santa Monica, CA 90404
Tel: (310) 828-5337
Fax: (310) 828-2556
E-mail: jwinikof@ucla.edu

Specialties: Construction consulting, engineering, safety and management; Construction defects and damages, costs to repair, policy coverage; Construction claims, delay impact analysis, CPM scheduling, contract disputes, damage calcs; Earthquake damage analysis and appraisal; Fire and flood damage appraisals; Safety Engineering, building codes and safety regulation compliance; Construction accidents (falls from height, scaffolds, ladders, use of tools and equipment); Slips, Trips and Falls (stairs, ramps, walkways). All California and other states. In business since 1969. Calif . Contractor's License B-1. Licensed Safety & Civil Engineers. Have testified in over 150 trials. **Degrees/licenses:** MD, Licensed State of California.

See primary listing under MEDICINE & HEALTH: Internal Medicine

Medical/Hospital Malpractice

Dominick Addario, MD
Psychiatry
3010 First Avenue
San Diego, CA 92103
Tel: (619) 295-2189
Fax: (619) 295-2362
E-mail: info@addario.com
Web Site: http://www.addario.com

Specialties: Medical and Hospital Malpractice, Brain Injury, Personal Injury, Harassment, Trauma, WC Disability, Will Contests-Competence, Fiduciary/HMO/provider-contract issues. Extensive IME experience Defense/

Plaintiff. Keynote Speaker, Expert Testimony. References from major firms on request. Diplomate, Amer. Board of Psychiatry and Neurology; Distinguished Fellow, American Psychiatric Association; Qualified Medical Examiner, State of California; Clinical Professor of Psychiatry, University of California, School of Medicine, San Diego. Offices also in San Francisco Bay Area, Palm Springs, Los Angeles and Riverside County. **Degrees/licenses:** MD, QME (CA); See above.

See primary listing under PSYCHIATRY: General

Robert G. Brueckner, MPH, LCHE

President
Health Care Administration
Legal Consultants
3131 Westberry Square, Ste. E
Joplin, MO 64804
Tel: (417) 623-5650
Fax: (417) 623-5650
E-mail: bbrueckner@earthlink.net
Web Site:
www.healthcarelegalconsulting.com

Specialties: Over 30 years experience in health care executive management, including CEO of two large nonprofit community/tertiary hospitals. Masters Degree in Public Health/Health Care Administration, UC - Berkeley. Plaintiff and Defense. Extensive experience in JCAHO; Operating Policies, Procedures, and Standards of Care; Physician Credentialing, Privileges, and Peer Review; Hospital and Medical Staff Bylaws, Rules and Regulations; Physician Contracts; Third-party Payor/Managed Care Relationships; EMTALA; Hospital/Physician Joint Ventures; Hospital/System Affiliations. Assistance in Case Screening for Merit; Identification of Issues; Case Development; Depositions; Trial Testimony. Life Diplomate, American College of Healthcare Executives. **Degrees/licenses:** BA, MPH, LCHE.

See primary listing under MEDICAL-LEGAL: General

Alvin C. Burstein, MD

Well Being Systems
5070 N. 40th St., Ste. 220
Phoenix, AZ 85018-2135
Tel: (602) 957-2368
Fax: (602) 957-0050
E-mail: aburstein@wbsaz.com

Specialties: Adult Psychiatry; Geriatric Psychiatry; Standard of care for psychiatric units, hospitals, geriatric psych. units, managed care companies, psychiatrists; Analyze interactions psychiatric, medical, side effects, substance abuse, intoxication issues; Psychopharmacology; Explain clinical issues for case presentation; private practice of psychiatry, Medical Director of psych. HMO, and psychiatric hospital and Geriatric Psych. Unit; Excellent reputation, teacher, communicator. Associate Professor of Psychiatry. **Degrees/licenses:** MD, AZ; Board Certified.

See primary listing under PSYCHIATRY: General

Mark W. Gordon, MD

Mark W. Gordon, MD, PA
2301 N. University Drive
Pembroke Pines, FL 33024
Tel: (954) 964-1490
Fax: (954) 963-3453
E-mail: drmark@dslx.net

Specialties: Extensive experience in evaluation of hospital liability in medical negligence issues. Deposition and trial work, both defense and plaintiff. Local and national peer review, private and government payment reviews, state and federal. See other listings for further qualifications - Surgery, General & Hospital Staff Issues. **Degrees/licenses:** BS, MD.

Douglas E. Heritage, MD, FACOG

2026A Opitz Blvd.
Woodbridge, VA 22191
Tel: (703) 491-7155
Fax: (703) 690-3958
E-mail: obgynexp@aol.com
Web Site: http://drheritage.com

Specialties: Private practice of Obstetrics & Gynecology since 1978; Special qualifications

(Listing continued on next page)

Medical/Hospital Malpractice *(cont.)*

Douglas E. Heritage, MD (cont.)
in GYN laser surgery, laparoscopic surgery, pelvic microsurgery and hysteroscopic surgery. Extensive experience in fetal monitoring, treatment of endometriosis, abnormal PAP smears. Twenty years experience malpractice case review, testimony for plaintiff and defendant. Board certified American Board OB-GYN 1980, voluntary recertified 1999, 2001, 2003, and 2005. Fellow, American College of Obstetricians & Gynecologists. Member American Society of Reproductive Medicine. Past Chairman Department OB-GYN Potomac Hospital. Recipient multiple continuing education awards from AMA, ACOG, Medical Society of Virginia. **Degrees/ licenses:** BS, MD.
See primary listing under MEDICINE & HEALTH: Obstetrics & Gynecology

Leonard Kalfuss, MD

Bone & Joint Medical Clinic
225 S. Civic Dr., Ste. 1
Palm Springs, CA 92262
Tel: (760) 327-8595
Fax: (760) 327-8597
E-mail: DrLKalfuss@dc.rr.com

Specialties: Forensic Orthopedics - 35 years. AME, IME, QME. Testimony experience: trial, deposition, complex cases for plaintiff/ defense, P.I.-medical record review malpractice. Available throughout California. Prompt response and reports. **Degrees/licenses:** BSc, MD, FICS; Board Certified Orthopedic Surgery, Forensic Medicine.
See primary listing under MEDICINE & HEALTH: Orthopedic Surgery

Joseph B. Marzouk, MD

350 30th St., Ste. 511
Oakland, CA 94609
Tel: (510) 835-6225
(510) 834-2800
Fax: (510) 834-8206
E-mail: jobm@aol.com
Web Site: www.infectiousdiseasemd.com

Specialties: Infectious diseases - infections of all medical specialties; Hepatitis; Infection control; HIV/AIDS; Food poisoning; Independent Medical Evaluations; Case reviews, depositions, trials; Plaintiff and defense work; Multiple presentations to various audiences on infectious disease topics; Author, Infectious Disease chapter in "Lawyer's Medical Encyclopedia;" Board Certified in Infectious Diseases, Internal Medicine, Infection Control. HIV Specialist. CV available on request. **Degrees/licenses:** MD (AZ, CA).

See primary listing under MEDICINE & HEALTH: Infectious Diseases

Medstuff

William W. Filler, Jr., MD, FACOG
Gilbert J. Martinez, MD, JD
42525 Chaparral Dr.
Temecula, CA 92592-8955
Tel: (951) 303-1429
Fax: (951) 303-9357
E-mail: bfiller@medstuff.com
Web Site: http://www.medstuff.com

Specialties: Medstuff specializes in providing medical expert witnesses for plaintiff or defense, matching the right experts for your particular needs. William W. Filler, Jr., MD, FACOG: Expert in all related OB/Gyn matters; Board Certified. Gilbert J. Martinez, MD, JD: Board Certified Family Practitioner. See website at www.medstuff.com for details.

See primary listing under MEDICINE & HEALTH: General

Eliezer Nussbaum, MD, FCCM, FCCP, FAAP

Director, Pediatric Pulmonology
Miller Children's Hospital at
Long Beach Memorial Medical Center
University of Calif., Irvine
2801 Atlantic Avenue
Long Beach, CA 90801-1428
Tel: (562) 933-8740
Fax: (562) 933-8744
E-mail: enussbaum@memorialcare.org
Web Site:
http://member.expertpages.com/nussbaum

Specialties: Pediatrics; Pediatric Pulmonary; Pediatric Critical Care; Trauma and Emergency Medicine; Professor of Pediatrics at University of California, Irvine; Chief of Pediatric Pulmonary Medicine; Medical Director of Pediatric Pulmonary and Cystic Fibrosis Center at Miller Children's Hospital at Long Beach Memorial Medical Center; Certified by American Board of Pediatrics; Pediatric Pulmonology; Pediatric Critical Care Medicine. Experienced expert witness. Fluent English and Hebrew. **Degrees/licenses:** MD, FCCM, FCCP, FAAP.

See primary listing under MEDICINE & HEALTH: Pediatrics, Pulmonary, Critical Care

Richard Alan Ofstein, MD

Radiologist
122 Ocean Park Blvd., #512
Santa Monica, CA 90405
Tel: (310) 581-9805
E-mail: rofstein@aol.com
or rofstein@ucla.edu

Specialties: Neuroradiology. Interpretation and appropriate utilization of Magnetic Resonance Imaging (MRI), Computed Tomography (CT), and general radiology. Board Certification Diagnostic Radiology and Certificate of Added Qualifications in Neuroradiology. Subspecialty expertise in neuro- and musculoskeletal pathology including trauma- and sports-related injuries. Founding Publisher & Editor of two internationally-recognized publications, "Magnetic Resonance Update" and "Consultations in Radiology & Imaging," published since 1989. Topics include Head Trauma, Cervical Spine Injuries, Back Pain, Knee Injuries, Shoulder Pain, and Temporomandibular Joint (TMJ) Dysfunction. Private practice. University Appointment as Assistant Clinical Professor of Radiology, UCLA School of Medicine, 1988-2002. **Degrees/licenses:** MD (1980); CA Med. Lic. G44857; Cert. of Added Qualifications in Neuroradiology.

See primary listing under MEDICINE & HEALTH: Radiology, Neuroradiology

Julius S. Piver, MD, JD

6602 Melody Lane
Bethesda, MD 20817
Tel: (301) 365-4020
(240) 381-3600
Fax: (301) 469-5469
E-mail: jpmdjd@comcast.net
Web Site: http://www.obgyn-dr.com

Specialties: Practicing gynecologist, Board Certified Obstetrics & Gynecology, with 19 years expert witness/consultant experience in OB/GYN negligence cases, Plaintiff/Defense. 4000+ deliveries, 1000+ hysterectomies, 1500+ laparoscopies. Oversaw 30,000 deliveries as Clinical Chairman of Obstetrics for 5 years at major DC hospital. Consulting on Quality of Care & Standard of Care Issues such as breast cancer, shoulder dystocia, informed consent, laparoscopy complications, tubal ligation issues, cesarean section, hysterectomy, fetal monitoring, appendicitis, placental abruption, ectopic pregnancy, ureteral/bladder injury, sexual assault, neuropathies. **Degrees/licenses:** MD, JD, BdCert Ob/Gyn, FACOG, FACS, FAAGL, FACLM.

See primary listing under MEDICINE & HEALTH: Obstetrics & Gynecology

Medical/Hospital Malpractice *(cont.)*

Jack H. Raber, Pharm. D.

Principal
Clinipharm Services
P.O. Box 3206
Seal Beach, CA 90740
Tel: (562) 596-8753
Fax: (707) 897-1657
E-mail: Clinipharm@aol.com
Web Site: www.clinipharmservices.com

Specialties: Liability and risk management assessment, pharmacy malpractice, pharmacy-related hospital malpractice, institutional pharmacy law. Available for research, consultation, and trial testimony (plaintiff, defense, administrative law hearings). **Degrees/licenses:** Pharm.D., University of Southern California, 1975; California RPh 29591.

See primary listing under MEDICINE & HEALTH: Pharmacy

Anthony J. Scarcella, MD, JD

380 S. State Road 434
Suite 1004, #388
Altamonte Springs, FL 32714
Tel: (407) 616-7295
Fax: (407) 299-8735
E-mail: ascarcellamd@aol.com
Web Site: http://www.ermedicineexpert.com

Specialties: Board Certified Emergency Medicine with extensive experience in Medical Record Review for lawyers as well as insurance companies. Disability Analysis and Verification, Malpractice Consulting and Expert Witness Services. **Degrees/licenses:** MD Certified - American Board of Emergency Medicine.

See primary listing under MEDICINE & HEALTH: Emergency Medicine

Jeffrey M. Sherwood, MD, FACS

P.O. Box 1071
Water Mill, NY 11976
Tel: (888) 343-7642
Fax: (631) 726-9323
E-mail: jms12544@yahoo.com

Specialties: General Surgery, Laparoscopic Surgery & Breast Surgery. Over 10 years experience reviewing cases for both defendants' and plaintiffs' attorneys. Board Certified; Fellow, American College of Surgeons; Member, Society of Laparoscopic Surgeons. **Degrees/licenses:** MD, New York State Medical License.

See primary listing under MEDICINE & HEALTH: Surgery, General

Stephen B. Shohet, MD

Professor of Medicine
1925 Gough Street
San Francisco, CA 94109
Tel: (415) 922-3070
Fax: (415) 922-3113
E-mail: sbshohet@aol.com

Specialties: Expert witness for hematology, including bleeding, thrombosis, clotting, Heparin, and platelet problems; anemias, Sickle Cell Disease, and red cell disorders; leukemias, lymphomas and white cell diseases. Professor Emeritus of Medicine and Laboratory Medicine at University of California, San Francisco, with substantial testimony experience for both plaintiffs and defense. Also consultation for biomedical instrument and patent issues. Numerous publications. Medical licenses in California and Massachusetts. **Degrees/licenses:** AB, MD; Medical Lic. in CA & MA.

See primary listing under MEDICINE & HEALTH: Hematology

Alvin Stein, MD, FACS

President
Stein Orthopedic Assoc., PA
4101 NW 4th Street, Ste. 401
Plantation, FL 33317
Tel: (954) 581-8585
Fax: (954) 581-5580
E-mail: nobones@aol.com
Web Site: http://www.proloshot.com

Specialties: A board certified orthopedic surgeon and pain management specialist with extensive experience in chart review for standard of care issues, utilization issues, and worker compensation claims. ABQAURP certified. Available for IMEs or chart reviews, plaintiff or defense, for an honest evaluation. Over 35 years of experience in practice of medicine. Rapid response and thorough analysis of the issues in any case. Available to testify if needed. References available. **Degrees/licenses:** MD, FACS.

See primary listing under MEDICAL-LEGAL: Medical Record Review

Martin H. Williams, PhD

Clinical & Forensic Psychologist
P.O. Box 62439
Sunnyvale, CA 94088
Tel: (888) 225-9957
Fax: (888) 225-9957
E-mail: mw@drmwilliams.com
Web Site: http://drmwilliams.com

Specialties: Dr. Williams is a psychologist and psychotherapist who testifies on malpractice and emotional damages. He is an expert on sexual harassment, boundary violations, therapist patient sex, malingering, post traumatic stress disorder and borderline personality disorder. He has published in refereed journals on harmfulness of therapist-patient sexual involvement, ethics, risk management and malpractice. He is in full-time clinical practice, is licensed in California and testifies nationally. Offices in Los Angeles, San Jose, Orange County and San Diego. **Degrees/licenses:** PhD in Psychology (1975); Calif. Licensed Psychologist (1976).

See primary listing under MEDICINE & HEALTH: Psychology

Medical/Hospital/HMO Malpractice

Robert J. Bargar, MD, SM

137 Pine Ridge Road
Newton, MA 02468
Tel: (617) 527-5225
Fax: (617) 965-9355
E-mail: nelsonbargar@msn.com
Web Site: http://member.expertpages.com/robertbargar

Specialties: Quality Assurance and Utilization Review (Board Certified); Public Health/Preventive Medicine (Board Certified); Medical Management (Board Certified); Physician Billing and Fraud; Health Insurance Administration; Claims Review; Evaluation of medical care involving multiple providers of different specialties and the institutions at which they practice. Qualified as expert by U.S. Dept. of Labor & U.S. Dept. of Justice. Member American College of Physician Executives & National Association of Physician Broadcasters. **Degrees/licenses:** MD Tufts, SM & AB Harvard, Med. & Ins. Adv. Lic. MA.

Nursing

Chisolm Legal Nurse Consulting

Daniel Chisolm, RN, BSN
Certified Legal Nurse Consultant
11 Wayside Road
Asheville, NC 28805
Tel: (828) 236-0031
Fax: (828) 236-0031
E-mail: ncexpertnurse@yahoo.com
Web Site: http://www.ncexpertnurse.com

Specialties: Daniel W. Chisolm is a Registered Nurse with over 10 years experience in Critical Care, ICU, MICU, Recovery Room, ER, and general nursing. He is actively practicing bedside nursing. Mr. Chisolm is experienced with all nursing issues. He is also working with patients on ventilators, cardiac monitors, feeding tubes, IV therapy, arterial lines, respiratory failure and cardiac arrest. Experience includes care to cardiology, respiratory, renal, neuro-

(Listing continued on next page)

Nursing *(cont.)*

Chisolm Legal Nurse Consulting (cont.)
logical and hepatic patients. Services include providing expert testimony, screening cases for merit, analyzing medical records for deviations from standards of care, nursing research. **Degrees/licenses:** Registered Nurse, Certified Legal Nurse Consultant.

See primary listing under MEDICAL-LEGAL: Nursing Malpractice

Nursing Malpractice

Laura Burchell-Henson, RN

Registered Nurse
Medi-Legal Consultants, Inc.
P.O. Box 1229
Lakeside, CA 92040
Tel: (619) 749-5476
(619) 933-5021
Fax: (619) 749-5185
E-mail: medi-legal@cox.net
Web Site: http://www.medi-legal.org

Specialties: Registered Nurse & Respiratory Therapist who has been retained in more than 200 medical related cases since April 1999 to include criminal, personal injury, medical malpractice & products liability cases. Has testified in trial/depo 40 times. Twenty years of clinical experience includes ICU, ER, homecare, long-term care, Med-surg, obstetrics, psychiatric, administration and surgery. Services offered include testimony, medical records review, comprehensive reports, standards of care, trial testimony, locating other experts, identify defendants, assess damages/injuries and causation. **Degrees/licenses:** RN, RCP, CCRN, CLNC, SANE.

Chisolm Legal Nurse Consulting

Daniel Chisolm, RN, BSN
Certified Legal Nurse Consultant
11 Wayside Road
Asheville, NC 28805
Tel: (828) 236-0031
Fax: (828) 236-0031
E-mail: ncexpertnurse@yahoo.com
Web Site: http://www.ncexpertnurse.com

Specialties: Daniel W. Chisolm is a Registered Nurse with over 10 years experience in Critical Care, ICU, MICU, Recovery Room, ER, and general nursing. He is actively practicing bedside nursing. Mr. Chisolm is experienced with all nursing issues. He is also working with patients on ventilators, cardiac monitors, feeding tubes, IV therapy, arterial lines, respiratory failure and cardiac arrest. Experience includes care to cardiology, respiratory, renal, neurological and hepatic patients. Services include providing expert testimony, screening cases for merit, analyzing medical records for deviations from standards of care, nursing research. **Degrees/licenses:** Registered Nurse, Certified Legal Nurse Consultant.

MED-LINK Consultation

Dorothy A. Pollock, RN
3362 Budleigh Drive
Hacienda Heights, CA 91745-6409
Tel: (626) 333-5110
Fax: (626) 968-0064
E-mail: dorothypollock@adelphia.net

Specialties: RN with 36 years experience, 31 years in surgery with emphasis on: trauma, orthopedics, neurology, cardiovascular, ophthalmology, ENT, Gynecology, Laparoscopy, Endoscopy, Urology, Plastics, Laser and Pain Management. Member of Association of peri-Operative Registered Nurses (AORN); American Association of Legal Nurse Consultants (AALNC); Secretary/Treasurer 2004-05. Past President of AALNC-LA. Services offered: Nursing SOC; IME/DME Accompaniment; Chronologies. Expert Witness for both Plaintiff & Defense. Federal, Civil and Criminal Courtroom experienced. **Degrees/licenses:** RN, BS Health Care Admin., CNOR, LNCC, ACLS, PALS.

See primary listing under MEDICINE & HEALTH: Nursing

James M. Miller, PE, PhD

President
Miller Engineering Associates, Inc.
2392 Fuller Court
Ann Arbor, MI 48105
Tel: (734) 662-6822
Fax: (734) 747-9712
E-mail: jmiller@millerengineering.com
Web Site: www.millerengineering.com

Specialties: Nursing Malpractice; Nursing Management; Mechanical Design Safety: Power Tools & Machine Guarding; OSHA/ANSI/ASTM Compliance; Warnings, Labels, Instructions & User Manuals: Health Hazard Warnings; Design of User Manuals & Warnings; Consumer Product Safety: Human Factors & Ergonomics, Slips, Falls-Premise, Vehicle, Ladder; Child, Home Appliances, Furniture; Vehicles: Auto, Truck, ATV, Boat, Jet Ski, Snowmobile; Seat Belts & Air Bags; Chemical, Fire, Environmental & Waste Disposal: Fires & Explosions-Vapors/Electrical/Chemical; Chemical Labeling Requirements; MSDS; Groundwater & Soil Contamination; Agricultural & Construction Safety: Tractor, Implement, Harvester & Grain Storage; Pesticides, Herbicides, Fungicides. **Degrees/licenses:** James Miller, PE, PhD; Bradley Cook, PE; Rebecca Lehto, PhD, RN, OCN.

See primary listing under ACCIDENT PREVENTION & SAFETY: General

Ophthalmology

Robert G. Josephberg, MD

984 North Broadway, Ste. 511
Yonkers, NY 10701
Tel: (914) 965-2526
Fax: (914) 965-2527
E-mail: LisaRiRob@optonline.net
Web Site:
http://www.westchester-retina.eyemd.org

Specialties: Chief of Retina (WMC); Board Certified Ophthalmologist (1981); Fellowship trained retinal Surgeon, Baylor College of Medicine, Houston, TX (1981); Volunteer Surgeon (Project Orbis); Inventor, VISITREC Vitrectomy (Top Ten Award, American Academy of Ophthalmology); Assistant Clinical Professor, NY Medical College and NJ College of Medicine; Well published; Active in teaching; Has lectured extensively on retinal detachment, macular degeneration, diabetic retinopathy, endophthalmitis and complications of ophthalmic surgery; Member, American Academy of Ophthalmology, American Society of Retina Specialists, NY Ophthalmology and Medical Society, Florida Medical Association, NJ Ophthalmology Society, Westchester Medical Society, American Medical Association. **Degrees/licenses:** MD, BS, ABO; Med. Lic. in NY, NJ & FL.

See primary listing under MEDICINE & HEALTH: Ophthalmology

Orthopedic Consulting

John H. Devor, MD

970 Dewing Ave., Ste. 200
Lafayette, CA 94549
Tel: (925) 284-5100
Fax: (925) 284-5551
E-mail: jdevormd@yahoo.com

Specialties: General orthopedics; Occupational and forensic orthopedics; Neck and lower back problems; Medical-legal evaluations; Medical record review/analysis; Review of myelograms, MRIs and CT scans; Second opinions/case management; Expert witness testimony. **Degrees/licenses:** MD CA Lic. #A31476; Certified Independent Medical Examiner (ABIME #96-00423).

See primary listing under MEDICINE & HEALTH: Orthopedics

Suicidology

Addiction Forensics Group

Mace Beckson, MD
11301 West Olympic Blvd. #323
Los Angeles, CA 90064
Tel: (310) 966-1907
Fax: (310) 477-0661
E-mail: becksonmd@becksonmd.com
Web Site: http://www.becksonmd.com

Specialties: Alcohol/drugs; addiction; suicide; PTSD; sex offenders; child molestation; sexual abuse; adult victims of childhood abuse; rape; violence; stalking; threat assessment; risk assessment; sexual addiction; impaired physicians; Medical Board; psychiatric malpractice; therapist misconduct; boundary violations; brain injury; neuropsychiatry; disability; competence to stand trial; insanity defense; sentencing; involuntary hospitalization; civil commitment. UCLA full-time faculty; Assoc. Clin. Prof.; Board-certified in Addiction/Forensic Psych; Certified Addiction Medicine; Distinguished Fellow, APA; Med. Director, Psychiatric Intensive Care, VA; Addiction Psych. Cmtee, AAPL; Expert Reviewer, CA Med Board; Suicidal Behavior Root Cause Analysis Team, VA; Chair, Task Force on Adolescent Addiction, ASAP; Sex Offender Cmtee, AAPL. **Degrees/licenses:** MD, Board Certified: Psych, Addiction Psych, Forensics.

See primary listing under MEDICINE & HEALTH: Alcohol/Drugs

Ronald W. Maris, PhD

Professor Emeritus
Suicide Center
University of South Carolina
305 Sloan Bldg., 911 Pickens St.
Columbia, SC 29208
Tel: (803) 777-6870
(803) 240-3073 (Cell)
(803) 736-6042 or 736-0365 (Res.)
Fax: (803) 777-5251 or 865-3946 (Res.)
E-mail: maris@sc.edu or rwmaris@aol.com
Web Site: http://www.suicideexpert.com

Home Office
9 Poachers Lane
Columbia, SC 29223-3014

Specialties: Suicide Death Investigation; Suicide Risk Assessment & Suicide Prediction; Medical Malpractice; Drug Liability (especially SSRI cases); Contested Life Insurance; Equivocal Death Investigation (suicide v. homicide v. accident); Small Plane Crashes; Workplace Violence Assessment. Past-President American Association of Suicidology, Past Editor-in-Chief of Suicide Journal; Fellow in American Academy of Forensic Sciences (Psychiatry); Board certified Forensic Examiner and Fellow; Author/editor of 20 books (incl. National Book-of-the-Month); Assoc. Professor - Johns Hopkins School of Medicine; 5 post-doctoral fellowships in psychiatry. **Degrees/licenses:** PhD, Fellow - ACFE, Fellow - AAFS.

See primary listing under PSYCHIATRY: Suicidology

MEDICINE & HEALTH

General

Accredited Psychiatry & Medicine

Harvard Medical School
Alumni & Faculty Experts
Tel: (617) 492-8366
Fax: (617) 441-3195
E-mail: harold_bursztajn@hms.harvard.edu
Web Site: http://www.forensic-psych.com

Specialties: Psychiatry, Forensic Psychiatry, Legal Medicine & Analysis, Managed Care, Testamentary Capacity, Addiction, Product Liability, Neuropsychiatric, Medical Employment & Discrimination, Toxic Torts, Independent Medical Examinations & Testing, Professional Ethics, Expert Testimony, Custodial Issues, Criminal Justice & Public Safety, Diminished Capacity, PTSD. Plaintiff and defense expert with local and national references. Over twenty five years of service as a distinguished patient care-focused clinician and as senior clinical faculty at Harvard Medical School; Co-Director of the Program in Psychiatry and the Law and Associate Professor of Psychiatry at the Harvard Medical School. **Degrees/licenses:** BA, MD, Lic.: MA, NH, National Dual Medical Board Certification.

See primary listing under PSYCHIATRY: General

CERA, Inc., Medical Legal Support Services

Timothy D. Brooks, MD
Medical Director
P. O. Box 11247
Pensacola, FL 32524-1247
Tel: (888) 476-7707 (Toll Free)
(850) 476-7707
Fax: (850) 995-9440
E-mail: info@cerainc.com
Web Site: http://www.cerainc.com/

Specialties: CERA, Inc. is a physician owned and operated consulting group providing medical malpractice case screening, expert witness identification, and preparation of Life Care Plans. CERA's staff of physicians and nurses can review your case and offer a preliminary opinion on merit. We also have experts available in all areas of medicine to review your case and offer a formal opinion on standard of care for plaintiff or defense. CERA's services are rapid, accurate and cost effective. For a no-obligation consultation, please call Toll Free (888) 476-7707. **Degrees/licenses:** MD, RN, CLNC, CLCP, OTR.

See primary listing under MEDICAL-LEGAL: Medical Record Review

ForensisGroup, Inc.

Mercy Steenwyk
3452 E. Foothill Blvd., Ste. 1160
Pasadena, CA 91107
Tel: (626) 795-5000
(800) 555-5422
Fax: (626) 795-1950
E-mail: experts@forensisgroup.com
Web Site: http://forensisgroup.com

Specialties: Thousands of our clients have gained the technical advantage and the edge in their cases from our multidisciplined group of experts in hundreds of disciplines. We have some of the best and the brightest at competitive rates backed by 14 years of excellent track record and the support of our trained staff. We assist you until you have the right expert. Some of our areas of expertise are: Construction, Safety, Engineering, Product Liability, Accident Reconstruction, Automotive,

(Listing continued on next page)

General *(cont.)*

ForensisGroup, Inc. (cont.)
Environmental, Slip & Fall, Appraisal, Medical and other scientific disciplines. Unsurpassed standards. Clients actively evaluate our experts. **Degrees/licenses:** PE, GC, CSP, PhD, MD, GC, CIH, AIA.

See primary listing under ACCIDENT PREVENTION & SAFETY: General

Medstuff

William W. Filler, Jr., MD, FACOG
Gilbert J. Martinez, MD, JD
42525 Chaparral Dr.
Temecula, CA 92592-8955
Tel: (951) 303-1429
Fax: (951) 303-9357
E-mail: bfiller@medstuff.com
Web Site: http://www.medstuff.com

Specialties: Medstuff specializes in providing medical expert witnesses for plaintiff or defense, matching the right experts for your particular needs. William W. Filler, Jr., MD, FACOG: Expert in all related OB/Gyn matters; Board Certified. Gilbert J. Martinez, MD, JD: Board Certified Family Practitioner. See website at www.medstuff.com for details.

Pro/Consul Technical and Medical Experts

1945 Palo Verde Ave., Suite 200
Long Beach, CA 90815-3443
Tel: (800) 392-1119
(562) 799-0116
Fax: (562) 799-8821
E-mail: eexperts@msn.com
Web Site: http://www.expertinfo.com

Specialties: RIGHT EXPERT RIGHT AWAY!® 15,000 experts in 7,000 fields. Listed and recommended by the A. M. Best Company. Full-time research staff. We welcome your RUSH cases! TECHNICAL: Fast inspections. Categories from Accident Reconstruction to Zoology, also including appraisal, economics, employment, human factors, insurance, premises liability, security, and many more. MEDICAL: IME's. Inexpensive insurance medical records reviews by MDs. Categories from Addiction Medicine to Zooplasty, including board certified physicians in all fields, dentistry, geriatrics, neuropsychology, neurosurgery, nursing, orthopedics, psychiatry and many more. Reasonable fees. Free initial consultation. Free resume binder. Free CLE classes. **Degrees/licenses:** MD, PhD, DDS, DVM, DO, DPM, PE, CPA, ME, CE, CRC, MAI, et al.

See primary listing under ACCIDENT RECONSTRUCTION: General

Stephen Read, MD

2566 Overland Ave., Ste. 500B
Los Angeles, CA 90064
Tel: (310) 521-9747
Fax: (310) 521-8112
E-mail: readsmd@aol.com
Web Site: www.geriatricpsychiatrist.com

Specialties: Practicing psychiatrist for twenty years; qualified as medical psychiatric expert witness more than 300 cases in federal and multiple state courts; capacity, testamentary capacity, will contests; conservatorship, competence to testify; undue influence, elder abuse, financial abuse; skilled nursing homes; quality of care; psychotropic medications; dementia, Alzheimer's Disease, frontal lobe, stroke, vascular dementias, Parkinson's disease, hydrocephalus, depression, psychosis; personal injury; Americans with Disability Act (ADA). Associate Clinical Professor UCLA, board certified: Psychiatry, Forensic Psychiatry, Geriatric Psychiatry; medical staff at UCLA Neuropsychiatric Hospital, Los Angeles VA and Air Force Base. **Degrees/licenses:** MD; Board Cert.: Psychiatry, Geriatric Psych., Forensic Psych.

TASAmed

A Division of The TASA Group
1166 DeKalb Pike
Blue Bell, PA 19422-1853
Tel: (800) 659-8464
Fax: (800) 850-8272
E-mail: tasamed@tasanet.com
Web Site: http://www.tasanet.com

Specialties: FIND THE MEDICAL EXPERT YOU NEED with TASAmed, a co-division of TASA, North America's foremost Expert Referral Service. Thousands of top-caliber Local and National specialists for case review, IME's, consulting, and testifying in over 900 medical fields. Categories of expertise include Anesthesiology; Cardiology; Cosmetic Surgery; Dentistry; Elder Abuse; Emergency Care; Environmental Medicine; Forensic Pathology; Geriatrics; Nephrology; Obstetrics; Occupational Medicine; Oncology; Pediatrics; Psychiatry; Pulmonology; Radiology; Sports Medicine; Surgery; & More. SERVICES INCLUDE prompt customized searches, referrals, resumes, and your initial interview calls with experts. Exceptional personal service for over 44 years. **Degrees/licenses:** All prof. degrees, licenses, certifications represented.

See primary listing under EXPERT WITNESS REFERRALS: General

AIDS Medicine

Stephen W. Hosea, MD

320 W. Pueblo, Rm. 6S09
Santa Barbara, CA 93105
Tel: (805) 682-3610
Fax: (805) 682-3050
E-mail: shosea@sbch.org

Specialties: Harvard College BA, 1969; Harvard Medical School MD, 1973; Massachusetts General Hospital Medical Resident, 1973-75; National Institutes of Health, NIAID Clinical Associate, 1975-78; Yale University 1978-79, Infectious Disease Fellow; NIH, NIAID 1979-81, Senior Investigator; Private Practice Infectious Disease, 1981-present; Associate Academic Chief of Medicine, 1983-present; Director AIDS Clinic, 1984-present; Head of Infection Control at Santa Barbara Cottage Hospital, 1993-present. **Degrees/licenses:** MD (Internal Medicine, 1976; Infectious Diseases, 1980); FACP.

See primary listing under MEDICINE & HEALTH: Infectious Diseases

Joseph B. Marzouk, MD

350 30th St., Ste. 511
Oakland, CA 94609
Tel: (510) 835-6225
(510) 834-2800
Fax: (510) 834-8206
E-mail: jobm@aol.com
Web Site: www.infectiousdiseasemd.com

Specialties: Infectious diseases - infections of all medical specialties; Hepatitis; Infection control; HIV/AIDS; Food poisoning; Independent Medical Evaluations; Case reviews, depositions, trials; Plaintiff and defense work; Multiple presentations to various audiences on infectious disease topics; Author, Infectious Disease chapter in "Lawyer's Medical Encyclopedia;" Board Certified in Infectious Diseases, Internal Medicine, Infection Control. HIV Specialist. CV available on request. **Degrees/licenses:** MD (AZ, CA).

See primary listing under MEDICINE & HEALTH: Infectious Diseases

Alcohol/Drugs

Addiction Forensics Group

Mace Beckson, MD
11301 West Olympic Blvd. #323
Los Angeles, CA 90064
Tel: (310) 966-1907
Fax: (310) 477-0661
E-mail: becksonmd@becksonmd.com
Web Site: http://www.becksonmd.com

Specialties: Alcohol/drugs; addiction; suicide; PTSD; sex offenders; child molestation; sexual abuse; adult victims of childhood abuse; rape; violence; stalking; threat assessment; risk assessment; sexual addiction; impaired physicians; Medical Board; psychiatric malpractice; therapist misconduct; boundary violations; brain injury; neuropsychiatry;

(Listing continued on next page)

Alcohol/Drugs *(cont.)*

Addiction Forensics Group (cont.)
disability; competence to stand trial; insanity defense; sentencing; involuntary hospitalization; civil commitment. UCLA full-time faculty; Assoc. Clin. Prof.; Board-certified in Addiction/Forensic Psych; Certified Addiction Medicine; Distinguished Fellow, APA; Med. Director, Psychiatric Intensive Care, VA; Addiction Psych. Cmtee, AAPL; Expert Reviewer, CA Med Board; Suicidal Behavior Root Cause Analysis Team, VA; Chair, Task Force on Adolescent Addiction, ASAP; Sex Offender Cmtee, AAPL. **Degrees/licenses:** MD, Board Certified: Psych, Addiction Psych, Forensics.

Lawson F. Bernstein, MD

MD - Forensic Neuropsychiatry
P. O. Box 81977
Pittsburgh, PA 15217
Tel: (412) 600-7996
Fax: (412) 422-5203
E-mail: lawsonbernstein@hotmail.com
Web Site: http://www.ifbmdpc.com

Specialties: Board certified academically published forensic neuropsychiatrist. Expertise in brain injury, stroke, neurotoxicology, acute/chronic pain, dementia, alcohol & substance abuse, gambling addiction and multiple other areas of neurology/psychiatry. Extensive criminal/civil trial (50/50) Plaintiff/Defense experience, including death penalty cases/legal insanity/diminished capacity. From 1991-1994, Dr. Bernstein was Director of the Psychiatry Residency Training Program at the University of Pittsburgh Medical Center, one of the largest academic psychiatric training programs in the U.S. Dr. Bernstein is also a Board Examiner for the American Board of Psychiatry & Neurology Oral Examination. **Degrees/licenses:** Medical.

See primary listing under MEDICINE & HEALTH: Head Injury

Yale H. Caplan

Director and Principal
National Scientific Services
3411 Philips Dr.
Baltimore, MD 21208
Tel: (410) 486-7486
Fax: (410) 653-4824
E-mail: ForTox@aol.com

Specialties: Forensic toxicology; clinical toxicology; general toxicology; medico-legal aspects of alcohol and drugs; laboratory testing for alcohol, drugs and other chemicals; effects of alcohol and drugs on drivers (drunk and drugged driving); breath alcohol testing; evaluation of the role of alcohol, drugs and chemicals (poisons) in postmortem (death) investigations; drug abuse; pharmacology and use and effects of prescription and other medicines; employee and workplace drug testing; interpretation of toxicology reports and issues; formerly Chief Toxicologist for the State of Maryland and Director of Forensic Toxicology for a large national laboratory. **Degrees/licenses:** PhD; BS, Pharmacy (PD); D-ABFT; CPC.
See primary listing under MEDICINE & HEALTH: Forensic Toxicology

George S. Glass, MD

George S. Glass, MD, PA
4600 Post Oak Place, Suite 307
Houston, TX 77027
Tel: (713) 666-9811
Fax: (713) 627-3488

Specialties: Dr. Glass is a Distinguished Fellow of the American Psychiatric Association, A Board Certified Psychiatrist and Addictionologist. He has spent more than 30 years involved in the treatment of people with Substance Abuse Problems as well as in the development of Inpatient and Outpatient Psychiatric and Substance Abuse Treatment Programs and Employee Assistance Programs. He is a Consultant to the Texas Board of Medical Examiners, the Texas Bar Association, the FAA, the Airline Pilots Association, and numerous other companies. He has had Academic Appointments at both Baylor School of Medicine and the University of Texas Medical School in Houston. **Degrees/licenses:** MD, Board Certified Psychiatrist, Addictionologist.

Douglas Severance, MD

5601 Norris Canyon Rd., Ste. 330
San Ramon, CA 94583
Tel: (925) 275-0400
Fax: (925) 327-7155
E-mail: poprocks120@earthlink.net

Specialties: Certified by the American Society of Addictive Medicine. Twenty years of work in chemical dependency. Medical director of several detox/rehabilitation programs. Contracted as a chemical dependency expert in multiple cases. **Degrees/licenses:** BS, MD, ABFP, ASAM.

See primary listing under ALCOHOL/DRUGS: General

S. Franklin Sher, MD

Toxicology & Family Physician
& Surgeon
1150 Civic Drive
Walnut Creek, CA 94596
Tel: (925) 935-3113
Fax: (925) 935-4482
E-mail: franklinsher@yahoo.com

Specialties: Impaired performance from alcohol or drugs; pedestrian, bicyclist or operator of any motorized transport for commercial/personal use. Forty five years experience. Over 2000 court trials (including federal and state) as qualified expert in 31 California counties; Review police, coroner, accident, reconstruction reports; depositions, interviews, transcripts; hospital and physician's records. Literature search; analysis and evaluation of evidence; retrograde extrapolations, dose/drink calculations; changes in human factors from alcohol/drug impairment; influence of body trauma/blood losses on alcohol/drugs levels. Clients include Caltrans, Attorney General, many major Law Firms; Defense 85%, Plaintiff 15%. **Degrees/licenses:** BS, MD, FAAFP.

See primary listing under ALCOHOL/DRUGS: General

Allergy/Immunology

Florida Center for Allergy & Asthma Care & Research

Michael P. Pacin, MD
President & CEO
8970 SW 87th Ct., Ste. 100
Miami, FL 33176
Tel: (305) 279-3366
Fax: (305) 271-3355
E-mail: info@florida-allergy.com
Web Site: http://www.florida-allergy.com

Specialties: For over 30 years, Dr. Pacin has diagnosed and cared for adult and pediatric patients suffering from allergies, asthma, sinusitis, immune deficiencies, and allergic skin diseases such as urticaria, angioedema, and eczema. He sees patients for allergies related to pollens, molds, drugs, foods, latex, chemicals, animals, dust, and environmental allergens. Dr. Pacin received his MD from Washington University School of Medicine and completed his fellowship in Allergy & Immunology at the University of California Irvine. Dr. Pacin has also conducted extensive clinical trial research on medications to treat allergy related diseases. **Degrees/licenses:** MD, Board Certified Allergy/Asthma/Immunology.

Oscar L. Frick, MD, PhD

Professor Emeritus Pediatrics-
Allergy-Immunology
University of California, San Francisco
370 Parnassus Avenue
San Francisco, CA 94117
Tel: (415) 566-0733
Fax: (415) 476-4009
E-mail: oscarfrick@earthlink.net

Specialties: Anaphylactic shock from drugs, foods, immunotherapy, biologicals like latex and prosthetics; Allergies to foods, especially peanuts and genetically-modified foods; Asthma, skin eczema, allergic sinusitis, hay fever, gastrointestinal, chronic diarrhea and malnutrition; Allergic reactions to drugs, antibiotics, e.g., penicillin, anesthetics, anticonvulsants. Professor Emeritus Pediatrics, Allergy-Immunology. President, American

(Listing continued on next page)

Allergy/Immunology *(cont.)*

Oscar L. Frick, MD (cont.)
Academy of Allergy & Immunology. Chairman, FDA Panel Pulmon-Allergy, Drugs. **Degrees/licenses:** MD, PhD, Amer. Board Allergy & Immunology & Pediatrics.

Kenneth T. Kim, MD

Allergy, Asthma & Respiratory Care
Medical Center
2600 Redondo Ave., #400
Long Beach, CA 90806-2330
Tel: (562) 997-7888
Fax: (562) 997-8884
E-mail: andrean@wcctrials.com
Web Site: http://www.allergy-asthma.info

Specialties: Expert reviewer & witness, QME, WC, pediatric and adult asthma, atopic dermatitis, eczema, hives, chronic cough, food/drug allergy, insect stings, mold allergy, latex allergy, sick building syndrome, disability evaluations, occupational latex allergy, disability evaluations for occupational asthma. **Degrees/licenses:** MD Harvard; Assistant Clinical Professor, UCLA, UCI.

Alternative Medicine

Aldo M. Rosemblat, MD, PC

6316 Castle Place, Ste. 200
Falls Church, VA 22044
Tel: (703) 241-8989
Fax: (703) 532-6247

Specialties: Diplomate American Board of Neurological Surgery, American Academy of Pain Management, American Board of Forensic Examiners; Doctor of Integrative Medicine, Capital University of Integrative Medicine; Board Certified, American Board of Chelation Therapy; Board Certified Physician, American Naturopathic Certification Board; Licensed in Maryland, Virginia & the District of Columbia. **Degrees/licenses:** MD, FA-ADEP.

See primary listing under MEDICINE & HEALTH: Neurosurgery

Amputation & Artificial Limbs

Arlene F. Hoffman, DPM, PhD

California Pacific Medical Center
2100 Webster St., Ste. 202
San Francisco, CA 94115-2375
Tel: (415) 923-3535
Fax: (415) 923-3672

Specialties: Medical evaluation and treatment of podiatric injuries; Perioperative evaluation; Wound healing; Blood flow evaluation of the lower extremity; Use of pharmaceuticals and laboratory evaluation. PhD, Downstate Medical Center, SUNY; DPM, California College of Podiatric Medicine; Fellow, Stanford University College of Medicine. Previous/current positions: Professor; Chair, Exam Committee, American Board of Podiatric Orthopedics; Board Trustee, ABPOPPM, ASPM, ASPD, ASPA; Special Editor, "The Lower Extremity;" General Editor, "Journal of the American Podiatric Medical Association;" Editor, "Yearbook of Podiatric Medicine and Surgery." Recipient of the Meritorious Service Award, APMA. 35+ publications. **Degrees/licenses:** DPM, PhD.

See primary listing under MEDICINE & HEALTH: Podiatry

Rod S. O'Connor, CPO

Certified Prosthetist & Orthotist
O'Connor Orthopedics
412 Carl Karcher Way
Anaheim, CA 92801
Tel: (714) 635-2650
(714) 635-2669
(714) 635-2651
Fax: (714) 635-0223
E-mail: mxrod@pacbell.net

Specialties: Certified by the American Board for Certification in Orthotics & Prosthetics. Specialist in: all lower extremity prosthetics, all upper extremity prosthetics, myoelectrics (bionics), etc.; braces for spine, halos, extremity bracing, fracture bracing, etc. Member: American Board for Certification in Orthotics & Prosthetics, American Orthotic & Prosthetic

Association, American Academy of Orthotists & Prosthetists, NCOPE accredited residency site. **Degrees/licenses:** CPO, VAQP.

Anesthesiology

Linda M. Huffman, CRNA

402 Tod Lane
Youngstown, OH 44504-3425
Tel: (330) 743-9596
(330) 360-0163 (Cell)
Fax: (330) 743-9596

Specialties: Nurse anesthesia practice: general surgery, trauma, obstetrics; Anesthesia gas delivery systems; Monitoring devices and applications; Anesthesia devices and applications; Standards for machines and monitoring; Pulse oximetry, capnography, ventilatory monitoring; Safety standards for ambulatory care, post-anesthesia recovery transport monitoring; Safe Medical Device Act of 1990; AANA and OSHA recommendations for waste gas management; ASTM standards for safety and performance of anesthesia machines and monitoring systems; NIOSH standards. RN (AZ, IL, NM, OH, OR, TX, VA, WV); Certified in ACLS, BCLS and PALS; Board Certification: Council on Certification of American Association of Nurse Anesthetists. **Degrees/licenses:** CRNA (Certified Registered Nurse Anesthetist).

Audiology

Douglas G. Finn, MD, FACS

Otolaryngology
253 - 78th Street
Brooklyn, NY 11209
Tel: (718) 439-6687
Fax: (718) 439-6713
E-mail: douglasgfinn@aol.com
Web Site: http://www.douglasgfinn.com

Specialties: Otolaryngology - Head and Neck Surgery, Forensic Otolaryngology, Oncology Review, Sinus Disorders, Trauma and Accident Evaluation, Personal Injury, Workers' Compensation, Occupational and Post-Traumatic Hearing Loss and Disability Evaluation, Medical Record Review. President, Kings County Medical Society - Otolaryngology Section; American College of Surgeons; American Head and Neck Society; Triological Society; Clinical Associate Professor, New York Medical College. **Degrees/licenses:** BA, MD

See primary listing under MEDICINE & HEALTH: Otolaryngology

Sacramento Ear, Nose & Throat Surgical & Medical Group, Inc.

Jeffrey W. Dudley
CFO/Medical Group Administrator
3810 J Street
Sacramento, CA 95816
Tel: (916) 736-3399
Fax: (916) 736-9837
E-mail: jdudley@sacent.com
Web Site: http://www.sacent.com

Specialties: Twelve Board Certified, full-time practicing Otolaryngologists; Otology; Neurotology; Hearing Loss; Tinnitus; Audiology; Head and Neck Cancer; Endoscopic Sinus Surgery; Facial Plastic Surgery; Allergy; Voice Disorders; Sleep Disorders; Swallowing Disorders; Vertigo; Smell and Taste Disorders. **Degrees/licenses:** All Board Certified MDs.

See primary listing under MEDICINE & HEALTH: Otolaryngology

Brain Injury

Warren E. Cohen, MD, FAAP

302 Carvel Ave.
Cedarhurst, NY 11516
Tel: (516) 371-3691
Fax: (516) 371-1895
E-mail: weco@pop.net

Specialties: Birth injury, birth defects, birth asphyxia, cerebral palsy, mental retardation, genetic conditions, pediatric disorders, neurologic disorders; Extent of neurologic damage, long-term disability needs, expected lifespan; Causation of birth injuries and neurologic disability in childhood; genetic/congenital cause versus birth-related injury. Experienced

(Listing continued on next page)

Brain Injury *(cont.)*

Warren E. Cohen, MD (cont.)
witness, plaintiff/defendant. Board certified in Pediatrics, Pediatric Neurology, and Medical Genetics. Also certified in Neuro-rehabilitation. Experienced children's hospital medical director, United Cerebral Palsy medical director. Associate Clinical Professor, George Washington University School of Medicine. Training: Hosp. Albert Einstein College of Medicine, National Institutes of Health. **Degrees/licenses:** BS, MD, FAAP.

See primary listing under MEDICINE & HEALTH: Pediatric Neurology

Edward S. Kaplan, MD, FACS

424 Sweetbriar Road
Memphis, TN 38120-2503
Tel: (901) 767-6442
Fax: (901) 685-7809
E-mail: elkaplan@aol.com

Specialties: Neurosurgery, Board Certified, 1966; Yale University, BA, 1955, Phi Beta Kappa; Columbia University, MD, 1959; University of Minnesota, MS (Neurosurgery), 1964; Internship, Columbia-Presbyterian Hospital, 1960; Neurosurgical Residency, Mayo Clinic, 1960-64; University of Tennessee, Instructor, Neurology, 1964-1973, Clinical Assistant Professor, Neurosurgery, 1973-2001; Baptist Hospital, Memphis, TN, Active Staff, 1964-2000. Congress Neurological Surgeons; American Association Neurological Surgeons; Fellow American College Surgeons; AMA; TMA; Memphis Medical Society; Memphis Surgical Society. **Degrees/licenses:** BA, MD, MS, FACS, ABNS Cert., Med. Lic. in TN.

See primary listing under MEDICINE & HEALTH: Neurosurgery

Henry W. Lahmeyer, MD

Clinical Professor of Psychiatry
Chicago Medical School
Two Northfield Plaza, Ste. 100
Northfield, IL 60093
Tel: (847) 446-3531
Fax: (847) 446-3573
E-mail: henry@lahmeyermd.com
Web Site: www.lahmeyermd.com

Specialties: Twenty years experience in treating and evaluating brain injury due to trauma, stroke, toxins, dementia, infections, electrical current, mental retardation and learning disabilities. Testified over 200 times for plaintiff and defense in cases of brain trauma. Maintains active private practice and research program. Previously Professor at the University of Illinois and Northwestern University, currently Clinical Professor of Psychiatry, Chicago Medical School. Published over 70 articles and received over 40 research grants. **Degrees/licenses:** BA, MD; Board Cert. in Psych, Sleep Med. & Forensic Psych.

See primary listing under MEDICINE & HEALTH: Psychiatry

Ariel Sherbany, MD, PhD

Pediatric Neurologist
Pediatric Neurology of Hudson Valley, PLLC
55 Old Nyack Turnpike, Ste. 101
Nanuet, NY 10954
Tel: (845) 627-0723
Fax: (845) 627-1009
E-mail: neuroman31@aol.com
Web Site: http://www.pedneuro.net

Specialties: Neonatal Neurology, Epilepsy, Child Neurology. Board Certifications: Pediatrics, Neurology, Neurophysiology. Academic affiliations: Columbia University, New York Medical College, Assistant Professor. Licensure: New York, New Jersey. Training: New York University, Washington University, Columbia University. Publications, lectures. **Degrees/licenses:** BS, MD, PhD.

See primary listing under MEDICINE & HEALTH: Pediatric Neurology

Richard K. Smith, PhD

Clinical Director
Back in the Saddle
Long-term Residential Services
for Head Injured Adults
9775 Mockingbird Ave.
Apple Valley, CA 92308
Tel: (760) 240-3217 & (909) 980-3567
Fax: (760) 240-3274 & (909) 989-3932
E-mail: staff@thesaddle.com
Web Site: http://www.thesaddle.com

Specialties: Head injury, CVA, spinal and other catastrophic pictures. Vocational and transitional design for adult head injured at Rancho Los Amigos Med. Center. Co-director, Back in the Saddle, long-term community residential setting for brain damaged adults. Private practice: domestic violence, vocational rehabilitation and community re-entry. PhD (USIU, 1991); MS Rehabilitation Counseling, Calif. State Univ., Los Angeles (1974). Formerly: So. Calif. Head Injury Foundation Board of Directors; San Bernardino County Dept. of Mental Health Commission. Currently, member San Bernardino County Domestic Violence Consortium; National Brain Injury Foundation; American and Calif. Psychological Assoc. **Degrees/licenses:** PhD, Licensed Clinical Psych., Certified Rehab. Counselor (CRC).

See primary listing under EMPLOYMENT: Vocational Rehabilitation

Breast Implants

John L. Baeke, MD

Park Place Plastic Surgery
14950 Newton
Overland Park, KS 66223
Tel: (913) 685-0101
Fax: (913) 685-3666
E-mail: JBaeke@ParkPlaceUSA.net
Web Site: http://www.beautifulbreasts.com

Specialties: Plastic Surgery; Includes breast implant problems, breast reduction/lift & post-mastectomy reconstruction issues; Body contouring: abdominoplasty & liposuction; Cosmetic laser procedures: tattoo removal, skin resurfacing, pigmented & vascular lesions; Post-traumatic injury & wound care acute & chronic including bed sores. Experience with plaintiff & defendant case review, brief preparation & testimony. Univ. Kansas-honors. First place Guffey Competition. First place Calif. Society of Plastic Surgeons. Assoc. Prof. University of Kansas School of Med. Amer. Society of Laser Medicine & Surgery. Amer. Society of Cosmetic Breast Surgery. Assoc. Military Surgeons of U.S., Amer. Academy of Wound Management, AMA. **Degrees/licenses:** MD.

See primary listing under MEDICINE & HEALTH: Plastic & Reconstructive Surgery

Breast Surgery

C. Andrew Heiskell, MD, FACS

Medical Legal Consultants, Inc.
4000 Hampton Center, Ste. D
Morgantown, WV 26505
Tel: (304) 599-8665
Fax: (304) 599-8584
E-mail: info@heiskellmd.com
Web Site: http://www.heiskellmd.com

Specialties: Dr. Heiskell is a practicing General and Vascular Surgeon. Dr. Heiskell has been in private practice for 25 years and has been reviewing medical records for over 10 years, testifying on behalf of claimants, defendants and insurers in cases of general and vascular surgery, laparoscopic surgery, surgical malpractice and standards of care. He performs numerous operations yearly including hernia repairs, laparoscopic gallbladder surgery, surgeries of the breast, colon, stomach, pancreas, spleen, thyroid, carotid arteries and many other vascular procedures. **Degrees/ licenses:** BS, MD, Board Certified.

See primary listing under MEDICINE & HEALTH: Surgery, General

Breast Surgery *(cont.)*

Jeffrey M. Sherwood, MD, FACS

P.O. Box 1071
Water Mill, NY 11976
Tel: (888) 343-7642
Fax: (631) 726-9323
E-mail: jms12544@yahoo.com

Specialties: General Surgery, Laparoscopic Surgery & Breast Surgery. Over 10 years experience reviewing cases for both defendants' and plaintiffs' attorneys. Board Certified; Fellow, American College of Surgeons; Member, Society of Laparoscopic Surgeons. **Degrees/licenses:** MD, New York State Medical License.

See primary listing under MEDICINE & HEALTH: Surgery, General

Burn Surgery

Joel J. Teplinsky, MD, FACS, FICS

Plastic, Reconstructive,
Burn & Hand Surgeon
16161 Ventura Boulevard
Encino, CA 91436
Tel: (818) 784-7707
(818) 990-9433
Fax: (818) 784-7598

Specialties: Cosmetic, Reconstructive, Burn, Hand, Wounds (Chronic) Surgery. Diplomate, American Board of Plastic Surgery; UCLA, Department Plastic Surgery, Attending Staff; Past President, International College of Surgeons, U.S. Section; Past Director, Residency & Staff Education, Grossman Burn Center, Sherman Oaks Hospital; Past Director, Wound Care Center, Sherman Oaks Hospital. CV: University of Wisconsin BS '60, MD '65; Herrick Hospital, Berkeley, CA, Internship '66; UC San Francisco, Psychiatry Residency '67; Capt., U.S. Medical Corps, USAF '67-'69; Fresno County Hospital, General Surgery Residency '69-'72; Kaiser Hospital, Los Angeles, General Surgery Residency '72-'75; Baylor College of Medicine, Houston, TX, Plastic Surgery Residency '75-'77. **Degrees/ licenses:** BS & MD California.

See primary listing under MEDICINE & HEALTH: Plastic & Reconstructive Surgery

Cancer/Oncology

Ronald Citron, MD

4189 Silverado Trail
Calistoga, CA 94515-9610
Tel: (707) 942-5818
E-mail: rscitronmd@earthlink.net

Specialties: Causation analysis of missed cancer diagnosis. Diplomate, American Board of Internal Medicine; Diplomate, American Board of Medical Oncology; Diplomate, American Board of Forensic Examiners. **Degrees/licenses:** MD.

Richard J. Cohen, MD, FACP

Consultant in Medical Oncology/
Hematology
3838 California St., Ste. 707
San Francisco, CA 94118
Tel: (415) 668-0160
Fax: (415) 752-4635
E-mail: rcohen3@aol.com
Web Site: http://doctor.pol.net/rjcohen

Specialties: Board certified in Medical Oncology, Hematology and Internal Medicine. Clinical Professor of Medicine, Univ. of Calif. Med. Center, San Francisco. Special expertise in cancers of breast, colon, lung, lymphomas, melanoma, etc. Extensive experience as consultant and expert witness in Medical-Legal cases for both plaintiff and defense. **Degrees/ licenses:** MD, Fellow of the American College of Physicians.

See primary listing under MEDICAL-LEGAL: Cancer/Oncology

Cardiac Surgery

Joseph S. Carey, MD

Chair, Quality Improvement Committee;
Past President California Society
of Thoracic Surgeons
3475 Torrance Blvd., Ste. B
Torrance, CA 90503
Tel: (310) 540-1011
Fax: (310) 540-1028
E-mail: careyjs@earthlink.net
Web Site: http://www.casts.org or
http://www.ctsnet.org/home/jscarey

Specialties: Quality control in cardiovascular and thoracic surgery; Outcomes research and analysis; Risk Adjustment; Online data coding and reporting; President, California Society of Thoracic Surgeons, 1996-1998; Chair, Quality Improvement Committee, 1998-present. Member, National Society of Thoracic Surgeons Ethics and Database committees, 1996-present. Associate Clinical Professor of Surgery, UCLA School of Medicine; Chief, Thoracic Surgery, VA Hospital, Los Angeles, 1967-1983. Private practice, thoracic and cardiovascular surgery, 1983-present. Extensive publications in outcomes of coronary and heart valve surgery, blood vessel diseases and lung problems. Consultant to hospitals for quality reviews. Wide experience in practice standards and legal reviews. **Degrees/licenses:** MD, FACS, FACC, Assoc. Clinical Prof., UCLA.

Samuel H. Sadow, MD, FACS

529 South Flagler Drive, Suite 18-G
West Palm Beach, FL 33401
Tel: (772) 335-9800
Fax: (561) 833-8663
E-mail: ssadow5398@aol.com

Specialties: Extensive experience with litigation of Standards of Care, Causation, Plaintiffs/Defendants, Bylaws and Hospital Privileges issues. Private practice of Cardiovascular and Thoracic Surgery, 1985-present; Principal investigator for FDA Phase III Trials ATS Medical Heart Valve Study. MD 1973, Chicago Medical School. Re-Certified in Thoracic Surgery. **Degrees/licenses:** MD, FACS, Amer. Boards of Surgery & Thoracic Surgery.

See primary listing under MEDICINE & HEALTH: Cardiothoracic Surgery

Cardiology

Marvin Appel, MD, FACC, FCCP

Marvin Appel, MD, Inc.
2888 Long Beach Blvd., Ste. 215
Long Beach, CA 90806
Tel: (562) 290-8115
Fax: (562) 290-0345
E-mail: marvinappel@cox.net

Specialties: Invasive and non-invasive cardiology including interventional cardiology. Ongoing active clinical practice for 23 years. Extensive experience for plaintiff and defense. Assistant Clinical Professor of Medicine, USC School of Medicine. Hospital Medical Director of Cardiology Services. **Degrees/licenses:** MD, FACC, FCCP, PhD, Board Certified Internal Med & Cardiovascular Disease.

Stephen Hubbard, MD

4490 Eagle Harbor Dr. NE
Bainbridge Island, WA 98110
Tel: (206) 855-8132
Fax: (206) 855-8139
E-mail: stehub@pol.net
Web Site: http://stephenhubbardmd.com

Specialties: Interventional cardiologist with experience in chart review, depositions, testimony. Expertise in myocardial infarction management, chest pain evaluation, angiography, angioplasty, pacemakers, medical management of hypertension, hyperlipidemia, CHF, CAD, arrhythmias. Graduate of UCSF School of Medicine; board certified in Internal Medicine and Cardiovascular Disease. Fellow, American College of Cardiology. Recently retired from private practice and now Clinical Assoc. Professor at UW School of Medicine, attending at Harborview Medical Center. **Degrees/licenses:** MD, Lic. in WA; FACC; Boards: Int. Med., CV.

Cardiology *(cont.)*

Basil M. RuDusky, MD

Private Practice of Internal Medicine, Cardiology & Forensic Medicine
15 Public Square
Wilkes-Barre, PA 18701
Tel: (570) 824-7115
Fax: Call

Specialties: Over thirty years experience in all aspects of internal medicine and cardiovascular medicine. Senior consultant in medicine and cardiology to numerous corporations worldwide and government agencies. Vast experience in corporate, occupational, medical-legal, military, and governmental medicine. Author of numerous publications, including five "Firsts" in the world's medical literature. Over thirty years experience in forensic medicine, including precedent setting state supreme court decisions. Extensive curriculum vitae and bibliography on request. **Degrees/licenses:** BA, MD, FACA, FCCP, FACP, FACC, DABFM, FACFE.

Cardiothoracic Surgery

Joseph S. Carey, MD

Chair, Quality Improvement Committee; Past President California Society of Thoracic Surgeons
3475 Torrance Blvd., Ste. B
Torrance, CA 90503
Tel: (310) 540-1011
Fax: (310) 540-1028
E-mail: careyjs@earthlink.net
Web Site: http://www.casts.org or http://www.ctsnet.org/home/jscarey

Specialties: Quality control in cardiovascular and thoracic surgery; Outcomes research and analysis; Risk Adjustment; Online data coding and reporting; President, California Society of Thoracic Surgeons, 1996-1998; Chair, Quality Improvement Committee, 1998-present. Member, National Society of Thoracic Surgeons Ethics and Database committees, 1996-present. Associate Clinical Professor of Surgery, UCLA School of Medicine; Chief, Thoracic Surgery, VA Hospital, Los Angeles, 1967-1983. Private practice, thoracic and cardiovascular surgery, 1983-present. Extensive publications in outcomes of coronary and heart valve surgery, blood vessel diseases and lung problems. Consultant to hospitals for quality reviews. Wide experience in practice standards and legal reviews. **Degrees/licenses:** MD, FACS, FACC, Assoc. Clinical Prof., UCLA.
See primary listing under MEDICINE & HEALTH: Cardiac Surgery

Henry Fee, MD

Cardiothoracic Surgeon
2504 Samaritan Dr., #10
San Jose, CA 95124
Tel: (408) 358-8771
Fax: (408) 358-8621

Specialties: MD from Harvard Medical School (1969); General Surgery Internship from Johns Hopkins Hospital; General & Cardiothoracic Surgery at UCLA; Congenital Cardiac Fellowship at Harvard. Private practice Cardiothoracic at Good Samaritan Hospital, San Jose, CA (1980-present). **Degrees/licenses:** MD (1969), Cert. in Cardiothoracic Surgery (1974), Re-cert. 1986.

Thomas R. McLean, MD

Third Millennium Consultants, LLC
4970 Park
Shawnee, KS 66216
Tel: (913) 526-5526
Fax: (913) 962-0840
E-mail: tmclean@dnamail.com
Web Site: www.firms.findlaw.com/TMCLLC

Specialties: Clinical Assistant Professor of Surgery, University of Kansas School of Medicine. Board Certified by the America Board of Surgery, American Board of Thoracic Surgery and American Board of Surgery-Critical Care. Medical Director, Third Millennium Consultants, LLC, (Specializing in medical records review for Quality Assurance, Utilization Review and Litigation); Former Medical Director, Goodyear Tire Company, Topeka Plant. Former Regional Medical Consultant, Social Security Administration, Kansas City, Mo. Fellow American College of Surgeons, Cardiology and Chest Physicians. **Degrees/licenses:** MD, MS, Lic. in Kansas & Missouri.

Samuel H. Sadow, MD, FACS
529 South Flagler Drive, Suite 18-G
West Palm Beach, FL 33401
Tel: (772) 335-9800
Fax: (561) 833-8663
E-mail: ssadow5398@aol.com

Specialties: Extensive experience with litigation of Standards of Care, Causation, Plaintiffs/Defendants, Bylaws and Hospital Privileges issues. Private practice of Cardiovascular and Thoracic Surgery, 1985-present; Principal investigator for FDA Phase III Trials ATS Medical Heart Valve Study. MD 1973, Chicago Medical School. Re-Certified in Thoracic Surgery. **Degrees/licenses:** MD, FACS, Amer. Boards of Surgery & Thoracic Surgery.

Case Evaluations

Stanley M. Bierman, MD, FACP
Associate Clinical Professor
at UCLA (Hon.)
2080 Century Park E., #1008
Los Angeles, CA 90067
Tel: (310) 553-3567
Fax: (310) 553-4538
E-mail: sbiermanmd@aol.com

Specialties: Dermatologist with 43+ years of medical treatment, consulting and expert witness experience in the following areas: Skin Cancer including Melanoma; Sexually Transmitted Diseases (STD); Herpes Simplex Infections; Dermatology Standard of Care; Skin Allergies; Scars; Stress Induced Skin Disorders. Fellow, American College of Physicians; Diplomate, American Board of Forensic Examiners. **Degrees/licenses:** MD, FACP.

See primary listing under MEDICINE & HEALTH: Dermatology

Chiropractic Medicine

Accident and Injury Analytica
Kenneth W. Luther, DC, QME
649 W. Maple Ave.
El Segundo, CA 90245
Tel: (310) 322-2233
Fax: (310) 322-6955
E-mail: k.luther@reconanalysis.com
Web Site: http://www.reconanalysis.com

Specialties: Chiropractor with 25 years of extensive consulting and expert witness experience in the following areas: Physical Medicine; Chiropractic Medicine; Accident Reconstruction; Injury Reconstruction; Qualified Medical Evaluation; Forensic Analysis. **Degrees/licenses:** BS; DC; QME.

See primary listing under ACCIDENT RECONSTRUCTION: General

Evan S. Rost, DC
1 Madelyne Place
Fair Lawn, NJ 07410
Tel: (201) 791-0004
Fax: (201) 791-0045
E-mail: doc@expertchiropractor.com
Web Site: www.expertchiropractor.com

Specialties: Chiropractic; Chiropractic Medicine; Forensic Examiner. Member, American College of Forensic Examiners #14745; Member, National Forensic Center, Certified Chiropractic Peer Reviewer and Independent Examiner, Certified Chiropractic Insurance Consultant, both certifications by Texas Chiropractic College; Diplomate, American Board of Disability Analysts; Diplomate, American Academy of Certified Consultants and Experts; Diplomate, American Academy of Experts in Traumatic Stress; Cleveland Chiropractic College 1983. Membership: American Pain Society, Headache Cooperative of New England, Inc., Florida Chiropractic Association, Indiana State Chiropractic Association, Northern New Jersey Chiropractic Society, New York State Chiropractic Association. **Degrees/licenses:** DC, CCIC, ACD, DABDA, FAAIM; Lic.: NJ, NY, FL, RI, IN.

Colon & Rectal Surgery

Dennis A. Fried, MD

3061 Pignatelli Crescent
Mt. Pleasant (Charleston), SC 29466
Tel: (843) 568-9160
Fax: (803) 753-0862
E-mail: Friedmd@chscr.com

Specialties: 24 years private practice of colon and rectal surgery (colon, rectum, anus) including cancer, diverticulitis, colitis, Crohns, incontinence, hemorrhoids, fissures, fistulas, pilonidal, rectocele, enterocele, prolapse, colonoscopy, polyps, laparoscopy, sphincter-sparing surgery, sphincter repairs, obstetric trauma, colostomy, ileostomy. Board certified in general and colon/rectal surgery. **Degrees/licenses:** BS, MS, MD, FACS, FASCRS (South Carolina license).

C. Andrew Heiskell, MD, FACS

Medical Legal Consultants, Inc.
4000 Hampton Center, Ste. D
Morgantown, WV 26505
Tel: (304) 599-8665
Fax: (304) 599-8584
E-mail: info@heiskellmd.com
Web Site: http://www.heiskellmd.com

Specialties: Dr. Heiskell is a practicing General and Vascular Surgeon. Dr. Heiskell has been in private practice for 25 years and has been reviewing medical records for over 10 years, testifying on behalf of claimants, defendants and insurers in cases of general and vascular surgery, laparoscopic surgery, surgical malpractice and standards of care. He performs numerous operations yearly including hernia repairs, laparoscopic gallbladder surgery, surgeries of the breast, colon, stomach, pancreas, spleen, thyroid, carotid arteries and many other vascular procedures. **Degrees/licenses:** BS, MD, Board Certified.

See primary listing under MEDICINE & HEALTH: Surgery, General

Ronald Zelnick, MD

General and Colorectal Surgeon
210 Jupiter Lakes Blvd., #3105
Jupiter, FL 33458
Tel: (561) 575-7875
Fax: (561) 575-5874
E-mail: docrsz@aol.com

Specialties: General Surgery; Laparoscopic Surgery; Colon and Rectal Surgery; Breast Surgery. Board Certified and Recertified General Surgery and Colon And Rectal Surgery. Fellow American College of Surgeons; Fellow American Society of Colon & Rectal Surgeons. Actively practicing surgery in private practice, 14 years experience; Medical-legal experience. **Degrees/licenses:** MD, Florida License.

Cosmetic Surgery

John L. Baeke, MD

Park Place Plastic Surgery
14950 Newton
Overland Park, KS 66223
Tel: (913) 685-0101
Fax: (913) 685-3666
E-mail: JBaeke@ParkPlaceUSA.net
Web Site: http://www.beautifulbreasts.com

Specialties: Plastic Surgery; Includes breast implant problems, breast reduction/lift & post-mastectomy reconstruction issues; Body contouring: abdominoplasty & liposuction; Cosmetic laser procedures: tattoo removal, skin resurfacing, pigmented & vascular lesions; Post-traumatic injury & wound care acute & chronic including bed sores. Experience with plaintiff & defendant case review, brief preparation & testimony. Univ. Kansas-honors. First place Guffey Competition. First place Calif. Society of Plastic Surgeons. Assoc. Prof. University of Kansas School of Med. Amer. Society of Laser Medicine & Surgery. Amer. Society of Cosmetic Breast Surgery. Assoc. Military Surgeons of U.S., Amer. Academy of Wound Management, AMA. **Degrees/licenses:** MD.

See primary listing under MEDICINE & HEALTH: Plastic & Reconstructive Surgery

Todd C. Case, MD, FACS

President
Todd C. Case, MD, PC
5881 N. Misty Ridge Dr.
Tucson, AZ 85718-3434
Tel: (520) 615-0597
Fax: (520) 615-0599
E-mail: tccaseworks@aol.com

Specialties: Complete start-to-finish cost-effective litigation support for plaintiff and defense; Impartial analysis; Reports summarizing medical records, explaining medical terms and procedures, and reviewing duty, breach, causation and damages; Strategic planning; Database searches; Expert witness services. Dr. Case is ABPS certified; Past Chief, plastic surgery (Tucson Medical Center); A former director of division of plastic surgery; Received prestigious national award for research; Authored and presented numerous papers; Invited lecturer (Italy, India). Actively practicing; Interests in facial , breast and body surgery, including cosmetic and laser procedures, and treatment for lymphedema. **Degrees/licenses:** MD, FACS, ABPS, AOA; Lic. AZ, CA, TX.

See primary listing under MEDICINE & HEALTH: Plastic & Reconstructive Surgery

Critical Care

Martin C. Johnson, MD, FACS, FAAP, FACME

CEO/President
Pacific Northwest Neurosurgical Association
31870 SW Country View Lane
Wilsonville, OR 97070-7476
Tel: (503) 694-5900
Fax: (503) 694-5649
E-mail: martinc33@hotmail.com

Specialties: Neurosurgery, Pediatric Neurosurgery, Neurotrauma, Child Abuse, Pediatric Neurology, Neurology, Neurological Critical Care, Reconstructive Neurosurgery, Workers' Compensation (neurosurgical/spinal orthopedic, IME), Disability Evaluation (neurosurgical - spinal orthopedic), Col. AUSA (ret.). Board Certified: American Board Neurosurgery, American Board Pediatric Neurosurgery, American Board of Forensic Examiners. **Degrees/licenses:** ABB, MD, FACS, FAAP, FACFM.

See primary listing under MEDICINE & HEALTH: Neurosurgery

Michael E. Kalafer, MD

2444 Via Aprilia
Del Mar, CA 92014
Tel: (858) 212-4447
Fax: (801) 327-2009
E-mail: kalafer@san.rr.com

Specialties: Pulmonary Medicine; Critical Care Medicine; Internal Medicine; Lung Cancer; Hospital Medical Director; Long Term Acute Care; Elder Abuse. Cornell University BS; SUNY Syracuse MD; Mt. Sinai Hospital NY Internship; UCSD Residency & Pulmonary Fellowship; Associate Clinical Professor of Medicine UCSD. Society of Critical Care Medicine; American Thoracic Society, Fellow American College Chest Physicians. Twenty four years clinical practice of pulmonary, critical care & internal medicine. Experienced in Medical Malpractice, Personal Injury, Wrongful Death; plaintiff and defense. Emphasis on timely and thoughtful case review. **Degrees/ licenses:** BS, MD (CA), FCCP; Board Cert.: Pulmonary, Critical Care & Int. Med.

See primary listing under MEDICINE & HEALTH: Pulmonary Medicine

Dermatology

Stanley M. Bierman, MD, FACP

Associate Clinical Professor
at UCLA (Hon.)
2080 Century Park E., #1008
Los Angeles, CA 90067
Tel: (310) 553-3567
Fax: (310) 553-4538
E-mail: sbiermanmd@aol.com

Specialties: Dermatologist with 43+ years of medical treatment, consulting and expert witness experience in the following areas: Skin Cancer including Melanoma; Sexually Transmitted Diseases (STD); Herpes Simplex

(Listing continued on next page)

Dermatology *(cont.)*

Stanley M. Bierman, MD (cont.)

Infections; Dermatology Standard of Care; Skin Allergies; Scars; Stress Induced Skin Disorders. Fellow, American College of Physicians; Diplomate, American Board of Forensic Examiners. **Degrees/licenses:** MD, FACP.

Oscar L. Frick, MD, PhD

Professor Emeritus Pediatrics-
Allergy-Immunology
University of California, San Francisco
370 Parnassus Avenue
San Francisco, CA 94117
Tel: (415) 566-0733
Fax: (415) 476-4009
E-mail: oscarfrick@earthlink.net

Specialties: Anaphylactic shock from drugs, foods, immunotherapy, biologicals like latex and prosthetics; Allergies to foods, especially peanuts and genetically-modified foods; Asthma, skin eczema, allergic sinusitis, hay fever, gastrointestinal, chronic diarrhea and malnutrition; Allergic reactions to drugs, antibiotics, e.g., penicillin, anesthetics, anticonvulsants. Professor Emeritus Pediatrics, Allergy-Immunology. President, American Academy of Allergy & Immunology. Chairman, FDA Panel Pulmon-Allergy, Drugs. **Degrees/licenses:** MD, PhD, Amer. Board Allergy & Immunology & Pediatrics.

See primary listing under MEDICINE & HEALTH: Allergy/Immunology

Emergency Medical Services

Emergency Medical & Safety Services Consultants

Guy H. Haskell, PhD, NREMT-P
Executive Director
1040 Graywell Drive
Bloomington, IN 47401
Tel: (812) 320-3954
Fax: (812) 331-0962
E-mail: ghaskell@indiana.edu
Web Site: http://www.emsexperts.org

Specialties: Dr. Haskell has been involved in EMS since 1983, and has served as a paramedic in the field, emergency department, ICU, and Pediatric MICU. Editor and author, Haskell has worked to bridge the theories of academic emergency medicine with the practice of EMS. Haskell is active as a paramedic, educator, and consultant nationwide with an international reputation. He holds the Ph.D. from Indiana University and instructorships in the major EMS disciplines. Dr. Haskell serves as consultant and expert for plaintiff and defense, providing review, depositions, reports and trial testimony. **Degrees/licenses:** PhD, MA, NREMT-P, National Registry & IN.

See primary listing under MEDICINE & HEALTH: Emergency Medicine

Emergency Medicine

Burton Bentley II, MD, FAAEM

President
Emergency Medicine
Litigation Analysts, Inc.
5189 N. Marlin Canyon Place
Tucson, AZ 85750
Tel: (888) 335-3652
Fax: (520) 615-5413
E-mail: bentley@erexperts.com
Web Site: http://www.erexperts.com

Specialties: Immediate, cost-effective, impartial analysis of emergency medicine cases; Review of duty, breach, harm, and causation; Summary of medical records; Explanation of medical terms and processes; Strategic planning; Database searches referenced to your case; Provision of expert witness services by board-certified, actively practicing emergency physicians; Complete start-to-finish litigation support for both plaintiff and defense. **Degrees/licenses:** MD, ABEM, FAAEM.

Emergency Medical & Safety Services Consultants

Guy H. Haskell, PhD, NREMT-P
Executive Director
1040 Graywell Drive
Bloomington, IN 47401
Tel: (812) 320-3954
Fax: (812) 331-0962
E-mail: ghaskell@indiana.edu
Web Site: http://www.emsexperts.org

Specialties: Dr. Haskell has been involved in EMS since 1983, and has served as a paramedic in the field, emergency department, ICU, and Pediatric MICU. Editor and author, Haskell has worked to bridge the theories of academic emergency medicine with the practice of EMS. Haskell is active as a paramedic, educator, and consultant nationwide with an international reputation. He holds the Ph.D. from Indiana University and instructorships in the major EMS disciplines. Dr. Haskell serves as consultant and expert for plaintiff and defense, providing review, depositions, reports and trial testimony. **Degrees/licenses:** PhD, MA, NREMT-P, National Registry & IN.

Ronald Himmelman, MD

Emergency Physician
466 Madison Ave.
Glencoe, IL 60022
Tel: (847) 917-4306
Fax: (847) 786-4535
E-mail: ronnyhim@comcast.net

Specialties: Medical legal consultant and working emergency physician. Extensive experience with plaintiff and defense concerning all aspects of emergency medicine and medical toxicology. **Degrees/licenses:** MD, Board Certified in Emergency Medicine & in Toxicology.

Robert E. Leyrer, MD

1100 Via Tripoli
Punta Gorda, FL 33950
Tel: (941) 575-4124
Fax: (941) 575-4124
E-mail: releyrer@comcast.net

Specialties: Board Certified in emergency medicine, residency trained in emergency medicine and trauma. Actively practicing department medical director with over 15 years experience in emergency medicine and pre-hospital care. Medical director of EMS and paramedic training program. Fellow of American Academy of Emergency Medicine. Fellow of American College of Emergency Physicians. Ten years of expert witness experience. **Degrees/licenses:** MD.

Alan L. Nager, MD

Medical Expert
22287 Mulholland Hwy., Ste. 250
Calabasas, CA 91302
Tel: (818) 224-3938
E-mail: anagermd@msn.com

Specialties: Pediatric Emergency Medicine, encompassing all pediatric diseases and traumatic injuries as they present in the emergency department. Experience in clinical and administrative issues relating to Pediatric Emergency Medicine. Standards of care, causation, outcome, and prognosis. Provides record review, consultation, and testimony. Plaintiff or defense. HOSPITAL/ACADEMIC APPOINTMENTS: Assistant Professor of Clinical Pediatrics, Keck School of Medicine at University of Southern California; Attending Physician, Pediatric Emergency Department, Children's Hospital Los Angeles; Division Head, Division of Emergency and Transport Medicine, Children's Hospital Los Angeles. **Degrees/licenses:** MD, Bd Cert in Pediatrics & Pediatric Emerg Med; Fellow Amer Acad of Pediatrics.

See primary listing under MEDICINE & HEALTH: Pediatrics

Emergency Medicine *(cont.)*

Reed S. Oxman, MD, FACEP, DAAPM

Reed S. Oxman, MD, PC
226 W. Rittenhouse Sq., #911
Philadelphia, PA 19103-5743
Tel: (215) 546-8211
Fax: (888) 432-0237
E-mail: rsopa@aol.com
Web Site: http://member.expertpages.com/Reed-S.-Oxman,-M.D. or http://www.emergencymed-painmanagement.com

Specialties: Emergency Medicine Residency Trained, American Board of Emergency Medicine Board Certified, Fellow of the American College of Emergency Physicians (FACEP); Also Board Certified Diplomate of the American Academy of Pain Management (DAAPM). Roughly 50% defense and 50% plaintiff cases in the areas of ER Malpractice, Pain Management, Rape, Child Abuse, Elder Abuse, Personal Injury, Trauma, and Motor Vehicle Accidents. Licensed in 11 states. Roughly 85-90% of the cases that I have accepted beyond my initial evaluation have concluded with a favorable judgment. Published as first author in areas of medicine inside and outside my specialties. **Degrees/licenses:** BA, MD, FACEP, DAAPM; Lic. in PA, MD, NJ, OH, CT, GA, FL, MO, WI, IL, IN.

Anthony J. Scarcella, MD, JD

380 S. State Road 434
Suite 1004, #388
Altamonte Springs, FL 32714
Tel: (407) 616-7295
Fax: (407) 299-8735
E-mail: ascarcellamd@aol.com
Web Site: http://www.ermedicineexpert.com

Specialties: Board Certified Emergency Medicine with extensive experience in Medical Record Review for lawyers as well as insurance companies. Disability Analysis and Verification, Malpractice Consulting and Expert Witness Services. **Degrees/licenses:** MD Certified - American Board of Emergency Medicine.

Kenneth A. Stein, MD

14312 Aitken Hill Court
Chesterfield (St. Louis), MO 63017
Tel: (314) 495-7009
Fax: (708) 585-3348
E-mail: kenny@er-md.com
Web Site: http://www.er-md.com

Specialties: Attending Staff Physician in Emergency Medicine and Critical Care at St. Anthony's Medical Center and Assistant Clinical Professor at St. Louis University Health Sciences Center, Department of Surgery/Emergency Medicine Division. Furnishes an unbiased opinion on medical malpractice and negligence, emergency medicine and internal medicine, for plaintiff or defense. Survey of case for merit, medical chart review and analysis, formulation of case strategy, preparation for opposing expert deposition and cross-examination, medical literature search, expert witness testimony. **Degrees/licenses:** MD, Board Certified in Internal Medicine.

Bruce Wapen, MD

Emergency Medicine Expert
969-G Edgewater Blvd., #807
Foster City, CA 94404
Tel: (650) 577-8635
Fax: (650) 577-0191
E-mail: expertwitness@drwapen.com
Web Site: http://www.drwapen.com

Specialties: Board certified emergency physician and experienced public speaker offers consultation, chart review, and testimony as an expert witness for plaintiff or defense involving litigation arising from the Emergency Department. **Degrees/licenses:** MD, FACEP.

Endocrinology

Janet Winikoff, MD, FACE

2021 Santa Monica Blvd., Ste. 325 E.
Santa Monica, CA 90404
Tel: (310) 828-5337
Fax: (310) 828-2556
E-mail: jwinikof@ucla.edu

Specialties: Board Certified Internal Medicine - ABIM; Board Certified Endocrinology and Metabolism (Diabetes) - ABIM; Fellow,

American College of Endocrinology; Assistant Clinical Professor, UCLA School of Medicine. Twenty years experience teaching and clinical practice. Experienced medical reviewer, plaintiff and defense. **Degrees/licenses:** MD, Licensed State of California.

See primary listing under MEDICINE & HEALTH: Internal Medicine

Family Medicine

David A. Libert, MD, FAAFP, PA

First Choice Medical Center
697 Maitland Ave., Ste. 1001
Altamonte Springs, FL 32701
Tel: (407) 539-2111
Fax: (407) 539-1211
E-mail: dlibert@earthlink.net
Web Site: http://www.fcmedcenter.com

Specialties: Dr. Libert has been a practicing physician since 1985; Has held positions of team physician, practicing physician and medical director at several area medical centers; Extensive experience in family practice and disability medicine. Plaintiff and defense Medical-Legal Services: Medical Record Review & Analysis; Identification of Standards of Care, Causation & Damage Issues; Definitions of Medical Terms & Procedures; Collaboration for Interrogatory Development; Expert Witness Deposition & Trial Testimony. MD University of Florida 1982; Diplomate American Board of Family Practice. **Degrees/ licenses:** MD, FAAFP; Lic. in the State of Florida since 1983.

See primary listing under MEDICAL-LEGAL: Medical Malpractice

Medstuff

William W. Filler, Jr., MD, FACOG
Gilbert J. Martinez, MD, JD
42525 Chaparral Dr.
Temecula, CA 92592-8955
Tel: (951) 303-1429
Fax: (951) 303-9357
E-mail: bfiller@medstuff.com
Web Site: http://www.medstuff.com

Specialties: Dr. Gilbert J. Martinez is a board certified family practioner with 30+ years experience. His medical practice has included all phases of family practice, including hospital and nursing home practice with special experience in Workers' Compensation and personal injury. He has served as president and chief executive of medical provider groups for HMOs and PPOs. Since 1984, he has also been an attorney and member of the California Bar. Dr. Martinez retired from active practice of law in 1999. For CV, please refer to the MedStuff Web site at www.medstuff.com.

See primary listing under MEDICINE & HEALTH: General

Ron Surowitz, DO

Board Certified Family Physician
Surowitz Consulting, Inc.
2185 Radnor Court
North Palm Beach, FL 33408
Tel: (561) 746-7826
(561) 746-7811
(561) 627-5952
Fax: (561) 744-1970
E-mail: rsurowitz1@aol.com

Specialties: Malpractice consulting and expert witness services; Evaluate standard of care for family and general practice; Expert diagnostic opinions; Board Certified in Osteopathic Family Practice; Past President of the Florida Osteopathic Medical Association; 33 years of practice experience; Plaintiff and defense review to evaluate medical malpractice; Rapid response; Thorough analysis of issues. **Degrees/licenses:** DO, FAOCFP / Florida, Missouri, Michigan, California.

Family Practice

Elliot D. Felman, MD

2336 Santa Monica Blvd., Ste. 208
Santa Monica, CA 90404
Tel: (310) 453-0033
Fax: (310) 453-2114
E-mail: drfelman@earthlink.net

Specialties: Board Certified Family Practice. In practice over 25 years. Experienced in both Plaintiff and Defense Review, Deposition and Trial Testimony for evaluation of Medical Malpractice. Evaluation of Standard of Care for Family Practice, General Practice & Internal Medicine. Clinical faculty, UCLA Medical School. **Degrees/licenses:** MD.

See primary listing under MEDICAL-LEGAL: Medical Malpractice, Family Practice

Forensic Medicine

A.L. Dollinger, MD

Dollinger Pathology Medical Group
777 E Palm Drive
Hanford, CA 93230-2314
Tel: (559) 589-9712
Fax: (559) 589-9698

Specialties: Board Certifications: American Board of Pathology (Anatomic, Clinical & Forensic); American Board of Forensic Examiners; American Board of Forensic Medicine. Fellow College of American Pathologists. Fellow American Society of Clinical Pathologists. Fellow American Academy of Forensic Sciences. Member National Association of Medical Examiners. Fellow College of Forensic Examiners. CV available on request. **Degrees/licenses:** MD, FASCP, FCAP, FAAFS, BCFE, BCFM.

See primary listing under MEDICINE & HEALTH: Forensic Pathology

Sanford H. Edberg, MD, FCAP

Forensic Pathologist
14 Newgate Road
Pittsburgh, PA 15202
Tel: (412) 761-5370
Fax: (412) 766-8024
E-mail: sedberg1@earthlink.net

Specialties: Born New York City, 1931; New York Medical College, MD, 1954; Rotating internship, Beth Israel Hospital, 1954-1955; U.S. Navy General Medical Officer, 1955-1957; Pathology residency, Bronx Municipal Medical Center, 1958-1961; Assistant Medical Examiner, New York City, 1960-1966; Board Certified Anatomic, Clinical, Forensic Pathology; Medical License, PA, 8871E; Director of Laboratories, Suburban General Hospital, Pittsburgh, PA, 1972-1998; Clinical Associate Professor, Pathology, Pittsburgh University Medical School, 1985-present; Coroner, Allegheny County, 1981-1982; Expert witness, extensive court appearances, depositions, legal consultations, malpractice, death causes, accidents, pneumoconiosis. **Degrees/licenses:** MD, FCAP, Board Certified AP, CP, FP.

See primary listing under MEDICINE & HEALTH: Forensic Pathology

Ali Z. Hameli, MD

Consultant, Forensic Pathology
3005 Silverside Road
Wilmington, DE 19810
Tel: (302) 478-3341
Fax: (302) 478-3341

Specialties: Forensic Pathology, Forensic Medicine, Forensic Toxicology; Professional Consultation/Case Management in Forensic Medicine/Pathology/Toxicology; Case review, verbal/written reports, deposition/trial testimony. Chief Medical Examiner 1964-1997; Director, Forensic Sciences Laboratory 1970-1997, State of Delaware; Clinical Associate Professor, Forensic Pathology, Jefferson Medical College; President, National Association of Medical Examiners 1973-1975; Vice President, American Academy of Forensic Sciences, 1992-1993; President Medical Society of Delaware, 1990-1991; Consultant, U.S. Justice Department, identification of Josef Mengele, 1985; Consultant, Mayoral

Commission, MOVE Bombing, Philadelphia, 1985. Recipient of many prestigious awards. **Degrees/licenses:** MD, Board Certified, Anatomic & Forensic Pathology.

See primary listing under MEDICINE & HEALTH: Forensic Pathology

Basil M. RuDusky, MD

Private Practice of Internal Medicine, Cardiology & Forensic Medicine
15 Public Square
Wilkes-Barre, PA 18701
Tel: (570) 824-7115
Fax: Call

Specialties: Over thirty years experience in all aspects of internal medicine and cardiovascular medicine. Senior consultant in medicine and cardiology to numerous corporations worldwide and government agencies. Vast experience in corporate, occupational, medical-legal, military, and governmental medicine. Author of numerous publications, including five "Firsts" in the world's medical literature. Over thirty years experience in forensic medicine, including precedent setting state supreme court decisions. Extensive curriculum vitae and bibliography on request. **Degrees/licenses:** BA, MD, FACA, FCCP, FACP, FACC, DABFM, FACFE.

See primary listing under MEDICINE & HEALTH: Cardiology

Forensic Pathology

A.L. Dollinger, MD

Dollinger Pathology Medical Group
777 E Palm Drive
Hanford, CA 93230-2314
Tel: (559) 589-9712
Fax: (559) 589-9698

Specialties: Board Certifications: American Board of Pathology (Anatomic, Clinical & Forensic); American Board of Forensic Examiners; American Board of Forensic Medicine. Fellow College of American Pathologists. Fellow American Society of Clinical Pathologists. Fellow American Academy of Forensic Sciences. Member National Association of Medical Examiners. Fellow College of Forensic Examiners. CV available on request. **Degrees/licenses:** MD, FASCP, FCAP, FAAFS, BCFE, BCFM.

Sanford H. Edberg, MD, FCAP

Forensic Pathologist
14 Newgate Road
Pittsburgh, PA 15202
Tel: (412) 761-5370
Fax: (412) 766-8024
E-mail: sedberg1@earthlink.net

Specialties: Born New York City, 1931; New York Medical College, MD, 1954; Rotating internship, Beth Israel Hospital, 1954-1955; U.S. Navy General Medical Officer, 1955-1957; Pathology residency, Bronx Municipal Medical Center, 1958-1961; Assistant Medical Examiner, New York City, 1960-1966; Board Certified Anatomic, Clinical, Forensic Pathology; Medical License, PA, 8871E; Director of Laboratories, Suburban General Hospital, Pittsburgh, PA, 1972-1998; Clinical Associate Professor, Pathology, Pittsburgh University Medical School, 1985-present; Coroner, Allegheny County, 1981-1982; Expert witness, extensive court appearances, depositions, legal consultations, malpractice, death causes, accidents, pneumoconiosis. **Degrees/licenses:** MD, FCAP, Board Certified AP, CP, FP.

Ali Z. Hameli, MD

Consultant, Forensic Pathology
3005 Silverside Road
Wilmington, DE 19810
Tel: (302) 478-3341
Fax: (302) 478-3341

Specialties: Forensic Pathology, Forensic Medicine, Forensic Toxicology; Professional Consultation/Case Management in Forensic Medicine/Pathology/Toxicology; Case review, verbal/written reports, deposition/trial testimony. Chief Medical Examiner 1964-1997; Director, Forensic Sciences Laboratory 1970-1997, State of Delaware; Clinical Associate Professor, Forensic Pathology, Jefferson Medical College; President, National Association of Medical Examiners 1973-1975;

(Listing continued on next page)

Forensic Pathology *(cont.)*

Ali Z. Hameli, MD (cont.)
Vice President, American Academy of Forensic Sciences, 1992-1993; President Medical Society of Delaware, 1990-1991; Consultant, U.S. Justice Department, identification of Josef Mengele, 1985; Consultant, Mayoral Commission, MOVE Bombing, Philadelphia, 1985. Recipient of many prestigious awards. **Degrees/licenses:** MD, Board Certified, Anatomic & Forensic Pathology.

Laboratory Corporation of America

1912 Alexander Dr.
Research Triangle Park, NC 27709
Tel: (800) 533-0567, Dept. 6
Fax: (919) 361-7737
E-mail: ForensicIdentity@labcorp.com
Web Site: http://www.labcorp.com

Specialties: Independent DNA testing; Criminal DNA case review, consulting, expert witness testimony. Experienced personnel, 3500+ cases completed. Hundreds of courtroom testimonies for prosecution and/or defense. ASCLD/LAB, CAP and New York State Department of Health accredited.

See primary listing under LITIGATION SUPPORT: Forensic Science

Forensic Toxicology

Yale H. Caplan

Director and Principal
National Scientific Services
3411 Philips Dr.
Baltimore, MD 21208
Tel: (410) 486-7486
Fax: (410) 653-4824
E-mail: ForTox@aol.com

Specialties: Forensic toxicology; clinical toxicology; general toxicology; medico-legal aspects of alcohol and drugs; laboratory testing for alcohol, drugs and other chemicals; effects of alcohol and drugs on drivers (drunk and drugged driving); breath alcohol testing; evaluation of the role of alcohol, drugs and chemicals (poisons) in postmortem (death) investigations; drug abuse; pharmacology and use and effects of prescription and other medicines; employee and workplace drug testing; interpretation of toxicology reports and issues; formerly Chief Toxicologist for the State of Maryland and Director of Forensic Toxicology for a large national laboratory. **Degrees/licenses:** PhD; BS, Pharmacy (PD); D-ABFT; CPC.

Ali Z. Hameli, MD

Consultant, Forensic Pathology
3005 Silverside Road
Wilmington, DE 19810
Tel: (302) 478-3341
Fax: (302) 478-3341

Specialties: Forensic Pathology, Forensic Medicine, Forensic Toxicology; Professional Consultation/Case Management in Forensic Medicine/Pathology/Toxicology; Case review, verbal/written reports, deposition/trial testimony. Chief Medical Examiner 1964-1997; Director, Forensic Sciences Laboratory 1970-1997, State of Delaware; Clinical Associate Professor, Forensic Pathology, Jefferson Medical College; President, National Association of Medical Examiners 1973-1975; Vice President, American Academy of Forensic Sciences, 1992-1993; President Medical Society of Delaware, 1990-1991; Consultant, U.S. Justice Department, identification of Josef Mengele, 1985; Consultant, Mayoral Commission, MOVE Bombing, Philadelphia, 1985. Recipient of many prestigious awards. **Degrees/licenses:** MD, Board Certified, Anatomic & Forensic Pathology.

See primary listing under MEDICINE & HEALTH: Forensic Pathology

Karl Verebey, PhD, DABFT

President & Director
Forensic Toxicology Associates
638 Debchar Court
River Vale, NJ 07675
Tel: (908) 862-4404
(201) 391-0015
Fax: (908) 862-4405
E-mail: k.verebey@att.net
Web Site: http://home.att.net/~k.verebey

Specialties: Alcohol & Drugs of Abuse Testing: Disputes of laboratory results; Interpretation of laboratory and behavioral data; Psychopharmacology & Clinical Pharmacology: Interpretation of drugs and/or alcohol toxicity based on concentration and time/action parameters; Toxicology of alcohol, drugs and metals. Cornell University Medical College, PhD, Pharmacology, Biochemistry; Board Certified in Forensic Toxicology & Clinical Laboratory Sciences; High Complexity Laboratory Director, ABB. Over 30 years experience drug abuse pharmacology, alcohol & psychopharmacology. Former Chief Toxicologist, City of New York. Over 100 publications. Over 300 cases since 1981; in court testimony accepted in 7 states as an expert. **Degrees/licenses:** PhD; DABFT (Amer. Bd. of Forensic Tox.); HCLD (ABB); Clin. Lab Direc. NY, NJ, PA.

See primary listing under ALCOHOL/DRUGS: Driving Under the Influence

Gastroenterology

Albert M. Harary, MD

654 Madison Ave., Sixth Floor
New York, NY 10021
Tel: (212) 702-0123
Fax: (212) 355-4244
E-mail: docharary@aol.com

Specialties: Gastroenterology; Liver diseases; Gastrointestinal endoscopy; Internal medicine; Stress & digestive disorders. Affiliation: Private Practice; New York University School of Medicine (Clinical Assistant Professor of Medicine). **Degrees/licenses:** MD; FACP; Board Certified.

Perry Hookman, MD

Perry Hookman, MD, PA
5607 NW 24th Terrace
Boca Raton, FL 33496
Tel: (561) 241-8550
E-mail: hookman@hookman.com
Web Site: http://www.hookman.com

Specialties: Expert medical opinion from board certified physician in internal medicine and gastroenterology. Will review medical records, diagnoses & treatment of internal medicine and gastrointestinal diseases. In current active private medical practice & medical school teaching faculty. See publications on Dr. Hookman's website. **Degrees/licenses:** Perry Hookman, MD, FACP, FACG, FACPE.

See primary listing under MEDICAL-LEGAL: Medical Malpractice

Charles S. Narasi, MD, FACG

Gastroenterologist
2545 Sheridan Drive
Tonawanda, NY 14150
Tel: (716) 834-1466
Fax: (716) 834-1618
E-mail: charlesn@adelphia.net

Specialties: Board certified in the field of digestive diseases. In private practice for over thirty years. Fellow of American College of Gastroenterology and member of Speaker's Bureau. Former clinical instructor in medicine, University of Buffalo, School of Medicine. Former medical staff president of two local hospitals. Immediate Past President G. I. & Liver Society of WNY. Active member local and national medical societies. Member speaker's bureau pharmaceutical companies. Independent Medical Reviewer for insurance companies and attorneys. At request - records review for merit. **Degrees/licenses:** MD.

Gastroenterology *(cont.)*

Farshid Sam Rahbar, MD, FACP

2080 Century Park East, #1804
Los Angeles, CA 90067
Tel: (310) 553-4400
Fax: (310) 553-5590
E-mail: giexpert@yahoo.com
Web Site: http://www.DrRahbar.com

Specialties: Board-certified Internist & Gastroenterologist; AME; IME; Consultant, Expert Witness, Technical Support, Medical Records Review; Disability Evaluation; Medical Malpractice; Plaintiff & Defense; Digestive & Liver Disorders, Hepatotoxicity, Drug Induced Liver Disease, Nutrition/TPN, Food Poisoning, Endoscopy & Surgery, Complications; Chemical, Electrical & Toxic Exposure, Chemical Sensitivity; Internal Medicine. 15+ years Medical-Legal experience. Numerous Depositions, Court Testimony. Former Chief of Gastroenterology. **Degrees/licenses:** MD, FACP.

Meyer N. Solny, MD, FACG

One East 68th Street
New York, NY 10021
Tel: (212) 570-6945
Fax: (212) 472-7687
E-mail: drmns@msn.com

Specialties: Board-Certified Gastroenterologist and Gastrointestinal Endoscopy specialist, Columbia and Cornell trained clinician, with an active Internal Medicine/Gastroenterology practice for the past 25 years, on staff at New York Presbyterian Hospital and Weill Cornell College of Medicine. Experienced as a medico-legal consultant and expert witness for both plaintiff and defense. Skilled in the explanation of complex medical issues to juries in a clear, evidence-based manner. **Degrees/licenses:** MD, FACG.

Carlos M. Torres, MD

Director, Gastrointestinal
and Liver Pathology Division
Metroplex Pathology Associates
9050 Jasmine Lane
Irving, TX 75063
Tel: (214) 596-2233
Fax: (972) 929-9996
E-mail: ctorres@pathologypartners.com
Web Site: www.pathologypartners.com

Specialties: Board certified Anatomic Pathologist (Barnes Hospital/Washington University). Fellowship in Oncologic Surgical Pathology (M.D. Anderson Cancer Center). Fellowship in Gastrointestinal and Liver Pathology (Brigham and Women's Hospital/Harvard Medical School). **Degrees/licenses:** Medical Doctor, Anatomic Pathologist Boarded.

Hand Surgery

Darrell L. Henderson, MD

Plastic Surgeon
Plastic Surgery Associates
1101 South College Rd., Ste. 400
Lafayette, LA 70503
Tel: (337) 233-5025
Fax: (337) 233-5054
E-mail: plasticsx@aol.com
Web Site: http://www.psassoc.com

Specialties: Hand/wrist surgeon, general plastic surgeon; Six-year residency at Mayo Clinic; General Surgery, Plastic Surgery. Fellowship in surgery of the hand and wrist with Dr. Frackelton, Milwaukee, WS. Vast experience in forensic evaluations of injuries and the impact disability has on the ability to work and problems, future medical, surgeries and expenses caused by the injury. Qualified as defense and plaintiff expert in many federal and state courts in the U.S. and Australia. American Society of Plastic Surgeons, American Board of Plastic surgeons, American Board of Forensic Examiners. **Degrees/licenses:** MD.

See primary listing under MEDICINE & HEALTH: Plastic & Reconstructive Surgery

Head Injury

Lawson F. Bernstein, MD

MD - Forensic Neuropsychiatry
P. O. Box 81977
Pittsburgh, PA 15217
Tel: (412) 600-7996
Fax: (412) 422-5203
E-mail: lawsonbernstein@hotmail.com
Web Site: http://www.ifbmdpc.com

Specialties: Board certified academically published forensic neuropsychiatrist. Expertise in brain injury, stroke, neurotoxicology, acute/chronic pain, dementia, alcohol & substance abuse, gambling addiction and multiple other areas of neurology/psychiatry. Extensive criminal/civil trial (50/50) Plaintiff/ Defense experience, including death penalty cases/legal insanity/diminished capacity. From 1991-1994, Dr. Bernstein was Director of the Psychiatry Residency Training Program at the University of Pittsburgh Medical Center, one of the largest academic psychiatric training programs in the U.S. Dr. Bernstein is also a Board Examiner for the American Board of Psychiatry & Neurology Oral Examination. **Degrees/licenses:** Medical.

Health Care Plans

Healthcare Litigation Support

PO Box 833
Petersham, MA 01366
Tel: (978) 724-0299
E-mail: pgeorge@healthcarelitigation.com
Web Site: www.healthcarelitigation.com

Specialties: A team of experts (not a referral service)-physicians, healthcare administrators, reimbursement specialists, health organization experts, health insurance experts, and other healthcare personnel-with broad, extensive experience and expertise in medical and administrative malpractice issues, physician practice operations, hospital management, health insurance and TPA issues, Medicare and Medicaid, medical billing and collections, fraud and abuse, managed care and other areas. Review case for merit, analyze medical and administrative events, identify causation, address standards of care, and articulate complex issues to triers of fact. Additional offices Toledo, Kansas City and Washington, D. C. **Degrees/licenses:** MD, JD, MPH; JD; PhD; BA.

See primary listing under MEDICAL-LEGAL: General

Hematology

Stephen B. Shohet, MD

Professor of Medicine
1925 Gough Street
San Francisco, CA 94109
Tel: (415) 922-3070
Fax: (415) 922-3113
E-mail: sbshohet@aol.com

Specialties: Expert witness for hematology, including bleeding, thrombosis, clotting, Heparin, and platelet problems; anemias, Sickle Cell Disease, and red cell disorders; leukemias, lymphomas and white cell diseases. Professor Emeritus of Medicine and Laboratory Medicine at University of California, San Francisco, with substantial testimony experience for both plaintiffs and defense. Also consultation for biomedical instrument and patent issues. Numerous publications. Medical licenses in California and Massachusetts. **Degrees/licenses:** AB, MD; Medical Lic. in CA & MA.

Hypertension

Howard S. Shapiro, MD, FACP

Howard S. Shapiro, MD, PC
2140 Bloomfield Woods Court
West Bloomfield, MI 48323-1913
Tel: (248) 865-9448
(248) 613-9353
Fax: (248) 332-6850
E-mail: hshapiromd@aol.com
Web Site: www.howardshapiromd.com

Specialties: I have had extensive experience in clinical nephrology, renal transplantation, acute and chronic dialysis as well as with associated problems, including hypertension,

(Listing continued on next page)

Hypertension *(cont.)*

Howard S. Shapiro, MD (cont.)
hyperparathyroidism, sodium and potassium disorders and acid-base derangements. My experience includes the chairmanship of nephrology divisions at two major hospitals, the direction of a fellowship program, and of a renal transplantation program. I directed a hospital chronic dialysis program and later founded and directed a regional group of chronic dialysis units. In addition, I chaired the Medical Review Board and was President of the Michigan ESRD Network. **Degrees/licenses:** MD, FACP; Bd. Cert. in Internal Med. & Nephrology; See Web site for CV.

See primary listing under MEDICINE & HEALTH: Nephrology

Infectious Diseases

Stephen W. Hosea, MD

320 W. Pueblo, Rm. 6S09
Santa Barbara, CA 93105
Tel: (805) 682-3610
Fax: (805) 682-3050
E-mail: shosea@sbch.org

Specialties: Harvard College BA, 1969; Harvard Medical School MD, 1973; Massachusetts General Hospital Medical Resident, 1973-75; National Institutes of Health, NIAID Clinical Associate, 1975-78; Yale University 1978-79, Infectious Disease Fellow; NIH, NIAID 1979-81, Senior Investigator; Private Practice Infectious Disease, 1981-present; Associate Academic Chief of Medicine, 1983-present; Director AIDS Clinic, 1984-present; Head of Infection Control at Santa Barbara Cottage Hospital, 1993-present. **Degrees/licenses:** MD (Internal Medicine, 1976; Infectious Diseases, 1980); FACP.

Joseph B. Marzouk, MD

350 30th St., Ste. 511
Oakland, CA 94609
Tel: (510) 835-6225
(510) 834-2800
Fax: (510) 834-8206
E-mail: jobm@aol.com
Web Site: www.infectiousdiseasemd.com

Specialties: Infectious diseases - infections of all medical specialties; Hepatitis; Infection control; HIV/AIDS; Food poisoning; Independent Medical Evaluations; Case reviews, depositions, trials; Plaintiff and defense work; Multiple presentations to various audiences on infectious disease topics; Author, Infectious Disease chapter in "Lawyer's Medical Encyclopedia;" Board Certified in Infectious Diseases, Internal Medicine, Infection Control. HIV Specialist. CV available on request. **Degrees/licenses:** MD (AZ, CA).

Internal Medicine

William D. Barnhart, MD, MBA, FACP, FACFE

Internal Medicine/Geriatrics
2625 Harlem Blvd.
Rockford, IL 61103
Tel: (815) 962-4299
Fax: (815) 965-8641
E-mail: wbarnh9400@aol.com
Web Site: www.dr-barnhart.yourmd.com

Specialties: Twenty years experience in medical malpractice, personal injury and Workers' Compensation - defense and plaintiff. Medical Educator and practitioner in internal medicine, primary care, preventive medicine, clinical ethics and clinical geriatrics. Active medical school faculty member. Extensive trial experience and skills in discovery and evidence depositions. Member - ASIM, AMA, ACLM, ASLME, ACFM, and other national organizations. Presenter nationally, in medical ethics and law for physicians. Fellow of the Institute of Medicine of Chicago, the American College of Physicians, and the American College of Forensic Examiners. **Degrees/licenses:** MD, MBA, FACP, BCME, BCFM, FACFE.

See primary listing under MEDICAL-LEGAL: General

Albert M. Harary, MD

654 Madison Ave., Sixth Floor
New York, NY 10021
Tel: (212) 702-0123
Fax: (212) 355-4244
E-mail: docharary@aol.com

Specialties: Gastroenterology; Liver diseases; Gastrointestinal endoscopy; Internal medicine; Stress & digestive disorders. Affiliation: Private Practice; New York University School of Medicine (Clinical Assistant Professor of Medicine). **Degrees/licenses:** MD; FACP; Board Certified.

See primary listing under MEDICINE & HEALTH: Gastroenterology

Perry Hookman, MD

Perry Hookman, MD, PA
5607 NW 24th Terrace
Boca Raton, FL 33496
Tel: (561) 241-8550
E-mail: hookman@hookman.com
Web Site: http://www.hookman.com

Specialties: Expert medical opinion from board certified physician in internal medicine and gastroenterology. Will review medical records, diagnoses & treatment of internal medicine and gastrointestinal diseases. In current active private medical practice & medical school teaching faculty. See publications on Dr. Hookman's website. **Degrees/licenses:** Perry Hookman, MD, FACP, FACG, FACPE.

See primary listing under MEDICAL-LEGAL: Medical Malpractice

James F. Lineback, MD, FCCP

2100 N. Main St., Suite 202
Santa Ana, CA 92706
Tel: (949) 610-0036
Fax: (949) 721-9121
E-mail: linebackmd@cox.net

Specialties: Medical Practice in Pulmonary/Chest Medicine and Internal Medicine since 1983. Internal Medicine; Pulmonary/Chest Medicine; Occupational Medicine; Wrongful Death Cases; Patient Care Issues; Medical Causation; Standard of Care Issues; Diagnostic Dilemmas; Toxic Exposure; Medical Records Review; Courtroom Testimony. Associate Clinical Professor of Medicine at USC College of Medicine and UC Irvine College of Medicine, Lecturer in Physiology at UC Riverside College of Medicine.. **Degrees/licenses:** MS, MD, FCCP. Board Cert. Internal Medicine & Pulmonary Medicine.

Farshid Sam Rahbar, MD, FACP

2080 Century Park East, #1804
Los Angeles, CA 90067
Tel: (310) 553-4400
Fax: (310) 553-5590
E-mail: giexpert@yahoo.com
Web Site: http://www.DrRahbar.com

Specialties: Board-certified Internist & Gastroenterologist; AME; IME; Consultant, Expert Witness, Technical Support, Medical Records Review; Disability Evaluation; Medical Malpractice; Plaintiff & Defense; Digestive & Liver Disorders, Hepatotoxicity, Drug Induced Liver Disease, Nutrition/TPN, Food Poisoning, Endoscopy & Surgery, Complications; Chemical, Electrical & Toxic Exposure, Chemical Sensitivity; Internal Medicine. 15+ years Medical-Legal experience. Numerous Depositions, Court Testimony. Former Chief of Gastroenterology. **Degrees/licenses:** MD, FACP.

See primary listing under MEDICINE & HEALTH: Gastroenterology

Basil M. RuDusky, MD

Private Practice of Internal Medicine, Cardiology & Forensic Medicine
15 Public Square
Wilkes-Barre, PA 18701
Tel: (570) 824-7115
Fax: Call

Specialties: Over thirty years experience in all aspects of internal medicine and cardiovascular medicine. Senior consultant in medicine and cardiology to numerous corporations worldwide and government agencies. Vast experience in corporate, occupational, medical-legal, military, and governmental medicine. Author of numerous publications, including five "Firsts" in the world's medical

(Listing continued on next page)

Internal Medicine *(cont.)*

Basil M. RuDusky, MD (cont.)
literature. Over thirty years experience in forensic medicine, including precedent setting state supreme court decisions. Extensive curriculum vitae and bibliography on request. **Degrees/licenses:** BA, MD, FACA, FCCP, FACP, FACC, DABFM, FACFE.

See primary listing under MEDICINE & HEALTH: Cardiology

Steven M. Simons, MD

435 N. Roxbury #311
Beverly Hills, CA 90210
Tel: (310) 274-7303
Fax: (310) 274-8572
E-mail: simons@cshs.org
Web Site: http://www.simonsmd.com

Specialties: Internal Medicine, Pulmonary, Critical Care, Asthma, Pulmonary Embolism, Ventilator Management, Pneumonia, Pleural Effusion, COPD, Bronchoscopy. POSITIONS: Chief of Staff, Chief of Medicine, Chief of Pulmonary, Director Pulmonary Endoscopy, Med. Director Quality Mgt. - Cedars; Chief of Staff - Cedars Sinai Medical Center, Medical Director Medical Affairs - Cedars. CERTIFICATIONS: Amer. Board of Internal Medicine, Pulmonary Diseases, Critical Care, Quality Assurance. 29 Publications. PROFESSIONAL SOCIETIES: Amer. College of Physicians; Amer. College of Chest Physicians; Amer. Thoracic Society; CA Medical Assn.; LA County Medical Assn.; Council on Critical Care; Amer. College of Sports Medicine. EXPERIENCE: 20 years Expert Witness, approx. 50% defense, 50% plaintiff. **Degrees/licenses:** BS, MD, FACP, FCCP, Clinical Professor - UCLA; Lic. CA, NY.

See primary listing under MEDICINE & HEALTH: Pulmonary Medicine

Kenneth A. Stein, MD

14312 Aitken Hill Court
Chesterfield (St. Louis), MO 63017
Tel: (314) 495-7009
Fax: (708) 585-3348
E-mail: kenny@er-md.com
Web Site: http://www.er-md.com

Specialties: Attending Staff Physician in Emergency Medicine and Critical Care at St. Anthony's Medical Center and Assistant Clinical Professor at St. Louis University Health Sciences Center, Department of Surgery/ Emergency Medicine Division. Furnishes an unbiased opinion on medical malpractice and negligence, emergency medicine and internal medicine, for plaintiff or defense. Survey of case for merit, medical chart review and analysis, formulation of case strategy, preparation for opposing expert deposition and cross-examination, medical literature search, expert witness testimony. **Degrees/licenses:** MD, Board Certified in Internal Medicine.

See primary listing under MEDICINE & HEALTH: Emergency Medicine

Janet Winikoff, MD, FACE

2021 Santa Monica Blvd., Ste. 325 E.
Santa Monica, CA 90404
Tel: (310) 828-5337
Fax: (310) 828-2556
E-mail: jwinikof@ucla.edu

Specialties: Board Certified Internal Medicine - ABIM; Board Certified Endocrinology and Metabolism (Diabetes) - ABIM; Fellow, American College of Endocrinology; Assistant Clinical Professor, UCLA School of Medicine. Twenty years experience teaching and clinical practice. Experienced medical reviewer, plaintiff and defense. **Degrees/licenses:** MD, Licensed State of California.

Laparoscopic Surgery

C. Andrew Heiskell, MD, FACS

Medical Legal Consultants, Inc.
4000 Hampton Center, Ste. D
Morgantown, WV 26505
Tel: (304) 599-8665
Fax: (304) 599-8584
E-mail: info@heiskellmd.com
Web Site: http://www.heiskellmd.com

Specialties: Dr. Heiskell is a practicing General and Vascular Surgeon. Dr. Heiskell has been in private practice for 25 years and has been reviewing medical records for over 10 years, testifying on behalf of claimants, defendants and insurers in cases of general and vascular surgery, laparoscopic surgery, surgical malpractice and standards of care. He performs numerous operations yearly including hernia repairs, laparoscopic gallbladder surgery, surgeries of the breast, colon, stomach, pancreas, spleen, thyroid, carotid arteries and many other vascular procedures. **Degrees/licenses:** BS, MD, Board Certified.

See primary listing under MEDICINE & HEALTH: Surgery, General

Laurence A. Jacobs, MD, FACOG

Reproductive Endocrinologist/Infertility
Jacobs Medical LLC
3149 Dundee Rd., #271
Northbrook, IL 60062
Tel: (847) 215-8899
(847) 372-4364 (Cellular)
(847) 817-5869 (Pager)
Fax: (847) 215- 8996
E-mail: jacobsmd66@aol.com
Web Site:
http://www.laurencejacobsmd.com

Specialties: Complications from laparoscopic surgery, infertility, in vitro fertilization (IVF), miscarriages, ectopic pregnancies, multiple pregnancies, fertility drugs, birth defects, pelvic infections, hormone therapy, endometriosis, gynecologic surgery. Recently recognized in the national guide book "America's Top Doctors" published by Castle Connolly (top 1/2% of specialists nationwide). Identified by peer nomination as one of the country's leading medical specialists in infertility/reproductive endocrinology. Prestigious Mayo Clinic Infertility Fellowship, 1986-1988; Northwestern University Medical School and OB/GYN residency, 1971-1979. Dedicated, experienced expert witness serving defense/plaintiff. **Degrees/licenses:** MD, BA Northwestern; Board Cert. OB/GYN, 1981, FACOG.

See primary listing under MEDICINE & HEALTH: Obstetrics & Gynecology

Jeffrey M. Sherwood, MD, FACS

P.O. Box 1071
Water Mill, NY 11976
Tel: (888) 343-7642
Fax: (631) 726-9323
E-mail: jms12544@yahoo.com

Specialties: General Surgery, Laparoscopic Surgery & Breast Surgery. Over 10 years experience reviewing cases for both defendants' and plaintiffs' attorneys. Board Certified; Fellow, American College of Surgeons; Member, Society of Laparoscopic Surgeons. **Degrees/licenses:** MD, New York State Medical License.

See primary listing under MEDICINE & HEALTH: Surgery, General

Surgery, Trauma, Laparoscopy Expertise

Devesh Tiwary, MD, FACS
1682 Canopy Oaks Blvd.
Palm Harbor, FL 34683-6161
Tel: (727) 489-9327
(727) 687-6787 (Cell)
Fax: (727) 489-9327
E-mail: adt@tiwary.net
Web Site: http://www.mydoctor.com/tiwary

Specialties: Trauma, surgery: general, abdominal, breast, wound care, basic and advanced laparoscopy. Board Certified in Surgery; Advanced Trauma Life Support Certified. All education in United States; no accent; articulate and able to explain complex medical concepts simply. Graduate of Harvard

(Listing continued on next page)

Laparoscopic Surgery *(cont.)*

Surgery, Trauma, Laparoscopy Expertise (cont.)
Law School; locum tenens trauma surgeon. Prior experience: Mayo Clinic Jacksonville, private practice, indigent care hospital, former Chief of Surgery at major urban hospital. See CV at website (above). **Degrees/licenses:** MD, FACS, BA Biology, ATLS Certified.
See primary listing under MEDICINE & HEALTH: Surgery, General

Ronald Zelnick, MD

General and Colorectal Surgeon
210 Jupiter Lakes Blvd., #3105
Jupiter, FL 33458
Tel: (561) 575-7875
Fax: (561) 575-5874
E-mail: docrsz@aol.com

Specialties: General Surgery; Laparoscopic Surgery; Colon and Rectal Surgery; Breast Surgery. Board Certified and Recertified General Surgery and Colon And Rectal Surgery. Fellow American College of Surgeons; Fellow American Society of Colon & Rectal Surgeons. Actively practicing surgery in private practice, 14 years experience; Medical-legal experience. **Degrees/licenses:** MD, Florida License.
See primary listing under MEDICINE & HEALTH: Colon & Rectal Surgery

Malpractice

CERA, Inc., Medical Legal Support Services

Timothy D. Brooks, MD
Medical Director
P. O. Box 11247
Pensacola, FL 32524-1247
Tel: (888) 476-7707 (Toll Free)
(850) 476-7707
Fax: (850) 995-9440
E-mail: info@cerainc.com
Web Site: http://www.cerainc.com/

Specialties: CERA, Inc. is a physician owned and operated consulting group providing medical malpractice case screening, expert witness identification, and preparation of Life Care Plans. CERA's staff of physicians and nurses can review your case and offer a preliminary opinion on merit. We also have experts available in all areas of medicine to review your case and offer a formal opinion on standard of care for plaintiff or defense. CERA's services are rapid, accurate and cost effective. For a no-obligation consultation, please call Toll Free (888) 476-7707. **Degrees/licenses:** MD, RN, CLNC, CLCP, OTR.

See primary listing under MEDICAL-LEGAL: Medical Record Review

Life Management Services

a division of CERA, Inc.
Donna D. Archer, ORT/L, CLCP
Consultant
P. O. Box 11247
Pensacola, FL 32524-1247
Tel: (888) 476-7707 (Toll Free)
(850) 476-7707
Fax: (850) 995-9440
E-mail: darcher@cerainc.com
Web Site: http://www.lms.cerainc.com/

Specialties: Life Management Services is a division of CERA, Inc. CERA is a physician owned and operated consulting group providing medical malpractice support services including preparation of Life Care Plans. CERA's Life Care Planner is certified (CLCP) and has 30+ years experience in the field of rehabilitation. For a no-obligation consultation, please call Toll Free (888) 476-7707. **Degrees/licenses:** CLCP, OTR, MD, RN, CLNC.

See primary listing under MEDICAL-LEGAL: Life Care Planning

Manhattan Ophthalmology Associates

Spencer E. Sherman, MD
President & Medical Director
166 East 63rd Street
New York, NY 10021
Tel: (212) 753-8300
Fax: (212) 752-4285
E-mail: sesmdpc@aol.com
Web Site: http://www.nyeyelaser.com

Specialties: AB Princeton University - cum laude, 1958; MD Columbia College of Surgeons, 1962; Specializing in: cataract, glaucoma, refractive surgery, contact lenses; Residency 1965-68, Mt. Sinai Hospital NY (Ophthalmology); Attending surgeon: Mt. Sinai, Lenox Hill, Manhattan Eye & Ear, NY Eye & Ear (all in NY). Honors: honor award & service award (AAO), Sigma Xi (Princeton), named Top Doctors in U.S., Best Doctor in NY; Who's Who in America. Fellow of: American & International College of Surgeons; American Academy of Ophthalmology; International Society of Refractive Surgeons; New York Society of Ophthalmology, AMA. **Degrees/licenses:** MD, Lic. in NY, FL, CA & NJ.

See primary listing under MEDICINE & HEALTH: Ophthalmology

Medical Administration

John Goldenring, MD, MPH

10496 Canyon Lake Drive
San Diego, CA 92131
Tel: (858) 635-5500
Fax: (858) 635-5600
E-mail: jgoldenr@san.rr.com

Specialties: Pediatrics, Adolescents and Young Adult Medicine to ages 0-27; Child Physical and Sexual Abuse, Pediatric Urgent and Emergency Care; Administrative Medicine - HMO, IPA and Hospital; Preventive Medicine; STDs; Pediatric Toxins; Cross-Cultural Medicine; International Health. **Degrees/licenses:** MD, MPH CA Lic. #G37744, TX Lic. #J0955.

See primary listing under MEDICINE & HEALTH: Pediatrics

Medical Devices, Equip.

AINSLIE

Alan Broadwin
Principal
27 Pine Ridge Road
Larchmont, NY 10538-2616
Tel: (914) 833-2649
Fax: (914) 833-5037
E-mail: broadwin@ainslie.com
Web Site: www.lawinfo.com/biz/ainslie

Specialties: Design and litigation consultant; Patent and Technology evaluation; Regulatory Compliance Assessment of ISO and GMP Quality Systems; Evaluation of adequacy of medical devices and disposables; Assistance in discovery and depositions as fact or expert witness; Engineering and due diligence investigations; Surgeon/hospital interface; Review of clinical/technical reports. **Degrees/licenses:** BA, BSME Columbia; MSIE Stevens; ASQ CQA; RAB cert. auditor; RAC.

Jerome T. Anderson, CCE

Principal
Biomedical Consulting Services
3551 Camino Mira Costa, Suite R
San Clemente, CA 92672
Tel: (949) 234-0525
Fax: (949) 234-0526
E-mail: janderson@biomedconsulting.com
Web Site: www.biomedconsulting.com

Specialties: More than 30 years experience in medical technology, medical research, and clinical applications of medical devices and equipment. Established and managed medical equipment service businesses. Clinical experience in the use of medical devices for patient care and diagnosis. Have provided expert witness and investigative services to medical equipment manufacturers, hospital risk managers, insurance companies and attorneys for more than 25 years. Completed medical equipment planning and health care facility design for more than 80 projects. **Degrees/licenses:** BA, Certified Clinical Engineer, Certified Biomedical Equipment Technician.

Medical Devices, Equip.
(cont.)

J. Dennis Bruner, PhD, PE

J. Dennis Bruner, PhD, PE, PC
6054 S. Krameria St.
Englewood, CO 80111-4274
Tel: (303) 771-0047
(303) 771-9306
Fax: (303) 771-0047 *51
E-mail: dennisbruner@att.net

Specialties: Quality/Regulatory Compliance: FDA Medical Device Regulatory Compliance and Quality System Consulting. Expert Witness: Medical devices used in Cardiovascular Surgery, Hemodialysis, Surgical Blood Salvage, Physiologic Pressure Monitoring and Pulmonary Disease. Experience: 30+ years of medical device manufacturing (Quality, Regulatory Compliance, ISO 9001, CE Marking, Top Management) experience. Products Liability defense experience in over 20 medical device law suits. Memberships: NAFE (Sr. Member), NSPE, ASME, ASQ, RAPS. Board Certified Diplomate in Forensic Engineering by NAFE, a CASB Member Board. Post Doctoral Research: Harvard Medical School. **Degrees/licenses:** BS, MS, PhD, Mechanical/Biomed Engr., Reg. Prof. Engr.

See primary listing under ENGINEERING: Forensic

Chemir Analytical Services

Shri Thanedar, PhD
CEO
2672 Metro Blvd.
Maryland Heights, MO 63043
Tel: (800) 659-7659
Fax: (314) 291-6630
E-mail: info@chemir.com
Web Site: http://www.chemir.com

Specialties: Materials Identification - identify and quantify components in an unknown sample; Deformulation - reverse engineering of a product; Failure Analysis - material and product failures; Comparative Analysis - product contamination and "good vs. bad" product comparison. Experienced in the chemical analysis of polymers, medical devices, pharmaceuticals, implantables, packaging, and adhesives. Recent cases include patent infringement; product liability and failure; stability; insurance claim validation. Experienced PhD chemists available for consultation including expert witness and testimony to back up laboratory data. In business since 1959.

See primary listing under CHEMISTRY/ CHEMICALS: General

Joseph F. Dyro, PhD, CCE

21 Bob's Lane
Setauket, NY 11733
Tel: (631) 751-7244
Fax: (631) 751-7802
E-mail: dyro@alum.mit.edu
Web Site: http://www.dyro.org/brg.htm

Specialties: Medical Devices Product Liability, Patent Infringement; Forensic Clinical Engineering; Biomedical Instrumentation; Biomechanics; Electrocution and Shock Accident Reconstruction; Human Factors; Hospital Accident Analysis. Editor-in-Chief of The Clinical Engineering Handbook. Wrote FDA Infant Incubator Standard. MIT SB Electrical Engineering; University of Pennsylvania MS, PhD, Biomedical Engineering. Editor, "Journal of Clinical Engineering." American College of Clinical Engineering, President, 1992-94. Director Biomedical Engineering and Associate Research Professor of Anesthesiology, SUNY, Stony Brook University Hospital, 1980-94; Fellow, American Institute for Medical and Biological Engineering. Over 25 years litigation experience. Certified Clinical Engineer. **Degrees/licenses:** SBEE, MS, PhD, CCE.

See primary listing under ENGINEERING: Biomedical

L.A. Geddes

Forensic Engineer
400 North River Rd., Ste. 701
West Lafayette, IN 47906
Tel: (765) 743-1941
(765) 494-2997
Fax: (765) 494-1193
E-mail: geddes@ecn.purdue.edu

Specialties: Electrical engineer, physiologist, biomedical engineer, certified clinical engineer, professional engineer (Texas license 10170). Author of "Medical Device Accidents" (Lawyers & Judges Publ., Inc. Tucson, Arizona) and over 750 scientific publications and 20 books. Holds 22 U.S. and foreign patents. Fellow IEEE, AAAS, American College of Cardiology, Royal Society of Medicine. Numerous scientific and teaching awards. Expert witness in over 100 lawsuits, depositions and 6 court cases. **Degrees/licenses:** ME, PhD, DSc, Texas License 10170.

Jack Goldberg

President
Metrionix, Inc.
9340 Carmel Mountain Rd., Ste. E
San Diego, CA 92129-2161
Tel: (858) 780-9311
Fax: (858) 780-9312
E-mail: info@metrionix.com
Web Site: http://www.metrionix.com

Specialties: Metrionix, Inc. provides expert witness, consulting and design services with expertise in medical and scientific instruments, audio and acoustics. Mr. Goldberg has 30 years of engineering experience and has served as an expert in patent litigation, trade secrets, criminal earwitness, failure analysis, and product liability, many cases involving medical instruments. Detailed knowledge includes circuit and system design, measurement and control, embedded software, signal processing, vital signs, infusion pumps and hearing. Trial experience includes testimony for plaintiff in medical instrument patent case which successfully led to award exceeding $100M. **Degrees/licenses:** MIT: MS and BS Elec Eng & Comp Sci; Sr. member IEEE.

Linda M. Huffman, CRNA

402 Tod Lane
Youngstown, OH 44504-3425
Tel: (330) 743-9596
(330) 360-0163 (Cell)
Fax: (330) 743-9596

Specialties: Nurse anesthesia practice: general surgery, trauma, obstetrics; Anesthesia gas delivery systems; Monitoring devices and applications; Anesthesia devices and applications; Standards for machines and monitoring; Pulse oximetry, capnography, ventilatory monitoring; Safety standards for ambulatory care, post-anesthesia recovery transport monitoring; Safe Medical Device Act of 1990; AANA and OSHA recommendations for waste gas management; ASTM standards for safety and performance of anesthesia machines and monitoring systems; NIOSH standards. RN (AZ, IL, NM, OH, OR, TX, VA, WV); Certified in ACLS, BCLS and PALS; Board Certification: Council on Certification of American Association of Nurse Anesthetists. **Degrees/licenses:** CRNA (Certified Registered Nurse Anesthetist).

See primary listing under MEDICINE & HEALTH: Anesthesiology

Rod S. O'Connor, CPO

Certified Prosthetist & Orthotist
O'Connor Orthopedics
412 Carl Karcher Way
Anaheim, CA 92801
Tel: (714) 635-2650
(714) 635-2669
(714) 635-2651
Fax: (714) 635-0223
E-mail: mxrod@pacbell.net

Specialties: Certified by the American Board for Certification in Orthotics & Prosthetics. Specialist in: all lower extremity prosthetics, all upper extremity prosthetics, myoelectrics (bionics), etc.; braces for spine, halos, extremity bracing, fracture bracing, etc. Member: American Board for Certification in Orthotics & Prosthetics, American Orthotic & Prosthetic Association, American Academy of Orthotists

(Listing continued on next page)

Medical Devices, Equip.
(cont.)

Rod S. O'Connor (cont.)
& Prosthetists, NCOPE accredited residency site. **Degrees/licenses:** CPO, VAQP.

See primary listing under MEDICINE & HEALTH: Amputation & Artificial Limbs

Alexander G. Sensenbrenner, CBET

The Sensenbrenner Corporation
P. O. Box 5098
Crestline, CA 92325-5098
Tel: (909) 338-0858
Fax: (909) 338-9079
E-mail: wysiwyg51@earthlink.net

Specialties: Medical Devices and Systems to include anesthesia equipment; ventilators; respiratory therapy equipment; electrosurgical units; cautery; pulse oximetry; patient monitoring; telemetry; radiological/x-ray imaging; hyperbaric chambers; ultrasound imaging; medical gases; hospital beds; laboratory equipment; end tidal CO2 monitoring; surgical instrumentation; lasers; insufflators; endoscopic instrumentation; endoscopes; hysteroscopes; laparoscopes; cystoscopes; sterilization/decontamination equipment; infusion pumps; syringe pumps; infusion controllers; patient-controlled anesthesia pumps; perfusion pumps; clinical engineering practices; Joint Commission for the Accreditation of Healthcare Organizations standards compliance. **Degrees/licenses:** Certified Biomedical Equipment Technician.

Neil Sheehan

Consulting Engineer, Medical Products
One Southgate Street
Atherton, CA 94027
Tel: (650) 363-0913
Fax: (650) 363-0923
E-mail: neiljs@aol.com

Specialties: Thirty years of experience in all aspects of medical device design and development from individual contributor to Vice President of Engineering and Manufacturing; Emphasis on disposables and associated hardware of all kinds (intravenous systems and components, surgical devices, catheters, hemodialysis, electrodes, pipettors, breathing circuits, connector systems, et al.) including manufacturing processes; Thirty-six patents; Experienced successful expert witness in major patent infringement suits; Also numerous favorable product liability and contract cases; Demonstrative evidence and litigation graphics; Excellent, likable courtroom presence; Education: Villanova Univ.; Harvard Univ. (Grad. School); University of Calif., Berkeley (Pre-Med). **Degrees/licenses:** BSME, Summa Cum Laude, Alumni Achiev. Award; Sr. Member SPE.

Thielsch Engineering, Inc.

Ara Nalbandian, PE, Vice President
Bob Basile, PE
Florence Cone
195 Frances Avenue
Cranston, RI 02910
Tel: (401) 467-6454
Fax: (401) 467-2398
E-mail: nalbandiana@thielsch.com
Web Site: http://www.thielsch.com

Specialties: Providing assistance to medical device industry including attorneys, insurance companies and manufacturers in designing, developing, manufacturing, qualification testing, and failure cause and origin determinations. Engineering evaluation on all types of devices including medical implants, orthopedic, endoscopy, wound management and rehabilitation products. Failure analysis performed on heart valves, hip, knee, shoulder, small joints implants, surgical procedure devices and equipment. Engineering laboratory with mechanical and material testing, environmental chemical science, microbiological and NDT capabilities. Registered Professional Engineers in Rhode Island, Massachusetts, Maine, New Jersey, Georgia, Florida, Indiana and California. **Degrees/licenses:** BS, PE, BS Mech. Engr. MS (RI, MA, ME, NJ, GA, FL, IN & CA).

See primary listing under ENGINEERING: Consulting

David Yadin
President
Biomedical Engineering Consultants
1111 Hermann Dr., Ste. 12B
Houston, TX 77004
Tel: (713) 522-6666
Fax: (713) 522-6686
E-mail: ybdavid@
texaschildrenshospital.org
Web Site: http://www.biomedeng.com

Specialties: Testing, evaluating, servicing, & repairs of Medical Devices & accessories. Over 25 years of expertise practicing at the world's largest medical center. Failure analysis & electromagnetic (EMI) compatibility investigation & assessment of infusion pumps, anesthesia machines, lasers & telemedicine. Directing comprehensive biomedical engineering program within hospital & home-care environments. Member of regulatory agency (FDA) panel & standards developing association (NFPA). Past president & founder of American College of Clinical Engineering (ACCE). President, Center for Telemedicine Law (CTL). Registered professional engineer (PE), certified clinical engineer (CCE), certified healthcare safety executive (HSPC), Fellow American Institute of Medical & Biological Engineering (AIMBE). **Degrees/licenses:** BSc, MSc, EdD, PE, CCE, HSPC, FAIMBE, FACCE. See above.

MRI

Harold S. Parnes, MD
Medical Director
Omega Diagnostic Imaging, PC
1525 Voorhies Ave.
Brooklyn, NY 11235
Tel: (718) 332-1999
Fax: (718) 332-3236 or (718) 332-4192
E-mail: hparneurad@aol.com

Specialties: Board Certified Diagnostic Radiology and Neuroradiology, currently in private practice. Assistant Professor of Radiology at State University of New York Stony Brook. Attended seven year Accelerated Biomedical (1978-1985) Program SUNY Downstate; Intern - Internal Medicine, Resident and Chief Resident Radiology - Long Island College Hospital; Fellowship 2 years Neuroradiology SUNY Stony Brook; Director Neuroradiology 4 years Queens General Hospital in conjunction with Long Island Jewish and Mount Sinai Medical Centers. Senior member American Society of Neuroradiology; member Society Spine Radiology; member American Society of Pediatric Neuroradiology; member American Society of Head and Neck Radiology. Licensed in Pennsylvania, Florida, California, New Jersey. **Degrees/licenses:** MD, SUNY Downstate, 7 yr. Accel. Biomedical Program.

See primary listing under MEDICINE & HEALTH: Radiology, Neuroradiology

Nephrology

Michael Blumenkrantz, MD, FACP, FACN, CNSP
2080 Century Park E., Ste. 707
Los Angeles, CA 90067
Tel: (310) 289-9824
Fax: (310) 277-3659

Specialties: Medical Doctor with extensive consulting and expert witness experience (plaintiff and defense) in the following areas: Internal Medicine; Dialysis (Hemodialysis & Peritoneal CAPD); Obesity; Nutrition; Geriatrics; TPN; Critical Care; Hypertension; Med/Legal Quality Assurance; Medical Malpractice; Case Evaluation. Over 80 publications. Formerly full-time Associate Professor of Medicine at UCLA. Extensive research and consulting experience. Visiting professor numerous national and international meeting. Articulate presentor - extensive experience medical/legal testimony. **Degrees/licenses:** MD; FACP; FACN; CNSP; Dipl, Bds - Internal Med. Nephrology, & Nutrition.

Allan Ramsay, MD
Consultant Nephrologist
P. O. Box 245
Cooperstown, NY 13326
Tel: (607) 547-2283
Fax: (607) 547-5897

Specialties: Kidney Disease; Kidney Biopsy; Dialysis; Transplantation Acid-Base; Electrolytes; Publications: 35; Testimony: 21 cases. **Degrees/licenses:** MD, New York.

Nephrology *(cont.)*

Howard S. Shapiro, MD, FACP

Howard S. Shapiro, MD, PC
2140 Bloomfield Woods Court
West Bloomfield, MI 48323-1913
Tel: (248) 865-9448
(248) 613-9353
Fax: (248) 332-6850
E-mail: hshapiromd@aol.com
Web Site: www.howardshapiromd.com

Specialties: I have had extensive experience in clinical nephrology, renal transplantation, acute and chronic dialysis as well as with associated problems, including hypertension, hyperparathyroidism, sodium and potassium disorders and acid-base derangements. My experience includes the chairmanship of nephrology divisions at two major hospitals, the direction of a fellowship program, and of a renal transplantation program. I directed a hospital chronic dialysis program and later founded and directed a regional group of chronic dialysis units. In addition, I chaired the Medical Review Board and was President of the Michigan ESRD Network. **Degrees/ licenses:** MD, FACP; Bd. Cert. in Internal Med. & Nephrology; See Web site for CV.

Neurology

Lawson F. Bernstein, MD

MD - Forensic Neuropsychiatry
P. O. Box 81977
Pittsburgh, PA 15217
Tel: (412) 600-7996
Fax: (412) 422-5203
E-mail: lawsonbernstein@hotmail.com
Web Site: http://www.ifbmdpc.com

Specialties: Board certified academically published forensic neuropsychiatrist. Expertise in brain injury, stroke, neurotoxicology, acute/chronic pain, dementia, alcohol & substance abuse, gambling addiction and multiple other areas of neurology/psychiatry. Extensive criminal/civil trial (50/50) Plaintiff/ Defense experience, including death penalty cases/legal insanity/diminished capacity. From 1991-1994, Dr. Bernstein was Director of the Psychiatry Residency Training Program at the University of Pittsburgh Medical Center, one of the largest academic psychiatric training programs in the U.S. Dr. Bernstein is also a Board Examiner for the American Board of Psychiatry & Neurology Oral Examination. **Degrees/licenses:** Medical.

See primary listing under MEDICINE & HEALTH: Head Injury

Warren E. Cohen, MD, FAAP

302 Carvel Ave.
Cedarhurst, NY 11516
Tel: (516) 371-3691
Fax: (516) 371-1895
E-mail: weco@pop.net

Specialties: Birth injury, birth defects, birth asphyxia, cerebral palsy, mental retardation, genetic conditions, pediatric disorders, neurologic disorders; Extent of neurologic damage, long-term disability needs, expected lifespan; Causation of birth injuries and neurologic disability in childhood; genetic/congenital cause versus birth-related injury. Experienced witness, plaintiff/defendant. Board certified in Pediatrics, Pediatric Neurology, and Medical Genetics. Also certified in Neuro-rehabilitation. Experienced children's hospital medical director, United Cerebral Palsy medical director. Associate Clinical Professor, George Washington University School of Medicine. Training: Hosp. Albert Einstein College of Medicine, National Institutes of Health. **Degrees/licenses:** BS, MD, FAAP.

See primary listing under MEDICINE & HEALTH: Pediatric Neurology

Alan B. Grindal, MD

Consultative Neurological Services
915 Sirus Trail
Sarasota, FL 34232
Tel: (941) 379-5246
Fax: (941) 379-8380
E-mail: agrindal@comcast.net
Web Site: http://www.neurology-doctor.com

Specialties: Board Certified by the American Board of Psychiatry and Neurology, with 30 years clinical practice experience. Chosen by peers consecutively to "The Best Doctors in America" Southeast Region, 1997 to 2004. Areas of special interest include stroke, dementia, head trauma, multiple sclerosis, headache, Parkinson's Disease and epilepsy. Services provided for attorneys and insurance companies are medical-legal consultation, peer review, and expert witness testimony if needed. A complete CV, including experience, publications and presentations, is available. **Degrees/licenses:** MD University of Illinois, Board Certified, Lic. Florida.

David A. Lombardi, MD

1467 North Wanda Rd., #165
Orange, CA 92867
Tel: (714) 289-1240
Fax: (714) 289-1276
E-mail: dlombardi001@earthlink.net

Specialties: Board Certified Neurologist; Workers' Compensation experience since 1978; Qualified Medical Evaluator; Independent Medical Evaluator; Agreed Medical Evaluator; Defense Medical Evaluator; Court Expert Witness Testimony; Deposition Expert Witness Testimony; Director, Neurodiagnostic Lab and Neurovascular Unit; Chairman, Bioethics Committee and Director Stroke Response Team at Western Medical Center, Santa Ana, California. Northeastern University, BA, Biology; Boston University School of Medicine, MD; American Academy of Neurology, Orange County Medical Association, California Medical Association, National Stroke Association. **Degrees/licenses:** MD, QME, IME, AME, DME.

Diana L. Ross, MD

Pediatric and Adult Neurology
8499 Deer Path
West Chester, OH 45069
Tel: (513) 942-6938
Fax: (513) 777-0431
E-mail: DRoss45698@aol.com

Specialties: Board certified American Board of Psychiatry and Neurology, with special competence in child neurology. Board certified American Board of Pediatrics. 30 years' practice of pediatric and neurology in academic and private practice, with emphasis on headache, epilepsy and learning disability. 20 years' experience in medico-legal review from newborn to adult patients. Have reviewed both plaintiff and defense cases, including "bad baby," vaccine injury, vehicular injury, missed infection and brain tumor and genetic disorders, and brachial plexus injury. **Degrees/licenses:** MD, Licensed Ohio.

See primary listing under MEDICINE & HEALTH: Pediatric Neurology

Jonathan S. Rutchik, MD, MPH

Neurology
Occupational & Environmental Medicine
20 Sunnyside Ave., Ste. A-321
Mill Valley, CA 94941
Tel: (415) 381-3133
Fax: (415) 381-3131
E-mail: contactus@neoma.com
Web Site: http://www.neoma.com

Specialties: Neurology, Occupational/Environmental Medicine, Neurotoxicology, organic solvents, heavy metals, pesticides, neuropathy, brain trauma, disability, risk assessment, neuroepidemiology, product liability, utilization review, upper/lower extremity, head, neck, back injury, plaintiff, defense. **Degrees/licenses:** MD, MPH, CA QME; Licensed in CA, NY, MA, NJ.

Robert J. Shorr, MD

RJS Medical
18455 Burbank Blvd. #105
Tarzana, CA 91356
Tel: (818) 776-9555
Fax: (818) 776-8883
E-mail: Robert.Shorr@att.com

Specialties: Certified (Neurology), American Board of Psychiatry and Neurology: highly experienced in electrodiagnostic testing. Workers Compensation and Personal Injury specialist; California State Qualified Medical Examiner; more than twenty years experience as an Independent Medical Examiner, Defense Medical Evaluator; Court Expert Witness testimony; Plaintiff and Defense, BA, University of California, Berkeley, M.D., University of California, Academy of Neurology, Association of California

(Listing continued on next page)

Neurology *(cont.)*

Robert J. Shorr, MD (cont.)
Neurologist, American Medical Association, California Medical Association, Los Angeles County Medical Association, California Society of Industrial Medicine and Surgery. Locations: Tarzana (San Fernando Valley) and Lancaster (Antelope Valley), California. Several other locations available in Ventura and Santa Barbara counties. **Degrees/licenses:** MD; QME; IME; AME; DME.

Arthur Taub, MD, PhD, PC

Arthur Taub, MD, PhD
1 Bradley Road
Woodbridge, CT 06525
Tel: (203) 389-6046
Fax: (203) 389-6053
E-mail: atmd@ix.netcom.com

Specialties: Data analysis, examination of major abnormalities of the central, peripheral, and autonomic nervous systems, caused by aging, mechanical (e.g., automobile, railroad, aircraft, nautical, gunshot) or toxic e.g., hydrocarbons) trauma (personal injury), or medical malpractice (standard of care, cause in fact, and damages: physical, pain and suffering, cognitive/behavioral). More than two decades of close experience with the civil bar, and more recently, with the Public Defender (capital crimes). Full time Neurologic practice of complex matters of pain, cognition, and behavior. Clinical Full Professor (1975-2000), Yale University School of Medicine. **Degrees/licenses:** MD cum laude, Yale; PhD Neurophysiology, MIT.

Neuropsychology

Lawson F. Bernstein, MD

MD - Forensic Neuropsychiatry
P. O. Box 81977
Pittsburgh, PA 15217
Tel: (412) 600-7996
Fax: (412) 422-5203
E-mail: lawsonbernstein@hotmail.com
Web Site: http://www.ifbmdpc.com

Specialties: Board certified academically published forensic neuropsychiatrist. Expertise in brain injury, stroke, neurotoxicology, acute/chronic pain, dementia, alcohol & substance abuse, gambling addiction and multiple other areas of neurology/psychiatry. Extensive criminal/civil trial (50/50) Plaintiff/Defense experience, including death penalty cases/legal insanity/diminished capacity. From 1991-1994, Dr. Bernstein was Director of the Psychiatry Residency Training Program at the University of Pittsburgh Medical Center, one of the largest academic psychiatric training programs in the U.S. Dr. Bernstein is also a Board Examiner for the American Board of Psychiatry & Neurology Oral Examination. **Degrees/licenses:** Medical.

See primary listing under MEDICINE & HEALTH: Head Injury

Pro/Consul Technical and Medical Experts

1945 Palo Verde Ave., Suite 200
Long Beach, CA 90815-3443
Tel: (800) 392-1119
(562) 799-0116
Fax: (562) 799-8821
E-mail: eexperts@msn.com
Web Site: http://www.expertinfo.com

Specialties: RIGHT EXPERT RIGHT AWAY!® 15,000 experts in 7,000 fields. Listed and recommended by the A. M. Best Company. Full-time research staff. We welcome your RUSH cases! TECHNICAL: Fast inspections. Categories from Accident Reconstruction to Zoology, also including appraisal, economics, employment, human factors, insurance, premises liability, security, and many more. MEDICAL: IME's. Inexpensive insurance medical records reviews by MDs. Categories from Addiction Medicine to Zooplasty, including board certified physicians in all fields, dentistry, geriatrics, neuropsychology, neurosurgery, nursing, orthopedics, psychiatry and many more. Reasonable fees. Free initial consultation. Free resume binder. Free CLE classes. **Degrees/licenses:** MD, PhD, DDS, DVM, DO, DPM, PE, CPA, ME, CE, CRC, MAI, et al.

See primary listing under ACCIDENT RECONSTRUCTION: General

Ronald H. Roberts, PhD, ABPP

2000 Van Ness Ave., Ste. 512
San Francisco, CA 94109-3017
Tel: (415) 776-2000
Fax: (415) 776-2001

Specialties: Personal injury; Neuropsychology; Head injuries; Chronic pain; Toxic exposure; Mold exposure; Criminal Responsibility; Work stress; Discrimination; Post-traumatic stress; Disability injuries; Diplomate, American Board of Med. Psychotherapists; Diplomate, American Board of Disability Evaluators; Diplomate in Forensic Psychology, American Board of Professional Psychology; Diplomate, American Board of Vocational Neuropsychology. **Degrees/licenses:** PhD, PSY8334 CA.

See primary listing under MEDICINE & HEALTH: Psychology

Neurosurgery

Jordan K. Davis, MD

Spine Care Institute
1905 Clint Moore Rd., Ste. 309
Boca Raton, FL 33496
Tel: (561) 988-8577
Fax: (561) 912-9710
E-mail: spinelink@aol.com
Web Site: http://www.spinelink.com

Specialties: All aspects of complex Spine Reviews, Medical Malpractice, IME. Board Certified, Defense and Plaintiff, Articulate. **Degrees/licenses:** MD.

Martin C. Johnson, MD, FACS, FAAP, FACME

CEO/President
Pacific Northwest Neurosurgical Association
31870 SW Country View Lane
Wilsonville, OR 97070-7476
Tel: (503) 694-5900
Fax: (503) 694-5649
E-mail: martinc33@hotmail.com

Specialties: Neurosurgery, Pediatric Neurosurgery, Neurotrauma, Child Abuse, Pediatric Neurology, Neurology, Neurological Critical Care, Reconstructive Neurosurgery, Workers' Compensation (neurosurgical/spinal orthopedic, IME), Disability Evaluation (neurosurgical - spinal orthopedic), Col. AUSA (ret.). Board Certified: American Board Neurosurgery, American Board Pediatric Neurosurgery, American Board of Forensic Examiners. **Degrees/licenses:** ABB, MD, FACS, FAAP, FACFM.

Edward S. Kaplan, MD, FACS

424 Sweetbriar Road
Memphis, TN 38120-2503
Tel: (901) 767-6442
Fax: (901) 685-7809
E-mail: elkaplan@aol.com

Specialties: Neurosurgery, Board Certified, 1966; Yale University, BA, 1955, Phi Beta Kappa; Columbia University, MD, 1959; University of Minnesota, MS (Neurosurgery), 1964; Internship, Columbia-Presbyterian Hospital, 1960; Neurosurgical Residency, Mayo Clinic, 1960-64; University of Tennessee, Instructor, Neurology, 1964-1973, Clinical Assistant Professor, Neurosurgery, 1973-2001; Baptist Hospital, Memphis, TN, Active Staff, 1964-2000. Congress Neurological Surgeons; American Association Neurological Surgeons; Fellow American College Surgeons; AMA; TMA; Memphis Medical Society; Memphis Surgical Society. **Degrees/licenses:** BA, MD, MS, FACS, ABNS Cert., Med. Lic. in TN.

Neurosurgery *(cont.)*

Isabelle L. Richmond, MD, PhD

Neurosurgical Consultant
912 Cedar Meadow Drive
Nellysford, VA 22958
Tel: (434) 361-9392
Fax: (434) 361-1419
E-mail: irneuro@hotmail.com

Specialties: Personal Injury, Workers' Compensation, Medical Malpractice, Medical Billing Issues, Federal/Military case review. Strong academic/basic neuroscience background. 20 years+ clinical experience medical records review: causation, standard of care, peer review, credentialling. Timely, accurate, articulate reports/depositions facilitate resolution of medical issues. Certified mediator comfortable with alternative dispute resolution methods. MD Duke 1974; PhD neurobiology Cornell 1968; Residency UCSF 1979; ABNS Certified 1982; ATLS Instructor, Level I Trauma Center. Prof. Clinical Surgery USUHS (Col. USAR). Chairman Medical Costs Peer Review, Workers' Compensation Commission of Virginia, 1993-1999. **Degrees/licenses:** MD, PhD, FACS, ABNS Cert.; Med. Lic. in VA.

See primary listing under MEDICAL-LEGAL: Medical Record Review

Aldo M. Rosemblat, MD, PC

6316 Castle Place, Ste. 200
Falls Church, VA 22044
Tel: (703) 241-8989
Fax: (703) 532-6247

Specialties: Diplomate American Board of Neurological Surgery, American Academy of Pain Management, American Board of Forensic Examiners; Clinical Instructor Georgetown University Hospital; Expert Witness Testimony in Maryland, Virginia & the District of Columbia; Surgery of the brain, spine, spinal cord and peripheral nerves; Disability Evaluations for: Workers' Compensation, Personal Injury and Social Security pertaining to the neurological system and to the joint and muscular skeletal systems. **Degrees/licenses:** MD, FA-ADEP.

Nursing

Laura Burchell-Henson, RN

Registered Nurse
Medi-Legal Consultants, Inc.
P.O. Box 1229
Lakeside, CA 92040
Tel: (619) 749-5476
(619) 933-5021
Fax: (619) 749-5185
E-mail: medi-legal@cox.net
Web Site: http://www.medi-legal.org

Specialties: Registered Nurse & Respiratory Therapist who has been retained in more than 200 medical related cases since April 1999 to include criminal, personal injury, medical malpractice & products liability cases. Has testified in trial/depo 40 times. Twenty years of clinical experience includes ICU, ER, homecare, long-term care, Med-surg, obstetrics, psychiatric, administration and surgery. Services offered include testimony, medical records review, comprehensive reports, standards of care, trial testimony, locating other experts, identify defendants, assess damages/injuries and causation. **Degrees/licenses:** RN, RCP, CCRN, CLNC, SANE.

See primary listing under MEDICAL-LEGAL: Nursing Malpractice

Kathleen M. Martin, RN, MSN, MPA, LNHA

368 White Oak Ridge Road
Short Hills, NJ 07078
Tel: (973) 912-9154
Fax: (973) 912-9702
E-mail: martgatt@yahoo.com
Web Site:
http://www.jurispro.com/KathleenMartin

Specialties: Long Term Care nursing; general nursing; geriatrics; assisted living; Nursing standards & documentation; JCAHO, ANA, and State Dept. of Health standards; wound care issues; falls; physical & chemical restraint; clinical & managerial experience; Cert. In Life Care Planning; expert testimony, deposition and trial experience over 16 years. Affiliation: Plaza Regency at Park Ridge, NJ.

Administrator/Corporate Executive. Licensed LTC Administrator-NJ-5yrs. RN 27 years. **Degrees/licenses:** RN; MSN; MPA (Master in Public (Health Care) Admin).

MED-LINK Consultation

Dorothy A. Pollock, RN
3362 Budleigh Drive
Hacienda Heights, CA 91745-6409
Tel: (626) 333-5110
Fax: (626) 968-0064
E-mail: dorothypollock@adelphia.net

Specialties: RN with 36 years experience, 31 years in surgery with emphasis on: trauma, orthopedics, neurology, cardiovascular, ophthalmology, ENT, Gynecology, Laparoscopy, Endoscopy, Urology, Plastics, Laser and Pain Management. Member of Association of peri-Operative Registered Nurses (AORN); American Association of Legal Nurse Consultants (AALNC); Secretary/Treasurer 2004-05. Past President of AALNC-LA. Services offered: Nursing SOC; IME/DME Accompaniment; Chronologies. Expert Witness for both Plaintiff & Defense. Federal, Civil and Criminal Courtroom experienced. **Degrees/licenses:** RN, BS Health Care Admin., CNOR, LNCC, ACLS, PALS.

James M. Miller, PE, PhD

President
Miller Engineering Associates, Inc.
2392 Fuller Court
Ann Arbor, MI 48105
Tel: (734) 662-6822
Fax: (734) 747-9712
E-mail: jmiller@millerengineering.com
Web Site: www.millerengineering.com

Specialties: Nursing Malpractice; Nursing Management; Mechanical Design Safety: Power Tools & Machine Guarding; OSHA/ANSI/ASTM Compliance; Warnings, Labels, Instructions & User Manuals: Health Hazard Warnings; Design of User Manuals & Warnings; Consumer Product Safety: Human Factors & Ergonomics, Slips, Falls-Premise, Vehicle, Ladder; Child, Home Appliances, Furniture; Vehicles: Auto, Truck, ATV, Boat, Jet Ski, Snowmobile; Seat Belts & Air Bags; Chemical, Fire, Environmental & Waste Disposal: Fires & Explosions-Vapors/Electrical/Chemical; Chemical Labeling Requirements; MSDS; Groundwater & Soil Contamination; Agricultural & Construction Safety: Tractor, Implement, Harvester & Grain Storage; Pesticides, Herbicides, Fungicides. **Degrees/licenses:** James Miller, PE, PhD; Bradley Cook, PE; Rebecca Lehto, PhD, RN, OCN.

See primary listing under ACCIDENT PREVENTION & SAFETY: General

Obstetrics & Gynecology

Ezell S. Autrey, MD, FACOG

Physician - Obstetrics, Gynecology and Infertility
7777 Forest Lane, Suite C-512
Dallas, TX 75230
Tel: (972) 566-6400
Fax: (972) 566-6769

Specialties: Obstetrics and gynecology - High risk obstetrics. All gynecological laparoscopic procedures including hysterectomies, forceps and vacuum extracting of fetus. Vaginal birth after caesarean section, shoulder dystocia, Erb's palsy, Infertility, Birth related injuries, Case merit review, Fetal heart rate tracings, Informed consent ureteral injury, failed tubal ligation, menopause management, Postpartum depression. **Degrees/licenses:** MD, Texas State License, Board Certified.

Don C. Creevy, MD, FACOG

Obstetrician & Gynecologist
4370 Alpine Road
Portola Valley, CA 94028
Tel: (650) 851-3146
(650) 529-1300 (Home fax)
Fax: (650) 851-9747 (Office)

Specialties: Routine & High Risk Pregnancy Care (including multiple births); Primary Care & Gynecology; Gynecological Surgery; Midwifery Practices. Board Certified in Obstetrics & Gynecology. Stanford University School of Medicine, Adjunct Clinical Assistant Professor. Twenty-five years experience as Expert Witness for both defense and plaintiff. Experienced with Case Review, Deposition & Trial.

(Listing continued on next page)

Obstetrics & Gynecology
(cont.)

Don C. Creevy, MD (cont.)
Doctor of Medicine; Fellow, American College of Obstetricians & Gynecologists; California & Minnesota medical license. **Degrees/ licenses:** MD, FACOG; Lic. in CA & MN.

Dave E. David, MD
Obstetrician/Gynecologist
Tel: (781) 764-4747
Fax: (603) 215-4960
E-mail: doctor@drdavedavid.com

Specialties: Obstetrics, gynecology, childbirth, gynecologic surgery, women's health, pregnancy. Diplomate of the American Board of Obstetrics and Gynecology; Diplomate of the National Board of Medical Examiners; Medical-Legal consulting and expert witness work for twenty-one years nationwide. Created the nationally released, full-length videotape on pregnancy, "Making Womb for Baby." Appearances on national television and radio speaking on medical issues. **Degrees/licenses:** MD, licensed in Massachusetts.

Anthony R. DeSalvo, MD
1842 East Market St.
Warren, OH 44483
Tel: (330) 856-7212
Fax: (330) 856-6101
E-mail: Tony@DrDeSalvo.com
Web Site: http://www.DrDeSalvo.com

Specialties: Board Certified in Obstetrics and Gynecology, in full-time private practice, and a public speaker. Provides medical record and report review, medical literature search, peer review, second opinion, and expert witness testimony for attorneys in Medical Malpractice and Personal Injury, both plaintiff and defense. Issues addressed are general obstetrical and gynecological cases, high-risk obstetrics, cesarean section, prenatal care, miscarriage, traumatic birth injury, perinatal medicine, antenatal care, abortion problems, sterilization, contraception, menstrual disorders, menopause HRT, gynecological surgery, laser surgery, endometriosis, hysterectomy, hysteroscopy, bladder repair, and incontinence. **Degrees/licenses:** MD, FACOG, Board Certified Ob/Gyn.

William W. Filler, Jr., MD, FACOG
President & Medical Director
Medstuff
42525 Chaparral Dr.
Temecula, CA 92592-8955
Tel: (909) 303-1429
Fax: (909) 303-9357
E-mail: bfiller@medstuff.com
Web Site: http://www.medstuff.com

Specialties: William W. Filler, MD, FACOG is a Board Certified professor in active practice in obstetrics and gynecology. He has been a doctor for 45 years and has held academic rank in New York and Missouri, in addition to this current activity in Southern California. He has served as an expert witness in OB/Gyn for over 15 years in most states of the U.S. and Canada. He has represented both plaintiff and defense. References are available. For CV please see MedStuff Web site at www.medstuff.com or call telephone number above.

Douglas E. Heritage, MD, FACOG
2026A Opitz Blvd.
Woodbridge, VA 22191
Tel: (703) 491-7155
Fax: (703) 690-3958
E-mail: obgynexp@aol.com
Web Site: http://drheritage.com

Specialties: Private practice of Obstetrics & Gynecology since 1978; Special qualifications in GYN laser surgery, laparoscopic surgery, pelvic microsurgery and hysteroscopic surgery. Extensive experience in fetal monitoring, treatment of endometriosis, abnormal PAP smears. Twenty years experience malpractice case review, testimony for plaintiff and defendant. Board certified American Board OB-GYN 1980, voluntary recertified 1999, 2001, 2003, and 2005. Fellow, American College of Obstetricians & Gynecologists. Member American Society of Reproductive Medicine. Past Chairman Department OB-GYN Potomac Hospital. Recipient multiple continuing education awards from AMA, ACOG, Medical Society of Virginia. **Degrees/ licenses:** BS, MD.

Laurence A. Jacobs, MD, FACOG

Reproductive Endocrinologist/Infertility
Jacobs Medical LLC
3149 Dundee Rd., #271
Northbrook, IL 60062
Tel: (847) 215-8899
(847) 372-4364 (Cellular)
(847) 817-5869 (Pager)
Fax: (847) 215- 8996
E-mail: jacobsmd66@aol.com
Web Site: www.laurencejacobsmd.com

Specialties: Complications from laparoscopic surgery, infertility, in vitro fertilization (IVF), miscarriages, ectopic pregnancies, multiple pregnancies, fertility drugs, birth defects, pelvic infections, hormone therapy, endometriosis, gynecologic surgery. Recently recognized in the national guide book "America's Top Doctors" published by Castle Connolly (top 1/2% of specialists nationwide). Identified by peer nomination as one of the country's leading medical specialists in infertility/reproductive endocrinology. Prestigious Mayo Clinic Infertility Fellowship, 1986-1988; Northwestern University Medical School and OB/GYN residency, 1971-1979. Dedicated, experienced expert witness serving defense/plaintiff. **Degrees/licenses:** MD, BA Northwestern; Board Cert. OB/GYN, 1981, FACOG.

Julius S. Piver, MD, JD

6602 Melody Lane
Bethesda, MD 20817
Tel: (301) 365-4020
(240) 381-3600
Fax: (301) 469-5469
E-mail: jpmdjd@comcast.net
Web Site: http://www.obgyn-dr.com

Specialties: Practicing gynecologist, Board Certified Obstetrics & Gynecology, with 19 years expert witness/consultant experience in OB/GYN negligence cases, Plaintiff/Defense. 4000+ deliveries, 1000+ hysterectomies, 1500+ laparoscopies. Oversaw 30,000 deliveries as Clinical Chairman of Obstetrics for 5 years at major DC hospital. Consulting on Quality of Care & Standard of Care Issues such as breast cancer, shoulder dystocia, informed consent, laparoscopy complications, tubal ligation issues, cesarean section, hysterectomy, fetal monitoring, appendicitis, placental abruption, ectopic pregnancy, ureteral/bladder injury, sexual assault, neuropathies. **Degrees/ licenses:** MD, JD, BdCert Ob/Gyn, FACOG, FACS, FAAGL, FACLM.

David M. Priver, MD

Obstetrician & Gynecologist
OB/GYN Expert Witness Services
4282 Genesee Ave., Ste. 201
San Diego, CA 92117
Tel: (858) 268-7324
Fax: (858) 268-3894
E-mail: dpriver@aol.com
Web Site: www.OBGynExpertWitness.com

Specialties: Pregnancy Care; Complications of Pregnancy; Abortion; Complications of Abortion; Gynecology; Pelvic Surgery; Laparoscopy; Ultrasound; Hormone Therapy. IAST President, San Diego County Medical Society, 1996-1997. 30 years in private practice of OB/Gyn. **Degrees/licenses:** BA, MD, FACOG.

Jeffrey R. Richardson, MD, FACOG

3555 Loma Vista Rd., Ste. 115
Ventura, CA 93003
Tel: (805) 648-4425
Fax: (805) 648-4426
E-mail: jrr6004@cs.com
Web Site: http://member.expertpages.com/obgynxpertwitnes

Specialties: Twenty plus years experience in private practice of OB/Gyn, Primary Care, Infertility, Gyn Surgery, Gyn Cancers, High Risk Obstetrics, Office Practice, Cancer Screening, Teaching of Residents. **Degrees/licenses:** MD, FACOG, Board Certified OB/Gyn.

Obstetrics & Gynecology
(cont.)

C. Paul Sinkhorn, MD, FACOG
2642 Marley Drive
Riverside, CA 92506
Tel: (909) 241-2745
Fax: (951) 779-9189
E-mail: cpaulsinkhorn@earthlink.net
Web Site: http://www.expertdoc.net

Specialties: Board Cert Obstetrics/Gynecology; Clinical Assoc. Prof, OB/GYN, Univ. of Calif.-Riverside; Teaching Faculty Arrowhead Regional Medical Center (San Bernardino County); High-risk obstetrics; expert in laparoscopy, laser, cesarean, sterilization, contraception, infertility, hysteroscopy, hysterectomy, bladder repair, incontinence; Deposition/Trial experience; Tobacco and smoking liability; past-President Professional Liability Committee for Riverside County Medical Association; Peer reviewer and Hospital Medical Staff Surveyor for California Medical Association; American Association of Gyn. Laparoscopists; ACOG; AOA Honorary; Am. Soc. Forensic OB/GYNs (past president); approx 60-40 plaintiff/defense. **Degrees/licenses:** MD, FACOG; licensed CA & AR.

Occup./Environ. Medicine

John D. Bogden, PhD
Professor
UMDNJ - New Jersey Medical School
Department of Preventive Medicine
& Community Health
185 South Orange Avenue
P.O. Box 1709
Newark, NJ 07101-1709
Tel: (973) 972-5432
Fax: (973) 972-7625
E-mail: bogden@umdnj.edu

Specialties: Toxicology & Nutrition Consultant; Specialty is Mineral and Trace Element Nutrition & Toxicology: lead poisoning, chromium toxicity, mercury poisoning, overdoses of minerals and trace elements, vitamin and mineral supplements, air, soil and water pollutants, environmental toxins, occupational medicine, analyses of body tissues and fluids; Expert reports, deposition and court testimony experience; More than 100 publications in leading medical, nutrition, and toxicology journals. **Degrees/licenses:** MS, PhD, FACN, CNS.

See primary listing under ENVIRONMENTAL: Toxicology

James L. Pearle, MD
President
Western Pulmonary Medical Group, Inc.
220 Laguna Road, Ste. 2
Fullerton, CA 92835-2523
Tel: (714) 446-7454
Fax: (714) 879-1049
E-mail: jpearlemd@hotmail.com

Specialties: Asbestosis and Occupational Lung Diseases with national experience and publications; Medical Malpractice, Sleep Disorders; Hospitalist, Pulmonary, Critical Care, and Internal Medicine. Hospital Medical Director, Hospital Chief of Staff, Director of Hospital Respiratory Therapy Department, President of Medical Group, Independent Medical Examiner, Principal Investigator for Clinical Trials, Experienced in Hyperbaric Medicine. Over one hundred depositions and trials. Board certified in Internal Medicine and Pulmonary Disease. Fellow, American College of Chest Physicians. Former Assistant Professor, UCLA School of Medicine and UC Irvine School of Medicine. **Degrees/licenses:** BA, MD.

See primary listing under MEDICINE & HEALTH: Pulmonary Medicine

Jonathan S. Rutchik, MD, MPH

Neurology
Occupational
& Environmental Medicine
20 Sunnyside Ave., Ste. A-321
Mill Valley, CA 94941
Tel: (415) 381-3133
Fax: (415) 381-3131
E-mail: contactus@neoma.com
Web Site: http://www.neoma.com

Specialties: Neurology, Occupational/Environmental Medicine, Neurotoxicology, organic solvents, heavy metals, pesticides, neuropathy, brain trauma, disability, risk assessment, neuroepidemiology, product liability, utilization review, upper/lower extremity, head, neck, back injury, plaintiff, defense. **Degrees/licenses:** MD, MPH, CA QME; Licensed in CA, NY, MA, NJ.

See primary listing under MEDICINE & HEALTH: Neurology

Alan M. Steinman, MD, MPH

Rear Admiral (Ret.), USCG/USPHS
1135 Harrington Place
DuPont, WA 98327
Tel: (253) 229-4088
Fax: (253) 964-3549
E-mail: asteinman@aol.com

Specialties: Drowning, hypothermia, sea survival, maritime medicine, water survival, protective clothing, cold water immersion, water rescue, safety investigation, life jackets, life rafts; past Surgeon General of the U.S. Coast Guard; developed cold water survival time charts for USCG; widely published in areas of sea survival and hypothermia; chapter on immersion hypothermia in leading textbook of emergency medicine; lectures in drowning, hypothermia and sea survival; Board Certified in Occupational Medicine; MD from Stanford University; post-graduate training at Mayo Clinic and University of Washington; experience as expert witness in both state and federal courts. **Degrees/licenses:** MD, MPH, FACPM.

Oculoplastic Surgery

Eugene O. Wiggs, MD

55 Madison St., Ste. 355
Denver, CO 80206-5429
Tel: (303) 377-8155
(303) 377-2020
Fax: (303) 377-2022
E-mail: ewiggs@omni.com

Specialties: Oculoplastic surgery is a synthesis of ophthalmology and plastic surgery. This discipline treats problems of the eyelids, lacrimal system and orbit. Oculoplastic surgeons also treat patients with thyroid eye disease, facial nerve palsy and socket problems in the one-eyed patient. BA - Johns Hopkins; MD - Duke; Internship - Denver General; Residency - Wilmer Institute, Johns Hopkins Hospital; Fellowship, Dr. Byron Smith/MEETH. Numerous publications & presentations; Honor Award recipient, American Academy of Ophthalmology; Clinical Professor of Ophthalmology Emeritus, University of Colorado; Former President, Colorado Ophthalmological Society. **Degrees/licenses:** BA - Johns Hopkins; MD - Duke.

Ophthalmology

Andrew A. Dahl, MD, FACS

President
Ophthalmic Consultants
1 Gus Siko Rd.
Poughkeepsie, NY 12601
Tel: (845) 471-7808
Fax: (845) 471-7640
E-mail: AndrewDahl@pol.net
Web Site: www.andrewdahl.yourmd.com

Specialties: Alpha Omega Alpha Medical Honor Society. Former Faculty, Harvard Medical School. Twenty five years practice of Ophthalmology and Ophthalmic Surgery. Twenty-five years experience in forensic eye cases including medical malpractice and product liability. Medical record review and expert witness services. Chairman, Medical Society Peer Review Committee; Chairman, Institutional Review Board. **Degrees/licenses:** BA, MD, FACS, FAAO.

Ophthalmology *(cont.)*

Robert G. Josephberg, MD

984 North Broadway, Ste. 511
Yonkers, NY 10701
Tel: (914) 965-2526
Fax: (914) 965-2527
E-mail: LisaRiRob@optonline.net
Web Site:
http://www.westchester-retina.eyemd.org

Specialties: Chief of Retina (WMC); Board Certified Ophthalmologist (1981); Fellowship trained retinal Surgeon, Baylor College of Medicine, Houston, TX (1981); Volunteer Surgeon (Project Orbis); Inventor, VISITREC Vitrectomy (Top Ten Award, American Academy of Ophthalmology); Assistant Clinical Professor, NY Medical College and NJ College of Medicine; Well published; Active in teaching; Has lectured extensively on retinal detachment, macular degeneration, diabetic retinopathy, endophthalmitis and complications of ophthalmic surgery; Member, American Academy of Ophthalmology, American Society of Retina Specialists, NY Ophthalmology and Medical Society, Florida Medical Association, NJ Ophthalmology Society, Westchester Medical Society, American Medical Association. **Degrees/licenses:** MD, BS, ABO; Med. Lic. in NY, NJ & FL.

Manhattan Ophthalmology Associates

Spencer E. Sherman, MD
President & Medical Director
166 East 63rd Street
New York, NY 10021
Tel: (212) 753-8300
Fax: (212) 752-4285
E-mail: sesmdpc@aol.com
Web Site: http://www.nyeyelaser.com

Specialties: AB Princeton University - cum laude, 1958; MD Columbia College of Surgeons, 1962; Specializing in: cataract, glaucoma, refractive surgery, contact lenses; Residency 1965-68, Mt. Sinai Hospital NY (Ophthalmology); Attending surgeon: Mt. Sinai, Lenox Hill, Manhattan Eye & Ear, NY Eye & Ear (all in NY). Honors: honor award & service award (AAO), Sigma Xi (Princeton), named Top Doctors in U.S., Best Doctor in NY; Who's Who in America. Fellow of: American & International College of Surgeons; American Academy of Ophthalmology; International Society of Refractive Surgeons; New York Society of Ophthalmology, AMA. **Degrees/licenses:** MD, Lic. in NY, FL, CA & NJ.

Eugene O. Wiggs, MD

55 Madison St., Ste. 355
Denver, CO 80206-5429
Tel: (303) 377-8155
(303) 377-2020
Fax: (303) 377-2022
E-mail: ewiggs@omni.com

Specialties: Oculoplastic surgery is a synthesis of ophthalmology and plastic surgery. This discipline treats problems of the eyelids, lacrimal system and orbit. Oculoplastic surgeons also treat patients with thyroid eye disease, facial nerve palsy and socket problems in the one-eyed patient. BA - Johns Hopkins; MD - Duke; Internship - Denver General; Residency - Wilmer Institute, Johns Hopkins Hospital; Fellowship, Dr. Byron Smith/MEETH. Numerous publications & presentations; Honor Award recipient, American Academy of Ophthalmology; Clinical Professor of Ophthalmology Emeritus, University of Colorado; Former President, Colorado Ophthalmological Society. **Degrees/licenses:** BA - Johns Hopkins; MD - Duke.

See primary listing under MEDICINE & HEALTH: Oculoplastic Surgery

Optometry

Darrell Carter

Clinical Professor, Emeritus
University of California - Berkeley
P.O. Box 1025
Glen Ellen, CA 95442
Tel: (707) 935-8908
Fax: (707) 938-9372
E-mail: dbcarter@uclink.berkeley.edu

Specialties: Optometry; Optometric standard of care; Examination and prescription procedures - tonometry, ophthalmoscopy, visual fields, etc.; Detection and management of ocular diseases; Contact lens procedures; Ocular pharmacology; Vision loss and economic effects; Visibility in auto and other accidents. **Degrees/licenses:** AB-UCLA, OD-SCCO, MS & PhD - UC; Optometry Licenses CA & NV.

Orthopedic Surgery

Bryant A. Bloss, MD

4770 Covert Ave., Ste. 104
Evansville, IN 47714
Tel: (812) 479-8571
(800) 880-8571
Fax: (812) 474-6237
E-mail: babortho@evansville.net

Specialties: Orthopaedic Surgery, Carpal Tunnel, Sports Medicine, Bone & Joint reconstructive Surgery, Hand Surgery. Licensed in Indiana, Kentucky, Illinois, and Louisiana. Licensed: Fellow, American Academy of Orthopaedic Surgery. Certified: American Board of Independent Medical Examiners. **Degrees/licenses:** MD. Orthopaedic Surgeon/American Board of Independent Medical Examiners.

Stanley D. Gertzbein, MD

6560 Fannin, #1900
Houston, TX 77030
Tel: (713) 986-5714
Fax: (713) 986-5711
E-mail: bkdoctor@aol.com
Web Site: http://www.thespineinstitute.ws

Specialties: Spinal Surgery: internationally recognized orthopedic surgeon with 30 years experience, with the last 20 years devoted to the treatment of complex spinal trauma cases resulting from automobile and other accidents, as well as complex degenerative disorders of the spine and spinal tumors. Clinical Professor of Orthopedic Surgery, Baylor College of Medicine. **Degrees/licenses:** MD.

Leonard Kalfuss, MD

Bone & Joint Medical Clinic
225 S. Civic Dr., Ste. 1
Palm Springs, CA 92262
Tel: (760) 327-8595
Fax: (760) 327-8597
E-mail: DrLKalfuss@dc.rr.com

Specialties: Forensic Orthopedics - 35 years. AME, IME, QME. Testimony experience: trial, deposition, complex cases for plaintiff/defense, P.I.-medical record review malpractice. Available throughout California. Prompt response and reports. **Degrees/licenses:** BSc, MD, FICS; Board Certified Orthopedic Surgery, Forensic Medicine.

Alan J. Zimmerman, MD

17 Eden Road
Lido Beach, NY 11561
Tel: (516) 431-5559
Fax: (309) 422-7208
E-mail: J40sailor@aol.com

Specialties: Orthopedic Surgery; Extensive Experience Expert Witness Testimony, Records Review; Personal Injury, Medical Malpractice, Plaintiff/Defense. Chief of Orthopedic Surgery, Long Beach Medical Center; Assist. Professor Clinical Orthopedic Surgery, State University of New York at Stony Brook, Adjunct Clinical Assistant Professor of Surgery, New York College of Osteopathic Medicine; Listed in "Best Doctors, NY Metro Area;" Board Certified American Board of Orthopedic Surgery; Fellow, American Academy of Orthopedic Surgeons. **Degrees/licenses:** BS Cum Laude; MD.

Orthopedics

John H. Devor, MD

970 Dewing Ave., Ste. 200
Lafayette, CA 94549
Tel: (925) 284-5100
Fax: (925) 284-5551
E-mail: jdevormd@yahoo.com

Specialties: General orthopedics; Occupational and forensic orthopedics; Neck and

(Listing continued on next page)

Orthopedics *(cont.)*

John H. Devor, MD (cont.)
lower back problems; Medical-legal evaluations; Medical record review/analysis; Review of myelograms, MRIs and CT scans; Second opinions/case management; Expert witness testimony. **Degrees/licenses:** MD CA Lic. #A31476; Certified Independent Medical Examiner (ABIME #96-00423).

Richard S. Goodman, MD, JD, FAAOS, ACLM

Physician & Attorney
Richard S. Goodman, MD, JD
285 East Main Street
Smithtown, NY 11787
Tel: (631) 724-2727
Fax: (631) 724-2729
E-mail: rsgmdesq@ipninet.com

Second Office
70 Glen Cove Rd., Ste. LL1
Roslyn Heights, NY 11577

Third Office
743 Columbia Turnpike
East Greenbush, NY 12061

Specialties: Orthopedics, Sport Injuries, Pediatric Orthopedics, Review of Medical Records, Standards of Care - Motor Vehicle Accidents, Personal Injuries. Consultant, Social Security Administration & New York State Retirement Board. MD, JD, License in NY & CA. Admitted NYS bar. Consultant, Long Island Jewish Medical Center & North Shore University Medical Center. Certified - American Board of Orthopaedic Surgery; Fellow - American Academy of Orthopaedic Surgery; Fellow - American College of Legal Medicine; Certified - New York State Workers' Compensation Board. **Degrees/licenses:** MD, JD, Med. Lic. NY & CA; Cert. NYS Work. Comp. Board; Admitted NY Bar.

Wilson C. "Toby" Hayes, PhD

President
Hayes + Associates, Inc.
301 SW 4th St., Suite 160
Corvallis, OR 97333
Tel: (541) 754-9645
(541) 912-7222
Fax: (541) 754-9949
E-mail: wch@hayesassoc.com
Web Site: http://www.hayesassoc.com

Specialties: Expertise: injury biomechanics, accident reconstruction and failure analysis; personal injury, products liability, wrongful death, premises liability, medical malpractice; motor vehicle accidents; slips, trips, falls; sports injuries, recreation and safety equipment, industrial injuries, ergonomics and repetitive stress syndromes. Background: (1979-98) Director, Orthopedic Biomechanics Laboratory, Mueller Professor Biomechanics, Harvard Medical School/MIT; (1998-present) Professor Exercise and Sports Science/Mechanical Engineering, Oregon State University; Orthopedics & Rehabilitation, Oregon Health Sciences University. Awards: (1995) American Society Biomechanics Borelli; (1996) Bristol-Myers Squibb/Zimmer Research. Excellence Orthopedic Treatment. **Degrees/licenses:** BS, MS (Stanford '64, '66); PhD (Northwestern '70).

See primary listing under ACCIDENT RECONSTRUCTION: Biomechanics

Alvin Stein, MD, FACS

President
Stein Orthopedic Assoc., PA
4101 NW 4th Street, Ste. 401
Plantation, FL 33317
Tel: (954) 581-8585
Fax: (954) 581-5580
E-mail: nobones@aol.com
Web Site: http://www.proloshot.com

Specialties: A board certified orthopedic surgeon and pain management specialist with extensive experience in chart review for standard of care issues, utilization issues, and worker compensation claims. ABQAURP certified. Available for IMEs or chart reviews, plaintiff or defense, for an honest evaluation. Over 35 years of experience in practice of medicine. Rapid response and thorough analysis of the issues in any case. Available to testify if needed. References available. **Degrees/licenses:** MD, FACS.

See primary listing under MEDICAL-LEGAL: Medical Record Review

Otolaryngology

Douglas G. Finn, MD, FACS

Otolaryngology
253 - 78th Street
Brooklyn, NY 11209
Tel: (718) 439-6687
Fax: (718) 439-6713
E-mail: douglasgfinn@aol.com
Web Site: http://www.douglasgfinn.com

Specialties: Otolaryngology - Head and Neck Surgery, Forensic Otolaryngology, Oncology Review, Sinus Disorders, Trauma and Accident Evaluation, Personal Injury, Workers' Compensation, Occupational and Post-Traumatic Hearing Loss and Disability Evaluation, Medical Record Review. President, Kings County Medical Society - Otolaryngology Section; American College of Surgeons; American Head and Neck Society; Triological Society; Clinical Associate Professor, New York Medical College. **Degrees/licenses:** BA, MD

Michael H. Fritsch, MD, FACS

Spec. Defense
Indiana University Medical Center
702 Barnhill Drive, Ste. 0860
Indianapolis, IN 46202
Tel: (317) 274-8571
Fax: (317) 274-0764

Specialties: Otolaryngology - Head & Neck Surgery, Otology, Neurotology, Skull Base Surgery, Audiology, Sinus Surgery. Books written in fields of Otology and Sinus Surgery. Continuing contributions to world scientific literature. Board Certified in Otolaryngology - Head & Neck Surgery. **Degrees/licenses:** BMed., MD; Specialty Certified, three Post-Specialty Fellowships.

Sacramento Ear, Nose & Throat Surgical & Medical Group, Inc.

Jeffrey W. Dudley
CFO/Medical Group Administrator
3810 J Street
Sacramento, CA 95816
Tel: (916) 736-3399
Fax: (916) 736-9837
E-mail: jdudley@sacent.com
Web Site: http://www.sacent.com

Specialties: Twelve Board Certified, full-time practicing Otolaryngologists; Otology; Neurotology; Hearing Loss; Tinnitus; Audiology; Head and Neck Cancer; Endoscopic Sinus Surgery; Facial Plastic Surgery; Allergy; Voice Disorders; Sleep Disorders; Swallowing Disorders; Vertigo; Smell and Taste Disorders. **Degrees/licenses:** All Board Certified MDs.

Pain Management

Zvi Herschman, MD

346 Wilson Street
West Hempstead, NY 11552
Tel: (516) 486-7384
Fax: (516) 486-2743
E-mail: hesh346@juno.com

Specialties: Pain Management, Critical Care, Accident Reconstruction, Toxicology, Criminalistics, Anesthesiology. Dr. Herschman is a practicing Anesthesiologist, Board Certified in Anesthesiology, Pain Management, Critical Care. Consultant in Toxicology for 15 years. PhD Candidate at John Jay College of Criminal Justice - Trace Evidence, Toxicology. Well published, experienced with expert testimony and accident reconstruction. **Degrees/licenses:** MD, DABA.

Pain Management *(cont.)*

Reed S. Oxman, MD, FACEP, DAAPM

Reed S. Oxman, MD, PC
226 W. Rittenhouse Sq., #911
Philadelphia, PA 19103-5743
Tel: (215) 546-8211
Fax: (888) 432-0237
E-mail: rsopa@aol.com
Web Site: http://member.expertpages.com/Reed-S.-Oxman,-M.D. or http://www.emergencymed-painmanagement.com

Specialties: Emergency Medicine Residency Trained, American Board of Emergency Medicine Board Certified, Fellow of the American College of Emergency Physicians (FACEP); Also Board Certified Diplomate of the American Academy of Pain Management (DAAPM). Roughly 50% defense and 50% plaintiff cases in the areas of ER Malpractice, Pain Management, Rape, Child Abuse, Elder Abuse, Personal Injury, Trauma, and Motor Vehicle Accidents. Licensed in 11 states. Roughly 85-90% of the cases that I have accepted beyond my initial evaluation have concluded with a favorable judgment. Published as first author in areas of medicine inside and outside my specialties. **Degrees/licenses:** BA, MD, FACEP, DAAPM; Lic. in PA, MD, NJ, OH, CT, GA, FL, MO, WI, IL, IN.

See primary listing under MEDICINE & HEALTH: Emergency Medicine

Edson O. Parker, MD

P. O. Box 29209
Las Vegas, NV 89126
Tel: (702) 499-9994
Fax: (702) 474-9420
E-mail: eoparker@aol.com
Web Site: http://www.eoparker.com

Specialties: Medical expert with over twenty years experience in all aspects of Pain Medicine, from medication management to very invasive therapies with injections, spinal cord stimulators, spinal infusion pumps and neurolytic procedures. MD from Vanderbilt University School of Medicine 1978. Board certified by the American Board of Anesthesiology in both Anesthesiology and Pain Medicine and Diplomate of the American Board of Pain Medicine. Clinical Professor of Surgery at the University of Nevada School of Medicine. Experienced in performing case reviews, IME's and depositions in a thoughtful and thorough manner, with insightful analysis and conclusions. Areas of expertise include pain management, pain medications, pain medicine and medical malpractice. CV available upon request. **Degrees/licenses:** MD, Board Cert. Anesthesiology & Pain Medicine.

Steven Richeimer, MD

Director
USC Pain Center
137 N. Larchment Blvd., #448
Los Angeles, CA 90004
Tel: (323) 692-3611
Fax: (323) 935-0791
E-mail: steven@richeimer.com
Web Site: http://www.painlegal.com

Specialties: Psychiatry, Anesthesiology, and Pain Management: (1) Is there reasonable support for the claim of chronic pain? (2) Has appropriate treatment of the pain problem been provided? (3) Where can expert pain treatment be provided? (4) Is significant disability expected? (5) Did prior pain treatment meet community standards of care? Dr. Richeimer is the Director of the University of Southern California Pain Center. Triple board certifications in Psychiatry, Anesthesiology, and Pain Management; Trained at the UCSF, UCLA, and Harvard Medical Schools; Former Director of the UC Davis Pain Management Center. **Degrees/licenses:** MD, License: CA.

Alvin Stein, MD, FACS

President
Stein Orthopedic Assoc., PA
4101 NW 4th Street, Ste. 401
Plantation, FL 33317
Tel: (954) 581-8585
Fax: (954) 581-5580
E-mail: nobones@aol.com
Web Site: http://www.proloshot.com

Specialties: A board certified orthopedic surgeon and pain management specialist with extensive experience in chart review for standard of care issues, utilization issues, and worker compensation claims. ABQAURP certified. Available for IMEs or chart reviews, plaintiff or defense, for an honest evaluation. Over 35 years of experience in practice of medicine. Rapid response and thorough analysis of the issues in any case. Available to testify if needed. References available. **Degrees/licenses:** MD, FACS.

See primary listing under MEDICAL-LEGAL: Medical Record Review

Pathology

Carlos M. Torres, MD
Director, Gastrointestinal
and Liver Pathology Division
Metroplex Pathology Associates
9050 Jasmine Lane
Irving, TX 75063
Tel: (214) 596-2233
Fax: (972) 929-9996
E-mail: ctorres@pathologypartners.com
Web Site: www.pathologypartners.com

Specialties: Board certified Anatomic Pathologist (Barnes Hospital/Washington University). Fellowship in Oncologic Surgical Pathology (M.D. Anderson Cancer Center). Fellowship in Gastrointestinal and Liver Pathology (Brigham and Women's Hospital/Harvard Medical School). **Degrees/licenses:** Medical Doctor, Anatomic Pathologist Boarded.

See primary listing under MEDICINE & HEALTH: Gastroenterology

Pediatric Emergency Medicine

Alan L. Nager, MD
Medical Expert
22287 Mulholland Hwy., Ste. 250
Calabasas, CA 91302
Tel: (818) 224-3938
E-mail: anagermd@msn.com

Specialties: Pediatric Emergency Medicine, encompassing all pediatric diseases and traumatic injuries as they present in the emergency department. Experience in clinical and administrative issues relating to Pediatric Emergency Medicine. Standards of care, causation, outcome, and prognosis. Provides record review, consultation, and testimony. Plaintiff or defense. HOSPITAL/ACADEMIC APPOINTMENTS: Assistant Professor of Clinical Pediatrics, Keck School of Medicine at University of Southern California; Attending Physician, Pediatric Emergency Department, Children's Hospital Los Angeles; Division Head, Division of Emergency and Transport Medicine, Children's Hospital Los Angeles. **Degrees/licenses:** MD, Bd Cert in Pediatrics & Pediatric Emerg Med; Fellow Amer Acad of Pediatrics.

See primary listing under MEDICINE & HEALTH: Pediatrics

Pediatric Neurology

Warren E. Cohen, MD, FAAP
302 Carvel Ave.
Cedarhurst, NY 11516
Tel: (516) 371-3691
Fax: (516) 371-1895
E-mail: weco@pop.net

Specialties: Birth injury, birth defects, birth asphyxia, cerebral palsy, mental retardation, genetic conditions, pediatric disorders, neurologic disorders; Extent of neurologic damage, long-term disability needs, expected lifespan; Causation of birth injuries and neurologic disability in childhood; genetic/congenital cause versus birth-related injury. Experienced witness, plaintiff/defendant. Board certified in Pediatrics, Pediatric Neurology, and Medical Genetics. Also certified in Neuro-rehabilitation. Experienced children's hospital medical director, United Cerebral Palsy medical director. Associate Clinical Professor, George Washington University School of Medicine. Training: Hosp. Albert Einstein College of Medicine, National Institutes of Health. **Degrees/licenses:** BS, MD, FAAP.

Pediatric Neurology *(cont.)*

Diana L. Ross, MD
Pediatric and Adult Neurology
8499 Deer Path
West Chester, OH 45069
Tel: (513) 942-6938
Fax: (513) 777-0431
E-mail: DRoss45698@aol.com

Specialties: Board certified American Board of Psychiatry and Neurology, with special competence in child neurology. Board certified American Board of Pediatrics. 30 years' practice of pediatric and neurology in academic and private practice, with emphasis on headache, epilepsy and learning disability. 20 years' experience in medico-legal review from newborn to adult patients. Have reviewed both plaintiff and defense cases, including "bad baby," vaccine injury, vehicular injury, missed infection and brain tumor and genetic disorders, and brachial plexus injury. **Degrees/ licenses:** MD, Licensed Ohio.

Ariel Sherbany, MD, PhD
Pediatric Neurologist
Pediatric Neurology
of Hudson Valley, PLLC
55 Old Nyack Turnpike, Ste. 101
Nanuet, NY 10954
Tel: (845) 627-0723
Fax: (845) 627-1009
E-mail: neuroman31@aol.com
Web Site: http://www.pedneuro.net

Specialties: Neonatal Neurology, Epilepsy, Child Neurology. Board Certifications: Pediatrics, Neurology, Neurophysiology. Academic affiliations: Columbia University, New York Medical College, Assistant Professor. Licensure: New York, New Jersey. Training: New York University, Washington University, Columbia University. Publications, lectures. **Degrees/licenses:** BS, MD, PhD.

Pediatrics

John Goldenring, MD, MPH
10496 Canyon Lake Drive
San Diego, CA 92131
Tel: (858) 635-5500
Fax: (858) 635-5600
E-mail: jgoldenr@san.rr.com

Specialties: Pediatrics, Adolescents and Young Adult Medicine to ages 0-27; Child Physical and Sexual Abuse, Pediatric Urgent and Emergency Care; Administrative Medicine - HMO, IPA and Hospital; Preventive Medicine; STDs; Pediatric Toxins; Cross-Cultural Medicine; International Health. **Degrees/licenses:** MD, MPH CA Lic. #G37744, TX Lic. #J0955.

Martin C. Johnson, MD, FACS, FAAP, FACME
CEO/President
Pacific Northwest
Neurosurgical Association
31870 SW Country View Lane
Wilsonville, OR 97070-7476
Tel: (503) 694-5900
Fax: (503) 694-5649
E-mail: martinc33@hotmail.com

Specialties: Neurosurgery, Pediatric Neurosurgery, Neurotrauma, Child Abuse, Pediatric Neurology, Neurology, Neurological Critical Care, Reconstructive Neurosurgery, Workers' Compensation (neurosurgical/spinal orthopedic, IME), Disability Evaluation (neurosurgical - spinal orthopedic), Col. AUSA (ret.). Board Certified: American Board Neurosurgery, American Board Pediatric Neurosurgery, American Board of Forensic Examiners. **Degrees/licenses:** ABB, MD, FACS, FAAP, FACFM.

See primary listing under MEDICINE & HEALTH: Neurosurgery

Alan L. Nager, MD

Medical Expert
22287 Mulholland Hwy., Ste. 250
Calabasas, CA 91302
Tel: (818) 224-3938
E-mail: anagermd@msn.com

Specialties: Pediatric Emergency Medicine, encompassing all pediatric diseases and traumatic injuries as they present in the emergency department. Experience in clinical and administrative issues relating to Pediatric Emergency Medicine. Standards of care, causation, outcome, and prognosis. Provides record review, consultation, and testimony. Plaintiff or defense. HOSPITAL/ACADEMIC APPOINTMENTS: Assistant Professor of Clinical Pediatrics, Keck School of Medicine at University of Southern California; Attending Physician, Pediatric Emergency Department, Children's Hospital Los Angeles; Division Head, Division of Emergency and Transport Medicine, Children's Hospital Los Angeles. **Degrees/licenses:** MD, Bd Cert in Pediatrics & Pediatric Emerg Med; Fellow Amer Acad of Pediatrics.

Pediatrics, Pulmonary, Critical Care

Eliezer Nussbaum, MD, FCCM, FCCP, FAAP

Director, Pediatric Pulmonology
Miller Children's Hospital at
Long Beach Memorial Medical Center
University of Calif., Irvine
2801 Atlantic Avenue
Long Beach, CA 90801-1428
Tel: (562) 933-8740
Fax: (562) 933-8744
E-mail: enussbaum@memorialcare.org
Web Site: http://member.expertpages.com/nussbaum

Specialties: Pediatrics; Pediatric Pulmonary; Pediatric Critical Care; Trauma and Emergency Medicine; Professor of Pediatrics at University of California, Irvine; Chief of Pediatric Pulmonary Medicine; Medical Director of Pediatric Pulmonary and Cystic Fibrosis Center at Miller Children's Hospital at Long Beach Memorial Medical Center; Certified by American Board of Pediatrics; Pediatric Pulmonology; Pediatric Critical Care Medicine. Experienced expert witness. Fluent English and Hebrew. **Degrees/licenses:** MD, FCCM, FCCP, FAAP.

Pharmacology

Lawson F. Bernstein, MD

MD - Forensic Neuropsychiatry
P. O. Box 81977
Pittsburgh, PA 15217
Tel: (412) 600-7996
Fax: (412) 422-5203
E-mail: lawsonbernstein@hotmail.com
Web Site: http://www.ifbmdpc.com

Specialties: Board certified academically published forensic neuropsychiatrist. Expertise in brain injury, stroke, neurotoxicology, acute/chronic pain, dementia, alcohol & substance abuse, gambling addiction and multiple other areas of neurology/psychiatry. Extensive criminal/civil trial (50/50) Plaintiff/Defense experience, including death penalty cases/legal insanity/diminished capacity. From 1991-1994, Dr. Bernstein was Director of the Psychiatry Residency Training Program at the University of Pittsburgh Medical Center, one of the largest academic psychiatric training programs in the U.S. Dr. Bernstein is also a Board Examiner for the American Board of Psychiatry & Neurology Oral Examination. **Degrees/licenses:** Medical.

See primary listing under MEDICINE & HEALTH: Head Injury

Esam Z. Dajani, PhD, FACG

President
IDDC Corporation
1549 RFD
Long Grove, IL 60047-9532
Tel: (847) 634-9586
E-mail: EsamD@aol.com
Web Site: http://www.edajani.com

Specialties: Clinical pharmacology, toxicology, drug development, regulatory affairs, pharmaceutical R & D and contract research

(Listing continued on next page)

Pharmacology *(cont.)*

Esam Z. Dajani (cont.)
organizations (CROs). Dr. Dajani has expertise in alcohol, drugs (prescription & OTC), driving under the influence, industrial chemicals, health & beauty products, product liability, labeling and medical malpractice. He provides research, analysis, merit statement, and testimony for plaintiff and defense. Dr. Dajani directed clinical research at major pharmaceutical companies and held academic appointments. He is currently serving as the president of a CRO group and Adjunct Professor of Medicine at Loyola University. He has 260 publications, presentations and patents. **Degrees/licenses:** BS, MS & PhD (Pharmacol. & Toxicol.). Licensed Pharmacist.

See primary listing under ALCOHOL/DRUGS: General

Daniel J. O'Brien, PhD

President
D.J. O'Brien & Associates, Inc.
1953 E. Frontier Lane
Olathe, KS 66062
Tel: (913) 764-8957
Fax: (913) 780-0632
E-mail: bentleyob@aol.com

Specialties: Pharmacology, Toxicology, Drug Warnings and FDA Regulations. Causation of adverse health effects of prescription and OTC drugs, chemicals, health and beauty products, biologicals and consumer products; warnings and labeling, regulatory requirements. Following receipt of a PhD in Pharmacology and Toxicology from Indiana University School of Medicine, Dr. O'Brien spent twenty years in management positions with major corporations in the drug and chemical industries. Such positions included Director, FDA Regulatory Affairs for a pharmaceutical company and Manager, Corporate Government Regulatory Affairs for a Chemical Company. Twenty plus years of consulting. Board Certifications. **Degrees/licenses:** BS, MS, PhD; BCFE, BCFM.

Rodney Richmond

PharmacoLegal Associates
Tel: (866) 288-8386
Fax: (866) 288-8386
E-mail: PharmacoLegal@aol.com
Web Site: http://www.PharmacoLegal.net

Specialties: Medication use (errors, overdosage/toxicity, underdosing, adverse reactions, drug interactions) for attorneys, insurers, patients, healthcare facilities; Pharmaceutical Care Standards (nursing homes/long-term care, acute care, hospice, home health); Geriatric Drug Therapy Management (Alzheimer's, Parkinson's, psychoactive medications, psychotropic drug reactions, polypharmacy); Clinical Pharmacy Services (drug information services, patient assessment & counseling); Drug Safety/Misadventure (interactions, adverse reactions, errors, death/overdose, product liability); Pharmacology (causal relationship drug exposure and subsequent effects, pharmacoepidemiology, pharmacokinetics); Pharmacy Operations (3rd party payment, managed care, controlled substances/narcotics, drug distribution systems, pharmacoeconomics). **Degrees/licenses:** MS Pharmacy; Reg. Pharm.; CGP; Fellow, Am. Soc. Consultant Pharm.

Pharmacy

Jack H. Raber, Pharm. D.

Principal
Clinipharm Services
P.O. Box 3206
Seal Beach, CA 90740
Tel: (562) 596-8753
Fax: (707) 897-1657
E-mail: Clinipharm@aol.com
Web Site: www.clinipharmservices.com

Specialties: Liability and risk management assessment, pharmacy malpractice, pharmacy-related hospital malpractice, institutional pharmacy law. Available for research, consultation, and trial testimony (plaintiff, defense, administrative law hearings). **Degrees/licenses:** Pharm.D., University of Southern California, 1975; California RPh 29591.

Rodney Richmond

PharmacoLegal Associates
Tel: (866) 288-8386
Fax: (866) 288-8386
E-mail: PharmacoLegal@aol.com
Web Site: http://www.PharmacoLegal.net

Specialties: Medication use (errors, overdosage/toxicity, underdosing, adverse reactions, drug interactions) for attorneys, insurers, patients, healthcare facilities; Pharmaceutical Care Standards (nursing homes/long-term care, acute care, hospice, home health); Geriatric Drug Therapy Management (Alzheimer's, Parkinson's, psychoactive medications, psychotropic drug reactions, polypharmacy); Clinical Pharmacy Services (drug information services, patient assessment & counseling); Drug Safety/Misadventure (interactions, adverse reactions, errors, death/overdose, product liability); Pharmacology (causal relationship drug exposure and subsequent effects, pharmacoepidemiology, pharmacokinetics); Pharmacy Operations (3rd party payment, managed care, controlled substances/narcotics, drug distribution systems, pharmacoeconomics). **Degrees/licenses:** MS Pharmacy; Reg. Pharm.; CGP; Fellow, Am. Soc. Consultant Pharm.

See primary listing under MEDICINE & HEALTH: Pharmacology

Physical Medicine/ Rehabilitation

John Scott Stephens, MS, PT

Carolina Rehabilitation, Inc.
809 Inlet View Dr.
Wilmington, NC 28409-2106
Tel: (910) 385-7149 (Cellular)
(910) 285-1650 (Office)
Fax: (910) 285-1675
E-mail: rehabservi@aol.com

Specialties: Physical therapist with thirty plus years clinical experience. Developed private practice to 20 offices including supervision of physical therapists, occupational therapists and speech-language therapists. Patient population served includes age ranges from birth through geriatrics. Positions held include founding president of Federation of State Boards of Physical Therapy, 1986-90; President, Virginia Physical Therapy Association, 1990-92; Chair, Practice Committee for Orthopaedic Section of the American Physical Therapy Association (APTA), 1992-1997; Board of Directors of APTA, 1994-97. Candidate for APTA vice-president, 1997. Case review experience for plaintiffs, defendants and insurers. $300/hour plus expenses. **Degrees/licenses:** NC/VA licensed physical therapist, BA UVA, MS Duke.

Plastic & Reconstructive Surgery

John L. Baeke, MD

Park Place Plastic Surgery
14950 Newton
Overland Park, KS 66223
Tel: (913) 685-0101
Fax: (913) 685-3666
E-mail: JBaeke@ParkPlaceUSA.net
Web Site: http://www.beautifulbreasts.com

Specialties: Plastic Surgery; Includes breast implant problems, breast reduction/lift & post-mastectomy reconstruction issues; Body contouring: abdominoplasty & liposuction; Cosmetic laser procedures: tattoo removal, skin resurfacing, pigmented & vascular lesions; Post-traumatic injury & wound care acute & chronic including bed sores. Experience with plaintiff & defendant case review, brief preparation & testimony. Univ. Kansas-honors. First place Guffey Competition. First place Calif. Society of Plastic Surgeons. Assoc. Prof. University of Kansas School of Med. Amer. Society of Laser Medicine & Surgery. Amer. Society of Cosmetic Breast Surgery. Assoc. Military Surgeons of U.S., Amer. Academy of Wound Management, AMA. **Degrees/licenses:** MD.

Plastic & Reconstructive Surgery *(cont.)*

Todd C. Case, MD, FACS

President
Todd C. Case, MD, PC
5881 N. Misty Ridge Dr.
Tucson, AZ 85718-3434
Tel: (520) 615-0597
Fax: (520) 615-0599
E-mail: tccaseworks@aol.com

Specialties: Complete start-to-finish cost-effective litigation support for plaintiff and defense; Impartial analysis; Reports summarizing medical records, explaining medical terms and procedures, and reviewing duty, breach, causation and damages; Strategic planning; Database searches; Expert witness services. Dr. Case is ABPS certified; Past Chief, plastic surgery (Tucson Medical Center); A former director of division of plastic surgery; Received prestigious national award for research; Authored and presented numerous papers; Invited lecturer (Italy, India). Actively practicing; Interests in facial , breast and body surgery, including cosmetic and laser procedures, and treatment for lymphedema. **Degrees/licenses:** MD, FACS, ABPS, AOA; Lic. AZ, CA, TX.

Cadvan O. Griffiths Jr., MD, LLB, FCLM

11645 Wilshire Blvd., Ste. 600
Los Angeles, CA 90025-6807
Tel: (310) 477-5558
Fax: (310) 274-7564
E-mail: cadvan@aol.com
Web Site: http://www.plasticsurgery.org

Specialties: Medical-legal consultation and malpractice review related to cosmetic and reconstructive surgery; Head, neck, hands, and extremities; QME; IME; AME; Certified American Board of Plastic Surgery; Certified Medical Review Officer; Member International Society of Aesthetic Plastic Surgery; Society of Head and Neck Surgeons; American Society of Plastic and Reconstructive Surgeons; American Arbitration Association; Society of Surgical Oncologists; Assoc. member American Bar Association; Consumer Attorney's Assn. **Degrees/licenses:** MD, LLB, FCLM.

Darrell L. Henderson, MD

Plastic Surgeon
Plastic Surgery Associates
1101 South College Rd., Ste. 400
Lafayette, LA 70503
Tel: (337) 233-5025
Fax: (337) 233-5054
E-mail: plasticsx@aol.com
Web Site: http://www.psassoc.com

Specialties: Hand/wrist surgeon, general plastic surgeon; Six-year residency at Mayo Clinic; General Surgery, Plastic Surgery. Fellowship in surgery of the hand and wrist with Dr. Frackelton, Milwaukee, WS. Vast experience in forensic evaluations of injuries and the impact disability has on the ability to work and problems, future medical, surgeries and expenses caused by the injury. Qualified as defense and plaintiff expert in many federal and state courts in the U.S. and Australia. American Society of Plastic Surgeons, American Board of Plastic surgeons, American Board of Forensic Examiners. **Degrees/licenses:** MD.

Martin C. Johnson, MD, FACS, FAAP, FACME

CEO/President
Pacific Northwest Neurosurgical Association
31870 SW Country View Lane
Wilsonville, OR 97070-7476
Tel: (503) 694-5900
Fax: (503) 694-5649
E-mail: martinc33@hotmail.com

Specialties: Neurosurgery, Pediatric Neurosurgery, Neurotrauma, Child Abuse, Pediatric Neurology, Neurology, Neurological Critical Care, Reconstructive Neurosurgery, Workers' Compensation (neurosurgical/spinal orthopedic, IME), Disability Evaluation (neurosurgical - spinal orthopedic), Col. AUSA (ret.). Board Certified: American Board Neurosurgery, American Board Pediatric Neurosurgery, American Board of Forensic Examiners. **Degrees/licenses:** ABB, MD, FACS, FAAP, FACFM.

See primary listing under MEDICINE & HEALTH: Neurosurgery

Joel J. Teplinsky, MD, FACS, FICS

Plastic, Reconstructive,
Burn & Hand Surgeon
16161 Ventura Boulevard
Encino, CA 91436
Tel: (818) 784-7707
(818) 990-9433
Fax: (818) 784-7598

Specialties: Cosmetic, Reconstructive, Burn, Hand, Wounds (Chronic) Surgery. Diplomate, American Board of Plastic Surgery; UCLA, Department Plastic Surgery, Attending Staff; Past President, International College of Surgeons, U.S. Section; Past Director, Residency & Staff Education, Grossman Burn Center, Sherman Oaks Hospital; Past Director, Wound Care Center, Sherman Oaks Hospital. CV: University of Wisconsin BS '60, MD '65; Herrick Hospital, Berkeley, CA, Internship '66; UC San Francisco, Psychiatry Residency '67; Capt., U.S. Medical Corps, USAF '67-'69; Fresno County Hospital, General Surgery Residency '69-'72; Kaiser Hospital, Los Angeles, General Surgery Residency '72-'75; Baylor College of Medicine, Houston, TX, Plastic Surgery Residency '75-'77. **Degrees/licenses:** BS & MD California.

Eugene O. Wiggs, MD

55 Madison St., Ste. 355
Denver, CO 80206-5429
Tel: (303) 377-8155
(303) 377-2020
Fax: (303) 377-2022
E-mail: ewiggs@omni.com

Specialties: Oculoplastic surgery is a synthesis of ophthalmology and plastic surgery. This discipline treats problems of the eyelids, lacrimal system and orbit. Oculoplastic surgeons also treat patients with thyroid eye disease, facial nerve palsy and socket problems in the one-eyed patient. BA - Johns Hopkins; MD -Duke; Internship - Denver General; Residency - Wilmer Institute, Johns Hopkins Hospital; Fellowship, Dr. Byron Smith/MEETH. Numerous publications & presentations; Honor Award recipient, American Academy of Ophthalmology; Clinical Professor of Ophthalmology Emeritus, University of Colorado; Former President, Colorado Ophthalmological Society. **Degrees/licenses:** BA - Johns Hopkins; MD - Duke.

See primary listing under MEDICINE & HEALTH: Oculoplastic Surgery

Podiatry

Arlene F. Hoffman, DPM, PhD

California Pacific Medical Center
2100 Webster St., Ste. 202
San Francisco, CA 94115-2375
Tel: (415) 923-3535
Fax: (415) 923-3672

Specialties: Medical evaluation and treatment of podiatric injuries; Perioperative evaluation; Wound healing; Blood flow evaluation of the lower extremity; Use of pharmaceuticals and laboratory evaluation. PhD, Downstate Medical Center, SUNY; DPM, California College of Podiatric Medicine; Fellow, Stanford University College of Medicine. Previous/current positions: Professor; Chair, Exam Committee, American Board of Podiatric Orthopedics; Board Trustee, ABPOPPM, ASPM, ASPD, ASPA; Special Editor, "The Lower Extremity;" General Editor, "Journal of the American Podiatric Medical Association;" Editor, "Yearbook of Podiatric Medicine and Surgery." Recipient of the Meritorious Service Award, APMA. 35+ publications. **Degrees/licenses:** DPM, PhD.

Psychiatry

Alvin C. Burstein, MD

Well Being Systems
5070 N. 40th St., Ste. 220
Phoenix, AZ 85018-2135
Tel: (602) 957-2368
Fax: (602) 957-0050
E-mail: aburstein@wbsaz.com

Specialties: Adult Psychiatry; Geriatric Psychiatry; Standard of care for psychiatric units, hospitals, geriatric psych. units, managed care companies, psychiatrists; Analyze interactions psychiatric, medical, side effects, substance abuse, intoxication issues; Psychopharmacol-

(Listing continued on next page)

Psychiatry *(cont.)*

Alvin C. Burstein, MD (cont.)
ogy; Explain clinical issues for case presentation; private practice of psychiatry, Medical Director of psych. HMO, and psychiatric hospital and Geriatric Psych. Unit; Excellent reputation, teacher, communicator. Associate Professor of Psychiatry. **Degrees/licenses:** MD, AZ; Board Certified.

See primary listing under PSYCHIATRY: General

Brian Crowley, MD

5225 Connecticut Ave., N.W., Suite 215
Washington, DC 20015
Tel: (202) 537-3300
Fax: (301) 365-8644
E-mail: bcrowleymd@aol.com
Web Site: www.drcrowley.yourmd.com

Specialties: Forensic Psychiatry, Civil & Criminal: Malpractice; Fitness for Duty; Independent Medical Examinations; Testamentary Capacity and Undue Influence; Personal Injury; Suicide; Stalking; Sexual Harassment/Abuse; Sexual Misconduct by Professionals; Posttraumatic Stress Disorder; Professional Ethics & Peer Review; Hospital and Outpatient Treatment Standards; Recovered Memories; Workplace Violence; Dangerousness Assessments; Sanity; Trial Competency; Diminished Capacity. Doctor Crowley, a Yale Medical School graduate, is Past Chief of Psychiatry at his hospital. He is past President, Washington Psychiatric Society; Distinguished Life Fellow, American Psychiatric Association; Fellow, American Academy of Psychoanalysis, and has often testified as an expert in federal and state courts. Available as Expert nationally. **Degrees/licenses:** MD, DLFAPA; Licensed in Maryland & DC.

Henry W. Lahmeyer, MD

Clinical Professor of Psychiatry
Chicago Medical School
Two Northfield Plaza, Ste. 100
Northfield, IL 60093
Tel: (847) 446-3531
Fax: (847) 446-3573
E-mail: henry@lahmeyermd.com
Web Site: www.lahmeyermd.com

Specialties: Civil & Criminal. Psychopharmacology, suicide, sleep disorders, depression, alcohol abuse, closed head injury, and post-traumatic stress disorder. Criminal cases have involved issues of criminal responsibility, Sexual Violent Persons Act commitment, competency to stand trial, to waive Miranda Rights, or to give a confession. Previously Professor at Northwestern University. Published over 70 articles and received over 40 research grants. Has testified or given depositions in many state jurisdictions and Federal Courts for both the plaintiff and defense in civil cases and for both the prosecution and defense in criminal cases. Maintains active clinical and research practice. **Degrees/licenses:** BA, MD; Board Cert. in Psych, Sleep Med. & Forensic Psych.

Ned P. Masbaum, MD

PO Box 3010
Carmel, IN 46082
Tel: (317) 846-7727
Fax: (317) 575-1898
E-mail: NPM.FORNPSYCH@att.net
Web Site: www.FORNPSYCH.com

Specialties: Psychiatry; Forensic Psychiatry; Medical-Legal Consultation; Competency; Insanity defense; Post-traumatic Stress Disorder; Spousal Abuse; Criminal prosecution or defense; Civil cases. **Affiliation:** Private Practice, Medical Staff, Clarian✱Methodist Hospital. Board Certified, American Board of Psychiatry & Neurology, in Psychiatry & Forensic Psychiatry. **Degrees/licenses:** MD; Licensed (IN).

Psychology

Academic Guidance Services (since 1960)

6399 Wilshire Blvd., Suite 515
Los Angeles, CA 90048
Tel: (310) 435-1129
(949) 833-9444
Fax: (213) 483- 4839
E-mail: davidhung8@cs.com
Web Site: http://childtreatment.com or
http://specialedu.net

Specialties: Educational evaluation, IEP analysis, appropriateness of school and home; Family dispute re: school and home placement, family counseling, child rearing practices, behavior management, diagnoses; Treatment of learning disabilities, attention deficit and hyperactivity disorders (ADHD), dyslexia; School selection, intensive tutoring of academic skills, individual school for credits. **Degrees/licenses:** PhD (Psychology); MA (Psychology); BSc.

See primary listing under EDUCATION/SCHOOLS: Consulting

R. Mark Binderman, PhD

Clinical Psychologist
3615-F Chain Bridge Road
Fairfax, VA 22030-3237
Tel: (703) 691-1010
Fax: (202) 645-8733
E-mail: rmbin@verizon.net

Specialties: Forensic psychological evaluations: sex offenders, recidivism risk; violence risk assessment; competence; sentencing; diagnosis, treatment recommendations. Testified before state and federal courts. Participation in over 100 cases. Advanced training and certification in violence, and in sex offenders. Testified on sexual sadism/homicide cases, and on assassination attempt case. Published chapters: "Identifying Violence Risk Factors" and "Understanding the Violence Risk Assessment Guide." Authority on relationship of mental illness to violence. **Degrees/licenses:** PhD, Psychology, 1974; Lic. in VA, Wash. DC, TN.

General & Forensic Psychiatry

Pogos Hagop Voskanian, MD
Assistant Professor of Psychiatry
Director, MCP-Hahnemann Univ.
Psychiatry & Law Program
1240 Serota Place
Philadelphia, PA 19115
Tel: (215) 938-7227
Fax: (215) 938-7474
E-mail: drvoskanian@aol.com
Web Site: www.forensic-psychiatrist.com

Specialties: Forensic Psychiatric Evaluations, Consultations and Expert Witness Testimony in civil and criminal cases... for plaintiff, defense, prosecution, courts, insurance companies and governmental agencies. Dr. Voskanian is certified by the American Board of Psychiatry and Neurology in Psychiatry and Forensic Psychiatry. In private practice, Dr. Voskanian specializes in comprehensive evaluations in a wide range of forensic issues including: Insanity Defense, Capital Sentencing, Disability Determinations, Workers' Compensation, Psychiatric Harm, Personal Injury, Psychiatric Malpractice, Discrimination, Sexual Harassment, ADA, Americans with Disabilities Act, various civil and criminal competencies, etc. **Degrees/licenses:** MD - Univ. of Mass.; Board Cert. in Psychiatry & Forensic Psychiatry.

See primary listing under PSYCHIATRY: General

John Watts Podboy

PO Box 488
Kenwood, CA 95452
Tel: (707) 833-6023
Fax: (707) 833-5224

Specialties: Forensic psychology; Psychodiagnostics; Forensic consultant to State & Federal Courts throughout California. Licensed Psychologist in private practice
Biographical Information: John Watts Podboy was born 1943 York PA; PhD 1975 (Rehabilitation Psychology) University of Arizona; Pre-Doctoral Clinical Internship, St. Mary's Hospital, affiliate of University of Arizona Medical School, Department of

(Listing continued on next page)

Psychology *(cont.)*

John Watts Podboy (cont.)
Psychiatry 1972 - 1973; MS 1971 (Counseling) San Diego State College; BA 1966 (Psychology) Dickinson College. Licensed Psychologist (CA). 1982 - Present: Private Practice, Clinical Psychology, Comprehensive psychodiagnostics, forensic consultations to State & Federal Courts; Consulting Clinical Psychologist, Sonoma County Probation Department. 1979 - 1982: Staff Psychologist, California Department of Developmental Services, Sonoma State Hospital, Eldridge, California. Fellow: American College of Forensic Psychology. Fellow & Diplomate: American Board of Medical Psychotherapists. Member: American Psychological Association; Western Psychological Association; California State Psychological Association; Redwood Psychological Society (President - 1982); American College of Forensic Examiners; The American Society of Criminology; Society of Police & Criminal Psychology; The New York Academy of Sciences. Numerous lectures & symposia incl: The Diagnosis of Specific Learning Disabilities Among a Juvenile Delinquent Population; Behavioral Science Consultation with the Prosecution & Defense in Death Penalty Cases. 25 publications including: Allegations of Child Sexual Abuse Present New Perils for Clinicians; Learning Handicap: The Underdiagnosed Disability; Utilization of a Hospital Staff Counseling Service; The Psychologist in the Courtroom - Current Perspectives on Stereotyped Views. Appearances & testimony in more than 2000 Superior Court proceedings; Expert witness in more than 200 homicide cases.
Degrees/licenses: PhD (Rehabilitation Psychology); MS (Counseling); BA (Psychology).

Ronald H. Roberts, PhD, ABPP

2000 Van Ness Ave., Ste. 512
San Francisco, CA 94109-3017
Tel: (415) 776-2000
Fax: (415) 776-2001

Specialties: Personal injury; Neuropsychology; Head injuries; Chronic pain; Toxic exposure; Mold exposure; Criminal Responsibility; Work stress; Discrimination; Post-traumatic stress; Disability injuries; Diplomate, American Board of Med. Psychotherapists; Diplomate, American Board of Disability Evaluators; Diplomate in Forensic Psychology, American Board of Professional Psychology; Diplomate, American Board of Vocational Neuropsychology. **Degrees/licenses:** PhD, PSY8334 CA.

Ralph S. Welsh, PhD, ABPP

Clinical Psychologist
P.O. Box 720
Georgetown, CT 06829-0720
Tel: (203) 743-1724
(203) 417-4330 (Cell)
Fax: (203) 938-9179
E-mail: rswelsh@mail.com

152 Deer Hill Ave.
Danbury, CT 06810

Specialties: Family, emigration, and personal injury law. Over 20 years of experience psychologically evaluating individuals for the state, the federal government, and for private attorneys. Thousands of hours on the stand providing expert testimony. Am particularly adept with emigration problems. Have written extensively in the area of child maltreatment and delinquency and recently received an award from the Connecticut Psychological Association for outstanding achievement in professional psychology. Have taught at two major universities. Work well with MDs. Will travel as needed. **Degrees/licenses:** BS, MS, PhD, ABPP, DBFE, Lic. State of CT.

Martin H. Williams, PhD

Clinical & Forensic Psychologist
P.O. Box 62439
Sunnyvale, CA 94088
Tel: (888) 225-9957
Fax: (888) 225-9957
E-mail: mw@drmwilliams.com
Web Site: http://drmwilliams.com

Specialties: Dr. Williams is a psychologist and psychotherapist who testifies on malpractice and emotional damages. He is an expert on sexual harassment, boundary violations, therapist patient sex, malingering, post traumatic stress disorder and borderline personality disorder. He has published in refereed journals on harmfulness of therapist-patient sexual involvement, ethics, risk management and malpractice. He is in full-time clinical practice, is licensed in California and testifies nationally. Offices in Los Angeles, San Jose, Orange County and San Diego. **Degrees/ licenses:** PhD in Psychology (1975); Calif. Licensed Psychologist (1976).

Pulmonary Medicine

Michael E. Kalafer, MD

2444 Via Aprilia
Del Mar, CA 92014
Tel: (858) 212-4447
Fax: (801) 327-2009
E-mail: kalafer@san.rr.com

Specialties: Pulmonary Medicine; Critical Care Medicine; Internal Medicine; Lung Cancer; Hospital Medical Director; Long Term Acute Care; Elder Abuse. Cornell University BS; SUNY Syracuse MD; Mt. Sinai Hospital NY Internship; UCSD Residency & Pulmonary Fellowship; Associate Clinical Professor of Medicine UCSD. Society of Critical Care Medicine; American Thoracic Society, Fellow American College Chest Physicians. Twenty four years clinical practice of pulmonary, critical care & internal medicine. Experienced in Medical Malpractice, Personal Injury, Wrongful Death; plaintiff and defense. Emphasis on timely and thoughtful case review. **Degrees/ licenses:** BS, MD (CA), FCCP; Board Cert.: Pulmonary, Critical Care & Int. Med.

James F. Lineback, MD, FCCP

2100 N. Main St., Suite 202
Santa Ana, CA 92706
Tel: (949) 610-0036
Fax: (949) 721-9121
E-mail: linebackmd@cox.net

Specialties: Medical Practice in Pulmonary/ Chest Medicine and Internal Medicine since 1983. Internal Medicine; Pulmonary/Chest Medicine; Occupational Medicine; Wrongful Death Cases; Patient Care Issues; Medical Causation; Standard of Care Issues; Diagnostic Dilemmas; Toxic Exposure; Medical Records Review; Courtroom Testimony. Associate Clinical Professor of Medicine at USC College of Medicine and UC Irvine College of Medicine, Lecturer in Physiology at UC Riverside College of Medicine.. **Degrees/licenses:** MS, MD, FCCP. Board Cert. Internal Medicine & Pulmonary Medicine.

See primary listing under MEDICINE & HEALTH: Internal Medicine

James L. Pearle, MD

President
Western Pulmonary Medical Group, Inc.
220 Laguna Road, Ste. 2
Fullerton, CA 92835-2523
Tel: (714) 446-7454
Fax: (714) 879-1049
E-mail: jpearlemd@hotmail.com

Specialties: Asbestosis and Occupational Lung Diseases with national experience and publications; Medical Malpractice, Sleep Disorders; Hospitalist, Pulmonary, Critical Care, and Internal Medicine. Hospital Medical Director, Hospital Chief of Staff, Director of Hospital Respiratory Therapy Department, President of Medical Group, Independent Medical Examiner, Principal Investigator for Clinical Trials, Experienced in Hyperbaric Medicine. Over one hundred depositions and trials. Board certified in Internal Medicine and Pulmonary Disease. Fellow, American College of Chest Physicians. Former Assistant Professor, UCLA School of Medicine and UC Irvine School of Medicine. **Degrees/licenses:** BA, MD.

Steven M. Simons, MD

435 N. Roxbury #311
Beverly Hills, CA 90210
Tel: (310) 274-7303
Fax: (310) 274-8572
E-mail: simons@cshs.org
Web Site: http://www.simonsmd.com

Specialties: Pulmonary, Internal Medicine, Critical Care, Asthma, Pulmonary Embolism, Ventilator Management, Pneumonia, Pleural Effusion, COPD, Bronchoscopy. POSI-

(Listing continued on next page)

Pulmonary Medicine *(cont.)*

Steven M. Simons, MD (cont.)
TIONS: Chief of Staff, Chief of Medicine, Chief of Pulmonary, Director Pulmonary Endoscopy, Med. Director Quality Mgt. - Cedars; Chief of Staff - Cedars Sinai Medical Center, Medical Director Medical Affairs - Cedars. CERTIFICATIONS: Amer. Board of Internal Medicine, Pulmonary Diseases, Critical Care, Quality Assurance. 29 Publications. PROFESSIONAL SOCIETIES: Amer. College of Physicians; Amer. College of Chest Physicians; Amer. Thoracic Society; CA Medical Assn.; LA County Medical Assn.; Council on Critical Care; Amer. College of Sports Medicine. EXPERIENCE: 20 years Expert Witness, approx. 50% defense, 50% plaintiff. **Degrees/licenses:** BS, MD, FACP, FCCP, Clinical Professor - UCLA; Lic. CA, NY.

Quality Assurance

Joseph S. Carey, MD

Chair, Quality Improvement Committee;
Past President California Society of Thoracic Surgeons
3475 Torrance Blvd., Ste. B
Torrance, CA 90503
Tel: (310) 540-1011
Fax: (310) 540-1028
E-mail: careyjs@earthlink.net
Web Site: http://www.casts.org or http://www.ctsnet.org/home/jscarey

Specialties: Quality control in cardiovascular and thoracic surgery; Outcomes research and analysis; Risk Adjustment; Online data coding and reporting; President, California Society of Thoracic Surgeons, 1996-1998; Chair, Quality Improvement Committee, 1998-present. Member, National Society of Thoracic Surgeons Ethics and Database committees, 1996-present. Associate Clinical Professor of Surgery, UCLA School of Medicine; Chief, Thoracic Surgery, VA Hospital, Los Angeles, 1967-1983. Private practice, thoracic and cardiovascular surgery, 1983-present. Extensive publications in outcomes of coronary and heart valve surgery, blood vessel diseases and lung problems. Consultant to hospitals for quality reviews. Wide experience in practice standards and legal reviews. **Degrees/licenses:** MD, FACS, FACC, Assoc. Clinical Prof., UCLA.

See primary listing under MEDICINE & HEALTH: Cardiac Surgery

Radiation Oncology

Randy V. Heysek, MD

CEO/President
Central Florida Cancer Institute
P.O. Box 90758
Lakeland, FL 33804-0758
Tel: (863) 284-6952
Fax: (863) 284-6951
E-mail: rheysekmd@aol.com
Web Site: http://www.cfcancerinst.com

Specialties: Board Certified, American Board of Radiology. Active practice in central Florida. University of Maryland, Cancer Center, specialty training; University of Florida, Medical School; University of Colorado, BA, Phi Beta Kappa. **Degrees/licenses:** MD, BA, FACRO.

Radiology, Neuroradiology

Richard Alan Ofstein, MD

Radiologist
122 Ocean Park Blvd., #512
Santa Monica, CA 90405
Tel: (310) 581-9805
E-mail: rofstein@aol.com or rofstein@ucla.edu

Specialties: Neuroradiology. Interpretation and appropriate utilization of Magnetic Resonance Imaging (MRI), Computed Tomography (CT), and general radiology. Board Certification Diagnostic Radiology and Certificate of Added Qualifications in Neuroradiology. Subspecialty expertise in neuro- and musculoskeletal pathology including trauma- and sports-related injuries. Founding Publisher & Editor of two internationally-recognized publications, "Magnetic Resonance Update" and "Consultations in Radiology & Imaging," published since 1989. Topics include Head Trauma, Cervical Spine Injuries, Back Pain, Knee Injuries, Shoulder Pain, and Temporomandibular Joint (TMJ) Dysfunction. Private practice. University Appointment as Assistant Clinical Professor of Radiology, UCLA School of Medicine, 1988-2002. **Degrees/licenses:** MD (1980); CA Med. Lic. G44857; Cert. of Added Qualifications in Neuroradiology.

Harold S. Parnes, MD

Medical Director
Omega Diagnostic Imaging, PC
1525 Voorhies Ave.
Brooklyn, NY 11235
Tel: (718) 332-1999
Fax: (718) 332-3236 or (718) 332-4192
E-mail: hparneurad@aol.com

Specialties: Board Certified Diagnostic Radiology and Neuroradiology, currently in private practice. Assistant Professor of Radiology at State University of New York Stony Brook. Attended seven year Accelerated Biomedical (1978-1985) Program SUNY Downstate; Intern - Internal Medicine, Resident and Chief Resident Radiology - Long Island College Hospital; Fellowship 2 years Neuroradiology SUNY Stony Brook; Director Neuroradiology 4 years Queens General Hospital in conjunction with Long Island Jewish and Mount Sinai Medical Centers. Senior member American Society of Neuroradiology; member Society Spine Radiology; member American Society of Pediatric Neuroradiology; member American Society of Head and Neck Radiology. Licensed in Pennsylvania, Florida, California, New Jersey. **Degrees/licenses:** MD, SUNY Downstate, 7 yr. Accel. Biomedical Program.

Radiology/Nuclear Medicine

Comprehensive Radiology Review, PLLC

A. Robert Tantleff, MD
57 Starling Court
East Hills, NY 11576
Tel: (516) 626-3688
Fax: (516) 626-6151
E-mail: artan@optonline.net
Web Site:
www.comprehensiveradiologyreview.com

Specialties: Board Certified Diagnostic Radiology/Radiographic Imaging (MRI, CAT Scan, Ultrasound, Nuclear Medicine, Angiography). Independent radiology review, IME, peer review, second opinion radiology interpretation, medical record review. Workers' Compensation, personal injury, long-term disability, medical malpractice. No geographical limits. 30 years in medical practice. Testimony experience. Available to insurance companies, plaintiff and defense attorneys, physicians and hospitals. **Degrees/licenses:** MD Summa Cum Laude, State Univ. of NY, Downstate Med. Ctr.

John H. Harris, Jr., MD, DSc, FACR

Emeritus Professor of Radiology
University of Texas-Houston Med. School
200 Alta Vista Dr.
Sedona, AZ 86351-6910
Tel: (928) 284-9392
Fax: (928) 284-9170
E-mail: jhharris@myexcel.com

Specialties: Dr. Harris, as the principal author of the "Radiology of Emergency Medicine," 4th ed., and "Radiology of Acute Cervical Spine Trauma," 3rd ed., is an internationally recognized authority in Emergency Radiology with special interest in cervical spine injury; Experienced expert medical witness; Awarded 1st Gold Medal, American Society of Emergency Radiology; Awarded 2001 Gold Medal of the American College of Radiology; Associate, American Academy of Orthopedic Surgeons; Honorary Member, American

(Listing continued on next page)

Radiology/Nuclear Medicine
(cont.)

John H. Harris, Jr. (cont.)
College of Emergency Physicians; F (Hon.)-Royal Australasian College of Radiologists. **Degrees/licenses:** MD, DSc, D-ABR; F-ASER; F-ACR; Arizona & Texas Med. Lic.

Rheumatology

Jeff Sarkozi, MD, FRCPC, FACR

The CA Institute for Fibromyalgia,
Arthritis & Rheumatology
801 North Tustin Ave., Suite 503
Santa Ana, CA 92705
Tel: (714) 973-4636
Fax: (714) 973-4776

Specialties: Fibromyalgia, Arthritis, Occupational, Industrial, and Environmental Rheumatology/Arthritis, Syndromes of Chronic Fatigue and Pain, Rheumatoid Arthritis, Osteoarthritis, Neck Pain, Back Pain, Lupus, Scleroderma, Raynaud's Syndrome, Spondylitis, Myositis. Consulting/Expert experience includes consultation, case review, analysis, IME/AME, deposition, trial experience. On behalf of silicone implant manufacturers and physicians involved in silicone implant litigation, on behalf of manufacturers involved in "phen-fen" litigation, plaintiff for 1-tryptophan EMS, industry/defendant and selected plaintiffs for industrial/occupational/environmental/post-traumatic claims of fibromyalgia and syndromes of chronic fatigue and pain, arthritis, connective tissue and other rheumatologic diseases. Multiple US/foreign Patents for ergonomic engineering. **Degrees/licenses:** MD, FRCPC (Brd. Cert. Rheumatology & Int. Med.); FACR (Lic. CA, NY).

Surgery, General

Mark W. Gordon, MD

Mark W. Gordon, MD, PA
2301 N. University Drive
Pembroke Pines, FL 33024
Tel: (954) 964-1490
Fax: (954) 963-3453
E-mail: drmark@dslx.net

Specialties: General Surgery, Gastrointestinal Endoscopy and Colon-Rectal Surgery; Private practice since 1975. Trustee/Director of large physician self-insurance trust 1984-1990: member claims committee, chairman audit committee. Records review, IMEs, utilization issues. Twenty years experience in case review, evaluation and trial participation, both defense and plaintiff. Certified American Board of Surgery. Fellow, American College of Surgeons. Society of American Gastrointestinal Endoscopic Surgeons. American Society of Colon and Rectal Surgeons. Clinical Associate Professor, Nova Southeastern University. Extensive hospital staff leadership positions and professional societies. CV on request. **Degrees/licenses:** BS, MD.

See primary listing under MEDICAL-LEGAL: Medical/Hospital Malpractice

C. Andrew Heiskell, MD, FACS

Medical Legal Consultants, Inc.
4000 Hampton Center, Ste. D
Morgantown, WV 26505
Tel: (304) 599-8665
Fax: (304) 599-8584
E-mail: info@heiskellmd.com
Web Site: http://www.heiskellmd.com

Specialties: Dr. Heiskell is a practicing General and Vascular Surgeon. Dr. Heiskell has been in private practice for 25 years and has been reviewing medical records for over 10 years, testifying on behalf of claimants, defendants and insurers in cases of general and vascular surgery, laparoscopic surgery, surgical malpractice and standards of care. He performs numerous operations yearly including hernia repairs, laparoscopic gallbladder surgery, surgeries of the breast, colon, stomach, pancreas, spleen, thyroid, carotid arteries and many other vascular procedures. **Degrees/licenses:** BS, MD, Board Certified.

Thomas R. McLean, MD

Third Millennium Consultants, LLC
4970 Park
Shawnee, KS 66216
Tel: (913) 526-5526
Fax: (913) 962-0840
E-mail: tmclean@dnamail.com
Web Site: http://www.firms.findlaw.com/TMCLLC

Specialties: Clinical Assistant Professor of Surgery, University of Kansas School of Medicine. Board Certified by the America Board of Surgery, American Board of Thoracic Surgery and American Board of Surgery-Critical Care. Medical Director, Third Millennium Consultants, LLC, (Specializing in medical records review for Quality Assurance, Utilization Review and Litigation); Former Medical Director, Goodyear Tire Company, Topeka Plant. Former Regional Medical Consultant, Social Security Administration, Kansas City, Mo. Fellow American College of Surgeons, Cardiology and Chest Physicians. **Degrees/licenses:** MD, MS, Lic. in Kansas & Missouri.

See primary listing under MEDICINE & HEALTH: Cardiothoracic Surgery

Jeffrey M. Sherwood, MD, FACS

P.O. Box 1071
Water Mill, NY 11976
Tel: (888) 343-7642
Fax: (631) 726-9323
E-mail: jms12544@yahoo.com

Specialties: General Surgery, Laparoscopic Surgery & Breast Surgery. Over 10 years experience reviewing cases for both defendants' and plaintiffs' attorneys. Board Certified; Fellow, American College of Surgeons; Member, Society of Laparoscopic Surgeons. **Degrees/licenses:** MD, New York State Medical License.

Surgery, Trauma, Laparoscopy Expertise

Devesh Tiwary, MD, FACS
1682 Canopy Oaks Blvd.
Palm Harbor, FL 34683-6161
Tel: (727) 489-9327
(727) 687-6787 (Cell)
Fax: (727) 489-9327
E-mail: adt@tiwary.net
Web Site: http://www.mydoctor.com/tiwary

Specialties: Trauma, surgery: general, abdominal, breast, wound care, basic and advanced laparoscopy. Board Certified in Surgery; Advanced Trauma Life Support Certified. All education in United States; no accent; articulate and able to explain complex medical concepts simply. Graduate of Harvard Law School; locum tenens trauma surgeon. Prior experience: Mayo Clinic Jacksonville, private practice, indigent care hospital, former Chief of Surgery at major urban hospital. See CV at website (above). **Degrees/licenses:** MD, FACS, BA Biology, ATLS Certified.

Ronald Zelnick, MD

General and Colorectal Surgeon
210 Jupiter Lakes Blvd., #3105
Jupiter, FL 33458
Tel: (561) 575-7875
Fax: (561) 575-5874
E-mail: docrsz@aol.com

Specialties: General Surgery; Laparoscopic Surgery; Colon and Rectal Surgery; Breast Surgery. Board Certified and Recertified General Surgery and Colon And Rectal Surgery. Fellow American College of Surgeons; Fellow American Society of Colon & Rectal Surgeons. Actively practicing surgery in private practice, 14 years experience; Medical-legal experience. **Degrees/licenses:** MD, Florida License.

See primary listing under MEDICINE & HEALTH: Colon & Rectal Surgery

Thoracic Surgery

Joseph S. Carey, MD

Chair, Quality Improvement Committee;
Past President California Society
of Thoracic Surgeons
3475 Torrance Blvd., Ste. B
Torrance, CA 90503
Tel: (310) 540-1011
Fax: (310) 540-1028
E-mail: careyjs@earthlink.net
Web Site: http://www.casts.org or
http://www.ctsnet.org/home/jscarey

Specialties: Quality control in cardiovascular and thoracic surgery; Outcomes research and analysis; Risk Adjustment; Online data coding and reporting; President, California Society of Thoracic Surgeons, 1996-1998; Chair, Quality Improvement Committee, 1998-present. Member, National Society of Thoracic Surgeons Ethics and Database committees, 1996-present. Associate Clinical Professor of Surgery, UCLA School of Medicine; Chief, Thoracic Surgery, VA Hospital, Los Angeles, 1967-1983. Private practice, thoracic and cardiovascular surgery, 1983-present. Extensive publications in outcomes of coronary and heart valve surgery, blood vessel diseases and lung problems. Consultant to hospitals for quality reviews. Wide experience in practice standards and legal reviews. **Degrees/licenses:** MD, FACS, FACC, Assoc. Clinical Prof., UCLA.

See primary listing under MEDICINE & HEALTH: Cardiac Surgery

Samuel H. Sadow, MD, FACS

529 South Flagler Drive, Suite 18-G
West Palm Beach, FL 33401
Tel: (772) 335-9800
Fax: (561) 833-8663
E-mail: ssadow5398@aol.com

Specialties: Extensive experience with litigation of Standards of Care, Causation, Plaintiffs/Defendants, Bylaws and Hospital Privileges issues. Private practice of Cardiovascular and Thoracic Surgery, 1985-present; Principal investigator for FDA Phase III Trials ATS Medical Heart Valve Study. MD 1973, Chicago Medical School. Re-Certified in Thoracic Surgery. **Degrees/licenses:** MD, FACS, Amer. Boards of Surgery & Thoracic Surgery.

See primary listing under MEDICINE & HEALTH: Cardiothoracic Surgery

Toxicology

Lawson F. Bernstein, MD

MD - Forensic Neuropsychiatry
P. O. Box 81977
Pittsburgh, PA 15217
Tel: (412) 600-7996
Fax: (412) 422-5203
E-mail: lawsonbernstein@hotmail.com
Web Site: http://www.ifbmdpc.com

Specialties: Board certified academically published forensic neuropsychiatrist. Expertise in brain injury, stroke, neurotoxicology, acute/chronic pain, dementia, alcohol & substance abuse, gambling addiction and multiple other areas of neurology/psychiatry. Extensive criminal/civil trial (50/50) Plaintiff/Defense experience, including death penalty cases/legal insanity/diminished capacity. From 1991-1994, Dr. Bernstein was Director of the Psychiatry Residency Training Program at the University of Pittsburgh Medical Center, one of the largest academic psychiatric training programs in the U.S. Dr. Bernstein is also a Board Examiner for the American Board of Psychiatry & Neurology Oral Examination. **Degrees/licenses:** Medical.

See primary listing under MEDICINE & HEALTH: Head Injury

Alan Buchwald, MD Inc.

Alan Buchwald, MD
P.O. Box 2009
Santa Cruz, CA 95063
Tel: (831) 761-0260
Fax: (831) 761-0260
E-mail: albuchwald955@pol.net
Web Site: http://doctor.medscape.com/
alanbuchwaldmd

Specialties: Medical toxicology; Poisoning; Overdose; Envenomation; Industrial/occupational; Environmental, Hazardous materials; Agricultural; Food toxicology; Indoor air problems; Fellow American Academy of Emergency Medicine; Board Certified - American Board of Emergency Medicine and American Board of Medical Toxicology; Subspecialty Certification in Medical Toxicology, ABEM; Medical Director - Occupational Health Center, Dominican Santa Cruz Hospital; Affiliations - American Academy of Clinical Toxicology, American College of Occupational and Environmental Medicine, British Toxicology Society, Royal Society of Medicine (London), Aerospace Medicine Association (Space Medicine Branch); Categories - General consulting, personal injury, Workers' Compensation. **Degrees/licenses:** BA, MS, MD, ACMT, QME.

Dermigen, Inc.

Earl F. Walborg, Jr., PhD
President
912 A Garwood St.
P.O. Box 727
Smithville, TX 78957
Tel: (512) 237-5357
Fax: (512) 237-5363
E-mail: ewalborg@dermigen.com
Web Site: http://www.dermigen.com

Specialties: Earl F. Walborg, Jr., PhD, President of Dermigen, Inc., coordinates the consulting services of scientific experts with a broad range of expertise in toxicology. Dermigen consultants are drawn from academia, contacts resulting from Dr. Walborg's research career with M.D. Anderson Cancer Center (1965-1985), and his more recent involvement in consulting and management of toxicological research. Dermigen consultants possess particular expertise in the carcinogenic potential of pesticides, petrochemicals, specialty organic chemicals, pharmaceuticals and electromagnetic fields. Consulting services include the preparation of position papers on the relevant science and expert testimony. **Degrees/licenses:** PhD.

See primary listing under ENVIRONMENTAL: Toxicology

H.H. Miller Consulting

Harold H. Miller
2816 Ironwood Drive
Grand Prairie, TX 75052
Tel: (972) 660-1614
E-mail: hhpm@sbcglobal.net

Specialties: Consulting services, Toxicology, Pharmacology, Expert Testimony, Quality Assurance, Quality Control, Hazardous Materials, Facility Inspections and Regulatory Affairs. Dr. Miller has academic training in chemistry, medical technology and pharmacology. Assistant Professor in college of pharmacy, Toxicologist with major petrochemical company and Director of Toxicology with national reference laboratory. Experienced in assessment of effects of prescribed medications, drugs of abuse and alcohol, in relation to alleged malpractice, accidents and investigations. Numerous inspections of facilities for regulatory compliance. Experienced as expert witness in administrative hearings, depositions and courtroom testimony. **Degrees/licenses:** BA Chemistry; MT (ASCP) Medical Technology; PhD Pharmacology.

Ronald Himmelman, MD

Emergency Physician
466 Madison Ave.
Glencoe, IL 60022
Tel: (847) 917-4306
Fax: (847) 786-4535
E-mail: ronnyhim@comcast.net

Specialties: Medical legal consultant and working emergency physician. Extensive experience with plaintiff and defense concerning all aspects of emergency medicine and medical toxicology. **Degrees/licenses:** MD, Board Certified in Emergency Medicine & in Toxicology.

See primary listing under MEDICINE & HEALTH: Emergency Medicine

Toxicology *(cont.)*

Marvin Kaminsky, PhD, DABT
President
Toxcor Associates, Inc.
P.O. Box 454
Flanders, NJ 07836
Tel: (973) 252-0204
Fax: (973) 252-4424
E-mail: kaminsky@toxcor-associates.com
Web Site: http://toxcor-associates.com

Specialties: Over 25 years experience in toxicology and product safety evaluation and assessment of pharmaceuticals, consumer healthcare and personal care products, cosmetics, chemicals, and household products. Expert witness and scientific support in product liability and toxic injury litigation. Board certified. Member of: Society of Toxicology, American College of Toxicology, American Chemical Society, American College of Forensic Examiners, and International Society of Regulatory Toxicology and Pharmacology. **Degrees/licenses:** PhD, Diplomate Amer. Bd. of Toxicology, Cert. Amer. Bd. of Forensic Examiners.

H.M. Mehendale
The University of Louisiana at Monroe
College of Health Sciences
Department of Toxicology
Monroe, LA 71209-0495
Tel: (318) 342-1691
Fax: (318) 342-1686
E-mail: mehendale@ulm.edu
Web Site: http://www.ulm.edu/pharmacy/mehendale/default.htm

Specialties: Toxicology; Chemical toxicology; Pesticides, solvents, other industrial chemicals; Cancer; Regulatory affairs; Occupational or accidental exposures and short- or long-term hazards; Hazardous wastes; Forensic Toxicological analysis of extraneous evidence; Body fluids and tissues, drugs, and intoxicants; Exposure to single or combinations of chemicals; Extensive experience in toxicological data interpretations; Board certified by American Board of Toxicology; Fellow, Academy of Toxicological Sciences; Published over 250 original research papers, review articles and book chapters. **Degrees/licenses:** BS, MS, PhD, D-ABT, F-ATS.

Harry A. Milman, PhD
Expert in Toxicology,
Carcinogenesis, Pharmacology,
and "Pharmacy Standard of Care"
ToxNetwork.com
14317 Bauer Drive
Rockville, MD 20853
Tel: (301) 871-6715
Fax: (301) 871-5586
E-mail: hmilman@toxnetwork.com
Web Site: http://www.toxnetwork.com

Specialties: Toxicology, carcinogens, drugs, and "Pharmacy Standard of Care." 35+ years experience in toxicology, carcinogenesis, pharmacology, and pharmacy as a Consultant/Expert Witness (since 1998), at the National Cancer Institute/NIH (10 years), at the Environmental Protection Agency (18 years), and as a licensed pharmacist (35 years). Published 5 books, >70 papers, and numerous governmental reports in toxicology and carcinogenesis. Litigation experience includes deposition and jury trial testimony; occupational cancer/toxicology; medical malpractice; product liability; carcinogens; toxic chemicals; sewer gas; DUI; morphine intoxication; and "Pharmacy Standard of Care." Member Society of Toxicology, ASPET, AGT. **Degrees/licenses:** BS, MS, PhD (Pharmacology - 1978).

See primary listing under ENVIRONMENTAL: Toxicology

Daniel J. O'Brien, PhD
President
D.J. O'Brien & Associates, Inc.
1953 E. Frontier Lane
Olathe, KS 66062
Tel: (913) 764-8957
Fax: (913) 780-0632
E-mail: bentleyob@aol.com

Specialties: Pharmacology, Toxicology, Drug Warnings and FDA Regulations. Causation of adverse health effects of prescription and OTC drugs, chemicals, health and beauty products, biologicals and consumer products; warnings and labeling, regulatory requirements. Following receipt of a PhD in Pharmacology and Toxicology from Indiana University School of Medicine, Dr. O'Brien spent twenty years in management positions with major corporations in the drug and chemical industries. Such positions included Director, FDA Regulatory Affairs for a pharmaceutical company and Manager, Corporate Government Regulatory Affairs for a Chemical Company. Twenty plus years of consulting. Board Certifications. **Degrees/licenses:** BS, MS, PhD; BCFE, BCFM.

See primary listing under MEDICINE & HEALTH: Pharmacology

Richard A. Parent, PhD, DABT, FATS, RAC, ERT

Consulting Toxicologist & President
Consultox Limited
P.O. Box 1239
Damariscotta, ME 04543
Tel: (207) 563-2300
Fax: (207) 563-8990
E-mail: rparent@consultox.com
Web Site: http://www.consultox.com

Specialties: Dr. Parent has been actively involved in litigation support for both plaintiff and defense since 1984. His credentials have been accepted in all local, state, and federal courts in which he has testified. He is doubly board certified in Toxicology (DABT, FATS), is a recognized expert toxicologist in Europe (ERT), and has published over 85 scientific studies in the peer-reviewed literature. Recent activities have involved vinyl chloride, pesticides, lindane, PCBs, dioxins, PPA, creosote, health surveys, ephedrine, welding fumes, tobacco smoke, metals, Fen-Phen, alcohol defense, benzene, diesel fumes, trichloroethylene, technical management of complex toxic tort litigation and health assessment through personal sampling. **Degrees/licenses:** PhD, DABT, FATS, RAC, ERT (Europe).

Princeton-Somerset Group, Inc.

Dennis M. Stainken, PhD
Principal
4 Carroll Drive
Hillsborough, NJ 08844
Tel: (908) 369-6890
(800) 597-8836
Fax: (908) 369-6881
E-mail: prinsomgrp@aol.com

Specialties: Expert Witness, Toxicology, Health Issues, Chemical Exposure, Mold Issues, Worker Exposure, Contamination Issues, Causation Assessment, Property Damage/Contamination & Remediation, Sewage, Gasoline & Oil Issues & Age Determination, Chemicals/Products, Risk Assessment, Indoor Air Quality/Health Effects, Toxic Tort Causation or Defense, Chemistry, Site Assessment, Regulatory Issues, Environmental Toxicology; Environmental Issues, Wetland/Ecological. Services nationwide, 30+ years of industrial & government experience in pollution under NPDES, CERCLA, RCRA, SDWA & CWA. Former Regulator, Professor, Consultant. 75+ publication. National expert in Environmental Toxicology, Fate & Effect of Pollutants. Board Certified Medical Investigator - IV. **Degrees/licenses:** BS, MS, PhD, NJ Lic. UST, Calif. REA; Diplomate, Am. Bd. Foren. Exam., CSE, PWS.

See primary listing under ENVIRONMENTAL: Consulting

Jonathan S. Rutchik, MD, MPH

Neurology
Occupational
& Environmental Medicine
20 Sunnyside Ave., Ste. A-321
Mill Valley, CA 94941
Tel: (415) 381-3133
Fax: (415) 381-3131
E-mail: contactus@neoma.com
Web Site: http://www.neoma.com

Specialties: Neurology, Occupational/Environmental Medicine, Neurotoxicology, organic solvents, heavy metals, pesticides, neuropathy, brain trauma, disability, risk assessment, neuroepidemiology, product liabil-

(Listing continued on next page)

Toxicology *(cont.)*

Jonathan S. Rutchik, MD (cont.)
ity, utilization review, upper/lower extremity, head, neck, back injury, plaintiff, defense. **Degrees/licenses:** MD, MPH, CA QME; Licensed in CA, NY, MA, NJ.

See primary listing under MEDICINE & HEALTH: Neurology

Toxicology Consultants Roundtable

John A. Budny, PhD
Director, Publicity
Tel: (818) 706-2410
Web Site: http://lawinfo.com/biz/toxicology/index.html

Specialties: Call for a nationwide FREE LIST OF EXPERIENCED TOXICOLOGY EXPERTS; Contact them directly; No fee. **Degrees/licenses:** Over 50 PhD's, MD's & DVM's + Board Certifications.

Urology

Richard C. Davi, MD, FACS

Urologic Surgeon
Expert Witnessing & Litigation Consulting
1541 Brickell Ave., Ste. 3604
Miami, FL 33129
Tel: (305) 342-6262
Fax: (305) 854-9069
E-mail: docrich2@bellsouth.net

Specialties: Urologic Oncology, Infertility, Lithotripsy/Stone Disease, Vasectomy, Prostate Diseases, Bladder Diseases, Incontinence, Sexually Transmitted Diseases, Interstitial Cystitis, Female Urology, Pediatric Urology (limited). Georgetown University, Georgetown University School of Medicine, University of Miami Residency, New York State and Florida Board of Medicine, American Board of Urology, FACS. **Degrees/licenses:** MD (New York & FL), Amer. Board of Urology, FACS.

Richard D. Kane, MD

Urologist/President
Wake Urological Assoc.
4301 Lake Boone Trail, Ste. 300
Raleigh, NC 27607
Tel: (919) 782-1255
Fax: (919) 782-6056
E-mail: wakeurol@aol.com

Specialties: Impotence; Incontinence; Renal and Ureteral Calculi; Prostate Cancer; Bladder Cancer; Penile Prosthesis complications and repairs; Surgical complications of prostate treatment; Testicular Torsion; Vasectomy complications. Northwestern University, MD; Duke University, General Surgery, Urology; Extensive expert witness testimony and/or case reviews; Private practice with appointment as clinical professor of Urology, University of North Carolina. **Degrees/licenses:** BS, MD, Board Certified.

Edward Moss, MD

Urologist
Edward Moss, MD
108-28 68 Drive
Forest Hills, NY 11375
Tel: (718) 520-0028
Fax: (718) 520-1544
E-mail: ENM50@aol.com
Web Site: http://www.mossurology.com

Specialties: Urologist - Board Certified, academic appointment 20+ years experience: adult urology, M/F, kidneys, ureters, bladder, prostate and male sexual organs. Cancer prostate, bladder, kidneys, impotence, incontinence and stone disease. Telephone consultations, written reports/prompt service. **Degrees/licenses:** MD, New York State License.

Vascular

Arlene F. Hoffman, DPM, PhD

California Pacific Medical Center
2100 Webster St., Ste. 202
San Francisco, CA 94115-2375
Tel: (415) 923-3535
Fax: (415) 923-3672

Specialties: Medical evaluation and treatment of podiatric injuries; Perioperative evaluation;

Wound healing; Blood flow evaluation of the lower extremity; Use of pharmaceuticals and laboratory evaluation. PhD, Downstate Medical Center, SUNY; DPM, California College of Podiatric Medicine; Fellow, Stanford University College of Medicine. Previous/current positions: Professor; Chair, Exam Committee, American Board of Podiatric Orthopedics; Board Trustee, ABPOPPM, ASPM, ASPD, ASPA; Special Editor, "The Lower Extremity;" General Editor, "Journal of the American Podiatric Medical Association;" Editor, "Yearbook of Podiatric Medicine and Surgery." Recipient of the Meritorious Service Award, APMA. 35+ publications. **Degrees/licenses:** DPM, PhD.

See primary listing under MEDICINE & HEALTH: Podiatry

Vascular Surgery

C. Andrew Heiskell, MD, FACS

Medical Legal Consultants, Inc.
4000 Hampton Center, Ste. D
Morgantown, WV 26505
Tel: (304) 599-8665
Fax: (304) 599-8584
E-mail: info@heiskellmd.com
Web Site: http://www.heiskellmd.com

Specialties: Dr. Heiskell is a practicing General and Vascular Surgeon. Dr. Heiskell has been in private practice for 25 years and has been reviewing medical records for over 10 years, testifying on behalf of claimants, defendants and insurers in cases of general and vascular surgery, laparoscopic surgery, surgical malpractice and standards of care. He performs numerous operations yearly including hernia repairs, laparoscopic gallbladder surgery, surgeries of the breast, colon, stomach, pancreas, spleen, thyroid, carotid arteries and many other vascular procedures. **Degrees/licenses:** BS, MD, Board Certified.

See primary listing under MEDICINE & HEALTH: Surgery, General

Samuel H. Sadow, MD, FACS

529 South Flagler Drive, Suite 18-G
West Palm Beach, FL 33401
Tel: (772) 335-9800
Fax: (561) 833-8663
E-mail: ssadow5398@aol.com

Specialties: Extensive experience with litigation of Standards of Care, Causation, Plaintiffs/Defendants, Bylaws and Hospital Privileges issues. Private practice of Cardiovascular and Thoracic Surgery, 1985-present; Principal investigator for FDA Phase III Trials ATS Medical Heart Valve Study. MD 1973, Chicago Medical School. Re-Certified in Thoracic Surgery. **Degrees/licenses:** MD, FACS, Amer. Boards of Surgery & Thoracic Surgery.

See primary listing under MEDICINE & HEALTH: Cardiothoracic Surgery

Robert Wagmeister, MD

2001 Santa Monica Blvd., #1170-W
Santa Monica, CA 90404
Tel: (310) 828-5626
Fax: (310) 828-2826
E-mail: rwagmd@aol.com

Specialties: Vascular Surgery: diseases, trauma, & surgery of the circulation, both arterial and venous. Includes carotid artery, aneurysms, bypass surgery, dialysis surgery, amputations, pulmonary embolus, spine access, phlebitis. Birthdate: May 16, 1949. MD, Tufts Medical School, 1974. Special Certification in Vascular Surgery given by American Board of Surgery. Memberships: Southern California Vascular Surgery Society; Society for Vascular Surgery; Society for Clinical Vascular Surgery; Peripheral Vascular Surgery Society. Extensive experience in medical malpractice cases; numerous cases each year; depositions; expert witness; court appearance as required. **Degrees/licenses:** MD, FACS.

METEOROLOGY/ CLIMATOLOGY

General

Climatological Consulting Corporation

Contact: Lee E. Branscome, PhD, CCM
7338 155th Place North
Palm Beach Gardens, FL 33418
Tel: (561) 744-4889
Fax: (561) 744-5098
E-mail: lbranscome@ccc-weather.com
Web Site: http://www.ccc-weather.com

Specialties: Climatological Consulting Corporation, headed by Dr. Lee E. Branscome, specializes in forensic meteorology and climatology with an emphasis on aviation and marine weather, severe storms and hurricanes, floods, fog, air quality, and weather satellite and radar analysis. A staff of meteorologists in the Palm Beach Gardens, FL office is complemented by a nationwide team of Associates. Testifying experts are Certified Consulting Meteorologists by the American Meteorological Society. **Degrees/licenses:** MSs, PhDs, CCMs. Resumes available on request.

Compu-Weather Experts, Inc.

2566 Route 52
Hopewell Junction, NY 12533
Tel: (800) 825-4445
Fax: (800) 825-4441
E-mail: experts@compuweather.com
Web Site: http://www.compuweather.com

Specialties: Admiralty, tides, lighting conditions, pollution, lightning strike verification, slip and fall cases, severe weather, climate analysis; Services: Official weather records, Plain-English written reports, Depositions, Site visits, Expert testimony; A complete forensic meteorology and expert service with twenty (20) professional meteorologists on staff; We offer fast efficient service, the most extensive in-house archive of past-weather records, and experienced experts to answer your questions and testify in "plain-English;" Rush service available. **Degrees/licenses:** BA, BS, MA, MS, PhD, Consulting Meteorologists.

Cox Weather Services

Robert B. Cox
Consulting Meteorologist
125 Frisbie Street
Middletown, CT 06457
Tel: (888) 248-9347
Fax: (888) 248-9347
E-mail: bob@coxweatherservices.com
Web Site: www.coxweatherservices.com

Specialties: Forensic meteorology - determining past weather conditions for any U. S. location. Involved in over 700 cases since 1999. Expert witness testimony. Customized weather forecasting. Broadcast meteorologist. **Degrees/licenses:** BS, Meteorology.

See primary listing under LITIGATION SUPPORT: Weather

Expert Weather Investigations (EWI)

Thomas E. Downs,V
Forensic Meteorologist
450 Seventh Ave., Ste. 1308
New York, NY 10123
Tel: (212) 594-3348
Fax: (212) 629-5825
E-mail: info@expertweather.com
Web Site: http://www.expertweather.com

Specialties: Specialists in acquiring and analyzing past weather records (Establish liability or non-liability); Comprehensive reports and graphics using the latest scientific methods (Utilize demonstrative evidence); Highly competent testimony from qualified and credentialed experts (Maximize recovery). Meteorological assistance with Personal Injury/Slip & Fall, Auto accidents, Claim investigations, Construction delays, Structure damage, Agricultural losses, Working conditions, Health concerns, Audibility & Illumination conditions, etc. Scientific analysis of Snow, Ice, Rain, Wind, Extreme Cold and Heat, Fog, Thunderstorms, Hurricanes, Sun Angle, Air Pollution. Background affiliations: New York State Climatologist's

Office, Northeast Regional Climate Center (NCDC/NOAA). **Degrees/licenses:** CCM, PhD, BS, MS, AMS, NYAS, NCIM; Cornell, MIT, NYU, CCNY, NWS.

Falconer Weather Information Service, LLC

Phillip D. Falconer, CCM
7 Via Maria Drive
Scotia, NY 12302
Tel: (800) 428-5621
Fax: (518) 399-5320
E-mail: pfalcone@nycap.rr.com
Web Site: http://www.wxscape.com/FWIS

Specialties: Acquisition and analysis of past weather records; Evaluation of weather conditions relating to accidents; Preparation of easy-to-read, interpretive reports on weather incidents anywhere within the United States. Official weather record certification and rush services available. Previously qualified as expert meteorologist by both education (BS, Penn State, 1971; MS, University of Wisconsin, 1973) and over twenty-five years of professional experience and training. Numerous technical and popular articles and presentations on weather topics. Professional member: American Meteorological Society; National Council of Industrial Meteorologists. AMS Certified Consulting Meteorologist (no. 411). **Degrees/licenses:** BS, MS, CCM.

Forensic Meteorology Associates, Inc.

Walter A. Lyons, PhD, CCM
President
46050 Weld County Road 13
Ft. Collins, CO 80524
Tel: (970) 568-7664
Fax: (970) 482-8627
E-mail: walt.lyons@forensic-weather.com
Web Site: http://www.forensic-weather.com

Specialties: Litigation support and expert witness; Reconstruction of weather events including lightning strike verification; Severe weather impacts: Tornadoes, microbursts, hurricanes and winter storms; Coastal and mountain meteorology; Local scale weather systems and microclimates; Air pollution and related issues; Extensive in-house weather data archives and technical library for fast responses; Technical communication to lay audiences; Advanced computer graphics, simulation and visualization facilities; Video presentations; Nationwide service. Member: National Council of Industrial Meteorologists; 35 years experience in university and industrial research and television weathercasting. DEGREES/LICENSES: PhD (University of Chicago); Certified Consulting Meteorologist (No. 163); Fellow and 2005 President of the American Meteorological Society. **Degrees/ licenses:** PhD, CCM. See Above.

MET Associates

David L. Mitchell, PhD
Managing Director
& Consulting Forensic Meteorologist
P.O. Box 70
Dayton, TX 77535-0070
Tel: (936) 257-1633 (office)
(713) 301-0242 (mobile)
Fax: (936) 258-4237
E-mail: mitchelldl@metassociates.net
Web Site: http://www.metassociates.net

Specialties: Forensic Meteorology, Air Quality Modeling and Weather Event Reconstruction and Analysis for insurance claims; Litigation Support Services and Expert Witness Testimony in the areas of Toxic Tort, Air Pollution Modeling, Weather related events including flooding, wind damage and weather related losses. David L. Mitchell is an authority on the numerical modeling of geophysical data with a doctorate in Meteorology from Purdue University. Dr. Mitchell has over 25 years of technical modeling experience in industry and consulting. He is an expert on Atmospheric Fluid Dynamics, Air Dispersion Modeling and Air Pollution Meteorology. He holds Texas Board of Professional Geoscientists License No. 1330. **Degrees/licenses:** PhD, MS, Purdue University; BS, Baylor University; Cert. Prof. Geoscientist.

General *(cont.)*

Murray & Trettel, Inc.

Mark T. Carroll
Vice President/Consulting Meteorologist
600 N 1st Bank Drive, Ste A
Palatine, IL 60067-8185
Tel: (847) 963-9000 Ext. 130
Fax: (847) 963-0199
E-mail: mt@weathercommand.com
Web Site: www.weathercommand.com

Specialties: Since 1946. Sixteen full-time meteorologists. Forensic meteorology specialists. Written "plain-English" opinions, depositions, site visits and expert testimony on all weather related incidents including but not limited to slip and fall, aviation, rail, vehicle, wind damage, etc. Climatological studies. Lightning verification, radar and satellite analysis. Staff includes members of the American Meteorological Society (AMS), National Weather Association, Midwestern Regional Climate Center Advisory Panel, Northern Illinois University Advisory Panel, Nuclear Utility Meteorological Users Group, Illinois Association of Environmental Professionals. **Degrees/licenses:** MS, BS.

MINING

General

Walt Pachucki

President
TEAM Engineering & Management, Inc.
P.O. Box 1265
Bishop, CA 93515
Tel: (760) 872-1033
Fax: (760) 872-2131
E-mail: team@qnet.com

Specialties: Mining related accident reconstruction; Mineral processing related accident reconstruction; Mining related injury cases; Mining equipment maintenance issues; Mining Engineering; Mineral processing equipment cases; Heavy equipment maintenance evaluations; Heavy equipment failure analysis. MEMBER: National Society of Mining Engineers; Society of Mining Engineers of the American Institute of Mining and Metallurgical Engineers; California Mining Association; Nevada Mining Association; American Board of Forensic Examiners. **Degrees/licenses:** BSc Mining Eng., Calif. EPA Reg. Environmental Assessor.

Joseph G. Wargo

Consultant - Geology, Mineral Exploration
21 Birchwood Place
Moraga, CA 94556
Tel: (925) 376-1091
Fax: (925) 376-0959
E-mail: jwargo@aol.com

Specialties: Geology; Mineral property exploration; Economic geology; Negotiations; Evaluation of geologic and exploration data; Expert testimony; Mining history. "Qualified Person" per Canada NI 43-101. **Degrees/licenses:** PhD; Registered Geologist (CA #328); Certified Professional Geologist (#54).

See primary listing under GEOLOGY: Economic & Mineral Geology

Heavy Equipment Maintenance Mgt.

Walt Pachucki

President
TEAM Engineering & Management, Inc.
P.O. Box 1265
Bishop, CA 93515
Tel: (760) 872-1033
Fax: (760) 872-2131
E-mail: team@qnet.com

Specialties: Mining related accident reconstruction; Mineral processing related accident reconstruction; Mining related injury cases; Mining equipment maintenance issues; Mining Engineering; Mineral processing equipment cases; Heavy equipment maintenance evaluations; Heavy equipment failure analysis. MEMBER: National Society of Mining Engineers; Society of Mining Engineers of the American Institute of Mining and Metallurgical Engineers; California Mining Association;

Nevada Mining Association; American Board of Forensic Examiners. **Degrees/licenses:** BSc Mining Eng., Calif. EPA Reg. Environmental Assessor.

See primary listing under MINING: General

MOTION PICTURES

General

Capt. Hugh M. Stephens, CSP, PE

President
Nautical Holdings Corp.
464 Main St., Suite 307
Port Washington, NY 11050
Tel: (516) 944-9600 (Winter)
(207) 622-9409 (Summer)
(504) 812-3786 (Cell)
E-mail: stephenssos2@aol.com

Specialties: Commercial merchant vessels, including supply, ROV and "frac" boats and ferries, Dynamic Positioning/Recreational Boating/Motion picture accident/Personal injury investigation. Collisions, Marine tankers, Confined space/Rescue/Slips/Falls, Marina casualties. Pres./Founder Marine Safety Engineering Firm. Positions in steamship industry: V.P. Operations, Marine Mgr., Marine Supt., Port Captain. Dredging & Repair Supt. Yacht Broker/Manager. Chartering Supervisor, Universal Marine Executive, Kevin Costner's feature film "Waterworld." Vice President No. Atl., Council American Master Mariners. Member Natl. Cargo Bureau, Commodore, Cobbosseecontee Yacht Club, Manchester, ME, Standing Committee Marine Society - NY. Certified Safety Professional, Professional Engineer - Safety Engineering (CA). **Degrees/licenses:** USCG Unlimited Ocean Master & First Class Pilot, Radar Operator, STCW95, GMDSS.

See primary listing under MARITIME & ADMIRALTY: Consulting

PACKAGING

General

Sterling Anthony

100 Renaissance Center - 43176
Detroit, MI 48243
Tel: (313) 531-1875
Fax: (313) 531-1972
E-mail: sterlinganthony@msn.com

Specialties: Personal injury and product liability cases requiring expertise in: package research & development; package design; labeling & warnings; palletizing & unitizing; regulatory compliance; performance testing. Experienced in consumer and industrial products. Thirty-year career as an industry employee, university instructor, consultant, and expert. Many publications and speaking engagements. Hold professional certifications in packaging, material handling, material management, purchasing, product & inventory control, and transportation. Member of the Human Factors and Ergonomics Society. **Degrees/licenses:** BS Packaging; MBA; PhD courses in Marketing & Logistics.

Chemical Accident Reconstruction Services, Inc.

Michael Fox, PhD
Founder
9121 E. Tanque Verde Rd., #105
Tucson, AZ 85749-8391
Tel: (800) 645-3369
Fax: (520) 749-0861
E-mail: services@chemaxx.com
Web Site: http://www.chemaxx.com

Specialties: Complex industrial chemical accidents, fires and explosions as well as chemical-related consumer product injuries. The founder of the company has his PhD in Physical Chemistry, is a Certified Fire & Explosion Investigator and Certified or Accredited in Hazardous Chemicals, OSHA Process Hazard Analysis Team Leader, DOT Hazardous Materials, Corrosion, Metallurgy, Failure

(Listing continued on next page)

General *(cont.)*

Chemical Accident Reconstruction Services, Inc. (cont.)
Analysis and Aerosols. Other specialties include: Propane, plastics, water chemistry, skin burns, acids, alkalis, carbon monoxide, flammable liquids, gasoline, scanning microscopy, MSDSs, natural gas, solvents, warning labels, PEX, welding, construction, chemical packaging & transport. For more specialties see web site. **Degrees/licenses:** PhD, Physical Chemistry; See certifications above.

See primary listing under CHEMISTRY/ CHEMICALS: General

Plastic Containers

Plastic Technologies, Inc.

Thomas E. Brady, PhD
President, CEO & Founder
1440 Timberwolf Drive
Holland, OH 43528-0964
Tel: (419) 867-5400
Fax: (419) 867-7700
E-mail: info@plastictechnologies.com or
t.brady@plastictechnologies.com
Web Site: www.plastictechnologies.com

Specialties: Plastic packaging, containers, closures, processing, orientation, blow molding, injection molding, recycling, design, testing, failure analysis, plastic materials analysis, PET, PVC, PE, PP. Legal: patents, litigation, licensing, technology transfer, court experience. Business: 30 years experience, patents, publications, R&D, manufacturing, business development; small business start up, operations, customer service. Personal: VP of Technology at Fortune 100 Company, Founder and President of leading PET R&D company and world class recycling company, Entrepreneur of the Year 1989, Small Business Man of the Year 1996, Amer. Management Award 1995, Ohio Technology Board. **Degrees/licenses:** BS, MS Dartmouth; PhD Univ. of Michigan.

Plastic Containers and Closures

GE Campbell & Associates

Ed Campbell, CPP
Sole Proprietor
1583 Spinnaker Dr., Ste. 212
Ventura, CA 93001
Tel: (805) 650-7388
E-mail: gecanda@idock.com
Web Site:
http://www.blowmolding.org/package.htm

Specialties: Ed Campbell has more than 40 years of experience in the field of blow molding plastic bottles in research and development, manufacturing, quality control and engineering of blow molding and packaging. He has 14 patents in plastic container packaging and blow molding technology. Mr. Campbell is the Sole Proprietor of G.E. CAMPBELL & ASSOCIATES, an international consulting firm catering to the unique needs of the plastic container packaging industry. In addition to plastic containers (blow molded bottles), Ed is also an expert in plastic closures, particularly regulated closures for child resistance and tamper evidency. **Degrees/licenses:** BS, Certified Packaging Professional (CPP).

PARKS & RECREATION

General

InterCity Testing & Consulting

167 Willis Avenue
Mineola, NY 11501
Tel: (516) 747-8400 (NY)
(800) 822-1515 (Outside NYS)
Fax: (516) 746-0121/0111 (NY)
Tel: (561) 745-7940 (FL)
Fax: (561) 745-7939 (FL)
E-mail: exptl@aol.com
Web Site: http://www.InterCityTesting.com

3550 Watt Ave., Ste. 5
Sacramento, CA 95821
Tel: (916) 481-3093
(800) 500-5561 (Toll Free)
Fax: (916) 481-3095

Specialties: Visit our web site for condensed expert CV's in: Amusement Parks & Rides; Automotive Safety & Accident Reconstruction; Biomedical/Biomechanical Injury Analysis; Biomechanics; Boating & Marine Safety; Chemicals & Chemical Engineering; Civil Engineering/Structural Failures; Construction Accidents; Electrical & Mechanical Engineering; Firearms & Explosives; Fire Investigations; Flammable Fabrics; Helmets/ Motorcycle, Bicycle, Sports & Industrial; Machine Guarding; Medical Devices; Medical Emergency/EMT; Metallurgy & Material Sciences; Parks & Playgrounds; Slips, Trips & Falls; Sports/Recreation/Aquatics; Toxicology; Transportation & Highway Safety; Warnings & Instructions. INTERCITY IS NOT AN EXPERT REFERRAL SERVICE. **Degrees/licenses:** PE's / degrees thru PhD's in above specialties.

See primary listing under ACCIDENT RECONSTRUCTION: General

Safety Play, Inc.

Scott Burton
— Free Air Fare —
Main Office:
10460 Roosevelt Blvd., #295
St. Petersburg, FL 33716
Tel: (888) 878-0244 (Toll Free)
(727) 522-0061
Fax: (727) 522-0061
E-mail: safetyplay@mindspring.com
Web Site:
http://www.mindspring.com/~safetyplay

California Office:
7095 Hollywood Blvd., #1308
Los Angeles, CA 90028

Specialties: Free air fare (minor restrictions apply, one round trip). Instructor for safety courses. Expert in playground, sports, and recreation accidents including playgrounds, soccer, trampolines, water, baseball, football, softball, basketball, volleyball, fitness equipment, exercise trails, etc. Investigation of warnings, ADA compliance, supervision, hazards, layout, design, surfacing, and inspections for risk management, parks and recreation, schools, facilities, amusement parks, resorts, day care centers, hotels, restaurants, etc. Voting member on ASTM committees creating national standards and CPSC guidelines. Ex-manufacturer who is experienced in expert testimony, manufacturing, design, planning, inspections, installations, recreational safety courses and manuals. Created Safety Signs and inspection tools. **Degrees/licenses:** Certified Playground Safety Inspector, Instructor, Bus. Deg.

See primary listing under RECREATION: General

PHOTOGRAPHY

Nighttime

Harris Visibility Studies, Inc.

James L. Harris, Sr.
2699 Camino Artemisa
Alpine, CA 91901
Tel: (619) 659-3827
Fax: (619) 659-3824
E-mail: JSr@hvsi.com

Specialties: Visibility issues in aviation (mid-airs & wirestrikes), automobile, motorcycle, pedestrian, and railroad crossing accidents; Sun/moon calculations, measurements of natural and artificial lighting including street lights and headlights; Characteristics of the human visual system such as foveal and peripheral contrast detection thresholds, fixations and visual search, the role of expectancy and its impact on perception-reaction; Nighttime photography using technique published in the Journal of Forensic Sciences; Quality computer animations and static simulations designed to accurately illustrate visibility issues; Defense against inaccurate computer animations. **Degrees/licenses:** BSEE.

See primary listing under ACCIDENT RECONSTRUCTION: Visibility

PRODUCT LIABILITY

General

A. C. T. International

Bernd S. Givon, PE & Associates
8306 Wilshire Blvd., #88
Beverly Hills, CA 90211
Tel: (310) 652-3221
Fax: (310) 652-3291
E-mail: actintl@netscape.com

Specialties: Forty-five years experience in consumer products evaluation, testing, failure analysis, industrial, commercial & domestic accident reconstruction; Investigate misuse, abuse, hazards & safety; Slip, trip & fall; Chairs, appliances, office & juvenile furniture; Playground and exercise equipment injuries; Bicycles and wheelchairs; Toys; Conveyors, power tools & ladders; Glass breakage; Textiles and fabric flammability, burn & scalding mishaps; Building materials; Gates, doors, windows & hardware; Damage assessment; Automotive accessories defects; Critique instructions & warnings; Detailed CV & fee schedule available upon request. **Degrees/licenses:** PhD, MS Mech Eng., PE (CA & NJ).

See primary listing under ENGINEERING: Forensic

Paul Doppelt

Consultant
PD Consultant, Inc.
9330 Karlov
Skokie, IL 60076
Tel: (847) 674-6242
(847) 674-6236
Fax: (847) 674-6242
E-mail: pauldinc@aol.com

Specialties: Over 30 years experience evaluating children's products for safety and overall design integrity, including such product categories as toys, plush dolls, juvenile products, child car seats, tricycles, children's bicycles, wheeled riding vehicles, and indoor and outdoor playground equipment. Can also provide analysis of the product's user instructions, warnings, and age grading. Member of the ASTM committees on toy safety, juvenile products safety and playground equipment safety. Participant in the development of the CPSC's regulations on toy safety. Member of the Midwest Society of Professional Consultants. **Degrees/licenses:** BS Mech. Engr. (Design), IL Inst. of Tech.

See primary listing under ACCIDENT PREVENTION & SAFETY: Children's Products

ForensisGroup, Inc.

Mercy Steenwyk
3452 E. Foothill Blvd., Ste. 1160
Pasadena, CA 91107
Tel: (626) 795-5000
(800) 555-5422
Fax: (626) 795-1950
E-mail: experts@forensisgroup.com
Web Site: http://forensisgroup.com

Specialties: Thousands of our clients have gained the technical advantage and the edge in their cases from our multidisciplined group of experts in hundreds of disciplines. We have some of the best and the brightest at competitive rates backed by 14 years of excellent track record and the support of our trained staff. We assist you until you have the right expert. Some of our areas of expertise are: Construction, Safety, Engineering, Product Liability, Accident Reconstruction, Automotive, Environmental, Slip & Fall, Appraisal, Medical and other scientific disciplines. Unsurpassed standards. Clients actively evaluate our experts. **Degrees/licenses:** PE, GC, CSP, PhD, MD, GC, CIH, AIA.

See primary listing under ACCIDENT PREVENTION & SAFETY: General

GTS Global Turbine Specialists

Arthur Eckstat, BSME, MBA, DBA
President
P.O. Box 130
Chandler, AZ 85244-0130
Tel: (602) 670-9651
Fax: (480) 380-2551
E-mail: GTSeckstat@qwest.net
Web Site: http://www.JurisPro.com/mem/ArthurEckstat

Specialties: Dr. Eckstat provides consulting, forensic investigation and expert witness services for Industrial and Consumer Products ranging from appliances to watercraft, including firearms. He was honored as a Contributor to Aviation History at the Smithsonian National Air & Space Museum in Washington, DC. After two days of direct testimony and cross-examination in a lawsuit against two Fortune 100 companies, the lead attorney stated that Arthur Eckstat was the best witness he'd had in over 20 years of practice. Just his Initial Expert Report is usually sufficient to result in a settlement. **Degrees/licenses:** BSME, MBA, DBA.

Marvin Kaminsky, PhD, DABT

President
Toxcor Associates, Inc.
P.O. Box 454
Flanders, NJ 07836
Tel: (973) 252-0204
Fax: (973) 252-4424
E-mail: kaminsky@toxcor-associates.com
Web Site: http://toxcor-associates.com

Specialties: Over 25 years experience in toxicology and product safety evaluation and assessment of pharmaceuticals, consumer healthcare and personal care products, cosmetics, chemicals, and household products. Expert witness and scientific support in product liability and toxic injury litigation. Board certified. Member of: Society of Toxicology, American College of Toxicology, American Chemical Society, American College of Forensic Examiners, and International Society of Regulatory Toxicology and Pharmacology. **Degrees/licenses:** PhD, Diplomate Amer. Bd. of Toxicology, Cert. Amer. Bd. of Forensic Examiners.

See primary listing under MEDICINE & HEALTH: Toxicology

Richard G. Pearson, PhD, F.Erg.S., CPE

Sage Forensics
5441 Blue Sage Drive
Raleigh, NC 27606
Tel: (919) 828-2443
Fax: (919) 836-8971
E-mail: rpearson@sageforensics.com
Web Site: http://www.sageforensics.com

Specialties: Forensic Consultant in Human Factors and Safety; Industrial and Consumer Products: design, safety, liability; Failure to Warn: signs, product labels, user manuals, instructions; Occupational Accidents: agriculture, construction, electrical; OSHA/Industry Standards; Machine Guarding; Highway Accidents: driver perception and reaction

(Listing continued on next page)

General *(cont.)*

Richard G. Pearson, PhD (cont.)
time; Human performance, attention, fatigue, human error. Professor Emeritus, Industrial Engineering, North Carolina State University; Consultant: National Institute of Occupational Safety and Health, Dupont, GE, Westinghouse; Fellow, four professional societies; Member ASTM, SAE, NSC. Over 60 publications. **Degrees/licenses:** MS, PhD, Cert. Prof. Ergonomist, F.Erg.S. (United Kingdom).

See primary listing under ACCIDENT PREVENTION & SAFETY: Human Factors

Marc H. Richman

One Richmond Square
Providence, RI 02906
Tel: (401) 751-9656
Fax: (401) 751-9210
E-mail: MHRichman@aol.com
Web Site:
www.marchrichmanengineering.com

Specialties: Product liability: adequacy of warnings & instructions; Design & manufacturing defects; Safety & guarding; Causation; Normal & foreseeable uses; Alternative designs. Affiliation: Brown University (Professor Emeritus, Engineering); Marc H. Richman, Inc. (President). **Degrees/licenses:** ScD; PE.

See primary listing under ENGINEERING: Metallurgical

Technology Associates

Dr. I.U. Ojalvo
President
137 E. 36th St., Ste. 7K
New York, NY 10016
Tel: (800) 358-9909
Fax: (888) 358-9901
E-mail: iuo@Technology-Assoc.com
Web Site: www.Technology-Assoc.com

1011 High Ridge Rd., 2nd Floor
Stamford, CT 06905
Tel: (203) 329-9909

5030 Champion Blvd., PMB 315
Boca Raton, FL 33496
Tel: (800) 358-9909

Specialties: Machinery; Fall downs; Structures; Construction; Ladders; Shopping Carts; Warnings; Human factors; Biomechanics; Sports & Playgrounds; Swimming pools; Codes & standards; Computer animation; Vehicles; Roadways; Pedestrians; Electric shock; etc. (over 1,400 cases); Testing; Consulting and testimony for defendants & plaintiffs in metropolitan NY area, New England, Florida & surrounding areas; Professors and licensed Professionals in Mechanical, Biomechanical and Electrical Engineering with many publications; Additional specialties in fires, floods, whiplash and other forms of soft tissue and skeletal injuries; Clients include most major insurance companies, municipalities and numerous private law firms (See listings under Accident Reconstruction & Engineering). **Degrees/licenses:** BS, MS, PhD, Lic. PE, Fellow ASME, US Fulbright.

See primary listing under ACCIDENT RECONSTRUCTION: General

See display advertisement on page 18

David Yadin

President
Biomedical Engineering Consultants
1111 Hermann Dr., Ste. 12B
Houston, TX 77004
Tel: (713) 522-6666
Fax: (713) 522-6686
E-mail:
ybdavid@texaschildrenshospital.org
Web Site: http://www.biomedeng.com

Specialties: Testing, evaluating, servicing, & repairs of Medical Devices & accessories. Over 25 years of expertise practicing at the world's largest medical center. Failure analysis & electromagnetic (EMI) compatibility investigation & assessment of infusion pumps, anesthesia machines, lasers & telemedicine. Directing comprehensive biomedical engineering program within hospital & home-care environments. Member of regulatory agency (FDA) panel & standards developing association (NFPA). Past president & founder of American College of Clinical Engineering (ACCE). President, Center for Telemedicine Law (CTL). Registered professional engineer (PE), certified clinical engineer (CCE), certified healthcare safety executive (HSPC), Fellow American Institute of Medical & Biological Engineering (AIMBE). **Degrees/licenses:** BSc, MSc, EdD, PE, CCE, HSPC, FAIMBE, FACCE. See above.

See primary listing under MEDICINE & HEALTH: Medical Devices, Equip.

Petroleum Products

Dellem Associates, Inc.

Larry S. Weaver
President
14023 No. Dale Mabry Hwy
Tampa, FL 33618-2401
Tel: (813) 963-5353
Fax: (813) 962-3164
E-mail: lweaver@dellem.com
Web Site: http://www.dellem.com

Specialties: Fuel storage facilities (specializing in Aviation Fuel facilities both on and off airports), including the construction, maintenance and operation of various types of petroleum facilities and the training and testing of personnel in handling petroleum products. Specifically for Aviation Fuel, we provide verification of specifications; determination of composition and potential sources of contamination; aircraft fueling procedures; operational safety and training of personnel. Member, ASTM Tech J - Development of aviation fuel specifications. **Degrees/licenses:** United States Naval Academy, BS; New York University, MBA.

Jewitt & Associates Fuels Technology

Carlton H. Jewitt
President
17572 Plumera Ln.
Fort Myers, FL 33917
Tel: (239) 731-2124
Fax: (239) 731-2124
E-mail: chjewitt@strato.net

Specialties: Thirty nine year career in petroleum fuels technology and technical services. Professional experience includes management, research, environmental, health and safety. Managed fuels technical services group providing support throughout Ashland Petroleum Division to key operating groups including Supply and Distribution, Trucks and Terminals, Refinery Sales, Marine, Pipeline, Bulk Plants and retail operations of Ashland and SuperAmerica. Conventional, reformulated, racing gasolines; diesel, aviation and renewable fuels; fuel oils. Ashland Petroleum representative (1/81 - 9/95) to the Coordinating Research Council Oil/Auto Research Committee. Former Chairman (6/85 - 12/95) ASTM Diesel Fuels Subcommittee. Accomplished technical writer. **Degrees/licenses:** BS Chemistry; ASTM & SAE Fuels Technical Committees.

Petroleum Products *(cont.)*

Maurice E. Le Pera

President
Le Pera and Associates
1050 Kiln Drive
Harrisonburg, VA 22801-8577
Tel: (540) 432-0991
Fax: (540) 432-0989
E-mail: melepera@aol.com
Web Site: http://www.melepera.com

Specialties: Petroleum product applications; gasoline; diesel fuels; turbine fuels; alternate fuels; engine and gear oils; hydraulic and brake fluids; greases; lubricants; preservatives; antifreeze and coolants; automotive applications; specification development; utilization criteria; quality assurance and testing; engineering evaluations; field problem solving; product substitutions; compatibility assessments; engine performance testing; validation of product claims; energy conservation and pollution prevention; recycling and reclamation; storage procedures. University of Delaware, BS chemistry; University of Delaware Graduate School, MS course work completed; Recipient of DOD Defense Standardization and Meritorious Civilian Service Awards; Numerous publications; member of professional societies. **Degrees/licenses:** BS.

PSYCHIATRY

General

Accredited Psychiatry & Medicine

Harvard Medical School
Alumni & Faculty Experts
Tel: (617) 492-8366
Fax: (617) 441-3195
E-mail: harold_bursztajn@hms.harvard.edu
Web Site: http://www.forensic-psych.com

Specialties: Psychiatry, Forensic Psychiatry, Legal Medicine & Analysis, Managed Care, Testamentary Capacity, Addiction, Product Liability, Neuropsychiatric, Medical Employment & Discrimination, Toxic Torts, Independent Medical Examinations & Testing, Professional Ethics, Expert Testimony, Custodial Issues, Criminal Justice & Public Safety, Diminished Capacity, PTSD. Plaintiff and defense expert with local and national references. Over twenty five years of service as a distinguished patient care-focused clinician and as senior clinical faculty at Harvard Medical School; Co-Director of the Program in Psychiatry and the Law and Associate Professor of Psychiatry at the Harvard Medical School. **Degrees/licenses:** BA, MD, Lic.: MA, NH, National Dual Medical Board Certification.

Dominick Addario, MD

Psychiatry
3010 First Avenue
San Diego, CA 92103
Tel: (619) 295-2189
Fax: (619) 295-2362
E-mail: info@addario.com
Web Site: http://www.addario.com

Specialties: Medical and Hospital Malpractice, Brain Injury, Personal Injury, Harassment, Trauma, WC Disability, Will Contests-Competence, Fiduciary/HMO/provider-contract issues. Extensive IME experience Defense/ Plaintiff. Keynote Speaker, Expert Testimony. References from major firms on request. Diplomate, Amer. Board of Psychiatry and Neurology; Distinguished Fellow, American Psychiatric Association; Qualified Medical Examiner, State of California; Clinical Professor of Psychiatry, University of California, School of Medicine, San Diego. Offices also in San Francisco Bay Area, Palm Springs, Los Angeles and Riverside County. **Degrees/ licenses:** MD, QME (CA); See above.

Lawson F. Bernstein, MD

MD - Forensic Neuropsychiatry
P. O. Box 81977
Pittsburgh, PA 15217
Tel: (412) 600-7996
Fax: (412) 422-5203
E-mail: lawsonbernstein@hotmail.com
Web Site: http://www.ifbmdpc.com

Specialties: Board certified academically published forensic neuropsychiatrist. Expertise in brain injury, stroke, neurotoxicology, acute/chronic pain, dementia, alcohol & substance abuse, gambling addiction and multiple other areas of neurology/psychiatry. Extensive criminal/civil trial (50/50) Plaintiff/ Defense experience, including death penalty cases/legal insanity/diminished capacity. From 1991-1994, Dr. Bernstein was Director of the Psychiatry Residency Training Program at the University of Pittsburgh Medical Center, one of the largest academic psychiatric training programs in the U.S. Dr. Bernstein is also a Board Examiner for the American Board of Psychiatry & Neurology Oral Examination. **Degrees/licenses:** Medical.

See primary listing under MEDICINE & HEALTH: Head Injury

Samuel Black, MD

924 Westwood Blvd., Ste 660
Los Angeles, CA 90024
Tel: (310) 208-5892
Fax: (310) 208-2302
E-mail: samblackmd@aol.com

Specialties: General psychiatry, sexual harassment, wrongful termination, medical malpractice, stress disorders, psychopharmacology, child custody. Review of medical records, IME. No charge for initial phone contact. References, CV and rates sent on request. Assistant Clinical Prof. UCLA School of Medicine; Attending Staff, Cedars-Sinai Medical Center; Major, US Army Medical Corps. Both defense and prosecution; experienced in-court appearance. 30 years in practice. **Degrees/licenses:** Doctor of Medicine, Board Certified, Psychiatry.

Alvin C. Burstein, MD

Well Being Systems
5070 N. 40th St., Ste. 220
Phoenix, AZ 85018-2135
Tel: (602) 957-2368
Fax: (602) 957-0050
E-mail: aburstein@wbsaz.com

Specialties: Adult Psychiatry; Geriatric Psychiatry; Standard of care for psychiatric units, hospitals, geriatric psych. units, managed care companies, psychiatrists; Analyze interactions psychiatric, medical, side effects, substance abuse, intoxication issues; Psychopharmacology; Explain clinical issues for case presentation; private practice of psychiatry, Medical Director of psych. HMO, and psychiatric hospital and Geriatric Psych. Unit; Excellent reputation, teacher, communicator. Associate Professor of Psychiatry. **Degrees/licenses:** MD, AZ; Board Certified.

Brian Crowley, MD

5225 Connecticut Ave., N.W., Suite 215
Washington, DC 20015
Tel: (202) 537-3300
Fax: (301) 365-8644
E-mail: bcrowleymd@aol.com
Web Site: www.drcrowley.yourmd.com

Specialties: Forensic Psychiatry, Civil & Criminal: Malpractice; Fitness for Duty; Independent Medical Examinations; Testamentary Capacity and Undue Influence; Personal Injury; Suicide; Stalking; Sexual Harassment/ Abuse; Sexual Misconduct by Professionals; Posttraumatic Stress Disorder; Professional Ethics & Peer Review; Hospital and Outpatient Treatment Standards; Recovered Memories; Workplace Violence; Dangerousness Assessments; Sanity; Trial Competency; Diminished Capacity. Doctor Crowley, a Yale Medical School graduate, is Past Chief of Psychiatry at his hospital. He is past President, Washington Psychiatric Society; Distinguished Life Fellow, American Psychiatric Association; Fellow, American Academy of Psychoanalysis, and has often testified as an expert in federal and state courts. Available as Expert nationally. **Degrees/licenses:** MD, DLFAPA; Licensed in Maryland & DC.

See primary listing under MEDICINE & HEALTH: Psychiatry

General *(cont.)*

General & Forensic Psychiatry

Pogos Hagop Voskanian, MD
Assistant Professor of Psychiatry
Director, MCP-Hahnemann Univ.
Psychiatry & Law Program
1240 Serota Place
Philadelphia, PA 19115
Tel: (215) 938-7227
Fax: (215) 938-7474
E-mail: drvoskanian@aol.com
Web Site: www.forensic-psychiatrist.com

Specialties: Forensic Psychiatric Evaluations, Consultations and Expert Witness Testimony in civil and criminal cases... for plaintiff, defense, prosecution, courts, insurance companies and governmental agencies. Dr. Voskanian is certified by the American Board of Psychiatry and Neurology in Psychiatry and Forensic Psychiatry. In private practice, Dr. Voskanian specializes in comprehensive evaluations in a wide range of forensic issues including: Insanity Defense, Capital Sentencing, Disability Determinations, Workers' Compensation, Psychiatric Harm, Personal Injury, Psychiatric Malpractice, Discrimination, Sexual Harassment, ADA, Americans with Disabilities Act, various civil and criminal competencies, etc. **Degrees/licenses:** MD - Univ. of Mass.; Board Cert. in Psychiatry & Forensic Psychiatry.

George S. Glass, MD

George S. Glass, MD, PA
4600 Post Oak Place, Suite 307
Houston, TX 77027
Tel: (713) 666-9811
Fax: (713) 627-3488

Specialties: Dr. Glass is a Distinguished Fellow of the American Psychiatric Association, A Board Certified Psychiatrist and Addictionologist. He has spent more than 30 years involved in the treatment of people with Substance Abuse Problems as well as in the development of Inpatient and Outpatient Psychiatric and Substance Abuse Treatment Programs and Employee Assistance Programs. He is a Consultant to the Texas Board of Medical Examiners, the Texas Bar Association, the FAA, the Airline Pilots Association, and numerous other companies. He has had Academic Appointments at both Baylor School of Medicine and the University of Texas Medical School in Houston. **Degrees/licenses:** MD, Board Certified Psychiatrist, Addictionologist.

See primary listing under MEDICINE & HEALTH: Alcohol/Drugs

Gilbert W. Kliman, MD

Medical Director
The Psychological Trauma Center
a division of Preventive Psychiatry
Assoc. Med. Group, Inc.
2105 Divisadero Street
San Francisco, CA 94115
Tel: (415) 292-7119
Fax: (415) 749-2802
E-mail: gil.kliman@cphc-sf-org

Specialties: Our center's mission includes evaluation of allegations within the justice system concerning psychological injuries to children. Defense or plaintiff initiated cases accepted without prejudice. Board certified child psychiatrists, psychologists, social workers, MFTs, educators and interns provide objective interdisciplinary evaluations and authoritative testimony nationwide including federal courts. Expertise includes institutional neglect and abuse of children, psychological trauma, malpractice, therapeutic residential care, and childhood posttraumatic disorders. Scientific bulletins, rates, case experience, CV's, attorney references, CLE videotapes, and sample retainer are on www.gilbertkliman.yourmd.com. **Degrees/licenses:** MD, Diplomate Am. Bd. Psychiatry, A. Ac. Child & Adol. Psych.

Jerald H. Ratner, MD

9750 NW 33rd St., Ste. 211
Coral Springs, FL 33065
Tel: (954) 752-9450
Fax: (954) 752-9888

Specialties: Independent Medical Examinations, Malpractice, Competency, Malingering, Medical Records Review, Psychotropic Drug Reactions. Former Chairman of Psychiatry at two hospitals; Fellow, College of Physicians of Philadelphia; Board Certified in Psychiatry; Diplomate, American Board of Forensic Medicine; Diplomate, American Board of Forensic Examiners; Fellow, American Psychiatric Association. **Degrees/licenses:** MD, DABFM, DABFE, FCPP, DABPN, FAPA.

Martin H. Williams, PhD

Clinical & Forensic Psychologist
P.O. Box 62439
Sunnyvale, CA 94088
Tel: (888) 225-9957
Fax: (888) 225-9957
E-mail: mw@drmwilliams.com
Web Site: http://drmwilliams.com

Specialties: Dr. Williams is a psychologist and psychotherapist who testifies on malpractice and emotional damages. He is an expert on sexual harassment, boundary violations, therapist patient sex, malingering, post traumatic stress disorder and borderline personality disorder. He has published in refereed journals on harmfulness of therapist-patient sexual involvement, ethics, risk management and malpractice. He is in full-time clinical practice, is licensed in California and testifies nationally. Offices in Los Angeles, San Jose, Orange County and San Diego. **Degrees/licenses:** PhD in Psychology (1975); Calif. Licensed Psychologist (1976).

See primary listing under MEDICINE & HEALTH: Psychology

Norman L. Wilson, MD, PC

Psychiatrist
Norman L. Wilson, MD, PC
3000 Connecticut Ave. N. W. #306
Washington, DC 20008
Tel: (202) 362-8660
Fax: (202) 483-3314
E-mail: wilsonwash@aol.com
Web Site:
http://www.drnormanwilson.yourmd.com

Specialties: Group & individual psychotherapy; Post-Traumatic Stress and Dissociative disorders; Psychopharmacology; Sexual harassment; Criminal responsibility; Compentency; Diminished capacity; Independent medical (psychiatric) evaluations; Forensic evaluations and testimony; Litigation support. Has testified in civil and criminal cases in D. C. Maryland, VA and FL, and has reviewed cases in PA and OH. Worked part-time with D. C. Forensic Services for fifteen years. Assistant Clinical Professor in Psychiatry, George Washington University. Former Chairman, Department of Psychiatry at Washington Hospital Center. Board-certified in psychiatry by the American Board of Neurology and Psychiatry. Distinguished Life Fellow of the American Psychiatric Association. Certified consultant in hypnosis by the American Society for Clinical Hypnosis. BS degree in Biophysics from Yale (Magna Cum Laude); MD degree in Medicine from Harvard Medical School. **Degrees/licenses:** MD (DC medical license #MD4506) (VA medical license #010135855).

Adolescent/Child

Vivian Alvarez, PhD

Clinical and Forensic Psychologist
Vivian Alvarez, PhD
12304 Santa Monica Blvd, Suite 210
Los Angeles, CA 90025
Tel: (310) 473-1210
Fax: (310) 473-7750
E-mail: vivianalvarez@netzero.net

Specialties: Psychological Evaluation and psychotherapy of children, adolescents, and adults. Specializing in post-trauma reactions (vehicular accidents, dog bites, fire/explosion, crime, assault); child sexual abuse; child suggestibility; wrongful death of parent or spouse; sexual harassment; learning disabilities; psychoeducational evaluations; special education issues. Bilingual (Spanish and English) and bicultural. Currently Assistant Clinical Professor, UCLA Dept. of Psychiatry and Biobehavioral Sciences; Clinical Psychologist, L.A. County Dept. of Mental Health; Many depositions and trial testimony for plaintiff and defense. Member: Phi Beta Kappa; Member: American Psychological Association; Member: American College of Forensic Examiners; Member: American Professional Society on the Abuse of Children. **Degrees/licenses:** PhD in Clinical Psychology (UCLA); Licensed Psychologist PSY10817.

Adolescent/Child *(cont.)*

Lawson F. Bernstein, MD

MD - Forensic Neuropsychiatry
P. O. Box 81977
Pittsburgh, PA 15217
Tel: (412) 600-7996
Fax: (412) 422-5203
E-mail: lawsonbernstein@hotmail.com
Web Site: http://www.ifbmdpc.com

Specialties: Board certified academically published forensic neuropsychiatrist. Expertise in brain injury, stroke, neurotoxicology, acute/chronic pain, dementia, alcohol & substance abuse, gambling addiction and multiple other areas of neurology/psychiatry. Extensive criminal/civil trial (50/50) Plaintiff/Defense experience, including death penalty cases/legal insanity/diminished capacity. From 1991-1994, Dr. Bernstein was Director of the Psychiatry Residency Training Program at the University of Pittsburgh Medical Center, one of the largest academic psychiatric training programs in the U.S. Dr. Bernstein is also a Board Examiner for the American Board of Psychiatry & Neurology Oral Examination. **Degrees/licenses:** Medical.

See primary listing under MEDICINE & HEALTH: Head Injury

Child Abuse

Vivian Alvarez, PhD

Clinical and Forensic Psychologist
Vivian Alvarez, PhD
12304 Santa Monica Blvd, Suite 210
Los Angeles, CA 90025
Tel: (310) 473-1210
Fax: (310) 473-7750
E-mail: vivianalvarez@netzero.net

Specialties: Psychological Evaluation and psychotherapy of children, adolescents, and adults. Specializing in post-trauma reactions (vehicular accidents, dog bites, fire/explosion, crime, assault); child sexual abuse; child suggestibility; wrongful death of parent or spouse; sexual harassment; learning disabilities; psychoeducational evaluations; special education issues. Bilingual (Spanish and English) and bicultural. Currently Assistant Clinical Professor, UCLA Dept. of Psychiatry and Biobehavioral Sciences; Clinical Psychologist, L.A. County Dept. of Mental Health; Many depositions and trial testimony for plaintiff and defense. Member: Phi Beta Kappa; Member: American Psychological Association; Member: American College of Forensic Examiners; Member: American Professional Society on the Abuse of Children. **Degrees/licenses:** PhD in Clinical Psychology (UCLA); Licensed Psychologist PSY10817.

See primary listing under PSYCHIATRY: Adolescent/Child

Lawson F. Bernstein, MD

MD - Forensic Neuropsychiatry
P. O. Box 81977
Pittsburgh, PA 15217
Tel: (412) 600-7996
Fax: (412) 422-5203
E-mail: lawsonbernstein@hotmail.com
Web Site: http://www.ifbmdpc.com

Specialties: Board certified academically published forensic neuropsychiatrist. Expertise in brain injury, stroke, neurotoxicology, acute/chronic pain, dementia, alcohol & substance abuse, gambling addiction and multiple other areas of neurology/psychiatry. Extensive criminal/civil trial (50/50) Plaintiff/Defense experience, including death penalty cases/legal insanity/diminished capacity. From 1991-1994, Dr. Bernstein was Director of the Psychiatry Residency Training Program at the University of Pittsburgh Medical Center, one of the largest academic psychiatric training programs in the U.S. Dr. Bernstein is also a Board Examiner for the American Board of Psychiatry & Neurology Oral Examination. **Degrees/licenses:** Medical.

See primary listing under MEDICINE & HEALTH: Head Injury

Forensic Psychiatry

Lawson F. Bernstein, MD

MD - Forensic Neuropsychiatry
P. O. Box 81977
Pittsburgh, PA 15217
Tel: (412) 600-7996
Fax: (412) 422-5203
E-mail: lawsonbernstein@hotmail.com
Web Site: http://www.ifbmdpc.com

Specialties: Board certified academically published forensic neuropsychiatrist. Expertise in brain injury, stroke, neurotoxicology, acute/chronic pain, dementia, alcohol & substance abuse, gambling addiction and multiple other areas of neurology/psychiatry. Extensive criminal/civil trial (50/50) Plaintiff/ Defense experience, including death penalty cases/legal insanity/diminished capacity. From 1991-1994, Dr. Bernstein was Director of the Psychiatry Residency Training Program at the University of Pittsburgh Medical Center, one of the largest academic psychiatric training programs in the U.S. Dr. Bernstein is also a Board Examiner for the American Board of Psychiatry & Neurology Oral Examination. **Degrees/licenses:** Medical.

See primary listing under MEDICINE & HEALTH: Head Injury

Ned P. Masbaum, MD

PO Box 3010
Carmel, IN 46082
Tel: (317) 846-7727
Fax: (317) 575-1898
E-mail: NPM.FORNPSYCH@att.net
Web Site: http://www.FORNPSYCH.com

Specialties: Psychiatry; Forensic Psychiatry; Medical-Legal Consultation; Competency; Insanity defense; Post-traumatic Stress Disorder; Spousal Abuse; Criminal prosecution or defense; Civil cases. Affiliation: Private Practice, Medical Staff, Clarian✱Methodist Hospital. Board Certified, American Board of Psychiatry & Neurology, in Psychiatry & Forensic Psychiatry. **Degrees/licenses:** MD; Licensed (IN).

See primary listing under MEDICINE & HEALTH: Psychiatry

Forensic Psychology

Vivian Alvarez, PhD

Clinical and Forensic Psychologist
Vivian Alvarez, PhD
12304 Santa Monica Blvd, Suite 210
Los Angeles, CA 90025
Tel: (310) 473-1210
Fax: (310) 473-7750
E-mail: vivianalvarez@netzero.net

Specialties: Psychological Evaluation and psychotherapy of children, adolescents, and adults. Specializing in post-trauma reactions (vehicular accidents, dog bites, fire/explosion, crime, assault); child sexual abuse; child suggestibility; wrongful death of parent or spouse; sexual harassment; learning disabilities; psychoeducational evaluations; special education issues. Bilingual (Spanish and English) and bicultural. Currently Assistant Clinical Professor, UCLA Dept. of Psychiatry and Biobehavioral Sciences; Clinical Psychologist, L.A. County Dept. of Mental Health; Many depositions and trial testimony for plaintiff and defense. Member: Phi Beta Kappa; Member: American Psychological Association; Member: American College of Forensic Examiners; Member: American Professional Society on the Abuse of Children. **Degrees/ licenses:** PhD in Clinical Psychology (UCLA); Licensed Psychologist PSY10817.

See primary listing under PSYCHIATRY: Adolescent/Child

R. Mark Binderman, PhD

Clinical Psychologist
3615-F Chain Bridge Road
Fairfax, VA 22030-3237
Tel: (703) 691-1010
Fax: (202) 645-8733
E-mail: rmbin@verizon.net

Specialties: Forensic psychological evaluations: sex offenders, recidivism risk; violence risk assessment; competence; sentencing; diagnosis, treatment recommendations. Testified before state and federal courts. Participation in over 100 cases. Advanced training and

(Listing continued on next page)

Forensic Psychology *(cont.)*

R. Mark Binderman, PhD (cont.)
certification in violence, and in sex offenders. Testified on sexual sadism/homicide cases, and on assassination attempt case. Published chapters: "Identifying Violence Risk Factors" and "Understanding the Violence Risk Assessment Guide." Authority on relationship of mental illness to violence. **Degrees/licenses:** PhD, Psychology, 1974; Lic. in VA, Wash. DC, TN.

See primary listing under MEDICINE & HEALTH: Psychology

John Watts Podboy

PO Box 488
Kenwood, CA 95452
Tel: (707) 833-6023
Fax: (707) 833-5224

Specialties: Forensic psychology; Psychodiagnostics; Forensic consultant to State & Federal Courts throughout California. Licensed Psychologist in private practice. See Dr. Podboy's biographical information under his primary listing of MEDICINE & HEALTH: Psychology on page 387. **Degrees/licenses:** PhD (Rehabilitation Psychology); MS (Counseling); BA (Psychology).

See primary listing under MEDICINE & HEALTH: Psychology

Head Injury

Martin Blinder, MD

Assistant Clinical Professor, Psychiatry
50 Idalia Road
San Anselmo, CA 94960
Tel: (415) 453-8920

Specialties: Extensive experience with nationwide court appearances in the following areas: Criminal responsibility; Eye witness identification; Head injuries; Malingering; Psychiatric malpractice; Sexual harassment/molestation; Testamentary capacity and undue influence; Wrongful termination. Professional Experience: (Adjunct) Assistant Professor of Law, Hastings; Supervising Psychiatist, Inpatient Psychiatric Service, UC Hospital; Psychiatric Consultant; FAA, U. S. Department of Justice, USPHS, U. S. Postal Service, Government of New Zealand; Qualified Medical Examiner, CA Department of Industrial Relations. Fellow, APA. Professional Societies: AMA, CMA, NCPS. More than 100 publications, including 6 books. **Degrees/licenses:** BA, Cornell University; MD, Chicago Medical School; Lic. (CA, GA, HI, KY).

See primary listing under IDENTIFICATION: Eyewitness

Post-Traumatic Stress

Addiction Forensics Group

Mace Beckson, MD
11301 West Olympic Blvd. #323
Los Angeles, CA 90064
Tel: (310) 966-1907
Fax: (310) 477-0661
E-mail: becksonmd@becksonmd.com
Web Site: http://www.becksonmd.com

Specialties: Alcohol/drugs; addiction; suicide; PTSD; sex offenders; child molestation; sexual abuse; adult victims of childhood abuse; rape; violence; stalking; threat assessment; risk assessment; sexual addiction; impaired physicians; Medical Board; psychiatric malpractice; therapist misconduct; boundary violations; brain injury; neuropsychiatry; disability; competence to stand trial; insanity defense; sentencing; involuntary hospitalization; civil commitment. UCLA full-time faculty; Assoc. Clin. Prof.; Board-certified in Addiction/Forensic Psych; Certified Addiction Medicine; Distinguished Fellow, APA; Med. Director, Psychiatric Intensive Care, VA; Addiction Psych. Cmtee, AAPL; Expert Reviewer, CA Med Board; Suicidal Behavior Root Cause Analysis Team, VA; Chair, Task Force on Adolescent Addiction, ASAP; Sex Offender Cmtee, AAPL. **Degrees/licenses:** MD, Board Certified: Psych, Addiction Psych, Forensics.

See primary listing under MEDICINE & HEALTH: Alcohol/Drugs

Vivian Alvarez, PhD

Clinical and Forensic Psychologist
Vivian Alvarez, PhD
12304 Santa Monica Blvd, Suite 210
Los Angeles, CA 90025
Tel: (310) 473-1210
Fax: (310) 473-7750
E-mail: vivianalvarez@netzero.net

Specialties: Psychological Evaluation and psychotherapy of children, adolescents, and adults. Specializing in post-trauma reactions (vehicular accidents, dog bites, fire/explosion, crime, assault); child sexual abuse; child suggestibility; wrongful death of parent or spouse; sexual harassment; learning disabilities; psychoeducational evaluations; special education issues. Bilingual (Spanish and English) and bicultural. Currently Assistant Clinical Professor, UCLA Dept. of Psychiatry and Biobehavioral Sciences; Clinical Psychologist, L.A. County Dept. of Mental Health; Many depositions and trial testimony for plaintiff and defense. Member: Phi Beta Kappa; Member: American Psychological Association; Member: American College of Forensic Examiners; Member: American Professional Society on the Abuse of Children. **Degrees/licenses:** PhD in Clinical Psychology (UCLA); Licensed Psychologist PSY10817.

See primary listing under PSYCHIATRY: Adolescent/Child

Lawson F. Bernstein, MD

MD - Forensic Neuropsychiatry
P. O. Box 81977
Pittsburgh, PA 15217
Tel: (412) 600-7996
Fax: (412) 422-5203
E-mail: lawsonbernstein@hotmail.com
Web Site: http://www.ifbmdpc.com

Specialties: Board certified academically published forensic neuropsychiatrist. Expertise in brain injury, stroke, neurotoxicology, acute/chronic pain, dementia, alcohol & substance abuse, gambling addiction and multiple other areas of neurology/psychiatry. Extensive criminal/civil trial (50/50) Plaintiff/Defense experience, including death penalty cases/legal insanity/diminished capacity. From 1991-1994, Dr. Bernstein was Director of the Psychiatry Residency Training Program at the University of Pittsburgh Medical Center, one of the largest academic psychiatric training programs in the U.S. Dr. Bernstein is also a Board Examiner for the American Board of Psychiatry & Neurology Oral Examination. **Degrees/licenses:** Medical.

See primary listing under MEDICINE & HEALTH: Head Injury

George S. Glass, MD

George S. Glass, MD, PA
4600 Post Oak Place, Suite 307
Houston, TX 77027
Tel: (713) 666-9811
Fax: (713) 627-3488

Specialties: Dr. Glass is a Distinguished Fellow of the American Psychiatric Association, A Board Certified Psychiatrist and Addictionologist. He has spent more than 30 years involved in the treatment of people with Substance Abuse Problems as well as in the development of Inpatient and Outpatient Psychiatric and Substance Abuse Treatment Programs and Employee Assistance Programs. He is a Consultant to the Texas Board of Medical Examiners, the Texas Bar Association, the FAA, the Airline Pilots Association, and numerous other companies. He has had Academic Appointments at both Baylor School of Medicine and the University of Texas Medical School in Houston. **Degrees/licenses:** MD, Board Certified Psychiatrist, Addictionologist.

See primary listing under MEDICINE & HEALTH: Alcohol/Drugs

Norman L. Wilson, MD, PC

Psychiatrist
Norman L. Wilson, MD, PC
3000 Connecticut Ave. N. W. #306
Washington, DC 20008
Tel: (202) 362-8660
Fax: (202) 483-3314
E-mail: wilsonwash@aol.com
Web Site:
http://www.drnormanwilson.yourmd.com

Specialties: Group & individual psychotherapy; Post-Traumatic Stress and Dissocia-

(Listing continued on next page)

Post-Traumatic Stress *(cont.)*

Norman L. Wilson, MD (cont.)

tive disorders; Psychopharmacology; Sexual harassment; Criminal responsibility; Compentency; Diminished capacity; Independent medical (psychiatric) evaluations; Forensic evaluations and testimony; Litigation support. Has testified in civil and criminal cases in D. C. Maryland, VA and FL, and has reviewed cases in PA and OH. Worked part-time with D. C. Forensic Services for fifteen years. Assistant Clinical Professor in Psychiatry, George Washington University. Former Chairman, Department of Psychiatry at Washington Hospital Center. Board-certified in psychiatry by the American Board of Neurology and Psychiatry. Distinguished Life Fellow of the American Psychiatric Association. Certified consultant in hypnosis by the American Society for Clinical Hypnosis. BS degree in Biophysics from Yale (Magna Cum Laude); MD degree in Medicine from Harvard Medical School. **Degrees/ licenses:** MD (DC medical license #MD4506) (VA medical license #010135855).

See primary listing under PSYCHIATRY: General

Sexual Harassment

Samuel Black, MD

924 Westwood Blvd., Ste 660
Los Angeles, CA 90024
Tel: (310) 208-5892
Fax: (310) 208-2302
E-mail: samblackmd@aol.com

Specialties: General psychiatry, sexual harassment, wrongful termination, medical malpractice, stress disorders, psychopharmacology, child custody. Review of medical records, IME. No charge for initial phone contact. References, CV and rates sent on request. Assistant Clinical Prof. UCLA School of Medicine; Attending Staff, Cedars-Sinai Medical Center; Major, US Army Medical Corps. Both defense and prosecution; experienced in-court appearance. 30 years in practice. **Degrees/licenses:** Doctor of Medicine, Board Certified, Psychiatry.

See primary listing under PSYCHIATRY: General

Suicidology

Ronald W. Maris, PhD

Professor Emeritus
Suicide Center
University of South Carolina
305 Sloan Bldg., 911 Pickens St.
Columbia, SC 29208
Tel: (803) 777-6870
(803) 240-3073 (Cell)
(803) 736-6042 or 736-0365 (Res.)
Fax: (803) 777-5251 or 865-3946 (Res.)
E-mail: maris@sc.edu or rwmaris@aol.com
Web Site: http://www.suicideexpert.com

Home Office
9 Poachers Lane
Columbia, SC 29223-3014

Specialties: Suicide Death Investigation; Suicide Risk Assessment & Suicide Prediction; Medical Malpractice; Drug Liability (especially SSRI cases); Contested Life Insurance; Equivocal Death Investigation (suicide v. homicide v. accident); Small Plane Crashes; Workplace Violence Assessment. Past-President American Association of Suicidology, Past Editor-in-Chief of Suicide Journal; Fellow in American Academy of Forensic Sciences (Psychiatry); Board certified Forensic Examiner and Fellow; Author/editor of 20 books (incl. National Book-of-the-Month); Assoc. Professor - Johns Hopkins School of Medicine; 5 post-doctoral fellowships in psychiatry. **Degrees/licenses:** PhD, Fellow - ACFE, Fellow - AAFS.

PUBLISHING

General

Bay Sherman Craig & Goldstein, LLP

Peter M. Craig
Hal Jaffe
11845 W. Olympic Blvd. #845
Los Angeles, CA 90064
Tel: (310) 477-1400
Fax: (310) 479-0720
E-mail: craigp@bscgllp.com
Web Site: http://magazineconsulting.com or http://baysherman.com

Specialties: All aspects of publishing litigation support and expert witness services including valuations, forensic accounting and financial analysis, damages, mergers and acquisitions; Experienced in testimony; Over 50 years combined experience; Published book on magazine finance, accounting and valuation; Over 150 seminars on various publishing financial topics. **Degrees/licenses:** BS, CPA.

Philip K. Ruggles

Printing Management Services
PO Box 46
San Luis Obispo, CA 93406
Tel: (805) 543-5968
Fax: (805) 543-9579
E-mail: pruggles@charter.net

Specialties: Litigation/consulting services for printing, publishing & allied graphic imaging industries; Damage evaluation for insurance; Quality systems; Safety issues; Training; Extensive knowledge of graphic arts business practices & manufacturing methods; Print estimating & costing methods; Evaluation of marketing, selling & pricing for traditional & digital products & services; Computer management systems for print manufacturing & printing company operation; Print production workflow; Prepress, litho sheetfed & web print production; Postpress production; Distribution of printed goods; Digital print production; Affiliation: Distinguished Emeritus Professor, California Polytechnic State University (Graphic Communication/Printing Management); Textbook author. **Degrees/licenses:** BS; MS.

See primary listing under GRAPHIC ARTS/PRINTING: General

REAL ESTATE

General

Advisors/Experts @ MCS Associates

Norman Katz
Managing Partner
18881 Von Karman Ave., Ste. 1175
Irvine, CA 92612-1569
Tel: (949) 263-8700
Fax: (949) 263-0770
E-mail: info@mcsassociates.com
Web Site: http://www.mcsassociates.com

Specialties: Nationally recognized banking, financial services, real estate consulting group; Experienced expert witnesses and consultants include bankers, lenders, insurance managers, brokers, agents, economists, securities brokers, trust fiduciaries, appraisers, accountants. Expertise: Bank operations, check fraud; Lending policies, procedures; Loan administration, foreclosures, bankruptcy; Lender liability; D&O Liability; Insurance (Life, Disability, Property & Casualty, Reinsurance, Surplus) underwriting, claims handling, bad faith; Broker duties, agency management; Title insurance & escrow; R/E brokerage, leasing, property management, appraisal, development, construction defects; Business valuation, lost profits, damages assessment; Forensic accounting; Securities brokerage, trading, investment suitability; Economic & statistical analysis. **Degrees/licenses:** MBA, PhD, CPA, CLU, CPCU, CFP, CFA, CREA, MAI, ASA.

See primary listing under FINANCE: Commercial Banking

General *(cont.)*

B & F Experts, Inc.

Financial Institutions, Business, Mortgage, Finance, Banking
J. F. "Chip" Morrow
Principal
Nationwide from San Antonio, TX
Tel: (866) 365-7212 (Toll Free)
Fax: (866) 869-4062 (Toll Free)
E-mail: jfmorrow@earthlink.net
Web Site: http://www.jfmorrow.com

Specialties: 35+ years management for financial institutions and business. 31+ years bank and mortgage lending experience funding 10+ billion. 18+ years President, CEO &/or Director. 7+ years mortgage company director and 22+ years mortgage lending. 15+ years leadership in state/national financial trade associations. 150+ nationwide cases: approximately 50% defendants and 50% plaintiffs. 40% cases for financial institutions, 40% against and 20% non-financial institution. Prepared court presentations, court testimonies, reports, declarations, findings, affidavits and other for Federal, bankruptcy and state courts. Cases involving financial institutions, businesses, lending, mortgage, lender liability, D/O, checks, operations and others.

See primary listing under FINANCE: General

Steven Cohen, Esq.

President
Cohen & Associates, Inc.
2530 Wilshire Blvd, 3rd Floor
Santa Monica, CA 90403
Tel: (310) 315-5404
Fax: (310) 315-5408
E-mail: scohen@litigationbusters.com
Web Site: http://www.litigationbusters.com

Specialties: Real Estate/Construction Specialist and Attorney with extensive experience in the following areas: Construction Defects; Construction Contract Disputes; Mold Inspection/Remediation; Risk Analysis; Mechanical Defects; Electrical Defects; Structural Defects; Real Estate; HOA, DRE, CSLB Rules & UBC Compliance. General/Electrical Contractor; Graduate level certified in Dispute Resolution. **Degrees/licenses:** Atty; JD-MBA; RE Broker; Gen/Electric Contractor.

See primary listing under CONSTRUCTION: General

ForensisGroup, Inc.

Mercy Steenwyk
3452 E. Foothill Blvd., Ste. 1160
Pasadena, CA 91107
Tel: (626) 795-5000
(800) 555-5422
Fax: (626) 795-1950
E-mail: experts@forensisgroup.com
Web Site: http://forensisgroup.com

Specialties: Thousands of our clients have gained the technical advantage and the edge in their cases from our multidisciplined group of experts in hundreds of disciplines. We have some of the best and the brightest at competitive rates backed by 14 years of excellent track record and the support of our trained staff. We assist you until you have the right expert. Some of our areas of expertise are: Construction, Safety, Engineering, Product Liability, Accident Reconstruction, Automotive, Environmental, Slip & Fall, Appraisal, Medical and other scientific disciplines. Unsurpassed standards. Clients actively evaluate our experts. **Degrees/licenses:** PE, GC, CSP, PhD, MD, GC, CIH, AIA.

See primary listing under ACCIDENT PREVENTION & SAFETY: General

Samuel K. Freshman, BA, JD

President
Standard Management Company
6151 W. Century Blvd., Suite 300
Los Angeles, CA 90045
Tel: (310) 410-2300
Fax: (310) 410-2919
E-mail:
sfreshman@standardmanagement.com

Specialties: Attorney, Real Estate Broker, Banker, Professor, Legal Malpractice, Arbitration, Brokerage, Malpractice, Leases, Syndication, Construction, Property Management, Finance, Due Diligence, Conflict of Interest, Title Insurance, Banking, Escrow. 32 years State & Federal Courts. 29 articles. Mediator,

Fidicuary Duties, Lease Inerpretation, Banking Title Company President. **Degrees/licenses:** BA, JD, California Bar, U. S. Supreme Court & District Court, U. S. Tax Court.

E. Robert Miller, CPM, CIPS, ACD, CMC

President
E. Robert Miller & Associates
330 Primrose Rd., Ste. 606
Burlingame, CA 94010
Tel: (650) 373-0705
Fax: (650) 373-0709
E-mail: elymiller@hotmail.com
Web Site: http://www.erobertmiller.com

Specialties: Expert in property management issues for all types of commercial and residential real estate. Experienced in arbitration, litigation, lease terms, personal injury, property damage, security, standards of care, due diligence. Over 175 case assignments; Past President, 83,000 apartment units, 14 million sq. feet office building, shopping centers, industrial buildings; Who's Who in California; Property Manager of the Year; IREM Academy of Authors; Past National President, Institute of Real Estate Management; Past Secretary General, World Property Management Committee; NAR Board of Directors. Published over 30 articles in national management and financial publications; Instructor: IREM, NAR, Colleges. **Degrees/licenses:** BS, Univ. of Wisconsin; CPM, CIPS, ACD, CMC; Broker.

See primary listing under REAL ESTATE: Property Management

Appraisal

BTI Appraisal

Ben F. Tunnell III
Chairman
605 West Olympic Blvd., Ste. 820
Los Angeles, CA 90015
Tel: (213) 532-3800
Fax: (213) 532-3807
E-mail: ben@btiappraisal.com
Web Site: http://www.btiappraisal.com

Specialties: BTI Appraisal offers litigation and appraisal experience, nationally and internationally, since 1974 in the areas of: Real Estate, Machinery & Equipment, and Business Valuation. We represent attorneys, insurance companies, governments, financial institutions and corporations for insurance claims, condemnations, and IRS and SEC issues. Well-written and documented reports reduce litigation costs and speed dispute resolution. Our work has passed the most rigorous scrutiny of the IRS, the SEC, government condemning agencies and state and federal courts. The collective experience of our nationally regarded professionals can address projects of all sizes and locations.

See primary listing under APPRAISAL & VALUATION: General

Commercial

Peter R. Roca

CEO & President
Global Real Estate Services Group, Inc.
8511 Valley Sage Rd.
Agua Dulce, CA 91390-2854
Tel: (661) 268-1592
Fax: (661) 268-1593
E-mail: Peter@GlobalServicesGroup.com
Web Site: http://GlobalServicesGroup.com

Specialties: Real Property Transaction Matters; Property Management & Leasing Practices; Deposition Preparation; Brokerage Practices; Standards of Care; Analysis of Deposition and Trial Testimony of Witnesses & Experts; Document Review; Disclosure

(Listing continued on next page)

Commercial *(cont.)*

Peter. R. Roca (cont.)
Requirements; Strategy Recommendations; Deposition and Trial Testimony; Assistance in Preparation of Deposition and Trial Plans for the Examination of Witnesses & Experts; Assistance with Pleadings, Motions, Briefs, and Declarations; Agency; Lease Audits; Customs & Practices. 24 years experience; Published Author; Real estate Review; Taught Real Estate related material at University level; Past President, BOMA San Diego. Will travel anywhere. Reasonable fee structure/rates. **Degrees/licenses:** JD, MBA, CCIM, CPM, RPA, FMA; Calif. R/E Broker, Receiver.

See primary listing under REAL ESTATE: Property Management

Consulting

Charles B. Warren, ASA

Principal
Warren & Warren
2033 Powell Street
San Francisco, CA 94133
Tel: (415) 433-0959
Fax: (415) 982-1441
E-mail: cbw@apo.com
Web Site: http://www.slip.net/~cjwarren

Specialties: Land economic studies, feasibility, cost/benefit analysis, entitlements research, remote sensing and imagery - acquisition and interpretation, seismic analysis. **Degrees/ licenses:** BA, Univ. of Calif.-Berkeley; Post Grad. Studies; Cert. General Appraisal Lic.

See primary listing under APPRAISAL & VALUATION: Real Estate

Finance

JRB Associates

John R. Britt
24208 Heritage Lane
Newhall, CA 91321-3536
Tel: (661) 255-0090
Fax: (661) 255-0091
E-mail: jrbassoc@earthlink.net
Web Site: http://www.bankingexpert.com

Specialties: Lender liability; Credit; Loan review and analysis; Bank operations; New accounts; Deposit and check fraud; Code of conduct; Branch administration; Board of Directors; Personnel; Previous experience as senior executive of major bank and President and CEO of two independent banks; Claremont McKenna College, BA, Business and Economics; Graduate, Pacific Coast Banking School, University of Washington; Deposition and trial experience since 1989; Board Certified Forensic Examiner and Fellow, American Board of Forensic Examiners. Forty years experience in the financial services industry. **Degrees/licenses:** BA: Business & Economics.

See primary listing under FINANCE: Commercial Banking

Lender Liability

B & F Experts, Inc.

Financial Institutions, Business,
Mortgage, Finance, Banking
J. F. "Chip" Morrow
Principal
Nationwide from San Antonio, TX
Tel: (866) 365-7212 (Toll Free)
Fax: (866) 869-4062 (Toll Free)
E-mail: jfmorrow@earthlink.net
Web Site: http://www.jfmorrow.com

Specialties: 35+ years management for financial institutions and business. 31+ years bank and mortgage lending experience funding 10+ billion. 18+ years President, CEO &/or Director. 7+ years mortgage company director and 22+ years mortgage lending. 15+ years leadership in state/national financial trade associations. 150+ nationwide cases: approximately 50% defendants and 50% plaintiffs. 40% cases for financial institutions, 40% against and 20% non-financial institution. Prepared court presentations, court testimonies, reports, declarations, findings, affidavits and other for Federal, bankruptcy and state courts. Cases involving financial institutions, businesses, lending, mortgage, lender liability, D/O, checks, operations and others.

See primary listing under FINANCE: General

Lending

B & F Experts, Inc.

Financial Institutions, Business,
Mortgage, Finance, Banking
J. F. "Chip" Morrow
Principal
Nationwide from San Antonio, TX
Tel: (866) 365-7212 (Toll Free)
Fax: (866) 869-4062 (Toll Free)
E-mail: jfmorrow@earthlink.net
Web Site: http://www.jfmorrow.com

Specialties: 35+ years management for financial institutions and business. 31+ years bank and mortgage lending experience funding 10+ billion. 18+ years President, CEO &/or Director. 7+ years mortgage company director and 22+ years mortgage lending. 15+ years leadership in state/national financial trade associations. 150+ nationwide cases: approximately 50% defendants and 50% plaintiffs. 40% cases for financial institutions, 40% against and 20% non-financial institution. Prepared court presentations, court testimonies, reports, declarations, findings, affidavits and other for Federal, bankruptcy and state courts. Cases involving financial institutions, businesses, lending, mortgage, lender liability, D/O, checks, operations and others.

See primary listing under FINANCE: General

Property Inspection

Steven Cohen, Esq.

President
Cohen & Associates, Inc.
2530 Wilshire Blvd, 3rd Floor
Santa Monica, CA 90403
Tel: (310) 315-5404
Fax: (310) 315-5408
E-mail: scohen@litigationbusters.com
Web Site: http://www.litigationbusters.com

Specialties: Real Estate/Construction Specialist and Attorney with extensive experience in the following areas: Construction Defects; Construction Contract Disputes; Mold Inspection/Remediation; Risk Analysis; Mechanical Defects; Electrical Defects; Structural Defects; Real Estate; HOA, DRE, CSLB Rules & UBC Compliance. General/Electrical Contractor; Graduate level certified in Dispute Resolution. **Degrees/licenses:** Atty; JD-MBA; RE Broker; Gen/Electric Contractor.

See primary listing under CONSTRUCTION: General

Property Management

Paul Kastes, CPM, LCAM

President
Principals Management Group, Inc.
2897 Avon Ct.
Palm Harbor, FL 34684
Tel: (813) 601-9727
Fax: (727) 773-1627
E-mail: paulkastescpm@aol.com
Web Site: www.pinellas.com/~principals

Specialties: Real Estate Property Management for income producing properties including apartments, office buildings, malls, etc. Over 30 years of "hands on" property management experience. Present portfolio includes properties in several states. As an active member of the real estate profession, I bring current, valid, and real world experience to assist both plaintiff and defense attorneys. I have provided testimony in premises liability cases including murders,

(Listing continued on next page)

Property Management *(cont.)*

Paul Kastes (cont.)
rapes, assaults, slip and falls, and contractual issues. Current references and CV on request. Certified Property Manager (CPM), Licensed Condominium Association Manager (LCAM), Certified Protection Officer Instructor (CPOI). **Degrees/licenses:** See above.

E. Robert Miller, CPM, CIPS, ACD, CMC

President
E. Robert Miller & Associates
330 Primrose Rd., Ste. 606
Burlingame, CA 94010
Tel: (650) 373-0705
Fax: (650) 373-0709
E-mail: elymiller@hotmail.com
Web Site: http://www.erobertmiller.com

Specialties: Expert in property management issues for all types of commercial and residential real estate. Experienced in arbitration, litigation, lease terms, personal injury, property damage, security, standards of care, due diligence. Over 175 case assignments; Past President, 83,000 apartment units, 14 million sq. feet office building, shopping centers, industrial buildings; Who's Who in California; Property Manager of the Year; IREM Academy of Authors; Past National President, Institute of Real Estate Management; Past Secretary General, World Property Management Committee; NAR Board of Directors. Published over 30 articles in national management and financial publications; Instructor: IREM, NAR, Colleges. **Degrees/licenses:** BS, Univ. of Wisconsin; CPM, CIPS, ACD, CMC; Broker.

Peter R. Roca

CEO & President
Global Real Estate Services Group, Inc.
8511 Valley Sage Rd.
Agua Dulce, CA 91390-2854
Tel: (661) 268-1592
Fax: (661) 268-1593
E-mail: Peter@GlobalServicesGroup.com
Web Site: http://GlobalServicesGroup.com

Specialties: Real Property Transaction Matters; Property Management & Leasing Practices; Deposition Preparation; Brokerage Practices; Standards of Care; Analysis of Deposition and Trial Testimony of Witnesses & Experts; Document Review; Disclosure Requirements; Strategy Recommendations; Deposition and Trial Testimony; Assistance in Preparation of Deposition and Trial Plans for the Examination of Witnesses & Experts; Assistance with Pleadings, Motions, Briefs, and Declarations; Agency; Lease Audits; Customs & Practices. 24 years experience; Published Author; Real estate Review; Taught Real Estate related material at University level; Past President, BOMA San Diego. Will travel anywhere. Reasonable fee structure/rates. **Degrees/licenses:** JD, MBA, CCIM, CPM, RPA, FMA; Calif. R/E Broker, Receiver.

Title

Petru Corporation

Timothy B. Truwe
President
250 S. Hallock Drive, Suite 100
Santa Paula, CA 93060
Tel: (805) 933-1389
Fax: (805) 933-1380

Specialties: Title, resource, and land consulting company with extensive consulting and expert witness experience in the following areas: Title Research; Title Engineering; Oil, Gas, Mineral & Geothermal; Regulatory Compliance; Due Diligence; Water Rights; Subdivision Map Act; Rights-of-Way; Title Insurance. Petru Corporation has provided its services on multi-million dollar projects and complex litigation. **Degrees/licenses:** Reg. Land Professional; Reg. Environmental Assessor.

RECREATION

General

Daniel P. Connaughton, EdD

P.O. Box 118208
Gainesville, FL 32611
Tel: (352) 392-0584 ext. 1296
Fax: (352) 392-7588
E-mail: danc@hhp.ufl.edu
Web Site: http://www.sportliability.com

Specialties: Consultant, researcher, and expert witness in personal injury cases involving sports, recreation, physical education, aquatics, diving, and fitness & health club activities. University professor & fitness program director. Teach "Legal Issues in Exercise & Sport." Dissertation: "Negligence Liability in Aquatics" (drowning, near-drowning, & spinal cord injuries). Doctorate in Physical Education, MS in Recreation, MS & BS in Exercise Science. Experienced participant, coach, administrator, & educator of many sports, recreation & aquatic activities. Certifications: ASEP Coaching Instructor, ACSM Health/Fitness Instructor, CSCS, numerous Red Cross Instructor certifications, Certified Park & Recreation Professional, Pool Operator. **Degrees/licenses:** EdD, MS, BS; EMT; Certifications: ACSM, NSCA, NRPA, ASEP, NSPF.

See primary listing under RECREATION: Sports

Marc A. Rabinoff

President
Rabinoff Consulting Services, Inc.
7600 W. Coal Mine Ave., Unit "A"
Littleton, CO 80123
Tel: (303) 972-3428
Fax: (303) 972-3428
E-mail: marc62aus@aol.com

Specialties: Personal injuries: gymnastics & trampolines, aquatics, health clubs, playgrounds, weight rooms, athletics, physical education and educational administration; Sports facilities (injuries & risk management); Product liability (sports injuries). Affiliation: Metropolitan State College of Denver (Professor and Chair, Department of Human Performance, Sport & Leisure Studies). **Degrees/licenses:** EdD.

Recreation & Sports Forensic of Recreation Safety Institute

Arthur H. Mittelstaedt, Jr., EdD
Paul Bosch, MPA, Assoc. Executive Director
Box 392
Ronkonkoma, NY 11779
Tel: (516) 883-6399
Fax: (516) 883-1814

Specialties: Educational & recreational facility negligence cases: pools, waterfronts, playgrounds, parks, camps, amusements, gyms, sports fields, fitness centers, golf courses. **Degrees/licenses:** All staff hold appropriate degrees & licenses for their specialties.

Reiner Associates, Inc.

Bert Reiner
President
10643 Angelo Tenero
Las Vegas, NV 89135
Tel: (702) 838-8997
(860) 716-4075 (Cell)
Fax: (702) 838-8669
E-mail: bert@reinerinc.com
Web Site: www.reinerinc.com/expert.html

Specialties: Playground equipment, infant/juvenile furniture, sporting goods, swimming pools, bicycles, toys. Multifunctional engineering consulting firm providing in-depth expert testimony & research-development, engineering, model-making, quality assurance & manufacturing. 30+ years experience in design of toys, sporting goods, swimming pools, playground equipment & juvenile furniture. Standards: UL, CSA, ASTM, ANSI, CPSC. **Degrees/licenses:** BSME; Member: TIA, ASME, ACFE, IEEE, SPE.

General *(cont.)*

Safety Play, Inc.

Scott Burton
— Free Air Fare —
Main Office:
10460 Roosevelt Blvd., #295
St. Petersburg, FL 33716
Tel: (888) 878-0244 (Toll Free)
(727) 522-0061
Fax: (727) 522-0061
E-mail: safetyplay@mindspring.com
Web Site:
http://www.mindspring.com/~safetyplay

California Office:
7095 Hollywood Blvd., #1308
Los Angeles, CA 90028

Specialties: Free air fare (minor restrictions apply, one round trip). Instructor for safety courses. Expert in playground, sports, and recreation accidents including playgrounds, soccer, trampolines, water, baseball, football, softball, basketball, volleyball, fitness equipment, exercise trails, etc. Investigation of warnings, ADA compliance, supervision, hazards, layout, design, surfacing, and inspections for risk management, parks and recreation, schools, facilities, amusement parks, resorts, day care centers, hotels, restaurants, etc. Voting member on ASTM committees creating national standards and CPSC guidelines. Ex-manufacturer who is experienced in expert testimony, manufacturing, design, planning, inspections, installations, recreational safety courses and manuals. Created Safety Signs and inspection tools. **Degrees/licenses:** Certified Playground Safety Inspector, Instructor, Bus. Deg.

TASA

(Technical Advisory Service for Attorneys)
1166 DeKalb Pike
Blue Bell, PA 19422-1853
Tel: (800) 523-2319
Fax: (800) 329-8272
E-mail: experts@tasanet.com
Web Site: http://www.tasanet.com

Specialties: Save search time! Contact TASA first. Benefit from 44 years of referral expertise. We assess your needs and refer experienced Local, Regional, or National professionals for Consulting and Litigation in Recreation areas you require involving Amusement Parks; Aquatics; Athletic Equipment; Bicycles; Boating; Climbing; Diving; Golf; Health and Fitness Clubs; Hotels; Motorcycles; Personal Injury; Playground Equipment; Public Lands and Waters; Resorts; Safety; Schools; Skiing; Snowboarding; Sports; Sports Administration; Supervision; and Hundreds More. SERVICES INCLUDE prompt customized searches, referrals, resumes, and your initial interview calls with experts. Exceptional personal service. **Degrees/licenses:** All prof. degrees, licenses, certifications represented.

See primary listing under EXPERT WITNESS REFERRALS: General

Aquatics

Gerald M. Dworkin

Consultant, Aquatics Safety & Water Rescue
Lifesaving Resources, Inc.
10 Main Street
P.O. Box 905
Harrisville, NH 03450
Tel: (603) 827-4139
Fax: (603) 827-4134
E-mail: admin@lifesaving.com
Web Site: http://www.lifesaving.com

Specialties: Drowning, Near Drowning, and Aquatic Injury Prevention and Emergency Management; Hazard and Risk Assessment, Victim and Incident Recognition, Emergency Protocols, and Aquatic Facility Operations; Lifeguard, Public Safety and Rescue Training and Supervision for Swimming Pools, Lakes, Oceans, Rivers and Waterparks, including specialties for Ice, Cold Water and Swiftwater Rescue. Authored numerous articles and several textbooks on Aquatics Safety, Water Rescue, and Pre-hospital Emergency Medical issues. Noted speaker and educator on Aquatics Safety and Water Rescue for Public Safety, Rescue and Aquatic Recreation organizations. Professional Firefighter, EMT, Lifeguard Instructor and Supervisor. **Degrees/licenses:** BS, EMT,NFPA FFIII, CPR/CPR Instruct, Lifeguard/Lifeguard Instruct, EMS Instruct.

Alan M. Steinman, MD, MPH

Rear Admiral (Ret.), USCG/USPHS
1135 Harrington Place
DuPont, WA 98327
Tel: (253) 229-4088
Fax: (253) 964-3549
E-mail: asteinman@aol.com

Specialties: Drowning, hypothermia, sea survival, maritime medicine, water survival, protective clothing, cold water immersion, water rescue, safety investigation, life jackets, life rafts; past Surgeon General of the U.S. Coast Guard; developed cold water survival time charts for USCG; widely published in areas of sea survival and hypothermia; chapter on immersion hypothermia in leading textbook of emergency medicine; lectures in drowning, hypothermia and sea survival; Board Certified in Occupational Medicine; MD from Stanford University; post-graduate training at Mayo Clinic and University of Washington; experience as expert witness in both state and federal courts. **Degrees/licenses:** MD, MPH, FACPM.

See primary listing under MEDICINE & HEALTH: Occup./Environ. Medicine

Boating

Fisher Maritime Consulting Group

Dr. Kenneth W. Fisher
President
147 Columbia Tpke., #203
Florham Park, NJ 07932
Tel: (800) 732-3476
(973) 660-1116
Fax: (973) 660-1144
E-mail: email@fishermaritime.com
Web Site: http://www.fishermaritime.com

Specialties: Ships, Offshore, Workboats, Barges, Inland, Boating; Design, Construction, Conversion, Repair, Dismantling; Shipyard Site Contamination, Marinas, Asbestos, Personal Watercraft. We assist owners and shipyards in developing, asserting and rebutting ship construction, conversion and repair claims. We analyze operational casualties and personal injury claims including allegations of unseaworthiness, negligent vessel design or operations, product failures, collisions, explosions, improper construction and maintenance in boat and marine accidents. We provide analytical defensive support for marine equipment manufacturers, and we assist plaintiffs to establish a basis for recovery of losses stemming from manufacturers of defective products. **Degrees/licenses:** Naval Architects, MSc, PhD, USCG Licensed.

See primary listing under MARITIME & ADMIRALTY: General

Boating *(cont.)*

Don Green

Marine Consultant
KDON Marine Consulting
8876 Gulf Freeway, Ste. 120
Houston, TX 77017
Tel: (713) 944-0966
(800) 444-3926
(281) 414-1954
Fax: (713) 944-2546
E-mail: don@kdoncorp.com
Web Site: http://www.kdoncorp.com

Specialties: Nationally recognized maritime expert. Retired Coast Guard Commander. Marine accident reconstruction, marine investigations, Coast Guard rules and regulations, boating accidents, collisions, allisions, fires, personal injuries. Litigation support. Accepted as a marine safety expert in federal and state courts. **Degrees/licenses:** MA, BS, Master 1600 Tons Oceans; Second Mate.

See primary listing under MARITIME & ADMIRALTY: General

Hector V. Pazos, PE

Ocean-Oil Expert Witness, Inc.
& Yachts Unlimited, Inc.
P.O. Box 47188
St. Petersburg, FL 33743-7188
Tel: (727) 347-2556
(504) 367-4072
Fax: (727) 343-9717 or (504) 367-3790
E-mail: Oceanoilpazos@cs.com or
Hectorpazos75597@aol.com
Web Site: http://www.siterrific.com/pazos

Specialties: Expert Witness; Accident investigation and marine/boating accident reconstruction; Design and construction defects of pleasure yachts, power boats, racing and cruising sailboats, high performance racing boats, personal water craft (wave runners), fishing vessels; Personal injury; Product liability; Fires and explosions; Slip and fall; Noise and vibrations; Diving and CO accidents; Marine surveying. Expert witness testimony provided in over 400 cases. Analysis, investigation and expert reports provided in over 1,200 cases. Owned and operated boats of 85', 65', 64', 49', 24' and 17' in length. Have sailed entire Caribbean Islands and countries with own 38' sailboat. **Degrees/licenses:** MS Naval Architect, Marine & Mechanical Engineer, PE.

See primary listing under MARITIME & ADMIRALTY: General

Mike Russell, U.S. Coast Guard (Ret)

Turnaround Maritime Services
P.O. Box 580128
Houston, TX 77258-0128
Tel: (281) 326-3191
Fax: (281) 326-3191
E-mail: MRuss6@aol.com

Specialties: Code of Federal Regulations, Coast Guard policies & regulations, marine industry standards, tankship, towboat, barge, passenger, airboat, amphibious & barge fleeting operations; tankship & tank barge pollution prevention & safety. Case review of vessel, longshoreman & stevedore personal injuries, marine collisions, fires, explosions, groundings, sinkings, boating, offshore platform & drilling rig incidents. Eighteen years in marine safety. Enforced Coast Guard regulations as former Chief, Inspections & Investigations. Reviewed over 760 marine casualties & personal injuries. Former towboat company safety director. Accepted as an expert in both state & federal courts. **Degrees/licenses:** BS.

See primary listing under MARITIME & ADMIRALTY: General

Capt. Mitchell S. Stoller

President
MAREX
30021 Tomas St., Ste. 300
Rancho Santa Margarita, CA 92688
Tel: (949) 858-5475
Fax: (949) 858-5477
E-mail: marexco@aol.com

Specialties: Expert Witness to the marine industry. Experience in Federal and State court, judicial arbitration, mediation services, and represents both plaintiff and defense. Consultant to the United States Coast Guard. Captain Stoller is the President and founder of Marex, a marine consulting company designed to market the safety expertise that enabled him to become the youngest captain of Exxon Shipping Company, U.S.A. He also holds an outstanding tanker safety operational record both at the Company and as a Los Angeles Harbor Pilot. Capt. Stoller has written and/or consulted on Safety and procedural manuals for numerous shipping companies and has been retained in over 800 blue/brown water cases across the nation from jet skis to pleasure crafts to super tankers. **Degrees/licenses:** Unlimited Master Mariner's Lic., Extensive Pilotage Lic., BS Nautical Sci.

See primary listing under MARITIME & ADMIRALTY: General

Bowling

Byron J. Sharp

President
Bevron Consulting Group, Inc.
P.O. Box 163839
Miami, FL 33116-3839
Tel: (305) 255-4144
Fax: (305) 253-3973
E-mail: imsharp@prodigy.net

Specialties: Providing expert witness and consulting services with reference to all subject matters of operation and risk management in the Roller Skating, Ice Skating, Bowling and Video Game Arcade Industries. Designed & constructed numerous Roller Skating Centers and converted several Roller Skating Centers to Ice Skating Centers. Over twenty-five years of experience as owner and chief executive officer of various recreational facilities with full and final responsibility for all aspects of their operation.

See primary listing under RECREATION: Skating (Roller & Ice)

Fitness Equipment/Products

Frank J. Smith

Owner
Elite Fitness Consulting Services
1021 Highland Park
Fallbrook, CA 92028-5421
Tel: (760) 728-5212
Fax: (760) 728-5239
E-mail: fitwitness@aol.com
Web Site: http://www.fitwitness.com

Specialties: Twenty five years in Fitness Equipment design, use and operation; Fitness Center design; Certification of Instructors; Sauna Room design and operation; Steam Room design and operation; Flooring applications to fitness; designing Programs for Fitness Equipment Users; Lecturer on Fitness and Fitness Equipment use. Seven years as a consultant to the "President's Council on Physical Fitness and Sports." Published in the following areas: Fitness and Use of Equipment, Fitness Center design, Training Charts and Instruction Materials, Rehabilitation Programs, Instructional Videos. Designed Institutional and Retail Marketing Programs for Fitness Equipment. Fee: $150.00 per hr. **Degrees/licenses:** BA Education, Univ. of Washington; Provisional Teaching Cert., Education.

See primary listing under ACCIDENT PREVENTION & SAFETY: Exercise Equipment

Golf

Gerald W. Pirkl

Owner
The Pirkl Association
33752 Bridgehampton Drive
Dana Point, CA 92629-2186
Tel: (949) 248-7098
Fax: (949) 248-7098
E-mail: pirklg@cox.net
Web Site: http://golfexpertwitness.com

Specialties: Golf Course Architect with over 35 years experience on over 100 projects,

(Listing continued on next page)

Golf *(cont.)*

Gerald W. Pirkl (cont.)
in Golf Course Planning, Design, Layout, Construction Supervision and Expert Witness Service. Registered Landscape Architect with an engineering background. Member of the American Society of Golf Course Architects, United States Golf Association, American Society of Landscape Architects, Golf Course Superintendents Association, Etc. Expert areas of litigation — cart paths, errant golf balls, adjoining property conflicts, course design & layout, fencing & netting, course construction, etc. (over 150 cases). **Degrees/licenses:** Reg. Landscape Architect (Lic. #12242); Cert. Engr. Tech. (#14100).

Horses - Equestrian

Kathy Kusner
1049 N. Stanley Ave., #6
West Hollywood, CA 90046
Tel: (323) 654-7266
Web Site: http://kathykusner.com

Specialties: Horses: Show Horses (Hunters and Jumpers); Racing; Rental Horses and Pleasure Horses; Cross Country Riding; All levels of Riding, Training and Instruction; Stable Management; Horse and Equipment Appraisal; Horse Behavior; Safety Procedures; Industry Standards; Accident Prevention and Reconstruction. Rider in three Olympic Games - Tokyo, Mexico City, and Munich (silver medal), and two Pan American Games - Sao Paulo (gold medal) and Winnipeg (silver medal). First licensed female jockey. Gives clinics nationally and internationally on training, riding, and showing. Named Horsewoman of the Year; inducted into the Show Jumping Hall of Fame and was chosen as one of the 50 most influential horsemen of the 20th Century. Horse Expert Witness since 1983.

See primary listing under ANIMALS: Horses

Playgrounds

Recreation & Sports Forensic of Recreation Safety Institute
Arthur H. Mittelstaedt, Jr., EdD
Paul Bosch, MPA, Assoc. Executive Director
Box 392
Ronkonkoma, NY 11779
Tel: (516) 883-6399
Fax: (516) 883-1814

Specialties: Educational & recreational facility negligence cases: pools, waterfronts, playgrounds, parks, camps, amusements, gyms, sports fields, fitness centers, golf courses. **Degrees/licenses:** All staff hold appropriate degrees & licenses for their specialties.

See primary listing under RECREATION: General

Skating (Roller & Ice)

Byron J. Sharp
President
Bevron Consulting Group, Inc.
P.O. Box 163839
Miami, FL 33116-3839
Tel: (305) 255-4144
Fax: (305) 253-3973
E-mail: imsharp@prodigy.net

Specialties: Providing expert witness and consulting services with reference to all subject matters of operation and risk management in the Roller Skating, Ice Skating, Bowling and Video Game Arcade Industries. Designed & constructed numerous Roller Skating Centers and converted several Roller Skating Centers to Ice Skating Centers. Over twenty-five years of experience as owner and chief executive officer of various recreational facilities with full and final responsibility for all aspects of their operation.

Snow Sports

James W. Isham

President
Isham & Associates
P.O. Box 2619
Taos, NM 87571
Tel: (505) 776-8268
Fax: (505) 776-2131
E-mail: jisham@newmex.com
Web Site: http://www.skiisham.com

Specialties: 40 years experience in all facets of ski area operations. 24 years experience as ski area litigation expert. Experienced in plaintiff and defense testimony. Skier-skier collisions; Snow Tubing; Ski school practices; Slope layout, grooming, signage, hazards; Skier responsibility. PSIA certification - examiner status; Honorary lifetime membership recognition; National Ski Patrol; Published "Risk Management;" PSIA, NZSIA, NSAA; National lecturer, national publications. 20 years experience in all facets of expert testimony - mediation/arbitration experience. **Degrees/licenses:** PSIA, NZSIA, CSIA; Texas Tech.; Cert. in Tennis, Snow Skiing & Golf.

Sports

Daniel P. Connaughton, EdD

P.O. Box 118208
Gainesville, FL 32611
Tel: (352) 392-0584 Ext. 1296
Fax: (352) 392-7588
E-mail: danc@hhp.ufl.edu
Web Site: http://www.sportliability.com

Specialties: Consultant, researcher, and expert witness in personal injury cases involving sports, recreation, physical education, aquatics, diving, and fitness & health club activities. University professor & fitness program director. Teach "Legal Issues in Exercise & Sport." Dissertation: "Negligence Liability in Aquatics" (drowning, near-drowning, & spinal cord injuries). Doctorate in Physical Education, MS in Recreation, MS & BS in Exercise Science. Experienced participant, coach, administrator, & educator of many sports, recreation & aquatic activities. Certifications: ASEP Coaching Instructor, ACSM Health/Fitness Instructor, CSCS, numerous Red Cross Instructor certifications, Certified Park & Recreation Professional, Pool Operator. **Degrees/licenses:** EdD, MS, BS; EMT; Certifications: ACSM, NSCA, NRPA, ASEP, NSPF.

Gerald W. Pirkl

Owner
The Pirkl Association
33752 Bridgehampton Drive
Dana Point, CA 92629-2186
Tel: (949) 248-7098
Fax: (949) 248-7098
E-mail: pirklg@cox.net
Web Site: http://golfexpertwitness.com

Specialties: Golf Course Architect with over 35 years experience on over 100 projects, in Golf Course Planning, Design, Layout, Construction Supervision and Expert Witness Service. Registered Landscape Architect with an engineering background. Member of the American Society of Golf Course Architects, United States Golf Association, American Society of Landscape Architects, Golf Course Superintendents Association, Etc. Expert areas of litigation — cart paths, errant golf balls, adjoining property conflicts, course design & layout, fencing & netting, course construction, etc. (over 150 cases). **Degrees/licenses:** Reg. Landscape Architect (Lic. #12242); Cert. Engr. Tech. (#14100).

See primary listing under RECREATION: Golf

Byron J. Sharp

President
Bevron Consulting Group, Inc.
P.O. Box 163839
Miami, FL 33116-3839
Tel: (305) 255-4144
Fax: (305) 253-3973
E-mail: imsharp@prodigy.net

Specialties: Providing expert witness and consulting services with reference to all subject matters of operation and risk management in the Roller Skating, Ice Skating, Bowling and Video Game Arcade Industries. Designed &

(Listing continued on next page)

Sports *(cont.)*

Byron J. Sharp (cont.)
constructed numerous Roller Skating Centers and converted several Roller Skating Centers to Ice Skating Centers. Over twenty-five years of experience as owner and chief executive officer of various recreational facilities with full and final responsibility for all aspects of their operation.

See primary listing under RECREATION: Skating (Roller & Ice)

RESEARCH & TESTING

General

R.F. Schiffmann Associates, Inc.

Robert F. Schiffmann
President
149 West 88 Street
New York, NY 10024-2401
Tel: (212) 362-7021
Fax: (212) 769-4630
E-mail: microwaves@juno.com
Web Site: www.microwaveinnovations.com

Specialties: Microwave Heating; Microwave Ovens; Microwave Foods; Microwave Packaging; Microwave Cookware; Microwave oven accidents and injuries; Microwave fires; Microwave patents and infringement; Industrial Microwave Processing Systems. Independent consultant since 1971; Contract R&D Laboratory; Teach two international courses on Microwave Technology annually; Lecture worldwide on Microwave Technology; Fellow of the International Microwave Power Institute (IMPI); Past Chairman, President & Board member of IMPI for 18 years; Over 30 U.S. patents; Scientific Lecturer on Microwave Technology for Institute of Food Technologists; Extensive Expert Witness Testimony. **Degrees/licenses:** BS, MS, FIMPI.

See primary listing under ACCIDENT RECONSTRUCTION: Microwave Heating

SECURITIES LAW

Civil/Criminal

Elaine E. Lukic, JD, LLM, LLM

P. O. Box 9038
Breckenridge, CO 80424
Tel: (970) 453-4788
(303) 809-3425
Fax: (970) 453-4580
E-mail: elainelukic@aol.com
Web Site: http://www.denverattorney.net

Specialties: 18 years experience as securities broker, insurance, Series 7, 64, 24, RIA, management, compliance. Securities case evaluation, strategy, damage calculations, expert reports and testimony. Criminal defense: securities fraud/theft/organized crime, COCCA, RICO. Civil: NASD arbitrations, DOJ, SEC. Private, state litigation and investigations and transaction experience. Excellent references, CV. Former prosecutor. NATIONWIDE. Admitted Colorado state and federal courts, 1998, US Tax Court 2001. DEGREES/LICENSES: JD, (cum laude) Thomas Cooley Law School; LLM (with distinction), Securities Regulation, Georgetown Law School; LLM, Tax, University of Denver Law. **Degrees/licenses:** See above.

SECURITY

General

Norman D. Bates, Esq.

President
Liability Consultants, Inc.
Boston - Tucson
Corporate Office
39 Union Avenue
Sudbury, MA 01776-2263
Tel: (978) 440-9906
(888) 872-5222 (Toll Free)
Fax: (978) 440-9907
E-mail: liabilityc@liabilityconsultants.com
Web Site:
http://www.liabilityconsultants.com or
http://www.crimebrief.com

Specialties: Specializing in security and the law, Norman D. Bates, Esq. Provides services on a wide range of crime and security management problems to real estate companies, hotels, hospitals, colleges, schools, parking facilities and public and private corporations. Expert in premises liability, negligent hiring, training and supervision and workplace violence. Maintains resource library and database of inadequate security cases and provides training seminars to wide range of professionals. Consulting services include CRIMEBRIEF®, a site-specific crime analysis system useful both for premises liability and due diligence. Over 800 cases reviewed nationwide, both plaintiff and defense. Frequently quoted on national T.V and in Press. Member, MA Bar Association. **Degrees/licenses:** Juris Doctor, Suffolk Law School, BS Criminal Justice, Northeastern University.

John H. Christman, CPP

Principal
John H. Christman - Security Consultant
2055 Oxford Ave.
Cardiff, CA 92007
Tel: (760) 632-1979
E-mail: john@securityexpert.com
Web Site: http://www.SecurityExpert.com

Specialties: Analysis of security/loss prevention programs and operations; Consultation; Expert opinion and testimony for all civil litigation involving PI claims resulting from security operations including shoplifting, investigations, dishonest employee terminations, guard operations & premises liability. Over thirty years management experience (VP level) in security, including department stores, supermarkets and drug stores. Former federal & local law enforcement. Published author and lecturer at college/security seminar/conference level. Twelve years on National Retail Federation LP Board of Directors. Member: American Society for Industrial Security and International Association of Professional Security Consultants. **Degrees/licenses:** BA, CPP, Licensed Private Investigator (CA).

James M. Dallas, CPP, ACFE, PI

Private Investigator
Dallas Security, Inc.
222 S. Easton Road, Suite 215
Glenside, PA 19038
Tel: (215) 576-7336
Fax: (215) 576-0680
E-mail: jdallas@dallassecurity.com
Web Site: http://www.dallassecurity.com

Specialties: 30+ years Security & Investigative experience in all phases to all industries and environments. Premises Liability foreseeability and adequacy studies. Guard Force management training and negligence. Investigative Negligence - Negligent hiring or retention. Bars, Restaurants, Hotels, Casinos, Multi-tenant residential or commercial properties, Retail and convenience stores, Shopping centers and malls, Parking lots and structures, Workplace violence. Bouncers - Doormen, Pre-employment screening background investigations. **Degrees/licenses:** CPP, ACFE, PI.

General *(cont.)*

Dalton Affiliates

Dennis R. Dalton, PhD
2280 Country Lane
Auburn, CA 95603
Tel: (530) 889-0588
Fax: (530) 889-9162
E-mail: daltonaffiliates@direcway.com

Specialties: Security expert in Premises Liability and Guard Operations; Mkts: Retail, Finance, Property Management and Entertainment; Assistance in Case Preparation; Discovery, Interrogatories, Depositions and Testimony; Former Corporate Security Manager and Police Officer; Nationally Known Consultant; Extensively Published; Frequent Lecturer; Numerous Awards; Professional Associations: ASIS, IAPSC and AMA. **Degrees/licenses:** BS, MA, PhD.

Thomas G. Davis

President
Security Litigation Group, Inc.
6099 Riverside Dr., Suite 102
Dublin, OH 43017
Tel: (614) 793-1614
Fax: (614) 793-1965
E-mail: thomdavis@securitylitigation.com
Web Site: http://www.securitylitigation.com

Specialties: Wide range of premises security and safety issues, including adequate/inadequate security/safety; negligent hiring, supervision and retention; management/policy concerns; violent criminal acts; contract security company operations; and alcohol-related incidents. His areas of expertise include lodging facilities, residential communities, office buildings, nightclubs/bars, senior living/nursing homes, childcare activities, hospitals, banks, casinos, racetracks, shopping/strip malls, parking facilities, universities/colleges, transportation companies, and retail establishments. Thom Davis has been retained as an expert in more than 350 cases in 45 states and the Caribbean since 1990. He has conducted several thousand safety/security evaluations of various properties and has been involved in law enforcement and safety and security management since 1971. **Degrees/licenses:** Certified Hotel Administrator (CHA), Certified Lodging Security Director (CLSD).

ECJM Consultants, Inc.

Edward Mamet, CPP, CFE
Captain, New York City Police Dept. (Ret.)
P.O. Box 1559
Cooper Station
New York, NY 10276
Tel: (212) 475-8215
Fax: (646) 349-3238
E-mail: ecjm2@msn.com
Web Site:
http://member.expertpages.com/edmamet

Specialties: Retired New York City Police Department Captain Edward Mamet founded ECJM Consultants Inc. after completing forty years service. His group provides high quality police and security related issues. ECJM Consultants Inc. specializes in law enforcement and security liability matters, supporting both plaintiff and defense attorneys. ECJM consultants are retired New York City Police Department command level officers whose combined experience exceeds 125 years in law enforcement and security. Law enforcement areas include negligent investigation, excessive force, in-custody death, high speed chases, false arrest, police misconduct, negligent hiring, training, supervision and retention. **Degrees/licenses:** AAS, Police Science; BS, Criminal Justice; MPA.

See primary listing under LAW ENFORCEMENT: Police Practices/Procedures

Lance R. Foster, CPP, CFE

Security Consultant
Security Associates, Inc.
619 Riviera Dr.
Tampa, FL 33606
Tel: (813) 254-3654
Fax: (813) 251-2210
E-mail: seccon@aol.com
Web Site: http://www.seccon.com

Specialties: Security management; premises liability; negligent security; banks; apartments; parking facilities; guard operations; retail stores; hotels; office buildings; restaurants;

ATMs; malls; commercial properties; casinos; security equipment; special events; fraud. Former homicide detective, bank director of security and college criminology instructor. Practicing consultant. Highly qualified and experienced. Editorial advisor and contributing author to Hospitality Law newsletter. Certified as a protection professional (CPP) and fraud examiner (CFE). **Degrees/licenses:** BS-Law Enforcement & Security; MEd-Education.

William T. "Bill" Gaut

9063 Autumn Haze Dr.
Naples, FL 34109-1501
Tel: (239) 593-8033
Fax: (239) 593-8033
E-mail: WTGaut@aol.com
Web Site: http://www.wtgaut.com

Specialties: Case Review and Expert Opinion in the areas of: Wrongful Death; Criminal Case Review; Security Industry Consultation; Security Management; Security Guard Training; Security Guard Operations; Premise Liability; Foreseeability Expectations; Police Management and Procedures; and Litigation Support. Thirty (30) years extensive experience in the fields of Criminal and Civil Investigation, Courtroom Testimony, Security Management and Training Standards, and Litigation Support. SEE WEB SITE FOR DETAILS: Criminal Justice College Professor, Captain of Detectives (135), Lead Homicide Detective, Certified Security Instructor, District Attorney Special Services Director, Multi-State Approved Security Training School Owner, and Corporate CEO. **Degrees/licenses:** AA-Cr Jus; BS-Cr Jus; MS- Pub & Priv Adm (MPA/MBA).

See primary listing under SECURITY: Premises Liability

Richard W. Kobetz

Executive Protection Institute
P.O. Box 802
Berryville, VA 22611-0802
Tel: (540) 554-2540
Fax: (540) 554-2558
E-mail: rwk@crosslink.com
Web Site: www.personalprotection.com

Specialties: Security negligence & liability; Hotels, motels, condos, resorts, recreational areas, parking lots, apartments; Security adequacy; Reasonable standards; Supervision & training of Security Officers; Use of force & proper measures & operations. **Degrees/licenses:** MS, MPA, DPA, CST, PPS.

See primary listing under LAW ENFORCEMENT: Police Practices/Procedures

Frank H. Saunders

Owner
Frank Saunders & Associates
PO Box 1730
Capitola, CA 95010
Tel: (831) 462-4851
(800) 526-5177, Ext. 820
Fax: (831) 462-3813
E-mail: fhs8686@aol.com
Web Site: www.expertwitness.com/saunders

Specialties: Law enforcement: Practices & procedures; Wrongful deaths; Use of deadly & non-lethal force: batons, mace, o.c. spray, handcuffs, flash-bang devices, bean-bag rounds, tazers, stun-guns, handling of mentally ill, tactical deployment, control holds (including carotid restraint); Excessive force or police brutality; Cord cuffing (hog tying); Positional asphyxia; Negligent hiring, retention & training; High speed pursuit conduct; Failure to protect; Jail procedures & prisoner safety; Barricaded suspects; Hostage protection; Crime scene investigations; Officer safety; Reaction & control of drug and/or alcohol intoxicants; Internal affairs & related agency investigations; Security: Event & crowd control; Store agent or citizen arrest procedures; Private guard security for location & transportation means or procedures; Building safety; Industrial & internal theft security; Use of canine or

(Listing continued on next page)

General *(cont.)*

Frank H. Saunders (cont.)
guard dog security & procedures; Court qualified 400+ times in 18 states and New Zealand. Licensed Private Investigator (CA); Certified Field Training Officer (FTO); Medal of Valor Recipient. **Degrees/licenses:** Los Angeles Police Department Academy Graduate.

See primary listing under LAW ENFORCEMENT: General

Ira S. Somerson, BCFE, CPP

Loss Management Consultants, Inc.
650 Sentry Parkway, Ste. One
Blue Bell, PA 19422
Tel: (800) 848-4308
(610) 279-5450
Fax: (610) 279-3548
E-mail: iss@securityoffice.com
Web Site: http://www.securityoffice.com

Specialties: Pre-Trial Support Services, Extensive Security Research Library Facilities, Reports/Opinions, and Expert Testimony at Deposition & Trial re: Foreseeability Analysis; Adequacy of Security Analysis; Risk Assessment; Crowd Control; Crime Prevention; Security Guard Operations; Alarm Company and Central Station Operations; Standard Security Practices; Safeguarding Intellectual Property; Business Investigations; Violence in the Workplace; Secuirty Training; Evaluations in Retail Operations; Convenience Stores; Service Stations; Fast Food Restaurants; Shopping Centers and Malls; Parking Facilities; Hospitality Industry; Colleges and Universities; High Rise Residential and Office Buildings; Healthcare Industry; Other Commercial, Industrial, and Residential Environments. **Degrees/licenses:** BCFE, CPP, Cert. Municipal Police Instruct. (PA).

Negligence

David L. Johnston, CPP, CFE

301 N. Harrison St., Ste. 114
Princeton, NJ 08540
Tel: (800) 578-0997
Fax: (856) 786-6777
E-mail: dljcpp@comcast.net
Web Site:
http://www.expertpages.com/cv/johnston

Specialties: Negligence/Forseeability/adequacy of Security Matters involving Business, Industry and Higher Education - Specializing in College & University Security Operations; Warehousing & Distribution Centers; Manufacturing Operations; Parking Garages & Lots; Retail Security & Shoplifting; Apartment & Multi-Family Dwellings; Office Buildings & High-Rise; White Collar Crime/Internal Frauds & Defalcations; Pre-Employment Screening; Adequacy of Security Training; Disaster Management/Business Continuity; Sexual Harassment Matters. Thirty years experience as Director in major corporations and universities. **Degrees/licenses:** BS, MA, CPP, CFE, CDRP, PTS, PEA.

See primary listing under SECURITY: Premises Liability

Ira S. Somerson, BCFE, CPP

Loss Management Consultants, Inc.
650 Sentry Parkway, Ste. One
Blue Bell, PA 19422
Tel: (800) 848-4308
(610) 279-5450
Fax: (610) 279-3548
E-mail: iss@securityoffice.com
Web Site: http://www.securityoffice.com

Specialties: Pre-Trial Support Services, Extensive Security Research Library Facilities, Reports/Opinions, and Expert Testimony at Deposition & Trial re: Foreseeability Analysis; Adequacy of Security Analysis; Risk Assessment; Crowd Control; Crime Prevention; Security Guard Operations; Alarm Company and Central Station Operations; Standard Security Practices; Safeguarding Intellectual Property; Business Investigations; Violence in the Workplace; Secuirty Training; Evaluations in Retail Operations; Convenience Stores; Service Stations; Fast Food Restaurants; Shopping Centers and Malls; Parking Facilities; Hospitality Industry; Colleges and Universities; High Rise Residential and Office Buildings; Healthcare Industry; Other Commercial, Industrial, and Residential Environments. **Degrees/licenses:** BCFE, CPP, Cert. Municipal Police Instruct. (PA).

See primary listing under SECURITY: General

Premises Liability

Randall Atlas, PhD, AIA, CPP

Atlas Safety & Security Design, Inc.
770 Palm Bay Lane, Ste. 4-I
Miami, FL 33138
Tel: (305) 756-5027
(800) 749-6029
Fax: (305) 754-1658
E-mail: ratlas@ix.netcom.com
Web Site: http://www.cpted-security.com

Specialties: Providing expert services in Architecture, Security Systems Design, Criminal Justice Facility Design & Accessibility, and Premises Liability involving Hotels, Office Buildings, Parking Lots/Garages, Shopping Centers, Gas Stations, Apartment Buildings, and University/School Campuses; Slip and Fall Forensic Analysis; Inmate Suicide Negligence; Building Code Review; Stair, Step and Ramp Design; Prison Violence and Jail Conditions; Americans with Disabilities (ADA) Compliance for Accessibility; Registered Architect (FL); Certified Protection Professional (CPP); Adjunct Professor in Architecture & Criminal Justice at Florida Atlantic University & Florida International University; Author of over 50 articles and books on bldg. security/safety and suicide prevention, Amer. with Disabilities Act. **Degrees/licenses:** PhD Crim.; Masters, Architecture; AIA, CPP; Lic. Architect (FL), NCARB Regis.

Norman D. Bates, Esq.

President
Liability Consultants, Inc.
Boston - Tucson
Corporate Office
39 Union Avenue
Sudbury, MA 01776-2263
Tel: (978) 440-9906
(888) 872-5222 (Toll Free)
Fax: (978) 440-9907
E-mail: liabilityc@liabilityconsultants.com
Web Site:
http://www.liabilityconsultants.com or
http://www.crimebrief.com

Specialties: Specializing in security and the law, Norman D. Bates, Esq. Provides services on a wide range of crime and security management problems to real estate companies, hotels, hospitals, colleges, schools, parking facilities and public and private corporations. Expert in premises liability, negligent hiring, training and supervision and workplace violence. Maintains resource library and database of inadequate security cases and provides training seminars to wide range of professionals. Consulting services include CRIMEBRIEF®, a site-specific crime analysis system useful both for premises liability and due diligence. Over 800 cases reviewed nationwide, both plaintiff and defense. Frequently quoted on national T.V and in Press. Member, MA Bar Association. **Degrees/licenses:** Juris Doctor, Suffolk Law School, BS Criminal Justice, Northeastern University.

See primary listing under SECURITY: General

James M. Dallas, CPP, ACFE, PI

Private Investigator
Dallas Security, Inc.
222 S. Easton Road, Suite 215
Glenside, PA 19038
Tel: (215) 576-7336
Fax: (215) 576-0680
E-mail: jdallas@dallassecurity.com
Web Site: http://www.dallassecurity.com

Specialties: 30+ years Security & Investigative experience in all phases to all industries and environments. Premises Liability

(Listing continued on next page)

Premises Liability *(cont.)*

James M. Dallas (cont.)
foreseeability and adequacy studies. Guard Force management training and negligence. Investigative Negligence - Negligent hiring or retention. Bars, Restaurants, Hotels, Casinos, Multi-tenant residential or commercial properties, Retail and convenience stores, Shopping centers and malls, Parking lots and structures, Workplace violence. Bouncers - Doormen, Pre-employment screening background investigations. **Degrees/licenses:** CPP, ACFE, PI.

See primary listing under SECURITY: General

William T. "Bill" Gaut

9063 Autumn Haze Dr.
Naples, FL 34109-1501
Tel: (239) 593-8033
Fax: (239) 593-8033
E-mail: WTGaut@aol.com
Web Site: http://www.wtgaut.com

Specialties: Case Review and Expert Opinion in the areas of: Wrongful Death; Criminal Case Review; Security Industry Consultation; Security Management; Security Guard Training; Security Guard Operations; Premise Liability; Foreseeability Expectations; Police Management and Procedures; and Litigation Support. Thirty (30) years extensive experience in the fields of Criminal and Civil Investigation, Courtroom Testimony, Security Management and Training Standards, and Litigation Support. SEE WEB SITE FOR DETAILS: Criminal Justice College Professor, Captain of Detectives (135), Lead Homicide Detective, Certified Security Instructor, District Attorney Special Services Director, Multi-State Approved Security Training School Owner, and Corporate CEO. **Degrees/licenses:** AA-Cr Jus; BS-Cr Jus; MS- Pub & Priv Adm (MPA/MBA).

David L. Johnston, CPP, CFE

301 N. Harrison St., Ste. 114
Princeton, NJ 08540
Tel: (800) 578-0997
Fax: (856) 786-6777
E-mail: dljcpp@comcast.net
Web Site:
http://www.expertpages.com/cv/johnston

Specialties: Negligence/Forseeability/adequacy of Security Matters involving Business, Industry and Higher Education - Specializing in College & University Security Operations; Warehousing & Distribution Centers; Manufacturing Operations; Parking Garages & Lots; Retail Security & Shoplifting; Apartment & Multi-Family Dwellings; Office Buildings & High-Rise; White Collar Crime/Internal Frauds & Defalcations; Pre-Employment Screening; Adequacy of Security Training; Disaster Management/Business Continuity; Sexual Harassment Matters. Thirty years experience as Director in major corporations and universities. **Degrees/licenses:** BS, MA, CPP, CFE, CDRP, PTS, PEA.

Paul Kastes, CPM, LCAM

President
Principals Management Group, Inc.
2897 Avon Ct.
Palm Harbor, FL 34684
Tel: (813) 601-9727
Fax: (727) 773-1627
E-mail: paulkastescpm@aol.com
Web Site: www.pinellas.com/~principals

Specialties: Real Estate Property Management for income producing properties including apartments, office buildings, malls, etc. Over 30 years of "hands on" property management experience. Present portfolio includes properties in several states. As an active member of the real estate profession, I bring current, valid, and real world experience to assist both plaintiff and defense attorneys. I have provided testimony in premises liability cases including murders, rapes, assaults, slip and falls, and contractual issues. Current references and CV on request. Certified Property Manager (CPM), Licensed Condominium Association Manager (LCAM),

Certified Protection Officer Instructor (CPOI). **Degrees/licenses:** See above.

See primary listing under REAL ESTATE: Property Management

E. Robert Miller, CPM, CIPS, ACD, CMC

President
E. Robert Miller & Associates
330 Primrose Rd., Ste. 606
Burlingame, CA 94010
Tel: (650) 373-0705
Fax: (650) 373-0709
E-mail: elymiller@hotmail.com
Web Site: http://www.erobertmiller.com

Specialties: Expert in property management issues for all types of commercial and residential real estate. Experienced in arbitration, litigation, lease terms, personal injury, property damage, security, standards of care, due diligence. Over 175 case assignments; Past President, 83,000 apartment units, 14 million sq. feet office building, shopping centers, industrial buildings; Who's Who in California; Property Manager of the Year; IREM Academy of Authors; Past National President, Institute of Real Estate Management; Past Secretary General, World Property Management Committee; NAR Board of Directors. Published over 30 articles in national management and financial publications; Instructor: IREM, NAR, Colleges. **Degrees/licenses:** BS, Univ. of Wisconsin; CPM, CIPS, ACD, CMC; Broker.

See primary listing under REAL ESTATE: Property Management

Ira S. Somerson, BCFE, CPP

Loss Management Consultants, Inc.
650 Sentry Parkway, Ste. One
Blue Bell, PA 19422
Tel: (800) 848-4308
(610) 279-5450
Fax: (610) 279-3548
E-mail: iss@securityoffice.com
Web Site: http://www.securityoffice.com

Specialties: Pre-Trial Support Services, Extensive Security Research Library Facilities, Reports/Opinions, and Expert Testimony at Deposition & Trial re: Foreseeability Analysis; Adequacy of Security Analysis; Risk Assessment; Crowd Control; Crime Prevention; Security Guard Operations; Alarm Company and Central Station Operations; Standard Security Practices; Safeguarding Intellectual Property; Business Investigations; Violence in the Workplace; Secuirty Training; Evaluations in Retail Operations; Convenience Stores; Service Stations; Fast Food Restaurants; Shopping Centers and Malls; Parking Facilities; Hospitality Industry; Colleges and Universities; High Rise Residential and Office Buildings; Healthcare Industry; Other Commercial, Industrial, and Residential Environments. **Degrees/licenses:** BCFE, CPP, Cert. Municipal Police Instruct. (PA).

See primary listing under SECURITY: General

SEXUAL HARASSMENT

General

Lawson F. Bernstein, MD

MD - Forensic Neuropsychiatry
P. O. Box 81977
Pittsburgh, PA 15217
Tel: (412) 600-7996
Fax: (412) 422-5203
E-mail: lawsonbernstein@hotmail.com
Web Site: http://www.ifbmdpc.com

Specialties: Board certified academically published forensic neuropsychiatrist. Expertise in brain injury, stroke, neurotoxicology, acute/chronic pain, dementia, alcohol & substance abuse, gambling addiction and multiple other areas of neurology/psychiatry. Extensive criminal/civil trial (50/50) Plaintiff/Defense experience, including death penalty cases/legal insanity/diminished capacity. From 1991-1994, Dr. Bernstein was Director of the Psychiatry Residency Training Program at the University of Pittsburgh Medical Center, one of the largest academic psychiatric training programs in the U.S. Dr. Bernstein is also a Board Examiner for the American Board of

(Listing continued on next page)

General *(cont.)*

Lawson F. Bernstein, MD (cont.)

Psychiatry & Neurology Oral Examination. **Degrees/licenses:** Medical.

See primary listing under MEDICINE & HEALTH: Head Injury

STATISTICS

General

The Center for Forensic Economic Studies

Jerome M. Staller, PhD, President
Brian P. Sullivan, PhD, VP
Pia Di Girolamo, PhD, Sr. Economist
Lawrence M. Santucci, MA, Sr. Economist
Donald F. Gurian, CPA,
Sr. Business Consultant
1608 Walnut Street, Ste. 801
Philadelphia, PA 19103
Tel: (215) 546-5600
Fax: (215) 732-8158
E-mail: cfes@cfes.com
Web Site: http://www.cfes.com

Specialties: Economic & Statistical Analysis in Personal Injury, Commercial, Employment and Civil Rights matters; Business Valuations. PhD-level economists & full-time support staff. **Degrees/licenses:** Staff members hold PhDs.

See primary listing under ECONOMICS: General

Edward C. Keller Jr.

Professor of Biology
West Virginia University
236 Grand St.
Morgantown, WV 26505
Tel: (304) 292-4554
Fax: (304) 293-6363
E-mail: ekeller@wvu.edu
Web Site: www.us.wvu.edu/~scidis/keller/

Specialties: Litigative & regulatory statistics; Ecological data handling techniques; Sampling design. **Degrees/licenses:** PhD, ScD, FAAAS.

SURVEYS & OPINION RESEARCH

General

Cogan Research Group

Dr. Sandra R. Cogan
President
3528 Torrance Blvd., Ste. 219
Torrance, CA 90503
Tel: (310) 316-4289
Fax: (310) 316-4939
E-mail: scogan@coganresearch.com
Web Site: http://coganresearch.com

Specialties: Conducts, critiques, and acts as an expert witness on surveys. Survey types: trademark; likelihood of confusion, secondary meaning, genericness, dilution; design patent infringement; misleading advertising; defamation of character; copyright infringement; and right of publicity. Has conducted over 150 surveys for trademark and unfair competition cases and testified in state and federal court. Taught Marketing at Loyola Marymount University, Cal State University Dominguez Hills, Pepperdine University; Taught Marketing Research at UCLA Extension. Teaches California State Bar accredited seminar, "Survey Research for Trademark Cases." **Degrees/licenses:** BS, Marketing; MBA, Doctorate of Business Admin.

See primary listing under MARKETING RESEARCH: General

TECHNOLOGY

Consulting

Barry Strock

President
Barry Strock Consulting Associates, Inc.
464 Pond Hill Rd.
Rensselaerville, NY 12147
Tel: (518) 797-3954
Fax: (518) 797-5282
E-mail: barry@strock.com
Web Site: http://www.strock.com

Specialties: Government Technology Procurement and Implementation Experts. Co-author "THE MUNICIPAL COMPUTER SYSTEMS HANDBOOK." 30 years government systems experience. 300 needs assessments, system procurements, implementations. Best practices for municipal systems; Financials, HRIS, CIS, CRM, Electric/Water Utilities, Police/Fire/EMS CAD/RMS, Courts, Housing Authorities, School Districts, Colleges, Health Care. Expert witness services, mediation, dispute resolution, legal oversight for over 100 clients. County, State, Federal court actions. College, attorney and hands-on educated and trained in contract law, public law, depositions, expert testimony. Specialize in City, County, Town, Village, Borough, State systems. Software, hardware, networks, telecom specialists. **Degrees/licenses:** BS, Finance/Economics; MPA/MURP; PhD, (abd) Health.

See primary listing under COMPUTERS/SOFTWARE: General

TRANSPORTATION

General

John Badger, CTL

508 Cushing Rd.
Newmarket, NH 03857-1738
Tel: (603) 292-5977
(203) 981-7219 (Cell)
E-mail: jbadger.1@comcast.net
Web Site: http://www.badgerconsulting.com

Specialties: Industrial Transportation, Distribution & Logistics specializing in Chemical Industry including Standards of Practice; Private Rail Fleet Management, Tankcar Design, Linings, Procurement, Operating Practices & Maintenance; Tanktruck, Tankcar Release Analysis, Investigation: Railroad Operating Practices, Procedures, Car Handling; Hazardous Materials Expertise, 49CFR FMCS Regulations/HAZMAT Compliance; Private Truck Fleet Operations; Freight Payment Analysis, Transaction Audit, Fraudulent Payment; Loss & Damage Analysis, Claim Management. Executive Consultant CG Ernst & Young, Genesis Solutions, RAS Associates, Daniel Penn Associates, etc. in all areas of supply chain. Former VP - Logistics, Olin Corporation; Former Chairman, CMA Distribution Committee; STB Rail Arbitrator. **Degrees/licenses:** BS, MA, ASTL-CTL, ATLLP, ICC/STB Practitioner.

ForensisGroup, Inc.

Mercy Steenwyk
3452 E. Foothill Blvd., Ste. 1160
Pasadena, CA 91107
Tel: (626) 795-5000
(800) 555-5422
Fax: (626) 795-1950
E-mail: experts@forensisgroup.com
Web Site: http://forensisgroup.com

Specialties: Thousands of our clients have gained the technical advantage and the edge in their cases from our multidisciplined group of experts in hundreds of disciplines. We have

(Listing continued on next page)

General *(cont.)*

ForensisGroup, Inc. (cont.)
some of the best and the brightest at competitive rates backed by 14 years of excellent track record and the support of our trained staff. We assist you until you have the right expert. Some of our areas of expertise are: Construction, Safety, Engineering, Product Liability, Accident Reconstruction, Automotive, Environmental, Slip & Fall, Appraisal, Medical and other scientific disciplines. Unsurpassed standards. Clients actively evaluate our experts. **Degrees/licenses:** PE, GC, CSP, PhD, MD, GC, CIH, AIA.

See primary listing under ACCIDENT PREVENTION & SAFETY: General

John C. Glennon, Chartered

6917 W. 76th Street
Overland Park, KS 66204
Tel: (913) 383-3856
Fax: (913) 383-2277
E-mail: experts@johncglennon.com
Web Site: http://www.johncglennon.com

Specialties: Motor Vehicle Accident Investigation; Accident Reconstruction; Vehicle Crush Analysis; Vehicular Mechanical and Structural Failure Analysis for Automobiles, Trucks, and Motorcycles; Testing Capabilities for Air Brakes, Hydraulic Brakes, Suspension Systems, Steering Systems, Tires, and Wheels; Determination if Proper Maintenance and Repair Procedures were Followed; Identification of Previous Body Structural Damage; Motor Carrier Safety and Compliance; Commercial Driver Responsibilities and Qualifications; Commercial Driver Hours of Service and Daily Logs; Proper Load Securement Procedures; Fleet Maintenance Requirements; Computer Animation; Forensic Mapping; Photo Modeling; Downloading of Crash Data Retrieval Systems (Automobile "BLACK BOX"). **Degrees/licenses:** D. Engr., PE, BS Automotive Technology, ASE Cert., CDL.

See primary listing under ACCIDENT RECONSTRUCTION: General

Management & Engineering

Innovation

An Engineering Firm
Ron Tolmei
Principal Investigator
1399 Ygnacio Valley Rd., Ste. 32
Walnut Creek, CA 94598
Tel: (925) 943-1604
Fax: (925) 943-1008
E-mail: rtolmei@earthlink.net

Specialties: Electrical/Electronic equipment design, medical electronics, computers, failure analysis, mass transit systems, patent infringement, auditing of engineering fees and charges; Modeling, simulations & technical exhibits. Negligence and liability assessments of design and manufacturing defects. Underwriters laboratories certification. Extensive experience with European product development for use in U.S.A. Expert analysis and testimony by former research, analysis and development director with 25 years professional experience at Johns Hopkins Applied Physics laboratory, Rockwell International (Rocketdyne), Bay Area Rapid Transit District (BART), Teknekron & Innovation. Authored patents, technical papers, articles and reports for publication in the United States and Europe. **Degrees/licenses:** BSEE, MSEE & PhD in Electronic Engineering.

See primary listing under ENGINEERING: Electronic

Railroad Engineering

Allan M. Zarembski, PhD, PE

President
ZETA-TECH Associates, Inc.
900 Kings Hwy. N., Ste. 208
Cherry Hill, NJ 08034
Tel: (856) 779-7795
Fax: (856) 779-7436
E-mail: zarembski@zetatech.com
Web Site: http://www.zetatech.com

Specialties: Railroad Engineering, vehicle/track dynamics, derailment analysis, failure analysis, track and track systems, track/train interaction, railroad operations analysis, costing, economics of railroad operations, maintenance, failure, railroad safety, risk analysis and risk management. Testifying before Federal and Local court, ICC. PhD Civil Engineering, Princeton University; MS, Princeton; MS, BS, New York University; Registered Prof. Engineer, 5 States. 120+ technical papers, 2 books, AMSE Rail Transportation Award 1992. **Degrees/licenses:** PhD, PE.

See primary listing under ACCIDENT RECONSTRUCTION: Railroads

Truck, Bus & Forklift Safety

V. Paul Herbert, CPSA

Director
Western Motor Carrier Safety Institute
954 Butterfly Valley Road
Quincy, CA 95971-9613
Tel: (530) 281-6565
(800) 875-7389
Fax: (530) 281-6566
E-mail: paulherbert@trucksafetyexpert.com
Web Site: http://www.trucksafetyexpert.com

Specialties: Truck and Bus Driver Selection, Training, Supervision and Qualification Standards; Commercial Vehicle Equipment, Inspection, Maintenance and Operation Standards; Commercial Vehicle Conspicuity/Visibility; Air Brake Systems, Coupling Devices - Fifth Wheels, Pintle Hooks, Steering Systems, Suspension Systems, Engines, Transmissions; Truck, Bus and Forklift Accident Analysis; Motor Carrier Safety Regulations; Loading/Load Securement Requirements; Hazardous Materials Transportation Regulations; Forklift, Loading Dock, Warehouse Operations. Certified Safety Coordinator, Certified Practicing Safety Administrator (CPSA), Certified Master Instructor (Commercial Drivers License), Certified National Safety Council DDC-8 Instructor, Certified Forklift Instructor, Former Truck Driver, Former State Trooper, Former Trucking Company Safety & Personnel Director. **Degrees/licenses:** See above for Qualifications & Certifications.

Trucking

John C. Glennon, Chartered

6917 W. 76th Street
Overland Park, KS 66204
Tel: (913) 383-3856
Fax: (913) 383-2277
E-mail: experts@johncglennon.com
Web Site: http://www.johncglennon.com

Specialties: Motor Vehicle Accident Investigation; Accident Reconstruction; Vehicle Crush Analysis; Vehicular Mechanical and Structural Failure Analysis for Automobiles, Trucks, and Motorcycles; Testing Capabilities for Air Brakes, Hydraulic Brakes, Suspension Systems, Steering Systems, Tires, and Wheels; Determination if Proper Maintenance and Repair Procedures were Followed; Identification of Previous Body Structural Damage; Motor Carrier Safety and Compliance; Commercial Driver Responsibilities and Qualifications; Commercial Driver Hours of Service and Daily Logs; Proper Load Securement Procedures; Fleet Maintenance Requirements; Computer Animation; Forensic Mapping; Photo Modeling; Downloading of Crash Data Retrieval Systems (Automobile "BLACK BOX"). **Degrees/licenses:** D. Engr., PE, BS Automotive Technology, ASE Cert., CDL.

See primary listing under ACCIDENT RECONSTRUCTION: General

V. Paul Herbert, CPSA

Director
Western Motor Carrier Safety Institute
954 Butterfly Valley Road
Quincy, CA 95971-9613
Tel: (530) 281-6565
(800) 875-7389
Fax: (530) 281-6566
E-mail: paulherbert@trucksafetyexpert.com
Web Site: http://www.trucksafetyexpert.com

Specialties: Truck and Bus Driver Selection, Training, Supervision and Qualification Standards; Commercial Vehicle Equipment, Inspection, Maintenance and Operation Standards; Commercial Vehicle Conspicuity/Visibility; Air Brake Systems, Coupling

(Listing continued on next page)

Trucking *(cont.)*

V. Paul Herbert (cont.)

Devices - Fifth Wheels, Pintle Hooks, Steering Systems, Suspension Systems, Engines, Transmissions; Truck, Bus and Forklift Accident Analysis; Motor Carrier Safety Regulations; Loading/Load Securement Requirements; Hazardous Materials Transportation Regulations; Forklift, Loading Dock, Warehouse Operations. Certified Safety Coordinator, Certified Practicing Safety Administrator (CPSA), Certified Master Instructor (Commercial Drivers License), Certified National Safety Council DDC-8 Instructor, Certified Forklift Instructor, Former Truck Driver, Former State Trooper, Former Trucking Company Safety & Personnel Director. **Degrees/licenses:** See above for Qualifications & Certifications.

See primary listing under TRANSPORTATION: Truck, Bus & Forklift Safety

National Transportation Consultants, Inc.

Joseph Y. Morrison
President
1109 South 10th Street
Noblesville, IN 46060
Tel: (317) 770-0953
Fax: (317) 770-0954
E-mail: jmorrison@ntconsult.com
Web Site: http://www.ntconsult.com

Specialties: Over 150 years of transportation safety experience. Motor Carrier Safety Regulations; Safety Program Development; DOT Audits; Hazardous Materials Training; Accident Investigation and Reconstruction. Member of Commercial Vehicle Safety Alliance; Indiana Motor Truck Association; American Society of Safety Engineers; IACAI; IATAI, ACTAR.

VOCATIONAL REHABILITATION

General

Joseph R. Mulhern, EDD, CRC

Vocational/Economic Expert
MCS Rehabilitation
6130 Elton Ave. #110
Las Vegas, NV 89107
Tel: (702) 216-0330
Fax: (702) 216-0331

Specialties: Loss of capacity to work and earn money. **Degrees/licenses:** EDD, CRC.

WAREHOUSING

General

Distribution Assistance

Arthur T. Silk
President
P O Box 1418
East Dennis, MA 02641-1418
Tel: (508) 385-9802
Fax: (508) 385-9802
E-mail: atsilk@gis.net
Web Site: www.distributionassistance.com

Specialties: Established in 1985, we are a management consulting logistics/expert witness firm devoted to helping clients create and improve cost effective/service enhancing solutions to issues in the areas of contract logistics, contract carrier transportation, customer service, distribution operations, import/export, incentive programs, inventory management, logistics audits and benchmarks, material handling, on time delivery, operating services, plant facilities, productivity improvements, safety, supply chain, third party logistics, traffic/transportation and warehousing. Industries serviced include active wear, athletic shoes/sneakers, automotive parts, beer/wine/ liquor, beverage, books, building products, clothing, consumer products, contract warehousing, distributors, drug stores, electronic parts, footwear, food, hardware, import/export, insurance, leather, non-profit, optical, paper, packaging, refrigerated/frozen retail, software, supermarket, suppliers, third party and wholesalers. **Degrees/licenses:** AB Honors-Boston College; MBA-Harvard Graduate School of Business Admin.

WARNINGS & INSTRUCTIONS

General

Sterling Anthony
100 Renaissance Center - 43176
Detroit, MI 48243
Tel: (313) 531-1875
Fax: (313) 531-1972
E-mail: sterlinganthony@msn.com

Specialties: Personal injury and product liability cases requiring expertise in analyzing the adequacy of warnings & instructions, especially when the medium of communication is the package/label. Experienced in consumer and industrial products. Thirty-year career as an industry employee, university instructor, consultant, and expert. Many publications and speaking engagements. Hold professional certifications in packaging, material handling, material management, purchasing, product & inventory control, and transportation. Member of the Human Factors and Ergonomics Society. **Degrees/licenses:** BS Packaging; MBA; PhD courses in Marketing & Logistics.

See primary listing under PACKAGING: General

Subject Index

A

SUBJECT INDEX

B

C

SUBJECT INDEX

SUBJECT INDEX

D

SUBJECT INDEX

SUBJECT INDEX

E

SUBJECT INDEX

SUBJECT INDEX

F

SUBJECT INDEX

G

H

SUBJECT INDEX

I

J

K

L

SUBJECT INDEX

SUBJECT INDEX

M

SUBJECT INDEX

N

O

P

SUBJECT INDEX

SUBJECT INDEX

Q

R

S

SUBJECT INDEX

SUBJECT INDEX

T

U

V

W

X - Y - Z

SUBJECT INDEX

Notes

Notes

Notes

Notes

Notes

Notes